N.P. 42B

JAPAN PILOT

VOLUME III

**Seto Naikai
(The Inland Sea of Japan)**

SEVENTH EDITION
1981

PUBLISHED BY THE HYDROGRAPHER OF THE NAVY

A

China Pilot	Fourth edition 1864
China Sea Directory Volume IV	First published. 1873
China Sea Directory Volume IV	Second edition 1884
China Sea Directory Volume IV	Third edition 1894
Japan Pilot	First published. 1904
Japan Pilot	Second edition 1914
Japan Pilot Volume II	Third edition 1926
Japan Pilot Volume II	Fourth edition 1940
Japan Pilot Volume II	Fifth edition 1953
Japan Pilot Volume III	Sixth edition. 1966

PREFACE

The Seventh Edition of Japan Pilot Volume III has been prepared by Captain P. G. R. Mitchell, MVO, RN, and contains the latest information received in the Hydrographic Department to the date given below.

This edition supersedes the Sixth Edition (1966) and Supplement No. 9 (1979) which are cancelled.

Information on currents has been revised by the Meteorological Office, Bracknell.

The following sources of information, other than Hydrographic Department publications and Ministry of Defence papers, have been consulted:

British

Ports of the World (1980)
Guide to Port Entry (1979/80)
Port Dues, Charges and Accommodation (1978/79)
Whitaker's Almanac (1980)

Japanese

Japanese Notices to Mariners
Japanese Sailing Directions, Pub No. 103, March 1978
Japanese Sailing Directions, Supplement No. 2, 1980
Japan Port Information 1979–1980
Japanese Light List, 1980
Relevant Japanese Charts
New Official Guide, Japan, 1975.

United States of America

USHO Pub. No. 156, *Sailing Directions for Japan*, 1972, corrected to Change No. 36/80.

D. W. HASLAM
Rear Admiral
HYDROGRAPHER OF THE NAVY

Hydrographic Department
Ministry of Defence
TAUNTON
Somerset
England
6th February 1981

CONTENTS

CHAPTER 1

CHAPTER 2

CHAPTER 3

CHAPTER 4

CHAPTER 5

CHAPTER 6

DIAGRAMS

EXPLANATORY NOTES

Admiralty Sailing Directions amplify charted detail and contain information needed for safe navigation which is not available from Admiralty charts, or other hydrographic publications. They are intended to be read in conjunction with the charts quoted in the text.

Sailing Directions are kept up to date by supplements published at intervals of 1½ to 2 years, each new supplement cancelling the previous one. In addition, a small number of Notices to Mariners are published specially to correct Sailing Directions for important information which cannot await the next supplement. A list of such notices in force is published at the end of each month in the weekly edition of *Admiralty Notices to Mariners*. Those still in force at the end of the year are reprinted in the *Annual Summary of Admiralty Notices to Mariners*.

This volume should not be used without reference to the latest supplement and those Notices to Mariners published specially to correct Sailing Directions.

References to hydrographic and other publications

The Mariner's Handbook gives general information affecting navigation and is complementary to this volume.

Ocean Passages for the World and *Routeing Charts* contain ocean routeing information and should be consulted for other than coastal passages.

Admiralty List of Lights should be consulted for details of lights, light-vessels, lighthouse-buoys and fog signals, as these are not fully described in this volume.

Admiralty List of Radio Signals should be consulted for information relating to coast and port radio stations, radio details of pilotage services, radiobeacons and direction finding stations, meteorological services and radio navigational aids, as these are only referred to briefly in this volume.

Annual Summary of Admiralty Notices to Mariners contains in addition to the temporary and preliminary notices, and notices affecting Sailing Directions only in force, a number of notices giving information of a permanent nature covering radio messages and navigational warnings, distress and rescue at sea and exercise areas.

The International Code of Signals should be consulted for details of distress and life-saving signals, international ice-breaker signals as well as international flag signals.

Remarks on subject matter

Buoys are generally described in detail only when they have special navigational significance, or where the scale of the chart is too small to show all the details clearly.

Chart references in the text normally refer to the largest scale Admiralty chart but occasionally a smaller scale chart may be quoted where its use is more appropriate.

Firing, practice and exercise areas. Except for submarine exercise areas, details of firing, practice and exercise areas are not mentioned in Sailing Directions, but signals and buoys used in connection with these areas are sometimes mentioned if significant for navigation. Attention is invited to the Annual Notice to Mariners on this subject.

Names have been taken from the most authoritative source. Where an obsolete name still appears on the chart, it is given in brackets following the proper name at the principal description of the feature in the text and where the name is first mentioned.

Tidal information relating to the daily vertical movements of the water is not given; for this *Admiralty Tide Tables* should be consulted. Changes in water level of an abnormal nature are mentioned.

Wreck information is included where drying or submerged wrecks are relatively permanent features having significance for navigation or anchoring.

Units and terminology used in this volume

Latitude and Longitude given in brackets are approximate and are taken from the chart quoted.

Bearings and directions are referred to the true compass and when given in degrees are reckoned clockwise from 000° (North) to 359°. The bearings of all objects, alignments and light sectors are given as seen from seaward. Courses always refer to the course to be made good.

Winds are described by the direction from which they blow.

Tidal streams and current are described by the direction towards which they flow.

Distances are expressed in sea miles of 60 to a degree of latitude and sub-divided into cables of one tenth of a sea mile.

Depths are given below chart datum, except where otherwise stated.

Heights of objects refer to the height of the structure above the ground and is invariably expressed as "... m in height".

Elevations, as distinct from heights, are given above Mean High Water Springs or Mean Higher High Water whichever is quoted in *Admiralty Tide Tables*, and expressed as, "an elevation of ... m". However the elevation of natural features such as hills may alternatively be expressed as "... m high" since in this case there can be no confusion between elevation and height.

Metric units are used for all measurements of depths, heights and short distances, but where feet/fathoms charts are referred to, these units are given in brackets for depths and heights printed on the chart.

Time is expressed in the four-figure notation beginning at midnight and is given in local time unless otherwise stated. Details of local time kept will be found in *Admiralty List of Radio Signals*.

Bands is the word used to indicate horizontal marking.

Stripes is the word used to indicate markings which are vertical, unless stated to be diagonal.

Conspicuous objects are those which stand out clearly from the background or other objects and are easily identifiable from a few miles offshore in normal visibility. They will usually be marked "conspic" on the chart if the scale is large enough.

Prominent objects are those which are easily identifiable, but do not justify being classified as conspicuous.

ABBREVIATIONS

The following abbreviations are used in the text

Units

°C	degrees Celius	kw	kilowatt(s)
dwt	deadweight tonnage	m	metre(s)
fm	fathom(s)	mb	millibar(s)
ft	foot (feet)	MHz	megahertz
grt	gross register tonnage	mm	millimetre(s)
hp	horse power	MW	megawatt(s)
kHz	kilohertz	No	ordinal number
km	kilometre(s)	nrt	nett register tonnage
kn	knot(s)		

Directions

N	north (northerly, northward, northern, northernmost)	S	south
		SSW	south-south-west
NNE	north-north-east	SW	south-west
NE	north-east	WSW	west-south-west
ENE	east-north-east	W	west
E	east	WNW	west-north-west
ESE	east-south-east	NW	north-west
SE	south-east	NNW	north-north-west
SSE	south-south-east		

Times

ETA	estimated time of arrival	GMT	Greenwich Mean Time
ETD	estimated time of departure		

Radio

D/F	direction finding	MF	medium frequency
R/T	radio telephony	HF	high frequency
W/T	radio (wireless) telegraphy	VHF	very high frequency
LF	low frequency	UHF	ultra high frequency

Vessels and cargo

Aux Y	Auxiliary Yacht	LASH	Lighter Aboard Ship
HMS	Her (His) Majesty's Ship	LNG	Liquified Natural Gas
MV	Motor Vessel	LPG	Liquified Petroleum Gas
MY	Motor Yacht	Ro-Ro	Roll-on, Roll-off
RMS	Royal Mail Ship	ULCC	Ultra Large Crude Carrier
SS	Steamship	VLCC	Very Large Crude Carrier

Tides

HW	High Water	MLHW	Mean Lower High Water
LW	Low Water	MLWS	Mean Low Water Springs
MSL	Mean Sea Level	MLWN	Mean Low Water Neaps
MHWS	Mean High Water Springs	MLLW	Mean Lower Low Water
MHWN	Mean High Water Neaps	MHLW	Mean Higher Low Water
MHHW	Mean Higher High Water	HAT	Highest Astronomical Tide
MHW	Mean High Water	LAT	Lowest Astronomical Tide

Navigation

ODAS	Ocean Data Acquisition System	SINS	Ships Inertial Navigation System
Satnav	Satellite navigation		

Organisations

IALA	International Association of Lighthouse Authorities	IMCO	Inter-governmental Maritime Consultative Organisation
IHO	International Hydrographic Organisation	NATO	North Atlantic Treaty Organisation
		RN	Royal Navy

Rescue and distress

AMVER	Automated Mutual Assistance Vessel Rescue System	RNLI	Royal National Lifeboat Institution
		SAR	Search and Rescue

GLOSSARY

Japanese words found on charts and in sailing directions

Japanese	English
asai	shallow
asase	ledge, shoal
bae (see hae)	bank, shoal
bakufu	waterfall
bana (see hana)	cape, point
bashi	bridge
bise	shoal
byōchi	anchorage
chiisai	little, small
chiku	district
chō	town, ward
chū	middle
da	ricefield
dai	large, great
daiba	fort
dake (see take)	hill, mountain
dashi	shoal
fukai	deep
futō	wharf
ga	of (in names)
gaikō	outer harbour
gake	cliff
gan	rock
gampeki	quay
gata	lagoon
gawa (see kawa)	river
genya	moor
guchi (see kuchi)	mouth of channel
gun	district
guntō	island group
guri	reef, rock
gyokō	fishing harbour
hae (see bae)	bank, shoal
hakuchi	roadstead
hama	beach, coast
hana	cape, point
hantō	peninsula
hashi	bridge
hatoba	wharf
heigen	plain
higashi	east
hikui	low
hira, hiro, hiroi	flat, level
hoku	north
ikari	anchor
ike	lake, pond
ishi	rock, above-water
iso	reef, rock
iwa	rock
jima (see shima)	island
jōrikusho	landing place
jū	middle
kai	sea
kaiho	fort
kaikyō	strait
kaiwan	gulf
kaku	point
kawa	river
ken	prefecture
ki	tree
kita	north
ko	lagoon, lake

Japanese	English
kō	harbour, port
ku	district, area
kubi	head, neck (used for cape)
kuchi	mouth of channel
kuri	reef, rock
kuro, kuroi	black
kyukō	old harbour
machi	town
matsu	cape, point
michi	road
mijikai	short
minami	south
minato	harbour, port
minatomachi	port
mine	peak
misaki	cape, point
monoageba	landing stage
mori	forest, wood
mura	village
myaku	chain (of hills, reefs)
nada	sea, stretch of water
nagai	long
naikō	inner harbour
naka	middle
nan	south
ne	rock
nishi	west
no	of (possessive)
nobori	ascent, rise
numa	marsh, swamp
ō	great, large
o	little
oka	hill, land, mound
oki	offing
okii	great, large
ressho	chain of islets
retsugan	chain of rocks
rettō	chain of islands
sai	west
saki	cape, point
sambashi	pier
san	mount, mountain
satai	sandbank
sawa	marsh, swamp
se	bank, islet, reef, shoal
sei	west
sen	peak
sendan	shoal
seto	strait
sha	sandbank
shi	city
shima	island
shimo	lower
shinkō	new harbour
shio	current, tide
shō	bank, reef, shoal
shotō	archipelago
shū	county, province
sima (see shima)	island
son	village
sone	rock, shoal
su	bank
suidō	channel
suna	sand
syotō (see shotō)	archipelago

Japanese	English	Japanese	English
ta	ricefield	wan	bay
tai	bank		
takai	high, tall	yama	mountain
take	hill, mountain		
taki	waterfall	zaki (see saki)	cape, point
tō	island, islet	zan (see sen)	peak
torii	gateway of Shinto temple	ze	shoal
tottei	pier	zeikanjo	Custom house
tsu	harbour, port	zen	mountain
		zone	shoal
uchi	in, inside	zowai	rock, shoal
umi	sea		
unga	canal		
ura	cove		

ORTHOGRAPHY

Transcription of Japanese

There are several systems in use for the transcription of Japanese characters into roman letters. The Modified Hepburn System is used by British and American Government agencies; therefore Admiralty charts and publications have names and geographic terms in this system. No single system has been established by the Japanese for national use. Their Post Office uses the Modified Hepburn System, while the Japanese Hydrographic Office uses a system known as Kokuteisiki for the romanization of names on their charts and in their English language version of the Notices to Mariners.

To convert from Kokuteisiki and other variants into Modified Hepburn the following table may be used:

Table for conversion from various Japanese systems into Modified Hepburn

Variant	Modified Hepburn	Variant	Modified Hepburn
di	ji	ssi	sshi
du	zu	ssy-	ssh-
dy-	j-	sy-	sh-
dzu	zu-	ti	chi
gw-	g-	tti	tchi
hu	fu	ttu	ttsu
io	yō	tty-	tch-
iu	yū	tu	tsu
kw-	k-	ty-	ch-
-nb-	-mb-	-wo (after vowel)	-ō
-nm-	-mm-	ye	e
-np-	-mp-	zi	ji
si	shi	zy-	j-

REPRINTED BOOK

ORIGINAL INDEX CHARTS

HAVE BEEN CANCELLED

SEE SUPPLEMENT

While, in the interests of the safety of shipping, the Hydrographic Department makes every endeavour to include in its hydrographic publications details of the laws and regulations of all countries appertaining to navigation, it must be clearly understood:

(a) *that no liability whatever can be accepted for failure to publish details of any particular law or regulation, and*

(b) *that publication of the details of a law or regulation is solely for the safety and convenience of shipping and implies no recognition of the international validity of the law or regulation.*

JAPAN PILOT

VOLUME III

CHAPTER I

NAVIGATION AND REGULATIONS
COUNTRY AND PORT INFORMATION
NATURAL CONDITIONS

NAVIGATION AND REGULATIONS

GENERAL DESCRIPTION AND LIMITS

Charts 532, 651, 951, 2874, 2875

1.1

This volume contains a description of **Seto Naikai** or **Inland Sea** (formerly sometimes known as **Seto Uchi**) which extends about 240 miles from W to E, and 10 to 30 miles from N to S, and is bounded N by the W part of the S coast of Honshū, and S by the N coasts of Kyūshū and Shikoku.

Seto Naikai is approached from W by way of Kanmon Kaikyō (33° 55' N, 130° 55' E) which leads into Suō Nada; from S through Bungo Suidō (33° 00' N, 132° 15' E) which leads into Iyo Nada; and from SE through Kii Suidō (33° 50' N, 135° 00' E) which leads into both Harima Nada and Ōsaka Wan. The sea, which contains an immense number of islands and islets, is famous for its scenic beauty and the greater part of it has been designated a National Park.

In addition to the major port complex of Kanmon Kō at the W end and Kōbe Kō and Ōsaka Kō at the E end, there are a number of large ports lying along the shores of Seto Naikai on both sides.

1.2

The limits of the book are defined as follows:

(a) Kuro Shima (34° 05' N, 130° 52' E), SW across the NW approach to Seto Naikai, to Myōken Saki (33° 56' N, 130° 41' E)

(b) thence along the NE coast of Kyūshū to Tsurumi Saki (32° 56' N, 132° 05' E), across Bungo Suidō to Komo Saki (32° 54' N, 132° 28' E)

(c) thence along the W, N and NE coasts of Shikoku to Kamoda Misaki (33° 50' N, 134° 45' E)

(d) thence ENE across the entrance to Kii Suidō to Hino Misaki (33° 53' N, 135° 04' E)

(e) thence NNE along the E coast of Honshū to Ōsaka (34° 40' N, 135° 25' E)

(f) thence W along the S coast of Honshū to Kuro Shima.

NAVIGATIONAL HAZARDS

Charts 2874, 2875

1.3

The number of vessels involved in marine accidents in Japanese coastal waters is very great; many of these accidents involve foreign vessels and are due to collision or stranding. In addition to the precautions required by the ordinary practice of seamen and the need to observe the various rules and regulations, particular attention should be paid to the factors outlined in the following paragraphs.

Risk of collision. Owing to the density of traffic, one of the greatest hazards to safe navigation in Japanese waters lies in the risk of collision, especially in poor visibility. In addition to the large numbers of vessels of all sizes using the shipping routes round the coasts, heavy concentrations of fishing vessels are to be encountered particularly in the various channels and narrows at about the time of slack water; however none will be found when the tidal stream is at strength.

Tows which sometimes consist of as many as ten vessels and may be as much as 400 m in length, may be encountered.

Numerous ferries and small motor vessels plying between the mainland and off-lying islands, cross the shipping routes; many of the small motor vessels exhibit side lights but neither masthead nor stern lights, and at night are easily mistaken for sailing vessels.

1.4

Accident areas. Care is needed in the following areas where the channels are narrow, tidal streams strong and where the traffic is particularly heavy:

(a) W approaches to, and in Kanmon Kaikyō (33° 55' N, 130° 55' E)

(b) Tsurushima Suidō (33° 55' N, 132° 40' E)

(c) Kurushima Kaikyō (34° 06' N, 133° 00' E)

(d) Bisan Seto (34° 22' N, 133° 50' E)

(e) Akashi Kaikyō (34° 37' N, 135° 00' E)

(f) Tomogashima Suidō (34° 17' N, 135° 00' E)

1.5

Weather. In all parts of the area covered by this volume a typhoon may occur in any month but the danger is greatest in the typhoon season from summer through to autumn (see 1.86).

Fog occurs in spring and early summer (see 1.93).

Shelter. On the approach of a tropical depression or typhoon, vessels intending to seek shelter are recommended to do so in a suitable harbour in good time. Details of refuge harbours are given at 1.67.

1.6

Fishing. Fishing vessels are very numerous in all parts of Seto Naikai during the fishing season and present a considerable hazard to navigation (see also 1.3). The fishing season is at its height from April to August which nearly corresponds to the period in which fog is more prevalent.

The majority of fishing vessels likely to be encountered are small craft of less than 5 tons. The principal methods of fishing are trawling, troll-lining, drift-netting, hand-lining and potting.

Fish havens consisting of concrete blocks, scrap metal (including motor vehicles) or sunken hulks, dumped on the seabed, are to be found in coastal waters and particularly near the approaches to harbours. Concentrations of fishing vessels can be expected in their vicinity.

Fixed fishing nets extending up to 2 miles, and sometimes 5 miles, from the shore are to be found off all coasts of Japan and its islands.

Details of fish havens and fixed fishing nets, in or near the approaches to harbours and which may be a hazard to navigation, are given in the appropriate chapters of this book.

Fish farming and the cultivation of oysters, seaweed and pearls are carried out in many of the shallow bays around the coast of Japan.

1.7

Areas dangerous due to mines. There are a number of areas within Seto Naikai and its approaches, which are declared dangerous due to mines laid during the war of 1939–1945. Due to the lapse of time, the risk in these areas to surface navigation is now considered no more dangerous than the ordinary risks of navigation; but a very real risk still exists with regard to anchoring, fishing or any form of submarine or seabed activity.

The areas are complex and are not mentioned in the text of this volume. They are given in detail on Charts S532, S2874 and S2875 which should be consulted. These charts are special editions of Charts 532, 2874 and 2875.

1.8

Harbour works. Extensive reclamation and harbour construction, often marked by temporary lights, light-buoys or buoys, is in progress in the vicinity of many of the ports covered in this volume. Charted navigational aids may be difficult to identify when rapid development has taken place and the information given by radar may be confusing.

1.9

Bridge works. In 1980, a large scale, long term, bridge building programme to link the S coast of Honshū to the N coast of Shikoku was in progress in three separate areas, as follows:

(a) Onomichi (34° 24' N, 133° 12' E) to Inabari (34° 04' N, 133° 00' E); bridges spanning Kurushima Kaikyō and the other straits to the NE.

(b) Ko Shima (34° 28' N, 133° 48' E) to Sakaide (34° 19' N, 133° 50' E); bridges spanning the W part of Bisan Seto, and Shimotsui Seto.

(c) Kōbe (34° 41' N, 135° 08' E) to Naruto (34° 11' N, 134° 36' E); bridges spanning Akashi Kaikyō and Naruto Kaikyō.

Temporary lights and light-buoys mark the areas where construction work is taking place and due care should be taken when navigating in the vicinity (see also 9.4 and 11.59). Information regarding the work is promulgated in Navigational Warnings.

1.10

Ferries. There is a network of both car and passenger ferry services running E and W along the whole length of Seto Naikai and also N and S linking Honshū, Shikoku and the many islands. The services to the islands are particularly frequent in the tourist season.

Railway ferries linking Honshū and Shikoku make frequent crossings between Nigata Kō (34° 13' N, 132° 40' E) and Horie Kō (33° 54' N, 132° 45' E), and between Uno Kō (34° 29' N, 133° 57' E) and Takamatsu Kō (34° 21' N, 134° 04' E).

Car ferries up to 10 000 tons and with a speed of 20 knots, passenger ferries up to 4000 tons, hydrofoils and hovercraft, operate on the numerous ferry routes that criss-cross Seto Naikai. These ferry routes do not necessarily follow the main traffic routes.

ROUTES

Charts 2874, 2875

Recommended routes

1.11

The recommended tracks usually followed by large vessels proceeding through Seto Naikai from Kanmon Kaikyō in the W to Ōsaka Wan in the E, are marked by fairway light-buoys and are shown on the charts. These routes, details of which are given at the paragraph reference quoted, lead as follows:

Suō Nada. Between the E entrance to Kanmon Kaikyō (33° 57' N, 131° 02' E) and Hime Shima (33° 44' N, 131° 40' E), 35 miles ESE (see 3.1).

Iyo Nada and Aki Nada. Between Hime Shima and Kurushima Kaikyō (34° 06' N, 133° 00' E), 71 miles ENE, where there are two through routes, namely;

A N route via Heigun Seto (33° 50' N, 132° 11' E) and Kudako Suidō (33° 59' N, 132° 34' E); and the main or S route through Tsurishima Suidō (33° 55' N, 132° 39' E) (see 5.3, 6.2).

Note. The N route is only 2 miles shorter than the S route, but the tidal streams in it are stronger. With a favourable stream, large vessels can take advantage of this route but it is much used by small vessels and tows and is not recommended at night.

Between Hayasui Seto (33° 19' N, 132° 00' E), the N entrance to Bungo Suidō, and Hime Shima, 30 miles NW (see 5.2).

Between Hayasui Seto and Tsurishima Suidō, 50 miles NE (see 5.4).

Hiuchi Nada and Bingo Nada. Between the W approach to Kurushima Kaikyō (34° 06' N, 133° 00' E) and the W end of Bisan Seto (34° 17' N, 133° 32' E) via Kurushima Kaikyō and thence through Hiuchi Nada and Bingo Nada (see 7.1, 8.2).

An alternative route through Mihara Seto (34° 20' N, 133° 05' E), via Oge Seto (34° 11' N, 132° 55' E) and Mekari Seto (34° 19' N, 133° 14' E), leads into Bingo Nada (see 7.21). This route is seldom used by large vessels unless bound for Onomichi-Itozaki Kō (34° 24' N, 133° 10' E).

Harima Nada and Ōsaka Wan. Between the E end of Bisan Seto (34° 24' N, 134° 14' E) and Akashi Kaikyō

(34° 37' N, 135° 00' E), 40 miles NE (see 10.2) and into Ōsaka Wan (12.1).

1.12

Caution. It should be noted that recommended tracks are based solely on navigational considerations and do not in any way imply a right not to conform with the *International Regulations for Preventing Collisions at Sea (1972).* Local shipping does not necessarily follow these tracks.

Compulsory traffic routes

1.13

Compulsory traffic routes prescribed by the Maritime Traffic Safety Law (1.27) are in force in the following straits:

(a) Kurushima Kaikyō (34° 06' N, 133° 00' E) (7.2)

(b) Bisan Seto (34° 22' N, 133° 50' E) (9.2) where there is also a route to Mizushima Kō (34° 28' N, 133° 45' E), and routes between Uno Kō (34° 29' N, 133° 57' E) and Takamatsu Kō (34° 21' N, 134° 03' E)

(c) Akashi Kaikyō (34° 37' N, 135° 00' E) (10.76)

These routes are shown on the larger scale charts and are described, together with the special regulations pertaining to each route, at the paragraph reference quoted above. These traffic routes are not IMCO adopted.

Small vessel route

1.14

Small vessels and tows usually take the following route E/W through Seto Naikai:

(a) From Kanmon Kaikyō, S of Motoyamano Su (33° 53' N, 131° 15' E) and along the N shore of Suō Nada

(b) thence through Hanaguri Seto (33° 47' N, 132° 00' E), Heigun Suidō (33° 50' N, 132° 12' E), and Nuwashima Suidō (33° 59' N, 132° 32' E) or Kudako Suidō (33° 59' N, 132° 34' E), and into Aki Nada

(c) thence through Mihara Seto (34° 18' N, 133° 00' E), along the N shore of Bingo Nada

(d) thence through Shiraishi Seto (34° 25' N, 133° 31' E) and Shimotsui Seto (34° 26' N, 133° 48' E), along the N side of Bisan Seto and through Katsurashima Suidō (34° 28' N, 133° 57' E) or Ishima Suidō (34° 29' N, 134° 02' E), and into Harima Nada

(e) thence N of Ieshima Guntō (34° 41' N, 134° 32' E), through Akashi Kaikyō (34° 37' N, 135° 00' E) and into Ōsaka Wan.

SETO NAIKAI DISTANCE TABLE

1.15   Distances in miles

	Kanmon Kaikyō (Moji Ku)	He Saki	Hayasui Seto (Bungo Suidō)	Motoyama-no Su (S of Ube Kō)	Hime Shima	Kominase Shima (E part of Iyo Nada)	Tsurushima Suidō	Kurushima Kaikyō	Bisan Seto (Nabe Shima)	Naruto Kaikyō	Akashi Kaikyō	Kōbe Kō	Ōsaka Kō
He Saki	7												
Hayasui Seto (Bungo Suidō)	73	66											
Motoyama-no Su (S of Ube Kō)	19	12	—										
Hime Shima	41½	34½	31½	23									
Kominase Shima (E part of Iyo Nada)	78½	71½	—	60	37								
Tsurishima Suidō	95	88	52	76½	53½	16½							
Kurushima Kaikyō	118½	111½	112	100	77	40	23½						
Bisan Seto (Nabe Shima)	165	158	198½	146½	123½	86½	70	46½					
Naruto Kaikyō	209	202	242½	190½	167½	130½	114	90½	44				
Akashi Kaikyō	227	220	260	208½	185½	148½	132½	108	62	30			
Kōbe Kō	239½	232½	273	221	198	161	144½	121	74½	—	12½		
Ōsaka Kō	248½	241½	282	230	207	170	153½	130	83½	—	21½	13½	
Tomogashima Suidō (Kii Suidō)	249	242	282½	230½	207½	170½	154	130½	84	19½	22	26	31

Note: Using other than the main straits, the following corrections should be applied:

Kaminoseki Kaikyō: − 1·5 miles   Kudako Suidō: − 2·5 miles

Hanaguri Seto: − 3 miles   Mihara Seto: + 4 miles

CHARTING INFORMATION

1.16

Admiralty charts of the area covered by this volume are based on Japanese charts.

In general, the Admiralty charts of Japanese ports used by foreign shipping are on a scale adequate for vessels under pilotage, and there are larger scale charts for most of the major ports commensurate with their importance or intricacy.

For ports and harbours used only by local shipping, Admiralty charts are not on a scale large enough to meet more detailed needs and recourse must be had, where necessary, to charts published by the Japanese Maritime Safety Agency.

The modified Hepburn System is used for the transliteration of Japanese place-names on Admiralty charts, but the Japanese Hydrographic Office use the Kokuteisiki System for selected names and words on their charts. Some of the more common differences in transliteration between the various Japanese systems and the modified Hepburn System are given on p xiii.

SUBMARINE CABLES AND PIPELINES

1.17

Submarine cables and pipelines. Submarine cables and pipelines are indicated on the charts, but they are only described in this volume if they lie in the vicinity of a recommended anchorage or in an area which might be used as an anchorage.

Caution. Every care should be taken to avoid anchoring or trawling in the vicinity of submarine cables or pipelines; damage to cables may cause serious interference with communications or power supplies, while damage to pipelines may cause leaks of oil or inflammable gases.

Further details regarding the International Convention for the protection of Submarine Cables, and also of the dangers involved in cutting to clear anchors or fishing gear in the event of fouling a cable or pipeline, are given in *The Mariner's Handbook*.

RADIO FACILITIES

1.18

Port Radio stations. There are port radio stations at the following ports in Seto Naikai:

Fukuyama	Kōbe	Ōsaka
Hiroshima	Moji	Sakaide
Kita-Kyūshū	Ōita	Shimonoseki

See *Admiralty List of Radio Signals Volume 6*.

Radio navigational warnings. Urgent warnings are broadcast by Japanese **coast radio stations** in English. Information that is not required by foreign shipping, is broadcast in Japanese only. See *Admiralty List of Radio Signals Volume 5*.

Fog warnings are broadcast in English when the visibility reduces to less than 1 mile in the following areas:

Kanmon Kaikyō	Himeji Kō
Kurushima Kaikyō	Wakayama-Shimotsu Kō
Bisan Seto	Ōsaka Kō
Akashi Kaikyō	Kōbe Kō
Naruto Kaikyō	
Tomogashima Suidō	

See *Admiralty List of Radio Signals Volume 5*.

Radio weather bulletins. The majority of Japanese radio stations transmit weather bulletins in Japanese and English, as follows:

(i) Storm warnings on receipt, and independently of other meteorological information.
(ii) Weather forecasts at routine times.
(iii) Facsimile transmissions of weather maps, surface currents, wave height prognoses and other information of interest to mariners are available from a few stations.

Details of radio weather services including the areas covered, are given in *Admiralty List of Radio Signals Volume 3 and 3A*.

Traffic advisory service. Details of broadcasts in Japanese and English, and radar assistance to shipping in Ōsaka Wan, are given at 12.25 and in *Admiralty List of Radio Signals Volume 6*.

Tidal stream signals, indicating the direction and rate of the tidal stream in Kurushima Kaikyō, are transmitted from Ōhama Tidal Stream Signal Station (34°05' N, 133° 00' E). See 7.6 and *Admiralty List of Radio Signals Volume 5*.

Electronic navigational aids

1.19

Position fixing systems. The following electronic position fixing systems are available in the area covered by this volume:

Decca—Kyūshū Chain (Chain 7c)
Loran A
Loran C—North west Pacific Chain (Rate 9970)
Omega

For details see *Admiralty List of Radio Signals Volume 5 and 5A*.

Radiobeacons. The only radiobeacon operating within the area covered by this volume is at Hino Misaki (33° 53' N, 135° 03' E) at the entrance to Kii Suidō. See *Admiralty List of Radio Signals Volume 2 and 2A*.

Racons and **ramarks** are established at some sites within the area. See *Admiralty List of Radio Signals Volume 2*.

BUOYS AND LIGHTS

1.20

Buoyage. The system of buoyage in use in Japanese waters is shown on the diagram.

In Seto Naikai, the convention observed in connection with the lateral marking of channels is that the W entrance to Kanmon Kō is the sea outlet and Kōbe Kō is considered to be the head waters.

The direction of buoyage for lateral marks is that the *starboard hand* of a channel or fairway is that on the right hand side, and *port hand* is that on the left hand side, of a vessel entering from seaward.

When lit, buoys marking the port hand of channels and fairways usually exhibit green flashing or white flashing lights; buoys marking the starboard hand usually exhibit red flashing lights. Group flashing lights of the appropriate colour are often exhibited by the outermost pair of buoys, and by buoys moored at turning points in a channel and at the junction of two channels.

In Japanese waters, lights and light-buoys which are not maintained or approved by the Maritime Safety Agency are depicted on Japanese and recent British Admiralty charts without a magenta flare symbol, but merely with "Lt" alongside. Mariners are cautioned that

DIAGRAMS ILLUSTRATING THE SYSTEM
OF BUOYAGE USED IN JAPANESE WATERS

FAIRWAYS AND CHANNELS

	PORT HAND MARKS	STARBOARD HAND MARKS
TOPMARK		
BUOY OR BEACON		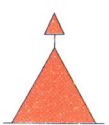 
	ODD NUMBER IN WHITE	EVEN NUMBER IN WHITE
COLOUR	BLACK	RED
LIGHT	WHITE OR GREEN	RED

MIDDLE GROUND MARKS

	BIFURCATION (OUTER END)	JUNCTION (INNER END)
TOPMARK		
BUOY		
COLOUR	BLACK AND WHITE BANDS	RED AND WHITE BANDS

MID-CHANNEL MARKS

TOPMARK	
BUOY OR BEACON	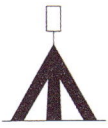 
COLOUR	BLACK AND WHITE STRIPES

ISOLATED DANGER MARKS

TOPMARK	
BUOY OR BEACON	 
COLOUR	RED AND BLACK STRIPES

WRECK MARK

BUOY	
	WRECK IN WHITE ONE SIDE JAPANESE EQUIVALENT OTHER SIDE
COLOUR	GREEN

several important channels in major harbours are marked by such navigational aids.

The shape of buoys and light-buoys in Japanese waters has no special significance and does not indicate the side on which a buoy should be passed.

The majority of light-buoys consist of a base on which is fixed a lattice structure; a light, and sometimes a topmark, is situated on the top of the structure. On British Admiralty charts of Japanese waters, these buoys may be charted by using the symbol for either a can or pillar light-buoy.

Caution. The buoyage in use in certain ports does not always conform to the standard system. Details are given in the appropriate part of the book.

1.21

Light-structures. In Japanese harbours, light-structures marking the entrances to artificial harbours and basins normally consist of round concrete towers from 8 m to 11 m in height; those to be left on the port hand when entering are painted white and those to be left on the starboard hand when entering are painted red.

PILOTAGE

Charts 532, 651, 951, 2874, 2875

1.22

Arrangements for pilots should be made through agents in Japan. If this is not possible pilots may be requested by radio, addressed to the pilots association or the harbour master of the particular port, well in advance of arrival.

Pilots Associations are established in Seto Naikai and cover the following areas:

Pilots Association	*Areas covered*
Naikai (Inland Sea)	Seto Naikai excluding approaches to Kanmon Kaikyō, Bungo Suidō, part of Ōsaka Wan, and Kii Suidō
Kanmon	Kanmon Kō and approaches
Ōsaka Wan	Tomogashima Suidō, Ōsaka Wan excluding the area covered by the Hanshin Pilots Association
Hanshin	NE part of Ōsaka Wan comprising Kōbe Kō, Nishinomiya Kō, Amagasaki Kō and Ōsaka Kō
Komatsushima	Komatsushima Kō
Wakayama-Shimotsu	Wakayama-Shimotsu Kō

1.23

Boarding points. Association pilots board vessels in the following positions:

Pilots Association	*Boarding points*
Naikai	Vessels via Kanmon Kaikyō—½ mile SE of He Saki Light (33° 57' N, 131° 02' E)
	Vessels via Bungo Suidō—3 miles SSE of Seki Saki Light (33° 15' N, 131° 54' E)
	Vessels via Kii Suidō—4 to 5 miles SSW of Kōbe Light (Wada Misaki) (34° 39' N, 135° 10' E)
	Vessels from Kōbe/Ōsaka—1 mile S of Kōbe Light (Wada Misaki)
Kanmon	Vessels from W—in the vicinity of Mutsure Shima (33° 58' N, 130° 52' E)
	Vessels from Seto Naikai—½ mile SE of He Saki Light (33° 57' N, 131° 02' E). (Change-over point with Naikai pilots)
Ōsaka Wan	Vessels via Kii Suidō—7 miles S of Tomogashima Light (34° 17' N, 135° 00' E)
	Vessels from W—4 to 5 miles SSW of Kōbe Light (Wada Misaki) (34° 39' N, 135° 10' E). (Change-over point with Nakai pilots)
	Vessels in Kōbe/Ōsaka—in vicinity of harbour outer limit or in berth
Hanshin	In vicinity of Kōbe Kō or Ōsaka Kō quarantine anchorage, as appropriate
Komatsushima	Off Komatsushima Kō, in position ¼ mile NW of Wadano Hana Light (34° 00' N, 134° 38' E)
Wakayama-Shimotsu	In vicinity of quarantine anchorage off Shimotsu Ku (34° 07' N, 135° 07' E)

1.24

The **Nakai Pilots Association (Inland Sea Pilots)** provides a 24 hour pilotage service through Seto Naikai and to various harbours on either side where local pilots are not available. Vessels approaching Seto Naikai and requiring a pilot should carry out the following procedure:

(a) Send ETA 24 hours in advance either through the agent or direct to Naikai Pilots (see *Admiralty List of Radio Signals Volume 6*).

(b) Confirm ETA 6 hours before arrival and notify any subsequent changes immediately.

(c) When within VHF radio range, confirm ETA with either Shimonoseki, Ōita or Kōbe port radio station as appropriate.

(d) When nearing the pilot boarding point, display International Code Flag G by day, and flash the letter G (− − ·) on a powerful light and sound the whistle at night.

(e) Entering from Bungo Suidō in bad weather, proceed to a position S of Tsuta Shima (33° 14' N, 131° 54' E) and await a pilot there.

1.25

Pilotage is compulsory in Kanmon Kō and Kōbe Kō.

In view of the complexity of the Maritime Traffic Safety Law, the high density of traffic and the caution about harbour works given at 1.8, pilotage in Seto Naikai is recommended; it is compulsory in Kurushima Kaikyō (7.1) and Bisan Seto (9.3).

Details of pilotage facilities at the various ports are given in the appropriate part of this book. See also *Admiralty List of Radio Signals Volume 6*.

Japanese pilot boats normally have a green or black hull, with PILOT in white on both sides, and a white super-structure. Exceptions to the general rule in the case of major ports are indicated in the text.

The signals for a pilot are those laid down in the International Code of Signals.

Each licensed pilot is provided with a copy of the

Japanese pilot regulations, and is instructed to produce it when required by those employing him.

Members of the Japan Pilots Association have been instructed to obtain the signature of the Master and/or Agent to a form of indemnity with regard to liability in the event of loss or damage to the vessel.

LAWS AND REGULATIONS

Japanese Maritime Safety Laws and Regulations
1.26

The laws and regulations which apply to vessels in the coastal waters and ports of Japan are contained in the English translation of the Japanese publication *Japan Maritime Safety Laws and Regulations*, dated May 1980.

Summaries of the more important of these laws and regulations, are given in the following paragraphs, 1.27–1.40.

A copy of *Japan Maritime Safety Laws and Regulations*, together with the latest amendments, should be obtained at the first opportunity after arrival in Japanese waters. An illustrated pamphlet entitled *Maritime Traffic Safety Law* and written in English, is available from the Maritime Safety Agency.

Maritime Traffic Safety Law
1.27

A **Maritime Traffic Safety Law,** designed to increase the safety of vessels in congested areas by prescribing special regulations and enforcing the use of certain traffic routes, applies within Seto Naikai. The Law does not apply within port and harbour limits which are covered by the Port Regulations Laws (1.37), nor within certain inshore areas normally navigated only by fishing vessels.

The Maritime Traffic Safety Law also covers Ise Wan and Tōkyō Wan (see Japan Pilot Volume II).
1.28

General regulations. The general regulations affecting all areas governed by the Maritime Traffic Safety Law are summarised as follows:

(a) The various Regional Maritime Safety Headquarters direct and control the flow of traffic. Certain speed limits are in force.

(b) All vessels of 50 m or more in length are required to use the traffic routes. In general, transit of a traffic route must be completed before sunset.

(c) A vessel of 200 m or more in length and a vessel carrying a dangerous cargo are required to report their intentions to the appropriate authority and comply with subsequent instructions (see 1.31–1.36 for details). A vessel of 200 m or more in length, in general, has the right of way within the route.

(d) A vessel, other than those engaged in fishing, cable-laying, surveying, minesweeping or construction work, when entering, leaving or crossing a traffic route, should keep out of the way of a vessel navigating along the traffic route.

(e) A vessel engaged in fishing, cable-laying, surveying, minesweeping or construction work, when entering, leaving or crossing a traffic route, or when stopped within a traffic route,

should keep out of the way of a vessel of 200 m or more in length which is navigating along the traffic route.

(f) At the intersection or junction of a traffic route, all vessels should keep out of the way of a vessel of 200 m or more in length, navigating along the traffic route.

(g) When risk of collision exists between a vessel engaged in fishing, cable-laying, surveying, minesweeping or construction work, which is entering, leaving or crossing a traffic route, and a vessel less than 200 m in length which is navigating along the traffic route, the International Regulations for Preventing Collisions at Sea should be observed.

(h) A vessel crossing a traffic route should cross it as nearly as possible at right angles.

(i) A vessel is not allowed to anchor within traffic routes except in emergency.

(j) In the event of a marine accident, the vessel involved is to inform the Maritime Safety Agency promptly and take steps to ensure that other traffic is not hazarded.

1.29

Signals displayed by vessels. When vessels join or leave certain traffic routes, and when they cross these routes, they are required to display a code of flag signals by day and make sound signals at night, to indicate their intentions. Details of these signals are given in the appropriate chapter of this book.
1.30

Shapes and lights. The following shapes and lights are required to be shown by certain vessels when navigating within the areas in which the Maritime Traffic Safety Law applies:

Type of Vessel	By Day	At Night (*in addition to lights required by Rule 23 of Rules for Preventing Collisions at Sea*)
Vessels of length 200 m or more	2 black cylinders, disposed vertically, (but separately from the cylinder required by Rule 28 of *Rules for Preventing Collisions at Sea*)	All round green flashing light showing between 180 and 200 flashes every minute
Vessels carrying dangerous cargo (as in 1.31(b))	International 1st Substitute over Flag B	All round red flashing light showing between 120 and 140 flashes every minute
Vessels engaged in construction work	White diamond over 2 red balls, disposed vertically	Two all round green lights disposed vertically in a lower position than steaming light
Vessels engaged in emergency operations	Red cone, point up	All round red flashing light showing between 180 and 200 flashes every minute

			No.	Item	Category of vessel to which item applies (see 1.31)

Special patrol vessels in traffic routes | Streamer, 2 m in length, red and white in stripes | All round green flashing light showing between 120 and 140 flashes every minute

No.	Item	Category of vessel to which item applies (see 1.31)
	(1) Addressee (abbreviated form)	(a), (b) and (c)
	(2) Name of vessel and gross tonnage	(a), (b) and (c)
	(3) Length of vessel in metres	(a)
	(4) Maximum draught in metres to 0·01 m	(a)
	(5) Type of dangerous cargo and amount of each type	(b)
	(6) Length of tow as described in (c)	(c)
	(7) Description of object being towed or pushed	(c)
	(8) Port of destination	(a), (b) and (c)
	(9) Traffic route, or section thereof, to be navigated (abbreviated form)	(a), (b) and (c)
	(10) Estimated date and time of entry into traffic route	(a), (b) and (c)
	(11) Estimated date and time of departure from traffic route	(a), (b) and (c)
	(12) Vessel's call sign or call name	(a), (b) and (c)
	(13) Method of communication if vessel has no radio	(a), (b) and (c)
	(14) Name and address of agent through whom instructions may be forwarded (applicable only if report is made by letter or telegram)	(a), (b) and (c)

Notes:
(i) If any item is NOT applicable insert NA.
(ii) If more than one traffic route is to be navigated, items (1), (9), (10), (11) should be reported in sequence of traffic routes.
(iii) Vessels described in 1.31(b)(ii) should indicate the amount of dangerous cargo as 0.
(iv) If two or more adjacent traffic routes are to be navigated, it is sufficient only to report the estimated date and time of departure from the final traffic route.

Example—M.V. SAFETY FIRST (gross tonnage 43 724 length overall 227 m, draught 12·50 m, call sign 9ZZZ, cargo 52 835 tons crude oil) intends to navigate Akashi Kaikyō traffic route (estimated time of entry is 5th 0930 and departure 5th 1000), then successively enter Bisan Seto East traffic route at 1300, Bisan Seto North Traffic route at 1445, Mizushima traffic route at 1500, departing thence 5th at 1600 to enter Mizushima port. The vessel designates Japan Shipping Agency Ltd, as conveyor or instructions from the shore authorities.

The corresponding message reads as follows:

NOTIFICATION
(1) GOKAN TAKAMATSU
(2) SAFETY FIRST 43 724
(3) 227
(4) 12·50
(5) CRUDE OIL 52 835
(6) NA
(7) NA
(8) MIZUSHIMA
(9) AKASHI, BISANEAST, BISANNORTH, MIZUSHIMA
(10) 5th 0930 1300 1445 1500
(11) 5th 1000 1600
(12) 9ZZZ
(13) NA

1.31

Reports. The following categories of vessels are required to report to shore authorities before navigating any of the traffic routes prescribed in the Maritime Traffic Safety Law. On receipt of the report, instructions for safe navigation will, when necessary, be passed to the vessel concerned:
(a) Vessels 200 m or more in length
(b) Vessels carrying a dangerous cargo as follows:
(i) Vessels of 1000 gross tons or more, carrying inflammable liquids or high pressure gas in bulk
(ii) Vessels in (i) which have unloaded but which are still subject to risk of fire or explosion
(iii) Vessels over 300 gross tons or more, carrying 80 tons or more of explosives or 200 tons or more of organic peroxide
(c) Vessels towing or pushing when the total length of tow including the length of the towing vessel, is 200 m or more.

1.32

Time of reporting. Reports should be made as follows:
Initial Report:
Vessels described in 1.31(a) and (c): by 1200 on the day before entering the traffic route.
Vessels described in 1.31(b): 3 hours before estimated time of entering the traffic route.
Amending Report:
Vessels described in 1.31(a): 3 hours before estimated time of entering the traffic route.
Vessels described in 1.31(b): immediately.
Except in emergency, the times are those by which the report should be received by the appropriate Maritime Safety Office.

1.33

Method of reporting. The Initial Report should be made to the Regional Maritime Safety Headquarters (RMSHQ) or Maritime Safety Office (MSO) by radio through a coast ratio station or by radio telephone; see *Admiralty List of Radio Signals Volume 6* for details.

In certain large Japanese ports where an Agent is available to convey instructions from the RMSHQ or MSO to the vessel, the report may be made by letter, telegram or telephone.

An Amending Report, if required, should be made by radio or telephone.

Information on traffic routes and details of shore authorities, which may be required to assist in the preparation of reports, are listed in the table at 1.36. For convenience, the traffic routes described in Japan Pilot Volume II are also included.

1.34

Contents of reports. The Initial Report should start with the word NOTIFICATION which should be followed by numbered items as follows:

(14) JAPAN SHIPPING AGENCY LTD., 1 MINATO I-CHOME KURASIKI

Note: Item (14) is NA if radio communications are used.

An Amending Report should start with the word AMENDMENT which should be followed by numbered items listed below (see Example).

No.	Item
(1)	Addressee and traffic route.
(2)	Name of vessel and gross tonnage.
Nos. corresponding to Initial Report	Amendments required.

Note—Radiotelephone should be used if practicable: ask for the Traffic Route Control Officer.

Example—Transit of Akashi Kaikyō traffic route by SAFETY FIRST will be delayed by an hour: estimated time of entry 5th 1030, estimated time of departure 5th 1100.

The corresponding message reads as follows:

AMENDMENT
(1) GOKAN AKASHI
(2) SAFETY FIRST 43 724
(10) 5th 1030
(11) 5th 1100

1.35

Instructions from shore authorities. On receipt by the RMSHQ or MSO of the Report from the vessel, instructions will be issued to the vessel, usually by the same method of communication by which the Report was made; in some circumstances a vessel may be directed to contact a coast radio station for further instructions.

The following are examples of the matters with which the instructions may deal:

(a) Change in the time of entry into a traffic route.
(b) Change in the speed of the vessel in a traffic route.
(c) Restrictions on navigation in the event of low visibility, or accident.
(d) Maintenance of watch on radiotelephone. Normally a vessel should maintain watch on radiotelephone from 3 hours before entering a traffic route until the time of finally leaving it.
(e) In some circumstances, vessels of 200 m or more in length and vessels carrying a dangerous cargo, may be required to hire an escorting vessel which may be equipped with appropriate fire-fighting facilities. Instructions may also be issued by special patrol vessels in the traffic routes.

1.36

Table listing traffic routes, details of authorities to whom reports should be addressed, and radio stations through which reports should be passed:

	Name of Traffic Route (TR)	Abbreviated name of TR	Coast radio station (Alternative station)	Name of Addressee (Abbreviated Name)	Address	Telephone
(i)	Uraga Suidō TR	URAGA	Yokohama (Kushiro)	Chief, Tōkyō Wan Traffic Advisory Service Centre (TOKYOWAN)	Kamoi Yokosuka-shi Kanagawa	0468-42-1155
(ii)	Naka-no-se TR	NAKANOSE	as in (i)	as in (i)	as in (i)	as in (i)
(iii)	Irago Suidō TR	IRAGO	Nagoya (Shiogama)	Commander, 4th RMSHQ (YONKAN)	2-3-12 Irifune Minato-Ku Nagoya 455	052-661-1611
(iv)	Akashi Kaikyō TR	AKASHI	Kōbe (Moji)	Commander, 5th RMSHQ (GOKAN)	1-chome Kaigan-dori Ikuta-Ku Kōbe 650	078-391-6551
(v)	Bisan Seto East TR Bisan Seto North TR Bisan Seto South TR Ukō East TR Ukō West TR Mizushima TR	BISANEAST BISANNORTH BISANSOUTH UKOEAST UKOWEST MIZUSHIMA	Kōbe (Kagoshima)	Chief, Takamatsu MSO (TAKAMATSU)	1-30 Asahishinmachi Takamatsu-shi 760	0878-21-7011
(vi)	Kurushima Kaikyō TR	KURUSHIMA	Hiroshima (Naha)	Chief, Imabari MSO (IMABARI)	1-2 Katahara-machi Imabari-shi	0898-32-0708
			Details of call signs and frequencies are given in *Admiralty List of Radio Signals Volume 6.*			Ask for Traffic Route Control Officer

Port Regulations Law
1.37

The regulations for vessels in Japanese ports, including specified ports, are contained in the **Port Regulations Law**. The Law applies within harbour limits.

A summary of the more important articles in the Port Regulations Law is given in the following paragraphs. Additional local regulations are in force in Kanmon Kō, Takamatsu Kō, Kōbe Kō and Ōsaka Kō and are referred to in the appropriate part of this book.

Arrival, departure, and movement within a port
(a) A vessel which has entered, or intends to depart from, a specified port shall make a report to the Port Captain. The entry report shall include:
  (i) name of vessel, type, nationality and port of registry
  (ii) gross tonnage, length, draught and speed
  (iii) name and address of owner or operator
  (iv) port of departure and last port of call
  (v) time and purpose of entry, and anchorage area
  (vi) description and quantity of cargo
  (vii) any information which may affect the safety of other vessels.
  The departure report shall include (i), (ii), (iii) and (vi) above, and the estimated time of departure, the next port of call and final destination.
(b) Except in emergency, a vessel shall not enter a specified port between sunset and sunrise unless permission to do so has previously been obtained from the Port Captain.
(c) Unless arrangements for berthing have been made in advance, the Port Captain will normally allocate an anchorage.
(d) Except in emergency, a vessel shall not shift berth without the permission of the Port Captain.
(e) A vessel wishing to put her main engines out of action shall inform the Port Captain, who may allocate her a special berth.
(f) A vessel shall not anchor in a fairway; near a wharf, pier, mooring buoy or dock; or near the entrance to a river, canal, waterway or basin.

Traffic rules
(a) A vessel approaching or leaving a specified port shall use the prescribed fairway.
(b) A vessel entering or leaving a fairway shall keep clear of vessels in the fairway.
(c) Overtaking in a fairway is not allowed.
(d) A vessel approaching the entrance to a specified port shall remain outside until a departing vessel is clear of the entrance.
(e) A vessel in or near a specified port shall proceed at such a speed as not to endanger other vessels.

Dangerous cargo
(a) A vessel having an explosive or dangerous cargo onboard shall inform the Port Captain, and shall remain outside the harbour limits until instructions have been received.
(b) A dangerous cargo shall not be loaded or discharged until permission of the Port Captain has been received.

Maintenance of channel
Discharge of ballast, oil residue, garbage and other waste material is prohibited within $5\frac{1}{2}$ miles of a port.

Fire warning
When a fire breaks out in a vessel which is not underway, she shall sound five long blasts on the whistle or siren, repeated at suitable intervals.

Prevention of Marine Pollution and Maritime Disaster Law
1.38

The regulations for vessels in Japanese waters are contained in the **Prevention of Marine Pollution and Maritime Disaster Law.**

Tankers are required to comply with these laws before arrival and while in harbour; and to report having done so. Any neglect resulting in oil pollution, however small, is to risk heavy fines and delays.

There are a number of depots throughout Japan where quantities of dispersants and clean-up equipment are stock-piled. Within the limits of this volume these depots are situated at the following ports:

Himeji	Matsuyama	Tokuyama-Kudamatsu
Imabari	Mizushima	Ube
Iwakuni	Ōita	Wakayama-Shimotsu
Kanmon	Ōsaka	

International regulations concerning pollution of the sea are given in *The Mariner's Handbook*.

Quarantine Law
1.39

The regulations for vessels in Japanese waters are contained in the **Quarantine Law.**

Quarantine examination can be carried out at the following Japanese ports in the area covered by this volume:

Fukuyama	Matsuyama	Saiki
Hannan	Mishima-Kawanoe	Sakaide
Hiroshima	Mizushima	Tokuyama-Kudamatsu
Iwakuni	Niihama	Ube
Kanmon	Ōita	Wakayama-Shimotsu
Kōbe	Ōsaka	
Kure	Saganoseki	

A vessel from a foregin port must obtain quarantine clearance (free pratique) before berthing in a Japanese port or communicating with the shore.

1.40

Radio pratique. Subject to a vessel holding a valid Japanese Sanitary Inspection Certificate, free pratique may be granted by radio which will allow the vessel to enter port and berth without the need for further clearance. The certificate is valid for one year.

Radio pratique is available at all the ports listed at 1.39 except Mishima-Kawanoe and Sakaide.

Application for a sanitary inspection may be made through the Agent at any of the ports where quarantine examinations are carried out.

A request for radio pratique should be addressed to the port to be visited, submitted through the Agent, not less than 12 hours and not more than 36 hours before arrival.

The request should be prefixed with the abbreviation RPM, followed by:
(2) Name of vessel
(3) The number (in full 7 digits) of the Japanese Sanitary Inspection Certificate
(4) Port and date of departure
(5) Intermediate ports of call
(6) Name of Japanese port of entry and estimated date and time of arrival
(7) Issuing authority and date of De-ratisation Certificate and whether De-ratting or Exemption.
(8) Number of crew and passengers (latter denoted by word PAX).
(9) Whether or not any person or goods were received from another vessel within 15 days prior to arrival in Japan; if affirmative, (a) name of other vessel, port of departure, sailing

date and ports of call, (b) date of transfer, number of persons and description of goods transferred.

(10) Whether any person suffered from any infectious disease within 15 days prior to arrival in Japan.

(11) Any case of death, other than by accident, within 15 days of arrival; if affirmative, name, age, date of death, cause or symptoms.

(12) Any sign of rats showing symptoms of pestilence or suspected of such, within 15 days prior to arrival.

(13) Whether cargo suspected of, or had been in contact with, an infectious disease carrier.

(14) Crew members or passengers who are not in possession of properly recorded and internationally recognised Smallpox Vaccination Certificate.

(15) Whether or not there is a doctor on board.

(16) Name of Master.

Example RPM—SAFETY FIRST—0840105—NEW YORK 1ST SEP—HONOLULU 16TH SEP—TOKYO 25TH SEP 1000—YOKOHAMA 1ST AUG 78 EXEMPTION—CREW 35 PAX30—9 TO 15 NONE—JOHN BROWN.

Radio Pratique will not be granted if a vessel comes from a notified epidemic area or when any crew member is suffering from a suspected or undiagnosed illness.

SIGNALS

Traffic and port signals
1.41

Traffic signals, tidal stream signals and port entry signals are described in this volume under the port or area concerned.

Weather signals
1.42

Two systems of visual storm signals are in use in Japanese ports, namely the General Storm Signals and the Local Storm Signals. General storm signals indicate the position of a cyclonic centre, the direction of its motion, etc; local storm signals indicate that gales or storms of dangerous intensity may be expected at the port where they are displayed. In some ports general and local storm signals are displayed side by side.

1.43

General storm signals. The general storm signals are hoisted at the yardarm and masthead of the storm signal mast. The symbols, which are generally painted red, but may be painted white to suit local conditions, and their code numbers, are as in Diagram 1.

Day signals
(a) Three symbols hoisted vertically at one yardarm of the storm signal mast, indicate the number of the district in which the cyclonic centre is situated; the symbols should be read from the top down. See Chartlet 1 on Diagram 1.

(b) Two symbols at the other yardarm indicate the direction of motion. See Table A.

(c) The rate of progression is indicated by the varying distances between the two symbols and from the yardarms. See Table B.

(d) One symbol at the masthead indicates the time at which the centre was located and the intensity of the storm. See Table C.

Night signals
(a) Three lights disposed vertically at one yardarm indicate the district in which the cyclonic centre is situated. See Chartlet II on Diagram 2.

(b) One light at the masthead indicates the subdivision of the district in which the cyclonic centre is situated. See Table D.

(c) Two lights disposed vertically at the other yardarm indicate the direction of motion of the cyclonic centre. See Table E.

1.44

Local storm signals. Storm warning signals are shown when the wind is expected to attain the force stated, within the next 24 hours inside a sea area of radius 20 miles from the storm signal station.

Day signals normally consist of three elements indicating wind force, wind direction, and change in wind direction; they are disposed vertically in that order. The signals indicating wind force may sometimes be used alone.

At night, wind force and direction is indicated by red and white lights; there is no signal to indicate a wind of force 6–7.

Details of both day and night signals are as in Diagram 3.

1.45

Special weather signals, giving warning of abnormal conditions likely to cause damage, are made by means of drogues and cylinders by day, and by coloured lights at night.

Details of the signals and their meanings are given in Diagram 3.

1.46

Weather forecast signals. At certain stations, signals made to indicate the probable weather for the current day are hoisted at midnight and hauled down at noon. At stations forecasting the weather for the following day, signals are displayed from noon to noon.

In the forecast made by flags, the wind direction is indicated by a triangular flag, the weather conditions by a square flag, and the change in temperature by a long triangular flag.

At night, the signals are made by coloured lights; those exhibited between sunset and midnight refer to the following day, and those exhibited between midnight and sunrise refer to the same day.

Details of the signals and their meanings are given in Diagram 4.

1.47

Tsunami warning signals are as follows:

Warning of Tsunami threat—Single strokes on a bell

Warning of weak Tsunami—Double stroke on a bell

Warning of large Tsunami—Strokes on a bell in groups of three, or blasts on a siren of about 5 seconds duration

Dispersal of a Tsunami—Single strokes on a bell alternating with double strokes.

GENERAL STORM SIGNALS (DAY)

Symbols and Code Numbers

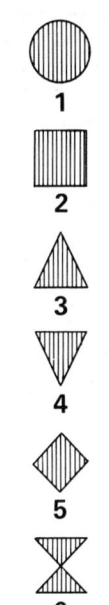

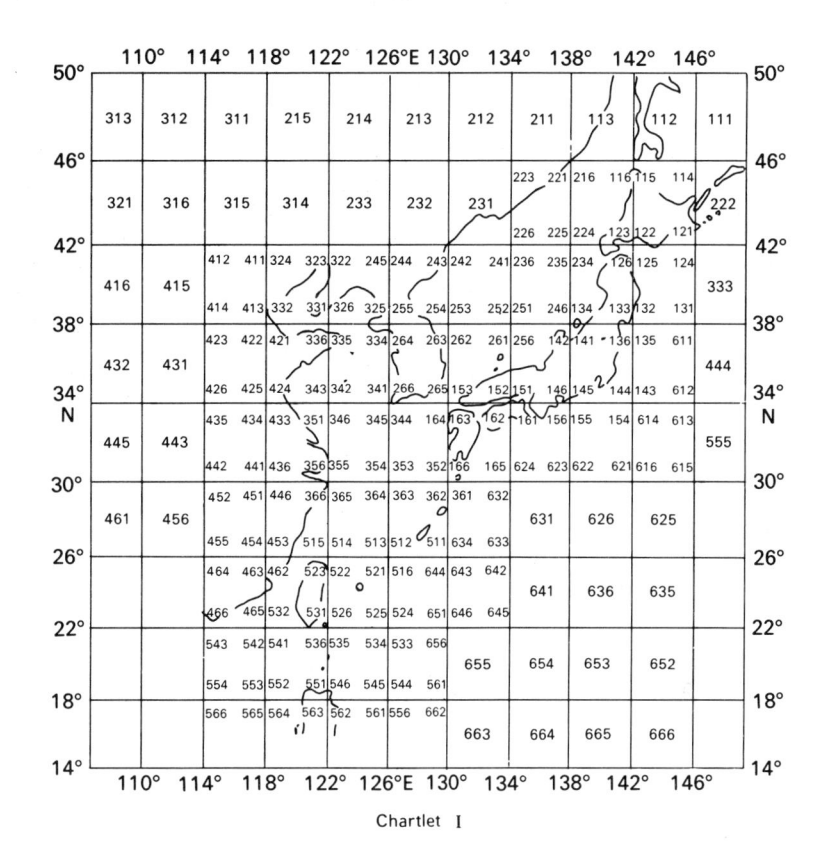

Chartlet I

Table A – Direction of Motion

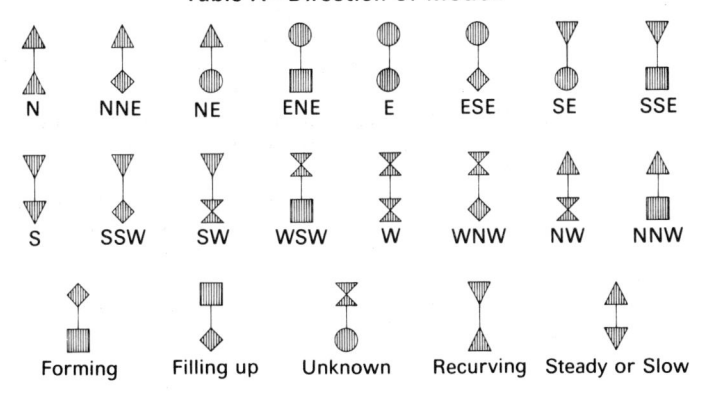

N   NNE   NE   ENE   E   ESE   SE   SSE

S   SSW   SW   WSW   W   WNW   NW   NNW

Forming   Filling up   Unknown   Recurving   Steady or Slow

Table C – Intensity and Time

Symbol	Intensity	Time
	Not indicated	0600, this morning.
	Violent	0600, this morning.
	Not indicated	1200, noon today.
	Violent	1200, noon today.
	Not indicated	1800, last night.
	Violent	1800, last night.

Table B – Rate of Progression

Direction symbols separated by the normal distance.	Moving in an E direction, velocity not known.
Direction symbols separated by twice the normal distance.	Moving in an E direction, 10 to 20 miles per hour.
Twice normal distance between yardarm and upper symbols.	Moving in an E direction, 20 to 30 miles per hour.
Twice normal distance between yardarm and upper symbol. Also twice normal distance between two symbols.	Moving in an E direction, over 30 miles per hour.

Table C

Table A
Table B

Chartlet I

The signal reads: At 0600 this morning a violent typhoon in district 523 was moving NE at a rate of 10 to 20 miles per hour.

Example

(1.43)   Diagram 1.

GENERAL STORM SIGNALS (NIGHT)

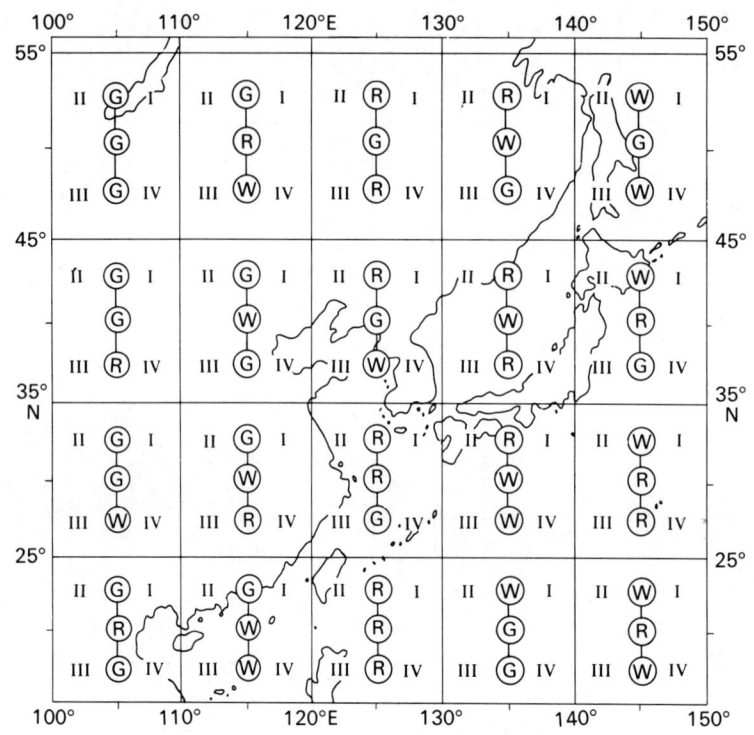

The letters W,R,G, denote White, Red and Green respectively.

Chartlet II

Table D – Sub-Division Light

White	Red	Green	No Light
Quadrant I	Quadrant II	Quadrant III	Quadrant IV

Table E – Direction of Motion Lights

Green over White	White over Red	White over White	Red over Red	Red over Green	Red over White	Green over Green	White over Green
N	NE	E	SE	S	SW	W	NW

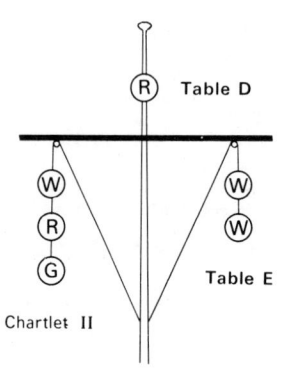

R Table D

W W
R W
G

Table E

Chartlet II

The signal reads: A typhoon or cyclone in the district bounded by the parallels of latitude 40° and 45°N, and the meridians of longitude 140° and 145°E is moving E.

Example

(1.43) Diagram 2.

LOCAL STORM SIGNALS

By Day		At Night	
Signal	Forecast	Signal	Forecast
Windforce		Ⓦ	Force 8-11 from any direction
	Force 6-7	Ⓡ	
	Force 8-11	Ⓡ	Force 8-11 from NW quadrant
	Force 12 and above	Ⓦ Ⓦ	Force 8-11 from SW quadrant
Wind direction			
	From NW quadrant	Ⓡ Ⓦ	Force 8-11 from NE quadrant
	From SW quadrant		
	From NE quadrant	Ⓦ Ⓡ	Force 8-11 from SE quadrant
	From SE quadrant	Ⓡ	Force 12 and above from any direction
Change in wind direction			
	Wind will veer		**Key**
	Wind will back		Ⓦ White light
			Ⓡ Red light

SPECIAL WEATHER SIGNALS

By Day	At Night	Significance	
Red drogue	Ⓡ Ⓡ	Strong winds	
Blue drogue	Ⓑ Ⓑ	Heavy rain	
Green drogue	Ⓖ Ⓖ	Heavy snow	Abnormal conditions likely to cause damage
Red and blue drogue	Ⓡ Ⓑ	Wind and rainstorms	
Red and green drogue	Ⓡ Ⓖ	Wind and snowstorms	
Red cylinder	Ⓡ Ⓡ Ⓡ	Rainstorms or snowstorms	Likely to cause excessive damage
Blue cylinder	Ⓑ Ⓑ Ⓑ	Heavy rainstorms or heavy snowstorms	

Key

Ⓡ Red light
Ⓑ Blue light
Ⓖ Green light

(1.44, 1.45) Diagram 3.

WEATHER FORECAST SIGNALS

Day Signals

Wind

Triangular Flag	Wind direction
White	N
White above green horizontally	NE
Green	E
Red above green horizontally	SE
Red	S
Red above blue horizontally	SW
Blue	W
White above red horizontally	NW

Weather

Square Flag	Weather
White	Fair
Red	Cloudy
Blue	Rain
Green	Snow
White above red horizontally	Clear, occasional cloud
White above blue horizontally	Clear, occasional rain
White above green horizontally	Clear, occasional snow
Red above white horizontally	Cloud, occasionally clear
Red above blue horizontally	Cloud, occasional rain
Red above green horizontally	Cloud, occasional snow
Blue above green diagonally	Rain or snow
White above green and blue horizontally	Clear, occasional rain or snow
Red above green and blue horizontally	Cloud, occasional rain or snow
Blue and green quarters	Fog

Temperature Change

Long Triangular Flag	Temperature Change
White	Becoming colder or cooler
Red	Becoming hotter or warmer

Night Signals

Lights	Significance	Lights	Significance
(W)	Clear weather	(Or) (G)	Cloudy, snow later
(Or)	Cloudy		
(B)	Rain	(B) (W)	Rain, clear later
(G)	Snow		
(W) (Or)	Clear, cloudy later	(B) (Or)	Rain, cloudy later
(W) (B)	Clear, rain later	(B) (G)	Rain, snow later
(W) (G)	Clear, snow later	(G) (W)	Snow, clear later
(Or) (W)	Cloudy, clear later	(G) (Or)	Snow, cloudy later
(Or) (B)	Cloudy, rain later	(G) (B)	Snow, rain later

Key

(W)	White light
(Or)	Orange light
(B)	Blue light
(G)	Green light

(1.46)　Diagram 4.

Special signals
1.48
Special flags. The following special flags are flown in Japanese Waters:

Maritime Safety Agency flag. A blue square flag with the white MSA emblem (compass star) in its centre. Flown by all MSA craft.

Department of Railways flag. White with two red horizontal bands connected by a vertical red stripe, the upper horizontal band is shorter than the lower, and neither band extends the whole length of the flag.

Customs flag. Square, white and blue diagonal, with a red circle in the centre.

Designation flag. Square red with two white squares, one in the middle of the upper edge and one in the middle of the lower edge. When displayed above an International Code Flag and/or Numeral Pendant, at a port signal station, indicates an anchor berth or mooring.

Berthing flag. Yellow and red swallow tailed. When displayed above an International Code Flag and/or Numeral Pendant at a port signal station, indicates an alongside berth.

Leaving flag. Red and yellow triangular.

1.49
Submarines of the Japanese Self Defence Force, when on the surface in traffic congested areas, exhibit an all round orange quick flashing light showing 90 flashes every minute, in addition and above the lights required by Rule 23 of the *Rules for Preventing Collisions at Sea.*

Details of shapes and lights required to be shown by certain vessels under the Maritime Traffic Safety Law are given at 1.30.

MARITIME SAFETY AGENCY AND RESCUE SERVICES

1.50
The **Maritime Safety Agency (MSA)** is responsible for all aspects of maritime control, administration and safety in Japanese waters which include the following:

(a) Enforcement of Japanese maritime laws and regulations
(b) Safe navigation
(c) Traffic control
(d) Search and rescue services
(e) Prevention of pollution
(f) Hydrographic services
(g) Fishery protection
(h) Law enforcement

Japan is divided into eleven maritime safety regions with a MSA Headquarters in Tōkyō; each of the regions has a Regional Maritime Safety Headquarters (RMSHQ) and there are Maritime Safety Offices (MSO) at many of the Japanese ports.

In the area covered by this volume, regional headquarters are located as follows:

RMSHQ	Place	Address	Telephone
5th	Kōbe	1-chome Kaigan-dori Ikuta Ku Kōbe	078-391-6551
6th	Hiroshima	3-10 Ujina-Kaigan Hiroshima-shi	0822-51-5111
7th	Moji	Nishi Kaigan-dori Moji Ku Kita-Kyūshū-shi	093-321-2931

The MSA operate numerous patrol vessels, survey vessels, tenders and aircraft.

1.51
Rescue. In Japanese waters, rescue services are a responsibility of the MSA, and ocean-going vessels should make contact with the nearest MSA coast radio station if the need arises. See *Admiralty List of Radio Signals Volume 1.*

The **Japanese Lifeboat Society** is mainly responsible for the rescue of life from small craft in local areas, and a list of their stations is published in the *Manual of Japanese Port and Harbour Regulations.* A wide range of life-saving equipment is kept at numerous other stations.

COUNTRY AND PORT INFORMATION

1.52

General information. Japan, Nippon or **Nihon** in Japanese, consists of the four principal islands of Hokkaidō, Honshū, Shikoku, and Kyūshū; over 3000 small adjacent islands and islets; and the Ryūkyū Islands or Nansei Shotō, including Okinawa and more than 200 other smaller islands. The total land area is 143 818 square miles with a population of about 116 million in 1979.

Tōkyō, the capital of Japan which in 1979 had a population of about 8·5 million, is situated in the SE part of Honshū.

Japan is described in three volumes of the Sailing Directions as follows:

Japan Pilot Volume I. NW, N and E coasts of Honshū and the coasts of Hokkaidō and adjacent islands.

Japan Pilot Volume II. SE coast of Honshū, the E, W and NW coasts of Kyūshū, the S coast of Shikoku, Nanpō Shotō, Nansei Shotō and Tsushima.

Japan Pilot Volume III. Seto Naikai or Inland Sea.

1.53

History. According to Japanese tradition Jimmu, the first emperor of Japan, ascended the throne in 660 BC. The dynasty founded by him still reigns and the monarchy is hereditary in the male heirs of the Imperial house. The history of the following centuries was one of inter-clan struggle until in the 12th Century Yoritomo made his family supreme and assumed the title of Shogun, Warlord. For the next 700 years Japan was ruled by military dictators. In the 17th Century, Portuguese traders and missionaries settled in Japan but subsequently the country adopted a policy of complete seclusion. In 1854, Commodore Perry, an American naval officer, forced the opening of foreign trade which marked the end of Japan's seclusion.

In 1867, the Shogunate was suppressed, an Emperor restored and a policy of expansion was followed. Formosa (now Taiwan) was acquired in 1894, Korea incorporated into the Japanese Empire in 1910, and in 1931, a long aggression against China was begun. Events of World War II in 1941, led to a decision by Japan to eliminate European and American power in the W Pacific; after a sweeping initial success against American, British and Dutch forces, Japan occupied the whole of SE Asia, the Eastern Archipelago and many of the Pacific Islands. From 1944 to 1945, allied forces gradually defeated the Japanese at sea and in the occupied territories, and in 1945 they surrendered in the face of overwhelming superiority in the air. Formosa was returned to the Chinese and Korea to the Koreans.

After a United States military occupation, Japan regained its independence in 1952 and a new Constitution was drawn up. In 1971, Japan signed an agreement with the United States ending the post war occupational rule by the US Forces of the Ryūkyū Islands.

1.54

Government. Japan has a parliamentary system of government with a popularly elected bicameral legislature known as the National Diet. The symbol of the state is the Emperor who performs only ceremonial functions. Executive authority resides in the Cabinet headed by the Prime Minister who is elected from the majority party in the National Diet. In 1978, the majority party was the Liberal Democratic Party which had been in power continuously from 1955.

Japan has a ground, maritime and air self-defence force of about 260 000 officers and men.

Language. The national language is Japanese which is used and understood by all including minority ethnic groups.

1.55

Physical features. The four main islands of Japan are mountainous; the greatest elevation being attained in the Japanese Alps, situated in the central part of Honshū, where Fuji San rises to 3775 m (12 386 ft).

The Japanese islands lie in a zone of extreme crustal instability in which constant re-adjustment appears to be occuring. There are numerous volcanic zones that include over 150 major volcanoes and thousands of hot springs. The islands experience numerous earthquakes and there are over 1500 quakes annually. Heavy quakes occur every few years and they usually result in considerable destruction and loss of life.

Owing to the mountainous nature of Japan, not more than 16 per cent of its area is available for cultivation; the soil is only moderately fertile but intensive cultivation produces good crops.

The rivers of Japan are comparatively short, and their flow is rapid; none is navigable by large ocean-going vessels. There are numerous lakes at various elevations, but most of them are small.

As might be expected from the mountainous nature of the country, large plains are few, but there are a number of small alluvial plains; the valleys of the larger rivers are especially fertile.

1.56

Flora and fauna. About 65 per cent of Japan's total area is covered with forests containing trees of many species which are typical of cool temperate climates; the coniferous pine and the Japanese cedar grow profusely throughout the country. Several of the species have industrial uses such as camphor, wax and lacquer trees. Bamboos, which grow in small groves, are also of commercial value.

Tropical species of trees and undergrowth grow on the S coasts of Kyūshū and Shikoku, and the islands to the S. Bananas and sugar canes are grown as food crops in these areas.

The flora of Japan is marked by a variety of species, different seasons presenting different colours with a change of foliage.

Animals generally are similar to those normally found in similar latitudes in other parts of the world; bears are to be found in Hokkaidō and the monkey is seen in deep forests or on mountains.

The seas around Japan abound with fish, commercially important of which are salmon, trout, tuna and herring. Whales, sea lions and seals are to be found and there are a great variety of molluscs and crustaceans.

Areas of outstanding natural beauty typical of Japanese scenery have been designated as **National Parks**; they occupy about 5 per cent of the entire area of Japan. **Marine Parks** have also been established to preserve the beautiful seascapes and marine life.

Game laws have been enacted in Japan, The hunting of seals and sea otters N of latitude 30° N is prohibited.

1.57

Mineral resources. The country has mineral resources including gold, silver, copper, lead zinc, iron, tungsten, manganese, chromite, coal and molybdenum.

Petroleum, iron ore and coal are among the principal imports to supplement deficiencies at home.

1.58

Trade and industry. Japan is one of the most highly industrialized nations in the world, with the full range of modern light and heavy industries which produce the entire spectrum of durable and non-durable goods for both producers and customers.

The chief imports consist of raw materials, foodstuffs, petroleum and chemicals.

The chief exports consist of ships, motor vehicles and motor cycles, synthetic textiles, canned fish and a wide variety of manufactured goods including radio equipment, cameras and watches.

1.59

Currency, weights and measures. The unit of currency in Japan is the *yen*. The *sen* is the hundredth part of a yen but is not in circulation.

The metric system of weights and measures is in force.

1.60

National holidays. The Japanese nation observes the following twelve national holidays (if a holiday falls on a Sunday, the following day is treated as a holiday).

1st January. . . . . New Year's Day
15th January . . . . Adults Day
11th February . . . . National Foundation Day
20th or 21st March . . . . Vernal Equinox Day
29th April. . . . . Emperor's Birthday
3rd May . . . . Constitution Memorial Day
5th May . . . . Children's Day
15th September . . . . Respect for the Aged Day

23rd or 24th September . . . Autumnal Equinox Day
10th October . . . . Sports Day
3rd November . . . . Culture Day
23rd November . . . . Labour Thanksgiving Day

1.61

Transport and communications. Japan has direct connections by regular air services between Tōkyō and the principal cities of the world. There are regular passenger services by sea from Australia, Asia and the South Pacific.

A regular domestic air service connects Tōkyō with the principal cities of Japan.

Japanese National Railways (JNR) maintains a rail network which covers the whole country; in addition JNR operates bus services over routes throughout Japan, and also a ferry service connecting the main island of Honshū with the other islands.

Shinkansen, the "new trunk rail line", is the nationwide, high-speed train service operated by the JNR.

There is a highly developed telecommunication system in Japan.

TERRITORIAL WATERS AND FISHING LIMITS

1.62

Seto Naikai is Japanese internal waters.

See also *Annual Summary of Admiralty Notices to Mariners.*

Port, Harbour or Anchorage	In Fairway	In Anchorage (i) Quarantine (ii) Outer (iii) Inner	Alongside Wharves	Remarks
†Aioi Kō (10.41) (34° 46' N, 134° 28' E)	8 m–10 m	(iii) 6 m–8 m	6 m–7 m	Shipbuilding Industrial port Sheltered anchorage
†Amagasaki Kō (12.53) (34° 41' N, 135° 23' E)	12 m	—	10 m–12 m	Industrial port
*Fukuyama Kō (8.43) (34° 26' N, 133° 27' E)	16 m	(i) 15 m–16 m	Up to 18 m	Industrial port
†Habu Kō (1.60) (34°17' N, 133°11' E)	10 m	—	4 m–10 m	Shipbuilding Industrial port
*Hannan Kō (12.15) (34° 28' N, 135° 21' E)	11 m–14 m	(i) 11 m–12 m	Up to 12.5 m	Commercial port
*Higashi-Harima Kō (10.65) (34° 43' N, 134° 50' E)	17 m	—	Up to 17 m	Industrial port
*Himeji Kō (10.54) (34° 46' N, 134° 38' E)				Industrial port divided into 5 separate harbours
Higashi Ku	14 m	—	14 m	
Shikama Ku	12 m	—	10 m–12 m	
Hirohata Ku	17 m	—	10 m–13·5 m	
Aboshi Ku	5 m	—	3 m–5 m	
Nishi Ku	10 m	—	10 m	
†Hirao Kō (3.35) (33° 54' N, 132° 03' E)	—	(ii) 7 m–13 m (iii) 5 m–9 m	4 m	Timber harbour Sheltered anchorage
*Hiroshima Kō (6.43) (34° 20' N, 132° 27' E)	8 m–17 m	(i) 16 m–17 m (ii) 16 m–18 m	9 m–9·5 m	Industrial and commercial port Sheltered anchorage
*Imabari Kō (7.17) (34° 04' N, 133° 01' E)	—	(ii) 10 m–20 m	8·5 m	Commercial port and tourist harbour
*Iwakuni Kō (6.29) (34° 10' N, 132° 15' E)	—	(i) 25 m (ii) 10 m–15 m	Oil Jetty—17 m 10 m–11 m	Industrial and commercial port Sheltered anchorage in NW winds
†Kanda Kō (3.47) (33° 48' N, 131° 01' E)	8 m–10 m	—	10 m	Coal shipment port Industrial harbour
*Kanmon Kō (2.26) (33° 54' N, 130° 55' E)	—	(i) (W) 10 m–28 m (E) 13·4 m	—	Major port complex on either side of Kanmon Kaikyō and comprises 5 separate ports Centre of large industrial zone
Kokura Ku (2.41)	12 m/8 m–10 m	(iii) Under 10 m	Up to 12 m	
Moji Ku (2.49)	—	(iii) 9 m–10 m	Up to 10·5 m	
Shimonoseki Ku (2.46)	—	—	Up to 9·5 m	
Tanoura Ku (2.55)	—	(iii) 10 m	10 m–12 m	
Wakamatsu Ku (2.30)	17 m/8 m–10 m	(iii) 10 m	Up to 12 m	
*Kōbe Kō (12.59) (34° 40' N, 135° 13' E)	4 Fairways— about 14 m	(i) 13 m–15 m (ii) 14 m	Sea-berth—12 m Up to 12 m	Large international trading port Sheltered anchorages

PRINCIPAL PORTS AND ANCHORAGES—*continued*

| Port, Harbour or Anchorage | Depths below Chart Datum | | | Remarks |
	In Fairway	*In Anchorage* (i) Quarantine (ii) Outer (iii) Inner	*Alongside* *Wharves*	
*Komatsushima Kō (11.16) (34° 00' N, 134° 36' E)	5 m–10 m	(ii) 7 m–8 m (iii) 6 m	8·5 m–10 m	Main linking port between E coast of Shikoku and Honshū
*Kure Kō (6.57) (34° 14' N, 132° 33' E)	Deep	(i) 21 m	8 m–14 m	Industrial port Shipbuilding and steelworks Sheltered anchorage Defence base
†Marugame Kō (9.26) (34° 18' N, 133° 47' E)	East—7·5 m West—10 m	—	7·5 m–10 m	Industrial port Ferry port
*Matsuyama Kō (5.28) (33° 51' N, 132° 42' E)	From N—50m	(i) 18 m–30 m	Oil Jetty—12·5m	Industrial port and tourist harbour
†Mishima-Kawanoe Kō (8.19) (34° 00' N, 133° 33' E)	9 m–15 m	(i) 15 m	14 m–15 m	Industrial port comprising harbours of Mishima and Kawanoe
†Mitajiri—Nakanoseki Kō (3.14) (34° 01' N, 131° 35' E)	7 m	—	4 m–7 m	Small industrial port comprising harbours of Mitajiri and Nakanoseki
*Mizushima Kō (9.43) (34° 30' N, 133° 45' E)	15·4 m	(i) 16 m–20 m	Oil Jetty—17 m Up to 10 m	Commercial and industrial port
*Niihama Kō (8.11) (33° 59' N, 133° 17' E)	7·4 m	(i) 12 m–15 m (ii) 5 m–20 m	9 m–14 m	Industrial port
*Ōita Kō (5.9) (33° 16' N, 131° 59' E)	—	(i) 43 m (ii) 35 m–53 m	Sea berth—30 m Up to 7 m	Industrial port New development in 1980
*Onomichi-Itozaki Kō (7.31) (34° 23' N, 133° 09' E)	—	(iii) 21 m–23 m	8 m–10 m	Industrial port Shipyards
*Ōsaka Kō (12.23) (34° 39' N, 135° 24' E) Ōsaka Ku (12.36) Sakai-Semboku Ku (12.28)	— 10 m 14 m/16 m	(i) 11 m–12 m — —	Oil Jetty—21 m Up to 12 m Up to 17 m	Large international trading port comprising the harbours of Ōsaka and Sakai
†Saganoseki Kō (5.7) (33° 15' N, 131° 52' E)	—	(i) 21 m–23 m	9 m–10 m	Small industrial harbour
†Saiki Kō (4.10) (32° 58' N, 131° 55' E)	—	(i) 20 m	8 m	Small industrial harbour Sheltered anchorage
*Sakaide Kō (9.28) (34° 20' N, 133° 51' E)	—	(i) 9 m–17 m	Sea berth—19·5 m 9 m–13 m	Commercial harbour
†Tachibana Kō (11.8) (33° 52' N, 134° 40' E)	—	(iii) 10·5 m	10·5 m–11 m	Small industrial harbour Sheltered anchorage
*Takamatsu Kō (9.57) (34° 21' N, 134° 03' E)	7 m–10 m	—	Up to 10 m	Rail and car ferry terminal linking N coast of Shikoku to Honshū
†Takehara Kō (6.83) (34° 19' N, 132° 55' E)	—	(ii) 15 m–22 m	7·5 m	Timber port. Ferry port

PRINCIPAL PORTS AND ANCHORAGES—continued

Port, Harbour or Anchorage	Depths below Chart Datum			Remarks
	In Fairway	*In Anchorage* (i) *Quarantine* (ii) *Outer* (iii) *Inner*	*Alongside* *Wharves*	
†Takuma Kō (9.22) (34° 15′ N, 133° 40′ E)	5·5 m	—	5·5 m–7·5 m	Timber and industrial harbour
*Tokuyama-Kudamatsu Kō (3.16) (34° 00′ N, 131° 48′ E)	Deep	(i) 10·5 m–11 m and 24 m	Oil Jetty—20 m 9 m–12 m	Industrial port comprising the harbours of Tokuyama and Kudamatsu
†Tsukumi Kō (4.14) (33° 05′ N, 131° 52′ E)	—	(iii) 10 m–19 m	15·5 m–18·5 m	Largest trading port in E Kyūshū. Sheltered anchorage
*Ube Kō (3.6) (33° 56′ N, 131° 14′ E)	Main fairway —9 m	(i) 8 m–9 m	Up to 10·5 m	Industrial port
*Uno Kō (9.76) (34° 29′ N, 133° 57′ E)	—	—	8 m–9·5 m	Rail ferry terminal linking S coast of Honshū to Shikoku. Shipbuilding
†Uwajima Kō (4.33) (33° 13′ N, 132° 33′ E)	Deep	(ii) 13 m	4 m–6 m	Timber harbour. Sheltered anchorage
*Wakayama-Shimotsu Kō (11.37) (34° 12′ N, 135° 08′ E)	—	(i) 21 m–26 m	—	A mainly industrial port comprising 4 harbours. Oil terminal in Shimotsu Ku
Arida Ku (11.40)	—	—	4 m–6 m	
Kainan Ku (11.49)	12 m	(ii) 5 m–20 m	Up to 13 m	
Shimotsu Ku (11.44)	12 m–16 m	(ii) 10 m–15 m	Oil Jetty—20 m	
Wakayamu Ku (11.51)	14 m–15 m	—	12 m–14 m	
†Yamaguchi Kō (3.10) (33° 59′ N, 131° 23′ E)	—	(iii) 5 m–7 m	—	Sheltered anchorage for small vessels

* indicates Specified Port
† indicates Open Harbour

Classification of Japanese ports
1.64
Specified ports. Specified ports in Japanese waters are defined as those suitable for deep-draught vessels and which are customarily used by foreign vessels.

Specified ports within the area covered by this volume are marked * in the list of Principal Ports and Anchorages (see 1.63).

All specified ports are subject to the Port Regulations Law (1.37).
1.65
Open harbours. Open harbours are established by Government ordinance and are harbours where foreign trade may be conducted.

Open harbours within the area covered by this volume are marked † in the list of Principal Ports and Anchorages (see 1.63). In addition, all specified ports within the area are classified as open harbours.

All open harbours are subject to the Customs Law (1.26).

1.66
Ports of entry and departure. All the ports listed at 1.63 are ports of entry and departure, with the exception of Takehara Kō. They have immigration facilities and are subject to the Immigration Control Law (1.26).
1.67
Harbours of Refuge. The following harbours in the area covered by this volume are considered to be refuge harbours in case of a typhoon:
- (a) *All classes of vessels*
  - Moji Ku (2.49)
  - Tokuyama-Kudamatsu Kō (3.16)
  - Kure Kō (6.57)
  - Kōbe Kō (12.59)
- (b) *Small vessels*
  - Uchinomi Kō (10.6)
  - Yura Kō (E side of Kii Suidō) (11.30)

The harbours listed in (b) are established by government decree with the principal object of providing sheltered anchorages for small vessels during typhoons;

they are not usually equipped for loading or discharge of ordinary cargoes, or for the embarkation or landing of passengers.

1.68

Japanese ports and harbours are further classified as follows; reference to these classifications is not made in this volume:

Principal ports. Ports, established by Government ordinance, which are concerned with national interests.

Local harbours. Harbours other than principal ports.

Fishing harbours. Harbours principally used by the fishing industry and which are designated as Types 1, 2, 3 and 4 Fishing harbours.

REPAIRS, FACILITIES AND SUPPLIES

Repairs

1.69

The principal underwater repair facilities available within the area covered by this volume are listed as follows. Only the largest dry dock in each port is mentioned; further details of these docks and other docks in the port concerned, are given in the appropriate part of this book.

Dry docks

Port	Length m	Width m	Depth m	Capacity grt
Aioi Kō (10.41)	340	56	8	150 000
Habu Kō (7.60)	282·5	46·5	8·8	79 000
Hashihama Wan (7.11)	127	18·9	4·8	6 200
Hiroshima Kō (6.43)	160	25	5·3	13 000
Imabari Kō (7.7)	161·5	25	5·5	10 000
Kōbe Kō (12.59)	301·5	43·7	9·5	85 000
Kure Kō (6.57)	331	43·9	12·8	91 000
Marugame Kō (9.26)	290	57	6·8	80 000
Mizushima Kō (9.43)	—	—	—	25 000
Onomichi-Itozaki Kō (7.31)	350	56	7·4	150 000
Ōsaka Ku (12.36)	193	25	8·1	24 000
Sakaide Kō (9.28)	450	72	9·2	270 000
Sakai-Semboku Ku (12.28)	400	55	6·5	90 000
Setoda Kō (7.52)	230	36	7·1	37 000
Shimonoseki Ku (2.46)	217	35	6·8	25 000
Tokuyama-Kudamastu Kō (3.16)	227	37	6·7	37 600
Uno Kō (9.76)	209	31·4	9·7	27 700
Yura Kō (11.30)	358	65	11.6	175 000

Facilities

1.70

De-ratting. In accordance with the International Health Regulations, de-ratting can be carried out, and Exemption Certificates issued, at the following ports:

Fukuyama	Niihama
Hannan	Ōita
Hiroshima	Ōsaka
Iwakuni	Saganoseki
Kanmon	Saiki
Kōbe	Sakaide
Kure	Tokuyama-Kadamatsu
Mishima-Kawanoe	Ube
Mizushima	Wakayama-Shimotsu

Exemption Certificates only, can be issued at Matsuyama.

1.71

Waste oil disposal facilities are available at the following Japanese ports in Seto Naikai:

Fukuyama	Kōbe	Sakaide
Habu	Matsuyama	Tokuyama-
Himeji	Mizushima	Kudamatsu
Hiroshima	Ōita	Tōyo
Iwakuni	Onoda	Ube
Kanmon	Onomichi-Itozaki	
Kikuma	Ōsaka	Wakayama-Shimotsu

1.72

Measured distances, the details of which are given at the paragraph references quoted, are established as follows:

Awaji Shima—E coast (12.8)
Ieshima Guntō—S side (10.53)
Itsuku Shima—SE side (6.35)
Mekko Hana (4.47)
Momo Shima—SW side (8.34)
Murasaki Hana (2.6)
Ōkado Hana (10.9)
Ō Kurokami Shima—W side (6.22)
Sada Misaki—7 miles NE (5.22)
Saiki Wan—N side (4.6)
Tsuda Wan (10.11)
Uwajima Wan (4.32)
Ya Shima/Heigun Shima (5.6)
Yuge Shima—E side (7.56)

1.73

Consular offices. There is a British Consul General at Ōsaka and a British Consul at Moji, Kita-Kyūshū.

Addresses	Telephone Nos
British Consulate-General	(06)231-3355/7
Hong Kong Bank Building	
45 Awajimachi 4-chrome	
Higashi Ku	
Osaka 541	
British Consulate	(093)331-1311/8
Holme Ringer & Co Ltd	
9–9 Minato-machi	
Moji Ku	
Kita-Kyūshū-shi 801	

Supplies

1.74

Fuel oil can be supplied at most major ports in Japan either by pipeline or barge. At some of these ports fuel may have to be lightered from the nearest fuel stock and up to 7 days notice may be required.

Details of the availability of fuel oil are given in the appropriate part of this book.

Fresh water can be supplied at most ports either at the berth or from water barge. Details are given in the appropriate part of this book.

NATURAL CONDITIONS

MARITIME TOPOGRAPHY

1.75

The Japanese islands and adjacent seas form part of the North West Pacific island and trench system. The continental shelf on the Pacific side of Japan is very narrow, being about 25 miles in width. Beyond the shelf is the continental slope, which is about 125 miles in width, and steepens abruptly at a depth of between 2000 m and 3000 m where it enters the Japan Trench (E of Japan) and the Sagami and Nankai Troughs (S of Japan). The Japan Trench trends in an almost N/S direction; it is about 560 miles long and 60 miles wide with a greatest depth of 8412 m.

1.76

Submarine earthquakes and tsunamis. Heavy submarine earthquakes occur in the West Pacific every few years. The majority of the epicentres of the more severe shocks are located beneath the deep trenches and give rise to **tsunamis** or **seismic sea-waves.**

Tsunamis occur on those coasts of Shikoku and Honshū which face the Pacific Ocean. In 1933, tsunamis originating with a major earthquake (magnitude 8·5 on the Richter scale) on the W slopes of the Japan Trench, raised mountainous waves, with surges up to 25 m high, along the shores of some of the Pacific facing bays and inlets of Japan. As recently as 1960, a seismic disturbance of exceptional severity off the coast of Chile generated a tsunami which created waves from 3 m to 6 m in height and caused much damage on the E coast of Honshū.

Submarine earthquakes with magnitudes over 8 have invariably been followed by tsunamis. Despite the enormous number of earthquakes of lesser magnitudes, very few of these have been associated with tsunamis. See also *The Mariner's Handbook.*

CURRENTS

1.77

Surface water movements in Seto Naikai are predominantly tidal.

The **Japan Current** or **Kuro Shio** flows NE, E of Kyūshū and S of Shikoku and Honshū, crossing the approaches to Bungo Suidō (32° 00' N, 132° 00' E) and Kii Suidō (33° 30' N, 135° 00' E), the two S entrances to Seto Naikai.

When the Japan Current is flowing normally, the weak tidal streams in Bungo Suidō are unaffected. In Kii Suidō the currents are weak; a NW flow predominates along its E shore, while a SW flow along its W shore in summer, changes to a NE flow in winter. The strength of these currents is less than ½ knot in winter increasing to ½ or ¾ knot in summer.

The occasional meandering of the Japan Current around large pools of cold surface water will lead to the formation of large semi-permanent eddies, lasting from two to nine years, in the area SE of Shiono Misaki (33° 26' N, 135° 45' E); (see Japan Pilot Volume II). On these occasions, a large anti-clockwise circulation develops which is liable to produce a strong W-going counter-current across and into the entrance to Kii Suidō. In summer, a small branch may also flow N from the main stream of the Japan Current into Bungo Suidō at a rate not exceeding ½ knot.

In the Sea of Japan, the **Tsushima Current** flows NE at a rate of ½ to 1 knot across the NW approaches to Kanmon Kaikyō (33° 55' N, 130° 55' E), the NW entrance to Seto Naikai. This can generate counter-currents and onshore sets, at times within the entrance of the strait.

Details of the currents off the coasts of Japan are given in Japan Pilot Volume I and Japan Pilot Volume II.

TIDES AND TIDAL STREAMS

1.78

In Seto Naikai, the tides and tidal streams depend principally on the passage of the tidal waves that enter by way of Bungo Suidō (33° 00' N, 132° 15' E) and Tomogashima Suidō (34° 17' N, 135° 00' E). The tidal stream sets N with the rising tide through these two entrances.

Tides. The tidal wave that passes through Bungo Suidō divides; one part progressing W across Suō Nada towards Kanmon Kaikyō, and the other progressing E across Iyo Nada, through the E part of Aki Nada, and into Hiuchi Nada and Bingo Nada; a branch enters Hiroshima Wan through Ōbatake Seto (33° 57' N, 132° 11' E) and Moroshima Suidō (33° 57' N, 132° 29' E). The tidal wave that passes through Tomogashima Suidō progresses through Ōsaka Wan and Akashi Kaikyō, across Harima Nada, and through Bisan Seto into Bingo Nada.

The diurnal inequalities in Seto Naikai are very remarkable; they are greater to the E of Bisan Seto than to the W of the strait, and are greatest of all near Akashi Kaikyō where single day tides occur on more than half the days of the month.

Tidal range. The range of the tide is greater in the W part of Seto Naikai than in the E part; the maximum range of about 4 m occurs in Bingo Nada.

1.79

Tidal streams. Throughout Seto Naikai, the tidal streams exhibit marked inequalities between those of the forenoon and those of the afternoon on any one day; for example, the W-going stream may attain a greater rate and continue for a longer period during the forenoon than during the afternoon of the same day. The greater the inequality of the tide, the greater is the inequality of the tidal stream; likewise the inequality of the tidal stream is greater E of Bisan Seto than W of the strait. It is, however, rarely so great that there are but one E-going and one W-going stream on any one day.

SEA AND SWELL

1.80

Sea and swell. Swell seldom causes any serious problems in the land-locked waters of Seto Naikai but unpleasant sea conditions develop in some areas exposed to strong NW to N winds funelling through gaps in the mountains. A prolonged spell of strong N winds will generate rough seas and some swell in the more exposed sea areas.

In the approaches to Bungo Suidō and Kii Suidō, rough seas are often experienced with strong S winds.

A confused sea, accentuated by tidal streams, may be encountered in the more tortuous channels.

Heavy seas and a confused swell will be encountered along the track of a typhoon or tropical revolving storm.

1.81

Sea temperature. The sea temperature is relatively high throughout the year due mainly to the influence of the Japan Current which flows along the S coasts of Japan.

The sea surface temperatures for February, May, August and November, based on ship observations, are shown on Diagrams 5 to 8. The temperatures in the land-locked waters of Seto Naikai are liable to vary considerably from the average, especially in mid-winter.

When the seasonal monsoons are particularly dominant or prolonged and there are long spells of hot or cold weather, abnormal sea temperatures of several degrees above or below the seasonal average occur, and they take a long time to return to normal.

CLIMATE AND WEATHER

1.82

The following paragraphs should be read in conjunction with the article on General Maritime Meteorology in *The Mariner's Handbook*.

Weather reports, forecasts and storm warnings are regularly broadcast on a regional basis; see *Admiralty List of Radio Signals*.

1.83

Seasonal aspects. The climate in Seto Naikai is largely controlled by the seasonal monsoons which blow in response to the fluctuation of pressure on the Asian Continent. The cold NW to N winds of winter are often fresh to strong and result in relatively low temperatures; snowfalls occur.

In contrast, the moist S winds of the summer months are usually light or moderate and are accompanied by average temperature for these latitudes.

Active depressions originating in S China, move E or NE across the area during the winter months bringing strong winds and rough weather, although gales are infrequent.

The average rainfall is considerable; most of the rain falls during the period from May to October with June and September being the wettest months.

The area is subject to typhoons (see 1.86). Fog is infrequent.

1.84

Pressure. The average distribution of pressure for January and July is shown in Diagrams 9 and 10. The seasonal pattern in winter is dominated by the large rise of pressure as the "Siberian High" reaches its maximum intensity over Mongolia by January; this gives a pronounced N gradient over the NW Pacific. The pressure gradient gradually weakens after February and becomes rather slack from late March to early May.

The collapse of the "Siberian High" is followed by the extension W of the Pacific anticyclone from late May onwards and brings a S to SE pressure gradient until September. From then onwards the "Siberian High" builds up again, and dominates the area over the winter months.

Monthly average pressure values range from about 1008 mb in mid-summer to about 1021 mb in mid-winter; day to day readings may, however, vary considerably from these values. Pressure as much as 20 mb above the average can occur when the pressure over Manchuria is particularly intense in winter, and falls of about 50 mb can accompany the more vigorous depressions.

The diurnal variation of pressure is about 2 mb with maxima at 1000 and 2200 local time and minima at 0400 and 1600.

1.85

Depressions. The extra-tropical depressions affecting this area have fairly active frontal systems. There are two main groups; those which originate in S China and move NE across Japanese waters, and those which move SE from Manchuria or Siberia then turn E or NE over or near the area, often deepening in the Seto Naikai region.

These depressions are usually associated with the polar front, the mean position of which is normally N of Japan in July and well to the S in January. As a consequence these depressions are most frequent from March to May (8 per month) and least frequent in July to September (2–3 per month). For actual tracks of some depressions see Diagram 11.

1.86

Typhoons. "Typhoon" is the name given to the most violent type of tropical revolving storms which affect the area. These storms are similar to the Bengal "cyclone" and the W Indian "hurricane".

Comprehensive information including precursory signs of tropical storms and the avoiding action to be taken, are given in *The Mariner's Handbook*.

Caution. Although warning of the position, intensity and expected movement of a typhoon is broadcast at frequent intervals, sometimes there is insufficient evidence for an accurate warning, or even a general warning, to be given and vessels must be guided by their own observations. The corrected barometer reading of 3 mb or more below the mean for that time of the year is a fairly reliable indication of the proximity of a storm.

In recent years weather satellites have resulted in considerable improvement in the guidance given in these warnings but on occasions the centres of the storms take such erratic tracks that prediction is very difficult.

Most tropical storms originate to E of the Philippines and then move NW to N towards China and Japan. The development zone is centred around 150°/170° E at about 5°/10° N in winter and moves NW some 10° of latitude and 20° of longitude by summer; in the second part of the year this zone retreats SE.

Many storm centres move NW initially, turning N and then recurving NE as they approach the coast of Japan. A few centres continue on a NW track towards Taiwan and the S China coast. Tracks of typhoons which have recently cross Seto Naikai are shown on Diagram 12.

The storms move rather slowly at first then gradually accelerate to about 15 knots before recurving. A speed of 20–30 knots is usual after recurving although speeds of 40 knots have been known.

A few typhoons or tropical storms cause severe damage and loss of life but many lose some of their violence before reaching Japanese waters. Even these modified storms give disturbed weather and strong winds.

The weakening storms, as they move N of about 30° N, can become linked to depressions further N and in these cases sometimes develop troughs of low pressure with frontal characteristics.

1.87

Frequency of typhoons. The frequency with which typhoons occur varies considerably from one year to another. A long term average gives about 12 per year, distributed as follows:

Aug, Sept, Oct   2 per month

Nov, Dec, Jan   ⎫
May, June, July ⎭ 1 per month

Feb, Mar, Apr   rare.

The frequency of typhoons recorded in the area

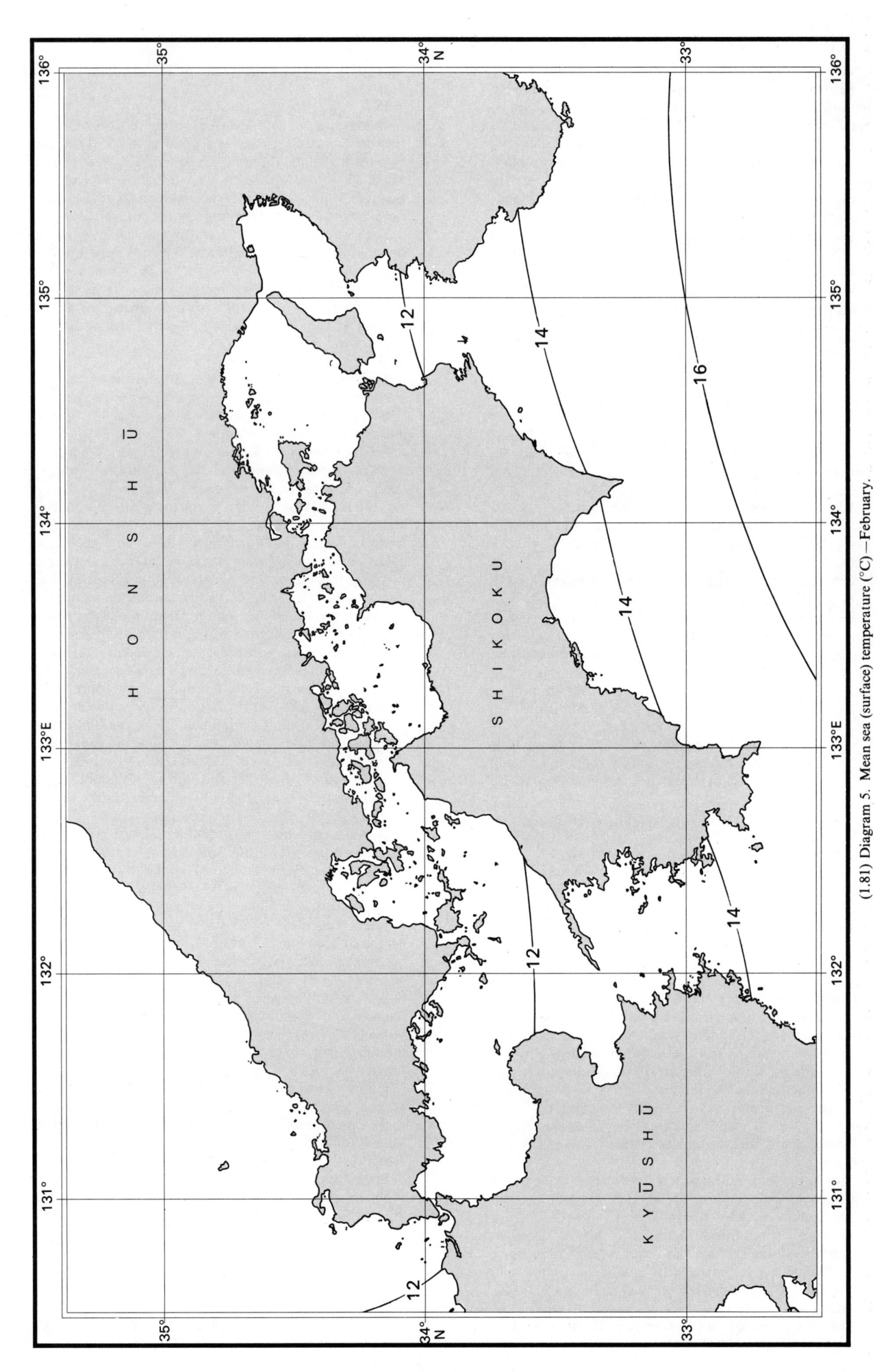

(1.81) Diagram 5. Mean sea (surface) temperature (°C)—February.

24

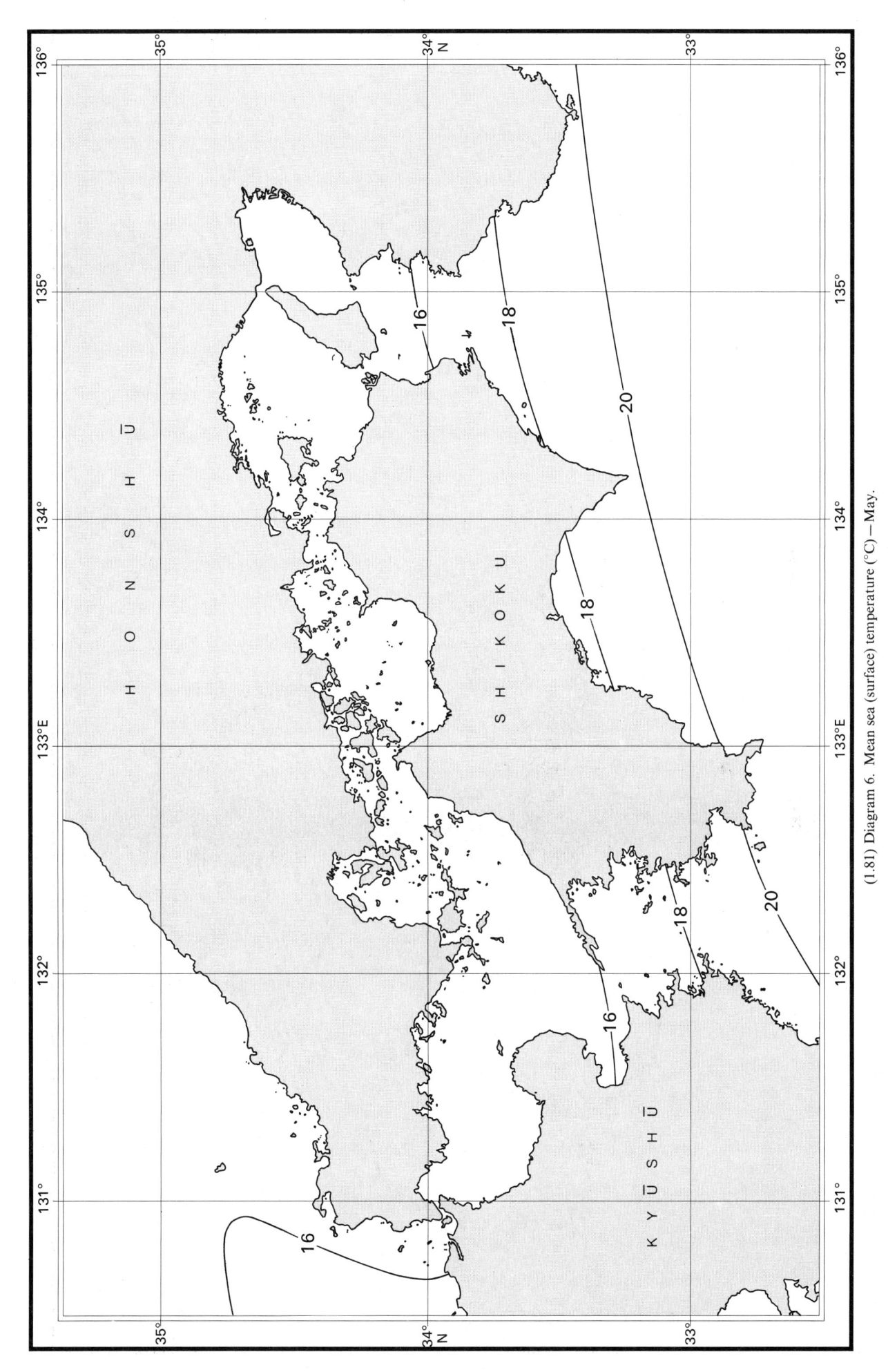

(1.81) Diagram 6. Mean sea (surface) temperature (°C) — May.

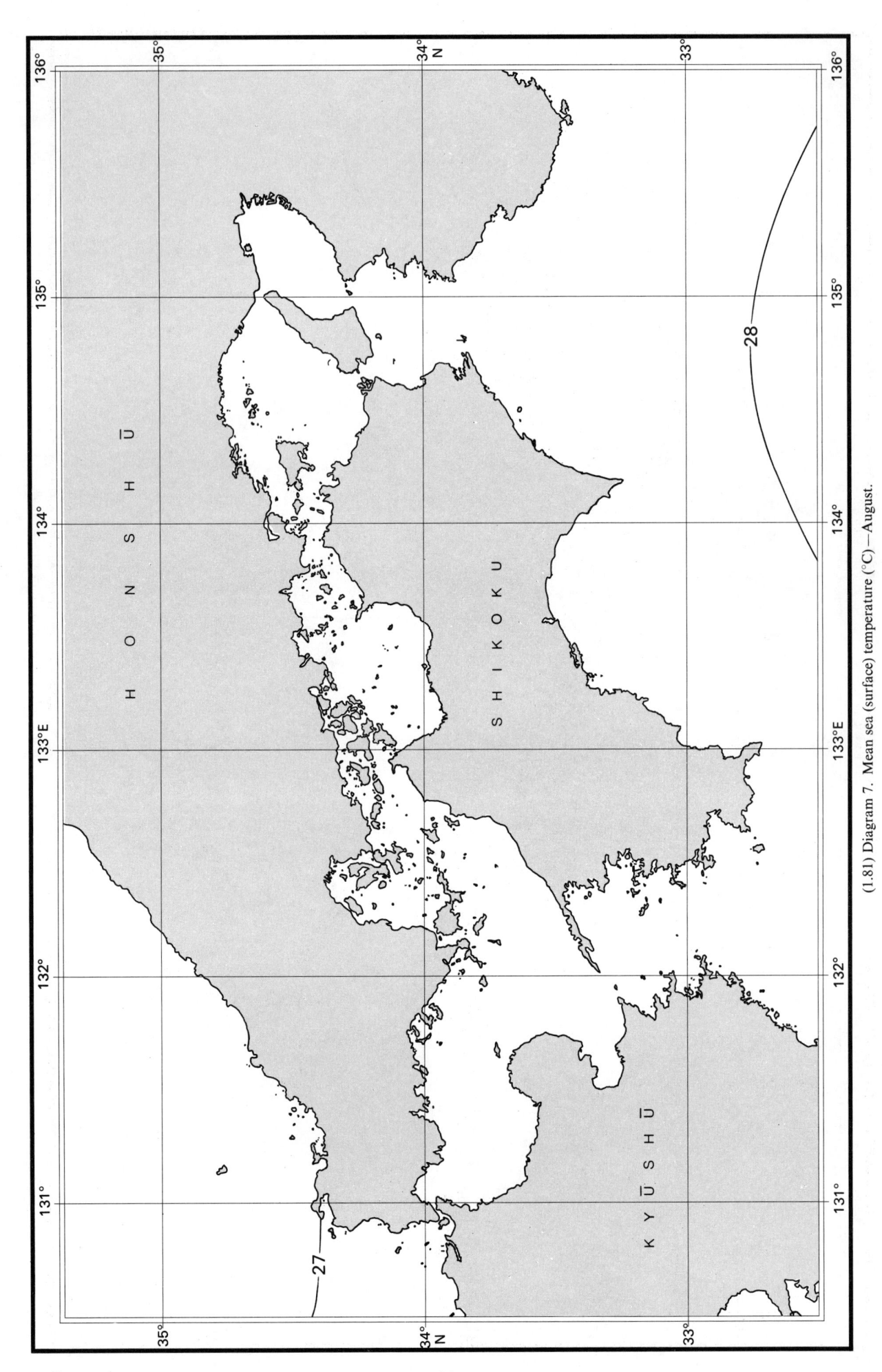

(1.81) Diagram 7. Mean sea (surface) temperature (°C)—August.

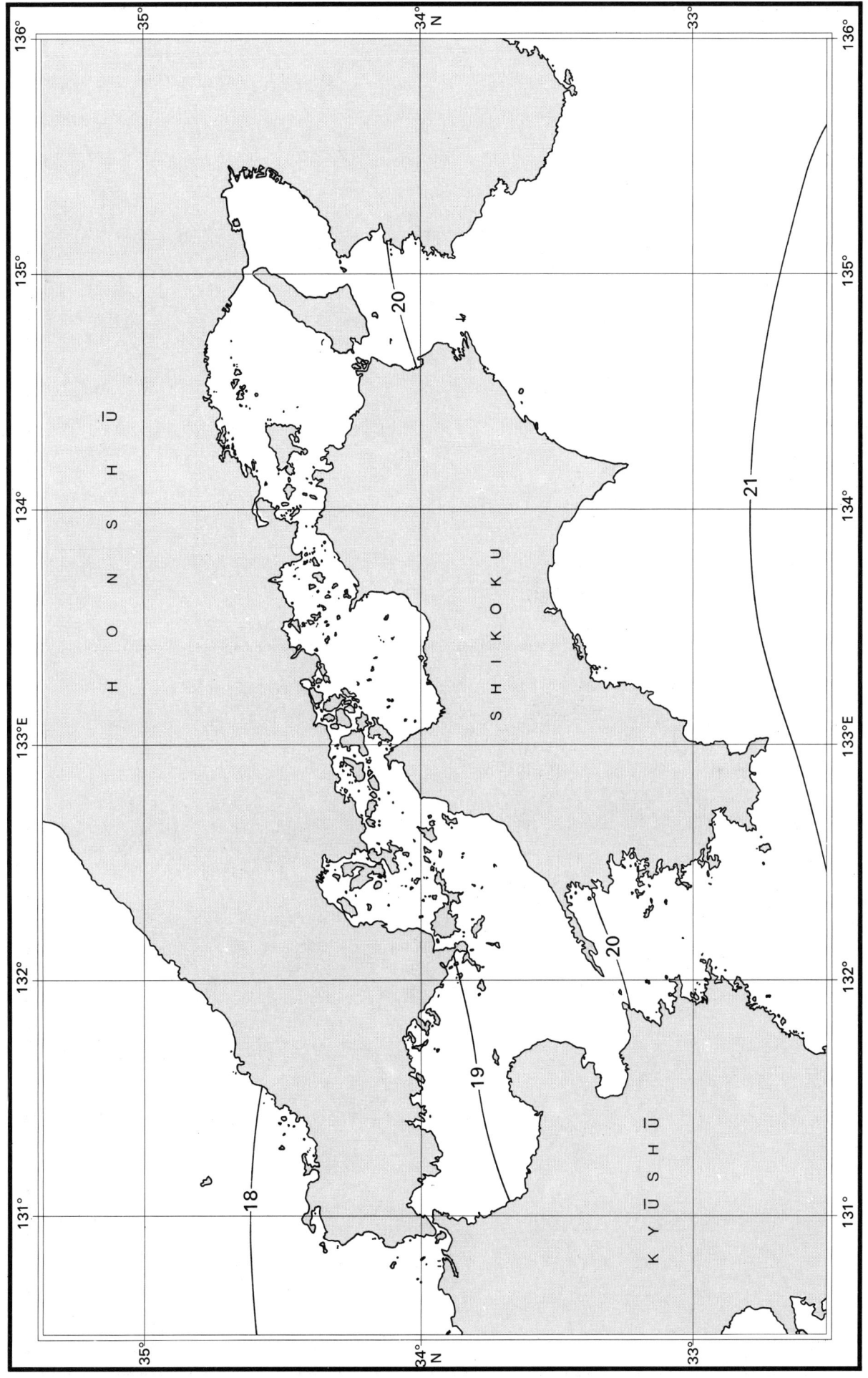

(1.81) Diagram 8. Mean sea (surface) temperature (°C) — November.

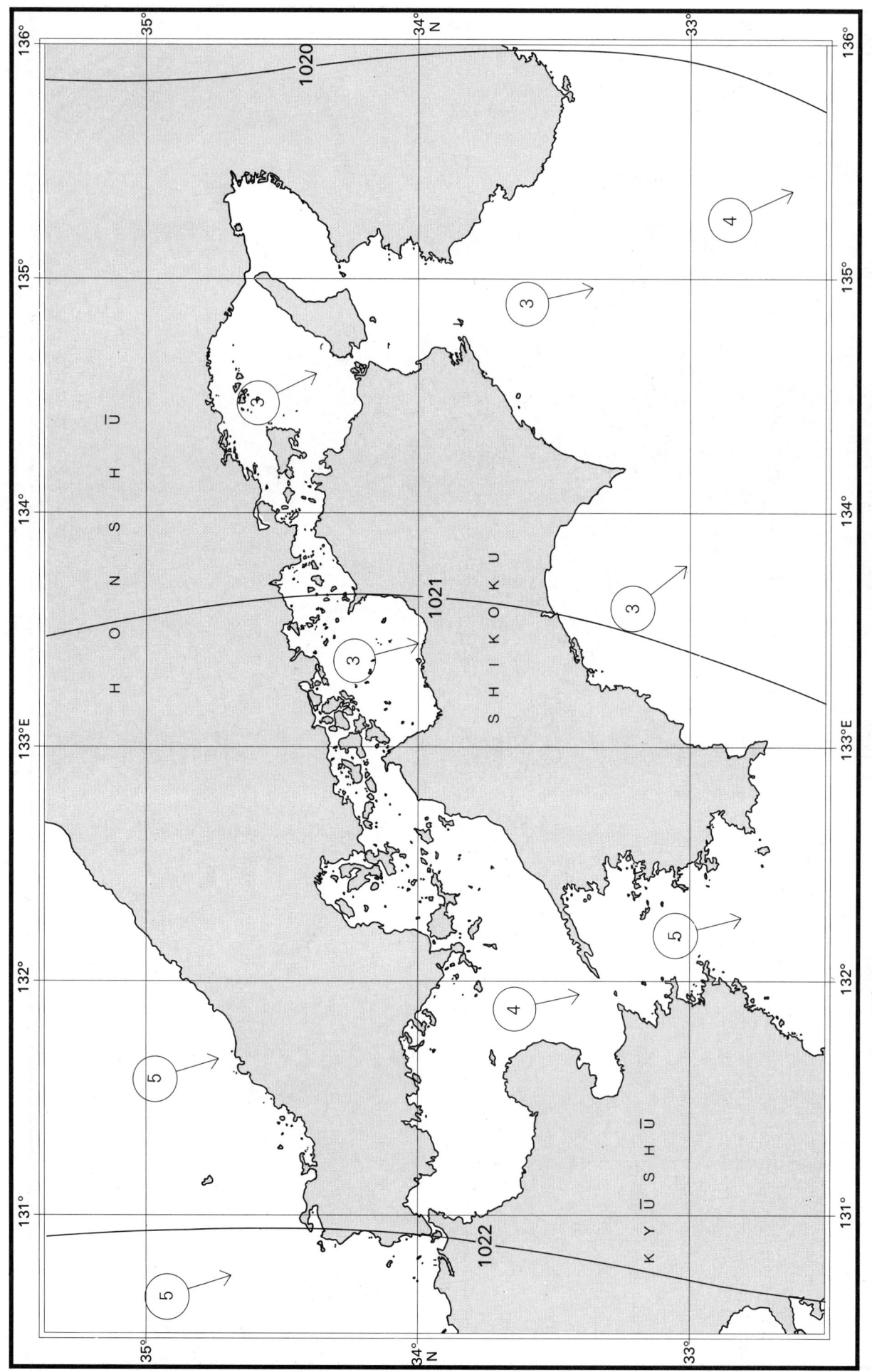

(1.84, 1.88) Diagram 9. Mean barometric pressure (mb) and dominant wind direction and force — January.

28

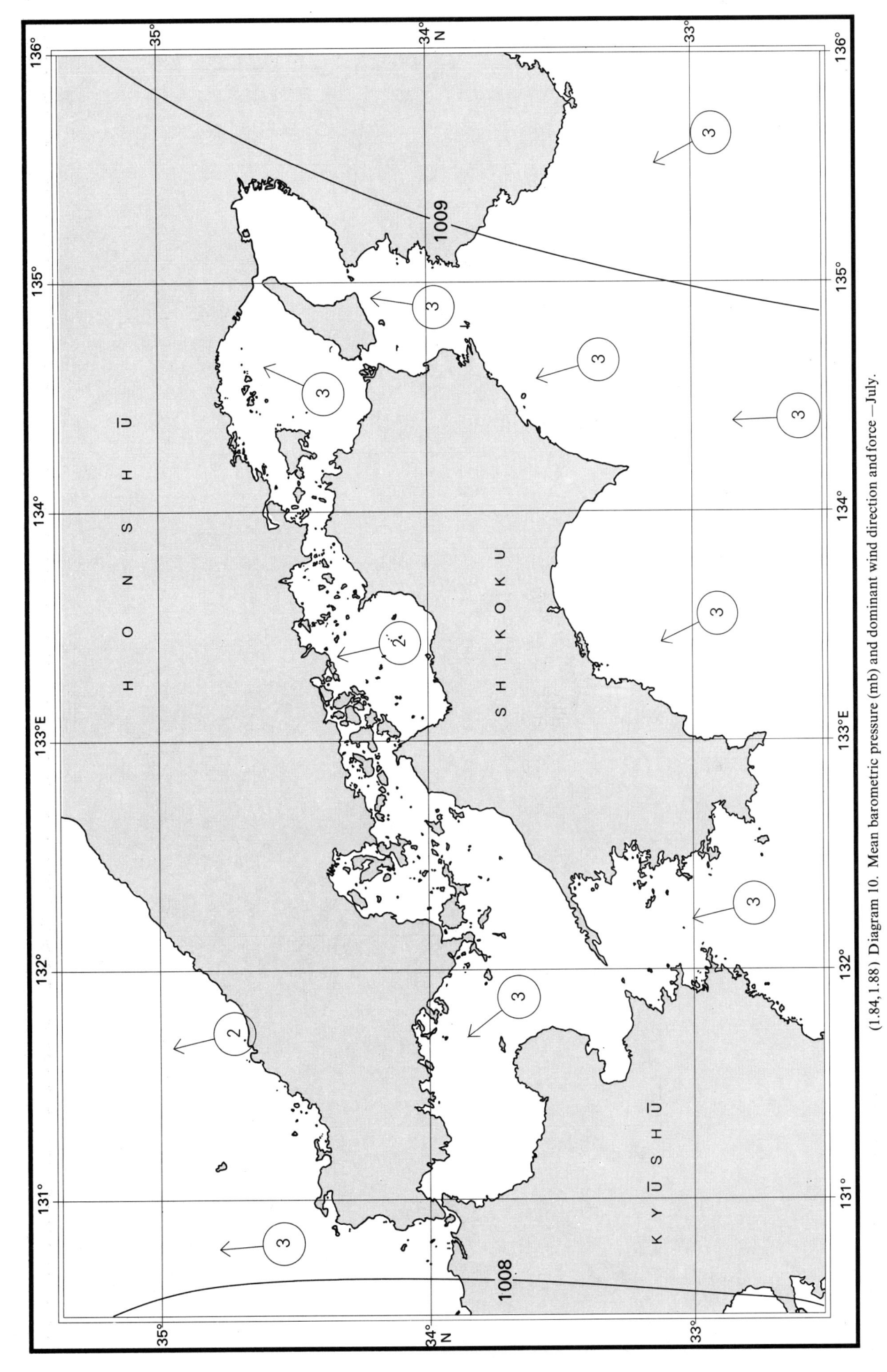

(1.84, 1.88) Diagram 10. Mean barometric pressure (mb) and dominant wind direction and force —July.

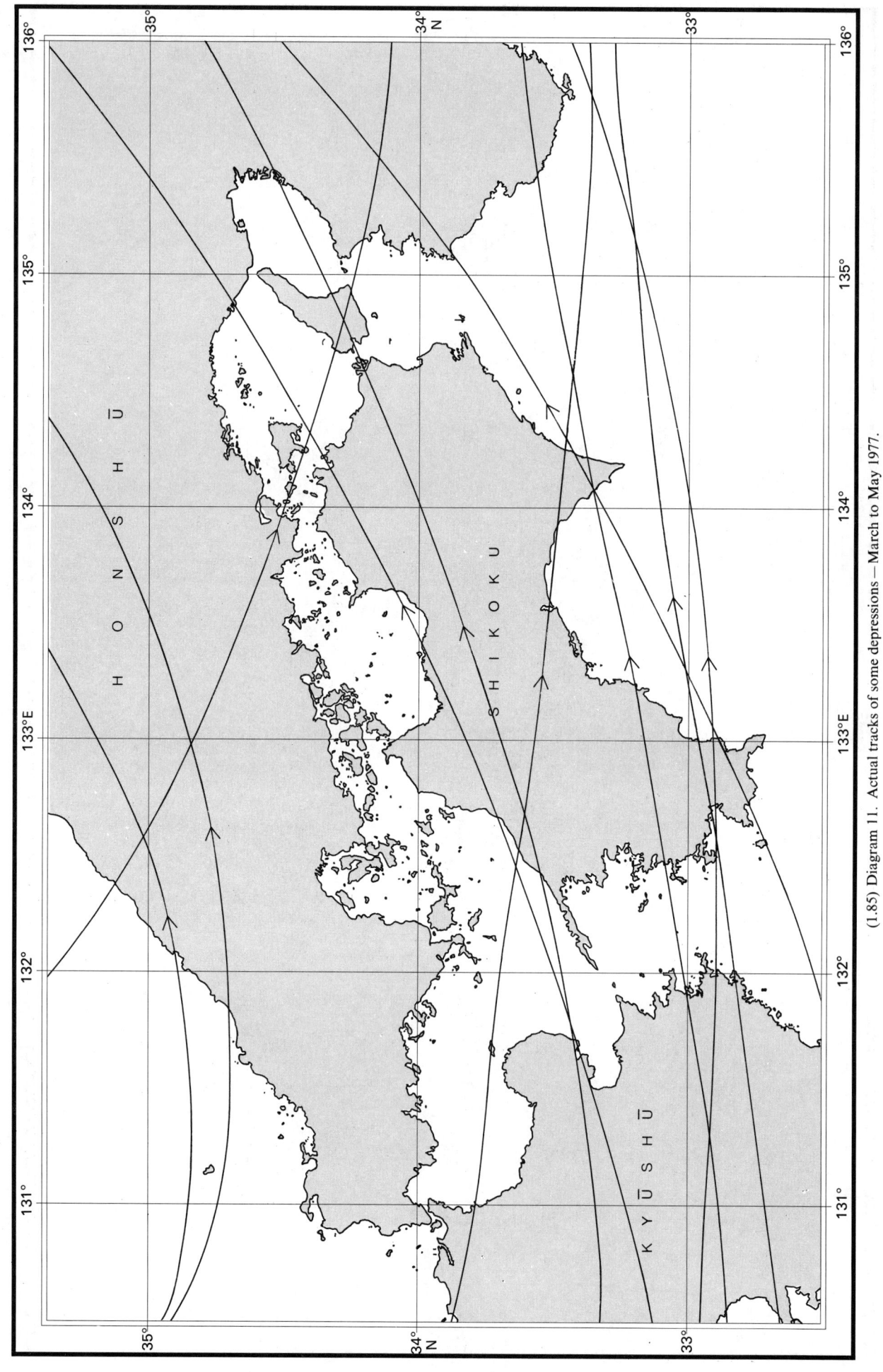

(1.85) Diagram 11. Actual tracks of some depressions — March to May 1977.

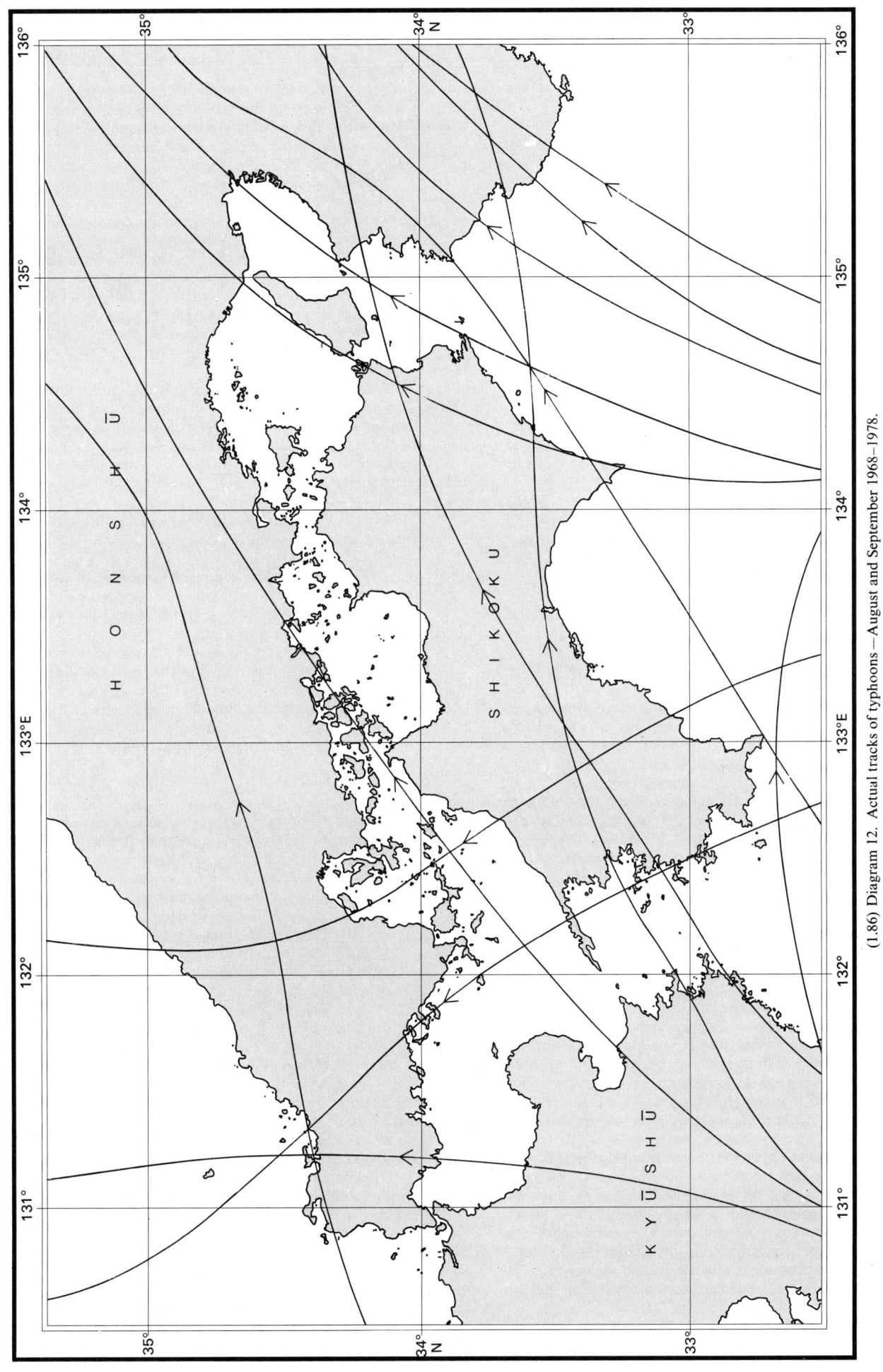

(1.86) Diagram 12. Actual tracks of typhoons—August and September 1968–1978.

covering the main islands of Japan (30°–45° N, 125°–150° E) and the two adjacent areas to the S, for the two periods 1968–1972 and 1973–1977, is as follows:

Area	30°–45° N 125°–150° E		20°–30° N 120°–130° E		20°–30° N 130°–150° E	
Period	1968–1972	1973–1977	1968–1972	1973–1977	1968–1972	1973–1977
Jan.	0	0	0	0	0	0
Feb.	0	0	1	0	0	1
Mar.	0	0	0	0	0	1
Apr.	0	0	1	0	2	1
May	1	1	2	2	3	4
June	0	0	1	2	1	1
July	7	9	7	9	9	9
Aug.	13	9	13	14	15	10
Sept.	9	8	9	6	14	8
Oct.	7	3	1	4	9	4
Nov.	2	3	2	3	6	4
Dec.	0	0	0	0	0	1
Total	39	33	37	40	59	44

It will be seen that over this recent decade there have been fewer typhoons than the long term averages. This decrease in activity and the corresponding decrease in fatalities was the subject of a special article published in a Japanese scientific journal in 1975.

1.88

Winds and gales. In Japanese waters the winter monsoon blows from about October to March. The direction is predominantly NW or N but there are frequent interruptions due to the movement of extra-tropical depressions across or near the area. The winds are relatively strong and reach gale force on occasions, usually in association with the passage of a depression.

In contrast, the summer monsoon, which blows in the months of June to August, is relatively weak and the direction is more variable although winds between SE and SW are somewhat more frequent. The winds are mostly light; strong winds are less frequent than in winter and gales are relatively infrequent.

When gales do occur in summer they are liable to be severe since most are associated with the presence of tropical storms or typhoons.

The dominant winds for January and July are shown on Diagrams 9 and 10, respectively.

In the periods between monsoons the winds are generally variable and light.

In the waters of Seto Naikai, the direction and force of the wind is likely to be considerably modified near the coasts and in the channels and narrows. These modifications are described in *The Mariner's Handbook*.

Land and sea breezes are a regular feature in settled weather from May to September. Katabatic winds blowing off the high ground on cold clear winter nights result in squalls along the coast close inshore.

1.89

Cloud. On average the drier winter months of October to January have least cloud, about 4 oktas, much of it occurring during the passage of depressions; June and the early part of July is usually the cloudiest period. There is another maximum around September during the autumnal and typhoon rains. Maximum cloud cover is most common around dawn, whilst on average the lowest amounts occur during the period from dusk to midnight.

The heavy thundery clouds which develop in summer afternoons usually disperse in the evening over land but some drift over coastal waters to persist throughout the night.

There are marked variations in cloud cover along irregular coastlines with the cloudiest parts being those exposed to the prevailing monsoon winds. Away from the coast the cloud cover is more uniform.

1.90

Rainfall. The annual rainfall in Seto Naikai varies between 1000 mm and 2000 mm.

The rainfall in the winter months is relatively low, but the summer is generally wet with two particularly wet periods. These are when the *bai-u* or *plum rains* occur in June and early July and again in September. Much of the rain is associated with the fronts of extra-tropical depressions, but some of the rain in the later period is contributed by the occasional downpours associated with tropical storms.

1.91

Snow. Seto Naikai, in common with Japan as a whole, has more snow than might be expected considering its latitude. The frequency is greatest in January and February with more than 5 days per month, and there are occasional snowfalls as early as November and into late spring.

Snow seldom lies for more than a day or two at sea level, but deep snow persists over most high ground for long periods in severe winters.

1.92

Thunderstorms. There is a predominance of summer thunderstorms over the mainly land-locked area of Seto Naikai. They can occur at any time of the year over the sea but they are rare in winter.

Summer storms, which are local and often violent, usually develop over the land during spells of hot weather and weak pressure gradients. They usually break out in the afternoon and disperse later in the day without much movement. Some storms however, drift out over the sea and may persist overnight.

Sudden squalls are a feature of the heavier thunderstorms.

1.93

Fog and visibility. Fog is rare at sea during the winter months when the N monsoon predominates. At this time of the year, radiation fog may occur particularly over low lying land along river estuaries, however it usually only lasts for a few hours around dawn.

In late spring and summer, sea fog can be formed when the S monsoon brings in warm humid air of tropical origin, but it is not too frequent owing to the relatively warm Japan Current over which it passes.

Visibility can be drastically reduced in heavy rainstorms and also in snowstorms off the coasts exposed to the N winds.

1.94

Air temperature. The seasonal range of temperature is large for these latitudes due to the very low temperatures experienced in winter during the N monsoon. January and February are normally the coldest months but sub-zero temperatures can occur at any time from mid November to mid April.

The inland waters of Seto Naikai enjoy some shelter from the N monsoon although the temperatures vary markedly owing to the irregularity of the coastline.

July and August are the warmest months; in summer, the hottest time of day usually occurs just before the onset of the sea breeze.

1.95

Humidity. In winter the cold air of Siberian origin has a low vapour content and low humidities generally are experienced over the whole area. Extremely low humidities are recorded in the lee of high ground as the air is dried after crossing the mountains.

In summer, the air brought in by the S monsoon is very moist due to the long sea fetch, and consequently high humidities are experienced. The highest humidities occur around dawn, followed by a fall as the temperature rises, but with the onset of a sea breeze the humidity again rises.

CLIMATIC TABLES

1.96

The Climatic Tables at 1.97 to 1.106 gives statistics for a number of land stations within the area. The averages at some stations are based on a limited number of years. The figures represent average conditions and percentage or monthly frequencies are shown where appropriate. It should be noted that there are significant variations from year to year in all seasons.

Weather records taken in the vicinity of a port may not be truly representative of the weather in the harbour area or approaches. The following factors should therefore be taken into account:

    (i) gales are more frequent at sea than at most land stations

    (ii) the average wind speed for a 24 hour period over the open sea is greater than that over the land

    (iii) there is a greater tendency for cloud to form over land by day and to disperse at night

    (iv) rainfall is greater over land, especially in hilly districts

    (v) the frequency of fog should be viewed with caution since most fogs over land occur around the dawn period but sea fog does not behave in this way

    (vi) temperature over land is more variable and has a greater range especially with clear skies.

Modifications of wind and weather in coastal waters are described in *The Mariner's Handbook*.

SHIMONOSEKI (33° 57' N, 130° 56' E) Height above MSL 3 m

WMO No. 47762   Climatic Table compiled from 10 to 30 years' observations, 1931 to 1960

Month	Average Pressure at M.S.L.	Mean daily max.	Mean daily min.	Mean highest in each month	Mean lowest in each month	Average humidity ⊖	Average humidity %	Average cloud cover ⊖	Precipitation	No. of days with 1 mm or more	N	NE	E	SE	S	SW	W	NW	Calm	Mean wind speed 0600	Mean wind speed 1400	No. of days with fog	No. of days with thunder	No. of days with snow
	mb	°C	°C	°C	°C	%	%	Oktas	mm											Knots				
January	1022	8	3	15	−2	66		6	69	12	5	10	19	3	3	8	25	27	1	10	12	1	⊕	8
February	1021	9	3	15	−1	67		6	83	9	5	15	25	3	3	7	20	23	1	9	11	2	⊕	7
March	1019	12	5	18	0	70		5	101	11	7	17	27	3	2	4	17	21	1	9	12	2	1	3
April	1016	17	10	23	5	73		5	142	10	3	17	35	2	1	4	17	19	1	8	12	2	1	⊕
May	1012	21	14	27	9	77		5	152	12	2	15	38	3	2	5	16	17	2	8	11	3	1	0
June	1008	25	18	29	14	82		6	288	11	3	11	39	3	3	5	14	19	3	8	11	2	1	0
July	1008	29	23	33	19	84		6	260	12	2	12	35	3	5	7	15	19	4	7	11	1	3	0
August	1009	30	24	34	21	80		4	138	8	3	13	39	4	4	6	11	15	4	8	11	1	3	0
September	1012	27	20	31	16	79		5	221	11	7	19	36	4	3	5	8	14	2	7	10	1	2	0
October	1018	22	15	27	10	73		4	97	7	9	21	31	3	3	5	13	11	2	7	10	1	⊕	0
November	1021	17	10	22	5	72		5	77	7	9	19	29	3	6	7	17	11	3	9	11	1	⊕	⊕
December	1022	11	6	17	1	68		6	73	9	7	11	21	3	3	9	21	27	0	9	11	1	⊕	3
Means	1016	19	13	34*	−3§	74		5	—	—	5	15	31	3	3	7	15	20	2	8	11	—	—	—
Totals	—	—	—	—	—	—			1701	119	—	—	—	—	—	—	—	—	—	—	—	18	12	21
Extreme values	—	—	—	37†	−6‡	—			—	—	—	—	—	—	—	—	—	—	—	—	—			
No. of years' observations	30	30				30	30		30	10	10									10		30	30	30

*Mean of highest each year   †Highest recorded temperature   ⊕ Rare

§Mean of lowest each year   ‡Lowest recorded temperature   ⊖ All observations

ŌITA (33° 14' N, 131° 37' E) Height above MSL 5 m

Climatic Table compiled from 10 to 30 years' observations, 1931 to 1960

Month	Average Pressure at M.S.L.	Temperatures Mean daily max.	Mean daily min.	Mean highest in each month	Mean lowest in each month	Average humidity 0600	1400	Average cloud cover 0600	1400	Precipitation mm	No. of days with 1 mm or more	Wind ⊖ N	NE	E	SE	S	SW	W	NW	Calm	Mean wind speed 0600	1400	No. of days with	No. of days with fog	No. of days with thunder	No. of days with snow
	mb	°C	°C	°C	°C	%	%	Oktas		mm											Knots					
January	1021	10	1	17	−4	77	56	5	5	41	5	11	5	3	5	23	8	17	23	6	5	7		1	0	5
February	1020	10	1	18	−4	77	58	4	5	79	6	16	9	3	5	22	7	10	20	7	5	7		1	⊕	4
March	1019	13	4	22	−3	82	59	5	5	96	10	16	13	5	6	20	7	7	18	10	5	7		1	⊕	1
April	1016	18	8	25	1	87	62	5	5	127	10	15	13	5	7	23	7	3	13	14	3	6		1	1	0
May	1013	22	12	28	5	91	64	5	5	146	12	15	15	5	11	25	5	4	9	11	3	6		2	⊕	0
June	1009	25	17	31	11	91	69	6	6	252	13	14	18	7	9	23	8	3	8	10	2	6		2	1	0
July	1009	30	22	34	19	94	71	5	5	258	12	11	16	7	11	25	11	4	6	7	2	5		2	3	0
August	1009	31	22	34	19	94	69	5	5	172	9	10	17	9	11	31	7	2	7	8	3	6		1	3	0
September	1012	27	19	32	13	91	68	5	5	243	11	13	15	7	9	33	7	3	9	5	3	6		⊕	2	0
October	1018	22	13	27	6	88	62	5	5	139	7	16	13	5	9	33	6	3	13	3	4	7		⊕	⊕	0
November	1021	17	8	23	2	86	60	5	5	66	6	15	10	3	7	35	7	5	15	2	4	6		1	⊕	1
December	1022	13	3	19	−2	80	57	4	5	47	4	11	5	2	5	31	9	11	21	1	5	7		⊕	⊕	1
Means	1016	20	11	35*	−6§	87	63	5	5	—	—	14	12	5	8	27	7	7	13	7	4	6		—	—	—
Totals	—	—	—	—	—	—	—	—	—	1655	105	—	—	—	—	—	—	—	—	—	—	—		12	10	12
Extreme values	—	—	—	36†	−7‡	—	—	—	—	—	—	—	—	—	—	—	—	—	—	—	—	—				
No. of years' observations	30	30	30	27	27	11	11	11	11	30	10	10										10–11		30	30	30

*Mean of highest each year †Highest recorded temperature ⊕ Rare
§Mean of lowest each year ‡Lowest recorded temperature ⊖ All observations

MATSUYAMA (33° 50' N, 132° 47' E) Height above MSL 32 m

WMO No. 47887

Climatic Table compiled from 10 to 30 years' observations, 1931 to 1960

Month	Average Pressure at M.S.L. (mb)	Temperature Mean daily max. (°C)	Temperature Mean daily min. (°C)	Temperature Mean highest in each month (°C)	Temperature Mean lowest in each month (°C)	Average humidity 0600 (%)	Average humidity 1400 (%)	Average cloud cover 0600 (Oktas)	Average cloud cover 1400 (Oktas)	Precipitation (mm)	Precipitation No. of days with 1 mm or more	Wind N	Wind NE	Wind E	Wind SE	Wind S	Wind SW	Wind W	Wind NW	Wind Calm	Mean wind speed 0600 (Knots)	Mean wind speed 1400 (Knots)	No. of days with fog	No. of days with thunder	No. of days with snow
January	1021	9	1	15	−3	80	55	5	6	49	8	7	6	17	12	4	5	20	21	7	4	7	1	⊕	6
February	1020	10	1	16	−3	82	55	5	6	65	7	9	7	17	9	5	7	16	19	10	3	7	1	⊕	5
March	1018	13	3	21	−2	84	55	5	5	91	10	11	7	15	9	7	9	15	19	10	3	7	1	1	2
April	1016	19	8	25	1	86	56	6	6	127	10	7	5	15	9	7	11	15	20	11	3	7	3	1	0
May	1013	23	13	28	6	88	59	5	6	124	11	7	6	14	11	7	13	15	19	12	2	6	3	⊕	0
June	1009	27	17	31	12	88	62	6	6	200	13	7	6	16	10	7	11	15	19	11	2	6	3	1	0
July	1009	31	23	35	19	89	64	6	5	208	12	7	5	16	10	7	11	13	19	13	2	6	2	3	0
August	1009	32	23	35	20	89	61	5	5	103	7	5	5	19	11	6	10	14	15	13	2	6	1	3	0
September	1012	28	19	33	13	91	63	5	5	177	10	7	7	19	15	7	7	9	15	12	3	6	1	1	0
October	1017	23	13	28	6	89	58	5	5	111	8	10	10	24	15	6	5	9	11	10	3	6	1	⊕	0
November	1020	18	8	23	2	86	58	5	5	67	6	9	9	26	14	4	4	11	15	11	3	6	1	⊕	⊕
December	1021	12	3	19	−1	81	57	5	5	60	5	7	7	23	15	5	5	15	17	7	4	6	1	1	2
Means	1015	20	11	35*	−4§	86	59	5	5	—	—	7	7	19	11	5	7	14	17	11	3	6	—	—	—
Totals	—	—	—	36†	−5‡	—	—	—	—	1379	108	—	—	—	—	—	—	—	—	—	—	—	19	11	15
Extreme values	—	—	—	35* / 36†	−4§ / −5‡	—	—	—	—	—	—	—	—	—	—	—	—	—	—	—	—	—	—	—	—
No. of years' observations	30	30	30	27	27	14		10		30	10	10									10		30	30	30

*Mean of highest each year
§Mean of lowest each year
†Highest recorded temperature
‡Lowest recorded temperature
⊕ Rare
⊖ All observations

HIROSHIMA (34° 22' N, 132° 26' E)   Height above MSL 29 m

WMO No. 47765   Climatic Table compiled from 10 to 30 years' observations, 1931 to 1960

Month	Average Pressure at M.S.L.	Temperature Mean daily max.	Temperature Mean daily min.	Temperature Mean highest in each month	Temperature Mean lowest in each month	Average humidity ⊖	Average humidity %	Average cloud cover ⊖	Precipitation Average	Precipitation No. of days with 1 mm or more	Wind ⊖ N	NE	E	SE	S	SW	W	NW	Calm	Mean wind speed 0600	Mean wind speed 1400	No. of days with fog	No. of days with thunder	No. of days with snow
	mb	°C	°C	°C	°C	%	%	Oktas	mm											Knots				
January	1021	9	0	15	− 4	72		5	45	8	36	22	2	3	5	7	11	11	3	6	8	1	0	10
February	1020	10	0	15	− 4	71		5	70	8	41	21	2	4	6	7	7	8	4	6	8	1	⊕	8
March	1019	13	3	19	− 2	71		5	106	10	37	21	2	4	7	11	7	5	4	6	8	2	⊕	4
April	1016	18	8	23	1	72		5	158	9	31	19	2	5	11	15	6	5	6	6	7	3	1	0
May	1013	22	13	27	6	75		5	154	11	27	19	3	5	13	17	6	3	8	5	7	2	1	0
June	1009	25	17	29	12	80		6	249	12	23	15	2	5	15	21	7	3	9	5	7	2	1	0
July	1009	29	22	33	19	82		6	250	13	15	13	3	8	21	22	5	2	10	4	6	3	3	0
August	1009	31	23	34	19	79		5	115	8	23	19	4	6	15	19	6	2	7	5	7	⊕	3	0
September	1012	27	19	32	13	80		5	215	12	37	21	2	3	11	12	4	3	6	6	8	1	1	0
October	1018	23	12	27	5	76		4	115	6	50	22	3	4	6	5	3	4	2	7	9	1	⊕	0
November	1021	18	7	22	1	75		4	67	5	51	25	2	3	3	3	4	4	1	7	9	1	⊕	⊕
December	1022	12	2	17	− 2	73		5	51	5	40	25	2	3	5	5	11	9	1	6	8	1	0	4
Means	1016	20	11	34*	− 5§	75		5	—	—	35	21	2	4	9	12	6	5	5	6	8	—	—	—
Totals	—	—	—	—	—	—		—	1595	107	—	—	—	—	—	—	—	—	—	—	—	18	10	26
Extreme values	—	—	—	37†	− 7‡	—		—	—	—	—	—	—	—	—	—	—	—	—	—	—			
No. of years' observation	30	20	20	30	30	30		30	30	10	10									10		20	30	30

*Mean of highest each year
§Mean of lowest each year
†Highest recorded temperature
‡Lowest recorded temperature
⊕Rare
⊖All observations

1.101

TADOTSU (34° 16' N, 133° 45' E)   Height above MSL 4 m

WMO No. 47890

Climatic Table compiled from 10 to 30 years' observations, 1931 to 1960

38

Month	Average Pressure at M.S.L. (mb)	Temperatures Mean daily max. (°C)	Mean daily min. (°C)	Mean highest in each month (°C)	Mean lowest in each month (°C)	Average humidity 0600 (%)	1400 (%)	Average cloud cover 0600 (Oktas)	1400 (Oktas)	Precipitation (mm)	No. of days with 1 mm or more	Wind ⊖ N	NE	E	SE	S	SW	W	NW	Calm	Mean wind speed 0600 (Knots)	1400 (Knots)	No. of days with fog	No. of days with thunder	No. of days with Snow
January	1021	9	2	13	−3	75	61	4	5	37	7	7	3	5	13	9	7	37	16	4	9	10	⊕	0	5
February	1020	9	2	16	−3	78	61	5	5	55	7	9	7	7	15	7	9	29	13	2	6	8	⊕	0	5
March	1018	12	4	19	−2	81	60	5	5	77	9	12	7	8	15	9	7	26	12	4	6	8	1	⊕	2
April	1016	17	8	24	2	84	61	5	5	89	9	15	9	7	16	9	8	23	8	6	4	7	1	⊕	0
May	1013	22	13	27	7	86	64	5	5	96	11	15	11	9	14	9	7	23	8	5	3	6	1	1	0
June	1009	25	18	30	13	87	69	6	6	151	11	17	11	9	9	9	5	24	9	7	3	6	1	1	0
July	1009	30	23	34	20	90	69	6	5	167	11	17	11	7	7	3	9	25	9	10	3	6	⊕	3	0
August	1009	32	24	35	20	89	64	5	5	91	7	15	7	11	17	8	9	19	9	4	3	7	⊕	4	0
September	1012	28	20	33	13	88	64	5	5	155	10	13	8	13	27	11	5	12	7	3	4	6	0	2	0
October	1018	22	13	27	7	87	62	5	5	114	7	13	8	9	29	13	4	11	9	2	5	6	0	⊕	0
November	1021	17	9	22	3	82	62	5	5	63	6	11	6	7	25	15	6	16	11	2	7	7	⊕	⊕	⊕
December	1021	11	4	17	0	78	63	4	5	43	5	7	3	4	19	12	7	31	18	0	8	9	⊕	⊕	2
Means	1015	20	12	36*	−3§	84	63	5	5	—	—	13	8	9	17	9	8	23	11	4	5	7	—	—	—
Totals	—	—	—	—	—	—	—	—	—	1137	101	—	—	—	—	—	—	—	—	—	—	—	4	11	14
Extreme values	—	—	—	38†	−5‡	—	—	—	—	—	—	—	—	—	—	—	—	—	—	—	—	—	—	—	—
No. of years' observations	30	30	30	27	27	14	10	10	10	30	10	10										10		30	30	30

*Mean of highest each year   †Highest recorded temperature   ⊕ Rare
§Mean of lowest each year   ‡Lowest recorded temperature   ⊖ All observations

OKAYAMA (34° 41' N, 133° 55' E)   Height above MSL 3 m

Climatic Table compiled from 10 to 30 years' observations, 1931 to 1960

Month	Average Pressure at M.S.L.	Temperature — Mean daily max.	Mean daily min.	Mean highest in each month	Mean lowest in each month	Average humidity 0600	Average humidity 1400	Average cloud cover 0600	Average cloud cover 1400	Precipitation	No. of days with 1 mm or more	Wind N	NE	E	SE	S	SW	W	NW	Calm	Mean wind speed 0600	Mean wind speed 1400	No. of days with fog	No. of days with thunder	No. of days with snow
	mb	°C	°C	°C	°C	%	%	Oktas		mm											Knots				
January	1021	9	−1	14	−5	84	53	4	6	36	6	9	4	3	2	2	8	30	23	17	2	7	1	⊕	7
February	1020	10	−1	15	−5	85	53	5	6	52	7	11	7	5	4	3	9	21	20	18	2	6	1	⊕	7
March	1018	13	2	20	−4	85	52	5	5	77	9	12	7	9	5	5	10	15	17	20	2	7	1	⊕	3
April	1016	19	7	25	0	87	52	5	6	100	10	9	7	17	8	5	11	13	13	19	2	6	1	1	⊕
May	1013	23	12	28	5	89	55	5	5	109	11	7	9	19	7	5	12	11	9	21	2	7	1	1	⊕
June	1009	26	17	31	11	88	57	6	6	159	12	9	8	17	8	5	13	11	7	23	2	6	1	2	0
July	1009	30	22	35	19	91	61	6	5	165	12	6	9	17	7	5	14	9	7	26	2	6	1	3	0
August	1009	32	23	35	19	88	60	5	5	99	7	9	8	19	8	5	11	7	7	25	2	7	1	3	0
September	1012	27	19	33	12	90	59	5	5	150	11	15	11	16	7	3	8	7	11	23	2	5	1	2	0
October	1018	22	11	27	5	91	57	5	5	94	7	17	11	9	5	4	5	11	17	20	1	5	1	⊕	0
November	1021	17	5	22	0	90	56	4	5	60	5	16	7	5	5	4	7	13	20	21	2	5	1	0	⊕
December.....	1021	12	1	18	−3	87	57	4	5	38	4	9	4	5	3	3	7	25	25	18	2	6	1	0	3
Means	1015	20	10	35*	−6§	88	56	5	5	—	—	11	8	11	6	5	10	14	15	21	2	6	—	—	—
Totals........	—	—	—	—	—	—	—	—	—	1139	101	—	—	—	—	—	—	—	—	—	—	—	13	12	19
Extreme values .	—	—	—	37†	−8‡	—	—	—	—	—	—	—	—	—	—	—	—	—	—	—	—	—			
No. of years' observations ...	29	10	10	27	27	12	10	29	10			10									10		29	29	30

*Mean of highest each year   §Mean of lowest each year

†Highest recorded temperature   ‡Lowest recorded temperature

⊕ Rare   ⊖ All observations

TOKUSHIMA (34° 04' N, 134° 35' E)   Height above MSL 2 m

WMO No. 47895   Climatic Table compiled from 10 to 30 years' observations, 1931 to 1960

40

Month	Average Pressure at M.S.L.	Temperature — Mean daily max.	Temperature — Mean daily min.	Temperature — Mean highest in each month	Temperature — Mean lowest in each month	Average humidity ⊖	Average humidity	Average cloud cover ⊖	Precipitation	Precipitation — No. of days with 1 mm or more	⊖ N	NE	E	SE	S	SW	W	NW	Calm	N	NE	E	SE	S	SW	W	NW	Calm	Mean wind speed ⊖	No. of days with	No. of days with fog	No. of days with thunder	No. of days with snow
	mb	°C	°C	°C	°C	%	%	Oktas	mm																				Knots				
January	1020	9	1	16	−3	67		4	40	6	8	3	1	1	2	10	45	27	5										10		⊕	0	5
February	1019	10	1	17	−2	68		5	61	7	13	4	3	3	2	7	37	27	5										9		⊕	0	4
March	1018	13	4	20	−1	70		5	95	10	13	5	5	6	4	7	27	28	5										8		1	⊕	2
April	1016	18	9	25	2	72		5	133	10	13	5	7	15	7	5	19	22	6										7		1	⊕	0
May	1013	23	13	29	6	76		6	126	11	9	6	11	19	7	6	15	19	8										6		1	⊕	0
June	1009	26	18	30	12	81		6	207	13	9	9	15	19	7	5	11	13	13										5		2	1	0
July	1009	30	23	34	19	84		6	197	11	9	8	15	23	7	3	7	10	17										5		1	3	0
August	1010	31	23	35	20	81		5	169	8	7	6	15	19	9	7	13	13	12										6		⊕	3	0
September	1012	27	20	32	13	80		6	257	13	9	5	8	11	8	9	22	19	9										6		⊕	2	0
October	1017	22	14	27	8	76		5	194	8	13	3	3	3	4	7	35	29	5										7		⊕	⊕	0
November	1020	17	9	23	4	73		4	94	6	13	3	2	3	3	8	37	29	4										8		⊕	⊕	⊕
December	1021	12	4	19	0	69		4	54	5	9	2	1	2	3	7	43	28	4										10		⊕	⊕	1
Means	1015	20	12	35*	−4§	75		5	—	—	11	5	7	11	5	7	25	21	8										7	—			
Totals	—	—	—	—	—			—	1625	107	—	—	—	—	—	—	—	—	—	—	—	—	—	—	—	—	—	—	—	—	8	10	12
Extreme values	—	—	—	38†	−6‡	—		—	—	—	—	—	—	—	—	—	—	—	—	—	—	—	—	—	—	—	—	—	—	—			
No. of years' observations	30	30				30	30	30	30	10	10																			10		30	30	30

*Mean of highest each year   †Highest recorded temperature   ⊕ Rare
§Mean of lowest each year   ‡Lowest recorded temperature   ⊖ All observations

WAKAYAMA (34° 14' N, 135° 10' E) Height above MSL 13 m

WMO No. 47777   Climatic Table compiled from 10 to 30 years' observations, 1931 to 1960

Month	Average Pressure at M.S.L.	Temperature Mean daily max.	Mean daily min.	Mean highest in each month	Mean lowest in each month	Average humidity 0600	1400	Average cloud cover 0600	1400	Precipitation mm	No. of days with 1 mm or more	Wind ⊖ N	NE	E	SE	S	SW	W	NW	Calm	N	NE	E	SE	S	SW	W	NW	Calm	Mean wind speed 0600	1400	No. of days with	No. of days with fog	No. of days with thunder	No. of days with snow
	mb	°C	°C	°C	°C	%	%	Oktas		mm																				Knots					
January	1020	9	1	16	−3	77	54	5	5	47	6	15	19	25	1	1	1	10	27	1										5	7		1	⊕	6
February	1019	10	1	17	−3	78	54	5	5	60	7	19	25	23	1	2	3	7	19	1										5	6		1	⊕	5
March	1018	13	4	21	−1	81	53	5	5	100	11	21	24	22	1	5	4	7	15	1										5	7		1	⊕	2
April	1016	19	9	25	2	82	54	6	6	125	10	17	20	21	3	8	9	10	11	2										5	7		1	1	0
May	1013	23	14	28	7	83	56	5	5	113	11	13	18	21	3	8	11	13	10	3										5	7		1	1	0
June	1009	27	18	31	13	85	62	6	6	199	11	11	13	19	3	9	19	16	8	2										4	7		⊕	1	0
July	1009	31	23	35	19	89	65	6	5	170	11	8	10	17	3	12	23	16	7	3										4	6		1	3	0
August	1010	32	23	36	20	89	62	5	5	121	7	11	13	23	3	8	18	15	7	2										5	7		⊕	3	0
September	1012	28	20	33	13	90	61	5	6	205	12	13	20	31	3	7	9	7	5	3										5	6		⊕	2	0
October	1017	23	13	28	7	89	59	5	5	147	8	19	27	36	2	1	2	5	8	2										5	6		1	1	0
November	1020	17	8	23	3	86	58	5	5	83	7	17	27	37	1	1	1	3	10	1										5	6		⊕	⊕	⊕
December	1021	12	4	19	0	81	58	5	5	63	6	15	22	27	1	1	1	7	25	0										5	6		1	⊕	1
Means	1015	20	11	36*	−3§	84	58	5	5	—	—	15	20	25	3	5	9	9	13	2										5	7		—	—	—
Totals	—	—	—	—	—	—	—	—	—	1435	106	—	—	—	—	—	—	—	—	—	—	—	—	—	—	—	—	—	—	—	—		7	11	15
Extreme values	—	—	—	38†	−5‡	—	—	—	—	—	—	—	—	—	—	—	—	—	—	—	—	—	—	—	—	—	—	—	—	—	—				
No. of years' observations	30	30	30	30	30	30		10–11		30	10	10																		10–11			30	30	30

*Mean of highest each year
§Mean of lowest each year
†Highest recorded temperature
‡Lowest recorded temperature
⊕ Rare
⊖ All observations

1.105

ŌSAKA (34° 41′ N, 135° 31′ E) Height above MSL 23 m

WMO No. 47772   Climatic Table compiled from 10 to 30 years' observations, 1931 to 1960

42

Month	Average Pressure at M.S.L.	Temperature				Average humidity		Average cloud cover	Precipitation		Wind distribution—Percentage of observations from																		Mean wind speed		No. of days with	No. of days with fog	No. of days with thunder	No. of days with snow
		Mean daily max.	Mean daily min.	Mean highest in each month	Mean lowest in each month	⊖	%	⊖	⊖	No. of days with 1 mm or more	⊖																			0600	1400				
											N	NE	E	SE	S	SW	W	NW	Calm	N	NE	E	SE	S	SW	W	NW	Calm						
	mb	°C	°C	°C	°C	%	%	Oktas	mm																				Knots					
January	1020	9	1	14	−4	69		4	43	7	17	9	4	7	7	12	26	10	9										5	9	9	⊕	6
February	1019	9	1	16	−3	69		5	58	7	21	15	5	5	7	11	18	9	9										4	9	8	⊕	6
March	1018	13	3	20	−2	69		5	96	11	25	15	4	5	5	9	17	10	9										4	9	6	⊕	3
April	1016	19	9	25	1	69		5	127	9	25	17	7	5	5	12	14	7	7										4	8	3	1	⊕
May	1013	24	14	29	7	70		5	122	11	19	22	8	5	5	11	17	5	8										3	8	3	1	0
June	1009	27	19	32	13	74		6	193	12	15	18	7	5	5	13	22	7	9										3	8	3	1	0
July	1009	31	23	35	19	76		5	177	10	13	15	6	5	7	15	23	5	9										3	8	2	3	0
August	1010	33	24	36	20	74		5	118	7	13	18	9	7	7	11	21	5	9										3	8	1	3	0
September	1012	29	20	33	13	76		5	171	12	23	24	8	7	7	8	9	5	9										3	7	2	2	0
October	1017	23	13	28	6	75		5	122	9	28	26	7	7	5	5	7	6	10										3	7	5	1	0
November	1020	17	7	23	1	75		4	81	7	25	18	7	7	5	6	9	8	13										3	7	11	⊕	⊕
December	1021	12	3	17	1	72		4	52	5	17	11	5	7	7	9	24	9	11										4	8	13	⊕	1
Means	1015	20	11	36*	−4§	72		5	—	—	21	17	7	7	7	10	17	7	9										3	8	—	—	—
Totals	—	—	—	—	—	—			1359	107	—	—	—	—	—	—	—	—	—	—	—	—	—	—	—	—	—	—	—	—	66	12	17
Extreme values	—	—	—	38†	−8‡	—			—	—																							
No. of years' observations	30	20	20	30	30	30		30	30	10						10														10		30	30	30

*Mean of highest each year   †Highest recorded temperature   ⊕ Rare
§Mean of lowest each year   ‡Lowest recorded temperature   ⊖ All observations

KŌBE (34° 41' N, 135° 11' E) Height above MSL 59 m

WMO No. 47770

Climatic Table compiled from 10 to 29 years' observations, 1931 to 1960

43

Month	Average Pressure at M.S.L.	Temperature Mean daily max.	Temperature Mean daily min.	Temperature Mean highest in each month	Temperature Mean lowest in each month	Average humidity 0600	Average humidity 1400	Average cloud cover 0600	Average cloud cover 1400	Precipitation	No. of days with 1 mm or more	Wind Θ N	NE	E	SE	S	SW	W	NW	Calm	N	NE	E	SE	S	SW	W	NW	Calm	Mean wind speed 0600	Mean wind speed 1400	No. of days with	No. of days with fog	No. of days with thunder	No. of days with snow
	mb	°C	°C	°C	°C	%	%	Oktas		mm																				Knots					
January	1020	8	1	14	−3	72	55	4	5	41	6	17	9	5	2	2	6	36	23	1										6	9		2	0	7
February	1019	9	1	15	−3	74	54	5	6	56	7	21	9	7	3	2	7	26	21	2										5	8		1	⊕	8
March	1018	12	4	19	−2	76	53	5	5	94	10	22	12	7	5	5	8	21	19	2										6	9		2	⊕	4
April	1016	18	9	24	2	76	52	5	5	123	10	17	15	11	7	6	11	18	14	1										6	9		1	1	⊕
May	1013	23	14	28	8	79	55	5	5	123	11	15	16	13	7	5	13	17	12	2										5	9		1	1	0
June	1009	26	18	30	13	82	58	6	6	181	12	13	15	12	7	7	15	20	11	2										5	8		1	1	0
July	1009	30	23	34	19	86	63	7	5	184	11	11	11	10	5	7	19	23	11	2										4	8		1	3	0
August	1010	31	24	35	20	83	58	5	5	136	8	15	13	11	8	9	15	17	11	1										5	9		⊕	3	0
September	1012	28	20	32	15	81	60	5	6	175	11	23	18	13	7	5	9	11	11	1										5	8		⊕	2	0
October	1017	22	14	27	8	79	58	5	5	105	7	34	17	11	7	3	5	9	15	0										5	7		⊕	⊕	0
November	1020	17	9	22	3	77	57	5	5	76	6	29	15	9	5	2	5	15	19	1										5	7		1	⊕	⊕
December	1021	11	4	17	0	75	56	4	5	44	5	19	10	5	3	2	7	32	24	1										5	8		2	⊕	1
Means	1015	19	12	35*	−4§	78	57	5	5	—	—	19	13	10	5	5	11	21	16	1	—	—	—	—	—	—	—	—	—	5	8		—	—	—
Totals	—	—	—	—	—	—	—	—	—	1337	105	—	—	—	—	—	—	—	—	—	—	—	—	—	—	—	—	—	—	—	—		12	10	21
Extreme values	—	—	—	37†	−6‡	—	—	—	—	—	—	—	—	—	—	—	—	—	—	—	—	—	—	—	—	—	—	—	—	—	—				
No. of years' observations	29	29	29	28	28	14	10–11			29	10					10														10–11			29	29	29

*Mean of highest each year
§Mean of lowest each year
†Highest recorded temperature
‡Lowest recorded temperature
⊕ Rare
Θ All observations

METEOROLOGICAL
CONVERSION TABLES AND SCALES

Fahrenheit to Celsius

°Fahrenheit

°F	0	1	2	3	4	5	6	7	8	9
					Degrees Celsius					
−100	−73·3	−73·9	−74·4	−75·0	−75·6	−76·1	−76·7	−77·2	−77·8	−78·3
− 90	−67·8	−68·3	−68·9	−69·4	−70·0	−70·6	−71·1	−71·7	−72·2	−72·8
−80	−62·2	−62·8	−63·3	−63·9	−64·4	−65·0	−65·6	−66·1	−66·7	−67·2
−70	−56·7	−57·2	−57·8	−58·3	−58·9	−59·4	−60·0	−60·6	−61·1	−61·7
−60	−51·1	−51·7	−52·2	−52·8	−53·3	−53·9	−54·4	−55·0	−55·6	−56·1
−50	−45·6	−46·1	−46·7	−47·2	−47·8	−48·3	−48·9	−49·4	−50·0	−50·6
−40	−40·0	−40·6	−41·1	−41·7	−42·2	−42·8	−43·9	−43·9	−44·4	−45·0
−30	−34·4	−35·0	−35·6	−36·1	−36·7	−37·2	−37·8	−38·3	−38·9	−39·4
−20	−28·9	−29·4	−30·0	−30·6	−31·1	−31·7	−32·2	−32·8	−33·3	−33·9
−10	−23·3	−23·9	−24·4	−25·0	−25·6	−26·1	−26·7	−27·2	−27·8	−28·3
0	−17·8	−17·2	−16·7	−16·1	−15·6	−15·0	−14·4	−13·9	−13·3	−12·8
10	−12·2	−11·7	−11·1	−10·6	−10·0	−9·4	−8·9	−8·3	−7·8	−7·2
20	−6·7	−6·1	−5·6	−5·0	−4·4	−3·9	−3·3	−2·8	−2·2	−1·7
30	−1·1	−0·6	0	+0·6	+1·1	+1·7	+2·2	+2·8	+3·3	+3·9
40	+4·4	+5·0	+5·6	6·1	6·7	7·2	7·8	8·3	8·9	9·4
50	10·0	10·6	11·1	11·7	12·2	12·8	13·3	13·9	14·4	15·0
60	15·6	16·1	16·7	17·2	17·8	18·3	18·9	19·4	20·0	20·6
70	21·1	21·7	22·2	22·8	23·3	23·9	24·4	25·0	25·6	26·1
80	26·7	27·2	27·8	28·3	28·9	29·4	30·0	30·6	31·1	31·7
90	32·2	32·8	33·3	33·9	34·4	35·0	35·6	36·1	36·7	37·2
100	37·8	38·3	38·9	39·4	40·0	40·6	41·1	41·7	42·2	42·8
110	43·3	43·9	44·4	45·0	45·6	46·1	46·7	47·2	47·8	48·3
120	48·9	49·4	50·0	50·6	51·1	51·7	52·2	52·8	53·3	53·9

Celsius to Fahrenheit

° Celsius

°C	0	1	2	3	4	5	6	7	8	9
					Degrees Fahrenheit					
−70	−94·0	−95·8	−97·6	−99·4	−101·2	−103·0	−104·8	−106·6	−108·4	−110·2
−60	−76·0	−77·8	−79·6	−81·4	−83·2	−85·0	−86·8	−88·6	−90·4	−92·2
−50	−58·0	−59·8	−61·6	−63·4	−65·2	−67·0	−68·8	−70·6	−72·4	−74·2
−40	−40·0	−41·8	−43·6	−45·4	−47·2	−49·0	−50·8	−52·6	−54·4	−56·2
−30	−22·0	−23·8	−25·6	−27·4	−29·2	−31·0	−32·8	−34·6	−36·4	−38·2
−20	−4·0	−5·8	−7·6	−9·4	−11·2	−13·0	−14·8	−16·6	−18·4	−20·2
−10	+14·0	+12·2	+10·4	+8·6	+6·8	+5·0	+3·2	+1·4	−0·4	−2·2
−0	32·0	30·2	28·4	26·6	24·8	23·0	21·2	19·4	+17·6	+15·8
+0	32·0	33·8	35·6	37·4	39·2	41·0	42·8	44·6	46·4	48·2
+10	50·0	51·8	53·6	55·4	57·2	59·0	60·8	62·6	64·4	66·2
20	68·0	69·8	71·6	73·4	75·2	77·0	78·8	80·6	82·4	84·2
30	86·0	87·8	89·6	91·4	93·2	95·0	96·8	98·6	100·4	102·2
40	104·0	105·8	107·6	109·4	111·2	113·0	114·8	116·6	118·4	120·2
50	122·0	123·8	125·6	127·4	129·2	131·0	132·8	134·6	136·4	138·2

MILLIBARS TO INCHES

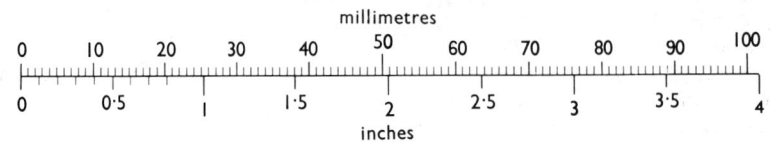

MILLIMETRES TO INCHES

(1) (for small values)

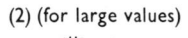

(2) (for large values)

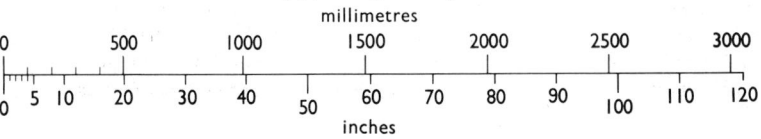

CHAPTER 2

KANMON KAIKYŌ AND APPROACHES

WEST APPROACHES TO KANMON KAIKYŌ

GENERAL INFORMATION

Charts 532, 524
2.1

Kanmon Kaikyō is the W entrance to Seto Naikai; it is much obstructed by islands, reefs and sandbanks, and at its narrowest part the fairway is only about 2 cables wide.

The area in the W approaches to Kanmon Kaikyō, W of a line joining Myōken Saki (33° 56' N, 130° 41' E) and Kuro Shima 13¼ miles NE, is described in Japan Pilot Volume II.

Areas dangerous due to mines. See 1.7.

A large number of **fish havens**, indicated on the charts, lie in the W approaches to Kanmon Kaikyō.
2.2

The coast on the S side of the W approach to Kanmon Kaikyō consists partly of large reclaimed areas and extends from Myōken Saki to Wakamatsu Ku (2.30), 7 miles E. A bank with depths of less than 20 m and on which are several islets and numerous rocks and shoals, extends 5 or 6 miles N from this stretch of coast and forms the W side of the fairway of Kanmon Kaikyō.

Landmarks. Hobashira Yama, with two summits 621 m and 616 m high, lies 7¼ miles SE of Myōken Saki and is prominent; a number of radio masts stand on the summits.

The two prominent chimneys (red and white) of **Wakamatsu Power Station,** with an elevation of 89 m, stand on **Jōno Saki,** 3 miles E of Myōken Saki.

ISLANDS IN THE WEST APPROACHES TO KANMON KAIKYŌ

Chart 524
2.3

Shira Shima (34° 00' N, 130° 43' E) and Futaoi Shima 6¼ miles NNE, are described in Japan Pilot Volume II.

Omiji Iwa (34° 00' N, 130° 49' E), 18 m high, lies on the SW side of the outer part of the fairway to Kanmon Kaikyō, 8 miles NE of Myōken Saki; a **light** is exhibited from a red round stone tower standing on the rock. **Okino Kuri,** with a depth of 1·2 m, and **Hiro Iwa,** 0·6 m high, lie within 7 cables NW and 4 cables WSW, respectively, of Omiji Iwa. A wave recorder marked by a *buoy* lies 1 mile WNW of the rock.

Shiru Su lies nearly 2 miles SW of Omiji Iwa at the NW end of an extensive shoal, with depths of less than 5 m, extending 4¼ miles NW from the entrance to Wakamatsu Ku. A **light** is exhibited from a white round metal tower with black bands standing on a bank of gravel and sand, 4 m high, situated in the middle of Shiru Su. A *light-buoy* is moored 1 miles SW of the bank.

Maruyama Dashi, with a least depth of 3·6 m over it, and **Yoko Se,** with a least depth of 2·7 m, lie, respectively, 2 miles and 3 miles SW of Shiru Su; they are each marked by a *light-buoy.*

Charts 1578, 524
2.4

Aino Shima (33° 59' N, 130° 49' E), covered with trees and 23 m high, lies ¼ mile S of Omiji Iwa.

Ainoshima Kō, protected by a breakwater, lies on the SW side of Aino Shima; a **light** is exhibited on the head of the breakwater.

Koshiki Iwa, a small square rock 3·6 m high, lies 6 cables ENE of the S extremity of Aino Shima and from it a shoal bank extends ¼ mile NW and 2 cables S. A *light-buoy* is moored 3 cables ENE of Koshiki Iwa and marks the W side of the N entrance to one of the two main channels leading to Kanmon Fairway.

Caution. Neither the passage between Koshiki Iwa and Aino Shima, nor the channel between Aino Shima and Shira Su, should be attempted without local knowledge.

Chart 1578
2.5

Mutsure Shima (33° 58' N, 130° 52' E), a flat-topped island surmounted by two clumps of trees and with numerous oil tanks on its SE side, lies 2 miles ESE of Aino Shima. It is situated on the NE part of a shoal on the SW part of which lie numerous rocks and reefs together with **Uma Shima, Hanare Shima, Kata Shima** and **Wagora Shima,** the last two being at the W and S extremities, respectively, of the shoal.

A **light** is exhibited from a white round stone tower standing on **Kita Saki,** the NE extremity of Mutsure Shima. A **signal station** from which berthing and anchoring signals are shown, stands near the lighthouse.

Quarantine anchorages. See 2.16.

Nisshin tanker berth consisting of dolphins and a mooring buoy, in a depth of 18 m, lies on the E side of Mutsure Shima; it is floodlit at night. Vessels berth heading either N or S; tugs are available.

Matsu Se, with a least depth of 8·4 m over it, lies ¼ mile N of the N end of Mutsure Shima and is marked 1 cable NE by a *light-buoy.* Another *light-buoy* marking the W extremity of the coastal bank, is moored 9 cables E of Matsu Se; a depth of 12·5 m is to be found 1 cable W of this buoy.

Densakuno Se, with a depth of 6 m over it, lies 2¼ cables N of Kata Shima (33° 58' N, 130° 51' E).

Katashima Suidō lies SW of Kata Shima and is marked by *light-buoys.*

KURO SHIMA TO KO SETO

Chart 524
2.6

The N side of the W approach to Kanmon Kaikyō, N of Kuro Shima (34° 05' N, 130° 52' E), is described in Japan Pilot Volume II.

Landmarks. Onigajo, 619 m high, 3 miles E of Kuro

Shima; **Sukizaki Yama,** 613 m high, 1¾ miles S of Onigajo; and **Yoshimiryūō San,** 462 m high, ½ mile W of Sukizaki Yama, are all sharp and prominent peaks.

Floodlights at **Hatabu** railway station, 1¼ miles SE of Kuro Saki (34° 00' N, 130° 55' E) (2.7), stand out well at night and are a good mark for vessels approaching Kanmon Kaikyō from W.

Ajiro Hana lies 1¾ miles SSE of Kuro Shima; **Kamo Shima,** 20 m high, lies on foul ground extending ½ mile SSE from the point.

Yoshimi Kō, protected by breakwaters, lies ½ mile ENE of Ajiro Hana; a **light** is exhibited at the head of the N breakwater. Several **submarine cables** are landed 1½ miles ESE of Ajiro Hana.

Murasaki Hana (34° 01' N, 130° 54' E), 2½ miles SSE of Ajiro Hana, is a low flat point densely covered with pine trees, from which a shoal spit extends 1¼ miles NW. **Kurumi Se,** a bank of pebbles, lies within 3 cables of the NW extremity of the spit; a **light** is exhibited from a white round concrete tower situated on the bank.

Yasuoka Kō, protected by two short breakwaters, lies at the head of a bight on the SE side of Murasaki Hana; a **light** is exhibited on the head of the W breakwater.

Measured distance. A measured distance of 2119 m is established in the vicinity of Murasaki Hana; the extremities are each marked by a pair of **beacons;** the running course is 354°.

Chart 1578

2.7

Kuro Saki (34° 00' N, 130° 55' E), 1½ miles S of Murosaki Hana, is a flat-topped cliff 71 m high; it is a good mark as the land N of it is low and cultivated.

Between Kuro Saki and the W entrance of Ko Seto 2½ miles S, the coast is foul for about 4 cables offshore.

Okino Se, with a least depth of 2·3 m, lies about ½ mile SW of Kuro Saki.

Ko Seto, a narrow tortuous channel which separates Hiko Shima (2.27) from the mainland, is entered 2½ miles S of Kuro Saki; a **bridge** with a vertical clearance of 42 m, spans the W entrance to the channel. Ko Seto gives access to Shimonoseki Gyokō (2.49) and, through a lock and a dredged channel, to the S part of Shimonoseki Ku.

A **light** is exhibited from a white round concrete tower standing close ENE of **Tarōgase Hana** on the S entrance point to Ko Seto.

Leading lights for the W approach to Ko Seto are exhibited from white round concrete towers (rectangular daymarks) situated 3 cables ESE of Tarōgase Hana Light-tower; the lights in line bear 130° and lead through the entrance which, in a depth of more than 5 m, has a navigable width of only 70 m.

The remains of a breakwater, with depths over it from 4·3 m to 5·2 m, lies 4 cables N of Tarōgase Hana Light-tower.

KANMON KAIKYŌ

GENERAL INFORMATION

Charts 524, 1578

2.8

Kanmon Kaikyō is about 15 miles long, and runs from Mutsure Shima (33° 58' N, 130° 52' E) (2.5) to He Saki (33° 57' N, 131° 02' E) (2.59). Navigation in the straits is difficult and the tidal streams are very strong particularly in Ō Seto (33° 54' N, 130° 55' E) and in Hayatomo Seto (33° 58' N, 130° 58' E), E of Kanmon Bridge. On occasions the visibility is poor.

Cautions. The traffic in Kanmon Kaikyō and its approaches is considerable; local shipping, vessels towing, and harbour craft are likely to be encountered in all parts of the straits particularly in fine weather and at slack water. The navigation lights of many of these vessels are very weak and are sometimes hardly visible.

In 1976, about 800 vessels were passing through the straits daily and of these the greatest number were small vessels of under 500 tons. About 70 per cent of the traffic passes through in daytime with the busiest periods being 0600–0900 and 1200–1400, and again just before and just after sunset.

Ferries up to 150 tons make about 70 return trips daily across the straits between Shimonoseki Ku, 1½ miles SW of Kanmon Bridge, and the ports on the S side.

At slack water, numerous fishing vessels will be encountered in the fairway but they easily avoid large ships which latter are advised to reduce speed and make use of the whistle rather than attempt large alterations of course.

Almost all the straits lie within the harbour limits of Kanmon Kō (2.26).

2.9

Weather. The wind is usually E in the morning until about 0900 and then W winds often set in during the middle part of the day.

Fog is most frequent in the straits from February to July. It most often starts about sunrise and when the wind is light, and disperses as the sun rises higher. It rarely occurs in wind speeds of over 10 knots.

When the wind is between E and S, smoke from the various factories on the Kyūshū side covers the straits, particularly the W part; on occasions it extends as far as Futaoi Shima (34° 06' N, 130° 48' E). However once the wind shifts to the W, the smoke clears and the visibility becomes good.

Under normal conditions the visibility is better in the afternoon than in the forenoon.

Tidal stream information

2.10

The tidal streams in Hayatomo Seto (33° 58' N, 130° 58' E) (2.55) run as follows:

In the middle of the channel the W-going and E-going stream attain their maximum rate at the time of HW and LW. The streams are weakest at about the middle of the interval between HW and LW.

Near the shore on either side of the fairway, the maximum rates occur about 30 minutes earlier than the middle.

The mean spring rate of both the E and W-going streams is about 7 knots but the greatest rate may exceed 8 knots. Slack water lasts no more than a few minutes.

On the down-stream side of Moji Saki (33° 57·5' N, 130° 57·9' E), the rates of and the area covered by eddies, increase after the main stream has attained its maximum rate.

2.11

Tidal streams in other parts of Kanmon Kaikyō run as follows:

E of Mutsure Shima (33° 58' N, 130° 53' E) (2.5). Tidal streams turn from ½ hour to 1 hour later than in Hayatomo Seto; their rates do not exceed 1 knot.

S of Oyamano Hana (33° 54·6' N, 130° 54·3' E) (2.29). Near the centreline of the fairway the tidal streams turn about 10 minutes later than in Hayatomo Seto and have rates from 5–5½ knots. Near the shore on either side of the fairway, the streams turn about 20 minutes earlier than in the centre.

Ō Seto (33° 54·6' N, 130° 55·8' E). In the main fairway, the tidal streams turn at about the same time as those in Hayatomo Seto and have rates from 6–8½ knots. Near the shore on either side, the streams turn 15–20 minutes earlier.

Between Ō Seto and Hayatomo Seto. In the main fairway, the tidal streams turn about ½ hour later than in Hayatomo Seto. The nearer to the shore on either side of the fairway, the earlier the tidal stream turns; in Moji Ku the stream turns about 3–4½ hours earlier than in Hayatomo Seto.

E of Hayatomo Seto. In the W part, the tidal streams turn in the main fairway 10–20 minutes later than in Hayatomo Seto, and about ½ hour earlier S of Manju Shima (33° 59·5' N, 131° 01·7' E).

2.12

Tidal stream signals. Tidal signal stations are situated as follows:

> Daiba Hana (33° 56·8' N, 130° 52·6' E) (2.27)—W entrance of Kanmon Fairway.
> Hinoyama Shita (33° 57·9' N, 130° 57·8' E) (2.55)—close E of Kanmon Bridge.
> He Saki (33° 57·3' N, 131° 01·6' E) (2.59)—E entrance of Kanmon Fairway.

Tidal stream signals are displayed from an electric signboard mounted on a quadrangular metal framework structure, and they indicate the direction of the tidal stream in Hayatomo Seto.

The signals consist of symbols as follows:

> (a) a letter **E** or **W** indicating the direction of the stream
> (b) an arrow pointing up indicating the first period of the stream
> (c) an arrow pointing down indicating the last period of the stream

The symbols are shown continuously by a white isophase light flashing every 2 seconds as follows:

Signal	Meaning
E↑	First period of E-going stream
EE	Middle period of E-going stream
E↓	Last period of E-going stream
W↑	First period of W-going stream
WW	Middle period of W-going stream
W↓	Last period of W-going stream

Arrival reports, Signals and Pilotage
2.13

Arrival reports. Vessels with a draught of 10 m or more, or over 30 000 grt, intending to enter Kanmon Kō or pass through Kanmon Kaikyō, should make a report to the Captain of the Port at Moji Maritime Safety Office not later than 3 hours before arrival off Mutsure Shima or He Saki as appropriate. The report may be made by radio or through the vessel's agent; see also *Admiralty List of Radio Signals Volume 6*.

The report should be prefixed NOTIFICATION ON ENTERING or NOTIFICATION ON PASSING THROUGH and should include the following information:

> (a) Vessels name, call sign, nationality, gross tonnage, draught and name of agent
> (b) ETA off Mutsure Shima or He Saki
> (c) Estimated date and time of entering Kanmon Kō

and berth allocated *or* estimated time of entering Kanmon Kaikyō and final destination

> (d) Amount and type of any dangerous cargo
> (e) Whether the vessel will be under pilotage
> (f) Whether Japanese charts are carried

Vessels using the anchorage areas N of Mutsure Shima (see 2.16) or the quarantine anchorages, should report the time and position of anchoring or of shifting berth.

2.14

Signals. When vessels other than small craft are underway within the harbour limits of Kanmon Kō, they should display International Code Pendant over Pendant 1 to indicate that they have right of way over small craft.

A vessel underway between Mutsure Shima and He Saki should display one of the followng signals to indicate her distination:

Destination	Signal
Kanmon Kaikyō	
—E entrance	First substitute over Flag E
Kanmon Kaikyō	
—W entrance	First substitute over Flag W
Moji Ku	First substitute over Flag M
Shimonoseki Ku	First substitute over Flag S
Tanoura Ku	First substitute over Flag T
Kokura Ku	First substitute over Flag K
Nishiyama Ku	First substitute over Flag N
Wakamatsu Ku	First substitute over Flag W
Vessel proceeding through Kanmon Kaikyō	Flags, K, P, K.

2.15

Pilotage. Pilotage for vessels of 10 000 grt or over passing through Kanmon Kaikyō is compulsory, but pilotage is recommended for all vessels without local knowledge.

Pilotage is compulsory in all the port areas outside the specified channels and fairways in Kanmon Kaikyō. Harbour pilots are not available after sunset.

The pilot will board vessels from W in the vicinity of Mutsure Shima (33° 58' N, 130° 52' E) and those from E off He Saki (33° 57' N, 131° 02' E).

The pilot boat is painted black with PILOT in white on the sides.

Naikai (Inland Sea) pilots take over from Kanmon Kaikyō pilots off He Saki. See also 1.22 and *Admiralty List of Radio Signals Volume 6*.

Chart 1578
Anchorages
2.16

Two **quarantine anchorages,** the limits of which are indicated on the chart, lie off the W entrance to Kanmon Kaikyō, E of Mutsure Shima (33° 58' N, 130° 52' E). There are shoals with depths of less than 10 m in the E anchorage.

There are anchorage areas N of Mutsure Shima for vessels with a draught of 10 m or more, or over 30 000 grt, as follows:

Vessels arriving by day. N of a line drawn 090° from Koshiki Iwa (33° 59' N, 130° 50' E).

Vessels arriving at night. The area between lines drawn 310° and 000° from a position 2600 m 000° from Mutsure Shima Light.

Vessels are requested not to anchor in the **main fairway** which is about 2½ cables wide; it is entered 9 cables NE of Mutsure Shima Light and leads S and SSW along the E side of the W quarantine anchorage to the harbour limit extending NW from Daiba Hana (33° 56·8' N, 130° 52·6' E).

Transfer of liquid cargo between tankers takes place E of Mutsure Shima.

Anchorages for vessels carrying **dangerous cargoes** have been established at Nishiyama Ku (2.28), Wakamatsu Ku (2.30), Kokura Ku (2.41), and Tanoura Ku (2.57).

A **quarantine anchorage,** the limits of which are indicated on the chart, lies off the E entrance to Kanmon Kaikyō, SE of He Saki (33° 57' N, 131° 02' E). A wreck with a depth of 15 m over it, lies in the N part of the anchorage.

Anchorage is **prohibited** in an area over the Kanmon railway tunnel, indicated on the chart, 7 cables NE of Yamasokono Hana (33° 54·7' N, 130° 55·5' E).

REGULATIONS FOR KANMON KAIKYŌ

2.17

The following regulations are in force for vessels proceeding through Kanmon Kaikyō:

(a) Vessels bound E through Hayatomo Seto must be N of a line joining Moji Saki Light-tower (33° 57·5' N, 130° 58·0' E) and the S extremity of Ganryū Shima, 2¼ miles SW, before reaching a line joining Shimonoseki rear leading light (33° 57·5' N, 130° 57·3' E) and **Misumi Yama,** 202 m high, 14 cables SSE.

Vessels bound W through Kanmon Kaikyō should enter Hayatomo Seto N of a line joining Moji Saki Light-tower and the summit of Manju Shima (33° 59·5' N, 131° 01·7' E), before reaching a line joining Hino Yama (33° 58·3' N, 130° 57·8' E) and He Saki Light-tower, 3 miles ESE.

Power-driven vessels of less than 100 grt are exempt from these rules; they should pass as close to Moji Saki as possible, those with the stream against them passing inshore of those with a following stream.

(b) Consequent on (a), large vessels bound E through Hayatomo Seto should keep power-driven vessels of less than 100 gross tons to starboard; bound W, they should keep them to port.

(c) Vessels proceeding through Hayatomo Seto against the stream should make good more than 3 knots over the ground.

(d) Vessels within ½ mile of Moji Saki should sound 3 prolonged blasts at frequent intervals.

(e) Vessels in Kanmon Kaikyō may overtake other vessels when there is adequate sea room.

Signals to be displayed by vessels underway within the harbour limits of Kanmon Kō are listed at 2.14.

DIRECTIONS FOR KANMON KAIKYŌ

Chart 1578
2.18

All vessels approaching or leaving Kanmon Kaikyō should establish communications with the signal stations at Mutsure Shima (2.5) and He Saki (2.59) and display their international signal letters.

The draught of vessels navigating Kanmon Kaikyō is limited to 10 m. Vessels with a draught of between 9·14 m and 10 m should pass through the straits between 1 hour before and 1 hour after HW.

Medium and small size vessels should aim to enter the strait during daylight hours about 1 hour before the tidal

stream in Hayatomo Seto turns from an adverse stream to a following one (see 2.10). The passage of the strait between midnight and dawn is not recommended as the W side is sometimes enveloped in mist.

A vessel should if possible avoid passing through the strait or in and out of the harbours on either side, with a following stream, but if this is unavoidable she should not do so when the stream is running at its greatest strength.

It is unsafe for large vessels to pass through the strait with an appreciable following stream, or at slack water when large numbers of local craft encumber the fairway. Provided they have sufficient power, the best time for large vessels to pass through Hayatomo Seto, the narrowest part, is with an adverse stream of between 2 and 4 knots. About 3¼ knots is reported to be advantageous, as by this time, few small craft will be in the fairway and the chance of meeting any vessel of appreciable size proceeding through the strait in the opposite direction will be minimal. Passage through the strait when a stream of 4 knots or more is running should not be attempted as powerful eddies may cause a dangerous sheer.

A speed of 10–12 knots through the water, increasing to 15 knots through Hayatomo Seto about 1 mile either side of Moji Saki, is recommended. If salvage operations are in progress, it will be necessary to reduce speed to not more than 5 knots.

2.19

The recommended tracks to be followed by vessels in the approaches to, and proceeding through Kanmon Kaikyō are shown on the chart. They should be adhered to as far as possible paying due regard to the regulations (2.17), other vessels in the channel, and to the tidal streams (2.10, 2.11).

West approaches to Kanmon Kaikyō
2.20

Vessels may pass either to the E or to the W of Mutsure Shima (33° 58' N, 130° 52' E) (2.5) depending on draught. Large vessels normally use the channel on the E side although in recent years, with the increase in the number of vessels passing through the straits, even large vessels use the channel on the W side.

E side of Mutsure Shima. The quarantine anchorage is on either side of the channel and large numbers of vessels may be found at anchor; some of these may be close to the fairway. In strong W winds, vessels tend to anchor in the W anchorage under the lee of Mutsure Shima (see also 2.16).

W side of Mutsure Shima. This channel leading through Katashima Suidō is narrow but is less tortuous than the channel E of Mutsure Shima. When rounding Kata Shima (2.5), care is needed to keep clear of Densakuno Se, 2½ cables N of Kata Shima, and the shoal water on the W side of the channel.

Kanmon Fairway—west part
2.21

The passage through Kanmon Fairway between Daiba Hana (2.27) and the W entrance of Ō Seto is not particularly difficult as the channel is wide and the tidal streams are weak. The shoal waters fronting Wakamatsu Ku (2.30) and Kokura Ku (2.41) on the SW side of the fairway are marked by *light-buoys.*

A good lookout must be kept for vessels entering and leaving the various fairways into Wakamatsu Ku and Kokura Ku, although vessels in Kanmon Fairway have right of way over vessels in these fairways (see 2.32 and 2.41).

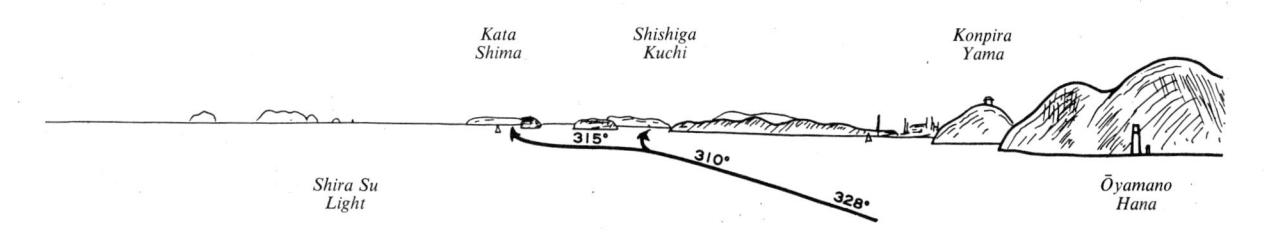

(2.21) Kanmon Kaikyō—W entrance from SE, seen from a position close SW of Ōyamano Hana
(33°54·7′N, 130°54·3′E).

(Original dated prior to 1978)

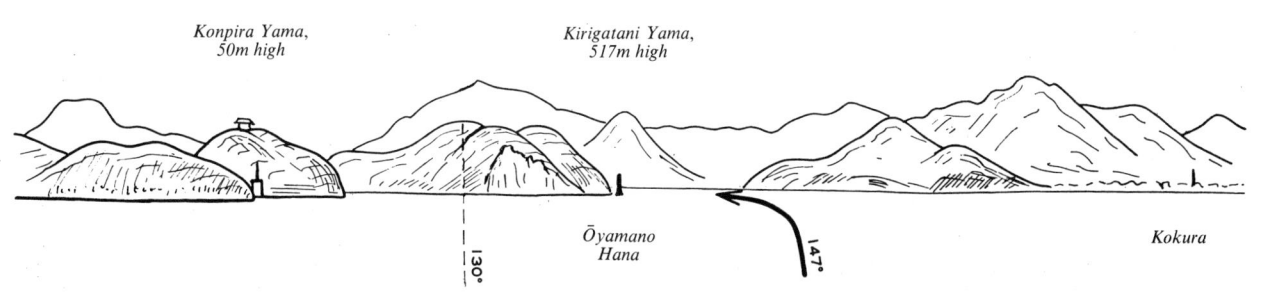

(2·22) Kanmon Kaikyō—Ō Seto from NW, seen from a position about 1 mile NW of
Ōyamano Hana *(33°54·7′N, 130°54·3′E).*

(Original dated prior to 1978)

(2.22) Kanmon Kaikyō—Ō Seto from NE, seen from a position about ¾ mile NE of
Ganryū Shima Light *(33°56′N, 130°56′E).*

(Original dated prior to 1978)

Ō Seto
2.22

Special caution must be exercised when rounding the S end of Hiko Shima in Ō Seto (2.47) which is a blind corner. Many accidents occur here and are mainly attributable to the frequent large alterations of course that have to be made, to the fact that vessels approaching one or another are on converging courses, to the frequent short cuts taken by small vessels making it impossible to pass port side to port side, and to the heavy traffic of harbour craft and ferries.

Eastbound. The S side of the fairway is marked by *light-buoys* but care is needed not to confuse these with numerous other light-buoys in the vicinity of the anchorage off Kokura Ku.

Shin-machi Oki Light-buoy, painted white on one side and red on the other and exhibiting a red or white flashing light every 3 seconds, is moored on the S side of the fairway 6½ cables SE of Kanenotsuru Misaki (33° 54·5′ N, 130° 54·8′ E) (2.29). The light-buoy rotates with the tidal stream; its red light and the red side of the buoy always face upstream.

Three sets of **leading lights, Ō Seto Nos. 1, 2** and **3**, are exhibited from white round metal towers (white triangular topmarks) situated on the SE side of Ō Seto, to assist E-bound vessels in rounding the bend. The use that can be made of these leading lights is best seen from the chart.

Westbound. It is advisable to alter course gradually round Hiko Shima; to avoid being set to the S, and to keep clear of the N edge of the fairway which is much used by small vessels.

Kanmon Fairway—east part
2.23

Between Yamasokono Hana (2.47) and Kanmon Bridge 3¼ miles NE, the E-going stream normally sets towards the Shimonoseki side. During the W-going stream, the effects of a SE-going stream flowing out from between Ganryū Shima (2.49) and Hiko Shima may be experienced on occasions when near Ganryū Shima.

Vessels bound for either Shimonoseki Ku (2.48) or Moji Ku (2.51) and proceeding with the tidal stream, usually turn in the fairway letting go an anchor.

Large numbers of small vessels and ferries cross the fairway between Shimonoseki Ku and Moji Ku.

Hayatomo Seto
2.24

Hayatomo Seto (2.55) is the narrowest and most congested part of Kanmon Kaikyō and vessels must navigate in accordance with the regulations (see 2.17).

Dangerous wrecks lie in the main fairway, respectively, 3 cables SW and 4 cables NE of Kanmon Bridge (2.55).

Hayatomo Seto Light-buoy, painted black on one side and white on the other and exhibiting a green or white flashing light every 3 seconds, is moored on the N side of the narrows 1 cable NE of the W end of Kanmon Bridge. The light-buoy rotates with the tidal stream; its green light and the black side of the buoy always face upstream.

A tidal stream meter is situated close NE of Hayatomo Seto Light-buoy.

Every endeavour should be made to keep in the main

(2.22) Kanmon Kaikyō—Ō Seto from NW
(Original dated prior to 1978)

(2.24) Kanmon Kaikyō—Hayatomo Seto from ENE
(Original dated prior to 1978)

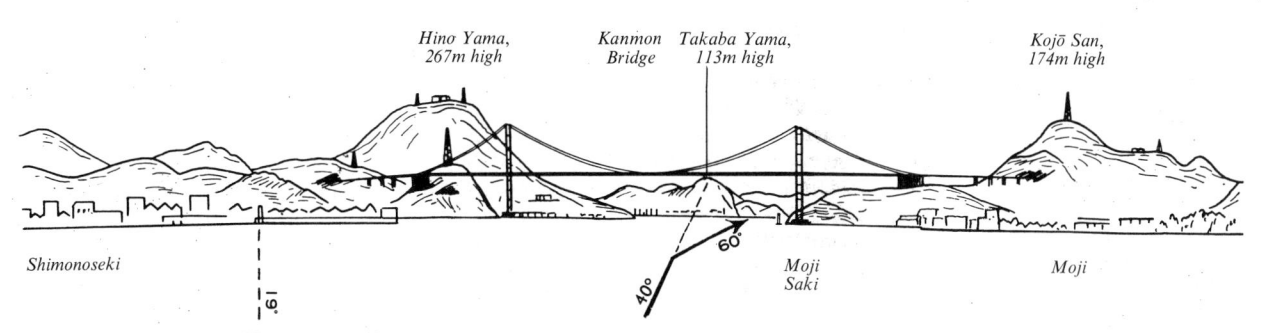

(2.24) Kanmon Kaikyō—Hayatomo Seto from SW, seen from a position about 1¾ miles SW of
Moji Saki *(33°57·5N, 130°58·0E)*.

(Original dated prior to 1978)

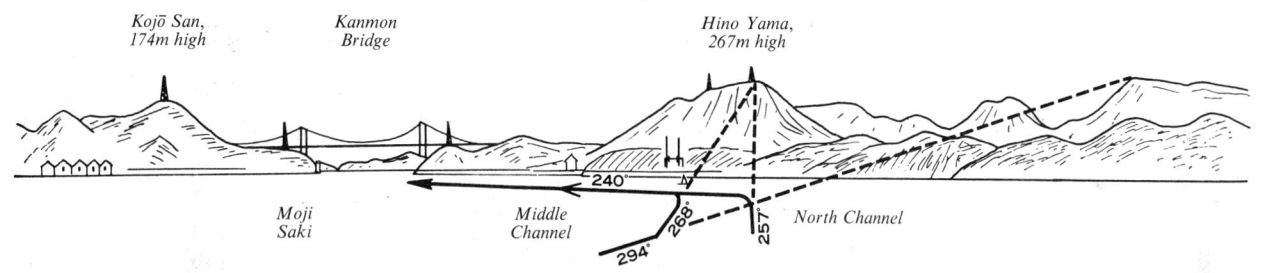

(2.24) Kanmon Kaikyō—Hayatomo Seto from E, seen from a position about 3½ miles ENE of
Moji Saki *(33°57·5N, 130°58·0E)*.

(Original dated prior to 1978)

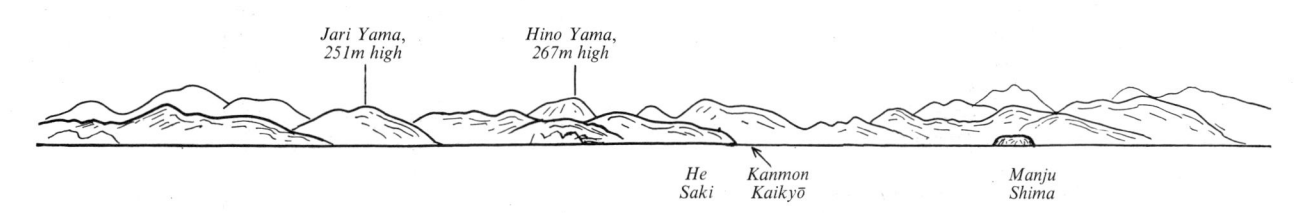

(2.25) Kanmon Kaikyō—SE approach, seen from a position about 8 miles SE of
He Saki *(33°57′E, 131°02′E)*.

(Original dated prior to 1978)

C

stream, which at strength is clearly defined and is easily followed when proceeding in the same direction; when proceeding against the stream, the utmost caution must be observed to avoid the eddies on either side. In order to avoid meeting other vessels in the narrows, close attention should be paid to sound signals (see 2.17).

A vessel proceeding against the stream should give way to those proceeding with it; under no circumstances should a vessel overtake or proceed abeam of another in the narrows.

Clearing line. The Shimonoseki Leading Lights (2.55) situated on Maru Yama, when in line bearing 240°, lead only about $\frac{1}{4}$ cable from the shore bank fringing Dannoura (33° 58' N, 130° 58' E).

Eastbound. E-bound vessels, proceeding with the stream, must avoid being set over towards the N shore at Dannoura into a position where they are starboard side to starboard side relative to W-bound vessels.

With an E-going stream, after passing Moji Saki (2.55), vessels should not alter course to starboard until He Saki bears more than 099°. An alteration too soon after passing Moji Saki may cause the stern to be caught in the E-going stream, the bow caught by an eddy, and the vessel swung violently to starboard.

Westbound. W-bound vessels, proceeding against the stream, may be set over towards the N shore at Dannoura; when attempting to get back into the fairway they must avoid creating the impression that it is intended to pass oncoming vessels to starboard.

East approaches to Kanmon Kaikyō
2.25

The majority of vessels, particularly those bound E, make use of Middle Channel (2.61).

Eastbound. E-bound vessels using North Channel (2.61) must exercise particular caution when crossing tracks of W-bound vessels entering the main fairway from Middle Channel.

At the E end of North Channel where there is a large alteration of course, particular attention must be paid to the tidal streams which on the SSE/NNW leg, set across the fairway.

Westbound. W-bound vessels, proceeding against the stream when leaving Middle Channel, will have the E-going stream on their port bow and may experience difficulty in turning to port and shaping course towards Hayatomo Seto. Consequently, care is necessary to ensure that the vessel is not being set over towards the NW shore.

KANMON KŌ

GENERAL INFORMATION
Chart 1578
2.26

Kanmon Kō, the whole of which is a specified port (see 1.64), occupies most of Kanmon Kaikyō. The port consists of six harbours; Nishuyama Ku (2.28), Wakamatsu Ku (2.30) and Kokura Ku (2.41) in the W part of the strait W of Ō Seto; Shimonoseki Ku (2.48), Moji Ku (2.51) and Tanaoura Ku (2.57) in the E part.

Kanmon Kō is a major port complex which is backed by the city of **Shimonoseki** on the N side, and by **Kita-Kyūshū,** an amalgamation of five cities, lying on the S side; the area is one of the great industrial zones of Japan.

In 1973, the population of Shimonoseki was 259 000 and that of Kita-Kyūshū was 1 050 000.

The harbour limits of Kanmon Kō are shown on the chart.

Arrival reports to be made and signals to be displayed in Kanmon Kō are described at 2.13 and 2.14.

Pilotage. See 2.15.

Regulations. General regulations prescribed by the Port Regulations Law are described at 1.37. Local regulations are in force in Wakamatsu Ku and these are described at 2.32.

Facilities. De-ratting. See 1.70.

A British Consul resides at Moji. See 1.73.

Communications. There are **port radio stations** at Kita-Kyūshū, Moji and Shimonoseki; see *Admiralty List of Radio Signals Volume 6.*

SOUTH WEST SIDE OF HIKO SHIMA

Chart 1578
2.27

Hiko Shima lies on the N side of Kanmon Fairway and is the S'most part of the city of Shimonoseki.

Takenoko Shima (33° 57' N, 130° 53' E) lies on a shoal which extends NW from the W end of Hiko Shima to which it is connected by a **bridge** with a vertical clearance of 15 m.

A **light** is exhibited from a white round structure on **Daiba Hana,** the SW extremity of Takenoko Shima. Tidal stream signals are displayed on Daiba Hana; (see 2.12).

Ichiga Se, with a depth of 8.7 m and marked close N by a *light-buoy,* and **Hira Se** with a least depth of 2 m and marked close SW by a *light-buoy,* lie, respectively, $2\frac{1}{4}$ cables NNW and $1\frac{1}{4}$ cables SW of Daiba Hana.

Haedomari, a fishing harbour protected by two breakwaters, lies on the E side of Takenoko Shima. A **light** is exhibited at the head of each breakwater.

Nishiyama Ku and Fukuura Wan
2.28

Nishiyama Ku, an industrial and timber harbour, lies on the W side of Hiko Shima $1\frac{1}{4}$ miles SE of **Shishiga Kuchi** (33° 56·6' N, 130°52·6' E), the W extremity of the island.

There is a **dangerous cargo** anchorage in Nishiyama Ku.

A pair of **leading beacons** (white metal framework; white triangular topmark), in line bearing 112°, is situated on the E side of Nishiyama Ku and lead into the bay.

A quayed basin with depths from 4 m to 4.9 m, lies in the N part of Nishiyama Ku; a **light** is exhibited at the W entrance point of the basin.

Mitsui Metals Wharf, with a depth of 12·5 m alongside, lies close W of the basin entrance.

Arata Breakwater lies $\frac{1}{4}$ mile SE of the basin entrance; a **light** is exhibited at its head.
2.29

Fukuura Wan is entered on the SE side of **Kabutoyama Misaki** (33° 55·1' N, 130° 54·1' E); it is much used as an **anchorage** for small vessels. A breakwater from which a **light** is exhibited, extends S from Kabutoyama Misaki and a *buoy* marks the edge of shoal water off the S entrance point of the bay.

A log pond protected by a short detached breakwater, lies within Fukuura Wan. A dolphin berth with a depth of 7.5 m alongside, and two red mooring buoys, lie close W of the detached breakwater.

In the outer part of the bay between the entrance and the dolphin berth, there are depths from 7 m to 7.5 m, but elsewhere the depths are less than 3 m.

Ōyamano Hana is a red cliffy point situated $\frac{1}{4}$ mile SSE of Kabutoyama Misaki; a **light** is exhibited from a white metal framework tower with a concrete base standing on the point.

Kanenotsuru Misaki (33° 54·5' N, 130° 54·8' E), the S extremity of Hiko Shima, is situated 4$\frac{1}{2}$ cables ESE of Ōyamano Hana; a **light** is exhibited from a white round stone tower standing on the point.

WAKAMATSU KU

Chart 1578 with plan
General information
2.30

Wakamatsu Ku (33° 56' N, 130° 52' E) lies in **Dōkai Wan** on the S side of the W part of Kanmon Kō. The harbour is divided into Nos. 1–6 Areas the limits of which are indicated on the chart.

The port consists of Anse Hakuchi (2.34), Main Harbour (2.35) and Seitetsu-Tobata Hakuchi (2.38). The towns of **Wakamatsu** and **Tobata** lie, respectively, on the W and E sides of Main Harbour, and the town of **Yawata,** where there are large steelworks, lies S of No. 2 Area.

Landmarks. Numerous tanks and chimneys stand along the shore. Several of the chimneys are conspicuous and their positions can best be seen on the chart; the higher chimneys are painted red and white.

Takatō Yama, with an elevation of 129 m, lies $\frac{3}{4}$ mile W of Wakamatsu Bridge (33° 54' N, 130° 49' E); it is a prominent hill on the summit of which there is a tower which is floodlit at night.
2.31

Pilotage. See 2.15.

Caution. The approaches to Wakamatsu Ku are exposed and with NW winds, heavy seas may build up in the shoal waters and caution should be exercised by deep-draught vessels when approaching the harbour. The entrance across the bar to Wakamatsu Fairway is difficult and during NW winds may be dangerous.

Anchorages. Nos. 5 and 6 Areas are designated as **dangerous cargo** anchorages.

Tidal streams. The tidal streams turn at about the time of HW and LW. The ebb stream in Main Harbour does not appear to exceed 1 knot and the flood stream is somewhat weaker.

Directions. W-bound vessels leaving Wakamatsu Fairway usually pass E of Funa Se (2.35).

E-bound vessels leaving any of the fairways in Wakamatsu Ku and observing a vessel approaching in Kanmon Fairway from SE, should alter course SE into the main fairway as early as safety permits in order that the two vessels may pass port to port.

Regulations
2.32

The following is a summary of the local regulations in force in Wakamatsu Ku:
 (a) A vessel under way in Kanmon Fairway has right of way over a vessel under way in either Anse Fairway, Wakamatsu Fairway or Tobata Fairway.
 (b) A vessel under way in Tobata Fairway or Okudōkai Fairway shall give way to a vessel under way in Wakamatsu Fairway.
 (c) A vessel of over 300 grt intending to enter Wakamatsu Fairway shall report her ETA by noon the previous day. Similarly before leaving through Wakamatsu Fairway or Okudōkai Fairway, she shall report her estimated time of getting under way by noon the previous day.
 (d) A vessel over 1000 grt intending to enter Seitetsu-Tobata Hakuchi shall report her ETA by noon the previous day. Similarly on leaving she shall report her estimated time of getting under way by noon the previous day.
 (e) A vessel over 300 grt leaving Main Harbour through Wakamatsu Fairway or leaving Seitetsu-Tobata Hakuchi through Tobata Fairway, shall hoist the appropriate flag signal by day, and at night exhibit 2 white lights vertically disposed, 30 minutes before getting under way. She shall also sound two prolonged blasts on the whistle.
 (f) In Wakamatsu Fairway and in Okudōkai Fairway, a vessel over 500 grt shall navigate in the central part of the fairway while a vessel of less than 500 grt shall navigate on her starboard side of the fairway.

Traffic signals
2.33

Signal stations are situated as follows:
 (a) Wakamatsu Outer signal station (33° 56·2' N, 130° 50·8' E)—on the N side of Wakamatsu Fairway
 (b) Tobata signal station (33° 55·2' N, 130° 51·8' E)—on the N entrance point of Seitetsu-Tobata Hakuchi Basin
 (c) Central signal station (33° 54·0' N, 130° 48·9' E)—close W of Wakamatsu Bridge
 (d) Maki Yama signal station (33° 53·1' N, 130° 48·9' E)—S of No. 3 Area
 (e) Dōhaku San signal station (33° 52·0' N, 130° 46·5' E)—S of Okudōkai Fairway

Traffic signals, controlling the traffic in Wakamatsu/Okudōkai Fairway and in Tobata Fairway, are displayed as follows:

Signal	Meaning
White light flashing every 2 seconds	Inward-bound traffic permitted
Red light flashing every 2 seconds	Outward-bound traffic permitted
White and red lights flashing alternately every 3 seconds	Outward-bound and inward-bound vessels of under 500 tons (100 tons in Tobata Fairway) permitted
Light exhibiting 3 red flashes and 3 white flashes every 6 seconds	All traffic prohibited except the one vessel permitted by the Captain of the Port

Anse Hakuchi
2.34

Anse Hakuchi (33° 57' N, 130° 50' E) in **No. 6 Area** was being developed in 1977; it lies N of the N'most reclaimed area off Wakamatsu Ku and is protected by a breakwater on its N side.

The harbour is approached from Kanmon Kaikyō through **Anse Fairway,** a buoyed channel dredged to a depth of 13 m. The fairway is entered between *No. 1* and *No. 2 Light-buoys.*

Berths. Anse No. 1 and **No. 2 Quays,** with depths of 13·5 m alongside, lie on the E part of the S side of Anse Hakuchi.

Anse Nos. 3 to **7 Quays,** with depths from 4·5 m to 7 m alongside, lie to the W of Anse No. 2 Quay.

In 1977, further reclamation work was in progress at the inner end of the harbour.

Main Harbour
2.35

Main Harbour is approached from Kanmon Kaikyō through **Wakamatsu Fairway,** a buoyed dredged channel with depths of 10 m in its outer part, which comprises all the waters inward of the fairway. The fairway is entered between *No. 1* and *No. 2 Light-buoys* which are moored ¼ mile SW of **Funa Se,** with a least depth of 7·2 m, which lies on the SW side of Kanmon Fairway; it is marked close N by a *light-buoy.*

In 1974, the least depth throughout the length of Main Harbour was 8 m.

North or **Dōkai Wan Entrance Breakwater** projects ENE from the reclaimed area on the N side of Wakamatsu Fairway; a **light** is exhibited from the head of the breakwater.

Leading lights are exhibited from white framework towers surmounted by white square daymarks. In line bearing 260°, the lights lead through the outer leg of Wakamatsu Fairway.

Shin Nippon Steel Jetty, a dolphin sea-berth with a depth of 7·4 m alongside, lies 4 cables WSW of the root of North Breakwater. A **light** is exhibited on the central dolphin and the approach to the berth is indicated by a **direction light,** the centre of the white sector bearing 309°.

2.36

Kita Minato, a tidal basin, lies in **No. 4 Area** and is entered from the W side of the fairway. There are depths from 0·6 m to 4·5 m at the inner end of this basin where there is quayage for vessels up to 1000 tons.

Wakamatsu Bridge, with a least vertical clearance of 38 m, crosses the fairway, 8 cables S of the entrance to Kita Minato. A fixed green **light** exhibited on the bridge marks its centre and a fixed red **light** marks each side of the channel.

No. 3 Area lies between the bridge and **Katsura Shima,** formerly an island but now the N extremity of reclaimed land, 1 mile SW. Numerous numbered mooring buoys lie on both sides of the channel in this area.

No. 2 Area, which contains **Yawata Basin,** is entered E of Katsura Shima and extends 1 mile S. It has depths from 5·5 m to 10·2 m and extensive quayage used exclusively for handling products of **Yawata Steelworks.** There are several lettered mooring buoys in the basin.

Okudōkai Fairway, a buoyed channel, leads from the entrance to Yawata Basin through No. 1 Area to the head of the harbour.

Berths in Main Harbour
2.37

Berths. The principal berths in Main Harbour are as follows:

Berth & Position	Depth m	Capacity tons
No. 5 Area		
Hibiki Nada Quay		
(33° 55·7' N, 130° 49·7' E)		
Berth 1	10	10 000
Hibiki Nada Dolphin Berth		
(33° 55·6' N, 130° 49·5' E)		
Berth 1, 2	10	10 000
No. 4 Area		
Uchiura Quay		
(33° 54·5' N, 130° 49·4' E)		
Berth 1–4	3–7	Up to 2 000
5	8–10	8 000
Tobata Shoko Wharf		
(33° 54·1' N, 130° 49·5' E)	6–8·5	Up to 10 000
No. 3 Area		
Wakamatsu Wharf		
(33° 53·7' N, 130° 48·5' E)	2–7	Up to 3 500
No. 2 Area		
Yawata Steel Quays		
(33° 52·6' N, 130° 48·5' E)		
Berth 1–20	4·5–10·5	Up to 7 000
No. 1 Area		
Scrap Iron Quay		
(33° 52·8' N, 130° 47·4' E)		
Berth 1, 2	8–9	7 000
Kurosaki Public Quay		
(33° 52·7' N, 130° 46·8' E)	6	4 000
Mitsubishi Coal Wharf		
(33° 52·5' N, 130° 46·1' E)	9–10	15 000

Seitetsu-Tobata Hakuchi
2.38

Seitetsu-Tobata Hakuchi (33° 55' N, 130° 52' E) is approached through **Tobata Fairway,** a buoyed channel, close S of the outer part of Wakamatsu Fairway. The fairway is entered between *No. 1* and *No. 2 Light-buoys* and in 1973 had a least depth of 17 m.

Leading lights are exhibited from white metal framework towers (triangular topmarks). In line bearing 213°, the lights lead through Tobata Fairway to the entrance of Seitetsu-Tobata Hakuchi.

Another set of **leading lights** are exhibited from white metal columns (triangular topmarks) situated at the head of Seitetsu-Tobata Hakuchi. In line bearing 246°, the lights lead into the basin.

A breakwater extends 2 cables NE from the S entrance point of Seitetsu-Tobata Hakuchi.

Shoketsu Hunadarami Basin is entered close N of the N entrance point of Seitetsu-Tobata Hakuchi and has a depth of 6 m in its entrance. **Shoketsu Quay** with depths from 4·4 m to 5 m alongside, lies on the W side of the basin and there are dolphin berths with depths of 5 m alongside, on both the E and W sides.

2.39

Berths. The principal berths in Seitetsu-Tobata Hakuchi are as follows:

Berth & Position	Depth m	Capacity tons
Kita-Kyūshū LNG Jetty		
S side of basin	15	64 000

Seitetsu-Tobata Hakuchi Quays
N and W sides of basin

Berth 1, 2	9·5–13	20 000
3	13	40 000
4	17	
6, 7	4·5–8	2 000
8	12	30 000
9	11	20 000

Regulation. A vessel not fitted with a funnel guard is prohibited from passing within 50 yards of Kita-Kyūshū LNG Jetty.

Facilities and supplies in Wakamatsu Ku
2.40

Facilities. There is a joint Harbour Office in Wakamatsu Ku which contains the offices of the Maritime Safety Agency, Customs and Immigration.

There are numerous tugs, lighters and harbour launches.

Repairs can be carried out at the Wakamatsu Shipyard in Kita Minato in No. 4 Area. There are several other small shipyards.

Ferry services link the Wakamatsu and Tobata sides of the main harbour, S of Wakamatsu Bridge.

Supplies. Fresh water is laid on to the principal quays. Fuel oil and water can be supplied by barge.

Communications. International airlines run from Fukuoka Airport about 40 miles SW. Domestic airlines run from Kita-Kyūshū Airport.

KOKURA KU

Chart 1578
2.41

Kokura Ku (33° 54' N, 130° 54' E), a commercial and industrial port, lies on the S side of the W part of Kanmon Kō, SE of Wakamatsu Ku. Extensive reclamation has been carried out and many factories are situated along the harbour front.

The port of Kokura Ku embraces all the quayed basins between the S side of Sakaikawa Fairway (33° 54·8' N, 130° 52·4' E) and **Akasaka** 2¼ miles SE.

Landmarks. The two power station chimneys on the S side of the inner part of Sakaikawa Fairway, and the chimneys of the Suminoto Ironworks on the SE side of Nichimei Hakuchi, are all painted red and white and are conspicuous.

Pilotage. See 2.15.

Anchorage. Kokura Ku is designated as a **dangerous cargo** anchorage.

Regulation. A vessel under way in Kanmon Fairway has right of way over a vessel under way in Kokura Ku fairways.

2.42

Sakaikawa Basin situated ¼ mile S of Seitetsu-Tobata Hakuchi (2.38), lies in the N part of Kokura Ku.

Sakaikawa Fairway, leading into this basin from Kanmon Fairway, has been dredged across **Ō Sone,** which has depths of less than 5 m, thence between *No. 1* and *No. 2 Light-buoys.* A depth of 7·5 m can be carried through the fairway to the head of the basin.

Berths. Tobata Sakai Kawa Public Quay, with depths from 1·4 m to 7·5 m alongside, lies at the inner end of the basin; a dolphin jetty and **Tobata No. 1 Quay** lie on the N side of the basin.

Hiagari N, Nos. 1–6 Quays, with depths of about 5 m alongside, lie in a small basin ¼ mile S of the entrance to Sakaikawa Fairway; Nos. 1 and 2 Breakwaters with a **light** at the head of each, lie on the N side of the entrance to the quays.

2.43

Nichimei (Hiagari) Hakuchi (33° 54' N, 130° 53' E) is approached from Kanmon Fairway through a buoyed channel dredged to 12 m. The channel is entered between *No. 1* and *No. 2 Light-buoys* and a breakwater projects 1½ cables ENE from the N entrance point of the harbour.

Mutsure Dashi, a number of detached patches with a least depth of 5·3 m, lies 3 cables N of the entrance to the channel to Nichimei Hakuchi.

Berths. Hiagari E, Nos. 1–5 Quays, with depths from 6·5 m to 10·5 m alongside, and **Hiagari E, No. 6** and **No. 7 Quays,** with depths from 11·5 m to 12 m alongside, lie on the N side of Nichimei Hakuchi and can accommodate vessels up to 27 000 tons.

Sumitamo Metal Industries No. 1 Quay, with a depth of 12 m alongside and which can accommodate vessels up to 60 000 tons, lies on the S side of Nichimei Hakuchi.

2.44

Sunatsu Hakuchi (33° 53·4' N, 130° 53·8' E) is approached from Kanmon Fairway through **Sunatsu Fairway,** a buoyed channel with depths from 8 m to 10 m; the fairway is entered between *No. 1* and *No. 2 Light-buoys.*

Leading lights are exhibited from white round towers (arrow topmarks); the front light is situated at the E entrance point of Sunatsu Hakuchi and the rear light at the head of the basin. In line these lights bear 232¼° and lead through Sunatsu Fairway.

A short breakwater with a **light** at its head, projects ¼ cable ENE from the W entrance point to the basin.

Murasaki Kawa discharges into a basin (33° 53·5' N, 130° 53·7' E) which is approached through a buoyed channel leading W from Sunatsu Fairway; there is a depth of 10 m in the channel and in the basin except at its head which is shoal. A transporter cable with a vertical clearance of 18 m spans the head of the basin.

Berths. Tōbu Quay and **Daikyō Dolphin Berth,** with depths from 5 m to 8 m alongside, lie on the E side of Sunatsu Hakuchi; **Seibu No. 1** and **No. 2 Quays** and **Sunatsu Ferry Quay,** with depths from 8 m to 8·5 m alongside, lie on the W side of the basin.

Sumitomo Metal Industries No. 1 and **No. 2 Quays,** with depths from 3·5 m to 10 m alongside, lie on the W side of Murasaki Kawa Basin. **Kokura Asano N Wharf** lies on the S side of the basin.

2.45

Takahama Basin, situated ¼ mile E of Sunatsu Hakuchi, is entered through a channel leading S from the NE end of Sunatsu Fairway. A **dolphin berth** with a depth of 5·4 m alongside, lies on the E side of the basin.

2.46

Facilities. There are offices of the Maritime Safety Agency, Customs and Immigration in Kokura Ku.

Three tugs and several lighters are available. Minor repairs can be undertaken.

Waste oil disposal facilities are available in Takahama Basin.

Supplies. Fresh water is available at the quays. Fuel oil can be supplied by lighter.

Communications. Car ferry services run from Nichimei Hakuchi to Tōkyō, Kōbe and Shimonoseki, and from Sunatsu Hakuchi to Matsuyama Kō on Shikoku.

SHIMONOSEKI KU

Chart 1578
2.47

Yamasonoko Hana (33° 54·7' N, 130° 55·5' E), on the NW side of **Ō Seto**, is the SE extremity of Hiko Shima (2.27). A **light** is exhibited from a white framework tower with a stone base standing on the point.

There are LNG berths close N of Yamasokono Hana and in the vicinity of **Deshimachi Hana,** the E extremity of Hiko Shima. The prohibition relating to such berths described at 2.39 applies.

A **submarine oil pipeline** extends ¼ cable from the shore 4 cables N of Yamasokono Hana, where there is an oil fuel storage area; a small red *buoy* marks the outer end of the pipeline.
2.48

Shimonoseki Ku (33° 56' N, 130° 56' E), a mainly commercial port, lies in the E part of Kanmon Kō on the NW side of Kanmon Fairway and fronts the city of Shimonoseki (2.26). It is linked to Kita-Kyūshū on the S side of the strait by road and rail tunnels and by Kanmon Bridge (2.55).

Landmarks. A tall white chimney stands near the root of No. 1 Pier (33° 56·5' N, 130° 55·6' E); a weather observatory with two radio towers is situated 9 cables N of the pier. **Weather signals** are displayed at the observatory (see 1.42).

Pilotage. See 2.15.
2.49

The SW part of Shimonoseki Ku is mostly shoal and in it lies **Ganryū Shima,** a low, flat islet in the E part of which is a shallow inlet. A **light** is exhibited from a prominent white round concrete tower with red bands standing on the E extremity of the island.

Koshiki Se, a group of rocks which dry 0·3 m, lies on a shoal bank extending NNE from Ganryū Shima and is marked by a red **beacon.** *Light-buoys* are moored, respectively, close E, N and W of Koshiki Se.

There are a large number of mooring buoys and piles in the area W of Ganryū Shima.

Leading beacons (red and white in bands) stand at **Enoura** on the NE side of Hiko Shima; in line, bearing 226¼°, these beacons lead in a least depth of 4·6 m, N of Ganryū Shima.

Close N of Enoura is the E entrance to Ko Seto (2.7) and a shallow channel leads through a lock to **Shimonoseki Gyokō,** an important deep-sea fishing harbour off the town of **Honmura.** Two **overhead cables** with a vertical clearance of 27 m, span the channel.

A basin with depths of about 9 m in its approach, lies ¼ mile N of Ganryū Shima. The basin is bordered on its N side by **Hosoe Wharf** and on its S side by **No. 2 Pier.** **No. 1 Pier** projects 2 cables from the W side of the basin.

Hanano-machi Basin lies between Hosoe Wharf and **Hanano-machi Wharf** 1¼ cables E and has depths of 2·5 m to 6 m. A breakwater with a light at its head, projects W from the E entrance point of Hanano-machi Basin.

East Harbour Quay lies 9 cables NE of No. 1 Pier, and **Sotohama-machi Breakwater,** which encloses a shallow basin and has a **light** at its head, is situated at the NE limit of Shimonoseki Ku, 3 cables farther NE.

2.50
Berths. The principal berths in Shimonoseki Ku are as follows:

Berth & Position	Depth m	Capacity tons
No. 2 Pier		
(33° 56·3' N, 130° 55·7' E)		
Berth 15	8–8·5	10 000
16, 17	8–9·5	15 000
No. 1 Pier		
(33° 56·5' N, 130° 55·7' E)		
Berth 9, 10	9	10 000
12, 13	7·5–8·5	10 000
Hosoe Wharf		
(33° 56·7' N, 130° 55·8' E)		Up to
Berth 18–22	5·5–10	15 000
Hanano-machi Wharf		
(33° 56·7' N, 130° 56·3' E)		
Berth 24, 25	11	5 000 dwt
26	6·5–7	5 000 dwt
East Harbour Quay		
(33° 57·0' N, 130° 56·6' E)		
Berth 1	5	1 000
2–4	5–8	4 000 dwt

Facilities. The offices of the Marine Safety Agency, Customs and Immigration are located in the Joint Harbour Office situated at the root of No. 1 Pier.

Eight tugs and 30 lighters are available.

Major repairs can be undertaken. There are a number of dry rocks at Enoura, the largest with a capacity of 25 000 tons.

Waste oil disposal facilities are available in the Hanano-machi Basin.

Supplies. Fresh water is available at the quays. Fuel oil can be supplied by lighter.

Climate. See table at 1.97.

Communications. There is a ferry service to Kita-Kyūshū on the other side of the strait, and to Pusan in Korea.

MOJI KU

Chart 1578
2.51

Moji Ku (33° 57' N, 130° 58' E) lies in the E part of Kanmon Kō on the SE side of Kanmon Fairway and fronts the city of **Moji** which lies within Kita-Kyūshū.

Pilotage. See 2.15.

Vessels may enter or leave the port area of Moji 24 hours a day, but alongside berthing and unberthing at night is at the discretion of the pilot.

Anchorages. Anchorage for large vessels, with good holding ground, sand and shell, is afforded off the Moji Ku quays in depths from 9 m to 11 m.

When a vessel is berthed at Moji Ku No. 1 and No. 2 Quays, no vessel is permitted to anchor in the area to the E of No. 9 Mooring Buoy. When there are no vessels alongside, temporary anchorage is permitted in the area but only if the vessel is leaving on the same day.

Foul areas lie 2 cables and 3¼ cables N of Shiroki Saki (2.53).

There are several numbered mooring buoys many of which exhibit a red **light,** in Moji Ku.
2.52

Directions. The **tidal streams** in Moji Ku are strong and very complicated especially during the W-going main stream when eddies are formed. Care is needed when berthing at buoys or alongside and the set of the tidal stream should be ascertained from the direction in which ships at anchor are swung.

Vessels anchoring must veer ample cable; a strict anchor watch and a lookout for dragging must be kept.

Vessels should avoid entering or leaving Moji Ku during the middle period of the tidal stream.

Vessels intending to secure to a buoy, should unshackle the anchor from the cable prior to entering harbour as the vessel's own cable is used for securing.

It is reported that when vessels are riding out storms secured to mooring buoys, they are better advised to ride to a short bridle rather than to a long one.

Landmarks. A warehouse, painted white, stands on No. 13 Berth and the 10-storied Harbour Office building stands on No. 1 Berth.

The three radio towers standing on **Hiroishi Yama**, 3 cables S of the No. 2 Berth, and a tall chimney close inland of No. 5 Berth, are prominent.

2.53

Kuzuha Basin or **No. 4 Basin** lies on the E side of Kanmon Fairway, 5 cables SE of Ganryū Shima (33° 56' N, 130° 56' E). The basin is divided into two sections by reclaimed land; a **light** is exhibited on the S end of Kuzuha Basin Breakwater. A berth for handling liquefied petroleum gas lies in the S basin. The prohibition relating to such berths described at 2.39, applies.

Shiroki Saki, on which there is a flagstaff, lies 8 cables NE of Ganryū Shima.

Kuzuha Quay on which lie **Berth Nos. 8–10** extends 3 cables SSW of Shiroki Saki.

Foreign Trade Quay on which lie **Berth Nos. 1–7** extends 7 cables NE of Shiroki Saki.

The ferry terminal lies 3 cables NE of the NE extremity of Foreign Trade Quay.

Kajiga Hana (33° 57' N, 130° 58' E) lies 1¼ miles NE of Shiroki Saki.

No. 2 Basin, protected by a detached breakwater and with depths from 2·5 m to 6 m, is entered close S of Kajiga Hana; a **light** is exhibited on the S end of the breakwater.

Shinhama Wharf on which lie **Berth Nos. 11–13** extends 3 cables S from the entrance to No. 2 Basin.

Berths. Details of berths in Moji Ku are as follows:

Name	Berth	Depth m	Capacity tons
Foreign Trade Quays	1–7	7·5–9·5	10 000
Kuzuha Quay	8–10	9·5–10·5	13 000
Shinhama Wharf	11–13	8–9·5	Up to 13 000

2.54

Facilities. The 7th Regional Maritime Safety Headquarters is situated in Moji.

A joint Harbour Office containing the offices of the Maritime Safety Agency, Customs, Quarantine and Immigration, lies near Berth No. 1. There is a **signal station** on the roof of the Harbour Office.

Tugs and lighters are available. Repairs can be undertaken.

There is a hospital and a medical clinic in Moji Ku.

Supplies. Fresh water is laid on to the principal quays and water boats are available. Fuel oil can be supplied by oilers.

Weather signals are shown (see 1.42).

KANMON KŌ—EAST ENTRANCE

Chart 1578
2.55

Moji Saki (33° 57·5' N, 130° 58·0' E) is a salient point ending in a low hillock whence the land rises steeply to **Kojō San**, 174 m high; a **light** is exhibited from a red round concrete tower standing on the point.

A metal tower stands near the summit of Kojō San and a pagoda, illuminated at night by mercury lights, stands 2¼ cables SE of it and is prominent.

Hayatomo Seto lies between Moji Saki and the coast of Honshū NW; the fairway in the narrows is reduced by shoals on either side to about 2½ cables.

Kanmon Bridge, a grey suspension bridge with a least vertical clearance of 62 m, built in 1973, spans Hayatomo Seto; a fixed green **light** exhibited on the bridge marks its centre and a fixed red **light** marks each side of the channel. The towers at each end of the bridge are prominent.

Overhead power cables with a vertical clearance of 72 m, span the channel close NE of the bridge.

Maru Yama, 60 m high, is situated on the NW side of Hayatomo Seto, ½ mile W of Moji Saki.

Shimonoseki Leading Lights are exhibited; the front light from a white round metal tower, 14 m in height, situated at the foot of Maru Yama; the rear light from a white metal framework tower, 6 m in height, surmounted by a white diamond, situated 1 cable WSW of the front light tower. These lights in line bear 240°.

Hinoyama Shita tidal signal station (see 2.12) stands on the N side of Hayatomo Seto, 3¾ cables N of Moji Saki.

Hino Yama, 267 m high and flat-topped, lies 4 cables N of Hinoyama Shita tidal signal station.

2.56

The coast on the N side of the E end of Kanmon Kaikyō between Kanmon Bridge, and **Kushi Saki**, a cliffy headland nearly 3 miles NE, is fringed with a shoal bank which gradually extends farther offshore. *Maeda Oki Light-buoy* is moored on the edge of this bank 1¼ miles ENE of the W end of the bridge.

Kamatokono Se, with a depth of 6·9 m, lies on the S side of the fairway 1 mile ENE of Moji Saki; a *light-buoy* is moored close W of the rock.

Two patches with a depth of 9·6 m and 9·7 m, respectively, lie about midway between Moji Saki and Kamatokono Se; a *light-buoy* is moored 1 cable WSW of the 9·6 m patch.

TANOURA KU

Chart 1578
2.57

Tanoura Ku (33° 58' N, 130° 59' E), which forms the E-most harbour of Kanmon Kō, is situated on the S side of the E end of Kanmon Kaikyō between Moji Saki and He Saki (2.59), 3 miles E. It is an industrial harbour with cement factories and an oil depot, and fronts the town of **Tanoura**.

Landmarks. Cement tanks and a crane painted red stand on Tanoura Wharf No. 4 Berth and are prominent.

Pilotage. See 2.15.

Anchorages. There is a **dangerous cargo** anchorage off Tanoura Ku; the transfer of liquid cargo between tankers takes place off the harbour.

2.58

Marubeni Ōkubo Jetty, an oil berth, lies $\frac{1}{2}$ mile ESE of Moji Saki and can accommodate tankers up to 40 000 tons.

Tanoura Wharf lies on reclaimed land lying between two shallow basins, 1 mile ESE of Moji Saki. **Tachinoura Wharf** extends $\frac{1}{2}$ mile NE from the E entrance point to the E'most basin.

In 1977, further reclamation work was in progress between Tachinoura Wharf and He Saki 1 mile ESE.

Berths. The principal berths in Tanoura Ku are as follows:

Berth & Position	Length m	Depth m	Capacity tons
Marubeni Ōkubo Jetty			
(33° 57·4' N, 130° 58·6' E)	—	10–12	40 000
Tanoura Wharf			
(33° 57·4' N, 130° 59·2' E)			
Berth 3, 4	405	8·5–10	10 000
5–8	728	8–9·5	10 000
Tachinoura Wharf			
(33° 57·8' N, 131° 00·0' E)			
Berth 2–6	925	10	15 000
7, 8	480	12	—
9	185	10	15 000

EAST APPROACHES TO KANMON KAIKYŌ

Chart 1578

2.59

The **Maritime Traffic Safety Law** (see 1.27) applies within Seto Naikai E of a line drawn NW from **Tobigasu Yama** (33° 57·5' N, 131° 00·2' E).

He Saki (33° 57·4' N, 131° 01·5' E) is the S arm of the E entrance to Kanmon Kaikyō; a **light** is exhibited from a white round stone standing on the point.

Haji Yama, 125 m high, lies close SW of He Saki and a red-coloured quarry lies on its S slope.

A **signal station,** from which berthing and anchoring signals are shown, and a tidal signal station (see 2.12) stand close to He Saki Light-tower. Vessels can communicate with the signal station at all times.

Quarantine anchorage. See 2.16.

2.60

Nakano Su, an extensive sandbank with depths of less than 5 m and a least depth of 2·8 m, lies in the E entrance to Kanmon Kaikyō about midway between He Saki (33° 57·4' N, 131° 01·5' E) and Manju Shima, 2$\frac{1}{4}$ miles N.

Light-buoys mark the E and W ends and the N and S sides of Nakano Su.

Tobiga Su, a sandbank with a least depth of 9·3 m, lies 1$\frac{1}{4}$ cables off the NE side of Tachinoura Wharf (2.58) 1 mile NW of He Saki. A *light-buoy* is moored 2$\frac{1}{4}$ cables NW of Tobiga Su.

Manju Shima (33° 59·4' N, 131° 01·7' E), 49 m high and thickly wooded, lies on the N side of the E approach to Kanmon Kaikyō; a **light** is exhibited from a white round concrete tower standing on the S side of the island. *Manju Shima Light-buoy* is moored 3$\frac{1}{2}$ cables SE of Manju Shima.

Kanju Shima, 30 m high and thickly wooded, lies on a shoal bank midway between Manju Shima and Kushi Saki (2.56). Several above and below-water rocks extend out to 1$\frac{1}{4}$ cables S and SE from Kanju Shima; *Toyohu Oki Light-buoy* is moored 4$\frac{1}{2}$ cables SSW of the islet.

Numerous **fish havens** lie on the edge of the coastal bank SW of Kushi Saki and S and SE of Kanju Shima.

2.61

North Channel, with a least depth of 10·4 m, leads from *Shimonoseki SE Fairway No. 1 Light-buoy* (33° 56·6' N, 131° 02·6' E), E and N of the light-buoys marking the N side of Nakano Su, to Hayatomo Seto.

Middle Channel, with a least depth of 12 m, leads from *Shimonoseki SE Fairway No. 1 Light-buoy*, N of Tobiga Su and S of Nakano Su, to Hayatomo Seto.

From Shimonoseki SE Fairway No. 1 Light-buoy, the recommended track E through Seto Naikai is marked by fairway light-buoys (see 3.1 and Chart 3225).

Charts 1578, 3225

2.62

Chōfu (33° 59·5' N, 130° 59·8' E) a suburb of Shimonoseki, lies close N of Kushi Saki (2.56).

A channel entered between *No. 1* and *No. 2 Light-buoys* situated 3 cables W of Manju Shima (2.60), leads from Kanmon Kaikyō to the N part of **Chōfu Hakuchi.** The fairway has depths of about 7 m and is buoyed.

No. 2 Breakwater lying in a NNE/SSW direction, lies 4 cables NW of Manju Shima; in 1965 another breakwater was under construction extending 3 cables NE from Kanju Shima.

Miyasaki Breakwater, at the head of which there is a **light,** protects a basin in the S part of Chōfu Hakuchi.

Reclaimed land projects ESE from the shore 4 cables NNE of Miyasaki Breakwater; a conspicuous power station chimney (red and white), with an elevation of 201 m, stands on the reclaimed land, and a wharf with a depth of 5·5 m alongside, lies on the S side.

In 1977, land was being reclaimed and an industrial site was under construction, 1 mile NNE of Chōfu Hakuchi.

CHAPTER 3

SUŌ NADA

GENERAL INFORMATION

Charts 2874, 3225

3.1

Suō Nada is the W part of Seto Naikai and lies between Honshū on the N and Kyūshū on the S side, from the E entrance to Kanmon Kaikyō in the W to a line joining Hime Shima (33° 44' N, 131° 40' E) and Iwai Shima (33° 47' N, 131° 58' E) in the E.

Route. The recommended track through Suō Nada leads ESE from *Shimonoseki SE Fairway No. 1 Light-buoy* (33° 57' N, 131° 03' E) and is indicated on the charts; the track is marked by fairway *light-buoys* moored about 5 miles apart.

The least depth of water along the recommended track through Suō Nada is 9·3 m and is found near the W end 1 mile SE of No. 2 Fairway Light-buoy; E of No. 3 Fairway Light-buoy the depths are over 17 m.

Anchorage can be obtained anywhere in the W part of Suō Nada.

Caution. Fishing nets, extending up to 5 miles from the shore, may be found between He Saki (33° 58' N, 131° 01' E) and Nakatsu Kō, 22 miles SSE.

Tidal streams in Suō Nada are weak and generally in the direction of the recommended track.

3.2

Seibu Sekiyū Sea-berth, an offshore oil terminal consisting of a mooring buoy available to vessels up to 250 000 grt, lies close S of the recommended track 6 miles S of Ube Kō (33° 56' N, 131° 13' E). A red **light** (Morse U) is exhibited and a fog signal is sounded from the buoy which is privately maintained.

A **submarine pipeline** is laid between the buoy and the shore NNW.

Pilotage. A berthing pilot can be embarked in the vicinity of the sea-berth. Tugs are available. There is communication with the shore by radio telephone.

Anchorage can be obtained SE of the buoy where the holding ground is reported to be good. Berthing at the buoy is carried out about 1 hour after HW and only by day.

SUŌ NADA—NORTH SIDE

KUSHI SAKI TO MOTOYAMA MISAKI

Chart 3225

3.3

A large shallow bay with a sandbank at its head, lies between Kushi Saki (33° 59' N, 131° 00' E) (2.56) and **Miya Saki** 7 miles E.

Landmark. Ryūō San, 134 m high with a clump of trees on its summit, surmounts a point situated 3 miles SSE of Miya Saki.

3.4

Onoda Kō (33° 58' N, 131° 10' E), protected by two breakwaters, is entered 1 mile N of Ryūō San; a **light** is exhibited at the head of the N breakwater. In 1973, the population of **Onoda,** which lies on the E side of the harbour, was 34 000.

Cement is the principal shipment from Onoda Kō.

Landmarks. Four power station chimneys, with an elevation of 76 m, on the S side of the harbour, and the several chimneys of Onoda Cement Works farther N, are good marks from seaward.

Tidal streams. Outside the harbour, the tidal stream is NW-going on the flood and SE-going on the ebb at a rate of 1 to 1¼ knots.

A narrow channel marked by *light-buoys* and with depths from 5 m to 7 m, leads to the harbour entrance; it is entered between *No. 1* and *No. 2 Light-buoys* moored 2¼ miles SW of Ryūō San. There are seaweed beds on both sides of the channel.

In 1979, reclamation work was in progress on the N side of the entrance to Onoda Kō. There are several mooring buoys in the N and E parts of the harbour.

Berths. There are two quays on the S side of the harbour with reported depths from 4 m to 7·5 m

alongside. A quay and a dolphin berth, with depths from 5 m to 6 m alongside, situated in the N part of the harbour, serve the cement works.

Facilities. Vessels up to 500 tons can be slipped at the inner end of the harbour.

Supplies. Fresh water is laid on to the quays and there is a small oiler.

Chart 676 plan of Ube Kō

3.5

Motoyama Misaki (33° 56' N, 131° 11' E), 1¼ miles SSE of Ryūō San, is a salient point terminating in a steep cliff on which stands a conspicuous tree. **Okino Se,** with a least depth of 0·9 m over it, lies 5 cables S of Motoyama Misaki and is marked close S by a *light-buoy.*

UBE KŌ

Charts 3225, 676 plan of Ube Kō

3.6

Ube Kō (33° 56' N, 131° 14' E), a specified port (see 1.64), lies at the mouth of **Kotō Kawa** between Motoyama Misaki and **Ube Misaki,** a low point on which there is an airfield, 4¼ miles E. Large quantities of fertiliser and cement are shipped out from Ube Kō. The harbour limits are shown on the charts.

The town of **Ube** which in 1973 had a population of 155 000, lies on the NE side of the harbour and in the past was the centre of considerable coal mining activities. The largest submarine coal mines in Japan are situated in this area.

Landmarks. Shimofuriga Take, 248 m high, lies 5¼ miles N of Ube Misaki. From SW it appears as three peaks and owing to the low lying land in the vicinity, it shows up well.

Several conspicuous chimneys, the higher of which are painted red and white and are marked by red obstruction lights, stand within the harbour area of Ube Kō; their positions can best be seen from the charts.

Pilotage. A harbour pilot is embarked in the quarantine anchorage.

Motoyamano Su, a sand spit with depths of less than 5 m, extends 3¼ miles SSW from Ube Misaki. A **light** is exhibited from a white concrete tower with black bands standing 6 cables NE of the S extremity of Motoyamano Su.

Numerous metal towers are situated in the vicinity of Motoyamano Su; they are marked by red lights.

A **quarantine anchorage** lies 1½ miles WNW of the light-tower on Motoyamano Su. An obstruction with a depth of 6·4 m lies near the NE corner of the anchorage.

Chart 676 plan of Ube Kō

Harbours

3.7

A buoyed channel dredged to a depth of 7·5 m, leads to **Seibu Sekiyū Pier** projecting S from reclaimed land 1¼ miles NE of Motoyama Misaki (33° 56' N, 131° 11' E); the channel is entered between *No. 1* and *No. 2 Light-buoys* moored 1½ miles SE of Motoyama Misaki.

Seven finger piers, with depths from 5·2 m to 6·2 m alongside, project E from the shore 3 cables NE of Motoyama Misaki.

West Harbour consists of two basins lying close E of the mouth of Kotō Kawa and entered through a buoyed channel with depths in its outer part from 4 to 6 m. *No. 1* and *No. 2 Light-buoys* are moored at the entrance of this channel 1½ miles ESE of Motoyami Misaki.

Main Harbour lies 2½ miles E of Motoyami Misaki and is entered between two reclaimed areas; on the SE side of the entrance a short breakwater projects WSW from the shore. A **light** is exhibited on each side of the entrance.

Main Fairway, buoyed and dredged to 9 m, leads from *No. 1 and No. 2 Light-buoys* moored 2½ miles SE of Motoyami Misaki, into Main Harbour.

East Harbour lies on the SE side of Main Harbour and is entered S of a reclaimed area. **East Fairway,** buoyed and dredged to 9 m, leads off Main Fairway into East Harbour. **Leading lights,** in line bearing 058°, lead through the channel into the harbour.

Vessels with a draught of 11 m and 7·6 m can use Main and East Fairways at HW and LW, respectively.

Chart 3225

A fishing harbour, protected by two breakwaters, lies ¾ mile SE of East Harbour; a **light** is exhibited on the head of the W breakwater. Seaweed beds containing thousands of steel piles, extend up to 2 cables offshore on either side of the entrance to the fishing harbour.

Chart 676 plan of Ube Kō

Berths and facilities

3.8

Berths. The principal berths in Ube Kō are as follows:

Name & Position	*Depth* *m*	*Capacity* *tons*
Seibu Sekiyū Pier		
(33° 56·3' N, 131° 12·1' E)		
W side	12	15 000
Main Harbour		
Shibanaka Wharf		
(33° 56·0' N, 131° 14·3' E)	7–9	20 000
Ube Kōsan		
(33° 56·4' N, 131° 14·2' E)		
No. 5 Quay	11	20 000
No. 6 Quay	11	—
Okinoyama Wharf		
(33° 56·5' N, 131° 14·2' E)	9·5	15 000
Ube Kōsan		
(33° 56·8' N, 131° 14·5' E)		
Nos. 1, 2 and 3 Quays	7–10	Up to 10 000
East Harbour		
Shibanaka E Wharf		
(33° 55·9' N, 131° 15·1' E)	8–9	5 000

Facilities. There are offices of the Maritime Safety Agency, quarantine, customs and immigration in Ube Kō.

Four tugs including one of 3000 h.p. are available.

Waste oil disposal facilities are available on the E side of Seibu Sekiyu Pier.

Minor repairs can be undertaken.

De-ratting: see 1.70.

Supplies. Fresh water can be supplied at the main quays.

Communications. Ube Airport lies on the E side of the harbour and from it there are domestic services to Tōkyō and Ōsaka.

UBE MISAKI TO NISHIDOMARI SAKI

Chart 3225

Ube Misaki to Kusayama Saki

3.9

The coast between Ube Misaki (33° 55' N, 131° 16' E) (3.6) and **Maruo Saki** a low point 5 miles ENE, is backed by low hills which have no distinguishing features; it is fringed with a shoal bank extending up to 1¾ miles offshore.

Kamega Se is the S'most of several groups of rocks extending E and SE of Ube Misaki; a **light** is exhibited from a black concrete column standing on this rock.

A number of **fish havens** and numerous laver beds lie off the coast between Ube Misaki and Maruo Saki.

Tokonami, a fishing harbour consisting of two basins protected by breakwaters, lies 2½ miles NE of Ube Misaki; a **light** is exhibited on the E breakwater of the W basin.

3.10

Maruo Kō (33° 58' N, 131° 21' E), a small harbour protected by breakwaters, lies close N of Maruo Saki; a **light** is exhibited on the head of the E breakwater.

Yamaguchi Kō, the depths in which are mostly shoal, is entered between **Tate Ishi** (33° 59' N, 131° 23' E), 3 m high, on the W side, and **Okino Se,** a 1·1 m patch, and **Hira Se,** 1 m high, on the E side; it is an open harbour (see 1.65).

A **light** is exhibited from a white round concrete tower standing on Tate Ishi, and a **beacon** on Okino Se is illuminated by an auxiliary **light** situated on Iwayano Hana (3.11) 4 cables NNE.

A large number of small vessels seek shelter in the inner part of Yamaguchi Kō in bad weather.

3.11

Aio Kō (33° 59' N, 131° 25' E) is entered between

Iwayano Hana (33° 59' N, 131° 24' E) and **Kusayama Saki**, a prominent point 115 m high, 2 miles E.

Take Shima, 35 m high to the tops of the trees, lies 1¼ miles SW of Kusayama Saki; a shoal bank extends 3 cables from its NW and N sides.

Iruka Se, a steep-to rock which dries 1·8 m, lies ½ mile SW of Take Shima and is marked close S by a *light-buoy*.

A number of **fish havens**, indicated on the chart, lie in the approaches to Aio Kō.

A yellow survey *light-buoy* is moored about midway between Iwayano Hana and Take Shima.

A **light** is exhibited from a white round concrete tower which stands on the summit of a hill on the E side of the entrance to Aio Kō. An auxiliary **light** shows over **Kamagino Se**, which dries 2·7 m, and **Okozeno Se**, which dries 1·8 m, situated, respectively, 4 cables S and 2 cables WSW of the light-tower; a **beacon** stands on each rock.

Anchorage for small vessels up to 50 tons is afforded in depths from 2 m to 5 m, in the entrance to the bay.

There are three basins used by fishing vessels in Aio Kō; a **light** is exhibited at the head of each of two breakwaters protecting the two basins on the E side of the harbour.

Charts 2874, 3225
Ōmi Wan to Nishidomari Saki
3.12

Ōmi Wan is entered between **Koiso Saki** (34° 00' N, 131° 29' E), 2¼ miles NE of Kusayama Saki, and **Chisō Hana**, 1¼ miles ESE; the depths in the bay are shoal and its shores consist mostly of sandy beaches.

Ōmi Wan Kohama Jetty with a **light** at its head, lies on the W side of the bay 4 cables N of Koiso Saki. There is a fishing harbour at **Ōmi**, protected by a breakwater, 1 mile farther NNW; a **light** is exhibited on the head of the breakwater.

Chart 2874

A **fish haven** lies ½ mile ESE of Ōmi Wan Kohama Jetty.

Nishinoura Kō (34° 00' N, 131° 31' E), protected by breakwaters, lies on the E side of Ōmi Wan ¼ mile N of Chisō Hana; a **light** is exhibited on the head of the S breakwater. A buoyed channel with a depth of 5·2 m leads to a pier, with a depth of 5 m alongside, within the harbour.
3.13

Saba Shima (33° 58' N, 131° 31' E), thickly wooded with pine trees and 30 m (100 ft) high, lies 2 miles S of Chisō Hana; a **light** is exhibited from a white square concrete tower which stands on the islet. A bank on which are two rocks the SE of which dries 2·1 m (7 ft), extends 3 cables ESE of Saba Shima.

Nishidomari Saki (34° 00' N, 131° 33' E) lies 1¼ miles ESE of Chisō Hana and is the W entrance point of Nakanoseki Kō (3.14). A **light** is exhibited from a white square concrete tower which stands on the slopes of the hills close NW of the point.

MITAJIRI-NAKANOSEKI KŌ

Charts 2874, 3153
3.14

Mitajiri-Nakanoseki Kō, an open harbour (see 1.65), consists of the harbours of Nakanoseki Kō and Mitajiri Kō which lie respectively, SW and NE of **Mukō Shima** (34° 00' N, 131° 35' E).

Landmark. Nishiki Yama, 353 m high, lies near the centre of Mukō Shima and is a good mark; two television masts lie close N of the summit.

Toiyaguchi Seto, a narrow channel about 1 mile long, separates Mukō Shima from the mainland; although the channel dries, it is used by small craft at HW. It is spanned by an opening **bridge** and an **overhead cable** with a vertical clearance of about 17 m.

Chart 2874

Nakanoseki Kō is entered between Nishidomari Saki (3.13) and **Ushiga Kubi** the SW extremity of Mukō Shima, 8 cables SE. **Kuro Se,** 2 m high, lies 1½ cables S of Ushiga Kubi and is marked close S by a *light-buoy*.

Fish havens and seaweed beds lie off the W entrance point to Nakanoseki Kō.

A fairway dredged to 7·5 m and marked by *light-buoys* leads to **Nakanoseki Quay,** with depths from 4·6 m to 7 m alongside, lying at the head of the harbour. *No. 1 Light-buoy* moored off the W extremity of Mukō Shima, marks the entrance to the fairway.

The town of **Nakanoseki** lies on the N side of the harbour.

Chart 3153
3.15

Mitajiri Kō is entered between **O Saki** (34° 01' N, 131° 36' E), the E extremity of Mukō Shima, and **Ryūgū Saki,** ½ mile NE. **Mitajiri Kō Light** is exhibited from a white round concrete tower which stands on Ryūgū Saki.

No. 2 Light-buoy is moored 2¼ miles SE of Ryūgū Saki.

A fairway, dredged to 7·2 m and marked by *light-buoys*, leads to **Heiwa Wharf** lying on the W side of the harbour. There are depths from 4 m to 7 m alongside the wharf and two mooring buoys are laid off its N end.

A shallow channel leads from Heiwa Wharf to the town of **Mitajiri** which forms part of the industrial city of **Hōfu** which in 1973 had a population of 102 000.

In 1979, land was being reclaimed to the NE of Heiwa Wharf.

Tidal streams. In Mitajiri Kō the flood stream is NW-going and the ebb stream is SE-going; the rate of the stream does not exceed ½ knot.

Fish havens and seaweed beds lie off the S coast of Mukō Shima and off the E entrance point to Mitajiri Kō.

Facilities. There is a customs office in Mitajiri Kō. There are no tugs.

Supplies. Fuel oil and fresh water can be supplied at Heiwa Wharf.

Hino Yama, 144 m high   Ōmi Yama 323 m high

Maruo Saki   Aio Kō   Akaishi Hana   Mukō Shima

(3.11) Suō Nada—N shore, seen from a position about 8 miles SSW of Maruo Saki (33° 58' N, 131° 21' E)
(Original dated prior to 1978)

61

TOKUYAMA—KUDAMATSU KŌ

Chart 3153 with plan
General information
3.16

Tokuyama-Kudamatsu Kō (34° 00' N, 131° 48' E), a specified port (see 1.64), comprises the area embraced by Tokuyama Wan and Kasado Wan; it is a good natural harbour with deep water and is a **harbour of refuge** (see 1.67).

The **harbour limits** are shown on the chart. The harbour is divided into Nos 1, 2, 3 and 4 Areas the limits of which are also shown on the chart.

Tokuyama and **Kudamatsu**, with a combined population of 156 000 in 1973, are both industrial centres with many factories.

Landmarks. Shikuma (Shikumaga) Take (34° 06' N, 131° 46' E) (see Chart 2874), 503 m (1649 ft) high, lies 7 miles N of the entrance to Tokuyama Wan; it is a densely wooded peak and is very prominent despite the fact that E and W of it there are higher mountains.

A chimney stands at an elevation of 231 m in the SW part of Ōshima Hantō (3.18) on the E side of the entrance to Tokuyama Wan, and is prominent from a distance. A large number of oil tanks, painted white, stand on the NW side of Ōshima Hantō 1¼ miles NNE of the chimney.

Pilotage. Pilotage is not compulsory. If required, the pilot will embark S of the entrance to Tokuyama Wan close E of Tokuyama No. 2 Light-buoy (34° 57' N, 131° 45' E).

Anchorages. The **quarantine anchorage** for Tokuyama-Kudamatsu Kō lies in Tokuyama Wan and is indicated on the chart. There is another quarantine anchorage (3.26) in No. 4 Area SE of Kasado Shima.

Deep-draught vessels should anchor S of the entrance to Tokuyama Wan.

Fish havens. A number of fish havens consisting of sunken hulks, concrete blocks or scrap metal, lie in the approaches to and around the islands enclosing Tokuyama-Kudamatsu Kō; the majority lie close inshore and their positions are best seen from the chart.

Typhoons. At the time of a typhoon vessels of less than 10 000 tons should seek sheltered anchorage in the W part of Tokuyama Wan or in the S part of Kasado Wan. Vessels of over 10 000 tons will be given guidance by the Captain of the Port for anchoring outside the harbour.

Approaches to Tokuyama Wan
3.17

The S approach to Tokuyama Wan is marked by *No. 1 Fairway Light-buoy* (Chart 2874) and *Tokuyama No. 2 Light-buoy*, moored 8 miles and 1 mile, respectively, S of the harbour entrance.

No Shima (33° 56' N, 131° 42' E), lies in the SW approach to Tokuyama Wan and is a flat-topped islet 75 m high. A **light** is exhibited at the S end of No Shima and an auxiliary **light** illuminates a **beacon** standing on **Omo Se,** which dries 3·1 m, 7 cables SSW.

A **light** is exhibited at the head of a breakwater at **No Shima Kō** on the W side of No Shima.

Hira Shima and **Oki Shima** lie within 6 cables N of No Shima, the three islands being joined by drying reefs.

Hiburi Saki (33° 55·6' N, 131° 49·2' E), an islet with two summits densely covered with pine trees, lies at the S extremity of Kasado Shima (3.24); a **light** is exhibited from a white round concrete tower which stands on the islet.

Tokuyama Wan (No. 3 Area)
3.18

Tokuyama Wan, the W part of Tokuyama-Kudamatsu Kō, is enclosed by a number of islands. The greater part of the bay lies in No. 3 Area.

On the SW and W sides of the bay, from S to N, lie **Su Shima** (33° 56' N, 131° 44' E), 83 m high, **Uma Shima** 164 m high, and **Otsu Shima,** 185 m high. Uma Shima and Otsu Shima are connected by a low isthmus. **Miyaichiko** and **Itsutsu Shima,** small islets, lie close off the W side of Otsu Shima.

No. 2 Light-buoy is moored on the W harbour limit 3 cables NW of the N extremity of Otsu Shima.

On the SE side of Tokuyama Wan, from W to E, lie **Iwa Shima,** consisting of two islets close together, **Sukumo Shima,** 137 m high, and **Ōshima Hantō.** A **light** is exhibited from a white round stone tower standing on the N islet of Iwa Shima.

Tidal streams. In Tokuyama Wan the tidal streams turn shortly after the times of HW and LW. In the main entrance to the bay between Su Shima and Iwa Shima, the spring rate of both streams is about 1¼ knots, but in the middle of the bay they do not exceed ½ knot.

On the rising tide the stream divides after passing through the main entrance; one branch flows N through Nakayano Seto and thence NE, and the other branch flows W through Senshima Suidō; the two branch streams meet N of Kurokami Shima where no stream is experienced.

3.19

Channels. The main deep-water channel into Tokuyama Wan from S lies between Su Shima and Iwa Shima; it is about 5 cables wide and has depths exceeding 30 m.

Except for a channel 1 cable wide with a depth of 6·4 m, the passage between Iwa Shima and Sukumo Shima is obstructed by reefs. A *buoy* (yellow can topmark) is moored 1½ cables NNE of Iwa Shima Light-tower.

Anchorages. Anchorage is possible almost anywhere in Tokuyama Wan taking care to avoid the various **submarine pipe-lines** and **submarine cables** indicated on the chart. The depths in the S part of the bay are from 11 m to 18 m, mud, and in the N part less than 10 m.

Berths. Idemitsu Sea-berth, consisting of seven mooring buoys (yellow lights), lies 6 cables NE of Iwa Shima. A **submarine pipeline** is laid between the sea-berth and the coast of Ōshima Hantō, ENE; two yellow conical *buoys* and a white spherical *buoy* are moored

Obira Yama
630 m high

Sukumo
Shima

| *Ryūgū* | *No Shima* | *Uma* | *Tokuyama* | *Ōshima* | *Kasado* |
| *Saki* | | *Shima* | *Wan* | *Hantō* | *Shima* |

(3.16) Tokuyama-Kudamatsu Kō from S, seen from a position about 10 miles SSE of No Shima (33° 56' N, 131° 42' E).
(Original dated prior to 1978)

near the seaward end of the pipeline. A *light-buoy* is moored on the N side of the sea-berth.

There is a depth of 20 m at Idemitsu Sea-berth which can accommodate vessels up to 200 000 dwt. Berthing must take place at HW slack and tug assistance is required.

Nishiga Mori Jetty, with a depth of 12 m alongside, projects N from the shore of Ōshima Hantō, 1¼ miles E of Iwa Shima. A **light** is exhibited from a grey column standing at the head of the pier and two mooring buoys lie off the pierhead.

Another pier with two mooring buoys off its head, suitable for a small vessel, lies on the S side of **Ryōdo Hana,** 5 cables NNE of Nishiga Mori Jetty.

Idemitsu Oil Installation lies on the NW side of Ōshima Hantō. **No. 5 Ōhura Jetty,** with a depth of 12 m alongside, lies 1½ miles NE of Idemitsu Sea-berth; **No. 3 Ōhura Jetty** with a depth of 11 m alongside, lies ½ mile farther NE. There are mooring buoys off these berths.

Two **submarine oil pipelines,** marked by yellow *buoys*, are laid NE from the N part of Idemitsu Oil Installation to Idemitsu Oil Refinery in Tokuyama.

3.20

Kurokami Shima, thickly wooded and 312 m high, and **Sen Shima,** 160 m high, lie on the NW side of Tokuyama Wan and are joined by a low isthmus.

Nakayano Seto, between the N end of Otsu Shima and the W side of Kurokami Shima, is encumbered by reefs at its S and N ends on which stand, respectively, **Kaba Shima,** 37 m high, and **Kaeru Shima,** 46 m high. The channel to the E of these two islets is deep.

The channel W of Kaba Shima is greatly reduced in width by rocks and shoals but a depth of 9 m can be carried through the fairway.

Okino Ikada, two islets, lie on a reef 1 cable off the S side of Kurokami Shima; a **beacon,** exhibiting a light, stands on each end of the reef.

Tokuyama Wan (No. 1 Area)

3.21

Senshima Suidō (34° 02' N, 131° 45' E), the N channel into No. 1 Area of Tokuyama Wan, is entered at *No. 3 Light-buoy* between the N side of Kurokami Shima and reclaimed land on the mainland to the N. The channel is buoyed and is dredged to a depth of 9 m.

Two **leading beacons** consisting of white metal posts (triangular topmarks) are situated on the W side of Sen Shima, and in line bearing 085¼°, lead through the first leg of Senshima Suidō.

Two **leading light-beacons,** consisting of white metal framework towers (triangular topmarks), stand on **Toyō Sōda Wharf** situated 4 cables NNE of **Matsuga Hana,** the NW extremity of Sen Shima. These light-beacons in line bearing 043½°, lead through the second leg of Senshima Suidō. Two **beacons** situated on the NE side of Kurokami Shima, in line astern bearing 223½°, also mark this alignment.

Toyō Sōda Basin lies on the W side of Toyō Sōda Wharf. A pair of **leading lights,** in line bearing 311½°, leads into a basin situated SW of Toyō Sōda Basin.

Tokuyama Sōda Nanyō Wharf lies on the E side of a basin entered 3 cables N of **Su Hana,** the NE extremity of Sen Shima; a pair of **leading lights,** in line bearing 004¾°, lead into this basin.

Okino Ikada, a reef partly above water, lies 1 cable E of Su Hana; a **light** is exhibited from a white round concrete tower standing on the reef.

3.22

A buoyed channel, dredged to 10 m, leads from No. 3 Area to **Harumi Wharf** situated ½ mile ESE of Okino Ikada; the channel is entered between *No. 1* and *No. 2 Light-buoys* moored ½ mile N of the NE limit of the quarantine anchorage. In 1978, the reclaimed area on the E side of this channel was being extended SSW.

The channel divides N of Harumi Wharf, one branch leading to the E end of Senshima Suidō and the other NNE to **Tokuyama Sōda Quay.** A pair of **leading beacons** (triangular topmarks), in line bearing 020¼°, leads to this quay.

A fairway, entered between *No. 1* and *No. 2 Buoys* moored close E of **Sa Shima** (34° 01' N, 131° 48' E), 75 m high, lying ½ mile off the NW side of the N part of Ōshima Hantō, leads to the E part of No. 1 Area. *No. 3 Buoy* is moored 7 cables NE of Sa Shima.

Nachi Wharf lies in the N corner of this part of No. 1 Area, 1¼ miles N of Sa Shima. The Harbour Office and port radio station are situated on this wharf.

Idemitsu Kōsan Oil Refinery, with numerous tanks and chimneys, extends along the shore situated to the SE of Nachi Wharf. Several piers project from this part of the shore and there is a boat harbour at **Kushigahama** on the E side of the bay.

3.23

Berths. The principal berths in Tokuyama-Kudamatsu Kō No. 1 Area are:

Berth & Position	*Depth* *m*	*Capacity* *tons*
Toyō Sōda Basin		
(34° 03·1' N, 131° 45·9' E)		
Cement Pier	12	15 000
No. 1 Container Wharf	9–10	15 000
Tokuyama Sōda Quay		
(34° 03·1' N, 131° 47·8' E)		
Salt Jetty	10	27 000
Minato-chō Wharf		
(34° 02·8' N, 131° 47·8' E)	5·5	3 000
Harumi Wharf		
(34° 02·4' N, 131° 47·6' E)	7–10	15 000
Nachi Wharf		
(34° 02·3' N, 131° 48·3' E)	7	5 000
Idemitsu Kōsan Refinery		
(34° 02·1' N, 131° 48·8' E)		
Central Pier	12	35 000

Kasado Wan (No. 3 Area)

3.24

Kasado Wan, the E part of Tokuyama-Kudamatsu Kō, lies between the SE side of Ōshima Hantō and the NW side of **Kasado Shima,** 2 miles SE.

The SW or main entrance to Kasado Wan is divided into two channels by a chain of islets and rocks; of these **Shimokōzu Se** (33° 57·5' N, 131° 47·0' E), dark and 2 m high, is the W'most rock of the chain.

Kamikōzu Se, light grey and 10 m high, lies on a shoal 3 cables ESE of Shimokōzu Se. **Furu Shima,** 58 m high and covered with pine trees, lies ½ mile E of Kamikōzu Se. **Myōken Dashi,** a rocky 3.6 m patch, and **Tsukuka Se,** a pinnacle rock with a depth less than 2 m, lie, respectively, 3 cables SW and 4 cables E of Furu Shima.

"A" light-buoy is moored 3 cables NNE of Furu Shima.

Within Kasado Wan, **Fuka Ura** with a fishing village at its head, is the W of two bays on the NW side of Kasado Shima; **fish havens** lie in the entrance to Fuka Ura. **Enoura** lies at the head of the E of the two bays.

Nakamo is a shoal that occupies a large portion of the N part of Kasedo Wan; its shoalest part has a depth of

5.7 m. At times Nakamo is thickly covered with seaweed.

Anchorages. Vessels can anchor anywhere in Kasedo Wan in depths from 11 m to 16 m, mud and good holding ground. Fuka Ura, in the S part of the bay, is a good anchorage.

Kasado Wan (No. 2 Area)
3.25

No. 2 Area of Tokuyama-Kudamatsu Kō lies in the NE part of Kasado Wan. The city of Kudamatsu (3.16) lies at the head of the bay. There are several factories, with numerous chimneys, in the city and an oil refinery at its SE end.

Suetake Kawa flows into the bay close W of the city. **Kudamatsu Gyokō**, protected by two breakwaters, lies on the W side of the mouth of Suetake Kawa; a **light** is exhibited at the head of the W breakwater.

Kudamatsu No. 2 Wharf and **Kudamatsu No. 1 Wharf** lie, respectively, on the W and E sides of the mouth of **Kirito Kawa** which flows into the bay 1 mile E of Suetake Kawa.

The controlling depth in the approach channel leading to the Kudamatsu wharves is 10·5 m.

Tokuyama-Kudamatsu Kō (No. 4 Area)
3.26

No. 4 Area of Tokuyama-Kudamatsu Kō lies to the E of Kasado Shima.

A **quarantine anchorage,** indicated on the chart, lies close off the E side of Kasado Shima.

Nippon Sekiyū New Oil Refinery lies on reclaimed land 7 cables NE of **Kamaishi Misaki** (33° 58' E, 131° 53' E), the NE extremity of Kasado Shima. **Nippon Sekiyū Sea-berth** projects from the S end of the oil refinery; **lights** are exhibited on the pierhead and from the dolphins at each end of the berth. The berth is protected by a submersible oil boom.

Two **leading beacons** (red and white columns, red triangular topmarks), in line bearing 019°, lead towards the sea-berth. *No. 1* and *No. 3 Light-buoys* are moored on the W side of the alignment, respectively, 7 cables S and 2 cables ENE of Kamaishi Misaki.

Tera Saki lies 8 cables NNW of Kamaishi Misaki and a *light-buoy* is moored close NE of it. **Nakano Se,** with a least depth of 11·3 m, lies 1 cable N of Tera Saki.

Nippon Sekiyū South Pier is situated on the mainland 5 cables N of Tera Saki; six red mooring buoys, some exhibiting red lights, lie off the pier.

Two **leading beacons** (white masts, triangular topmarks) stand close NW of Nippon Sekiyū South Pier and, in line bearing 322°, lead to the berth.
3.27

Berths. The principal berths in Tokuyama-Kudamatsu Kō Nos. 2 and 4 Areas are:

Berth & Position	Depth m	Capacity tons
Kudamatsu No. 2 Wharf		Up to
(34° 00·2' N, 131° 51·4' E)	4·5–10	10 000
Nippon Sekiyū West Pier		
(33° 59·5' N, 131° 52·2' E)	7–9	5 000
Hitachi (Hidatsu) Wharf		
(33° 59·0' N, 131° 52·7' E)	9·5	10 000
Nippon Sekiyū South Pier		
(33° 59·1' N, 131° 52·4' E)	13	50 000
Nippon Sekiyū Sea-berth		
(33° 58·6' N, 131° 53·4' E)	20	190 000 dwt

Miyano Seto
3.28

Miyano Seto, between **Seto Misaki** (33°59·2' N, 131°51·6' E), the N extremity of Kasado Shima, and **Miyanosu Hana,** a narrow tongue of land extending WSW from the mainland, is the SE approach to Kudamatsu. A **light** is exhibited from a white round concrete tower standing on Miyanosu Hana.

Miyano Seto is deep but only about 1 cable wide, it is spanned by a **bridge** with a vertical clearance of 24 m, and by an **overhead cable** with a vertical clearance of 27 m. The centre of the bridge, which is illuminated at night, is marked by red and green fixed lights.

Tidal streams in Miyano Seto are N-going on the rising tide and S-going on the falling tide, turning about 2 hours before HW and LW. The rate may reach 2 knots.

Hikari Kō
3.29

Hikari Kō (33° 57' N, 131° 56' E), a narrow basin, is entered on the E side of the mouth of **Shimata Kawa. Shin Nippon Steel Quay** lies in this basin.

Ōminase Shima, 83 m high, lies ¼ mile S of the entrance to Hikari Kō; a **light** is exhibited from a white round concrete tower on its S end. **Kominase Shima,** consisting of two islets, lies on a reef extending 4 cables NW from the N end of Ōminase Shima and is connected to it by a breakwater.

A small harbour protected by a breakwater lies 1¼ miles SE of Hikari Kō; a **light** is exhibited on the head of the breakwater.

Facilities in Tokuyama-Kudamatsu Kō
3.30

There are offices of the Maritime Safety Agency, Customs, Quarantine and Immigration in Tokuyama and offices of the Maritime Safety Agency and Customs in Kudamatsu.

There are eight tugs (200–5000 hp) and numerous harbour launches.

Repairs can be undertaken at **Kasado Dockyard** in Enoura (3.24) where there are three dry docks.

Waste oil disposal facilities are available at the Idemitsu Kōsan Refinery situated ¼ mile NE of Miyanosu Hana (3.28).

Medical and dental facilities are available.

De-ratting; see 1.70.

Supplies. Fresh water can be supplied at the main wharves. Fuel oil is available.

KINE SAKI TO KAMINOSEKI KAIKYŌ AND OFF-LYING ISLANDS

Chart 2874
Kine Saki to Sagono Seto
3.31

Murozumi Hantō (33° 55' N, 131° 58' E) lies 3 miles SE of the mouth of Shimata Kawa (3.29) and the intervening shore consists of a sandy beach backed by green pine trees. Murozumi Hantō is 116 m (380 ft) high, thickly covered with pine trees and is prominent.

Kine Saki is the SW extremity of Murozumi Hantō and **Zōbi Misaki** consisting of a spit of sand and gravel, is the NE extremity. **Murozumi Kō Light** stands on Zōbi Misaki.

Murozumi Kō (33° 55' N, 131° 58' E), on the E side of Murozumi Hantō, is entered N of Zōbi Misaki; it consists of a small bay open SE in which the depths are less than 12 m, sand and mud. It is suitable as a sheltered **anchorage** for vessels up to 500 tons.

The town of **Murozumi** lies at the head of the harbour and is well known as a tourist resort and has a flourishing fishing industry.

There is a landing jetty at the town with depths from 1·5 m to 2·5 m on its NW side.

There is a ferry service from Murozumi Kō to Ushi Shima 4½ miles SE.

A number of **fish havens** lie within ½ mile of Kine Saki and also close to the coast ESE of Zōbi Misaki.

3.32

Ushi Shima (33° 51' N, 132° 01' E), 154 m (504 ft) high with four thickly wooded summits of about equal height, lies 4½ miles SSE of Murozumi Hantō. A **light** is exhibited from a red round concrete tower standing on **Kaitsuke Hana,** the N extremity of the island.

Ushi Shima Kō lies in a bay on the NW side of Ushi Shima which is well protected from SE and affords **anchorage** in depths from 10 m to 23 m, mud. A breakwater with a **light** exhibited at its head, is situated on the S side of the bay.

Submarine cables, one of which is a power cable, are laid from the bay on the NW side of Ushi Shima to the mainland N.

Fish havens lie 2 cables WNW of Kaitsuke Hana and 1 cable N of the W extremity of the island.

O Shima (33° 52' N, 131° 59' E), consisting of two grassy islets joined by rocks which dry, lies 1 mile NW of Ushi Shima. The S and larger islet is 39 m (130 ft) high and is surmounted by a solitary pine tree.

3.33

Kandori Saki (33° 54' N, 132° 02' E) lies 3 miles SE of Murozumi Hantō (3.31). A shallow spit on which lie Uma Shima, Hane Shima and Sagō Shima, extends SE from the shore E of Kandori Saki.

Umashima Suidō, the channel between the mainland and **Uma Shima** (33° 54' N, 132° 03' E) is about ½ mile wide but is encumbered with rocks some of which dry; it leads to Hirao Kō (3.35) at the N end of Sagō Wan. A **light** is exhibited from a red round concrete tower standing on **Maru Iwa** one of the rocks in the middle of Umashima Suidō. A depth of 2·2 m can be carried through the channel about midway between the rocks and the mainland but local knowledge is necessary.

Yōgai Yama, the summit of Uma Shima, is 108 m (356 ft) high and thickly covered with pine trees.

Hane Shima is joined to Uma Shima by a drying bank, and the shallow channel between it and Sagō Shima to the S is only about 1 cable wide. An **overhead cable** with a vertical clearance of about 18 m, crosses this channel.

Sagō Shima (33° 52' N, 132° 04' E) has a ridge, 121 m (396 ft) high, running N and S through its centre and on it are a large number of pine trees. **Ikada Se,** a black rock 4 m high, lies on a shoal extending 3 cables SW from the SW point of the island; a **light** is exhibited from a black round concrete tower standing on the rock.

A narrow channel suitable for small craft with local knowledge, lies between Ikada Se and Sagō Shima.

Sagono Seto lies between the SE end of Sagō Shima and Koyamano Hana, the N point of Naga Shima, and is about 6 cables wide (see also 3.39). The channel is used by vessels entering or leaving Sagō Wan (3.35).

Charts 2874, 3602

Murotsu Hantō and Sagō Wan

3.34

Murotsu Hantō is a mountainous peninsula which

extends 7 miles SSE from the coast NE of Kandori Saki (33° 54' N, 132° 02' E) (3.33). The ridge in the N part of the peninsula is surmounted by large pine trees; in the S part of the peninsula **Ōza San,** 526 m high, is the highest mountain in the vicinity and from E appears treeless and conical.

Chart 2874

3.35

Sagō Wan is bordered on its W side by Uma Shima (33° 54' N, 132° 03' E) (3.33), Sagō Shima and Naga Shima, and on its E side by Murotsu Hantō. The sound affords good sheltered anchorage with a bottom of mud, clear of a **submarine cable** which runs NE from the NE extremity of Sagō Shima, to Murotsu Hantō.

Hirao Kō (33° 54' N, 132° 03' E), an open harbour (see 1.65), lies at the NW end of Sagō Wan but is only suitable for small vessels up to 100 tons. A narrow peninsula on which stand a factory and a shipbreakers yard, projects W from the NW side of Murotsu Hantō.

Sagōwan Hakuchi, on the S side of the peninsula, affords **anchorage** in depths from 7 m to 13 m mud; there are a number of red mooring buoys in the N part of this anchorage and **submarine cables** run from the N end of Uma Shima to the W end of the peninsula.

Befu Hakuchi, the inlet on the N side of the peninsula, affords sheltered **anchorage** in depths from 5·5 m to 9 m; there is a quay and landing jetties in this inlet.

Islands south west of Sagō Wan

3.36

Iwai Shima (33° 47' N, 131° 59' E), 6 miles SW of Sagono Seto (3.33) the SW entrance to Sagō Wan, is a mountainous island with a flattened summit 355 m (1167 ft) high in its E part, and a conspicuous densely wooded peak, 330 m high, in its W part.

Koiwai Shima, 208 m (681 ft) high, conical and thickly wooded, lies 1 mile NW of Iwai Shima; it is rocky and steep-to on all sides. **Fish havens** lie within 1½ miles on all sides of Koiwai Shima.

Magoiwai, a grassy islet 37 m (120 ft) high, lies close off the W end of Iwai Shima to which it is joined by reefs.

Eboshi Se, a rock awash, lies 1½ cables ESE of the E extremity of Iwai Shima and between the two there are several rocks which dry.

Fish havens lie within 1 mile NE, SE and S of Iwai Shima.

Hanaguri Seto, a deep-water channel nearly 1½ miles wide, lies between Iwai Shima and Naga Shima 2 miles E. A *light-buoy* is moored on the W side of the S approach to Hanaguri Seto.

3.37

Naga Shima, a large island, lies between Iwai Shima and the SW side of the S end of Murotsu Hantō. **Kamisakari Yama,** the summit, is 313 m (1029 ft) high and lies near the NE end of the island; its NW slope is bare of trees.

Hanaguri Shima (33° 47' N, 132° 02' E), thickly wooded and cliffy on all sides, lies on the E side of Hanaguri Seto close off the SW extremity of Naga Shima; a **light** is exhibited from a white round concrete tower standing on the W point of the islet.

The passage between Hanaguri Shima and Naga Shima is almost completely obstructed by reefs and only passable by fishing boats.

Amada Shima lies 1½ miles ESE of Hanaguri Shima; the passage between it and the S extremity of Naga Shima is obstructed by rocks. The S point of Amada

Shima consists of a steep red cliff, 66 m (219 ft) high; a **light** is exhibited from a white round metal tower standing on the point.

Foul ground extends 4 cables SW from the SW side of Amada Shima.

Fish havens lie within 8 cables NNW, 4 cables WSW, 6 cables SE and 4 cables NE of Amada Shima and off the SE coast of Naga Shima.

Chart 3602

Yoko Shima (33° 49' N, 132° 07' E) lies in the S approach to Kaminoseki Kaikyō (3.40) $\frac{3}{4}$ mile S of the E end of Naga Shima. It is 91 m high, covered with scrub and steep-to except within 1 cable of its SE side.

Fish havens lie within 2 miles SW and $\frac{3}{4}$ mile E of Yoko Shima.

Chart 2874

3.38

Kanō Shima (33° 49' N, 132° 03' E), situated 1 mile off the NW side of Naga Shima, consists of three thickly wooded islets the central and highest of which is 33 m (107 ft) high and prominent. **Fish havens** lie 1 mile ESE, $\frac{1}{2}$ mile NE and $1\frac{1}{2}$ miles ENE of Kano Shima.

A **light** is exhibited at the head of a breakwater at **Siraida** on the NW side of Naga Shima $1\frac{3}{4}$ miles E of Kanō Shima.

3.39

Koyamano Hana (33° 51' N, 132° 05' E) is the NW point of Naga Shima; a pine wood surmounting a hill 4 cables S of the point is very prominent. The wood and a cliff on the NW face of the hill, are good marks for identifying the S side of Sagono Seto.

Kame Iwa, 3 cables NE of Koyamano Hana, has three heads, the N'most of which is awash; a **light** is exhibited from a red round concrete tower with black bands, standing on the S'most head which dries 2·7 m (9 ft).

Clearing line. The N extremity of Ushi Shima (3.32), bearing about 277° and kept midway between Ikada Se (3.33) and the SW extremity of Sago Shima, leads close N of Kame Iwa.

Nakoya Saki, $1\frac{1}{4}$ miles SE of Koyamano Hana, is foul within $1\frac{1}{2}$ cables. **Nabe Shima,** 15 m high and coloured red, lies $1\frac{3}{4}$ miles farther SE; it is flat-topped, sparsely covered with shrubs and lies on the W side of the N approach to Kaminoseki Kaikyō (3.40).

Anchorages. Vessels with local knowledge can obtain anchorage sheltered from W winds either off **Shidai,** a village on the E side of the S part of Naga Shima, or in a bight off **Kamai** a village $1\frac{3}{4}$ miles farther NE.

Chart 3602

Kaminoseki Kaikyō

3.40

Kaminoseki Kaikyō is the strait between **Tōrono Hana** (33° 50' N, 132° 07' E), the E extremity of Naga Shima and the SW extremity of Murotsu Hantō (3.34). The fairway, in which there are depths from 9 m to 12 m, is reduced by shoals on either side to a width of about $\frac{1}{4}$ cable. Tōrono Hana is fringed by rocks within $\frac{1}{2}$ cable E.

Kaminoseki Kaikyō is spanned by **Kaminoseki Bridge** with a vertical clearance of about 23 m; a green fixed light marks the centre of the bridge and a red fixed light marks each side of the clear passage.

Murotsu Light is exhibited from a white round concrete tower which stands on a rocky projection on the N side of the strait close E of the bridge. The red sector of this light covers rocks lying within $1\frac{1}{2}$ cables of the shore 1 mile E of the light-tower, between the bearings of 250° and 274°.

Caution. The traffic through Kaminoseki Kaikyō is very heavy and care is needed particularly with respect to vessels towing. Ferries cross the strait between Kaminoseki Kō and Murotsu Kō close W of the bridge.

Tidal streams. The flood stream is E-going and the ebb stream is W-going, the turn of the tidal stream occurring about 1 hour after that in Ōbatake Seto. The spring rate is about $2\frac{1}{4}$ knots.

3.41

Leading lights are situated on the S side of Kaminoseki Kaikyō; the front light is exhibited from a white tower (triangular topmark), 11 m in height, and the rear light from a similar tower, 7 m in height, situated close SSE of the front light. The lights in line bear 154°.

Directions. Kaminoseki leading lights are principally used by E-bound vessels; W-bound vessels should make an early turn to starboard after passing through the narrowest part of the strait.

Taishi Yama, 62 m high, wooded and rather pointed, is situated 3 cables NW of the front leading light and is a good head mark for W-bound vessels. **Shiro Yama,** 57 m high and rather flat, lies $1\frac{1}{2}$ cables N of Taishi Yama.

Anchorage. During strong NW winds, temporary anchorage can be obtained in depths from 3 m to 20 m, sand, about 3 cables E of the Murotsu Light-tower, but in depths less than 6 m there are rocks on either side of the anchorage.

Submarine cables, indicated on the chart, run from a position 6 cables ENE of Murotsu Light-tower to Heigun Shima and Ya Shima.

Charts 2874, 3602

3.42

Kaminoseki Kō (33° 49·8' N, 132° 06·9' E), a small harbour protected by breakwaters, lies on the W side of Kaminoseki Kaikyō, N of the narrows; a **light** is exhibited at the head of the N breakwater.

There are depths from 5 m to 7 m within the harbour which is principally used by local fishing vessels. There is a jetty with a depth of 5 m alongside at the inner end of the basin.

Anchorage is afforded in depths of 20 m, about $\frac{1}{2}$ cable off the breakwaters at Kaminoseki Kō.

Fukuura Hakuchi, a small bay enclosed by mountains on three sides, is entered 4 cables NW of Kaminoseki Kō; it affords **anchorage** sheltered from SW winds and is also used by small vessels at the time of a typhoon.

3.43

Murotsu Kō (33° 50' N, 132° 07' E) lies on the E side of Kaminoseki Kaikyō, N of the narrows; part of the harbour is protected by **Shōwa-machi Breakwater,** on the head of which a **light** is exhibited, projecting SW from the shore $4\frac{1}{2}$ cables N of Murotsu Light-tower. The harbour is used by small vessels sheltering from strong E winds and by those awaiting a favourable tidal stream through the strait. **Anchorage** is afforded in depths from 5 m to 15 m, sand and mud.

In 1980, a breakwater extending SW and S from a point 1 cable N of the root of Shōwa-machi Breakwater, was under construction.

A quay used by the ferries is situated about 1 cable SE of the breakwater and there is a short pier $1\frac{1}{2}$ cables farther S.

Facilities. There is a Maritime Safety Agency office in Murotsu Kō.

SUŌ NADA—SOUTH SIDE

Chart 3225
He Saki to Inoura Kō
3.44
The coast between He Saki (33° 57' N, 131° 02' E) (2.59) and **Takeno Hana**, 3¼ miles SSW, is rocky and indented.

Hishakuda Kō (33° 54' N, 131° 00' E), a boat harbour protected by a breakwater, is entered 4 cables W of Takeno Hana; a **light** is exhibited at the head of the breakwater.
3.45
Shin-Moji Hakuchi is the area lying between Hishakuda Kō and Inoura Kō, 3¼ miles S. Extensive reclamation work has been carried out in the S part of Shin-Moji Hakuchi and a basin with depths from 5 m to 7·5 m, lies between reclaimed areas 2¼ miles SSW of Takeno Hana.

The basin is approached by a buoyed channel dredged to a depth of 6 m; the inner end of the channel is partially protected on its S side by a breakwater extending NE from the shore. *No. 1* and *No. 2 Light-buoys*, the outermost pair of channel buoys, are moored 1¼ miles SE of Takeno Hana.

Idemitsu Kōsan No. 1 and **No. 2 Dolphin Jetties**, with depths from 5·5 m to 6 m alongside, lie on the SE side of the basin; **Shin-Moji No. 1** and **No. 2 Quays** with depths from 3 m to 4·5 m alongside, lie at the head of the basin.

The Nagoya/Moji car ferry berths at a quay on the NW side of the basin.
3.46
Inoura Kō (33° 50' N, 130° 59' E), protected on its SE side by a breakwater, is entered close S of the reclaimed area forming the S side of Shin-Moji Hakuchi; a **light** is exhibited at the head of the breakwater.

The harbour is entered between *No. 1* and *No. 2 Light-buoys* moored off the head of the breakwater. Within the breakwater, in the channel leading to the inner harbour, there are depths of 2·7 m.

Landmark. There are some red cliffs on the W side of the harbour which are conspicuous from E.

Kanda Kō
3.47
Kanda Kō (33° 48' N, 131° 00' E), an open harbour (see 1.65) and an industrial port, lies 3 miles SSE of Inoura Kō and is divided into two basins by reclaimed land. It is protected by breakwaters and **Kōno Shima**, 29 m high and round topped. A **light** is exhibited at the head of each of the N and E breakwaters.

Landmarks. Two tall power station chimneys (red and white), with elevations of 202 m and 172 m, respectively, stand in the central part of the harbour and are conspicuous.

Pilotage is not compulsory but harbour pilots are available from sunrise to 1 hour before sunset in the anchorage close S of the entrance channel between *No. 3* and *No. 5 Light-buoys.*

A buoyed channel with depths from 9 m to 10 m, leads to the harbour entrance; *No. 1* and *No. 2 Light-buoys*, the outermost pair of channel buoys, are moored 3¼ miles ENE of Kōno Shima. A wave height survey platform, marked by a red light, stands 1¼ miles S of No. 1 Light-buoy.

In 1979, an area marked by framework towers exhibiting red lights and by numerous yellow *light-buoys*, was being reclaimed N of the entrance channel.

Within the entrance to Kanda Kō, a buoyed channel dredged to 10 m leads W to the N basin or **Hon Kō,** which is shallow at its head. The basin is spanned by an **overhead cable** with a vertical clearance of 56 m.

The S basin or **Minami Kō,** is approached by a buoyed channel, dredged to 7·5 m, lying between Kōno Shima and the reclaimed area W.
3.48
Berths. The principal berths in Kanda Kō are:

Berth & Position	Depth m	Capacity tons
Hon Kō		
Matsuyama Dolphin Berth (33° 47·8' N, 131° 00·3' E)	9·7	15 000
Matsuyama Timber Quay (33° 47·8' N, 131° 00·1' E)	10	15 000
No. 10 Quay (33° 47·5' N, 130° 59·9' E)	9·5–10	10 000
Minami Kō		
Nankō Quay (33° 46·1' N, 131° 00·1' E)	7·5	—
Ferry Quay (33° 46·3' N, 131° 00·0' E)	7·5	11 000

Facilities. There are offices of the Maritime Safety Agency and Customs in Kanda Kō. Immigration authorities will attend from Moji.

Two tugs are available.

Supplies. Fresh water is available on the principal quays. Fuel oil can be supplied by oiler from Moji.

Communications. There are ferry services to Ōsaka and Kōbe.

Chart 2874
Kanda Kō to Unoshima Kō
3.49
The shore between Kanda Kō (33° 48' N, 131° 00' E) (3.47) and Unoshima Kō, 12¼ miles SSE, is low and fringed with pine woods; it consists for the most part of sand and gravel and is fringed by a bank with depths of less than 10 m extending 3 miles offshore in places. Numerous **fishing stakes** lie in depths of less than 5 m along this stretch of coast.

Landmarks. Nuki Yama, a conspicuous, treeless, conical peak 711 m (2332 ft) high, is situated 4¼ miles WSW of Kanda Kō and is the highest peak in the neighbourhood.

Ehiko Yama (33° 30' N, 131° 00' E), 1199 m (3936 ft) high and the highest mountain inland on this stretch of coast, is situated 13 miles SW of Unoshima Kō. **Inuga Take,** 1129 m (3703 ft) high and somewhat pointed, and **Kunimi Yama,** 637 m (2089 ft) high, treeless and rather flat, lie between Ehiko Yama and Unoshima Kō.

Hachiman San, 658 m (2158 ft) high and prominent, lies 9¼ miles SE of Unoshima Kō.

Mino Shima, 60 m (196 ft) high and covered with pine trees, lies 2¼ miles S of Kanda Kō; a prominent wood surmounts a promontory ¼ mile S of Mino Shima.
3.50
Unoshima Kō (33° 38' N, 131° 08' E) is entered between a breakwater on its W side and a quayed breakwater on its E side; a **light** is exhibited on the head of the W breakwater. A detached breakwater extends 3 cables N from a position close W of the head of the W breakwater.

In 1979, a detached breakwater was under construction about 1½ cables N of the quayed breakwater on the E side of the harbour entrance.

A reclaimed area on which stands the **Buzen Power Station,** projects from the coast close W of the W breakwater. A **dolphin berth** with depths from 7·6 m to 8 m alongside, lies on the NE corner of this reclaimed area.

A *light-buoy* (red light) is moored 1½ miles NNE of the dolphin berth and *buoys* mark the channel to the berth.

Caution. A large number of fishing nets and seaweed beds extend seawards up to 4 miles off Unoshima Kō, except in the fairways; care is needed when entering or leaving harbour particularly at night.

Landmarks. A power station chimney (red and white), with an elevation of 200 m, stands on the reclaimed land to the W of the W breakwater and is a good mark. There are several factory chimneys on the S shore of the harbour.

Berths. The E breakwater is quayed on its W side and there are depths from 5·5 m to 7·5 m alongside the outer end.

A large number of fishing boats shelter in the harbour in bad weather.

Supplies. Fresh water and fuel oil can be supplied.

Nakatsu Kō

3.51

Nakatsu Kō consists of two fishing harbours, **Koiwai** and **Yoshitomi,** which lie at the mouth of **Yamakuni Kawa** (33° 37' N, 131° 11' E), and the main harbour, protected by two breakwaters, situated close NW of **Mamaga Saki,** 3 miles ESE. The town of **Nakatsu,** with a population of 55 000 in 1973, lies at the mouth of Yamakuni Kawa.

Landmarks. Two chimneys on the W side of the mouth of Yamakuni Kawa are good marks.

Fairways. The fairway to the fishing harbours lies between two training walls which are covered at HW. **Nakatsu Kō Light** is exhibited from a red round concrete tower standing at the N extremity of the W training wall about 1 mile offshore. The fairway is shallow but is used by local fishing boats at HW.

The main harbour of Nakatsu Kō is entered between the head of North Breakwater and the N end of East Breakwater which is detached; a **light** is exhibited at the head of North Breakwater.

The entrance to the fairway to the main harbour is marked by a *buoy* moored 3½ cables NE of the head of North Breakwater; the depths in the fairway are from 5·1 m to 6·6 m.

Berth. Public Quay with a depth of 5·5 m alongside its greater part, lies on the SE side of the main harbour.

Landmark. A silo on Public Quay is a good mark.

Nakatsu Hirasu, a bank of sand and gravel over which there are depths of less than 2 m, extends about 2½ miles offshore between the mouth of Yamakuni Kawa and the main harbour.

Fish havens lie 1 mile WNW and 2¾ miles ENE of Nakatsu Kō Light-tower.

Seaweed beds extend seawards up to 4 miles off Nakatsu Kō, except in the fairways.

Imazu Kō to Tsurugi Hana

3.52

Imazu Kō (33° 35' N, 131° 16' E), a small harbour, lies 2 miles SE of the main harbour of Nakatsu Kō. A **light** is exhibited from a white round concrete tower standing 1 mile NNE of Imazu Kō.

Ō Se, a bank of gravel, sand and shells, with depths of less than 5 m, extends about 1½ miles offshore 3½ miles E of Imazu Kō; two **fish havens** lie on the bank.

Nagasu Kō (33° 35' N, 131° 22' E) lies on the E side of the mouth of **Yakkan Kawa** and is protected on its W side by a breakwater. A training wall on which a **light** is exhibited, projects N from the harbour.

Takada Kō (33° 35' N, 131° 25' E) lies in the mouth of **Katsura Kawa** which flows into the sea 2½ miles E of Nagasu Kō. A training wall, 1¼ miles long, with a **light** exhibited from a red round concrete tower at its N end, lies on the E side of the river mouth.

3.53

Usuno Hana (33° 38' N, 131° 29' E), lies 5 miles NE of the mouth of Katsura Kawa and between them the shore is fronted by a sandbank which dries out about 1 mile; there are many **fish traps** on this bank.

Naga Saki, a salient cliffy point covered with pine trees, is situated 3½ miles NE of Usuno Hana; **Kakaji Light** is exhibited from a white round concrete tower standing on the point.

Near the extremity of Naga Saki lies a remarkable rock on which there are some pine trees which resembles a boat under sail when seen from E or W.

Kakaji Kō, a small harbour protected by breakwaters and used only by small vessels with local knowledge, lies in a bay on the W side of Naga Saki. A **light** is exhibited on the head of the N breakwater.

Fish havens lie 1¼ miles SW, 8 cables W, and up to 4 miles NE and 2¼ miles ENE of Naga Saki.

Biwa Saki, a cliffy point, lies 2 miles E of Naga Saki; a **light** is exhibited from a white round concrete tower standing on the point.

A **fish haven** lies 3¾ miles N of Biwa Saki.

3.54

Takedatsu Kō (33° 41' N, 131° 35' E) is entered between Biwa Saki and **Kame Saki,** 1 mile E. **Tarō Iwa,** a drying rock surmounted by a stone **beacon,** lies 2 cables off the E entrance point and is illuminated by an auxiliary **light** standing on Kame Saki. Care is necessary as the beacon is submerged at HW.

A breakwater with a **light** exhibited at its head, lies on the W side of Takedatsu Kō; small craft with local knowledge can anchor near the breakwater.

Imi Kō protected by breakwaters, lies on the W side of **Imi Saki,** 1 mile ESE of Kame Saki; a **light** is exhibited at the head of the N breakwater. A ferry runs from Imi Kō to Himeshima Kō (3.55), 3 miles NE.

Naga Se, 1¾ miles E of Imi Saki, is a rocky ledge which dries out about 2½ cables offshore, and from the extremity of which a shoal, with depths of less than 5 m, extends for a farther 1½ cables. Naga Se is marked close N by a *light-buoy* (black; white light group flashing 2 every 6 seconds).

Kumade (Kumage) Kō (33° 40' N, 131° 39' E) is entered 2½ miles ESE of Imi Saki; there is a small breakwater on its W side.

Tsurugi Hana, the E entrance point to Kumade Kō, and the coast SE, are described at 5·21.

Hime Shima

3.55

Hime Shima (33° 44' N, 131° 40' E) is separated from the S shore of Suō Nada by **Himeshima Suidō. Yahazu Yama,** the summit of Hime Shima, is a remarkable conical peak 265 m (868 ft) high.

The W part of Hime Shima forms a peninsula; Minami Ura lies on the S side and Kita Ura on the N side.

Minami Ura is shoal for about ½ mile offshore. Reefs extend ¾ mile S from **Mitsuishi Hana** the SW extremity of Hime Shima; **Heguri Dashi,** with a depth of 6·8 m (22 ft), lies 4 cables SE of the point.

Himeshima Kō (33° 43' N, 131° 39' E), a small harbour protected by breakwaters, lies at the head of Minami Ura and has a reported depth of 4 m; a **light** is exhibited at the head of the E breakwater.

There is a ferry service to Imi Kō (3.54).

Supplies. Fresh water and small quantities of fuel oil can be supplied in Himeshima Kō.

3.56

Kita Ura situated on the N side of Hime Shima, is shoal; on the E side of its entrance is **Uki Su,** a low islet 3 m high, close to which are foul ground and a drying reef.

Kitaura Kō (33° 44' N, 131° 39' E), protected by breakwaters, lies on the W side of Kita Ura; a **light** is exhibited on the head of the S breakwater.

A **light** is exhibited from a white round stone tower standing on the E extremity of Hime Shima.

Anchorages. With SE winds, anchorage can be obtained off the NW side of Hime Shima in a depth of 24 m, sand, with Mitsuishi Hana bearing 180° distant 8 cables. Vessels of shallow draught can anchor closer inshore.

With N winds, anchorage can be obtained off the SE side of Hime Shima in a depth of 15 m, sand, about 6 cables SW of the E extremity of the island.

Anchorage can be obtained off Minami Ura but the tidal streams are strong and the holding ground is not good.

Caution. Care is needed when anchoring as a large number of **fish havens,** consisting of sunken hulks, lie on all sides of Hime Shima within 1 mile offshore, and in Himeshima Suidō.

Submarine cables, the routes of which are shown on the chart, are laid across Himeshima Suidō.

Tidal streams in Himeshima Suidō turn about 3 hours before the stream in Kanmon Kaikyō and have a spring rate of 2¼ knots.

CHAPTER 4

BUNGO SUIDŌ

GENERAL INFORMATION

Chart 651
4.1

Bungo Suidō leads from the Pacific Ocean to Seto Naikai between the E side of Kyūshū and the SW end of Shikoku. The strait is entered from S between Tsurumi Saki (32° 56' N, 132° 05' E) and Kōmo Saki, 20 miles E; Hayasui Seto (33° 18' N, 131° 58' E) lies at its N end (see 4.18).

The area S of the line joining Tsurumi Saki and Kōmo Saki is described in Japan Pilot Volume II.

4.2

Shibiko Se (32° 56' N, 132° 16' E), an isolated rock with a depth of 14 m over it, lies in mid-channel 9¼ miles E of Tsurumi Saki.

Mizunoko Shima (33° 02' N, 132° 11' E), a dark islet 19 m high, lies in mid-channel 8¼ miles NE of Tsurumi Saki; a **light** is exhibited from a white round stone tower with black bands, standing on the islet and a **racon** transmits from the light-tower.

Mizunoko Shima is prominent and a good radar mark.

Ko Bae, a brown rounded rock 1 m high, lies 1½ cables S of Mizunoko Shima and **Hira Se,** with a depth of 1·8 m over it, lies 1½ cables SE of the islet.

Kanbei Se (33° 10' N, 132° 11' E), an isolated reef with a depth of 5·3 m over it, lies 8 miles N of Mizunoko Shima.

With the exception of the isolated dangers just described, the fairway through Bungo Suidō is deep.

4.3

Weather. In Bungo Suidō, the S monsoon winds are generally more frequent in summer and the N monsoon winds in winter. The monsoon wind is most developed on the Kyūshū side of the strait in the last ten days of July and first ten days of August when it blows strongly from the SE. However during this period a strong W wind known locally as *Haemaji*, accompanied by heavy rain, may blow and has been known to persist for one to two weeks.

In July and August morning and evening calms are frequent.

Fog is most frequent in June and July but is rare in January. It is generally either an early morning fog which disperses about 0900 or 1000, or a dense fog which blows in from S after rain.

4.4

Directions. Large vessels N-bound normally pass through a position about 1¼ miles W of Mizunoko Shima and steer 333° for the middle of Hayasui Seto (4.18) and thence join the recommended tracks shown on Charts 651 and 2874 (see also 5.2).

BUNGO SUIDŌ—WEST SIDE

Chart 651
4.5

Ō Shima (32° 58' N, 132° 05' E), 192 m high, is separated from the N side of the peninsula which terminates in Tsurumi Saki, by Motonoma Kaikyō. A **light** is exhibited on the head of a breakwater at **Bungo Kō** on the NW side of Ō Shima.

Motonoma Kaikyō is deep and very narrow but on account of drying rocks situated on either side, and the strength of the tidal streams, it is almost impassable. A **light** is exhibited from a red round concrete tower with black bands, situated on the S side of Motonoma Kaikyō.

Sakino Se consists of three islets lying 1¼ miles E of Ō Shima; the central one is dark and 34 m high and on it a **light** is exhibited from a white round concrete tower. **Kajikake Se,** a rock awash, lies 2 cables NW of Sakino Se.

There are tide rips in the vicinity of Sakino Se.

Rocks with depths of less than 2 m lie close off the E and W sides of Ō Shima. **Takate Shima,** 42 m high, lies ½ mile NNW of the N extremity of the island and between them is **Koma Shima,** 81 m high and flat-topped, and two smaller islets.

A **fish haven** lies 1¼ miles NNW of Takate Shima.

SAIKI WAN

Chart 651
4.6

Saiki Wan is entered between Takate Shima (32° 59' N, 132° 04' E) and Kamado Saki (4.12) 5 miles NNW. The several headlands within the bay are fringed with reefs and rocks and should be given a wide berth.

Landmarks. The following features near the coast bordering Saiki Wan may be identified:

Tosakajō Yama, on the S side of the bay 5 miles SW of Takate Shima, is 331 m high and somewhat prominent from N.

Tokurō Mine, a ridge surmounted by a row of trees, attains an elevation of 353 m 1 mile W of Tosakajō Yama.

Hiko Take, on the NW side of the bay 6¼ miles W of Kamado Saki, is 638 m high, prominent and the highest mountain in the vicinity.

Takahira Yama, on the N side of the bay 2 miles W of Kamado Saki, is a bare dome-shaped summit 340 m high.

Measured distance. A measured distance lies on the N side of Saiki Wan, marked as follows:

(a) E end. Two **beacons** standing on Kamado Saki.
(b) 1½ miles W of (a). Three **beacons.**
(c) 1 mile W of (b). Two **beacons.**
(d) W end. Two **beacons** 1 mile W of Takahira Yama.

The distances between the four groups of beacons are:
(a)–(b) 2493·4 m
(b)–(c) 1800·1 m
(c)–(d) 1644·0 m

The running courses are 085½° and 265½°.

Approaches to Saiki Kō

4.7

Sunokoshi (33° 00' N, 132° 01' E), a sandbank swept to a depth of 9 m, lies in the fairway of the entrance to Saiki Wan. Takega Shima in line with the NW extremity of Ya Shima, bearing 240°, leads very close NW of Sunokoshi.

Takega Shima, a remarkable bare islet 33 m high, lies on a rocky shoal 2¼ miles SW of Sunokoshi; a **light** is exhibited from a white round concrete tower on a square base standing on the islet.

Nagare Bae, a rock 1 m high on which stands a **tower,** lies ½ mile S of Takega Shima. **Nishino Se,** with a depth of 1·6 m over it, lies at the end of a shoal extending 1¾ cables SW of Nagare Bae; it is marked close W by a *light-buoy*.

Ya Shima (32° 58' N, 131° 57' E), situated 1¾ miles SW of Takega Shima, has two summits both about 99 m high; a **tower** stands on the S summit.

Ō Se, a 6·7 m patch, lies 2½ cables NW of the NW extremity of Ya Shima.

Mitsukuri Shima, 24 m high and surmounted by a **tower,** lies 6½ cables W of the NW extremity of Ya Shima with another islet close N of it. A reef on which there are several above-water rocks, extends SSE from Mitsukuri Shima to the shore; two of these rocks are surmounted by pine trees and are prominent.

Matsuura Kō (32° 56·7' N, 131° 58·0' E), protected by a breakwater, lies at the head of the inlet entered between Ya Shima and Mitsukuri Shima. A **light** is exhibited on the head of the breakwater.

4.8

Ōnyū Shima, a large island, occupies the greater part of the head of Saiki Wan. A **light** is exhibited from a white round tower on a square base situated on **Tōdō Hana** (32° 59' N, 131° 56' E) the S end of Ōnyū Shima. *No. 2 Light-buoy* (black; green light flashing every 2 seconds) is moored 3½ cables SE of Tōdō Hana.

Katajiro Shima, 45 m high with a densely wooded summit, lies ½ mile E of **Motoga Hana,** the E extremity of Ōnyū Shima. **Naka Bae,** a rock which dries 1·5 m, lies about midway between Motaga Hana and Katajiro Shima.

The NE extremity and N side of Ōnyū Shima are fringed with numerous rocks out to 3½ cables. Two islets, about 20 m high, lie on a shoal in the middle of the channel between the NW side of the N part of Ōnyū Shima and the mainland.

A *light-buoy* (black; green light group flashing 2 every 6 seconds) is moored close NW of a small group of rocks situated 2 cables NNE of the NW extremity of Ōnyū Shima.

4.9

Directions for Saiki Wan. Approaching Saiki Wan from S, pass E of Sakino Se (32° 58' N, 132° 06' E) (4.5) and steer for Kamado Saki (4.12) on a course of 315°. When Takate Shima is abeam to port, alter course to 265° to head for the S summit of Ōnyū Shima (4.8). When Takega Shima Light is abeam to port, alter course to about 250° and head for a red and white chimney standing on the W side of the mouth of Banshō Kawa (4.10). On approaching the entrance to Saiki Kō, adjust course as necessary to pass N of No. 2 Light-buoy. (4.8).

Approaching Saiki Wan from N, pass more than 2 miles E of Takago Iwa (33° 07' N, 132° 02' E) (4.12) and keep Takega Shima Light ahead bearing 210°. When the N edge of Ōnyū Shima is abeam to starboard, alter course to about 250° and enter harbour as previously directed.

Saiki Kō

4.10

Saiki Kō (32° 58' N, 131° 55' E), a former naval base but now an industrial port, lies S and W of Ōnyū Shima; it is an open harbour (see 1.65). The principal mouth of **Banshō (Banjō) Kawa** is situated at the S end of the harbour, 1 mile S of Tōdō Hana; **Me Shima** lies on the W side of the river. **Naga Shima,** close W of Me Shima, is separated from the towns of **Saiki** and **Katsura,** on the mainland, by **Nagashima Kawa,** a subsidiary mouth of Banshō Kawa.

The S harbour limit of Saiki Kō is a line drawn from the E entrance point of Banshō Kawa to the E extremity of Ōnyū Shima; the N limit is a line drawn NW from the N side of Ōnyū Shima.

Pilotage. Pilotage is not compulsory but pilots are available and will board in the quarantine anchorage.

Landmarks. Two prominent chimneys stand on the N part of Me Shima on the W side of the mouth of Banshō Kawa; the E'most chimney is 76 m in height and painted grey, and the W'most is 78 m in height and painted red and white.

Anchorages. A **quarantine anchorage** has been established 1 mile ENE of Tōdō Hana; it is a suitable anchorage for large vessels but in E to S winds at the time of a typhoon, vessels should shift berth to the W of Ōnyū Shima where there are depths from 17 m to 20 m. Two red mooring buoys are laid close NW of the quarantine anchorage.

In N winds, good anchorage is afforded in depths from 8 m to 14 m, sand and mud, to the W of Tōdō Hana.

Submarine cables and a **submarine pipeline** are laid across Saiki Kō from the SW side of Ōnyū Shima.

Tidal streams in the approach to Saiki Kō between Takega Shima and Tōdō Hana are E-going on the falling tide and W-going on the rising tide, but do not attain any great rate.

4.11

The **Kōkoku Rayon Factory** stands in the N part of Me Shima. **Kōkoku Rayon Dolphin Pier** (32° 58·3' N, 131° 55·2' E), with a depth of 8·5 m alongside, is situated at the NW corner of Me Shima; **Meshima Quay,** with a depth of 10 m alongside, lies on the N side of Me Shima close ESE of the dolphin pier.

A basin lies on the E side of the mouth of Nagashima Kawa and is protected on its E side by a breakwater at the head of which stands a **beacon,** and on its W side by a training wall with a **light** at its head.

Another basin, protected by breakwaters, lies on the W side of the mouth of Nagashima Kawa; a **light** is exhibited at the head of each breakwater. **Kazura Wharf,** with depths from 3 m to 4·5 m alongside, lies in this basin.

Nihon Cement Works (32° 59·5' N, 131° 53·6' E) lies on the N side of a cove 1¼ miles WNW of the SW extremity of Ōnyū Shima. Four piers extend SSE from the cement works; the E'most pier has depths of 9 m on its E side and the others have depths from 4·3 m to 6·1 m alongside.

There is a basin on the E side of the cement works with a quay on its W side with a depth of 8·5 m alongside.

Facilities. There are offices of the Maritime Safety Agency, Customs, Quarantine and Immigration in the joint Harbour Office situated close S of the basin on the E side of the mouth of Nagashima Kawa.

Several tugs and harbour launches are available.

There is a dry dock with a capacity of 2600 tons in **Saiki Shipyard** on the N side of Naga Shima; small repairs can be undertaken.

There is a hospital and medical clinic.

De-ratting; see 1.70.

Supplies. Fresh water is available at the principal berths, and by barge. There are several oilers.

Communications. There is a car ferry service to Ōnyū Shima.

APPROACHES TO TSUKUMI WAN AND USUKI WAN

Chart 651
4.12
Kamado Saki (33° 03' N, 132° 01' E) is a precipitous headland densely covered with shrubs and rising to an elevation of 201 m, ½ mile WSW of its extremity. Several above-water rocks lie within 1 cable of the headland and **Misago Bae,** pointed and 29 m high, is prominent from N and S.

Hoto Shima, almost connected to a point 2¼ miles NNW of Kamado Saki, has a pointed summit 183 m high and is sparsely covered with shrubs.

Hotoshima Kō (33° 06' N, 132° 00' E), protected by a short breakwater, lies on the SW side of Hoto Shima; a **light** is exhibited on the head of the breakwater. Another **light** is exhibited from a white round concrete tower 3 cables NNE of the head of the breakwater.

A reef on which lie several above-water rocks, extends 1 mile NE of Hoto Shima. **Takago Iwa** (33° 07' N, 132° 02' E), the most remarkable rock, is 35 m high and a **light** is exhibited from a white round concrete tower standing on it. **Fuka Se,** the outermost rock with a depth of 1·8 m, lies 2½ cables E of Takago Iwa.

Kitano Se with a depth of 3 m, lies 1 mile SE of Takago Iwa.

Overfalls occur off Takago Iwa. A **fish haven** lies ½ mile N of the NW extremity of Hoto Shima.

Jimuku Shima, 118 m high, lies 3 miles NNW of Hoto Shima. **Okimuku Shima,** 141 m high and thickly covered with trees, lies close NE of Jimuku Shima; several rocks which dry, lie within ½ mile SE of Okimuku Shima.

A **fish haven,** consisting of sunken hulks, lies ½ mile off the W side of Okimuku Shima.

TSUKUMI WAN

Chart 651
4.13
Tsukumi Wan is entered between **Kannon Saki** (33° 05' N, 131° 56' E) and **Kusuya Saki,** 2 miles NNW; the shores of the bay are mostly cliffy.

Shiro Iwa, a steep-to, white rock, 5 m high, lies ¼ mile N of Kannon Saki; a **light** is exhibited from a red round concrete tower with black bands, standing on the rock.

Kuro Iwa, a black rock 1 m high, lies 1¼ miles SW of Kusuya Saki; on its E side is a rock which dries 0·3 m. A *light-buoy* (red; red light group flashing every 6 seconds) is moored close E of Kuro Iwa.

Kuro Shima, 91 m high to the tops of the trees, lies 6 cables SW of Kuro Iwa, and a shallow ledge extends 1 cable from its N side.

Chinuzaki Hana (33° 05' N, 131° 53' E), 3 miles WSW of Kannon Saki, is the extremity of a promontory extending NW from the S shore of Tsukumi Wan. A **light** is exhibited from a white round concrete tower situated on the W extremity of the point.

Pearl beds lie on the W side of Kuro Shima and on the E and W sides of Chinuzaki Hana.
4.14
Tsukumi Kō (33° 05' N, 131° 52' E), an open harbour (see 1.65), lies at the head of Tsukumi Wan and is divided into two parts by a peninsula which connects the small island of **No Shima** with the shore. The harbour is a commercial and industrial port and is used principally for the shipment of limestone and cement products.

The towns of **Tsukumi** and **Tokuura** border the shore of the S and N parts of the harbour, respectively.

The harbour limit extends NW from Chinuzaki Hana to the N shore of the bay.

Landmarks. Several chimneys lie on the peninsula dividing the harbour; two of them are painted red and white and the highest has an elevation of 93 m.

A white cliff formed by limestone quarrying is situated on **Suishō Yama,** 256 m high, ¼ mile W of the harbour front, and stands out well from seaward.

Pilotage. Pilotage is not compulsory but is recommended for a first visit. Three pilots are available and they embark in the area S of Kuro Shima (33° 06' N, 131° 54' E).

A **direction light** is exhibited 2 cables S of the mouth of **Aoe Kawa** which flows into the S part of the harbour; the white light indicates the navigable fairway.

Anchorage. Good sheltered anchorage is afforded, except in NW and N winds, in depths from 10 m to 19 m, mud, in the inlet entered SW of Chinuzaki Hana; however in 1979, reclamation work was in progress on the NE side of the inlet.
4.15
Berths. Nittetsu Pier, with a depth of 10 m alongside, extends E from the N entrance point of Aoe Kawa and can accommodate a vessel of 23 000 grt.

Onoda Cement Works lies on the peninsula dividing the harbour. **Noshima Pier** with a depth of 16 m alongside and which can accommodate a vessel up to 50 000 grt, lies on the N side of the peninsula; **Noshima Wharf,** with a depth of 9 m alongside, lies on the S side.

Todaka Nos. 1 and **2 Piers** extend SE from reclaimed land on the N side of the inner end of the N harbour and have depths from 9 m to 10 m alongside.

Onoda Cement No. 2 Wharf, with a depth of 8 m alongside, lies on the S side of the inner end of the N harbour.

Facilities. There are offices of the Maritime Safety Agency and Immigration in the joint Harbour Office in Tsukumi Kō.

There are several tugs and launches.

Supplies. Fresh water is available at the principal quays and there are water boats.

USUKI WAN

Chart 651
4.16
Usuki Wan is entered between Kusuya Saki

(33° 07' N, 131° 55' E) (4.13) and **Kushiga Hana,** 5¼ miles NNW.

Landmark. Mominoki Yama, 483 m high with a pointed summit, lies 1¾ miles W of Kushiga Hana and is the highest mountain in the vicinity; its E slope is grassy but there are woods on the W side of its summit.

Tsukumi Shima, a well-wooded dark islet, 165 m high with a sharp summit, lies ¾ mile from the S shore of Usuki Wan, 3 miles WNW of Kusuya Saki. Two rocks, the N of which has a depth of 0·9 m over it, and the other dries 0·6 m, lie between Tsukumi Shima and the shore S; a **beacon** (white metal post) stands on the drying rock.

A **fish haven,** charted as an obstruction, lies 1 mile E of Tsukumi Shima.

Kuro Shima, 26 m high, lies close to the NW shore of Usuki Wan, 2¼ miles SW of Kushiga Hana. **Mitsugo Shima,** consisting of three black pointed islets the highest of which is 27 m high, lies ¾ mile S of Kuro Shima; a reef extends 2 cables S of the S'most islet.

Shitanoe Kō (33° 09' N, 131° 50' E), a natural harbour with depths from 5 m to 9 m, is entered 1 mile SW of Mitsugo Shima; it is only available to small craft with local knowledge. A **light** is exhibited from a white round concrete tower standing on the E entrance point of Shitanoe Kō.

4.17

Usuki Kō (33° 08' N, 131° 49' E) is the inner part of Usuki Wan. The commercial town of **Usuki** lies at the mouth of **Usuki Kawa** which flows into the head of the harbour. In 1973, the population of Usuki was 40 000.

A **light** is exhibited from a red tripod on a concrete base situated at the head of a training wall on the N side of the mouth of Usuki Kawa.

The channel in the mouth of Usuki Kawa has been dredged to 1·5 m but is liable to silt.

Sagari-matsu Basin, with depths from 3 m to 5 m, is situated 3 cables S of the head of the training wall. A **light** is exhibited on the head of the SE breakwater protecting the basin.

Usuki Steel No. 2 Quay, with a depth of less than 3 m alongside, lies on the S side of Sagari-matsu Basin. There are further berths on the E and W sides of the basin with reported depths of 4·5 m alongside.

Two mooring buoys, each suitable for a 10 000 ton vessel, are moored 1 mile ENE of Sagari-matsu Basin.

HAYASUI SETO

Chart 651

4.18

Hayasui Seto lies between **Seki Saki** (33° 16' N, 131° 54' E), the NE extremity of **Saganoseki Hantō,** a well-wooded peninsula, and Sada Misaki (4.20) 7 miles NE; the strait leads from Bungo Suidō into Iyo Nada which lies in the W part of Seto Naikai. A **light** is exhibited from a white round metal tower standing on Seki Saki.

Caution. There is considerable traffic in Hayasui Seto and its approaches and many fishing vessels may be encountered.

The **Maritime Traffic Safety Law** (see 1.27) applies within Seto Naikai, NW of a line joining Seki Saki and Sada Misaki.

Pilotage. Naikai (Inland Sea) pilots are embarked 3 miles SE of Seki Saki (see 1.22). Signals for a pilot should be directed at the **signal station** exhibiting a fixed red **light,** situated 2 cables WSW of Seki Saki Light-tower.

In bad weather, vessels embarking a pilot should move into calmer waters S of Tsuta Shima (33° 14' N, 131° 54' E), 4 miles WSW; there is a **signal station** on Tsuta Shima. Tidal streams up to 2 knots have been reported in the boarding area.

Landmarks. Kotōmi Yama, 196 m high, is the summit of Saganoseki Hantō; two conspicuous chimneys (red and white) stand, respectively, at elevations of 325 m and 292 m, 5½ cables W of the summit. A **weather station** with a flagstaff stands on **Tōmi Yama,** 5½ cables S of Kotōmi Yama.

4.19

Shita Ura on the S side of the isthmus between Saganoseki Hantō and the mainland, is the winter anchorage for Saganoseki Kō (5.7) which is situated on the N side of the isthmus.

Saganoseki Gyokō (33° 14' N, 131° 53' E), protected by two breakwaters, lies in the NW corner of Shita Ura; a **light** is exhibited on the head of the E breakwater.

Tsuta Shima, in the approach to Shita Ura, is 63 m high and has pine trees on its N and W extremities; it is fringed with rocks within 2 cables. A *light-buoy* (black; white light flashing every 3 seconds) is moored 2 cables S of the island.

A **fish haven,** consisting of sunken hulks, lies 4 cables SW of Tsuta Shima; another one lies close NE of the island.

4.20

Hira Se lies ¾ mile NNE of Seki Saki (33° 16' N, 131° 54' E); overfalls occur near it. A **light** is exhibited from a red round concrete tower with black bands surmounting the rock.

Gongen Bae, which dries 1·2 m, lies 7 cables NE of Hira Se. A rock with a depth of less than 2 m lies close SE of Gongen Bae.

Taka Shima, 145 m high and thickly covered with reeds, is situated 2 miles ENE of Seki Saki; a remarkable solitary pine tree stands on the W extremity of the island. The SW side of Taka Shima is fringed with rocks and reefs which dry out about 2½ cables.

Ashika Se (33° 17' N, 131° 58' E) is the outermost of three rocks which lie close off the E extremity of Taka Shima; a **light** is exhibited from a white concrete column standing on the rock. A shoal with a depth of 1·8 m over it, lies 1 cable NE of Ashika Se.

Ushi Shima, 21 m high, lies on a reef situated 8 cables N of the W extremity of Taka Shima; from it the reef extends 2 cables WNW and at its extremity there is a rock with a depth of less than 2 m over it.

Sada Misaki (33° 20' N, 132° 01' E), on the NE side of Hayasui Seto, is the SW extremity of a long and narrow peninsula. A **light** is exhibited from a white octagonal concrete tower standing on the cape. A **ramark** transmits from a position near the lighthouse.

There is a **signal station** at the lighthouse but it is only open by day.

Mi Shima, 29 m high, with two rocks awash, one close N of it and the other close S, lies at a short distance N of Sada Misaki.

Ōgon Bae which dries 1·5 m and is surmounted by a

beacon, lies 3 cables SSW of Sada Misaki. The beacon is illuminated by an auxiliary **light** exhibited from Sada Misaki Lighthouse.

A disused **dumping ground** for explosives, the limits of which are indicated on the chart, is situated in Hayasui Seto.

BUNGO SUIDŌ—EAST SIDE

KŌMO SAKI TO YURANO HANA

Chart 651

4.21

Kōmo Saki (32° 54' N, 132° 29' E) is a black cliff forming the SW extremity of a peninsula on the E side of the S entrance of Bungo Suidō. A **light** is exhibited from a white round concrete tower situated on Kōmo Saki.

Yoko Shima, 143 m high and densely covered with shrubs, lies 4 miles NW of Kōmo Saki; the S and W sides of the island are cliffy. A round-topped black rock, 11 m high, is one of a number of rocks lying on foul ground extending ½ mile N from the N end of Yoko Shima.

Ka Shima, 212 m high and densely wooded, lies 2½ miles NNW of Kōmo Saki; a **light** is exhibited from a white round concrete tower situated on the NE end of the island.

The S coast of Ka Shima consists of dark brown cliffs; foul ground extends about 4 cables SW from its SW extremity.

Ka Shima is part of the **Ashizuri National Park** and ferries run from it to the mainland.

Oji Shima, 99 m high and with a pointed summit, and **Koji Shima,** a bare rock 49 m high, lie together ¾ mile SSW of the W extremity of Ka Shima.

Kuro Bae, 9 m high, is the highest and S'most of a group of rocks lying 6 cables ESE of the N extremity of Ka Shima.

Tsubute Saki (32° 58' N, 132° 28' E), a steep-to promontory faced on its W side by a black cliff, lies 1½ miles NNE of Ka Shima.

A number of rocky islets lie within 1¼ miles off the coast between Tsubute Saki and **Hanaguri Saki,** a black cliffy point, 1¾ miles NE. **Kurobe Shima,** 11 m high, and **Tsuno Shima,** 23 m high, lying, respectively, ¾ mile NW and 1¼ miles NNW of Tsubute Shima, are the outermost of these islets.

4.22

Hirajō Byōchi (32° 58' N, 132° 31' E) is entered between Hanaguri Saki and **Hotoke Saki,** faced with a black cliff, 4 cables NNE. **Kogai Bae,** a rocky islet 13 m high, lies close off Hotoke Saki; a **light** is exhibited from a white round concrete tower on the islet.

A **light** is exhibited from a white round concrete tower on **Mabune,** a rock 17 m high, lying on the S side of Hirajō Byōchi 1 mile within the entrance.

Hirajō Byōchi affords sheltered **anchorage** to vessels with local knowledge.

Sōzu Kawa flows into the head of Hirajō Byōchi about ½ mile ESE of **Ō Shima,** a flat and well-wooded islet 34 m high.

Mishō Kō, known locally as **Nagasaki Kō,** lies on the N shore of Hirajō Byōchi close NE of Ō Shima; it is protected by a breakwater and used principally by small vessels loading timber.

The town of **Hirajō** lies on the N bank of Sōzu Kawa about ¾ mile within its shallow mouth.

4.23

Komatsu Saki (33° 01' N, 132° 29' E), a precipitous headland faced with red cliffs, lies 1¼ miles NNW of Hotoke Saki (4.22) and on it is a rounded hill 118 m high; a rock with a depth of 1·8 m over it, lies 1 cable S of the point.

Kashiwa Ura, a small cove, is entered close E of Komatsu Saki and affords **anchorage** to small vessels except during S winds.

Between Komatsu Saki and Yurano Hana 5½ miles W, there are a number of small bays most of which are exposed S and are too deep for anchoring.

Kuro Bae, a black flat rock 3 m high, lies on a reef 1½ miles WNW of Komatsu Saki; a **light** is exhibited from a white round concrete tower surmounting the rock.

Shioko Shima, a prominent islet with three summits, lies 5 cables NNW of Kuro Bae; between them there is a reef on which lie some drying rocks. The channel between Shioko Shima and the shore close N is foul.

Yurano Hana (33° 01' N, 132° 23' E) is a precipitous brown headland, the grassy summit of which is 248 m high; it is the W extremity of a narrow and irregular peninsula extending 7 miles W and SSW from the general line of the coast. A **light** is exhibited from a white concrete tower situated on the headland.

Ōsaru Shima, 81 m high, lies close off Yurano Hana. **Ko Saru Shima,** 62 m high, lies close off a point 1 mile SE of Yurano Hana, and **Okino Tsuru Se,** 7 m high, lies ½ mile S of Ko Saru Shima.

The **tidal streams** off Yurano Hana sometimes attain a rate of 2½ knots and cause overfalls.

SUGE SAKI TO IWAMATSU BYŌCHI

Chart 651

4.24

Suge Saki (33° 04' N, 132° 25' E) lies 3½ miles NNE of Yurano Hana; a **light** is exhibited from a white round concrete tower situated on the point.

Funakoshi Canal which runs through the isthmus, lies 1½ miles SE of Suge Saki. **Lights** are exhibited on the heads of breakwaters at the N and S ends of the canal. A **bridge** with a vertical clearance of about 17 m spans the canal.

Arashi Ura is entered 3½ miles E of Suge Saki and has depths from 27 m to 46 m, mud; it is well sheltered and free from dangers but local knowledge is required.

4.25

Oitsukami Shima (33° 06' N, 132° 20' E), 194 m high, lies 5 miles NW of Suge Saki; the W side of the island consists of high cliffs fringed with rocks.

Jinokuwa Bae and **Okinokuwa Bae,** respectively, 59 m and 50 m high, grassy and prominent, are the two largest of many rocks lying within 6 cables W of the W side of Oitsukami Shima.

Nedoko Iwa, two prominent rocks with grassy summits the E of which is 62 m high, lie on a reef extending 1 mile ESE of the E extremity of Oitsukami Shima. A channel 2 cables wide and about 18 m deep, lies between a rock which dries 0·3 m at the W end of the reef and Oitsukami Shima.

Nakano Se, a group of black rocks the highest of

which is 3 m high, lies ¼ mile N of the NW extremity of Oitsukami Shima; from it a reef with a depth of 6·4 m over its extremity, extends ¼ mile SE.

Aino Se, a steep-to rock with a depth of 9·1 m over it, lies ¾ mile N of Nakano Se.

Watarino Se, a detached rock which dries 0·9 m, lies 1¼ miles ENE of Nedoko Iwa; a metal **beacon** (black and red bands) marks the rock.

4.26

Takega Shima (33° 06' N, 132° 25' E), 171 m high with a wooded summit, lies 1¾ miles N of Suge Saki (4.24) and is prominent. A **light** is exhibited from a white round concrete tower standing on the cliffy W side of Takega Shima.

Clearing line. The W extremity of Kuro Shima (4.29) bearing about 358°, with Ōko Shima (4.30) partly open W of it, leads about midway between Watarino Se and Takega Shima.

Taka Shima, 71 m high, lies close NE of Takega Shima and is joined to it by a reef. **Mae Shima,** 29 m high and the highest and centre of three rocks joined together by ledges which dry in places, lies 9 cables SE of Taka Shima.

Hadaka Shima, 27 m high, lies 4 cables N of Taka Shima and about midway between them is a rock with a depth of 1·2 m over it. A shoal on which there are drying rocks, extends 3 cables E from Hadaka Shima.

Iwamatsu Byōchi

4.27

Kashiwa Saki (33° 07' N, 132° 27' E) lies 2 miles NE of Takega Shima; a **beacon** stands close S of the point.

Shōno Shima, a steep rocky islet 20 m high, lies near the extremity of a reef extending 3½ cables WNW from Kashiwa Saki; a curiously shaped rock is situated on its E summit. A **light** is exhibited from a white round concrete tower situated on the islet.

Iwamatsu Byōchi is a sheltered harbour entered between Kashiwa Saki and **Senoshita Hana** 9 cables NNW. A rock with a depth of 2·7 m lies 2 cables W of Senoshita Hana.

Landmark. Togega Mori, 204 m high, is situated close E of Senoshita Hana and is dark and densely covered with trees; it is a good mark.

Nakano Se, with a depth of 11·4 m, lies in the middle of Iwamatsu Byōchi 1½ miles E of Kashiwa Saki; with this exception, there are no dangers in the inlet at a greater distance than 1¼ cables offshore and the bottom is of mud or sand. However there are a large number of pearl and seaweed beds within the inlet.

Iwamatsu Kō (33° 07' N, 132° 30' E), protected from W by a breakwater, is situated on the N side of Iwamatsu Byōchi near its head; a **light** is exhibited on the head of the breakwater.

A fairway marked by **light-buoys** leads through the inlet to Iwamatsu Kō.

There are depths from 3 m to 4 m alongside a quay at the inner end of the harbour.

The town of **Iwamatsu** can be reached by small craft; it lies on the S bank about 1 mile from the mouth of **Iwamatsu Kawa** which flows into the head of Iwamatsu Byōchi.

HIBURI SHIMA TO KA SHIMA

Chart 651

4.28

Hiburi Shima (33° 10' N, 132° 17' E), sparsely covered with trees, is situated 4 miles NNW of Oitsukami Shima (4.25); it is divided into two parts by a narrow boat channel which can only be used at HW. The summit of the S part of the island is 194 m high, and 4 cables SE of it, is a hill 93 m high surmounted by a prominent solitary pine tree. The SW side of Hiburi Shima is mostly cliffy.

A **light** is exhibited from a white square concrete tower situated near the W extremity of Hiburi Shima.

Okino Shima, 73 m high, thickly wooded and pointed, lies in the middle of a group of rocky islets connected by reefs and sandbanks, within ¾ mile N of **Matsuga Hana,** the NW extremity of Hiburi Shima.

Yoko Shima, 120 m high and almost barren, lies close E of the SE extremity of Hiburi Shima; its S side is cliffy.

Kirino Se, a double-headed rock which dries 0·9 m and off which **overfalls** occur, lies 3 cables SE of the E extremity of Yoko Shima.

Kanbei Se, 4 miles W of Hiburi Shima, is described at 4.2.

Anchorage is afforded in **Ako Ura,** the W of the three bays on the N side of Hiburi Shima, although the greater part of the bay is deep; the anchorage becomes dangerous in winds between N and E.

Tidal streams in the deep channel between Hiburi Shima and To Shima are NW-going on the rising tide and SE-going on the falling tide and sometimes attain a rate of 2¼ knots.

4.29

Noto Saki (33° 09' N, 132° 26' E), a precipitous headland in the form of a small peninsula, lies 1½ miles NW of Senoshita Hana (4.27). A **light** is exhibited from a white round tower with red bands situated on the headland.

Landmark. Gongen Yama, 489 m high and wooded, is the highest peak in the neighbourhood and lies 2¼ miles E of Noto Saki.

Kuro Shima, 140 m high, lies on a shoal 1½ miles WNW of Noto Saki; its S side is cliffy.

Komobuchi Byōchi is entered between Noto Saki and **Chigiri Shima,** 94 m high and thickly wooded, 2 miles NW. **Saru Shima,** 50 m high, pointed and thickly wooded, lies close S of Chigiri Shima.

Urushi Shima, consisting of three rocky islets the highest of which is 40 m high, lies 7 cables E of Chigiri Shima; the two highest of these islets are black and have trees on their summits.

Komobuchi Byōchi divides at its head into two well-sheltered branches in which there are depths from 32 m to 55 m, mud. A **light** is exhibited from a white round concrete tower standing on **Ko Shima** which lies close off the W entrance point of the NW branch.

Hosoki Canal has been constructed across the narrow neck which forms the N side of the NW branch of Komobuchi Byōchi; it is 190 m long, about 20 m wide and has a depth of about 3 m. A **light** is exhibited on the W side of the N entrance to the canal.

There are a large number of fish and pearl beds in Komobuchi Byōchi.

4.30

To Shima (33° 12' N, 132° 22' E), 190 m high, lies 3 miles NW of the entrance to Komobuchi Byōchi and is separated from the peninsula forming the N side of Komobuchi Byōchi by **Fubushino Seto.**

Ōko Shima, an islet 54 m high, lies in the middle of the narrowest part of Fubushino Seto and a **light** is exhibited from a white round concrete tower on it.

The passage E of Ōko Shima is about 2 cables wide but the fairway is reduced to about 1 cable by **Iwashi Bae,** which dries 1·5 m, and lies within 1 cable of the S extremity of Ōko Shima.

The passage W of Ōko Shima is somewhat wider but is completely obstructed by a reef and is impassable. **Shiro Bae,** a white rock 5 m high, lies on this reef.

Steel pylons standing on Ōko Shima and which support **overhead cables,** are prominent.

Tidal streams. In the channel E of Ōko Shima, the tidal stream is N-going on the rising tide at a rate of 3¾ knots and S-going on the falling tide at a rate of 2½ knots; tide rips occur in the narrows.

Tōdo Shima, 123 m high and densely wooded, is joined to the SE extremity of To Shima by a rocky bank.

Kō Shima, a grassy round-topped islet 39 m high, lies close off the W extremity of To Shima; **overfalls** occur near the islet.

Honura Kō (33° 12' N, 132° 22' E), protected by breakwaters, lies on the E side of To Shima. A **light** is exhibited on the head of the S breakwater.

Ka Shima, 121 m high and wooded, lies 6 cables NW of the N extremity of To Shima; the passage between the two is encumbered with above-water rocks. A **light** is exhibited from a white square concrete tower on the N side of Ka Shima.

Okino Kaba, a line of four rocks the highest of which is 11 m high, is situated 1½ cables W of the W extremity of Ka Shima; they are steep-to on their W side.

UWAJIMA WAN

Chart 651

4.31

Uwajima Wan is entered between **Mizugaura Saki** (33° 12' N, 132° 28' E), 3½ miles E of Ōko Shima (4.30), and Ōra Shíma (4.36) 2¾ miles N.

Michi Shima, 26 m high, lies within 4 cables of the shore 1 mile W of Mizugaura Saki. A **light** is exhibited on the head of a breakwater extending E from Michi Shima.

Maru Se, a dangerous rock with a least depth of 1·3 m over it, lies in the middle of the entrance of Uwajima Wan, 1½ miles NNW of Mizugaura Saki. A *light-buoy* is moored close NW of Maru Se.

Yanoura Dashi with a depth of 5·9 m, lies 8 cables N of Mizugaura Saki and midway between them is **Yoko Se** with a depth of 8·2 m. A *light-buoy* moored 2 cables ENE of Mizugaura Saki, marks a group of rocks extending 1½ cables E of the headland.

Taka Shima, 74 m high, is situated close within the S part of the entrance to Uwajima Wan, 1 mile ENE of Mizugaura Saki; the channel between the point and the island is much encumbered with rocks. A **light** is exhibited from a black round concrete tower standing on **Bozu Bae** at the extremity of a rocky reef extending 2 cables SW from the SW extremity of Taka Shima.

Futanarabe Shima, two islets 14 m and 11 m high, lie on a rocky shoal situated in mid-channel between Mizugaura Saki and Bozu Bae.

No Shima, 50 m high, lies almost in the middle of the entrance to Uwajima Wan, 1 mile N of Taka Shima; there is a crumbling cliff on its S side. There are a number of above-water rocks within 3 cables N of the W part of the island.

4.32

Mizugaura Gyokō (33° 12·2' N, 132° 27·6' E), a small harbour protected by a breakwater, is entered close S of Mizugaura Saki. Two **lights,** disposed horizontally, are exhibited from a white triangular framework tower on the breakwater.

Nishi Uchi and **Higashi Uchi** are two inlets lying in the SE corner of Uwajimi Wan; a *light-buoy* (black and white in bands; white light flashing every 3 seconds) is moored off the point separating them. Good **anchorage** is afforded in both Nishi Uchi and Higashi Uchi.

Ku Shima (33° 14' N, 132° 31' E) is situated 3 miles NE of Mizugaura Saki and rises to **Toyaga Mori,** a prominent conical hill 319 m high; cultivated land extends right up to the top of the hill.

Measured distance. A measured distance of 2434 m, each end of which is marked by a pair of **beacons** (conical topmark, point up), is established between the NW extremity of Taka Shima and the W extremity of Ku Shima. The running course is 049¾°.

Uwajima Kō

4.33

Uwajima Kō (33° 13' N, 132° 33' E), a well-sheltered harbour with Ku Shima (4.32) lying across its entrance, is situated on the E shore of Uwajima Wan; it is an open harbour (see 1.65). The town of **Uwajima,** with a population of 65 000 in 1973, lies at the head of the harbour.

Landmarks. Tadanami Hana, a black rocky cliff the summit of which is densely wooded, lies ½ mile N of the N extremity of Ku Shima; from a distance it resembles a dark island and is a good mark. A **light** is exhibited from a white concrete column standing on **Hikide Hana,** the SW extremity of the promontory.

Gongen Mori, 309 m high and surmounted by a remarkable clump of pine trees, lies 8 cables E of Hikide Hana.

Kiriga Se, a pinnacle rock with a depth of 5 m over it, lies 7 cables W of Tadanami Hana and a *light-buoy* is moored on its S side.

Directions. Steer on the alignment of Gongen Mori and Hikide Hana, bearing 092°, which leads over 1 cable N of **Ō Se** (33° 14·5' N, 132° 26·6' E) with a depth of 12·8 m over it, 2½ cables N of the dangers N of No Shima (4.31), and 1 cable S of the light-buoy marking Kiriga Se.

When the N extremity of Ku Shima is abeam to starboard, alter course to 123° to bring the white keep of a castle standing on **Shiro Yama,** 94 m high, situated in the middle of the town of Uwijima, ahead.

When **Nerai Iwa,** 33 m high and lying 6 cables SE of Hikide Hana is abeam to port, alter course to about 130° and steer for the harbour entrance.

Anchorage. A good anchorage is afforded in a depth of about 13 m, mud, about 1½ cables NNW of the inner breakwater light (4.35). During strong NW winds small craft can shelter in **Ōura,** a cove in the NE corner of the harbour.

4.34

A **light** is exhibited from a white round concrete tower situated on **Dōga Saki** on the S side of the strait separating Ku Shima from the mainland to the S. **Ushiga Se,** with a depth of 1·8 m, lies on the S side of the strait 6 cables ENE of Dōga Saki.

Caution. There are a large number of pearl oyster beds around Ku Shima; the channel S of the island is also encumbered with them.

4.35

The inner harbour of Uwajima Kō consists of a basin protected by a short breakwater on its N side. A **light** is exhibited on the head of this breakwater.

In 1978, breakwater construction work was in progress on the N side of the existing breakwater and on the opposite shore, WNW.

Berths. Tsukiji Jetty, with depths from 5·5 m to 6 m alongside, and **Tsukiji Quay,** with a depth of 4 m alongside, both lie on the N side of the inner harbour; **Sakashimotsu Quay,** with a depth from 4·5 m to 5·5 m alongside, lies on reclaimed land on the S side of the harbour.

Facilities. There are offices of the Maritime Safety Agency and Customs in Uwajima Kō.

Repairs can be carried out in the **Uwajima Shipyard**; there are four other shipyards.

There is a civic hospital.

Supplies. Fresh water is laid on to the quays and there are ten small oilers.

Weather signals (see 1.42) are shown from a weather station on top of a hill in the NW part of the town.

Communications. There is a car ferry service from Uwajima Kō to Beppu Kō (5.16) and a passenger ferry service to the outlying islands.

Yoshida Kō and Ōra Shima

4.36

Yoshida Kō (33° 16' N, 132° 32' E) lies in the NE corner of Uwajima Wan and is entered close NW of Tadanami Hana (4.33). The harbour is well sheltered except in strong S winds. The town of **Yoshida** lies at the head of the harbour.

Landmark. Tōmi Yama, 343 m high to the tops of the trees, lies on the NE side of the harbour 2¼ miles NE of Tadanami Hana; it is a good head mark for entering.

Anchorage can be obtained in a depth of 25 m, mud, about ½ mile from the head of the harbour.

There is a floating jetty with reported depths of 4 m to 6 m alongside, at the inner end of the harbour which can accommodate two vessels of 1000 tons each.

Ōra Saki (33° 15' N, 132° 28' E), the S extremity of **Ōra Shima,** is the N entrance point to Uwajima Wan; a **light** is exhibited from a white round concrete tower standing on rocks extending 1½ cables SSW from Ōra Saki. **Kasa Se,** a steep-to rock with a depth of 2·2 m over it, lies 2 cables SSW of the point.

Yamashita Canal separates the N end of Ōra Shima from the mainland and is used by vessels up to 50 tons bound for Uwajima Wan from NW. A **light** is exhibited from a red round concrete tower at the W end of the canal.

HOKKEZU WAN AND OKUCHI WAN

Chart 651

Hokkezu Wan

4.37

Hokkezu Wan is entered between Ōra Saki (33° 15' N, 132° 28' E) (4.36) and **Hirabae Hana,** a prominent red point, 3¾ miles NW.

Landmarks. Takamori Yama, a prominent mountain 634 m high, is situated near the head of Hokkezu Wan, 6¼ miles ENE of Hirabae Hana.

Gongen Yama, 437 m high and thickly wooded, lies 1¾ miles N of Hirabae Hana and is good mark.

Mizuko Shima, 8 m high, lies near the middle of Hokkezu Wan 3¼ miles E of Hirabae Hana; a **light** is exhibited from a white round concrete tower standing on the rock.

Sujiga Ura, a small inlet on the S side of Hokkezu Wan, lies 3¼ miles NNE of Ōra Saki; it affords no more than sheltered anchorage for small craft. A remarkable rock, 3 m high, lies at the W entrance point to Sujiga Ura.

Anchorages. Tamatsu Kō (33° 19' N, 132° 31' E) lies at the head of Hokkezu Wan. The N shore of the harbour should not be approached within 3 cables, for it is foul in places. There is good anchorage in a depth of 14 m, mud, on the S side of the harbour.

Tawaratsu Hakuchi, a small bay on the N side of Hokkezu Wan, is entered 6 cables NE of Mizuko Shima. Anchorage can be obtained in a depth of 12 m off the village of **Waki** situated at its head; this is the best anchorage in Hokkezu Wan.

Good anchorage for small craft can be obtained in the two small bays lying immediately W of Tawaratsu Hakuchi.

Takayama Hakuchi, entered close E of Hirabae Hana, affords good sheltered anchorage for small vessels in its inner part in moderate depths, mud.

Okuchi Wan and approaches

4.38

Ō Saki (33° 19' N, 132° 22' E), a well-wooded promontory, lies 3 miles WNW of Hirabae Hana (4.37) and is fringed with reefs extending 1 cable offshore. A **light** is exhibited from a white square concrete tower standing on Ō Saki.

Yoko Se, a steep-to detached rock with a depth of 6·8 m over it, lies 2¼ cables SSE of Ō Saki.

Sanzō Baya consists of three rocks lying 3 cables SSW of Ō Saki; the N'most and highest rock is 4 m high, the S'most and lowest is 2 m high. An auxiliary **light** is exhibited from Ō Saki Light-tower and shows over Sanzō Baya.

Local vessels are reported to pass between Sanzō Baya and Ō Saki.

Yuriageno Se, with a depth of 7·3 m over it, lies 4½ cables WSW of the S'most rock of Sanzō Baya.

4.39

Okuchi Wan is entered between **Muro Hana** (33° 20' N, 132° 22' E), 1 mile NNE of Ō Saki, and **Gongen Saki,** a steep cliffy headland, 1½ miles farther NNE. Owing to numerous islets and reefs extending N from Muro Hana, the entrance to Okuchi Wan is not more than 6 cables wide.

Taka Shima, 35 m high and thickly wooded, lies 4 cables N of Muro Hana and is the largest of the islets in the entrance of Okuchi Wan. A **light** is exhibited from a white round concrete tower on the NW extremity of Taka Shima; another **light** is exhibited at the head of a breakwater extending 1½ cables S from the S end of the islet.

Mizukuri Shima, a remarkable rocky islet 18 m high with pine trees at its N end, lies 5 cables NE of Taka Shima; reefs on which lie several small rocks, extend 1 cable ENE from the islet.

Reefs run between Taka Shima and Mizukuri Shima and on them lie several rocky islets. There is a boat channel across the reefs.

Anchorages. On the S side of Okuchi Wan from W to E lie **Nakano Ura, Minae Ura** and **Kuranuki Ura.** These coves afford anchorage to vessels with local knowledge but in the greater part of each the depths are somewhat great and the anchorage space is limited. Nakano Ura, entered 1½ miles NNE of Ō Saki, is a safe anchorage.

4.40

Mikame Kō (33° 22·5' N, 132° 24·8' E) lies at the inner end of the N arm of Okuchi Wan; it is a good natural harbour sheltered from all winds. The town of **Mikame** lies at the head of the harbour.

Landmark. Dōga Mori, 327 m high, lies ½ mile N of Mikame. Care is needed not to mistake the floodlights on the S slopes of Dōga Mori for leading lights.

Fuku Shima (33° 21·3' N, 132° 24·3' E), an islet 28 m high and densely covered with brushwood, lies close WSW of the E entrance point to Mikame Kō; **Fuku Se,** with a depth of 8·2 m over it, lies 1 cable SW of the islet.

Goishi Bae, a double headed rock the N head of which is 1 m high and the S head dries 1·5 m, lies on the W side of Mikame Kō 6 cables N of Fuku Shima; **Jino Se,** a rocky reef with depths of less than 13 m over it, extends 2 cables SW from the rock.

A *light-buoy* (black; white light flashing every 3 seconds) is moored close SSE of Goishi Bae; in 1979, a breakwater, connecting the rock to the shore NW, was under construction.

There are fish beds on both sides of Mikame Kō.

There are two pontoon jetties and a berthing wall at Mikame.

Nakano Ura, a boat harbour, lies on the N side of Okuchi Wan 7 cables NNW of Fuku Shima.

4.41

Biri Shima, a narrow islet 73 m high, lies parallel to the coast close N of Gongen Saki (33° 22' N, 132° 23' E) (4.39); the channel between the islet and the mainland is 1 cable wide and deep.

Gorotoki Hana lies 1½ miles N of Gongen Saki and has no dangers more than 1 cable from it.

Landmark. Anakuchi Yama rises to an elevation of 352 m 9 cables E of Gorotoki Hana and is surmounted by a remarkable clump of pine trees.

A bay, open to the W, lies between Gorotoki Hana and **Tatsu Saki,** which has the appearance of an island, 1¾ miles N. **Tō Saki,** 7 m (22 ft) high, and other rocks, lie about midway between Gorotoki Hana and Tatsu Saki and divide the bay into two.

JINO Ō SHIMA TO SADA MISAKI

Chart 651

Jino Ō Shima and Ō Shima

4.42

Jino Ō Shima (33° 22' N, 132° 21' E), an uninhabited island 129 m high, lies 1½ miles WNW of Gongen Saki (4.39).

Ko Shima, 36 m high and covered with pine trees, lies on a shoal extending NE from the E extremity of Jino Ō Shima and is joined to it by a sandbank which dries. A **light** is exhibited from a white round concrete tower standing on the NE side of Ko Shima.

Gazeno Se, with a depth of 8·6 m over it, lies 1½ cables NNE of Ko Shima.

The **tidal streams** in the channel between Jino Ō Shima and the mainland E are not strong and probably are N-going on the rising tide and S-going on the falling tide; slack water would appear to last less than 1 hour.

Kazenashi Hana, faced with a high steep cliff which stands out well from a distance, is the S extremity of Jino Ō Shima; between it and **Sone Saki,** 5½ cables WNW, is an exposed bay encumbered with reefs and shoals.

Osomizu Hana is the W extremity of Jino Ō Shima; **Maru Se,** a detached rock with a depth of 0·9 m over it, lies 2 cables SW of the point.

Ō Shima, the S part of which consists of a flat-topped hill 167 m high, lies with its SE extremity 2 cables N of Osomizu Hana; between them lies **Sannō Shima,** 33 m high, which is connected to Osomizu Hana by a causeway and to Ō Shima by a concrete bridge.

The W side of Ō Shima is mainly cliffy and is fringed with rocks. **Awako Shima,** 37 m high and covered with grass and bushes, lies 1½ cables N of the NW extremity of Ō Shima; the channel between them is only suitable for small craft with local knowledge.

Okino Haya, a rock awash, is situated on the extremity of foul ground extending 2½ cables E from the NE extremity of Ō Shima.

Shitama Kō and approaches

4.43

Okino Kunugi Se (33° 24' N, 132° 19' E), a pinnacle rock with a depth of 8·6 m over it, lies nearly 1½ miles NW of Ō Shima (4.42); **Jino Kunugi Se,** with a depth of 14·6 m over it, lies 2½ cables SE of Okino Kunugi Se.

Clearing line. The W extremity of Sa Shima (33° 26' N, 132° 22' E) (4.44) in line with **Sanuki Mine,** 385 m high, on the N side of Yawatahama Kō, bearing 056°, leads almost 3½ cables NW of Okino Kunugi Se.

Watariga Haya, a rock which dries 0·9 m, lies 1 mile N of Ō Shima; several rocks lie within 1 cable W of it, and within 1½ cables S of them is a reef with a depth of 2·7 m. A *light-buoy* is moored close NW of Watariga Haya.

4.44

Shitama Kō (33° 26' N, 132° 24' E) is entered between Tatsu Saki (4.41) and Suwa Saki, 1½ miles N.

Ko Shima, 20 m high, lies on a reef extending from the SE shore of Shitama Kō, ½ mile NE of Tatsu Saki; **Ogami Se,** with a depth of 10·9 m over it, lies 2 cables NW of Ko Shima.

There are quays at **Shitama** at the head of Shitama Kō, and at **Gōda** close SW of Shitama, but with W winds vessels cannot lie alongside them.

Suwa Saki, the N entrance point of Shitama Kō, is the extremity of a narrow point consisting of four prominent rockheads; a white monument stands on the rockhead at the outer end.

Rocks extend about 1 cable W from the outer end of Suwa Saki, and **Zeku Iwa,** 3 m high, lies at their extremity. A **light** is exhibited from a white round concrete tower with black bands on Zeku Iwa.

Sa Shima (33° 26' N, 132° 22' E), 51 m high, lies with its E extremity ¾ mile W of Suwa Saki; the island is well-known as a tourist excursion centre. A **light** is exhibited from a white round concrete tower standing on the W summit of Sa Shima.

A reef extends 1½ cables E from the E end of Sa Shima and on its extremity is a rock with a depth of 2·2 m over it.

Tategami, consisting of a number of reefs and rocks, lies off the W end of Sa Shima; **Rokubu Iwa,** the somewhat prominent S'most rock, is 6 m high.

The village of **Yoshigaura** is situated about the middle of the N side of the island and has a quay.

Yawatahama Kō and Kawanoishi Kō

4.45

Yawatahama Kō (33° 27' N, 132° 25' E) is entered between Suwa Saki (4.44) and **Yano Saki** 1 mile N. The town of **Yawatahama,** which in 1973 had a population of 47 000, lies on the N side of the mouth of **Shin Kawa** which flows into the head of the harbour.

Yawatahama is noted for its production of cotton textiles, and large quantities of mandarin oranges are grown in the area.

The shores of Yawatahama Kō are fringed with scattered rocks. **Ō Se,** with a depth of 1·8 m over it, lies 1 cable offshore 2 cables SW of the mouth of Shin Kawa.

A breakwater extends W from a point on the N side of

the mouth of Shin Kawa, a river which almost dries. A **light** is exhibited on the head of the breakwater.

The harbour, which gradually narrows, is entered on the W side of the breakwater; there is a basin used by fishing vessels at its inner end.

Anchorage. Good anchorage, sheltered from winds from all directions, is afforded in depths from 12 m to 16 m, mud, W of the head of the breakwater.

Berths. Oki-Shinden 7 m Quay lies on the N side of the breakwater, and **Yawatahama Jetty,** with a depth of 5 m alongside, lies at the end of a projection at the inner end of the harbour. Fishing vessels use the quays lying between Oki-Shinden 7 m Quay and Yawatahama Jetty.

Facilities. Kurinoura Dock, with a capacity of 4000 tons, is situated on the S side of the mouth of Shin Kawa.

There is a civic hospital.

Supplies. Fresh water is laid on to the berths and there are several oilers.

Communications. There are car ferry services to Uwajima Kō (4.33), Usuki Kō (4.17) and Beppu Kō (5.16).

4.46

Kawanoishi Kō (33° 28' N, 132° 24' E) is entered between Yano Saki (4.45) and **Nihonmatsu Hana** 4 cables W. **Ko Shima,** a remarkable islet 14 m high on which there are some trees and a small shrine, lies close off Nihonmatsu Hana.

There are seaweed beds extending along both sides of the bay from September to April.

Anchorage, sheltered from winds from all directions, is afforded in depths from 11 m to 20 m, mud, in Kawanoishi Kō.

The town of **Kawanoishi** lies at the head of the harbour where there is a pontoon jetty with a reported depth of 10 m alongside, and two landing jetties with a reported depth of 3·5 m alongside.

Kuro Shima to Sada Misaki

4.47

Kuro Shima (33° 27' N, 132° 21' E), 126 m high, lies on the N side of the W approach to Yawatahama Kō. Reefs and rocks lie within 1¼ cables of the SW end of the island, and **Hiruko Iwa,** a remarkable black pointed rock 2 m high, lies close off the NE extremity.

Karasu Shima, a treeless islet 38 m high, lies about midway between Kuro Shima and Nihonmatsu Hana.

Muroga Hana, a prominent gravel point covered with pine trees, lies 1 mile NNE of Kuro Shima; a **light** is exhibited from a white round concrete tower on the point.

Iho Kō is entered on the E side of Muroga Hana; the depths in the bay are too great for convenient anchorage except for small vessels with local knowledge.

Mekko Hana (33° 27' N, 132° 19' E), a salient rocky point with two red summits, the S of which resembles an islet, lies 2¼ miles SW of Muroga Hana; a **light** is exhibited from a white round column standing on the point.

A **measured distance** of 2479·3 m, each end of which is marked by a pair of **beacons** (cone, point up, topmark), lies between the S extremity of Mekko Hana and the W extremity of Kuro Shima. The running course is 087½°.

Kuchō Wan is entered on the W side of Mekko Hana; its shores are fringed with reefs but landing can be effected at **Kuchō** at the head of the bay though the depths in its vicinity are shoal.

Landmark. A **Decca transmitting station** with a radio mast (orange and white) marked by red obstruction lights, stands at an elevation of 540 m, 4½ miles WSW of Mekko Hana.

Kajiya Saki (33° 22' N, 132° 09' E) lies 9¼ miles SW of Mekko Hana. A *light-buoy* is moored close S of a rock awash lying 1½ miles SW of Kajiya Saki.

4.48

Misaki Kō (33° 23' N, 132° 07' E) is entered close NW of **Dōji Hana** situated 2½ miles WSW of Kajiya Saki and at its head is the village of **Misaki.** Some rocks awash lie within 2 cables of Dōji Hana.

Inoura Naikō, protected by a breakwater, lies on the S side of Misaki Kō close within its entrance; a **light** is exhibited on the head of the breakwater.

Sada Naikō, a small cove, lies ½ mile NE of Inoura Naikō.

A **light** is exhibited at the head of No. 1 Breakwater situated at the head of Misaki Kō.

Anchorage is afforded in Misaki Kō except during W winds. However with W winds small craft can obtain shelter in either Inoura Naikō or Sada Naikō where there are landing jetties.

Communications. There are scheduled ferry services from Misaki Kō to Yawatatama Kō (4.45) and Saganoseki Kō (5.7).

Sada Misaki Kō (33° 22' N, 132° 03' E), protected by a short breakwater, lies 2¼ miles W of Dōji Hana; a **light** is exhibited on the head of the breakwater.

Sada Misaki is described at 4.20.

CHAPTER 5

IYO NADA

GENERAL INFORMATION

Chart 2874
5.1

Iyo Nada, situated in the W part of Seto Naikai, lies between the NW coast of Shikoku and the islands which lie in the approaches to Hiroshima Wan and Aki Nada. Iyo Nada is approached from W through Suō Nada (3.1), and from S through Bungo Suidō (4.1) via Hayasui Seto (4.18).

Routes
5.2

West side. The fairway on the W side of Iyo Nada from Hayasui Seto (33° 18' N, 132° 00' E) to Hime Shima (3.55), 30 miles NW, is marked by *Iyo Nada W Fairway Nos. 1–4 Light-buoys*, moored 5 miles apart; the depths in the fairway are over 30 m. Small vessels make use of Himeshima Suidō, S of Hime Shima.

Hime Shima is a good mark but the headlands on the coast bordering the W side of Iyo Nada are not easy to identify.

A *light-buoy*, used for fishing purposes, is moored $2\frac{1}{4}$ miles SSW of Iyo Nada W Fairway No. 2 Light-buoy.

Fish havens lie, respectively, 2 miles SW and 2 miles NW of Iyo Nada W Fairway No. 3 Light-buoy.
5.3

North side. The fairway on the N side of Iyo Nada from a position about midway between Hime Shima and Iwai Shima (33° 47' N, 131° 58' E) to the W entrance of Tsurushima Suidō (33° 55' N, 132° 39' E), is marked by *Iyo Nada Fairway Nos. 1–9 Light-buoys*. Apart from Ō Se (5.37), a rock with a depth of 11 m (36 ft) over it lying close S of Ya Shima (33° 38' N, 132° 09' E), the water is generally deep.

Fish havens situated SW of Hōjira Shima (33° 44' N, 132° 01' E) and S of Ya Shima have a least depth of 20 m. Fishing boats congregate in the vicinity of Ō Se.

There is a fairway through Heigun Suidō (33° 50' N, 132° 11' E) (5.39 and 5.40) marked by *Heigun Suidō Fairway Nos. 1–4 Light-buoys*; it is a busy channel much used by small vessels. The majority of W-bound small vessels enter this channel from Kudako Suidō (33° 58' N, 132° 34' E) (5.60) and leave either through Kaminoseki Kaikyō (33° 50' N, 132° 07' E) (3.40) or otherwise to the S of Iwai Shima.

The minimum depth of water in the centre of this fairway is 31 m, however the traffic is heavy and at night large vessels are recommended to use the main fairway S of Ya Shima.

5.4

South side. The fairway on the S side of Iyo Nada from Hayasui Seto to the W entrance of Tsurushima Suidō, runs NW of Ao Shima (33° 44' N, 132° 29' E) (5.53) and joins the N fairway at Iyo Nada Fairway No. 8 Light-buoy. The depths in the fairway are over 50 m and there are no dangers.

Landmarks. Ao Shima, Kominase Shima (5.53) 5 miles NW, and Yuri Shima (5.56) 7 miles NNE, are good marks but the mountains and headlands along the coast of Shikoku are distant and not easy to identify.

The recommended tracks to be followed in all the fairways just described are shown on Charts 2874, 3602 and 3603.

Tidal streams
5.5

Tidal streams in the vicinity of the fairways through Iyo Nada are as follows:

W side. NNW-going and SSE-going, turning almost at the same time as in Hayasui Seto. The rate of the stream decreases as one goes N from a spring rate of $1\frac{1}{2}$–2 knots, 6 miles NNW of Hayasui Seto, to a rate of $1-1\frac{1}{2}$ knots off Hime Shima.

N side. The area between the S side of Iwai Shima (33° 47' N, 131° 58' E) and the S side of Ya Shima, 8 miles ESE, is where the tidal streams flowing in and out of Suō Nada and of Ōbatake Seto (33° 57' N, 132° 11' E) meet and divide. Between Hime Shima and Ya Shima the tidal streams set across the main track; between Ya Shima and Kominase Shima the stream is N-going during the rising tide and S-going during the falling tide.

S side. In the E part of Iyo Nada between Hayasui Seto and Tsurushima Suidō the tidal streams are:

NE-going—2 hours after LW to 2 hours after HW.

SW-going—2 hours after HW to 2 hours after LW.

The spring rate is $1-1\frac{1}{2}$ knots but both direction and rate can vary markedly from day to day.

The stream turns later as one goes E; the turn is about 1 hour later off Ao Shima than it is in Hayasui Seto.

Chart 3602
5.6

Measured distances. Three measured distances, shown on the chart, are marked by **beacons** on Ya Shima, Heigun Shima, Kominase Shima and Ao Shima. The running courses are 071° and 251°.

IYO NADA—WEST SIDE

SEKI SAKI TO ŌITA KŌ
Charts 651, 2874
5.7

Seki Saki (33° 16' N, 131° 54' E) and Saganoseki Hantō are described at 4.18.

Saganoseki Kō (33° 15' N, 131° 52' E), an open harbour (see 1.65), lies in **Uwa Ura** on the N side of the isthmus joining Saganoseki Hantō to the mainland; **Saganoseki,** an industrial town, lies at the head of the harbour.

Landmarks. Two conspicuous chimneys, described at 4.18, are situated on a hill on the NE side of Saganoseki Kō and are good marks for identifying the harbour from seaward.

A fairway *light-buoy* is moored 1 mile N of the entrance to the harbour. **Fish havens** are situated within 1¼ miles N of the light-buoy.

A **quarantine anchorage** lies in the approach to the harbour, close SW of the fairway buoy.

Pilotage is not compulsory. Pilots are available between sunrise and 1 hour before sunset either in the quarantine anchorage or at Seki Saki pilot station.

The inner part of the harbour is protected by two short breakwaters, a **light** is exhibited from the head of the W breakwater.

Berths. Hiroura Wharf, owned by the **Nippon Mining Company,** lies on the N side of the harbour 2 cables within the entrance; it has depths from 9 m to 10 m alongside and can accommodate two vessels of 10 000 tons.

Inner Harbour Quay, with depths from 2·5 m to 4 m alongside, lies at the inner end of the harbour; a ferry pier lies on the S side of the harbour.

Facilities. There is a customs office and quarantine office in Saganoseki Kō.

Three tugs are available.

De-ratting; see 1.70.

Supplies. Fresh water is available at Hiroura Wharf.

Communications. There is a ferry service across Hayasui Seto from Saganoseki Kō to Misaki Kō (4.48), 15 miles ENE.

5.8

Iso Saki (33° 15' N, 131° 47' E), faced with red cliffs, lies 4 miles W of Saganoseki Kō, and **Babano Se,** with a depth of 4·5 m, is situated 9 cables NNE of the point.

Ōzai-Hiyoshibaru Hakuchi, the E part of Ōita Kō (5.9), lies within 2 miles W of Iso Saki. The harbour is protected by Middle Breakwater, 1 mile in length and which runs parallel with shore, and East Breakwater. A large area of reclaimed land faced with quays lies within the harbour.

In 1980, Middle Breakwater was being extended W, and further development work was being carried out within the harbour.

A *buoy* (red conical), exhibiting a red light, is moored 1 mile NNE of the entrance to Ōzai-Hiyoshibaru Hakuchi.

ŌITA KŌ

Charts 626, 651
5.9

Ōita Kō, a specified port (see 1.64), lies on the S side of the entrance to Beppu Wan (5.15); the port is in two parts, one fronting the town of **Tsurusaki** (33° 15' N, 131° 41' E) and the other fronting **Ōita** 4 miles W, with extensive reclaimed land lying between them.

Pilotage. Pilotage is not compulsory but is recommended. The pilot may be embarked in the quarantine anchorage provided at least 24 hours notice is given but he is usually embarked at the Seki Saki pilot station (4.18).

Anchorages. Anchor berths have been established as follows:

Berth No	Position	Depth m	Capacity tons
1	33° 16·4' N 131° 38·7' E	37–38	Up to 20 000
2	33° 17·1' N 131° 42·0' E	52–53	Over 100 000
3	33° 17·1' N 131° 42·4' E	48–50	50 000/100 000
4	33° 16·8' N 131° 42·7' E	45–46	20 000/50 000
5	33° 16·7' N 131° 43·1' E	35–40	Up to 30 000
6	33° 16·5' N 131° 43·4' E	35	Up to 30 000

The **quarantine anchorage** lies with its centre in position 33° 16·0' N, 131° 46·0' E in depths from 25 m to 43 m.

Shin Nittetsu anchorage lies with its centre in position 33°16·5' N, 131° 39·2' E.

Anchor berths are allocated by the Port Captain.

Landmarks. A conspicuous chimney (33° 16·0' N, 131° 40·5' E) with an elevation of 202 m, stands 6½ cables SSW of the entrance of Tsurusaki Hakuchi. Numerous other chimneys are situated in the port area and their positions can best be seen on the chart; the highest chimneys are painted red and white.

A silver painted radio tower, stands at an elevation of 126 m, 6 cables WSW of the entrance to Nishi Ōita Hakuchi (33° 14·9' N, 131° 35·3' E).

Chart 626
Tsurusaki Chiku
5.10

Tsurusaki Chiku (33° 17' N, 131° 41' E), consisting of two large basins, lies within the **Ōita Tsurusaki Industrial Zone** on the W bank of **Ōno Kawa.** In 1978, another industrial zone was being developed on the E side of Ōno Kawa (see 5.8).

Kyūshū Sekiyū Sea-berth (33° 16·7' N, 131° 41·4' E), with mooring dolphins at each end, is situated on the E side of the entrance to Tsurusaki Hakuchi; **lights** are exhibited on the pierhead and on the dolphins. There are depths from 20 m to 21 m alongside, and vessels of 250 000 dwt can be berthed. The berth is protected by a submersible oil boom. Vessels berth bows W; tugs are available.

Shōden Sea-berth (33° 16·6' N, 131° 40·5' E), with mooring dolphins at each end, is situated on the W side of the entrance to Tsurusaki Hakuchi; **lights** are exhibited on the pierhead and on the dolphins. There is a depth of 17 m alongside and vessels up to 70 000 dwt can be berthed.

Tsurusaki Hakuchi, the E of the two basins in Tsurusaki Chiku, is protected by a breakwater extending from each side of the entrance; a **light** is exhibited at the head of each breakwater. There are depths from 12·8 m to 13·6 m in the entrance.

Two fluorescent orange **beacons** (triangular topmarks) are situated at the head of Tsurusaki Hakuchi; in line they bear 160° and indicate the fairway through the middle of the basin. Anchorage is **prohibited** in this fairway.

There are a number of quays and dolphin berths within Tsurusaki Hakuchi on both sides of the basin, with depths from 3·5 m to 7 m alongside.

Onakashima Kawa, with depths from 3·7 m to 6·4 m, leads from the S end of Tsurusaki Hakuchi for ¼ mile S where it is spanned by a **bridge** with a vertical clearance of about 16 m. There are quays N of the bridge on both sides of the river, with depths from 3·7 m to 4·9 m alongside.

An **overhead cable** with a vertical clearance of 49 m, spans the entrance to Onakashima Kawa.

5.11

Otozu Hakuchi, the W of the two basins in Tsurusaki Chiku, is entered ¼ mile W of Tsurusaki Hakuchi and is protected by a breakwater extending from each side of the entrance; a **light** is exhibited at the head of each breakwater. There are depths from 12·8 m to 15·8 m in the entrance and from 13·4 m to 23·8 m within the basin, except within 2 cables from its head which is shoal.

Two **light-beacons** (white; triangular topmarks) are situated at the head of Otozu Hakuchi; in line they bear 162° and indicate the fairway through the middle of the basin. Anchorage is **prohibited** in this fairway.

Otozu Kawa, discharges into the SE corner of Otozu Hakuchi; an **overhead cable** with a vertical clearance of 34 m, spans the mouth of the river.

There is a dolphin **oil berth** on the W side of the entrance to Otozu Hakuchi, within the breakwaters, with a depth of 13 m alongside.

Shin Nippon Steel Product Quay, 1000 m in length and with depths from 6·5 m to 13 m alongside, lies along the W side of the basin and can accommodate vessels up to 50 000 dwt.

Ōita Chiku

5.12

Ōita Chiku (33° 15′ N, 131° 37′ E) is that part of Oita Kō which lies in the vicinity of the mouth of **Ōita Kawa,** 4 miles WSW of Tsurusaki Chiku. It fronts the town of Ōita which in 1973 had a population of 288 000.

Raw Material Sea-berth (33° 16′ N, 131° 38′ E), consisting of an L-shaped pier, projects from reclaimed land on the E side of the mouth of Ōita Kawa and can accommodate vessels up to 300 000 dwt. **Berths N1** and **N2,** with depths from 26 m to 30 m alongside, lie on the N side of the pierhead, and **Berths N3** and **N4,** with depths from 23 m to 29 m alongside, lie on the S side. Dolphins stand at each end of the pierhead.

Lights are exhibited on the pierhead and on the dolphins. A **direction light** is exhibited on the pier to facilitate the berthing of vessels on the S side of the pierhead.

5.13

Tsuru Hakuchi (33° 15·6′ N, 131° 37·5′ E), a small basin, lies on the E side of the mouth of Ōita Kawa. **Tsuru Berths A** and **B,** dolphin berths with depths of 6 m alongside, lie at the head of the basin.

Sumiyoshi Hakuchi, an L-shaped basin protected by two breakwaters, is entered 1 mile WSW of the mouth of Ōita Kawa; a **light** is exhibited at the head of each breakwater. There are depths from 9·4 m to 10·1 m in the outer part of the basin and from 4·9 m to 5·5 m in the inner part.

Sumiyoshi No. 1 Quay, with a depth of 9 m alongside, lies close within the breakwaters on **Sumiyoshi Wharf** situated on the E side of the basin, and can berth vessels up to 10 000 dwt.

Sumiyoshi Nos. 2–5 Quays, with depths from 3·5 m to 5 m alongside, border the inner part of the basin.

Nishi Ōita Hakuchi, protected by two breakwaters, is entered 1¼ miles WSW of the mouth of Ōita Kawa; a **light** is exhibited at the head of each breakwater. There are depths from 5·5 m to 7 m in the W part of the basin but the E part is shoal.

Namaishi Nos. 1–4 Quays, with depths from 2·5 m to 6 m alongside, lie on **Ikushi Wharf** situated on the S side of the basin.

5.14

Facilities at Ōita Kō. There are offices of the Maritime Safety Agency, Customs, Quarantine and Immigration in the joint Harbour Office situated on the E bank of the mouth of Otozu Kawa which flows into the head of Otozu Hakuchi.

Tugs are available. Harbour launches operate from a basin near the Harbour Office.

Waste oil disposal facilities are available at the inner end of Tsurusaki Hakuchi. Small repairs can be undertaken.

Hospitals are available.

Weather signals are shown (see 1.42).

De-ratting; see 1.70.

Climate; see table at 1.98.

Supplies. Fresh water is available on the quays. Fuel oil can be supplied by barge.

Communications. There is a **port radio station** at Ōita Kō; see *Admiralty List of Radio Signals Volume 6.*

There are car ferry services to several ports in Seto Naikai.

There is a hovercraft service to Ōita Airport situated on the coast in the vicinity of Gyōsha Saki Light (5.20), 16 miles N of Ōita Kō.

BEPPU WAN

Chart 651

5.15

Beppu Wan is entered between Tsurusaki Chiku (33° 17′ N, 131° 41′ E) (5.10) and Tōrō Hana (5.19), 6 miles NW.

The fairway into Beppu Wan from Iyo Nada is marked by *Beppu Fairway Nos. 1–4 Light-buoys,* shown on the chart.

Caution. There are a large number of **fishing nets** and **fish havens** within about ¼ mile of the shores of Beppu Wan between Ōita Kō and Hiji Kō in the NW corner of the bay.

Landmarks. Takasaki Yama, 627 m high, lies 3 miles W of Ōita Kō and is steep-sided, round-topped, wooded and prominent. **Tsurumi Take** 1374 m high, lies 5 miles WNW of Takasaki Yama and has a prominent building, marked by a red light, on its summit. Three **television towers,** marked by red lights, stand on the summit of a hill, 525 m high, 3 miles NNE of Tsurumi Take.

Shiro Yama, 350 m high, is situated on the N side of Beppu Wan 8 miles NE of Tsurumi Take and has a prominent clump of trees on its summit; there are higher mountains farther NW.

Beppu Kō

5.16

Beppu Kō (33° 18′ N, 131° 31′ E), situated at the W end of Beppu Wan, fronts the city of **Beppu** which in 1973 had a population of 124 000. Beppu is a tourist centre and is well-known for its hot springs and scenery.

Beppu Marine Tower, 94 m high, silver-painted and marked by a red light, and a large number of hotels, are situated in the town and are prominent. A white statue of Buddha stands about ¼ mile WNW of Beppu Marine Tower.

Beppu Hakuchi (33° 16·4′ N, 131° 30·6′ E) lies at the S end of Beppu Kō; a mole extends E from the central part of the town and there are depths from 3 m to 4·5 m on its

S side. There are two basins on the N side of the mole, the N'most of which is a **yacht harbour.**

Beppu Kokusai Kankō Hakuchi (33° 18·0' N, 131° 30·5' E), situated 1¼ miles N of Beppu Hakuchi, is the international tourist harbour of Beppu. It is protected on its S side by East Breakwater and on its E side by a detached breakwater nearly ¼ mile in length; a **light** is exhibited on the head of East Breakwater and on both ends of the detached breakwater.

The harbour is entered between the head of East Breakwater and the S end of the detached breakwater.

Nos. 1–3 Wharves lie within Kokusai Kankō Hakuchi and are much used by regular shipping services to all parts of Seto Naikai. There are depths from 3 m to 5 m alongside the quays on Nos. 1 and 2 Wharves and depths from 7 m to 8 m on the E side of No. 3 Wharf.

Kamekawa Hakuchi lies 1¼ miles N of Kokusai Kankō Hakuchi and affords anchorage about 2 cables offshore. There is a boat pool fronting **Kamekawa,** a suburb of Beppu; in 1978, a basin was under construction on its N side.

5.17

Hiji Hakuchi lies within the harbour limits of Beppu Kō and fronts the town of **Hiji** (33° 22' N, 131° 32' E); it affords **anchorage** in depths from 10 m to 40 m, sand and mud.

Ikari Se, which dries 0·9 m, lies 4 cables offshore in the W part of the anchorage, and rocks with a least depth of 3 m extend 1 cable SW from it. **Okino Se,** with a depth of 4·3 m over it, lies 2 cables offshore 8 cables SW of Ikari Se.

Hiji Kō (33° 22' N, 131° 32' E), protected by two breakwaters, lies in the NE part of Hiji Hakuchi and provides a good sheltered **anchorage** for small vessels; a **light** is exhibited from the head of the W breakwater. A short quay with a depth of 5·5 m alongside, is situated on the N bank of the mouth of **Kaneida Kawa** which flows into the NE part of the harbour.

Supplies. Fresh water can be supplied at Beppu Hakuchi and at Beppu Kokasai Kankō Hakuchi.

KUNISAKI HANTŌ—SOUTH AND EAST COASTS

Charts 2874, 651

5.18

Kunisaki Hantō, the peninsula on the NE side of Kyūshū, is surmounted by a number of dormant volcanoes. **Futago Yama,** the prominent summit of the peninsula, is 719 m (2361 ft) high; round this summit are a number of remarkable conical peaks.

Inomure Yama, the most W'ly mountain, lies 4½ miles WNW of Futago Yama and has two peaks the E of which rises to an elevation of 466 m (charted as 1496 ft) and is surmounted by a clump of trees. These mountains slope steeply to wooded coastal plains which terminate in headlands about 30 m high.

Chart 651

Tōrō Hana to Gyōsha Saki

5.19

The coast between **Tōrō Hana** (33° 21' N, 131° 36' E) and **Kanuki Saki** 3 miles NE, consists mostly of red cliffs backed by woods and fringed with reefs.

Kitsuki Wan is entered between Kanuki Saki and **Tsukuishi Hana,** 3½ miles NE; the head of the bay is fringed with a sandbank which dries out ½ mile in places. **Kamisorino Se,** with a depth of 3·9 m over it, lies on the W side of the entrance to Kitsuki Wan; a **fish haven** lies close S of Kamisorino Se.

Morie Kō (33° 25' N, 131° 40' E), a shallow harbour, lies on the NE side of Kitsuki Wan. A **light** is exhibited from a red round brick tower situated on the extremity of a sand spit extending W along the S side of Morie Kō. A radio tower (red and white in bands) 123 m in height and marked by red obstruction lights, stands ¾ mile ENE of the light-tower.

There is a good **anchorage** for small vessels in depths from 2 m to 3·5 m, mud, in Morie Kō, sheltered from all but S winds.

Fish havens are situated ¾ mile SE and 1¾ miles ESE of Morie Kō Light-tower. From September to April there are seaweed and oyster beds within 1½ miles offshore off the W and E entrance points to Kitsuki Wan.

5.20

The coast between Tsukuishi Hana (33° 24' N, 131° 42' E) (5.19) and Gyōsha Saki 4½ miles NNE, appears as a line of low hills and is foul for about 1 mile offshore in places; the outermost danger is **Natano Se** with a depth of 8·6 m over it. This stretch of coast should be given a wide berth as the tidal streams set onshore.

The town of **Aki** lies at the mouth of **Aki Kawa** which flows into the sea ½ mile SW of Gyōsha Saki. A *light-buoy* (pillar; white light flashing) is moored 1 mile SE of the entrance to the river and the channel to it is marked by further light-buoys.

Gyōsha Saki Light (33° 28' N, 131° 44' E) stands in the position of a former headland which has been overlaid by the development of Ōita Airport, nearby; an **aero light** is exhibited close NNW of it.

The E side of the airport is fringed with foul ground extending ½ mile offshore. A *light-buoy* is moored off the SE edge of the foul ground, and another *light-buoy*, used for meteorological purposes, is moored 6 cables NNE of the first buoy.

Chart 2874

Kurotsuno Hana to Tsurugi Hana

5.21

Kurotsuno Hana (33° 32' N, 131° 45' E), a low rocky point backed by a dense growth of dark green pine trees, lies 4½ miles N of Gyōsha Saki; it should be given a wide berth for numerous reefs lie in its vicinity.

Hogo Se, with a depth of 9·4 m (31 ft), lies 1½ miles ENE of Kurotsuno Hana and is sometimes marked by tide rips; about 6 cables NE of it there is a rock with a depth of 12·2 m (40 ft) over it. A rock with a depth of 4·3 m (14 ft) over it lies 9 cables SSW of Hogo Se, and another rock with a depth of 5·2 m (17 ft) over it, lies 1¼ miles SW of Hogo Se.

Kunisaki Kō (33° 34' N, 131° 44' E) lies at the mouth of **Tabuka Kawa. Ō Se,** a narrow reef with depths of less than 5 m, extends 6 cables ENE from the shore abreast the town of **Kunisaki**; a *light-buoy* (black; white light group flashing 2 every 6 seconds) is moored off the E extremity of Ō Se.

A basin enclosed by breakwaters lies in **Tabuka Hakuchi** on the N side of the river; a **light** is exhibited on the S breakwater. There are ferry quays, with a reported depth of 4·5 m alongside, in the basin.

From September to June seaweed beds lie in front of Kunisaki Kō and also N and S of it within 1 mile offshore.

Tomiku Kō (33° 36' N, 131° 43' E), a small basin protected by breakwaters, lies 2¾ miles NNW of Kunisaki Kō; a **light** is exhibited on the head of the N breakwater. **Me Se,** a rocky ledge which dries 0·6 m (2 ft), extends ⅓ mile offshore from a position close S of Tomiku Kō and forms a natural breakwater.

The shore from Tomiku Kō to **Tsurugi Hana,** 5 miles NNW, is fringed with a bank with depths of less than 5 m; there are no off-lying dangers.

The coast of Kunisaki Hantō, W of Tsurugi Hana, is described at 3.52–3.54.

IYO NADA—SOUTH EAST SIDE

SADA MISAKI TO MASAKI KŌ

Charts 2874, 651

5.22

The coast between Sada Misaki (33° 20' N, 132° 01' E) (4.20) and **Hasede Hana** 14 miles ENE, consists of the N side of a long narrow peninsula and is mostly cliffy and steep-to; there are no off-lying dangers.

Landmarks. Garan Yama, the highest mountain on the peninsula, is 413 m high and lies 6¼ miles ENE of Sada Misaki; it is prominent. A radio mast, described at 4.47, stands 5¼ miles ENE of Garan Yama.

A **light** is exhibited from a white concrete column on **Mimai Saki** situated 7 miles NE of Sada Misaki.

Measured distance. A measured distance of 2036·4 m, marked by two pairs of **beacons** which stand near the shore, lies on the N side of Garan Yama; the running courses are 053° and 233°.

Between Mimai Saki and Hasede Hana there are five bays all of which afford shelter except during N winds.

5.23

Mitsukue Kō (33° 27' N, 132° 16' E) is entered between Hasede Hana and **Fusuma Saki** ¼ mile NE; a **light** is exhibited from a white square concrete tower standing Fusuma Saki.

Anchorage is afforded in Mitsukue Kō in depths from 20 m to 30 m, mud, with good holding ground; in N winds a very heavy sea runs into the bay and anchoring is not possible.

From September to April there are seaweed beds on the E and S sides of Mitsukue Kō.

A cove protected by a breakwater and sheltered from all winds, lies on the W side of Mitsukue Kō and has a quay on its S side with reported depths from 4 m to 4·5 m; a **light** is exhibited on the head of the breakwater. **Anchorage** in a depth of 10 m is available in the cove to small vessels with local knowledge.

There is a Maritime Safety Agency office in Mitsukue Kō.

Chart 2874

5.24

The coast from Fusama Saki (33° 28' N, 132° 16' E) to the mouth of Hiji Kawa, 14 miles NE, is cliffy and steep-to.

An **atomic power station** is situated 3 miles ENE of Fusuma Saki and on its W side there is an unloading quay with depths from 5 m to 5·5 m alongside.

Hoboro Se, with a depth of 10·4 m (34 ft) over it, lies 1 mile offshore 9 miles NE of Fusama Saki. A **light** is exhibited on the head of a breakwater at **Kusho Kō,** 2 miles NE of Hoboro Se.

5.25

Hiji Kawa (33° 36' N, 132° 29' E) flows into the sea 14 miles NE of Fusama Saki. A bank which has been swept to a depth of 7·8 m (25 ft), extends 1¼ miles offshore in the vicinity of the mouth of Hiji Kawa. **Katayama Su** which has been swept to a depth of 3·7 m (12 ft), lies on the E part of this bank and its edge is marked by tide rips. The shoalest part of Katayama Su lies 4 cables N of the head of the W breakwater at Nagahama Kō.

There is a shallow bar across the entrance to Hiji Kawa and within its mouth the sandbanks are continually shifting; the river is spanned by a prominent **bridge** a short distance upstream.

5.26

The town of **Nagahama** lies on the E side of the mouth of Hiji Kawa; **Nagahama Kō,** protected by two breakwaters, lies close E of the town. A **light** is exhibited on the head of each breakwater.

Weather. A very cold wind known locally as *Kawa Arase,* is reported to spring up from the mouth of Hiji Kawa and blows from the middle of the night to early morning often carrying fog as far N as Ao Shima, 7 miles N. On a clear night or early on a fine morning, this fog may serve to identify Nagahama. This phenomenon may occur when the weather is not fine but to a lesser degree; in summer it always stops in the early morning.

Landmarks. A chimney (red) stands in Nagahama 5 cables SW of the light-tower on the head of N breakwater; another chimney (red and white) stands 4 cables ENE of the light-tower.

Berths. There are depths from 4 m to 6 m in the main part of Nagahama Kō. **East Quay** with a depth of 5 m alongside, lies on the S side of the harbour and there are a number of quays and jetties with depths up to 5 m alongside in the inner part of the harbour.

Onoda Cement Kuroda dolphin berth with a depth of 10 m alongside and which can accommodate a vessel up to 6000 tons, lies on reclaimed land about 2 cables NE of the harbour entrance. A wharf with a depth of 7·3 m alongside, lies 1 cable NE of the dolphin berth.

Supplies. Fresh water is available on several of the quays, and there is an oiler.

Communications. There are regular ferry services to Ao Shima about 7 miles N of Nagahama Kō, and to Kōbe Kō.

5.27

The coast between Nagahama Kō (33° 37' N, 132° 29' E) and Matsuyama Kō 20 miles NE, consists mostly of sandy beaches and there are no dangers more than ⅓ mile offshore.

Chart 3602

Toyota Kō (33° 39' N, 132° 35' E) protected by breakwaters, lies 5¼ miles ENE of Nagahama Kō; a **light** is exhibited on the head of the W breakwater.

Chart 3603

Gunchū Kō (33° 45' N, 132° 42' E), a small harbour protected by two breakwaters, is entered 13½ miles NE of Nagahama Kō; a **light** is exhibited on the head of the W breakwater. There are depths of less than 5 m in the harbour; a quay with depths from 4 m to 5 m alongside, lies on the E side.

Masaki Kō (33° 47' N, 132° 42' E), a small harbour protected by two breakwaters, lies 1¼ miles N of Gunchū Kō, and has depths of about 2·5 m within; a **light** is exhibited on the head of the W breakwater. A chimney (red and white), 60 m in elevation and marked by red obstruction lights, stands 4 cables NE of the light-tower.

MATSUYAMA KŌ

Charts 3603, 694 plan of Matsuyama Kō
5.28

Matsuyama Kō (33° 51' N, 132° 42' E), a specified port (see 1.64), lies on the E side of the S approach to Takahama Seto (5.33). Nishi-Habu Hakuchi, 2¼ miles S, Takahama Hakuchi, 1¼ miles N, and Matsuyama Kankō Hakuchi (5.34), 2 miles N, of the main harbour, also form part of Matsuyama Kō.

The harbour is divided into Nos. 1 and 2 Areas by a line drawn SE from Kuro Saki (33° 52' N, 132° 41' E) (5.35), the SE point of Gogo Shima.

Matsuyama, the largest city in Shikoku and a tourist centre, lies about 3 miles SE of the main harbour; in 1973, it had a population of 350 000.

Landmarks. Benten (Kiyomizu) Yama (33° 50·5' N, 132° 43·1' E), 128 m (422 ft) high and flat-topped, is prominent from a distance. The chimneys and oil tanks of Maruzen Sekiyu Refinery, ¼ mile NW of Benten Yama, are good marks.

Pilotage. Pilotage is not compulsory but is recommended; the pilot boards in the quarantine anchorage. No night berthing is permitted.

Anchorages. The **quarantine anchorages** for Matsuyama Kō, the limits of which are shown on the charts, lies 1½ miles SW of the S entrance to Takahama Seto.
5.29

Nishi-Habu Hakuchi lies on the N side of the mouth of **Shigenoba Kawa** (33° 49' N, 132° 41' E) and its entrance is protected from SW by a detached breakwater; a **light** is exhibited on the N end of the breakwater.

The area NE of the breakwater has been dredged to a depth of 10 m, and the NE side of the channel is marked by *No. 1* and *No. 3 Light-buoys* (black).

Habu Nos. 1, 2 and **3 Quays,** with a reported depth of 4 m alongside, lie within the harbour on the E side, and **No. 1** and **No. 2 Dolphin Jetties,** with a reported depth of 6 m alongside, lie on the N side.

Fish havens lie 4 cables W and between 3 and 5 cables NNW of the breakwater.

Chart 694 plan of Matsuyama Kō
5.30

Yoshidahama Basin (33° 50·4' N, 132° 42·0' E), protected by a breakwater, is entered 1¼ miles NNE of Nishi-Habu Hakuchi; a **light** is exhibited on the head of the breakwater. In 1978, a breakwater and another basin were under construction to the SW of Yoshidahama Basin.

Landmark. Kutsuna Yama, 57 m (186 ft) high to the tops of the trees, lies close NE of the entrance to Yoshidahama Basin and is a good mark.

Fish havens lie ¼ mile W and ¾ mile WSW of the head of the entrance to Yoshidahama Basin.

Sa Shima (33° 50·7' N, 132° 42·0' E), a gravel bank which dries about 1 m, lies 3 cables N of Yoshidahama Basin; a detached breakwater extends N and S along this bank.

Berths. Two piers, forming the **Nihon Sekiyu tanker berth,** project from the shore 1 cable E of the N end of the Sa Shima detached breakwater. Two mooring buoys and four dolphins are available at this berth where vessels up to 190 m in length and with a draught of 9·5 m

can be accommodated. Berthing should take place at the start of the N-going (flood) tidal stream; tug assistance is necessary. Berthing and unberthing is restricted to daylight hours only.
5.31

The **outer harbour** of Matsuyama Kō is protected by **No. 1 Breakwater** which extends 6 cables N from **Maruzen Sekiyu Refinery** situated 2 cables NE of Sa Shima. In 1978, **No. 2 Breakwater,** lying in a N and S direction, was under construction to the N of No. 1 Breakwater forming the W side of the entrance to the outer harbour.

Yokomakura Shō, with a least depth of 5·2 m (17 ft) over it, lies 6 cables WNW of the head of No. 1 Breakwater; a *light-buoy* is moored on the W side of the shoal.

Berths. The principal berths in the outer harbour are:

Berth & Position	Length m	Depth m	Capacity tons
No. 2 Wharf			
(33° 51·7' N, 132° 42·6' E)			
No. 3 Quay	390	7·5	5 000
No. 2 Quay	180	4–5·5	2 000
No. 1 Wharf			
(33° 51·4' N, 132° 42·7' E)			
No. 2 Quay	370	9·5–10	10 000
No. 1 Quay	237	5·5	3 000
Okaga Wharf			
(33° 51·0' N, 132° 42·6' E)			
No. 3 Quay	90	5·5	2 000
Maruzen Sekiyu Refinery			
Nos. 2 and 3 Piers		6–6·5	3 000
(33° 51·0' N, 132° 42·4' E)			
No. 2 Dolphin Jetty		11–12·5	45 000
(33° 51·1' N, 132° 42·2' E)			

The **inner harbour** of Matsuyana Kō is entered 5½ cables NE of the head of No. 1 Breakwater; a **light** is exhibited on the head of a short breakwater extending N from the W entrance point of the harbour. There is a ferry berth and passenger jetty within the harbour.

Facilities in Matsuyama Kō
5.32

There are offices of the Maritime Safety Agency, Customs, Quarantine and Immigration in the joint Harbour Office situated close SE of No. 1 Quay on Outer Harbour No. 1 Wharf.

Tugs are available. Minor repairs can be undertaken.

Waste oil disposal facilities are available at the Maruzen Sekiyu piers at the S end of the outer harbour.

Weather signals (see 1.42) are shown from a radio mast on the Harbour Office and from a position on the S side of the inner harbour.

There are two hospitals in the town.

Climate. See table at 1.99.

Supplies. Fuel oil and fresh water are available.

Communications. There are regular passenger and car ferry services to many ports in Seto Naikai. There are regular air services to Ōsaka and Tōkyō from **Matsuyama Airport,** 2 miles S of the harbour.

TAKAHAMA SETO

Charts 694 plan of Matsuyama Kō, 3603
5.33

Takahama Seto (33° 53' N, 132° 42' E) separates Gogo Shima (5.67) from the coast of Shikoku and is the N approach to Matsuyama Kō; it is not less than 4½ cables wide and about 50 m deep in the middle.

Caution. The traffic through and across Takahama Seto is heavy.

Tidal streams in Takahama Seto are N-going on the flood and S-going on the ebb, the turn occurring about 1½ hours earlier than in Tsurushima Suidō (5.64). The tidal streams are strong and may reach a rate of 5 knots.

Anchorage can be obtained in Takahama Seto, but to avoid the strong tidal streams and to keep clear of the fairway, vessels should anchor slightly W of the centre line of the strait.

Submarine cables, indicated on Chart 3603, are laid across Takahama Seto.

Takahama Seto—east side
5.34

Shijū Shima, a conical islet 15 m high with trees on top, lies on a shoal close off the E shore of the narrows at the S end of Takahama Seto.

Takahama Hakuchi (33° 52·8' N, 132° 42·1' E), within the harbour limits of Matsuyama Kō, is a bight on the N side of Shijū Shima. **Mitsubishi Cement Pier** with a depth of 7 m alongside, and another pier close N, lie in the bight; green and red lights are exhibited from the end of Mitsubishi Cement Pier.

Matsuyama Kankō Hakuchi (33° 53·1' N, 132° 42·3' E), the tourist harbour of Matsuyama Kō, lies close N of Takahama Hakuchi. **No. 1 Pier** with a depth of 13 m to 14·5 m alongside, **No. 2 Pier** with a depth of 6 m alongside, and **No. 1 Ferry Quay** with a depth of about 5 m alongside, lie in the S part of this bay.

Tsukumo Shima, 24 m high to the tops of the trees, lies off the middle of Matsuyama Kankō Hakuchi 9 cables NNE of Shijū Shima; a *light-buoy* is moored close SW of the islet.

Fish havens lie, respectively, 3½ cables and 5 cables S of Tsukumo Shima.

Chart 3603

Shiraishi Hana (33° 54' N, 132° 43' E) lies on the E side of the N entrance to Takahama Seto and close off it stands a remarkable white rock 6 m high. A rock with a depth of 1·4 m over it, lies 3½ cables SSW of Shiraishi Hana and there are rocky ledges to the E of a line joining the rock to the point.

Inunokashira Shima, 10 m high, lies ⅓ mile NNE of Shiraishi Hana. **Nakano Se** which dries 3·1 m and is surrounded by rocks awash, lies 2 cables SSE of Inunokashira Shima.

Tsugai Su, a shallow bank with a least depth of 3·4 m, lies 6 cables NE of Inunokashira Shima.

Chart 694 plan of Matsuyama Kō, 3603
Takahama Seto—west side
5.35

Gogo Shima (5.67) borders the W side of Takahama Seto, and **Kuro Saki** (33° 52·4' N, 132° 41·5' E) its SE extremity, is the W entrance point to the S entrance to the strait. **Shirano Hana** lies 6½ cables NNW of Kuro Saki; **Yura Wan** lies between Shirano Hana and **Kan Saki,** 1¼ miles NNE. In 1977, construction work was in progress on the NW shore of Yura Wan.

Okino Mo, a shoal with depths from 3·3 m to 11 m over it, lies across the entrance to Yura Wan.

Tsumuri Saki, the NE extremity of Gogo Shima, lies 1½ miles NNE of Kan Saki; it is thickly wooded with pine trees. A **light** is exhibited from a white round concrete tower standing on the point.

Anchorages. There is anchorage for small vessels, sheltered from NE winds, in the bay on the S coast of Gogo Shima. Anchorage can be obtained in **Tomari Wan,** entered close SSE of Shirano Hana, in a depth of 33 m about 3 cables offshore.

A good sheltered anchorage is afforded in Yura Wan to the N of Okino Mo, but clear of the **submarine cables** indicated on Chart 3603.

The W side of Gogo Shima is described at 5.67.

IYO NADA—NORTH SIDE

ISLANDS IN THE NORTH PART OF IYO NADA

Chart 2874
5.36

Hōjiro Shima (33° 44' N, 132° 01' E), an islet in the N part of Iyo Nada, consists of two grassy islets connected by reef which dries; the N islet is 33 m high and the S islet 22 m high. A **light** is exhibited from a white square concrete tower standing on the N islet.

Uwa Shima, 84 m (274 ft) high and wooded, lies ⅓ mile ENE of Hōjiro Shima; its W end is a long and narrow rocky headland, and close to its E end there is a prominent isolated rock.

Naka Se, a shoal the E head of which dries 0·9 m (3 ft), lies nearly midway between Hōjiro Shima and Uwa Shima.

Fish havens, consisting of sunken hulks, lie 6 cables SW, 1¼ miles W and 3 cables NW of Hōjiro Shima.

Chart 3602
5.37

Ya Shima is situated with **Hirane Saki** (33° 43' N, 132° 08' E), its S extremity, 5¼ miles ESE of Uwa Shima. The island is in three parts joined by narrow isthmuses; the S'most and largest part is 278 m high with a flattish

summit, and the N part is narrow and 66 m high. All three parts have numerous hillocks and are thickly covered with pine trees.

A **light** is exhibited from a white square tower standing on Hirane Saki.

Ō Se, 4 cables S of Hirane Saki, has a depth of 11 m over it, and is sometimes marked by tide rips.

Sengai Se, a group of drying rocks, lies 3 cables NW of the W extremity of the central part of Ya Shima and is marked close W by a *light-buoy*. **Tsubu Se,** a black rounded rock 2 m high, lies at the extremity of a chain of islets and rocks extending 2¼ cables NW from the N end of the central part of the island.

Three **beacons,** marking the W end of the W'most of three measured distances (see 5.6), stand on the hillside on the E side of the S part of the island.

Anchorage is afforded in depths from 6 m to 29 m, mud and sand, sheltered from E, in **Hon Ura,** a bay on the W side of the isthmus joining the S and central parts of Ya Shima; a heavy sea runs into the bay in NW winds and during N and S gales. Two **submarine cables** are landed in the NE corner of this bay and should be avoided when anchoring.

A **light** is exhibited on the head of a breakwater situated on the S shore of the bay.

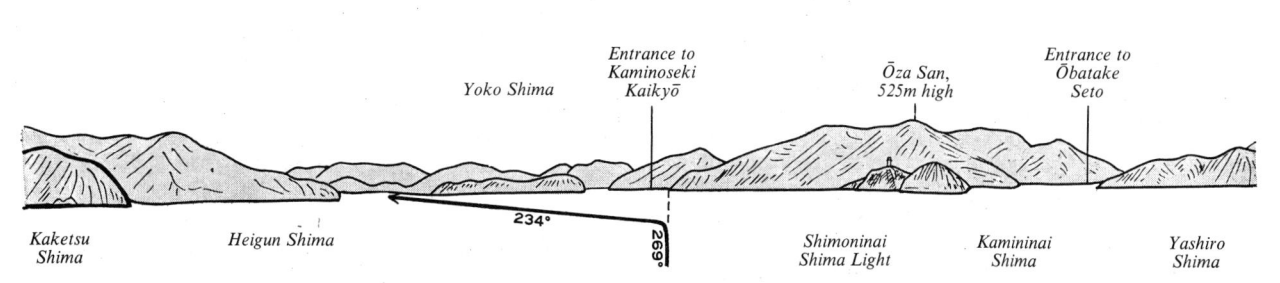

Fuka Yama, 461m high

Hirane Saki Light   *Ya Shima*   *Iyano Hana*   *Heigun Shima*

(5.37, 5.38) Iyo Nada—Ya Shima and Heigun Shima from SE, seen from a position about
3½ miles ESE of Iyano Hana *(33°46′N, 132°16′E)*.

(Original dated prior to 1978)

Okikamuro Shima

Heigun Shima   *Sakari Saki*   *Futagami Shima*   *Ōminase Shima*   *Yuri Shima*   *Kominase Shima*

(5.38) Iyo Nada—Islands E of Heigun Shima from SW, seen from a position about 5 miles
SW of Sakari Saki *(33°47′N, 132°17′E)*.

(Original dated prior to 1978)

Yoko Shima   *Entrance to Kaminoseki Kaikyō*   *Ōza San, 525m high*   *Entrance to Ōbatake Seto*

234°   269°

Kaketsu Shima   *Heigun Shima*   *Shimoninai Shima Light*   *Kamininai Shima*   *Yashiro Shima*

(5.39) Heigun Suidō from E, seen from a position about 4½ miles ENE of
Kaketsu Shima *(33°49′N, 132°16′E)*.

(Original dated prior to 1978)

5.38

Heigun Shima (Tō) is situated with **Kushi Saki** (33° 48' N, 132° 11' E), its SW extremity, 2½ miles NNE of Ya Shima. In the middle of the island are two round-topped mountains of almost the same height which are covered with shrubs and grass.

Handō Iwa, 1 mile S of Kushi Saki, is a precipitous rock 15 m high which resembles a boat under sail.

Anchorage, sheltered from winds between N and E, is afforded in depths from 7 m to 25 m in **Nishi Ura** a bay on the E side of Kushi Saki; **fish havens** lie across the entrance to Nishi Ura.

Mi Shima (33° 46' N, 132° 15' E) consisting of three islets covered with pine trees, lie 1 cable S of **Iyano Hana,** the S extremity of Heigun Shima, and are joined to it by a drying sandbank. A **light** is exhibited from a black round concrete tower standing on **Okino Se,** the W'most of two drying rocks lying 1½ cables SW of Mi Shima.

Two **beacons** marking the E end of the W'most and the W end of the central of three measured distances (see 5.6), stand close NNW of Iyano Hana.

Several **fish havens** lie along the S coast of Heigun Shima within ¼ mile of the shore.

Sakari Saki, the E extremity of Heigun Shima, is surmounted bya well-wooded conical hill which is a good mark. There are always tide rips off this point.

Aka Saki is the N extremity of Heigun Shima and close off it is a rock, 5 m high, which shows up well from W; the rocks in the vicinity of the point are tinged with red.

Kaketsu Shima (33° 49' N, 132° 16' E), 200 m high, lies 1 mile off the E coast of Heigun Shima; **Matsubushi Se,** with a depth of 3·5 m, lies ½ mile ENE of the NE extremity of Kaketsu Shima.

HEIGUN SUIDŌ

Chart 3602

5.39

Heigun Suidō is bordered on its S side by the N coast of Heigun Shima. The S approaches to Kaminoseki Kaikyō are described at 3.37.

Senba Saki (33° 50' N, 132° 09' E), the S extremity of Murotsu Hantō (3.34), stands at the W end of Heigun Suidō and has a remarkable steep cliff on its S side; its summit is covered with dense dark pine woods. A **light** is exhibited from a red round concrete tower standing on **Kojikake Iwa,** awash, situated 1 cable SE of Senba Saki.

Kurosaki Hana, 9 cables NE of Senba Saki, is a black rocky point which is prominent from SW.

Shimoninai Shima, 1 mile E of Kurosaki Hana, is a round island with a small flat summit 108 m high which resembles an inverted bowl; a **light** is exhibited from a white round concrete tower standing near the summit of the island. Shimoninai Shima lies at the S end of the S approach to Ōbatake Seto (5.42).

Minami Iso, with a depth of 12 m over it, lies 1 cable S of Shimoninai Shima.

Kamininai Shima, 6 cables E of Shimoninai Shima, is 108 m high and thickly covered with brambles; the S extremity of the island is a small black cliff partly whitened by guano. **Kura Iso,** with a depth of 1·7 m, lies 4 cables SSE of Kamininai Shima and is sometimes marked by tide rips.

5.40

Daiha (Hōshi) Saki (33° 51' N, 132° 13' E), the SW extremity of Yashiro Shima, lies ½ mile NE of Kamininai Shima. **Hōshi Iwa,** a prominent dark rock 6 m high and surmounted by a solitary pine tree, lies close S of Daiha Saki and is joined to it by a sandbank; a shoal extends 1 cable SE of it.

Daihanomozu, a detached rock with a depth of 4·5 m, lies 7 cables SE of Hōshi Iwa.

Clearing lines. Ōza San (33° 51' N, 132° 09' E) (3.34) in line with the S extremity of Shimoninai Shima bearing about 284°, leads about 1 cable S of Kura Iso (5.39). The N shoulder of Ōmi Yama (33° 56' N, 132° 25' E) (5.41) in line with Age Saki (5.49) bearing 061°, leads 2½ cables SE of the rock and 2½ cables SE of Daihanomozu.

The W extremity of Daiha Saki in line with Hiko Shima (5.42) bearing about 324°, leads about 2 cables W of Daihanomozu.

YASHIRO SHIMA

Chart 3602

5.41

Yashiro Shima, a large island, separates Iyo Nada from Hiroshima Wan to the N. Ōbatake Seto lies on the NW side of the island, Kushigase Seto and Moroshima Suidō on the E side.

Landmarks. Kanō San (33° 55' N, 132° 15' E), 694 m high, is situated in the middle of the W part of Yashiro Shima and from it mountain ranges extend S, N and E.

Genmei San, a rocky peak 623 m high, 1 mile S of Kanō San, and **Dake Yama,** a conical peak 624 m high to the tops of the trees, 1¼ miles E of Kanō San, are both good marks.

Shiroki Yama, 376 m high, lies in the middle of the central part of Yashiro Shima, 5½ miles ESE of Kanō San; it has pine woods on it and is a good mark from E and W. **Ōmi Yama,** 336 m high, is situated 4½ miles NE of Shiroki Yama.

YASHIRO SHIMA—WEST SIDE

Chart 3602

5.42

The S approach to Ōbatake Seto (33° 57' N, 132° 11' E) is entered between Kurosaki Hana (33° 50' N, 132° 10' E) (5.39) and Daiha (Hōshi) Saki 2½ miles ENE; Shimoninai Shima and Kamininai Shima lie in the entrance.

Hiko Shima, a rocky islet 14 m high, lies on the E side of the channel 2 miles NW of Daiha Saki; from W, three summits surmounted by tall pine trees can be seen and it is a good mark. A shoal bank on which there is a drying rock, extends 2 cables W from Hiko Shima.

Clearing line. The NE extremity of Kaketsu Shima (5.38) in line with Daiha Saki, bearing about 133°, and the two W extremities of Yashiro Shima in line bearing 356°, lead not less than 1 cable W of the shoal bank.

Himi Saki, a prominent treeless headland of a reddish colour, lies 6½ cables NNW of Hiko Shima.

No. 1 Fairway Light-buoy is moored in mid channel 1 mile WSW of Himi Saki, and *No. 2 Fairway Light-buoy* is moored 4 miles NNW of the point.

Karasu Shima (33° 55' N, 132° 08' E), 32 m high and thickly wooded, lies on a shoal 3 cables off the Murotsu Hantō shore, 2½ miles NW of Himi Saki. **Bōzu Iwa,** close to its NE extremity, is a remarkable white rock 4 m high; it shows up well from a distance.

Kuroshima Hana, a black rocky point covered with pine trees and which resembles an island, lies nearly 1½ miles NNW of Karasu Shima. A tall chimney which is prominent, stands 4 cables farther NNW.

Kuroshima Hana is fringed with rocks within 1¼ cables; **Koiketsugawano Su,** a narrow shoal with a least depth of 4·7 m, lies 4 cables E of the point.

Kasasa Shima (33° 56′ N, 132° 10′ E), 114 m high and flat-topped, lies 1¼ miles SW of the narrowest part of Ōbatake Seto; the island, fringed with a shoal bank, is thickly covered with pine trees and is dark in colour.

No Shima, an islet 37 m high and covered with brambles, lies 4 cables S of Kasasa Shima.

5.43

Yanai Kō (33° 57′ N, 132° 08′ E) is a bay entered to the N of Kuroshima Hana (5.42). **Hadaka Shima,** a rocky islet 14 m high with black cliffs, lies in the bay ¾ mile NE of Kuroshima Hana. A detached breakwater is situated close NE of Hadaka Shima and a short breakwater extends W from the islet; a **light** is exhibited at the end of each breakwater. In 1978, both breakwaters were being extended.

From September to April, seaweed beds are established for about ¾ mile S of Hadaka Shima and for about ½ mile E of Kuroshima Hana.

Anchorage is afforded in depths from 17 m to 18 m, mud, 2½ cables E of Hadaka Shima. There is a good anchorage for small vessels in depths from 3 m to 9 m, mud, to the N of the islet. A **fish haven** lies 8 cables E of Hadaka Shima.

Prefectural Quay, with a reported depth of 5·5 m on its S end, projects from the shore 2 cables N of Hadaka Shima; it can accommodate vessels up to 1000 tons. There is a ferry quay with depths from 3·5 m to 4 m alongside, to the W of Prefectural Quay.

There is a basin, which dries, on the N side of the mouth of **Katano Kawa** at the inner end of the harbour.

Facilities. There are three small tugs and some lighters.

There are car ferry and passenger ferry services to Matsuyama Kō (5.28) and other harbours along the coast.

5.44

Komatsu Kō (33° 56′ N, 132° 11′ E), situated on the NW coast of Yashiro Shima, is entered ¾ mile SE of Kasasa Shima. The greater part of the harbour has depths from 10 m to 20 m and is much used by vessels awaiting the tide in Ōbatake Seto, and as a sheltered **anchorage** at the time of a typhoon; the holding ground is good and the tidal streams weak.

Okino Mo, a bank with a least depth of 1·1 m over it, lies in the middle of the entrance to Komatsu Kō and is marked on its NE edge by a *light-buoy*. Okino Mo is covered with seaweed the greenish colour of which indicates its position.

Submarine cables, one of which is a power cable, run from the vicinity of the S entrance point of Komatsu Kō to Kasasa Shima.

From October to April, there are seaweed beds in the vicinity of the mouth of **Yashiro Kawa** which flows into the E part of the harbour.

There are three boat basins in the harbour protected by breakwaters.

Supplies. Fresh water and fuel oil can be supplied.

ŌBATAKE SETO AND APPROACHES

Chart 3602

5.45

Ō Iso (33° 57·0′ N, 132° 10·8′ E), a rock about 2 m high, lies 7 cables NE of the NE extremity of Kasasa Shima (5.42); a **light** is exhibited from a red round concrete tower with black bands standing on the rock.

A ledge, which dries, extends 1 cable SW from Ō Iso, and a chain of reefs extend 1½ cables NW; **Kaizenji Shō,** with a depth of 5 m, is the NW reef and is marked on its N side by a *light-buoy*.

Ōisono Su, with depths from 2·9 m to 4·4 m, sand, is an extensive shoal lying midway between Kasasa Shima and Ō Iso.

Ōbatake Kō consisting of a small basin and a pier, is situated on the mainland N of Ō Iso. Small vessels can obtain temporary **anchorage** out of the tidal stream N of a line joining Ōbatake Kō and Setoyama Hana, ½ mile E.

5.46

Ōbatake Seto (33° 57′ N, 132° 11′ E) is the channel between the NW coast of Yashiro Shima and the mainland of Honshū opposite; it is the shortest route between Suō Nada and Hiroshima Wan.

Ōbatake Seto is about 4 cables wide at its narrowest part between **Myōjin Hana,** a wooded point on the S side, and **Setoyama Hana,** wooded and backed by reddish cliffs, on the N side. A white stone *torii* stands on Myōjin Hana.

Ōshima Bridge, painted pale green and with a vertical clearance of 30 m, spans the channel; the navigable width of the fairway is restricted to that between the 3rd and 4th piers of the bridge. A green light on each side of the bridge marks the centre of the fairway and red lights mark the edges; a fog signal (siren) is sounded from No. 4 Pier.

An **overhead cable** with a vertical clearance of 46 m and supported by tall pylons on the shore either side, crosses Ōbatake Seto close E of the bridge.

Kōzu Shō, which dries 0·6 m, lies ½ cable W of the S pier of Ōshima Bridge; reefs and shoal water extend ½ cable N from it. No attempt should be made to pass between these rocks and the point.

Setoyama Hana on the N side of the narrows is fringed with rocks; although the channel between this point and the 3rd pier is over 100 m wide and has depths from 16 m to 20 m, it must not be used for navigation.

Caution. The traffic, particularly of small vessels, through Ōbatake Seto is heavy and large numbers of fishing vessels may be encountered. The ferry between Ōbatake Kō and Komutsu Kō crosses the channel W of the bridge.

5.47

Designated route. A vessel passing through Ōbatake Seto must follow the designated route and comply with the following regulations:

(a) A W-bound vessel is to keep N of the centre line of the channel which is marked at its E end by *No. 3 Fairway Light-buoy*; on reaching the bridge the vessel should pass between the 3rd and 4th piers. She may pass midway between these piers should there be no oncoming traffic.

(b) An E-bound vessel is to pass N of the light-buoy moored close N of Kaizenji Shō (5.45) and keep S of the centre line; on reaching the bridge the vessel should pass between the 3rd and 4th piers. She may pass midway between these piers should there be no oncoming traffic.

(c) A vessel is not to pass between Myōjin Hana and Ō Iso.

(d) A vessel navigating in Ōbatake Seto should proceed at reduced speed.

(e) A vessel is not to overtake or proceed abeam of another vessel in the vicinity of the bridge.

5.48

Migama Wan (33° 57′ N, 132° 12′ E) lies on the S side

of the E entrance to Ōbatake Seto, 1 mile E of the narrows; in the middle of the bay there is a detached shoal with a depth of 10 m over it.

Temporary **anchorage** is afforded in Migama Wan in depths from 10 m to 13 m, sand. From October to April there are seaweed beds at the inner end of the bay.

Tanojiri Hana, the E entrance point to Migama Wan, is densely covered with pine trees. **Submarine cables,** indicated on the chart, are laid across Ōbatake Seto from the vicinity of Tanojiri Hana.

Heburi Hana, covered with dense scrub, is situated 1 mile E of Tanojiri Hana. **Heburi Shima,** 2½ cables N of the point, consists of two islets joined by a reef which dries; on the S islet which is 33 m high, there is a prominent pine tree. The passage between the islets and Heburi Hana should not be attempted without local knowledge.

Harano (Hara) Su, a long and narrow shoal with a least depth of 9·1 m, lies in the NE approach to Ōbatake Seto 2½ miles NE of the narrows; the shoal is not marked by seaweed.

The bottom is foul ½ mile E and S of Harano Su.

No. 4 Fairway Light-buoy is moored 1½ miles NNE of Harano Su.

YASHIRO SHIMA—SOUTH SIDE

Chart 3602

5.49

Between Daiha (Hōshi) Saki (33° 51' N, 132° 13' E) (5.40) and **Hotoke Saki** 3 miles E, the S shore of Yashiro Shima forms a bight with a sandy beach. Hotoke Saki is dark and thickly covered with pine trees, and from W it appears as an island and is prominent.

Suzume Iwa, 7 m high and surmounted by a solitary pine tree, lies at the extremity of a reef extending 2 cables S from Hotoke Saki; it is not easily seen against the background of the point.

Kabōnomozu Shō, two rocks about 1 cable apart, lie 1¼ miles ENE of Daiha Saki and have a least depth of 8 m over them.

Age Saki, a thickly wooded narrow point, lies 7 cables E of Hotoke Saki; an islet lies close E of the point and is joined to it by a sandbank.

5.50

Agenoshō Wan is entered between Age Saki and **Izaki Hana,** 2½ miles ESE. **Tatsu Shima,** (33° 52' N, 132° 19' E), a wooded islet 87 m high, lies in the entrance to Agenoshō Wan ¾ mile WNW of Izaki Hana.

A **fish haven** lies in the approaches to Agenoshō Wan, 1¾ miles WSW of Tatsu Shima, and another lies close off the NW side of the island.

A **submarine cable,** indicated on the chart, is laid between Tatsu Shima and the coast N.

Ko Iso, a rock which dries 0·6 m, lies 2½ cables NE of the NE extremity of Tatsu Shima. **Oko Se,** a group of rocks the highest of which dries 1·8 m, lies 2½ cables SW of **Daizaburō Hana** a prominent point situated 1 mile NNE of Tatsu Shima.

From October to April there are seaweed beds in the vicinity of Daizaburō Hana and about ½ mile N of Age Saki.

5.51

Agenoshō Kō (33° 53·5' N, 132° 17·0' E) lies in the W part of Agenoshō Wan and is entered between Age Saki and **Ryū Saki** nearly 1½ miles NNE.

Kōno Yama, 103 m high and prominent, lies on the W side of Agenoshō Kō and divides the town into **Nishi Agenoshō** on the SW side and **Higashi Agenoshō** on the NE side.

Anchorages. There is a good anchorage in a depth of 20 m, mud, in the inner bay on the W side of Ryū Saki. Except during SE winds there is a good anchorage in a depth of 20 m, mud, to the N of Age Saki.

There are basins in both Nishi Agenoshō and Higashi Agenoshō mainly used by vessels up to 100 tons. A **light** is exhibited on the head of a short breakwater extending W from **Kame Shima,** a small islet joined to the shore lying off Higashi Agenoshō.

OFF-LYING ISLANDS SOUTH EAST OF YASHIRO SHIMA

Chart 3602

5.52

Okikamuro Shima (33° 51' N, 132° 22' E) is situated 1½ miles ESE of Izaki Hana (5.50) and is separated from the S coast of Yashiro Shima by a shallow channel; **Setono Ishi,** a rock which dries 0·9 m, lies on the S side of the middle of the channel. A **light** is exhibited from a red round concrete tower with black bands, surmounting Setono Ishi.

There is a maximum depth of only 2·7 m in the centre of the channel to the N of Setono Ishi; small vessels always pass through the channel, in which there is a least depth of 3·3 m, on the S side of the rock.

Overhead cables, with a vertical clearance of 44 m, cross the W entrance of the channel.

The summit of Okikamuro Shima is conical and 177 m high; it is dark and thickly covered with pine trees. A **light** is exhibited from a white round concrete column standing on a reef close off the SW extremity of the island.

Kajikake Shō, a reef with a depth of 5 m over it, extends 1¼ cables SE from the SE end of Okikamuro Shima, and foul ground, with a rock awash, extends 1 cable from its E end.

Tide rips occur within about ½ mile of the S side of Okikamuro Shima.

5.53

Sengai Se (33° 49' N, 132° 22' E), which dries 1·6 m, lies 1¼ miles S of Okikamuro Shima; a **light** is exhibited from a red round concrete tower with black bands standing on the rock. A rock with a depth of 0·7 m over it, lies 1½ cables SE of Sengai Se.

Ōminase Shima (38° 48' N, 132° 24' E) is situated 2 miles SE of Sengai Se; its summit is rather flat and densely covered with trees, but has two pointed peaks the S and higher of which is 230 m high. There is a steep fall towards the low N end of the island.

Tide rips sometimes occur within ½ mile N and ¼ mile S of the island.

Kominase Shima (33° 47' N, 132° 24' E), 1¼ miles S of Ōminase Shima, is 120 m high with a thickly wooded summit; the NE side of the island is cliffy and the SW side steep-to. A **light** is exhibited from a white round concrete tower situated on the S end of the island.

Three **beacons** marking the E end of the central and the W end of the E'most of three measured distances (see 5.6), stand near the summit of Kominase Shima.

Tide rips occur near a 0·3 m patch lying close off the NW extremity of the island and also off its SE side.

Charts 3602, 3603

Ao Shima (33° 44' N, 132° 29' E), 4¾ miles SE of Kominase Shima, is 90 m high towards its W end; there is a solitary pine tree near its E end. A **light** is exhibited from a white round concrete tower standing on the W summit of the island.

Three **beacons** marking the E end of the E'most of three measured distances (see 5.6), stand near the middle of the N side of Ao Shima.

A rock with a depth of 1·3 m over it, lies 2 cables E of the E extremity of Ao Shima.

YASHIRO SHIMA—SOUTH EAST SIDE

Chart 3602

5.54

Ushigakubi (33° 52' N, 132° 23' E), the SE extremity of Yashiro Shima, terminates in a low hill of a reddish grey colour and is sparsely covered with pine trees.

Yazaemon Se, with a depth of 16 m over it, lies 9 cables NE of Ushigakubi and is sometimes marked by tide rips.

Sasa Shima, 76 m high and covered with pine woods and shrubs, lies 2¾ miles NNE of Ushigakubi. A line of islets lie between Sasa Shima and the coast N.

Kodomari Wan is entered between Sasa Shima and **Ō Hana** ¾ mile NE; an 8 m patch lies in the entrance to the bay 4 cables NNE of Sasa Shima. Except during S winds, Kodomari Wan affords sheltered **anchorage** in depths from 12 m to 20 m.

Charts 3602, 3603

Yuu Ura (33° 56' N, 132° 26' E) is entered 1½ miles NE of Ō Hana; it affords **anchorage,** sheltered from N winds, to small vessels in a depth of 20 m, hard mud. **Yuta Kō,** protected by a breakwater, is situated at the head of the bay; a **light** is exhibited on the breakwater.

Setono Hana (33° 57' N, 132° 29' E), the E extremity of Yashiro Shima, has a level summit thickly covered with pine trees and is a good mark; its NE extremity is fringed with reefs extending ½ cable offshore.

5.55

Katayama Shima (33° 55' N, 132° 28' E) is situated 1¾ miles SSW of Setono Hana and is separated from the SE coast of Yashiro Shima by **Katayama Seto** a deep channel about 4 cables wide.

Katayama Shima is in two parts separated by a low isthmus; the NW and higher part of the island is 215 m high.

Tokkuri Se, which dries 2·4 m, lies ½ cable SW of **Tokkuri Hana** the SE extremity of Katayama Shima; tide rips occur off the point on the rising tide. **Ō Ishi,** a rock 1·5 m high, lies on a reef 4 cables NE of Tokkuri Hana and should be given a wide berth; a **light** is exhibited from a white round concrete tower standing on the rock.

Kamoji Shō (33° 53' N, 132° 29' E), a steep-to detached rock with a depth of 7·3 m over it, lies 2¼ miles SSE of Tokkuri Hana.

Clearing lines. Kamose Shima (5.56) in line with the W edge of Yoko Shima, bearing 055°, leads close N of Kamoji Shō; the W edge of Katayama Shima in line with **Taino Yama,** 212 m high, in the E part of Yashiro Shima, bearing about 340°, leads close W of the rock.

CHANNELS AND ISLANDS BETWEEN YASHIRO SHIMA AND GOGO SHIMA

Charts 3602, 3603

5.56

Yuri Shima (33° 51' N, 132° 32' E) is in two parts connected by a low sandy isthmus and appears as two islets from N or S; the E part, the highest, is 193 m high. A **light** is exhibited from a white round concrete tower standing on the S end of the island.

A rocky patch, with a depth of 4·1 m over it, lies 2 cables W of the W extremity of Yuri Shima.

Futagami Shima is situated with **Nō Saki** (33° 56' N, 132° 31' E) its W extremity, 5 miles N of Yuri Shima. **Kome Yama,** the summit, is 183 m high and lies near the middle of the S side of the island, with **Myōken Yama** lying close W of it; from S these two hills appear as prominent conical peaks of about the same elevation.

There are several rocks scattered close in to the coast of Futagami Shima.

Kamose Shima (33° 55' N, 132° 32' E), two steep-to islets 33 m high, lie close together ¾ mile S of Futagami Shima. **Kamoseno Okino Ishi,** a steep-to detached rock with a depth of 9·4 m over it, lies 3 cables S of Kamose Shima.

Yoko Shima, Naka Shima and **Koichi Shima,** all fringed with reefs, lie within 2¼ miles SE of the E extremity of Futagami Shima; they should not be approached within 1 cable. A **light** is exhibited from a white round concrete tower on the SE extremity of Koichi Shima.

5.57

Nasake Shima (33° 57' N, 132° 29' E) is separated from Setono Hana (5.54), the E end of Yashiro Shima, by **Kushigase Seto** which is about 2 cables wide; reefs fringe its sides reducing the width of the fairway to about 1 cable.

An **overhead cable,** with a vertical clearance of about 40 m, crosses Kuchigase Seto.

Nasake Shima is covered with a sparse growth of pine trees and its summit, 178 m high to the tops of the trees, appears as a sharp peak from E. The island is fringed with rocks and reefs on all sides which in places extend 1½ cables offshore. **Kanjō Shima,** 11 m high with pine trees on its summit, lies 1 cable S of the SE extremity of Nasake Shima.

Tateba Dashi, a detached rock with a depth of 3 m over it, lies ½ mile N of the N extremity of Nasake Shima.

Moroshima Suidō

5.58

Moroshima Suidō lies between the E side of Nasake Shima and the SW end of Tsuwaji Shima; its S part is divided into two by **Moro Shima** (33° 57' N, 132° 30' E), a round-topped island 116 m high and thickly covered with coarse grass.

Nenashi Shō lies on a shoal ½ mile SE of Moro Shima; a **light** is exhibited from a red round metal tower with black bands surmounting the rock.

Miruga Seto, the W part of Moroshima Suidō, is about 2½ cables wide and the only dangers in it are the reefs extending from the E extremity of Nasake Shima. It is the main route through Moroshima Suidō; however it is narrow and the tidal streams in it are strong, and large concentrations of fishing vessels may be encountered in its entrances. Passage through it therefore is not recommended for large vessels and for vessels without local knowledge.

Tidal streams in Miruga Seto are:

N-going—LW to HW in Hiroshima Wan

S-going—HW to LW in Hiroshima Wan

The mean spring rate is 4½ knots but the rate reaches 6 knots at times. On a rising tide the tidal stream sets towards the E extremity of Nasake Shima.

Igai Seto, the E-part of Miruga Seto, is about 4 cables wide but the fairway is reduced to 2 cables by shoals on each side.

Tsuwaji Shima is situated with **Karumo Hana** (33° 58' N, 132° 30' E), its SW extremity, ½ mile N of Moro Shima. The headlands on the W coast of Tsuwaji Shima are prominent; **Takenoko Shima,** 32 m high, lies in the middle of a small bay on the SW side of the island.

Aburatori Se, which dries 1·2 m, lies close off the SE coast of Tsuwaji Shima 1 mile NE of Karumo Hana; a **light** is exhibited from a white round concrete structure standing on the rock.

Nuwashima Suidō
5.59

Nuwashima Suidō (33° 59' N, 132° 32' E), a deep channel, lies between Tsuwaji Shima and **Nuwa Shima** to the E. An **overhead cable** with a vertical clearance of about 40 m, crosses the strait.

The width of the fairway in Nuwashima Suidō is reduced by shoals in its narrowest part to about 4 cables. **Shin Iso,** with a depth of 7·1 m over it, lies on the W side of its narrowest part off the NE extremity of Tsuwaji Shima, and **Okoze Iwa,** which dries 0·9 m, lies on the E side 2 cables NW of the NW extremity of Nuwa Shima. A **light** is exhibited from a red round concrete tower on a reef extending about 1 cable N from Okoze Iwa.

Futago Shima, situated ½ mile SW of the S extremity of Nuwa Shima, consists of two islets joined by a shoal; **Shimo Futago Shima,** the W islet, is 36 m high, and **Kami Futago Shima,** the E islet, is 43 m high. **Bishago Iwa,** which dries 0·6 m, lies at the extremity of a shoal bank which extends 1¼ cables W from Shimo Futago Shima.

Directions. The recommended track through Nuwashima Suidō is shown on the charts. Shimo Futago Shima in line with Kome Yama, 183 m high, 1½ miles farther S, bearing 175°, leads through the narrows clear of all dangers. Strong eddies may be encountered in the strait.

Kudako Suidō
5.60

Kudako Suidō (33° 58' N, 132° 34' E) lies between Nuwa Shima and Naka Shima to the E. Together with Tsurushima Suidō (5.64), this channel is one of those connecting Iyo Nada with Aki Nada; it is also a main channel between Iyo Nada and Hiroshima Wan and is wider and easier to navigate than Nuwashima Suidō, but is about 4½ miles longer.

Cautions. The traffic through Kudako Suidō is very heavy and particular care is needed at its N and S entrances where traffic meets from a number of directions.

From September to April seaweed beds are to be found in many places within 3 cables of the coasts of Nuwa Shima and Naka Shima.

Kudako Shima, 48 m high, lies in the middle of Kudako Suidō and divides the strait into two channels; **Heyano Seto,** the channel on the E side, is the principal one, but the channel on the W side is much used by small vessels and vessels towing. A **light** is exhibited from a white round stone tower standing on Kudako Shima.

Hokkoku Iwa with a depth of 1 m over it, lies 4½ cables SSW of Kudako Shima and is steep-to.

A **light** is exhibited from a white round concrete tower standing on **Heyano Hana** 8 cables E of Kudako Shima; a remarkable detached rock lies off the extremity of this point.

A **light** is exhibited from a white concrete column standing on **Kazakiri Hana,** the NE extremity of Nuwa Shima.

5.61

Directions. The recommended tracks in the approaches to and through Kudako Suidō are shown on the charts.

The SW extremity of Ō Tateba Shima (6.60) bearing 013°, or the W summit of Yoko Shima (33° 55·4' N, 132° 33·7' E) in line with the summit of Yuri Shima, bearing about 196°, lead through the fairway E of Kudako Shima, clear of the eddies.

To clear Hokkuku Iwa, a vessel passing N of Futagami Shima should keep Shimo Futogo Shima (33° 57' N, 132° 32' E) (5.59) bearing more than 266° and open S of Kami Futago Shima, until the SW extremity of Ō Tateba Shima bears less than 017° and is open E of the E side of Kudako Shima.

During the rising tide there is a considerable N-going stream in the position, S of Kudako Shima, where course must be altered; low powered E-bound vessels should exercise care at this turn.

Naka Shima
5.62

Naka Shima borders the E side of Kudako Suidō (5.60); **Aka Saki** (33° 56' N, 132° 36' E), its S extremity, is surmounted by a conical hill, 121 m high, which shows up well from S.

Fuguri Iwa, a black rock 2 m high, lies at the extremity of a reef extending 6 cables SE from Aka Saki; a **light** is exhibited from a black round concrete tower with white bands, standing on the rock.

Tobino Hana, a promontory, is situated about the middle of the NW side of Naka Shima, 1¼ miles NE of Heyano Hana (5.60).

Chart 3603

Kuzure Iwa, a steep-to detached rock 6 m high, lies 2½ cables offshore nearly 2 miles NE of Tobino Hana.
5.63

A **light** is exhibited from a white concrete column standing on **Shira Saki** (36° 01' N, 132° 39' E), the N extremity of Naka Shima.

Uta Saki, the NE extremity of Naka Shima, lies ½ mile SE of Shira Saki. A group of islets lie within 4 cables NE of Uta Saki; **Okinoko Shima,** 29 m high, is the NE'most and highest islet of this group.

Sekito Seto lies between the SE extremity of Naka Shima and Mutsuki Shima close E; the channel is deep but the fairway is very narrow owing to shoals on either side.

Sekito Seto is spanned by **overhead cables** with a least vertical clearance of about 20 m, at its narrowest part.

Nakashima Kō (33° 38' N, 132° 39' E), a shallow bay, lies on the W side of the N entrance to Sekito Seto. A harbour protected by two breakwaters, lies at the inner end of the bay and is used by the car ferry to Matsuyama Kō (5.28); a **light** is exhibited on the head of the S breakwater.

Taka Shima, on the W side of the S entrance to Sekito Seto, has two summits connected by a neck of sand and appears as two islets; the SE and somewhat higher summit is 37 m high. **Tono Shima,** a steep-to conical rock 37 m high, lies 4 cables SE of Taka Shima.

Anchorage is afforded in a bay on the S side of Naka Shima entered between Taka Shima and Aka Saki (5.62), the S extremity of Naka Shima 1½ miles W. The best berth is in depths from 11 m to 16 m, with Fuguri Iwa

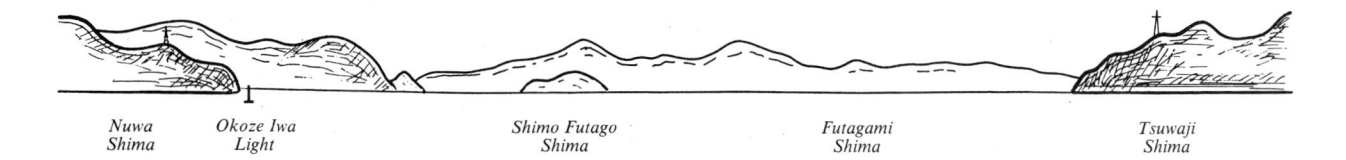

Nuwa
Shima   Okoze Iwa
Light   Shimo Futago
Shima   Futagami
Shima   Tsuwaji
Shima

(5.59) Nuwashima Suidō from N, seen from a position close NW of
Okoze Iwa Light *(33°59′N, 132°32′E)*.

(Original dated prior to 1978)

Tsuwaji
Shima   Ka Shima   Karoto Shima   Okoze
Iwa Light   Nuwa
Shima

(5.59) Nuwashima Suidō from S, seen from a position about 1 mile SSW of
Okoze Iwa Light *(33°39′N, 132°32′E)*.

(Original dated prior to 1978)

Naka
Shima   Yuri Shima

Heyano   Yoko   Kudako   Futagami   Nuwa
Hana Light   Shima   Shima Light   Shima   Shima

(5.60) Kudako Suidō from NE, seen from a position about 1½ miles NE of
Kudako Shima Light *(33°58′N, 132°34′E)*.

(Original dated prior to 1978)

Kudako   Kazakiri   Ōtabeba   Heyano Hana   Naka Shima
Shima Light   Hana Light   Shima   Light

(5.60) Kudako Suidō from S, seen from a position close SSE of Kudako Shima Light
(33°58′N, 132°34′E).

(Original dated prior to 1978)

(5.64) Tsurushima Suidō from NE, seen from a position about 3 miles NE of Hazuma Hana *(34°00′N, 132°47′E)*.

(Original dated prior to 1978)

(5.64) Tsurushima Suidō (W-bound), seen from a position about 1 mile SE of Ho Saki *(33°57′N, 132°41′E)*.

(Original dated prior to 1978)

Mutsuki Shima   Ho Saki   To Aki Nada   Hazuma Hana   Haizo Hana   Tsuru Shima Light

(5.64) Tsurushima Suidō (E-bound), seen from a position about 1½ miles W of
Tsuru Shima Light *(33°53′N, 132°38′E)*.

(Original dated prior to 1978)

Yuri Shima   Tsurushima Suidō   Tsuru Shima   Ko Fuji Yama, 281m high   Gogo Shima   Matsuyama Kō

(5.66) Tsurushima Suidō from SW, seen from a position about 5 miles SW of Yuri Shima
(33°51′N, 132°32′E).

(Original dated prior to 1978)

(5.62) bearing 225° and Tono Shima bearing 106° distant about 1 mile.

Care is needed to avoid anchoring near two **submarine cables** which are landed in the E part of the bay; and from September to April, **seaweed beds** which extend about 6 cables from the inner part of the bay.

TSURUSHIMA SUIDŌ

Chart 3603
5.64

Tsurushima Suidō (33° 56' N, 132° 40' E), the widest of the channels connecting Iyo Nada and Aki Nada, is bordered by Naha Shima, Mutsuki Shima and Nokutsuna Shima on its N side, and Tsuru Shima and Gogo Shima on its S side. The navigable width of the channel is about 1¼ miles and the depths in it are in general over 50 m.

Directions. The recommended tracks in the approaches to, and through Tsurushima Suidō are shown on the chart.

Recommended Traffic Separation Scheme. The 6th Regional Maritime Safety Headquarters requests that vessels should keep on the starboard side, at a distance of more than 150 m, of a line joining a fairway *light-buoy* moored 1 mile NW of Tsuru Shima Light (5.66) and *Aki Nada S Fairway No. 1 Light-buoy* moored in the E entrance to the strait.

Cautions. The passage through Tsurushima Suidō can be made both by day and at night by large vessels. However care is needed as in the W entrance the traffic from Iyo Nada meets the traffic from Heigun Suidō and Kudako Suidō, and in the E entrance numerous ferries and pleasure craft cross the route.

Concentrations of fishing vessels may be encountered at night in the straits and in the W approaches between Yuri Shima and Tsuru Shima.

Particular care is needed in fog when many accidents occur in the area.

Although a cross-set is seldom experienced, caution is necessary when the tidal stream is at strength.

5.65

Mutsuki Shima (33° 57' N, 132° 40' E), on the N side of the strait, is separated from Naka Shima by Sekito Seto (5.63); it has two summits and **Takamatsu Yama,** the E summit, is 217 m high and has a remarkable cliff half way up its S side.

Ho Saki, a salient point with a few pine trees on it, is the SE extremity of Mutsuke Shima; a **light** is exhibited on a black rock, 1 m high, close SE of the point.

Imoko Seto, a channel about ¼ mile wide, lies between Mutsuki Shima and Nokutsuna Shima to the E; **Imoko Shima,** a steep-to islet 40 m high, lies near the middle of the channel. An **overhead cable** with a least vertical clearance of 29 m, spans Imoko Seto.

Katano Iso, a rocky patch with a depth of 2·2 m lies on the E side of the N entrance to Imoko Seto.

Nokutsuna Shima lies 5 cables E of Mutsuki Shima and is fringed with shoals on all sides extending 1 or 2 cables offshore. Its summit, 95 m high, is a bare hill of a reddish-brown colour. A **light** is exhibited from a white round concrete tower standing on **Ushigakuchi Saki,** the SE extremity of the island.

Tano Shima, 38 m high and with a few pine trees on its summit, lies close off the NE extremity of Nokutsuna Shima.

There are depths of 13 m ¼ mile N of Nokutsuna Shima and a **fish haven** lies ¼ mile farther N.

5.66

Tsuru Shima (33° 53' N, 132° 38' E) is situated on the E side of the S entrance into Tsurushima Suidō; it has a wooded rounded summit 151 m high which slopes down to **Ikeno Hana** its low NW extremity. A **light** is exhibited from a white round stone tower standing in the N part of the island; a **racon** transmits from the light-tower.

Ko Seto, a channel about 6 cables wide, separates Tsuru Shima from the W extremity of Gogo Shima.

5.67

Gogo Shima, on the SE side of Tsurushima Suidō, is hilly and in the valleys are many orchards. **Ko Fuji Yama,** 281 m high and wooded, lies in the S part of Gogo Shima and is prominent.

Washigasu Wan (33° 54' N, 132° 40' E) lies on the W side of the middle part of Gogo Shima and affords **anchorage** out of the tidal stream and sheltered from winds from N, through E, to SE. The best berth is in a depth of 12 m about 2 cables WNW of **Kamose Shima,** 18 m high, situated 2 cables offshore on the E side of the bay.

From September to April, seaweed beds fringe the shores of the bay.

Submarine cables, the routes of which are indicated on the chart, are landed in a bay on the NW side of Gogo Shima.

Kotobiki Hana (33° 55' N, 132° 41' E) is situated at the N end of Gogo Shima and close off it is a remarkable rock 9 m high. Foul ground, on which lie an islet and a rock which dries 2·1 m, extends about 1¼ cables NW from Kotobiki Hana.

The E coast of Gogo Shima is described at 5.35.

CHAPTER 6

AKI NADA

GENERAL INFORMATION

Charts 2874, 3602, 3603
6.1

Aki Nada lies between the line of islands situated between Ōbatake Seto (33° 57' N, 132° 11' E) and Matsuyama Kō (33° 52' N, 132° 42' E), 27 miles E, and the coast of Honshū to the N. Hiroshima Wan forms the W part of Aki Nada.

Routes
6.2

S route. The S route through Aki Nada from Tsurushima Suidō (33° 55' N, 132° 40' E) to Kurushima Kaikyō (34° 08' N, 133° 00' E) is marked by *Aki Nada S Fairway Nos. 1–4 Light-buoys* and has a minimum depth of 21 m; it is the route normally used by large vessels.

A 16 m patch of fine sand covering a rock, lies 6 cables NW of the recommended track in position 34° 05·2' N, 132° 49·4' E, 2 miles SE of Itsuki Shima.

N route. The N route from Kudako Suidō (33° 59' N, 132° 35' E) to Kurushima Kaikyō is marked close NW of Ai Shima (34° 04' N, 132° 42' E) by *Aki Nada N Fairway No. 1 Light-buoy*, and is deep; it is used by large numbers of small vessels bound to and from Suo Nada via Heigun Suidō (33° 50' N, 132° 12' E). Vessels bound for ports in Hiroshima Wan via Hashirashima Suidō (34° 01' N, 132° 29' E) or Ondo Seto (34° 12' N, 132° 32' E) branch off from this route.

A large number of small vessels bound for Kudako Suidō from E, take a short cut by passing S of Itsuki Shima and between Ai Shima and Koai Shima.

The recommended tracks to be followed in the routes just described are shown on the charts.

Caution. *Ferries, many of which are hydrofoils, plying between Hiroshima Kō (34° 20' N, 132° 27' E) and Matsuyama Kō, cross the recommended tracks.*
6.3

Other routes. Vessels bound for ports in Hiroshima Wan from S may leave the main route through Iyo Nada at *Iyo Nada Fairway No. 9 Light-buoy* (33° 53' N, 132° 36' E) (5.3) and proceed through Kudako Suidō (5.60) the principal channel leading to Hiroshima Wan. The recommended track for this route and for the alternative route N of Futagami Shima (33° 56' N, 132° 33' E) are shown on Charts 3602 and 3603.

Ōbatake Seto (33° 57' N, 132° 11' E) (5.46), on the W side of Yashiro Shima, and Moroshima Suidō (5.58) and Nuwashima Suidō (5.59) off its E side, are alternative but narrower channels leading to Hiroshima Wan from Iyo Nada and are much used by small vessels.

Hashirashima Suidō (34° 01' N, 132° 29' E) (6.14) is the main channel into Hiroshima Wan from S, and from the E part of Aki Nada. Ondo Seto (34° 11' N, 132° 33' E) (6.56), a narrow channel used by small vessels, lies between the N end of Kurahashi Shima and the mainland and leads to Kure Kō and thence to Hiroshima Wan.

Tidal streams
6.4

Tidal streams. In the central part of Aki Nada in the area extending from Ai Shima to Kurushima Kaikyō (34° 08' N, 133° 00' E), the tidal streams are as follows:

LW	
+ 0200	NE-going
HW	SW-going
LW	
+ 0200	NE-going

The tidal stream turns about 20 minutes later than in Kurushima Kaikyō and the spring rate is about 2 knots.

In the SE part of Aki Nada, a N-going set may be experienced on the rising tide and a S-going set on the falling tide.

In Hiroshima Wan the tidal streams are generally less than 1 knot and turn about the time of HW and LW.

HIROSHIMA WAN

Chart 3602
6.5

Hiroshima Wan is a large bay in the W part of Aki Nada; Iwakuni Kō (34° 11' N, 132° 14' E) (6.29) lies on the W side of the bay, Hiroshima Kō (34° 21' N, 132° 28' E) (6.43) on its N side and Kure Kō (34° 14' N, 132° 33' E) (6.57) on its NE side. The S shore of the bay is formed by the N coast of Yashiro Shima (5.41).

Caution. There are many oyster and seaweed beds in Hiroshima Wan and care is needed. **Submarine cables,** the positions of which are indicated on the chart, are laid in the bay.

Routes leading to Hiroshima Wan from Iyo Nada and the E part of Aki Nada are described at 6.2 and 6.3.

HIROSHIMA WAN—SOUTH SIDE

Chart 3602
6.6

The S side of Hiroshima Wan is formed by the N coast of Yashiro Shima (5.41) off which lie a number of islands and islets.

Landmarks. Kanō San and Dake Yama which lie in

the middle of the W part of Yashiro Shima, and Ōmi Yama in the E part, are good marks; they are described at 5.41.

Mae Shima to Matsuga Hana

6.7

Mae Shima (34° 00' N, 132° 16' E), in two parts joined by a narrow isthmus on which stand some houses, is situated on the E side of the N approach to Ōbatake Seto (5.46). **Gyōja Yama,** in the S part, is 109 m high and somewhat pointed, and **Oban Yama,** in the N part, is 124 m high and thickly covered with pine trees.

Fuku Shima, a flat-topped islet 51 m high to the tops of the trees, lies 1 mile SW of Mae Shima.

6.8

Kuka Wan is entered between Heburi Hana (33° 58' N, 132° 14' E) (5.48) and **Ōsaki Hana** 2½ miles ESE; a **light** is exhibited from a white concrete tower standing on the point.

Landmark. Yakushi Yama, a sharp peak 277 m high, is situated 6 cables S of Ōsaki Hana and is a good mark for identifying the harbour.

Okino Mo, a shoal with a depth of 5 m and covered with seaweed, lies on the W side of an extensive bank, with depths of less than 10 m, which extends about 2 miles NNE from the entrance to Kuka Wan; it is reported that the bank is increasing in size.

Okino Iso, three detached rocks with a least depth of 0·1 m, lies 1 mile NNE of Ōsaki Hana.

Fish havens lie on Okino Mo and within 4 cables WNW of Ōsaki Hana. From October to April seaweed beds are to be found in the vicinity of Okino Mo and on the E and W sides of the bay.

Anchorage. Except with winds between NW and NE, anchorage is afforded in depths of about 10 m, 2½ cables offshore abreast Kuka Kō.

6.9

Kuka Kō, consisting of three basins protected by breakwaters, lies in the SE corner of Kuka Wan; a **light** is exhibited on the head of the breakwater protecting the W'most basin in which there is a car ferry terminal.

Small quantities of fuel oil and fresh water can be supplied in Kuka Kō and there are repair facilities for small vessels.

6.10

Hize Shima (33° 55' N, 132° 19' E), 68 m high and covered with shrubs and grass, lies in the middle of the entrance of a small bay entered 2 miles SE of Ōsaki Hana (6.8). **Anchorage** can be obtained in depths from 11 m to 16 m in the bay but two **submarine cables** are landed in its SE corner.

Waga Shima, 79 m high and surmounted by a solitary pine tree, lies near the middle of the entrance of a bay entered 4 miles SE of Ōsaki Hana. A sandbank on which stands two islets and some drying rocks, extends 6 cables N from the shore near the middle of the head of the bay; a detached rock with a depth of 0·9 m, lies 5 cables NNE of the extremity of this sandbank.

Matsuga Hana (33° 55' N, 132° 22' E), lies 4¼ miles ESE of Ōsaki Hana (6.8). **Nabe Shima,** 35 m high, steep-sided and covered with pine trees, is the larger of two islets lying within 2 cables NW of Matsuga Hana; **Tobisekuiai,** a rock with a depth of 3·2 m, lies at the extremity of a shoal extending about 4 cables NNW from Nabe Shima.

Off-lying islands north-west of Matsuga Hana

6.11

Uka Shima (33° 57' N, 132° 21' E), surmounted by a ridge 168 m high and thickly covered with pine trees, lies 1½ miles NNW of Matsuga Hana (6.10). The S point of this island is sandy and from it a drying spit extends about 2 cables S; **Kurohoguri,** a black rock 1·6 m high, stands on this spit.

Hando Shima, Oito Shima, Koito Shima and **Yahazu Se,** a dangerous rocky patch close SW of Hando Shima, lie between the S point of Uka Shima and the coast of Yashiro Shima to its S.

Directions. Hando Shima open N of Oito Shima, bearing about 243°, leads about 2 cables N of Tobisekuiai (6.10); a vessel proceeding W should not alter course S to round Oito Shima until the E extremity of Kashira Shima (6.12) is in line with the W extremity of Kurakake Shima, bearing 347°.

6.12

Kashira Shima (33° 58' N, 132° 21' E), N of Uka Shima and separated from it by a narrow and shallow channel spanned by an **overhead cable** with a vertical clearance of 16 m, has three dark summits the central and highest of which is 89 m high to the tops of the trees.

Kurakake Shima, 62 m high and thickly covered with pine trees, lies ¼ mile N of Kashira Shima; three beacons stand on its E side.

Kuro Shima, 117 m high and covered with pine trees, lies ¼ mile NW of Kurakake Shima; from N it appears conical and is easily identified. A rock which dries 1·2 m lies at the extremity of a reef which extends 1½ cables NE of Kuro Shima.

Iseko Shima, a sparsely wooded islet 39 m high, lies 1 mile N of Kuro Shima. The SE extremity of Iseko Shima is joined to the main part by a low sandy isthmus and appears as a separate islet; a **beacon** stands on the extremity and a reef extends 2 cables SE of it.

Ō Zone, a steep-to rock with a depth of 4·1 m, lies 2½ cables NE of Iseko Shima.

Zushiga Hana to Setono Hana

6.13

Zushiga Hana (33° 56' N, 132° 24' E) lies 2½ miles E of Oito Shima (6.11); a wooded hillock with a shrine on its E side, is situated on the point.

Michi Shima, 1 mile NW of Zushiga Hana, is flat-topped and surmounted by a solitary pine tree; a 3·6 m rocky patch lies 2 cables NW of the islet.

Charts 3602, 3603

Matsuga Hana (33° 57' N, 132° 27' E) (not to be confused with the Matsuga Hana described at 6.10) lies 2 miles ENE of Zushiga Hana and is at the extremity of a red-coloured ridge.

Anchorage, sheltered from winds between S and W, can be obtained in a depth of about 12 m about 1 cable offshore in the bay entered close E of Matsuga Hana.

Izumi Shima, a rocky islet 30 m high, lies ½ cable offshore 1¼ miles ESE of Matsuga Hana; several rocks lie on the N side of the islet, the outermost of which is 3 m high, white, pointed and remarkable.

Setono Hana, the E extremity of Yashiro Shima and Kushigase Seto are described at 5.54 and 5.57, respectively.

HASHIRASHIMA SUIDŌ

Charts 3602, 3603

6.14

Hashirashima Suidō (34° 01' N, 132° 29' E) is the principal channel into Hiroshima Wan from the S and E and is bordered on each side by a number of islands and rocks. *Hiroshima Wan No. 1 Fairway Light-buoy*

(34° 01' N, 132° 30' E) is moored in the S entrance to the strait and *Hiroshima Wan No. 2 Fairway Light-buoy* (34° 08' N, 132° 22' E) is moored 5 miles NW of the N entrance to the strait. The recommended track through Hashirashima Suidō is shown on the charts.

Hashirashima Suidō—west side
6.15

Fukura Shima (33° 59' N, 132° 26' E), 62 m high and covered with pine trees, lies on the W side of the S end of Hashirashima Suidō.

Naga Shima, also known as **Kottoi Shima,** is 68 m high and covered with pine trees, and lies 3 cables N of Fukura Shima; a reef extends about 2 cables N from the N end of the islet.

Tsuzaki Shima, a group of three islets thickly wooded with pine trees, lies ½ mile N of Naga Shima; the N islet, the highest of the three, is 52 m high.

Hashira Shima (34° 01' N, 132° 25' E), a dark, conical and prominent island 289 m high, is situated with its low sandy SE extremity 2 cables NW of Tsuzaki Shima; the channel between them is reduced in width by shoals on either side to about 1 cable.

Hashirashima Kō, protected by breakwaters, is situated on the E side of Hashira Shima; a **light** is exhibited on the head of the E breakwater. A **fish haven** lies ½ mile E of the breakwater head.

Ko Hashira Shima, 2 cables NE of the N extremity of Hashira Shima, has two wooded summits the E and higher being 96 m high.

Chart 3602

Ha Shima, ¼ mile NW of Hashira Shima, is in two parts joined by a low isthmus; the S part has a round wooded summit 137 m high to the tops of the trees. **Nakanoko Shima,** 20 m high, lies 3½ cables N of Ha Shima.

Te Shima, a wooded islet 89 m high, lies 1¼ miles N of Hashira Shima.

Hotaka Shima, on the W side of the N end of Hashirashima Suidō, lies 2¼ miles N of Hashira Shima and is 35 m high and is covered with pine trees. In the channel between the two islets there is a shoal on which are two rocks which dry 3·6 m. A reef extends about 1 cable NE from the NE extremity of Hotaka Shima.

Charts 3602, 3603
Hashirashima Suidō—east side
6.16

Yoko Shima (34° 02' N, 132° 30' E), on the E side of the S end of Hashirashima Suidō, is 94 m high. A chain of rocks extends about 6 cables NW from the middle of the NW side of the island and **Yokoshima Tsuzuki,** the highest rock on it which has three separate rounded summits, is 28 m high to the tops of the trees.

Kashinoko Shima, 20 m high and sparsely covered with pine trees, lies on a reef, parts of which dry, 1 mile NW of Yoko Shima.

Kuro Shima (34° 03' N, 132° 28' E) 72 m high and wooded, lies with its low sandy S extremity 2 cables NW of Kashinoko Shima.

Ebigahire, a group of rocks the highest of which dries 2·4 m, lies within 6 cables W of Kuro Shima.

Nishi Gobanno Bae, on the E side of the N end of Hashirashima Suidō, is the NW'most of the dangers to the NW of Yoko Shima; a **light** is exhibited from a red round stone tower standing on the rock. A rock which dries 0·3 m lies on a reef 3 cables E of Nishi Gobanno Bae.

The dangers lying between Yoko Shima and Nishi Gobanno Bae are covered by the red sector of Nishi Gobanno Bae Light; no attempt should be made to cross this area.

HIROSHIMA WAN—EAST SIDE

Charts 3602, 3603
6.17

Kurahashi Shima forms the S part of the E side of Hiroshima Wan; it is separated from the mainland of Honshū by Ondo Seto (6.56). Higashi Nōmi Shima (6.21), Nishi Nōmi Shima (6.23) and Eta Shima (6.40), all three islands joined together, form the N part.

Islands south of Kurahashi Shima
6.18

Shira Ishi (34° 02' N, 132° 33' E) or **Mitsu Ishi,** consists of three rocks lying in a N/S direction on a steep-to shoal situated 2½ miles S of the S extremity of Kurahashi Shima; the highest rock is 8 m (charted as 4·3 m) high and is white with guano. A **light** is exhibited from a red square concrete tower with black bands standing on the highest rock in the middle of the reef.

Ha Shima, 69 m high to the tops of the trees, lies 2 miles WNW of Shira Ishi; a shoal bank extends 1 cable S from it and rocks lie close off its N point.

Manaita Se, a detached reef which dries 0·3 m, lies ½ mile E of Ha Shima and is marked on its N side by a *light-buoy.*

Ka Shima (34° 03' N, 132° 32' E) is situated close SW of Karoto Shima the SE extremity of Kurahashi Shima; three prominent wooded peaks of about equal height stand in the S part of the island.
6.19

Karoto-ko Seto, spanned by a **bridge** with a vertical clearance of about 23 m, separates the N end of Ka Shima from Karoto Shima; the width of the channel is restricted by shoal banks on either side to about ½ cable.

On the W side of the S approach to Karoto-ko Seto, there is a remarkable white sandy beach. On the E side of the strait, the land is high and covered with pine trees.

A **light** is exhibited on the head of a breakwater at **Kurahashi Kō,** a basin situated on the W side, close N of the bridge.

Directions for Karoto-ko Seto. Shiri Ishi Light-tower, bearing 163° and slightly open E of the NE extremity of Nuwa Shima (34° 00' N, 132° 34' E), leads through

Naga
Shima

Hashira
Shima

Yoko Shima

Ha
Shima

Ka
Shima

275°

(6.14) Hashirashima Suidō from E, seen from a position about 7 miles E of Hashira Shima (34° 01' N, 132° 25' E)

(Original dated prior to 1978)

Karoto-ko Seto clear of all dangers, but local knowledge is necessary.

Tidal streams in Karoto-ko Seto are S-going from 1½ hours after LW to 1½ hours after HW, and N-going from 1½ hours after HW to 1½ hours after LW. The maximum spring rate is 2 knots in the middle of the channel.

Kurahashi Shima—south west side

6.20

Karoto Shima (34° 04' N, 132° 33' E), the E part of which is 101 m high, is joined to the SE extremity of Kurahashi Shima. A **light** is exhibited from a red round concrete tower with black bands standing on the W of two drying rocks of **Sengai,** situated 2 cables E of the E side of Karoto Shima.

A bight lies between Karoto Shima and Jōgeshi Hana 3½ miles NW and in it are several coves with villages at their heads. **Torii Dashi,** with a depth of 8·1 m, lies near the middle of the bight.

Jōgeshi Hana is the SW extremity of Kurahashi Shima and is a remarkable precipitous headland and its rocky outcrops can be seen from a distance.

Nabe Shima (34° 05' N, 132° 27' E), a flat-topped thickly wooded islet 17 m high, lies close inshore 3½ cables NW of Jōgeshi Hana and is easy to identify as its green colour is in strong contrast with the reddish coast of Kurahashi Shima.

Yamaura Take, 490 m high with a flattened summit, lies 1¼ miles NNE of Jōgeshi Hana and is the highest mountain on Kurahashi Shima.

Kuroshima Suidō, about 1¼ miles wide and free of dangers, lies between Kuro Shima (6.15) and the other dangers bordering the E side of Hashirashima Suidō, and Jōgeshi Hana.

Dentarō Hana (34° 06' N, 132° 27' E), the W extremity of Kurahashi Shima, lies on the S side of the approach to Hayase Seto (6.53) and has a dark and rounded summit; a **light** is exhibited from a white round concrete tower standing on the point.

Higashi Nōmi Shima and islands west

6.21

Higashi Nōmi Shima, the S'most part of a comparatively large island, is situated with **Oyake Hana** (34° 08' N, 132° 26' E), its SW extremity, 1½ miles NNW of Dentarō Hana (6.20). **Koshiki Se,** a steep-to rock awash, lies 1 cable SE of the point, and **Eboshi Iwa,** wedge-shaped and 7 m high, lies 1 cable W.

Naga Shima, 90 m high and surmounted by a thick growth of trees, lies ½ mile WNW of Oyake Hana. **Aino Iso,** with a depth of 0·9 m lies in the middle of the channel between Naga Shima and Oyake Hana.

Waga Shima lies close off the N side of Naga Shima and is joined to it by a breakwater which affords shelter to small craft.

Okino Shima, situated 1 mile N of Oyake Hana, is densely wooded and has three peaks the S'most and highest of which is 94 m high; a reddish brown cliff on the SW end of the island is prominent.

Chart 3602

6.22

Ō Kurokami Shima is situated 2 miles NW of Oyake Hana, and its summit, attaining an elevation of 459 m in its SW part, is steep on its SW side; the island is covered with scrub and being dark, is in strong contrast with neighbouring islands which are red in colour.

Measured distance. A measured distance of 2042·7 m marked by two sets of **beacons,** is situated on the W coast of Ō Kurokami Shima; the running course is 315°.

Anchorage may be obtained SW of Ō Kurokami Shima or SE of Naga Shima.

Umaga Se (34° 10' N, 132° 22' E), with a depth of less than 2 m, lies ½ mile W of the NW part of Ō Kurokami Shima and is marked close N by a *light-buoy*.

Shira Ishi (34° 10·5' N, 132° 21·0' E), consisting of two white rocks the S and higher of which is 7 m high, lies 1¾ miles W of the N extremity of Ō Kurokami Shima; reefs extend about ½ cable from the W and S side of the rocks. A **light** is exhibited from a red round stone tower with black bands standing on the N rock of Shira Ishi.

Charts 3602, 3603

Kanokawa Kō

6.23

Kanokawa Kō (34° 10' N, 132° 26' E), situated in **Kanokawa Uchi,** is entered between Ōya Hana and **Akabane Saki** ¾ mile ESE.

Nishi Nōmi Shima is the NW part of the island of which Higashi Nōmi Shima (6.21) is the S part. **Ōya Hana,** the S extremity of Nishi Nōmi Shima, is a narrow point from which a reef extends about 1 cable S.

Landmarks. Shindō Yama, 2¾ miles NNE of Ōya Hana, is a somewhat remarkable conical hill 285 m high, which is a good mark for passing through the channel between Ō Kurokami Shima and Okino Shima, and for entering Kanokawa Uchi.

A group of silver-coloured oil tanks stand on the W shore of Kanokawa Uchi to the N of Ōya Hana.

Pilotage. Pilotage is not compulsory for Kanokawa Kō, but if required pilots are available in the quarantine anchorage at Iwakuni Kō (6.29). Pilots will not berth or unberth vessels at night.

Vessels are required to call at Matsuyama Kō (33° 52' N, 132° 42' E), Iwakuni Kō (34° 12' N, 132° 14' E) or Kure Kō (34° 14' N, 132° 32' E) for quarantine clearance.

The E side of the fairway leading to Kanokawa Oil Terminal is marked by a line joining a *light-buoy* (red) moored 4 cables SSE of Ōya Hana, and *"B" Light-buoy* (red) moored 5½ cables NE of the point. A *light-buoy* (black) moored 1 cable E of Ōya Hana marks the W side of the fairway.

Rocky shoals, marked by a *buoy* (red and black) and a *light-buoy* (red), lie off the E side of Kanokawa Uchi between Akabane Saki and a point 6 cables N.

6.24

Mitsubishi Shoji Kanokawa Oil Terminal is situated on the W side of Kanokawa Uchi close NNE of Ōya Hana.

No. 1 Pier, at the N end of the terminal, provides a berth for tankers up to 12 m draught using three mooring buoys forward and three aft.

No. 3 Pier, 3½ cables S of No. 1 Pier, is a dolphin seaberth which can accommodate tankers up to 14 m draught; a **light** is exhibited at this pier.

Nos. 2 and **4 Piers,** on either side of No. 3 Pier, have depths of 7·5 m alongside and are used by coastal tankers up to 5000 tons.

Vessels berth heading N. In 1977, it was reported that tankers of 70 000 dwt and over are required to have a fire fighting vessel in attendance while in port.

A landing jetty and a boat basin protected by breakwaters, lie on the E side of the inner end of Kanokawa Uchi; a **light** is exhibited on the head of the S breakwater.

Facilities and supplies. Tugs are available from Kure Kō and normally join at the entrance to Kanokawa Uchi. Fuel oil and fresh water can be supplied.

Hiroshima port radio station covers Kanokawa Oil Terminal.

Chart 3602

Nishi Nōmi Shima—west side

6.25

Mitsuke Ishi (34° 11' N, 132° 25' E), with a depth of 1·3 m, lies 1¼ miles NW of Ōya Hana (6.23) and over it the water is of a greyish-white colour; a *light-buoy* is moored on its N side. **Kamada Se,** a steep-to rock with a depth of 1·2 m over it, lies 2 cables offshore 6 cables NE of Mitsuke Ishi.

A **light** is exhibited on the head of a breakwater at **Hata Kō,** 2 miles NNW of Ōya Hana: another **light** is exhibited on the head of **Korenage Breakwater** 1 mile farther NW.

Iruka Hana (34° 13' N, 132° 23' E) rises to a double summit, 129 m high, 4 miles NNW of Ōya Hana; a white round pillar stands close off the point.

Ko Kurokami Shima, a dark islet thickly covered with trees and 129 m high, lies 1½ miles NW of Iruka Hana; a white round pillar stands on the N end of the islet.

Manaita Shō, a group of rocks, lies 6 cables N of Ko Kurokami Shima; the E'most rock dries 1·2 m and the W'most is awash. A **light** is exhibited from a red round concrete tower with black bands standing on Manaita Shō.

A **light** is exhibited on the head of a breakwater at **Mino Kō,** 1½ miles N of Iruka Hana.

Kanne Hana (34° 16' N, 132° 23' E) lies on the N side of a promontory which forms the NW extremity of Nishi Nōmi Shima. A rock, 7 m high, lies 1 cable offshore 2 cables WSW of Kanne Hana.

HIROSHIMA WAN—WEST SIDE ŌBATAKE SETO TO IWAKUNI KŌ

Chart 3602

6.26

The W shore of Hiroshima Wan between the N entrance of Ōbatake Seto (33° 58' N, 132° 12' E) (5.46) and Iwakuni Kō, 14 miles N, is for the most part faced with stone embankments and fringed with sand banks which dry out about 4 cables off-shore in places. It is backed by hills of moderate height, the summits of which are thickly covered with scrub.

Landmark. Zenitsubo Yama, on which there is a **beacon,** is situated 3 miles N of Ōbatake Seto; it attains an elevation of 539 m and is somewhat higher than the hills in the vicinity.

Ōbatake Seto to Monzen Kawa

6.27

Yuu Kō (34° 02' N, 132° 13' E), a small harbour protected by a breakwater, lies 5 miles NNE of Ōbatake Seto; a **light** is exhibited at the head of the breakwater.

Omōdaka Hana lies 2¼ miles N of Yuu Kō at the SW end of the harbour limits of Iwakuni Kō; it is fringed with a sandbank which extends 1½ cables offshore.

Monzen Kawa (34° 07' N, 132° 14' E), the S branch of Nishiki Kawa, flows into the sea 2½ miles NNE of Omōdaka Hana.

Landmark. Atago Yama, 98 m high with a remarkable clump of pine trees on its summit, is situated 1½ miles NW of the mouth of Monzen Kawa; a red light is exhibited on the SE shoulder of the hill.

Chūkoku Electricity Wharf, with a depth of 5 m alongside, lies on reclaimed land 1¼ miles W of the mouth of Monzen Kawa. An approach channel with depths from 5·2 m to 6·7 m leads from E to the wharf and is entered between *No. 2 Light-buoy* and a black *buoy* (cylindrical topmark).

Two chimneys (red and white), marked by red obstruction lights, stand at an elevation of 99 m, in the vicinity of Chūkoku Electricity Wharf.

Off-lying islands east of Iwakuni Kō

6.28

Kabuto Shima (34° 07' N, 132° 19' E), a remarkable red, rocky islet with a pointed summit 101 m high, lies on the W side of the main fairway through Hiroshima Wan, 6 miles ENE of Omōdaka Hana (6.27). From November to March, laver beds lie up to 2 miles E of Kabuto Shima and are marked by *light-buoys* (orange light).

Himeko Shima, a rock 13 m high, lies on a shoal 2 miles NW of Kabuto Shima; a pointed rock 5 m high, lies close N of Himeko Shima and is joined to it by a drying reef. **Mano Iso,** with a depth of 17 m, lies nearly midway between Kabuto Shima and Himeko Shima.

Chart 3469 plan of Iwakuni Kō

Atada Shima (34° 11' N, 132° 19' E), 203 m high, is situated 4 miles N of Kabuto Shima; its coasts are mainly cliffy but there are some sandy beaches. **Atada Kō** lies on the NE side of the island; close off it and connected to it by a breakwater, lies **Inoko Shima,** 82 m high, with some prominent pine trees at its S end.

Danna Se, a steep-to rock with a depth of 6·6 m lies ½ mile W of the W side of Atada Shima.

IWAKUNI KŌ

Charts 3469 plan of Iwakuni Kō, 3602

6.29

Iwakuni Kō (34° 10' N, 132° 15' E), a specified port (see 1.64), lies on the W shore of Hiroshima Wan between the mouth of **Imazu Kawa** and **Shōzoku Hana,** 2½ miles N. Port facilities for both the US Forces and Japanese Self Defence Forces are situated to the S of Imazu Kawa. The harbour limits are shown on the charts.

The city of **Iwakuni,** which in 1973 had a population of 109 000, is an industrial centre. **Iwakuni Airport,** on which stand several radio towers, lies on reclaimed land between Monzen Kawa (6.27) and Imazu Kawa. **Iwakuni Airport Aerolight** is exhibited occasionally from a metal framework tower situated on the W side of the airfield.

Approaches to Iwakuni Kō

6.30

Landmarks. A large number of silver-painted oil tanks and chimneys stand in Kyōa Sekiyū Refinery situated on the S side of **Ōze Kawa** which flows into the sea close N of Shōzoku Hana (34° 12' N, 132° 15' E). A neon light is exhibited at a height of 65 m in a position 3 cables SW of Shōzoku Hana; a conspicuous chimney (red and white, with flare), stands at an elevation of 73 m, 6 cables WSW of Shōzoku Hana.

Pilotage. Pilotage is not compulsory. If required, pilots are available in the quarantine anchorage from 1 hour after sunrise to 1 hour before sunset.

Anchorages. The **quarantine anchorage,** shown on the charts, is situated 1¾ miles NE of the mouth of Imazu Kawa. Good sheltered anchorage is afforded in depths from 10 m to 15 m, mud, in the bight to the SW of the mouth of Monzen Kawa (6.27).

There are several mooring buoys in the harbour.

Prohibited area. Navigation is prohibited in the area between the line joining *Iwakuni Offing Nos. 1, 3* and *5 Light-buoys* and the coast to the W, except by permission of the Commander of Iwakuni Airport.

Directions. Approaching Iwakuni Kō from Hashirashima Suidō and on reaching Hiroshima Wan No. 2 Fairway Light-buoy (34° 08′ N, 132° 22′ E) (6.14), alter course to bring Iwakuni Ko N Breakwater Light (34° 11·4′ N, 132° 14·2′ E) ahead, bearing 298°, and proceed to the quarantine anchorage.

Approaching from Ōbatake Seto (5.46), steer to pass between Kabuto Shima (34° 07′ N, 132° 19′ E) and the light-buoys marking the E boundary of the prohibited area; thence steer for the quarantine anchorage.

Caution. When a tanker carrying liquefied gas is alongside the LPG Pier (34° 11·7′ N, 132° 14·7′ E), a red and white flag by day, or a red light at night, will be shown at the pierhead; other vessels must not approach within 50 m of the pier.

Chart 3469 plan of Iwakuni Kō
Harbour
6.31
A number of wharves, piers and basins are situated in Iwakuni Kō between the mouths of Imazu Kawa and Ōze Kawa. The timber ponds, basins and berths of the **Sanyō-Kokusaku Pulp Company** lie within 1¼ miles NNW of the mouth of Imazu Kawa and the **Kyōa Sekiyū Refinery** piers and jetties lie within ¼ mile SSW of Shōzoku Hana.

Iwakuni North Wharf, which is public, lies close E of the root of **Iwakuni Kō N Breakwater** which protects a small harbour situated 1 mile SSW of Shōzoku Hana; a **light** is exhibited on the head of the breakwater.

No. 2 and *No. 4 Light-buoys* mark the N side of a fairway leading to the Sanyō-Kokusaku Pulp Company **Timber Jetty** and **C1 Jetty.**

Berths and facilities
6.32
Berths. The principal berths in Iwakuni Kō are:

Berth & Position	Length m	Depth m	Capacity tons
Muronoki Public Wharf			
(34° 10·5′ N, 132° 14·8′ E)			
NW side	180	5·4	2 000
SE side	185	10	15 000
Sanyō-Kokusaku Pulp Co			
(34° 10·8′ N, 132° 14·5′ E)			
Timber Jetty	100	7·5–8	5 000
C1 Jetty	80	9–9·5	15 000
C2 Dolphin Berth	—	11·5	40 000
Iwakuni North Wharf			
(34° 11·6′ N, 132° 14·4′ E)			
No. 2 Quay	180	5·5	2 000
Shōzoku Wharf	185	10	15 000
Kyōa Sekiyū Refinery			
LPG Pier	140	8–10	3 000
(34° 11·7′ N, 132° 14·7′ E)			
No. 2 Products Jetty	110	9–9·5	5 000
(34° 11·8′ N, 132° 14·7′ E)			
No. 3 Products Pier	520	7·5–13	20 000
(34° 11·9′ N, 132° 14·9′ E)			
Crude Oil Dolphin Berth	—	17	150 000
(34° 12·0′ N, 132° 15·1′ E)			

6.33
Facilities. There are offices of the Maritime Safety Agency, Customs, Quarantine and Immigration in the joint Harbour Office located on **Shinkō Quay** situated 1¼ miles SSW of Shōzoku Hana.

Two large and four small tugs are available and they usually join in the quarantine anchorage.

Waste oil disposal facilities are available near the mouth of Ōze Kawa.

There is a hospital in Iwakuni.

De-ratting; see 1.70.

Supplies. Fresh water can be supplied at the principal berths and there are four oilers.

Communications. Hiroshima port radio station covers Iwakuni Kō.

The nearest airport is at Hiroshima about 30 miles by road.

HIROSHIMA WAN—WEST SIDE ŌTAKE KŌ AND KUBA KŌ

Charts 3469 plan of Iwakuni Kō, 3602
6.34
Ōtake Kō (34° 14′ N, 132° 14′ E), the harbour limits of which are shown on the charts, extends from the mouth of Ōze Kawa (6.30) to a point about 2¼ miles NNW, and consists of two main basins. The industrial town of **Ōtake** backs the harbour and there are numerous factories along the shore.

Ōtake Basin, within which there are quays with depths from 3·5 m to 4·5 m alongside, is entered 6 cables NNW of the mouth of Ōze Kawa. A **submarine pipeline,** the outer end of which is marked by a *buoy* (black and yellow), crosses the entrance to the basin.

Tobiishi Basin, protected from E by a breakwater, is entered nearly 1¼ miles NW of Ōtake Basin; a **light** is exhibited on the head of the breakwater. **Tobiishi Jetty,** with a reported depth of 4 m alongside, lies on the W side of the basin and is used by ferries.

Chart 3602
Kuba Kō (34° 15′ N, 132° 14′ E), protected by a breakwater, lies at the W entrance point of the S approach to Ōno Seto, 3 miles NNW of Shōzoku Hana; a **light** is exhibited on the head of the breakwater.

HIROSHIMA WAN—NORTH PART

Chart 3602
Itsuku Shima and Ōno Seto
6.35
Itsuku Shima or **Miya Shima** (34° 17′ N, 132° 19′ E), on the W side of the principal approach channels to Hiroshima Kō, is a comparatively large island which is separated from the W shore of Hiroshima Wan by Ōno Seto. The island is densely wooded and is a well known tourist resort; **Mi Sen,** the summit of the island, attains an elevation of 539 m.

The celebrated Itsukushima or Miyashima Shrine is situated on the NW coast of the island.

Measured distance. A measured distance of 2283·6 m has been established on the SE coast of Itsuku Shima; each end is marked by a pair of white **beacons.** The running courses are 048° and 228°.

Chart 3602, 3469 plan of Iwakuni Kō
Kuba Wan lies between the SW end of Itsuku Shima and Otake Kō (6.34) to the W; **Kabe Shima,** 45 m high, lies 4 cables W of the S extremity of Itsuku Shima.

Chart 3602

6.36

Ōno Seto (34° 17' N, 132° 17' E), the channel separating Itsuku Shima from the mainland, is about 3 cables wide at its narrowest part; but the fairway, through which a depth of 6 m can be carried, is reduced by shoals near the middle of the strait to a navigable width of less than 1 cable. The strait is tortuous and its navigation is very difficult; no attempt should be made to pass through without local knowledge. There are also a large number of oyster beds on either side of the channel further reducing its navigable width.

A **light** is exhibited from a white round concrete tower on **Shinkai Hana,** a point on the W side of the narrowest part of Ōno Seto. **Kame Se,** a reef situated on a shoal on the N side of a sharp bend in the fairway, lies ¾ mile NE of Shinkai Hana; a **light** is exhibited from a black square concrete tower standing on **Kame Ishi,** the E extremity of Kame Se.

Kurakake Shō, which dries 0·9 m, lies 2 cables N of Kame Se and is connected to the NW shore of the strait by a shallow spit.

6.37

Miyashima Kō (34° 18' N, 132° 19' E) lies in a bight on the NW side of Itsuku Shima, 1 mile SW of Hijiri Saki its N extremity. Most of the harbour has depths of less than 3 m and there are extensive drying banks in its SW part; a prominent red *torii*, the largest in Japan, stands on a drying sandspit in front of the Itsukushima Shrine (6.35).

Three piers are situated at the N end of Miyashima Kō and there are frequent ferry services from the piers to the mainland opposite.

Anchorage. Small vessels can obtain anchorage in Miyashima Kō, out of the tidal streams, in a depth of about 7 m, mud, 4 or 5 cables off the *torii* with the stone beacon off Hijiri Saki in line with Tsukune Shima (6.44), bearing about 061°.

Hijiri Saki is fringed with a shoal bank close N of which is a stone **beacon.** A **fish haven** lies 8 cables NNE of Hijiri Saki.

A **light** is exhibited on a breakwater at **Jigozen Kō** situated on the mainland 1¾ miles NNW of Hijiri Saki.

Miyashima Seto and Nasami Seto

6.38

Miyashima Seto (34° 17' N, 132° 22' E) lies between the E extremity of Itsuku Shima (6.35) and Ō Nasami Shima ¾ mile E; its N approach is divided into two channels by **Eno Shima,** an islet 39 m high, fringed with a shoal bank. A **light** is exhibited from a white round concrete tower standing on the summit of Eno Shima.

Directions. A vessel using Miyashima Seto should pass W of Eno Shima as there are many oyster beds between Eno Shima and Ō Nasami Shima.

Ō Nasami Shima, on the E side of Miyashima Seto, has two summits the E of which is 90 m high; shoals extend about 1½ cables W and N from the W extremity of the island. A **light** is exhibited from a black round concrete tower on **Nakano Se,** a rock 1 m high, lying off the S side of Ō Nasami Shima.

6.39

Nasami Seto (34° 16' N, 132° 23' E) lies between Nakano Se and Kanne Hana (6.25) and is 3 cables wide; the fairway is deep and free from dangers.

Ando Shima in the NE approach to Nasami Seto, lies 1½ miles ENE of Kanne Hana and is 10 m high; a shoal bank extends ½ cable from its SW side. A **light** is exhibited from a white round concrete tower standing on Ando Shima.

A number of **fish havens** lie close S and SW of Ando Shima.

A **light** is exhibited on the head of a breakwater ½ mile SE of Kanne Hana, and also on a breakwater at **Mitaka Kō** 1¼ miles farther E.

Caution. Oyster beds extend up to ½ mile offshore along the N coast of Nishi Nōmi Shima between Kanne Hana and the entrance to Tsukumo Seto (6.40); vessels using Nasami Seto are recommended to pass N of Ando Shima, at a moderate speed, to avoid disturbing the beds.

Eta Uchi

6.40

Tsukumo Seto (34° 15' N, 132° 26' E), the channel into Eta Uchi, is entered 2¾ miles ESE of Kanne Hana; it is sometimes obstructed by fishing nets, and oyster beds lie on either side, but otherwise it is straight and free from dangers.

Eta Uchi, an almost land-locked bay, lies between the NE side of Nishi Nōmi Shima and the SW side of **Eta Shima** which is the NE part of the island.

Matsuga Hana (34° 13·6' N, 132° 27·7' E) is a salient point about the middle of the S shore of Eta Uchi and there is a rock with a depth of less than 2 m, 1 cable N of it; a narrow reef with a depth of 1·8 m over its extremity, extends about ½ mile N from the shore 4 cables W of Matsuga Hana.

A **fish haven,** consisting of concrete blocks, lies 8 cables NNW of Matsuga Hana.

The buildings and radio masts of the **Japanese Maritime Defence Force College** stand on the E shore of Eta Uchi; a number of mooring buoys are situated off the college and there is a jetty.

Caution. Oyster beds extend up to ½ mile offshore on the W side of Eta Uchi between Tsukumo Seto and Matsuga Hana; vessels should proceed at moderate speed to avoid disturbing the beds.

Charts 3602, 3603

Ōsu Seto and approaches

6.41

Ōsu Seto (34° 17' N, 132° 26' E) is the principal channel leading to Kure Kō (6.57) and is about 4½ cables wide between **Shiinoki Hana,** a cliffy point at the W end of the N side of Eta Shima, and **Gehōno Hana,** the SE

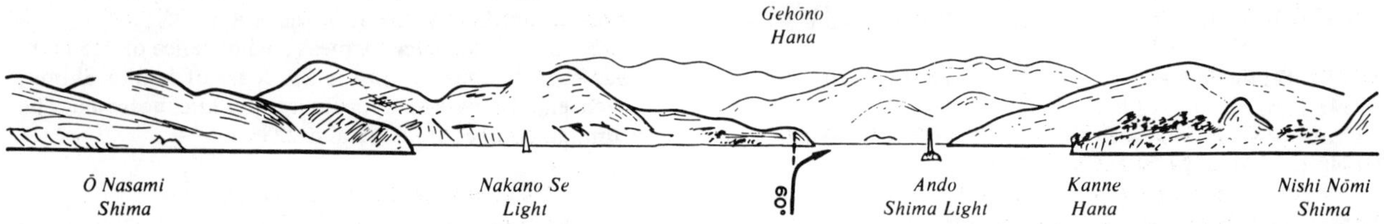

(6.39) Nasami Seto from SW, seen from a position close W of Kanne Hana (34° 16' N, 132° 23' E)

(Original dated prior to 1978)

extremity of Nino Shima. A reef extends about 1½ cables SE of Gehōno Hana.

Charts 3602, 3603, 3469 plan of Hiroshima Kō

Nino Shima, a well wooded and hilly island, lies about midway between the NW end of Eta Shima and Hiroshima Kō to the N. **Akinoko Fuji,** a prominent conical peak 276 m high and surmounted by a white mast exhibiting a red light, is situated in the N part of the island.

Dōgen Ishi, a detached rock with a depth of 2·9 m, lies 3 cables NE of Gehōno Hana; a **light** is exhibited from a white concrete column standing on the rock.

Misen Dashi, with a depth of 9·5 m, lies 6 cables ENE of Gehōno Hana. **Fish havens** are situated 1½ cables N and close SW of Misen Dashi.

Tōge Shima, a wooded islet 127 m high and steep-to except on its SE side, lies in the NE approach to Ōsu Seto, 1¼ miles NE of Gehōno Hana.

Charts 3602, 3603

6.42

The N coast of Eta Shima between Shiinoki Hana and Yakata Ishi 2 miles ENE, forms the S side of the E approach to Ōsu Seto.

A rocky shoal with a depth of 11·1 m, lies 4 cables offshore about midway between Shiinoki Hana and Yakata Ishi; a *light-buoy* is moored close NW of the shoal.

Kirikushi Wan is entered between the rocky shoal and Yakata Ishi 1 mile E; a *light-buoy* is moored on the edge of the shore bank at the head of the bay.

Anchorage. Kirikushi Wan affords anchorage to small craft in depths from 12 m to 14 m.

Yakata Ishi (34° 18' N, 132° 29' E) lies on the extremity of a reef which extends 1½ cables N from the N end of a low and narrow tongue of land which forms the NE extremity of Eta Shima; a **light** is exhibited from a red round stone tower situated on Yakata Ishi and is a good mark when entering Kure Kō.

HIROSHIMA KŌ

Charts 3602, 3469 plan of Hiroshima Kō

6.43

Hiroshima Kō (34° 20' N, 132° 27' E), a commercial and industrial harbour and a specified port (see 1.64), lies in the N corner of Hiroshima Wan. Within the harbour limits of Hiroshima Kō on the W side, lie the timber harbour of **Hatsukaichi Kō** (34° 21·0' N, 132° 20·7' E) and the fishing harbours of **Itsukaichi Gyokō** (34° 21·4' N, 132° 22·0' E) and **Kusatsu Gyokō** (34° 22·4' N, 132° 24·1' E). The harbour limits are shown on the charts.

Hiroshima, the most important city in this part of Japan, lies about 2 miles N of the harbour. Several branches of Ōta Kawa flow through the city, and the keep of the castle, in the middle of the city, is a prominent object. In 1973, the population of Hiroshima was 732 000.

Outer approaches

6.44

Ō Kakuma Shima (34° 19' N, 132° 24' E), 37 m high, lies in the SW approaches to Hiroshima Kō, 1 mile NW of the SW extremity of Nino Shima (6.41). **Ko Kakuma Shima,** 21 m high, lies 2½ cables N of Ō Kakuma Shima and is joined to it by reefs and shoals; a yellow *light-buoy* is moored close NE of the islet.

A **fish haven** lies 3 cables NE of Ko Kakuma Shima.

Tsukune Shima, a prominent rocky islet 20 m high and fringed with reefs, lies 1¾ miles NNW of Ō Kakuma Shima.

6.45

Landmarks. A radio tower (red and white) stands at an elevation of 122 m in Hatsukaichi Kō (34° 21' N, 132° 21' E).

Two television towers (red and white), standing at an elevation of 257 m and 258 m, and an observation platform, are situated on **Jō Yama** (34° 21·8' N, 132° 29·6' E) in the E part of Hiroshima Kō.

Directions. Large vessels approaching Hiroshima Kō from SW should either proceed through Nasami Seto (32° 16' N, 132° 23' E) (6.39), Ōsu Seto (32° 17' N, 132° 27' E) (6.41) and E of Toge Shima, to the quarantine anchorage; or through Miyashima Seto (32° 17' N, 132° 22' E) (6.38), W of Eno Shima, and NW of Ō Kakuma Shima and Ko Kakuma Shima, into No. 1 Fairway (6.47).

Pilotage is not compulsory but is recommended for vessels without local knowledge. Pilots are available at the quarantine anchorage. Requests for pilots should be made 72 hours in advance.

Cautions. Large numbers of small vessels cross the main shipping route between Hashirashima Suidō (34° 02' N, 132° 27' E) and the entrances to Miyashima Seto and Nasami Seto. Many fishing boats are likely to be encountered in Nasami Seto.

Oyster beds, and from October to March, seaweed beds, are situated around the islands in the harbour area and in the vicinity of the river mouths.

Chart 3469 plan of Hiroshima Kō

Outer harbour including Kaida Wan

6.46

Ujina Shima (34° 20·5' N, 132° 27·8' E), 56 m high at its N end, lies 1½ miles NNE of Nino Shima and is connected to the mainland N of it by a causeway. A **light** is exhibited from a red round concrete tower situated on the S end of Ujina Shima.

Kanawa Shima, ¾ mile E of Ujina Shima has two summits the S and higher of which is 171 m high to the tops of the trees; the sides of the island are fringed with shoal banks extending as much as 1 cable offshore in places. A rock 10 m high and surmounted by a **beacon** (diamond topmark), lies ½ cable off the NW extremity of the island, and a pile, 2 m high, is situated close NE of it.

Kaida Wan is situated on the E side of Hiroshima Kō; its entrance is spanned by **Hiroshima Bridge.** There is a vertical clearance of 30 m under the S part, 24 m under the middle part and 14 m under the N part of the bridge. Red and green lights, as indicated on the chart, are shown on the bridge.

An **overhead power cable** with a vertical clearance of 30 m, spans the entrance to Kaida Wan close E of the bridge; the cable is supported on each side by a conspicuous tower which is marked by a red light.

Prohibited areas, marked in places by *buoys* exhibiting flashing orange lights, are established on each side of a fairway leading to the head of Kaida Wan.

6.47

The outer harbour of Hiroshima Kō is divided into **Nos. 1, 2** and **3 Areas,** the limits of which are shown on the chart.

No. 1 Fairway leads to No. 1 Area from W, passing SE of Ujina Shima and N of Kanawa Shima. **No. 2 Fairway,** from Kure Kō, joins No. 1 Fairway SE of Ujina Shima.

Anchorages. The **quarantine anchorage,** shown on the chart, is centred ¼ mile NE of Tōge Shima (34° 18·7' N, 132° 27·9' E).

The following anchor berths have been established:

Berth	Bearing and distance from Ujina Shima Lt		Maximum draught	Maximum length
A	056°	2510 m	6 m	120 m
B	052°	2200 m	7 m	120 m
C	067°	2467 m	8 m	150 m
D	058°	1070 m	10 m	150 m
E	089°	900 m	12 m	150 m
F	116°	1160 m	12 m	150 m
G	127°	1640 m	12 m	150 m
H	133°	2160 m	12 m	150 m
I	158°	900 m		
J	162°	1 500 m		
K	122°	3280 m		
L	132½°	3430 m		
M	270°	3550 m		
N	262°	3820 m		
No. 1	150°	3000 m		
No. 2	160°	3000 m		
No. 3	200°	2000 m		
No. 4	230°	5000 m		
No. 5	240°	5000 m		

Anchorages A–H are discharging berths and anchorages I–N and Nos. 1–5 are waiting berths. Vessels at anchorages A–H should use two anchors.

Inner harbour and wharves
6.48
Ōta Kawa is one of the several rivers which flow into the sea W of Ujina Shima (6.46); a number of basins lying between reclaimed land are situated in this area but can accommodate small vessels only. A **light** is exhibited at the end of a short breakwater projecting from the SW end of **Deshima,** the E entrance point to Ōta Kawa; **Mitsubishi Shipyard** lies on the W side of the entrance.

An inner harbour lies close NW of Ujina Shima and is entered between two breakwaters; a **light** is exhibited at the head of each breakwater.

Foreign Trade Wharf fronts the SE side of the suburb of **Ujina** ¼ mile NE of Ujina Shima. The factories of **Tōyo Industries** front the shore between Foreign Trade Wharf and the N end of Hiroshima Bridge.

The mouth of **Enkō Kawa** is situated on the N side of Kaida Wan close E of Hiroshima Bridge. **Tōyō Bridge** with a vertical clearance of 22 to 33 m, and an **overhead cable** with a vertical clearance of about 39 m, cross the river close within its entrance.

Berths and facilities.
6.49
Berths. The principal berths within the harbour limits of Hiroshima Kō are as follows:

Berth & Position	Length m	Depth m	Capacity tons
Hatsukaichi 10 m Quay (34° 20·2' N, 132° 20·9' E)	370	10	15 000
Deshima W Quay (34° 21·1' N, 132° 26·8' E)	540	4–4·5	1 300
Deshima E Quay (34° 20·8' N, 132° 27·2' E)	160	6–7	5 000
Foreign Trade Wharf (34° 21·1' N, 132° 28·6' E) Nos. 1–4 Quays	700	9–9·5	10 000
Ube Kōsan Pier (34° 21·6' N, 132° 31·4' E)	20	8	500
Nishimoto Quay (34° 19·6' N, 132° 30·4' E)	77	6 (reported)	5 000

There are a large number of mooring buoys in the harbour.

6.50
Facilities. Offices of the Maritime Safety Agency, Customs, Quarantine and Immigration are located in the joint Harbour Office situated close W of the W end of Foreign Trade Wharf.

Numerous tugs and lighters are available.

Waste oil disposal facilities are available.

There are several hospitals in the city.

De-ratting; see 1.70.

There is a dry dock with a capacity of 10 000 tons at the Mitsubishi Shipyard and two dry docks, one of which has a capacity of 13 000 tons, at **Kanawa Dock** on the NE side of Kanawa Shima (6.46).

Supplies. Fresh water is available on all the public quays and there is a water boat.

Fuel oil is available by barge from Iwakuni; three days notice is required.

Communications. There is a **port radio station** at Hiroshima.

There are a large number of regular shipping services to ports in Seto Naikai and to the neighbouring islands.

There are regular domestic air services to Ōsaka and Tōkyō from **Hiroshima Airport.**

Climate. Weather signals are shown at Hiroshima Kō (see 1.42). See also table at 1.100.

APPROACHES TO KURE KŌ

Charts 3602, 3603, 3472
North approach to Kure Kō
6.51
The N approach to Kure Kō is entered between Yakata Ishi (34° 18' N, 132° 29' E) (6.42) and **Kannon (Kanon) Saki,** 1¼ miles NE. The W side of the approach is formed by the E coast of Eta Shima (6.40), and for about 3 miles S of Yakata Ishi it is cliffy.

Caution. Many fishing vessels are likely to be encountered in the vicinity of Yakata Ishi.

Landmark. Inoshishi Yama, 113 m high with a rounded summit, stands close inland of **Shibitono Hana** situated 3¼ miles SSE of Kannon Saki. It is a good mark for entering Kure Kō.

Chart 3472
6.52
Koyō Kō (34° 15' N, 132° 30' E) lies on the opposite shore to Shibitono Hana; **Ikada Se,** with a depth of less than 2 m, lies close N of the S entrance point to the harbour and is marked 1 cable NNE by a *light-buoy.*

Yoshiura Wan, within the harbour limits of Kure Kō, is entered between Shibitono Hana and **Mitsuishi Hana** ¼ mile SSE.

A black *buoy* is moored 2 cables SE of Shibitono Hana on the edge of the shore bank.

Tarōbō, a detached rock with a depth of 1·8 m, lies 3 cables W of Mitsuishi Hana and is marked close N by a *buoy.*

Oil Fuel Pier projects from the NW side of Yoshiura Wan 3 cables E of Shibitono Hana. There are mooring buoys off the head of the pier and also in the NE part of the bay.

Two floating docks are situated off the S shore of the bay; the largest has a capacity of 2000 tons.

Ō Urume Shima and **Ko Urume Shima** are prominent islets lying on a shoal bank which extends ½ mile SW from Mitsuishi Hana. An **overhead cable** runs from Mitsuishi Hana to both islets and the pylons supporting them are prominent.

A **signal station,** from which berthing and movement signals as well as weather signals (see 1.42) are shown, stands on Ko Urume Shima; a **light** is exhibited from the roof of the signal station which is painted white.

Charts 3602, 3603

South approach to Kure Kō

6.53

Hayase Seto (34° 09' N, 132° 30' E), between Kurahashi Shima and Higashi Nōmi Shima, is the S approach to Kure Kō and at its narrowest part the fairway is about ½ cable wide. The **tidal streams** in the narrows attain a spring rate of 4 knots and the passage should not be attempted without local knowledge. The channel is much used by small vessels some of which are up to 1000 tons.

Kajikakeno Hana, the SE extremity of Higashi Nōmi Shima, lies on the W side of the S entrance to Hayase Seto. **Oenoura Dashi,** with a depth of 4·6 m, lies 1 cable S of Kajikakeno Hana and is marked close SE by a *light-buoy*; **Shimono Su,** with a depth of 5·8 m lies 1½ cables E of the point.

Torigakubino Ishi Light is exhibited from a red round concrete tower situated at the head of a short breakwater extending NW from the SE entrance point to Hayase Seto.

There is a **fish haven** situated 2 cables S of Torigakubino Ishi Light.

Ryōshida (Jōshida) Kō (34° 08' N, 132° 30' E), a bay used by small vessels as a port of shelter in winds other than from SW to W, lies on the E side of the S entrance to Hayase Seto opposite Kajikakeno Hana. There is a basin protected by breakwaters at the inner end of the bay.

Hayase Bridge with a vertical clearance of about 36 m, and an **overhead cable** with a vertical clearance of 37 m, cross the narrows about ½ mile N of Torigakubino Ishi Light.

6.54

Hiki Shima (34° 10·3' N, 132° 29·1' E), on the W side of the N end of Hayase Seto, is a narrow steep-sided islet of a yellowish brown colour, 22 m high. **Ōgaki Kō Hiki Shima Light** is exhibited from a white round concrete tower situated at the head of a short breakwater extending NNW from the N extremity of Hiki Shima; another breakwater extends S from the S extremity of the islet.

Ushizono, a rock which dries 1·8 m, lies on a detached shoal 4 cables SSE of Hiki Shima; on it stands a **beacon** (red and black, round, concrete). A rock with a depth of 2·8 m lies ½ cable E of Ushizono.

Matsuga Hana, a salient point thickly covered with pine trees, is situated 3 cables NW of Hiki Shima; a **beacon** (black, round concrete) stands ½ cable NE of the point.

Kakinoura Gyokō lies between Matsuga Hana and **Hide Saki,** faced with a low brown cliff, 8 cables N; a reef extends 1 cable S from Hide Saki.

An **oil terminal** (34° 11·6' N, 132° 29·0' E), with numerous tanks, lies within ½ mile N of Hide Saki. A dolphin berth, with a depth of about 15 m alongside, is situated close off the coast 1½ cables NNE of Hide Saki, and a pier with a depth of 9 m alongside, lies 1½ cables farther NNE.

A wharf with a depth of about 15 m alongside, lies 9 cables NE of Hide Saki.

Vessels using these berths are required to call at Kure Kō for quarantine clearance. Vessels usually berth bows S with the assistance of tugs which come from Kure Kō. The port radio station at Hiroshima covers the berths.

Chart 3472

6.55

Mitsugo Shima (34° 11·5' N, 132° 30·9' E), consisting of two islets, lies on the E side of the N entrance to Hayase Seto (6.53). A narrow channel with a least depth of 9 m, lies between the S and largest islet of Mitsugo Shima, and the N coast of Kurahashi Shima.

An L-shaped jetty with a dolphin off each end and with a depth of 17 m alongside, is situated on the SW side of Mitsugo Shima. In 1970, a jetty was under construction on the NW side of the islet.

Ōdono Shō, with a depth of 0·9 m and marked close E by a *light-buoy*, lies 1 cable N of **Hitsukino Hana** the N extremity of Kurahashi Shima.

Charts 3472, 3603, 3602

Sauth east approach to Kure Kō

6.56

Ondo Seto (34° 12' N, 132° 32' E), a very narrow channel, separates the N end of Kurahashi Shima from the mainland; it is the shortest route leading into Kure Kō and thence Hiroshima Wan from the E and is the route normally used by small vessels. There is a blind bend in the channel, the tidal streams attain a spring rate of 4 knots and the volume of traffic both crossing and passing through it is large; it should only be used with local knowledge.

Ondo Bridge with a vertical clearance of 23 m and painted red, crosses Ondo Seto at its narrowest part. The width of the channel under the bridge is about 60 m; a green light on the bridge marks the centre of the channel and a red light marks either side.

An **overhead cable** with a vertical clearance of 31 m, crosses the channel 1½ cables N of the bridge.

Directions. The N and S approach to the narrows are each marked by a *light-buoy*; these buoys indicate the centre of the channel entrances and vessels should leave them on their port side.

Uchino Mo, with a least depth of 4·5 m, lies in the middle of the fairway in the E approach to Ondo Seto 3½ cables SE of the bridge. A **fish haven,** charted as an obstruction, lies 2 cables SW of Uchino Mo.

Ondo Light is exhibited from a white round concrete tower standing on **Sangenyano Hana,** the W entrance point of the N entrance to Ondo Seto.

KURE KŌ

Chart 3472

6.57

Kure Ku (34° 14' N, 132° 33' E), the main part of **Kure Kō** which is a specified port (see 1.64), is entered SE of Ō Urume Shima (6.52); it is a fine natural harbour enclosed on three sides by mountains. It is a former naval port and is now used as a base for the Japanese Self Defence Force; it is also an industrial port with large shipbuilding yards and steel works.

The harbour limits of Kure Ku are shown on the chart.

The city of **Kure** which lies at the head of the bay, had a population of 240 000 in 1973.

Pilotage is not compulsory. Harbour pilots are available in the quarantine anchorage.

Anchorages. The **quarantine anchorage,** indicated on the chart, lies outside the harbour limit across the entrance to the harbour.

The following anchor berths for discharging or awaiting an alongside berth, are established:

Anchor Berth	Bearing and distance from Ko Urume Shima Light	
Y1	348°	1170 m
Y2	019°	1330 m
C	176°	840 m
D	160°	1540 m

There are numerous lettered mooring buoys in the harbour; their positions are shown on the chart.

Nisshin Steel Works and **Ishikawajima-Harima Shipyard** where there are dry docks with facilities for building vessels up to 800 000 dwt, lie on the SE side of Kure Ku.

Kawaharaishi W Wharf lies ¼ mile WNW of the mouth of **Nikō Kawa** situated in the NE part of the harbour; **Muromachi Quays** lie in a basin on the E side of the mouth of the river.

Berths and facilities
6.58

Berths. The principal berths in Kure Ku are as follows:

Berth & Position	Length m	Depth m	Capacity tons
Kawaharaishi W Wharf (34° 14·4' N, 132° 32·4' E)	440	5–7·5	Up to 5 000

Berth & Position	Length m	Depth m	Capacity tons
Muromachi Quays (34° 14·3' N, 132° 33·3' E)	—	4·5–6·5	Up to 2 000
Central Ferry Quay (34° 14·3' N, 132° 33·5' E)	—	5	Up to 1 000
Shōwa (Shōa) Wharf (34° 13·6' N, 132° 33·2' E)			
No. 1 Quay	150	9	3 000
No. 2 Quay	170	9	10 000
Nisshin Steel Raw Materials Wharf (34° 13·0' N, 132° 32·1' E)	260	18	150 000

6.59

Facilities. The offices of the Maritime Safety Agency, Customs, Quarantine and Immigration are located in the joint Harbour Office situated on the E side of the mouth of Nikō Kawa.

Numerous tugs and lighters are available in Kure Ku.

Major repairs can be undertaken. No. 4 Dry Dock in Ishikawajima-Harima Shipyard has a capacity of 91 000 tons.

There are two hospitals in Kure.

De-ratting; see 1.70.

Supplies. Fresh water is available at the principal berths. Fuel oil is available.

Communications. Hiroshima port radio station covers Kure Ko.

There are large numbers of regular shipping services to other ports in Seto Naikai and to the neighbouring islands.

Weather signals (see 1.42) are shown at Ko Urume Shima signal station and from a radio tower standing near the Harbour Office.

AKI NADA—EAST PART

ISLANDS IN THE EAST PART OF AKI NADA
Charts 3602, 3603
6.60

Ō Tateba Shima (34° 02' N, 132° 36' E), 111 m high and covered with brambles, lies 1¾ miles N of the N entrance to Kudako Suidō (5.60); it should not be approached within 1 cable for it is fringed with shoals. **Ko Tateba Shima,** 61 m high, lies 3 cables NE of Ō Tateba Shima, and **Suzuki Iwa,** with a depth of 9·5 m, lies 2 cables farther E.

Chart 3603

Ai Shima (34° 04' N, 132° 43' E), 6 miles ENE of Ō Tateba Shima, is 55 m high; a **light** is exhibited from a white round concrete tower situated on its SE end.

Small vessels can obtain temporary **anchorage** in a shallow bay on the S side of Ai Shima.

Ō Ishi, a detached rock with a depth of 16 m, lies 4 cables SE of Ai Shima.

Koai Shima, 62 m high and thickly wooded, lies 1¼ miles SE of Ai Shima.

6.61

Shira Ishi (34° 06' N, 132° 45' E), two prominent rocks, lie 2½ miles NE of Ai Shima; the W rock is high and white, the E one is black.

Itsuki Shima (34° 07' N, 132° 48' E), an island with two summits, lies 2 miles NE of Shira Ishi; it is a good

mark and in its SW part is a hill 88 m high. A rock which dries 1·8 m, lies about 1 cable off the S side.

Yazaemon Shō, with a depth of 6·3 m, lies ¼ mile S of Itsuki Shima.

AKI NADA—SOUTH EAST SIDE

Chart 3603
Shiraishi Hana to Senbagadake Hana
6.62

Horie Wan, on the S side of Aki Nada, is entered between Shiraishi Hana (33° 54' N, 132° 43' E) (5.34) and a point 2½ miles ENE. Inunokashira Shima and Tsugai Su, which are situated on the E side of the N entrance to Takahama Seto and lie across the entrance to Horie Wan, are described at 5.34.

Landmark. The two chimneys of the **Shikoku Matsuyama Power Station** (33° 53·9' N, 132° 43·9' E) which lie on the W side of **Kuma Kawa** which flows into the sea 11 cables E of Shiraishi Hana, are conspicious.

Horie Kō (33° 54' N, 132° 45' E), protected by breakwaters, lies 2 miles E of Shiraishi Hana; a **light** is exhibited from the head of the E breakwater and on the SW head of the detached breakwater. The depths in the main part of the harbour are from 4 m to 7 m; the harbour is used by the train ferry to Nigata Ku (6.72) and the car ferry to Hiro Ku (6.69).

Anchorages. Horie Wan affords anchorage, except with winds between W and N, in a depth of 13 m, mud, S of a 8·5 m shoal, with Tsumuri Saki (33° 55' N, 132° 42' E) bearing 293° distant a little over 2 miles.

Temporary anchorage can be obtained in depths from 11 m to 16 m, S of **Ō Su,** a shoal with a least depth of 4·1 m, with Tsumuri Saki bearing about 262° distant 2¼ miles.

6.63

Ka Shima (33° 58' N, 132° 46' E), a round-topped thickly wooded islet 113 m high, lies close offshore 4 miles N of Horie Kō; **Koka Shima,** 28 m high, and **Chigiri Iwa,** 26 m high, lie close together on a shoal ½ mile W of Ka Shima. **Gyokurikando,** a group of rocks the E'most of which is 9 m high, lie 1½ cables SW of Koka Shima.

A **light** is exhibited on the head of a breakwater at the NE point of Ka Shima and an **overhead cable** with a vertical clearance of about 30 m, spans the channel between the islet and the coast E.

Hōjō Kō, protected by two breakwaters, lies on the coast 2 cables E of Ka Shima; a **light** is exhibited on the head of the N breakwater. There is a pontoon jetty with depths from 2·4 m to 3 m alongside, at the inner end of the harbour.

Hazumano Hana (34° 00' N, 132° 46' E), 1½ miles N of Ka Shima, is a prominent salient point which rises to a hillock on which there is a clump of pine trees. A **light** is exhibited from a white round concrete tower standing on Hazumano Hana.

Landmarks. Koshiore Yama, 213 m high, and **Eiryō Yama,** 301 m high, lie, respectively, 1¼ miles and 1¾ miles ESE of Hazumano Hana and are prominent.

Meishi Yama, 296 m high, and **Takahagi Yama,** 355 m high, lie, respectively, 1¼ miles NE and 1¾ miles ENE of Eiryō Yama; they are both prominent and conical with a thick growth of pine trees on their summits.

Takanawa Yama, the highest peak in the vicinity, attains an elevation of 985 m, 5¼ miles SE of Hazumano Hana.

Shiode Iso, 1 m high and surrounded by drying rocks, lies on the extremity of a shallow spit which extends ½ mile N from the shore 1½ miles NE of Hazumano Hana. A **light** is exhibited from a red concrete column standing on the rock.

Landmark. Senbagadake Hana, a dark precipitous rocky point, lies 1 mile E of Shiode Iso; the point is in marked contrast with the other greyish white headlands in the vicinity.

Charts 3603, 3604

Kikuma Kō and Kikuma Oil Terminal

6.64

Kikuma Kō (34° 02' N, 132° 50' E), protected by a breakwater lying parallel to the coast, is entered 2 miles NE of Senbagadake Hana; a **light** is exhibited at the head of the breakwater. Quays with depths from 3·5 m to 4 m alongside, are situated on the E side of the harbour.

Landmarks. Three silver-coloured television towers marked by red lights, stand on top of a hill, 450 m high, 3 miles ESE of the harbour entrance.

Kikuma Kawa flows into the sea close N of Kikuma Kō and a training wall on the S side of the river mouth forms the N boundary of the harbour.

6.65

Kikuma Oil Terminal (34° 03' N, 132° 51' E), with numerous prominent tanks and chimneys, stands on reclaimed land 1½ miles NE of Kikuma Kō. The lights of the terminal can be seen at a distance.

Heso Shima, a rocky islet which is 33 m high and prominent, lies 2 cables W of the S end of the terminal; a sandspit which dries extends ½ cable SE from the islet.

Aji Iwa, a rocky reef with a least depth of 2 m, lies 5 cables offshore, 8 cables N of Heso Shima; it is marked by a *light-buoy* at both its NE and W ends.

Pilotage is not compulsory. Pilots are available but will not berth or unberth vessels after sunset.

The berths cannot be used in heavy weather. Vessels usually berth on the flood stream which is NE-going, and lie heading SW.

Tugs are obtainable from Kure Kō or Matsuyama Kō.

6.66

Berths. No. 1 Pier, with depths from 6 m to 11·5 m alongside, projects from the shore from a position 2½ cables E of Heso Shima. **No. 2 Pier,** with depths from 5 m to 6·5 m alongside, lies about 1 cable N of No. 1 Pier.

Taiyō Sekiyū Dolphin Berth (34° 03·0' N, 132° 51·4' E), with depths from 16·5 m to 18 m alongside and connected to the shore by a jetty, lies 2 cables N of Heso Shima; **lights** are exhibited in the middle of the berth and at each end. The berth is suitable for tankers up to 88 500 dwt..

Taiyō Sekiyū Sea-berth, consisting of three *buoys* and five mooring buoys and suitable for tankers up to 130 000 dwt, lies in depths from 20 m to 30 m, 7 cables NE of Taiyō Sekiyū Dolphin Berth. A **submarine pipeline** is laid from the berth SSW to the shore.

There are numerous mooring buoys in the vicinity of No. 1 Pier and No. 2 Pier.

Facilities. Waste oil disposal facilities are available.

Supplies. Fresh water and provisions can be supplied.

Ke Shima to Kajitori Hana

6.67

Ke Shima (34° 04' N, 132° 53' E), a rounded islet 41 m high, lies 1½ miles NE of Kikuma Oil Terminal; it is fringed with reefs and is joined to the coast by rocks and shoals.

Obe Wan is entered between Ke Shima and **Misakino Hana** 2½ miles NNE. An extensive shoal with depths

(6.67) Ōge Seto and Kurushima Kaikyō from SW, seen from a position about 6 miles SW of Kajitori Hana (34° 07' N, 132° 54' E)

(Original dated prior to 1978)

from 10·4 m to 11 m, occupies the centre of the bay with deeper water closer inshore.

Yuzure Shima, consisting of several conical rocks the highest of which is 27 m high, lies in the S part of Obe Wan. **Katabira Iso,** an isolated rock 2 m high, lies ½ mile W of Yuzure Shima. Two mooring buoys lie close to the S shore of Obe Wan, 8 cables SSW of Yuzure Shima.

Obe Gyokō lies in the N part of the E shore of Obe Wan.

Anchorage. Obe Wan is open W but affords good anchorage in depths from 11 m to 15 m, mud, with Ke Shima bearing 225° and Misakino Hana bearing 315°.

Kajitori Hana (34° 07' N, 132° 54' E), ½ mile NNW of Misakino Hana, is the W extremity of a narrow hilly projection which forms the N side of Obe Wan; a **light** is exhibited from a white round concrete tower on the point.

Ōgan Shō, a detached rock with a depth of 9·4 m, lies 3½ cables NW of Kajitori Hana; heavy overfalls occur in its vicinity.

EAST SIDE OF KURAHASHI SHIMA

Charts 3602, 3603
6.68

Karoto Shima (34° 04' N, 132° 33' E) at the SE extremity of Kurahashi Shima, is described at 6.20.

Kamega Kubi (34° 07' N, 132° 36' E), the E extremity of Kurahashi Shima, lies at the end of a small but prominent peninsula.

Taino Uchi is entered 2 miles NW of Kamega Kubi and has in general depths of less than 10 m. A rock with a depth of 3·6 m lies nearly 3 cables N of the SE entrance point of the bay.

Nasake Shima (34° 10' N, 132° 35' E), 126 m high with some remarkable trees on its E side, lies within 1¼ miles NE of the NW entrance point of Taino Uchi; there are two islets between it and the point.

Okuno Uchi, with depths in general less than 10 m, is entered between the NW entrance point of Taino Uchi and **Ōura Saki** (34° 10' N, 132° 34' E), 1¼ miles NNE.

Ajiwa Shima, consisting of two islets, lies on the coastal bank within ¼ mile N of Ōura Saki; the edge of the bank close E of the rocks is marked by a red *buoy* (cone topmark). A detached rock with a depth of 0·6 m, lies 3 cables E of Ajiwa Shima and is marked on its N side by a *light-buoy.* There are oyster beds S of this rock and in Okuno Uchi.

Ondo Seto and its E approach are described at 6.56.

HIRO WAN

Charts 3602, 3603
6.69

Hiro Wan (34° 13' N, 132° 36' E), which is within the harbour limits of Kure Kō (6.57), lies on the N side of the E approach to Ondo Seto. **Hiro Ku,** on the N side of Hiro Wan, is the commercial port of the city of Kure.

Landmark. Noro Yama, 4 miles NNE of **Shimoneko Saki** the E entrance point of Hiro Wan, is 837 m high; it has a knob on its summit and is prominent.

A **quarantine anchorage** lies on the harbour limit 1¼ miles W of Shimoneko Saki.

A channel with a depth of 8 m and marked by two pairs of *light-buoys,* leads to the **Tōyō Pulp Wharf** on the E side of the mouth of **Hiro Higashi Ō Kawa** which flows into the NE corner of the bay. **Leading lights,** exhibited from white metal columns (triangular topmark), stand on the wharf and in line bearing 029°, lead through the channel; No. 1 and *No. 2 Light-buoys,* the outermost pair of light-buoys, are moored 7 cables SSW of the front leading light.

Berths. A **dolphin berth,** with depths from 8·5 m to 10 m alongside and with a mooring buoy at each end, lies close S of the front leading light and can accommodate a vessel up to 30 000 tons.

A quay with a depth of 4 m alongside, lies 1 cable NNE of the rear leading light, but in the channel W of the leading lights the depth is only 2·4 m.

An **overhead cable** with a vertical clearance of about 26 m, spans the channel 2 cables N of the rear leading light.

AKI NADA—NORTH EAST SIDE OFFLYING ISLANDS AND STRAITS

Chart 3603
Straits north west and east of Shimo Kamagari Shima
6.70

Shimo Kamagari Shima (34° 11' N, 132° 40' E) is situated 3 miles ESE of the entrance to Hiro Wan (6.69); a *light-buoy* is moored close off the SW extremity of the island.

Shimo Kuro Shima, 101 m high, and **Kami Kuro Shima,** 82 m high, lie within 1¼ miles of the S side of Shimo Kamagari Shima. **Hikube Shima,** a much smaller islet 14 m high, lies 4 cables NE of Kami Kuro Shima on the W side of the S approach to Sannose Seto (6.73). The depths in the vicinity of these islets are uneven and they should be avoided.

6.71

Neko Seto, a channel about ½ mile wide with a depth of about 50 m, separates Shimo Kamagari Shima from the mainland NW.

A **light** is exhibited from a black round concrete tower standing on **Kasane Iwa,** (34° 12' N, 132° 40' E), a point on the N side of Neko Seto. An **overhead power cable** with a vertical clearance of 38 m, spans the strait.

Meneko Shima, 20 m high and flat-topped, lies on the N side of the narrowest part of the strait close SW of **Kenreiga Hana** (34° 12·5' N, 132° 41·3' E). A **light** is exhibited from a white round concrete tower standing on the SW end of Meneko Shima; a 5·1 m patch lies close S of Kenreiga Hana.

Kashiwa Shima, 133 m high and covered with dense dark woods, lies on the N side of the E entrance to Neko Seto; the island shows up well against the background of the grassy hills in the vicinity.

Tidal streams. At the W entrance to Neko Seto the stream is E-going from 1½ hours after LW to 1½ hours after HW, and W-going from 1½ hours after HW to 1½ hours after LW. The tide turns about 30 minutes earlier in the E entrance. The spring rate in the narrows is about 5 knots.

6.72

Nigata Ku (34° 13' N, 132° 40' E) which is within the harbour limits of Kure Kō (6.57), lies in a bay on the N side of Neko Seto entered between Kasane Iwa (6.71) and Kenreiga Hana. At the head of the bay there are several white-painted hotels.

Anchorage. Nigata Ku affords good anchorage in depths over 13 m except in strong S winds.

There is a quay, with a reported depth of 5 m alongside, in Nigata Ku which is used by the train ferry to Horie Kō (6.62) in Shikoku.

From October to April, seaweed beds are situated on both the E and W sides of Nigata Ku.

6.73

Sannose Seto (34° 11' N, 132° 41' E), a channel 1 cable wide at its narrowest part, lies between Shimo Kamagari Shima (6.70) and Kami Kamagari Shima, E of it. The **tidal streams** in Sannose Seto have a spring rate of 6 knots and the passage of the strait should not be attempted without local knowledge.

In the N entrance to Sannose Seto, a spit with a depth of 8·7 m extends 1½ cables NE from the NE extremity of Shimo Kamagari Shima and a 6·6 m patch lies about 2 cables SE of the point. **Ko Shima,** 17 m high, with numerous above-water rocks and shoals within 1½ cables N and S of it, lies on the E side of the S entrance to the strait.

Kamagari Bridge with a vertical clearance of about 23 m, spans the strait near its S end. An **overhead cable** with a vertical clearance of about 33 m, spans the strait 2½ cables N of the bridge.

Several **fish havens,** consisting of sunken hulks or concrete blocks, lie in both the N and S entrances to Sannose Seto.

Kami Kamagari Shima and Toyo Shima

6.74

Kami Kamagari Shima (34° 11' N, 132° 44' E), on the E side of Sannose Seto, is covered in places with orange groves; **Shichikokumi Yama,** its summit, attains an elevation of 455 m near the centre of the island.

Komatsu Shima, 31 m high, and **Ōmatsu Shima,** 25 m high, lie close together on a rocky shoal off the middle of the N side of Kami Kamagari Shima.

Ni Shima, 4 m high, lies close off the NE extremity of Kami Kamagari Shima; a **light** is exhibited from a white square concrete tower standing on the rock. **Aka Ishi,** a detached rock with a depth of 0·9 m, lies 4 cables NW of Ni Shima; **Sasa Shima,** 22 m high, and a number of rocks and shoals, lie within 4 cables SE.

Anchorage. Temporary anchorage can be obtained during NE winds in depths from 10 m to 20 m, mud, off the S side of Kami Kamagari Shima.

6.75

Toyo Shima (34° 10' N, 132° 47' E), with two summits and covered with orange trees, is situated E of Kami Kamagari Shima and is seperated from it by a channel about 3 cables wide. Owing to the dangers in its S entrance and the strength of the tidal streams, this channel should not be attempted without local knowledge.

Okubi Shima, which lies across the S entrance to the channel between Kami Kamagari Shima and Toyo Shima, has a remarkable sharp wooded summit, 98 m high, at its NE end.

Daishi Shima, 31 m high and covered with pine trees, and **Futamado Shima,** consisting of two islets about 14 m high, lie on a reef in the channel between the NW end of Okubi Shima and Kami Kamagari Shima. **Kamo Se,** 15 m high, lies among other rocks close off the SW extremity of Okubi Shima; a **light** is exhibited from a white square concrete tower standing on Kamo Se.

Toyoshima Kō (34° 10' N, 132° 48' E), protected by a breakwater, lies on the E extremity of Toyo Shima; a **light** is exhibited on the head of the breakwater.

Ōsaki Shimo Shima and Okamura Shima

6.76

Ōsaki Shimo Shima (34° 10' N, 132° 50' E), E of Toyo Shima, is separated from it by a channel with a navigable width of about 1 cable and with a depth of over 20 m.

The narrowest part of the channel is spanned by an **overhead cable** with a vertical clearance of 48 m.

Mikado Shima, 108 m high and wooded, lies in the N approach to the channel; an **overhead cable** with a vertical clearance of about 23 m, spans the channel between the island and Ōsaki Shimo Shima to the S.

Suzume Shima, 5 m high, and **Okino Ishi,** with a depth of 1·8 m, lie on the E side of the S entrance to the channel between Toyo Shima and Ōsaki Shimo Shima.

Ippōji Yama, the flat summit of Ōsaki Shimo Shima, attains an elevation of 448 m 1 mile W of the E end of the island and from it there is a gradual slope to some cliffs at the W end of the island. At the E end of the island there is a bare hill with a double summit, the E slope of which descends to the town of **Mitarai.** There are orange groves all round the coasts of the island.

Charts 3603, 3604

6.77

Mitarai Seto (34° 11' N, 132° 52' E), leading N into Akashi Seto (6.79), lies between the NE side of Ōsaki Shimo Shima and the SW side of **Okamura Shima. Ko Shima,** 77 m high, and **O Shima,** 98 m high and lying close NNW of Ko Shima, divide the N part of the strait into two channels, and the channel W of O Shima is further divided by **Hera Shima,** 77 m high; all three of the islets are fringed with rocky shoals. A **light** is exhibited from a white column standing on the N end of O Shima.

Mitarai Seto should not be attempted without local knowledge. The channel passing E of Ko Shima and O Shima, carries a depth of over 10 m through it and is the one used by the ferries.

6.78

The main part of **Mitarai Kō,** the harbour limits of which enclose Mitarai Seto and the N coast of Ōsaki Shimo Shima, lies on the W side of the S part of Mitarai Seto; it is much used by small vessels taking shelter or awaiting the turn of the tidal stream.

A **light** is exhibited on the head of **Mitarai Breakwater** on the W side of the S entrance to Mitarai Seto; another **light** is exhibited on the head of **Ocho Breakwater,** ¼ mile NW.

Okino Su, with a depth of 3·3 m, lies 1¼ cables E of the head of Mitarai Breakwater.

Overhead cables span the channel on either side of Ko Shima (6.77); there is a vertical clearance of 39 m on the W side of the islet and 42 m on the E side.

Anchorage. Temporary anchorage is afforded in depths from 20 m to 30 m, sand, about 3 cables W of **Kannon Saki,** the S extremity of Okamura Shima.

Kubi Ura, within the harbour limits of Mitarai Kō, lies in the middle of the NW side of Ōsaki Shimo Shima; a breakwater, from the W end of which is exhibited a **light,** extends W from the E side of the bay.

Okamura Kō, at the head of a bay on the SE side of Okamura Shima, is protected by breakwaters but is only suitable for small craft.

Ōsaki Kami Shima and Akashi Seto

6.79

Ōsaki Kami Shima is a large island which forms the W side of the W entrance to Mihara Seto (7.21); **Kanno Mine** (34° 13' N, 132° 55' E), its summit, attains an elevation of 452 m in its SE part and is surmounted by some remarkable trees.

Akashi Seto is bordered on the S side by the N end of Mitarai Seto and the N coast of Okamura Shima, and on the N side by Ōsaki Kami Shima; it is about 4 cables wide at its narrowest and is deep in its centre.

Tidal streams. In Akashi Seto the tidal streams are E-going from ½ hour after LW to ½ hour after HW, and W-going from ½ hour after HW to ½ hour after LW; the spring rate is about 2 knots.

A **light** is exhibited on the head of a breakwater on the N side of Akashi Seto near its narrowest part. **Kurosu Shō,** a rock which dries 1·8 m, lies 3 cables W of the breakwater light and is surmounted by a black concrete **beacon.**

Numerous **fish havens** lie along the N side of Akashi Seto.

Ko Ōge Shima, on the S side of Akashi Seto, lies close E of Okamura Shima (6.77) and is separated from it by a narrow channel spanned by an **overhead cable** with a vertical clearance of 27 m. Ko Ōge Shima consists of quartz which has been much quarried especially on the S side of its summit where a large and prominent white cliff has been formed.

Ōge Seto and the E side of Ōsaki Kami Shima are described at 7.22 and 7.23.

YANAGINO SETO AND APPROACHES

Chart 3603

South west approach to Yanagino Seto

6.80

Yoko Shima (34° 14' N, 132° 46' E), 34 m high and well-wooded, lies on the NW side of the SW approach to Yanagino Seto (6.82); small vessels frequently shelter off its NE side but clear of a rock, 1 m high, lying 3 cables NE of the island.

Kuru Shima, 66 m high, lies 1¾ miles SE of Yoko Shima; from E or W it appears to have two peaks. A rock with a depth of 1·8 m lies 1 cable E of the islet.

Shimoikariiso, a detached rock 1 m high, lies 1¼ miles NE of Yoko Shima; a **light** is exhibited from a black round concrete tower surmounting the rock.

Uma Shima, 66 m high, lies between Shimoikariiso and the mainland WNW.

Uchinoumi Wan (34° 16' N, 132° 46' E) is entered between Uma Shima and **Ōshiba Shima,** a considerably larger islet, 1 mile NE; several islets and shoals encumber the entrance of the bay, the greater part of which is shoal.

Anchorage is afforded in Uchinoumi Wan in depths from 9 m to 15 m, mud, about 5 cables W of the W extremity of Ōshiba Shima, but owing to the shoals and numerous oyster beds and fish havens, local knowledge is necessary.

6.81

Mitsu Wan (34° 17' N, 132° 50' E) is entered between Ōshiba Shima and **Aka Saki,** a steep headland of a remarkable red colour, 2 miles NE; the SW part of the bay and the waters within 4 cables of the E shore, are encumbered with islets and shoals.

Ai Shima, flat-topped, 30 m high and covered with peach trees, and **Ryūō Shima,** 23 m high, lie on a bank with depths of less than 5 m extending 1¼ miles NE from the NE side of Ōshiba Shima.

Karafune Shima, 23 m high and covered with pine trees, lies 3 cables SSE of Aka Saki.

Akitsu Kō (34° 19' N, 132° 49' E), a small harbour protected by a breakwater, lies at the inner end of Mitsu Wan; a **light** is exhibited on the head of the breakwater.

Landmark. The three chimneys, each with an elevation of about 30 m, of the **Sankyō Chemical Works** standing at the head of Mitsu Wan, are good marks for identifying Akitsu Kō.

Mitsu Wan is encumbered with fishing stakes and oyster beds except in the fairway leading to Akitsu Kō; this fairway is situated somewhat towards the E side of the bay.

Facilities and supplies. There is a shipyard at Akitsu Kō which can effect repairs to vessels up to 800 tons. It is reported that fresh water and fuel oil are available.

Tsukuga Shima (34° 15' N, 132° 50' E), the W'most islet off the NW side of Ōsaki Kami Shima is 46 m high and lies on the SE side of the approach to Yanagino Seto. A reef which dries extends 4 cables N from the islet, and a **light** is exhibited from a red round concrete tower standing on the NW extremity of the reef.

Charts 3603, 3604

Yanagino Seto

6.82

Yanagino Seto (34° 17' N, 132° 53' E) is the channel between the various islands and islets on the NW side of Ōsaki Kami Shima and the mainland to the N. The minimum navigable width of the channel is about 5 cables and it is deep.

Tidal streams. In Yanagino Seto the tidal streams are E-going from about 1¾ hours after LW to 1¾ hours after HW and W-going from about 1¾ hours after HW until 1¾ hours after LW; the spring rate is about 2 knots.

Naga Shima (34° 16' N, 132° 52' E), **Usu Shima, Chigiri Shima** and **Ikino Shima** are the outermost islands from SW to NE of an archipelago which lies on the S side of Yanagino Seto within 1½ miles of the NW side of Ōsaki Kami Shima. No attempt should be made to pass between any of these islands without local knowledge as there are many rocks, shoals and obstructions in the several channels.

Landmarks. A factory standing on low ground in the N part of Chigiri Shima and a tall chimney on the summit of the island, are prominent.

A *light-buoy* is moored 1 cable off the NW extremity of Ikino Shima.

Tarōga Hana, on the N side of Yanagino Seto, is a salient point 1½ miles ENE of Aka Saki (6.81) and from it a shoal extends 2½ cables S; **Ikari Shima,** a pointed rock 7 m high, lies near the extremity of this shoal. A **light** is exhibited from a black round concrete tower standing on Ikari Shima.

Takehara Kō

6.83

Takehara Kō (34° 19' N, 132° 55' E), at the mouth of **Hon Kawa,** is an open harbour (see 1.65) lying 2½ miles NE of Tarōga Hana; the town of **Takehara** which in 1973 had a population of 38 000, lies about 1 mile upstream.

The S harbour limit of Takehara Kō is a line extending from Taroga Hana to the NW point of Aba Shima (6.84), thence 1¾ miles ENE to the shore.

A breakwater extends 2 cables ESE from the W side of the mouth of Hon Kawa; a **light** is exhibited on the head of the breakwater. There are reported depths of 3 m in the river.

Mitsu Ishi, with a depth of 3·7 m, and **Mote Shō,** with a depth of 0·6 m, lie in the SE approaches to Takehara Kō, respectively, 4 cables SSE and 9 cables SE of the breakwater light.

Clearing line. The S extremity of Aba Shima in line with **Jiō Yama,** a prominent hill 183 m high on the N end of Ōmi Shima, bearing about 107°, leads about 2 cables S of both Mitsu Ishi and Mote Shō.

Landmarks. A prominent structure on a pedestal

stands near the E entrance point of Hon Kawa. A power station chimney (red and white), which is prominent, stands near the E end of the harbour limit 2¼ miles ENE of the breakwater light.

Anchorages. There is an anchorage for large vessels in depths from 15 m to 17 m about 3 cables SW of the breakwater; timber vessels of about 10 000 tons are reported to anchor in a depth of 22 m, sand, about 8 cables farther SW.

Fish havens lie close to these anchorages, 2 cables SW and 7 cables SSW of the breakwater light.

There is a private quay with a depth of 7·5 m alongside, situated within the harbour limits 1¼ miles NE of Mitsu Ishi.

Chart 3604
North east approach to Yanagino Seto
6.84

Aba Shima (34° 19' N, 132° 57' E), a long and narrow island, lies across the E entrance to Yanagino Seto and has two summits; the S and highest one is 99 m high and thickly wooded. A shoal with depths of less than 10 m, extends about 8 cables off-shore from the E side of Aba Shima; **Okino Su,** a detached sandbank parts of which dry, lies on this shoal.

Kara Shima, small, steep-to, rounded and 24 m high, lies 6 cables S of Aba Shima and is surmounted by a solitary tree.

Sagumino Ishi, a rock with a depth of 4·6 m, is steep-to and lies 4 cables SW of Kara Shima.

Sagumino Mo, a detached mudbank with a depth of 1·4 m, lies 5 cables SSW of Kara Shima.

Sagumi Shima, 125 m high, lies close off the N extremity of Ōsaki Kami Shima.

Ōsaki Seto, the channel between Ikino Shima (6.82) and the NW coast of Ōsaki Kami Shima, is entered 3 cables WNW of Sagumi Shima. A mudbank with a least depth of 0·8 m extends about 4 cables E from the E side of Ikino Shima and forms the W entrance point to the strait; **Umano Se,** a rock drying 0·5 m, lies in the S part of this mudbank and is marked close S by a *light-buoy.*

Mebarusaki Kō (34° 17' N, 132° 56' E) is enclosed by Sagumi Shima, Ikino Shima and the N point of Ōsaki Kami Shima; it affords temporary **anchorage** to small vessels awaiting a favourable tidal stream through the straits.

CHAPTER 7

KURUSHIMA KAIKYŌ, MIHARA SETO AND ADJACENT ISLANDS

KURUSHIMA KAIKYŌ AND APPROACHES

REGULATIONS AND GENERAL INFORMATION

Chart 3604 with plan of Kurushima Kaikyō

7.1

Kurushima Kaikyō (34° 07' N, 133° 00' E) is the S'most and principal channel linking Aki Nada with Hiuchi Nada and Bingo Nada. There is considerable traffic in Kurushima Kaikyō and its approaches, and large numbers of fishing vessels may be encountered particularly at or near slack water; at night, the lights used by fishing vessels may hinder navigation.

Kurushima Kaikyō is entered from W between Ōsumi Hana (34° 08' N, 132° 56' E) (7.8) and the S extremity of Ōge Shima (7.22), 2½ miles N. Through the straits there are several channels of which Naka Suidō and Nishi Suidō, on the E and W sides, respectively, of Uma Shima (34° 07' N, 133° 00' E) (7.12) are suitable for large vessels. Higashi Suidō (7.15) is the E'most channel.

The water in the two main channels of the straits is deep except for Taka Se (34° 07·4' N, 133° 00·1' E) (7.14), with a depth of 19 m, situated in the N entrance to Naka Suidō.

The tidal streams are strong and complex in Kurushima Kaikyō (see 7.4).

Ō Shima, a large hilly island, lies on the NE side of Kurushima Kaikyō.

Landmarks. Towers, supporting overhead cables (see 7.11, 7.14 and 7.15) crossing the strait, are conspicuous.

Pilotage is compulsory in Kurushima Kaikyō for all vessels over 10 000 grt.

Traffic routes and regulations

7.2

Traffic routes prescribed by the **Maritime Traffic Safety Law** (1.27) and shown on the chart, are in force in Kurushima Kaikyō.

The **general regulations** for all traffic routes prescribed by the Law are given at 1.28; information and additional regulations for Kurushima Kaikyō are as follows:

(a) A vessel navigating with the tidal stream shall use Naka Suidō (7.14); a vessel navigating against the tidal stream shall use Nishi Suidō (7.12).

(b) A vessel is prohibited from entering, leaving or crossing the traffic route, if crossing the centre line is involved, between Line A (drawn E from Kono Se (34° 07·6' N, 132° 59·3' E) and Line B (joining Shiro Ishi (34° 06·2' N, 132° 59·2' E) and Jizō Hana); these lines are shown on the chart.

(c) When the tidal stream changes after a vessel is committed to using one of the channels, she should use the following sound signals at frequent intervals on approaching the channel and until she is finally clear of it:
(i) Naka Suidō—one prolonged blast
(ii) Nishi Suidō—two prolonged blasts
(iii) Kurushimano Seto—three prolonged blasts.

(d) The tidal stream signals described at 7.6 are the authority for determining the direction of the tidal stream; if the signals are not shown, the direction should be determined with the help of the tide tables.

(e) Local vessels using Kurushimano Seto (34° 07' N, 132° 58' E), the channel SW of O Shima (7.10), are allowed to navigate Nishi Suidō even when proceeding with the tidal stream provided they keep to the W of other vessels using Nishi Suidō.

(f) The following vessels are required to have an escort vessel with a fire fighting capability before navigating the straits:
(i) Vessels of 250 m or more in length
(ii) Vessels of 200 m or more in length which are carrying a dangerous cargo
(iii) Vessels of 25 000 grt or more which are carrying liquefied gas

(g) The following additional limitations and regulations apply to tankers using the strait:

(i) *Length overall*   *Maximum draught*

Laden tankers and tankers in ballast but not gas free	
200 m–230 m	12 m
230 m–285 m	11 m

Gas free tankers	
200 m–250 m	13 m
250 m–300 m	11 m

(ii) Tankers should only navigate Naka Suidō during daylight hours and when the favourable tidal stream is less than 3 knots

(iii) The draught of tankers on passage between Kurushima Kaikyō traffic route and Mizushima traffic route (9.6) should not be more than 11 m

(h) In low visibility, entry into the Kurushima Kaikyō traffic route is restricted as follows:

Type of Vessel	*Restriction*
(i) Vessels of 200 m or more in length	Entry prohibited when the visibility in the traffic route is less than 1 mile
(ii) Vessels of 50 000 grt or more carrying dangerous cargo	
(iii) Vessels of 25 000 grt or more carrying liquefied gas	
(iv) Vessels towing or pushing very long tows	
(v) Vessels carrying dangerous cargo (excluding those in (i), (ii) and (iii) above)	Entry prohibited when the visibility in the traffic route is less than ½ mile

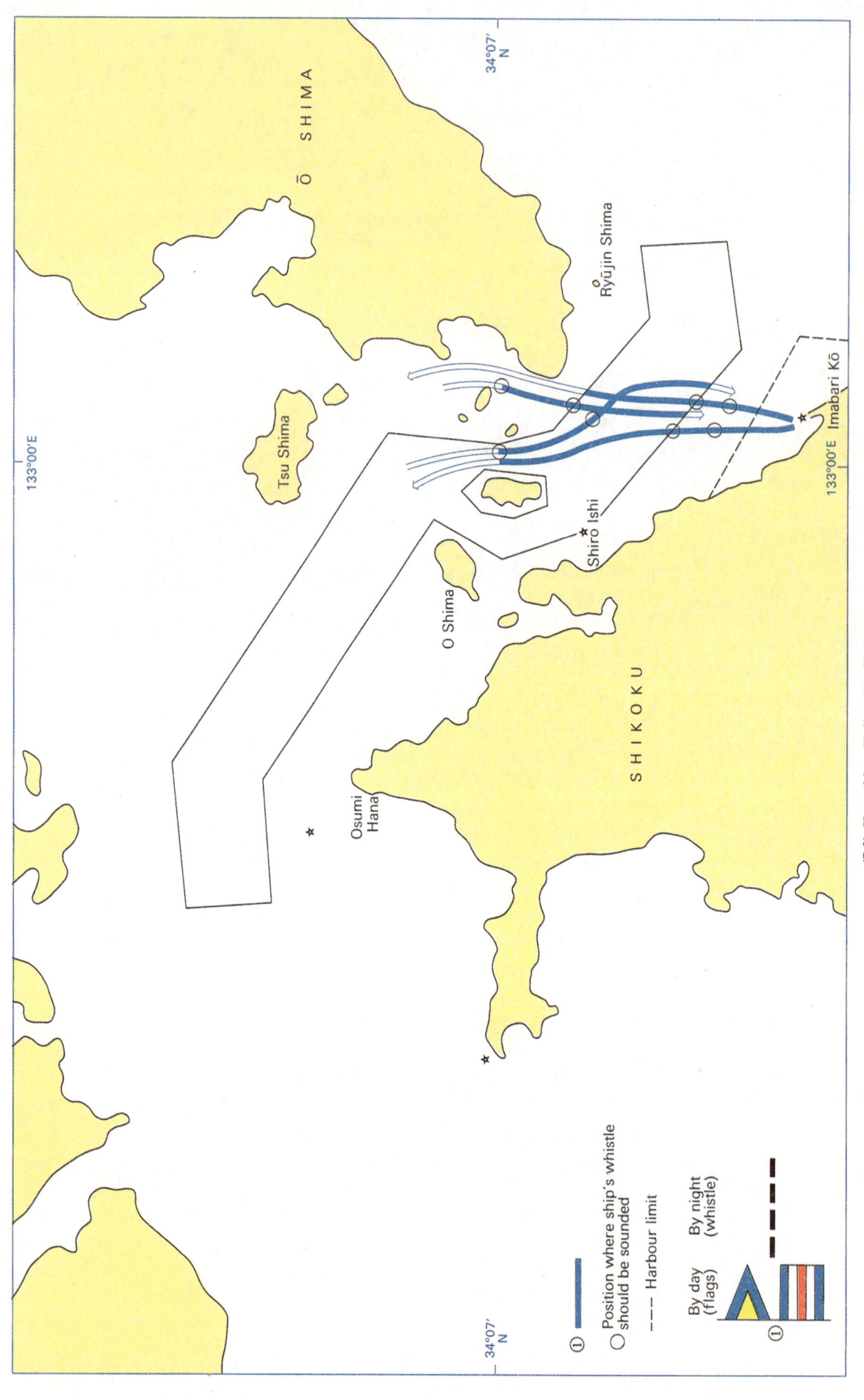

Ō SHIMA

Ryūjin Shima

Tsu Shima

O Shima

Shiro Ishi

SHIKOKU

Osumi
Hana

Imabari Kō

34°07'
N

34°07'
N

① ▬▬▬ Position where ship's whistle should be sounded
○ should be sounded
― ― ― Harbour limit

By day   By night
(flags)   (whistle)

①

(7.2) **Kurushima Kaikyō Traffic Route**

Signals to be shown by vessels. The chartlet (facing page) of the traffic route shows the flag signal to be displayed by day and the sound signal to be made at night by vessels which have to cross the traffic route or part of it, S of Line B (see chart), in order to indicate their intentions to other vessels. The flag signal should be displayed while the vessel is in the coloured part of the track; the sound signal should be made in the positions indicated on the chartlet by black dots.

Directions for Kurushima Kaikyō
7.3

In both the NW and SE approaches to the narrows in Kurushima Kaikyō, it is essential that the tracks of E-bound and W-bound vessels be well separated. While keeping within the traffic route, vessels using Naka Suidō should therefore keep as far as practicable from the Shikoku shore; vessels using Nishi Suidō should keep as near as practicable to the Shikoku shore but at the same time remembering that local vessels may be bound to or from Hashihama Wan (34° 06·8' N, 132° 58·4' E) and Kurushimano Seto.

Particular care is required during the S-going tidal stream when vessels on opposite courses will pass starboard side to starboard side; early action should be taken to ensure entering the traffic route on the correct side.
7.4

In the NW approach, *No. 2* and *No. 4 Light-buoys* are moored on the S edge of the traffic route; *No. 5 Light-buoy* is moored at the NE angle of the route ¼ mile S of Tsu Shima (34° 09' N, 133° 00' E) (7.9). In the SE approach, *No. 7 Light-buoy* and *No. 8 Light-buoy* are moored, respectively, on the N and S sides of the E end of the traffic route.

The numerous shore marks and the light-buoys are the best aids; the eye is the best guide during the strength of the stream.

A vessel passing through at about the time of slack water should pay close attention to the sound signals of other vessels and should make every endeavour to avoid meeting in the narrows; meeting in Naka Suidō is particularly dangerous.

The leading lights on Hinai Hana (34° 07·5' N, 130° 01·0' E), described at 7.15, may be of assistance to vessels approaching Naka Suidō from NW.

Tidal stream information
7.5

Tidal signal stations are established in Kurushima Kaikyō as follows:

NW entrance
Ōsumi Hana tidal signal station (7.8)—34° 08·2' N, 132° 56·5' E
Tsu Shima tidal signal station (7.9)—34° 08·8' N, 132° 59·6' E
Narrows
Nakato Shima tidal signal station (7.14)—34° 06·9' N, 133° 00·2' E
SE entrance
Ōhama tidal signal station (7.16)—34° 05·2' N, 132° 59·6' E
Nagaseno Hana tidal signal station (7.16)—34° 06·3' N, 133° 02·1' E

7.6

Tidal stream signals are displayed at the various tidal signal stations as follows; the signals invariably refer to the stream in Naka Suidō:

(a) *Ōsumi Hana and Nagaseno Hana tidal signal stations*

The signals are displayed continuously by a white isophase light every 4 seconds, on an indicator board, as follows:

Signal	Meaning
S or N	Direction of stream
0–9	Rate of stream in knots
↑	Increasing stream
↓	Decreasing stream
X	Last period of stream (for about 10 minutes before the turn).

Examples:

S 2 ↑	S-going stream, rate 2 knots, increasing
S X	Last period of S-going stream
N 6 ↓	N-going stream, rate 6 knots, decreasing
N X	Last period of N-going stream

Note: If the rate of the stream is unknown the figures will be omitted.

(b) *Tsu Shima and Ōhama tidal signal stations*
The signals are displayed by red and green lights, continuously, as follows:

Signal	Meaning
Green light flashing every 10 seconds	S-going stream
Green light group flashing 3 every 20 seconds	Last period of the S-going stream (for about 10 minutes before the turn)
Red light flashing every 10 seconds	N-going stream
Red light group flashing 3 every 20 seconds	Last period of the N-going stream (for about 10 minutes before the turn)

(c) *Nakato Shima tidal signal station*
The signals are displayed, by day, by a white beam having a red disc at one end and a black rectangle at the other, pivoted at the head of a white post, at an elevation of 37 m. At night, signals are displayed by red and green lights as in (b).

Signal	Meaning
Beam inclined at an angle of 30° from the vertical, black rectangle uppermost	S-going stream
Beam inclined at an angle of 70° from the vertical, black rectangle uppermost	Last period of the S-going stream (for about 10 minutes before the turn)
Beam inclined at an angle of 30° frm the vertical, red disc uppermost	N-going stream
Beam inclined at an angle of 70° from the vertical, red disc uppermost	Last period of the N-going stream (for about 10 minutes before the turn)

In addition, Ōhama tidal signal station transmits continuously a radio navigational message giving the direction of the stream in Naka Suidō; see *Admiralty List of Radio Signals Volume 5.*

Fog
7.7

Fog in Kurushima Kaikyō is most common from April to June and usually occurs in the latter half of the night in the four to six hours before sunrise but normally disperses by about 1100; its duration is longer in spring than in summer.

The presence of fog in the strait is sometimes very variable; it can be thick in the vicinity of one entrance while at the same time it is clear in the other.

KURUSHIMA KAIKYŌ—NORTH WEST ENTRANCE

Chart 3604 with plan of Kurushima Kaikyō
7.8

Ōsumi Hana (34° 08' N, 132° 56' E), the N'most headland in the W part of Shikoku, is a low point fringed by a reef on the S side of the NW entrance to Kurushima Kaikyō. **Ōsumi Hana tidal signal station** consisting of a white tower (metal framework) stands 1 cable S of the headland (see also 7.6).

Ikada Iso, 6 m high, lies on a shoal 4 cables WNW of Ōsumi Hana and from it a reef which dries extends 1¼ cables N; a **light** is exhibited from a round concrete tower situated on a flat-topped rock at the N extremity of this reef. Two white rocks lie within 1 cable SE of Ikada Iso.

A **fish haven** lies 1¼ miles W of Ōsumi Hana.

The coast between Ōsumi Hana and Namikata Kō (7.11) 1½ miles SE, is fringed with rocky shoals extending 2 cables offshore in places. **Mitsu Iso,** which dries 0·6 m, lies 4½ cables SE of Ōsumi Hana and a shoal bank with a depth of 3·9 m at its extremity, extends about 1 cable NE from it.

7.9

Tsu Shima (34° 09' N, 133° 00' E), on the E side of the W entrance to Kurushima Kaikyō, lies 3 miles ENE of Ōsumi Hana. **Ichinose Yama,** the summit of the island, is 176 m high and rather pointed; it is a good mark when approaching Kurushima Kaikyō from W.

Tsu Shima tidal signal station consisting of a white round concrete structure, stands on the SW end of Tsu Shima; signal lights are exhibited at an elevation of ·48 m, and an orange light, indicating the position of the station, is exhibited at an elevation of 54 m (see also 7.6).

Ōzukuma Shima, 34 m high and fringed with rocks on its W side, lies close off the SE extremity of Tsu Shima. An **overhead cable** with a vertical clearance of 32 m, spans the narrow channel between Ōzukuma Shima and Ō Shima to the SE. This channel is used by coastal ferries plying between Imabari Kō in Shikoku and Onomochi-Itozaki Kō in Honshū.

Tsukura Ura (34° 09' N, 133° 02' E) on the W side of Ō Shima, is entered 1 mile NE of Tsu Shima; the depths in the bay are less than 5 m. A **light** is exhibited from a red round concrete tower with black bands situated on **Watamaki Iso,** 3 cables NE of the S entrance point to the bay.

KURUSHIMA KAIKYŌ—THE NARROWS

Chart 3604 with plan of Kurushima Kaikyō
7.10

O Shima (34° 07' N, 132° 59' E), an islet 99 m high, partly cultivated and in part wooded, lies 2 miles SE of Ōsumi Hana (7.8).

Biwano Hana, a small wooded bluff, is connected to the SW end of O Shima by a narrow isthmus. **Naka Iso,** which dries 3·7 m, lies at the extremity of a spit extending ¼ cable SW from Biwano Hana; a **light** is exhibited from a black round concrete tower on Naka Iso.

Kono Se (34° 07·6' N, 132° 59·4' E), a detached rock which is steep-to on its E and W sides, lies on the W side of the N end of Nishi Suidō (7.12); a **light** is exhibited from a red round stone tower standing on the rock.

Caution. In 1979, Kono Se and the light-tower standing on it, were being removed; a **prohibited area** marked by *light-buoys* (yellow; yellow light flashing every 3 seconds) had been established around the work.

Kurushimano Seto and approaches
7.11

Kurushimano Seto, a deep but narrow channel, lies between Naka Iso (34° 07·1' N, 132° 58·6' E) (7.10), off the SW extremity of O Shima, and **Kuru Shima,** 38 m high and wooded, 2 cables SW.

Namikata Kō (34° 07·2' N, 132° 57·6' E), protected by two breakwaters, lies on the W side of the N approach to Kurushimano Seto, ¾ mile NW of Kuru Shima; a **light** is exhibited on the head of the E breakwater. **Hiro Se,** a reef which dries 1·2 m, lies 1¼ cables N of the head of the E breakwater; a **light** is exhibited from a red round concrete tower with black bands standing on the reef.

Overhead cables span the channels on each side of Kuru Shima; the vertical clearance is about 54 m NE and about 50 m SW of the island.

Hashihama Wan (34° 06·8' N, 132° 58·4' E) entered on either side of Kuru Shima, is designated as **No. 3 Area** within the harbour limits of Imabari Kō (7.17), 4 miles SSE. It is used by small local vessels as a temporary **anchorage** in depths from 10 m to 20 m, sand, with the head of a pier on the E side of Kuru Shima bearing 019°, and **Suishōno Hana,** the E entrance point to the inlet, bearing 053°.

Wanigasu Su, with a depth of 4·7 m, lies 2½ cables SW of Suishōno Hana; a mooring buoy is moored close to it.

The town of **Hashihama** lies on the W side of the inlet and can be reached by a boat channel.

Facilities. There are a number of dry docks in Hashihama Wan, the largest of which has a capacity of 10 000 tons. Several tugs are available.

Supplies. There are three oilers.

Nishi Suidō
7.12

Nishi Suidō separates **Uma Shima** (34° 07' N, 133° 00' E), with two summits the S and highest of which is 87 m high situated ½ mile SE of O Shima (7.10), from the coast of Shikoku.

Koura Saki Light is exhibited from a white round concrete tower standing on the NW extremity of Uma Shima; a **light** is exhibited from a white round concrete tower on **Uzu Hana,** a small peninsula at the SW extremity of the island.

Overhead cables. Four overhead cables, three of which are power cables, with a vertical clearance of about 75 m, span Nishi Suidō between the NW side of Uma Shima and O Shima. The cables are supported at each end by a metal tower (red and white), 80 m in height and marked by red obstruction lights.

Another overhead power cable with a vertical clearance of about 70 m, spans Nishi Suidō between the S end of Uma Shima and Shikoku, WSW. The towers supporting the cable at each end are conspicuous and

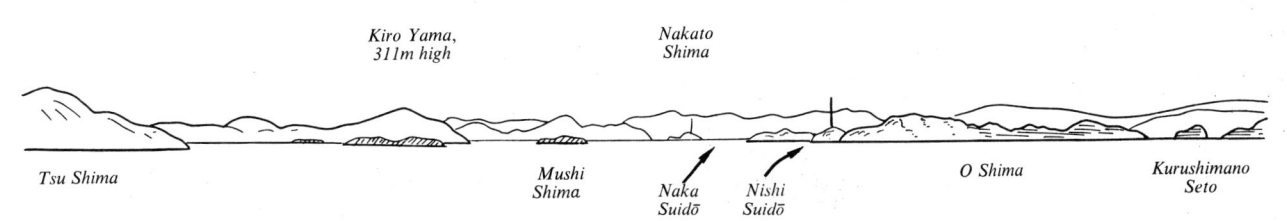

(7.8) W entrance to Kurushima Kaikyō from W, seen from a position about 1½ miles W of
Tsu Shima *(34°09′N, 133°00′E)*.

(Original dated prior to 1978)

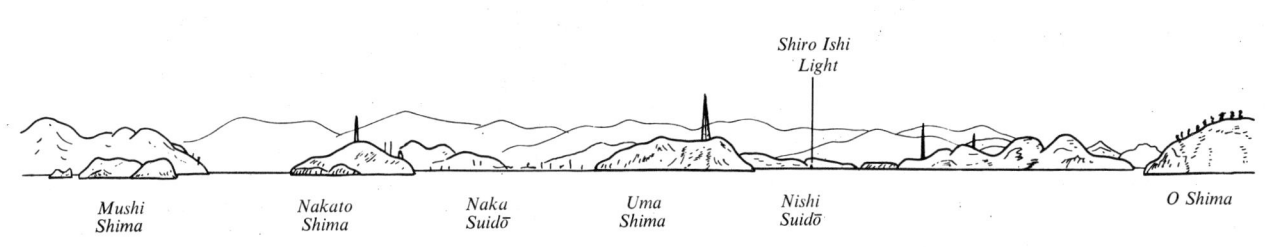

(7.10) The narrowest part of Kurushima Kaikyō from N, seen from a position about 1 mile N
of Uma Shima *(34°07′N, 133°00′E)*.

(Original dated prior to 1978)

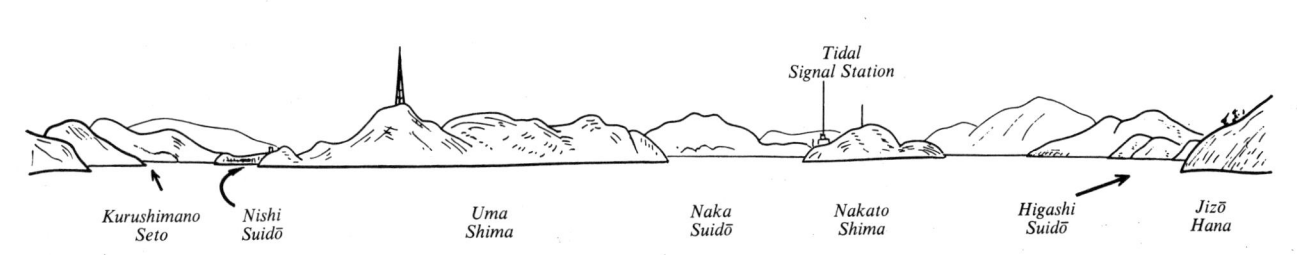

(7.10) The narrowest part of Kurushima Kaikyō from SE, seen from a position about 1 mile
SSE of Jizō Hana *(34°06′N, 133°01′E)*.

(Original dated prior to 1978)

stand at elevations of 200 m and 162 m, respectively; they are marked by red obstruction lights.

7.13

Ōiseno Shō (34° 06·7' N, 132° 59·0' E), with a depth of 4·4 m, and **Ama Se,** which dries 0·6 m, both lie about 1 cable off the coast of Shikoku on the W side of the S part of Nishi Suidō. A **light** is exhibited from a red round concrete tower standing on Ama Se.

Shiro Ishi, 2 m high and its upper part white, lies 1 cable offshore and 5 cables SSE of Ōiseno Shō; a **light** is exhibited from a red round concrete tower standing on the rock.

Mukuri, a detached rock with a depth of 4·7 m, lying 1¼ cables ESE of Shiro Ishi is the outermost danger on the SW side of Nishi Suidō.

Clearing line. Biwano Hana (7.10) bearing less than 325° and open NE of **Sashide Hana** (34° 06·8' N, 132° 58·9' E), leads not less than ½ cable NE of Mukuri.

Naka Suidō

7.14

Naka Suidō is the channel between the E side of Uma Shima (7.12) and **Nakato Shima** (34° 06·8' N, 133° 00·3' E), a round-topped island, 2¼ cables E. **Taka Se,** a rock with a depth of 19 m, lies in the fairway in the N entrance to Naka Suidō.

A rock with a depth of 1·7 m, lies within ¼ cable of the E coast of Uma Shima about 2¼ cables SE of the N extremity of the island. A **light** is exhibited from a white square concrete tower situated on **Nagase Hana,** the E extremity of Uma Shima, at the narrowest part of Naka Suidō.

Nakato Shima tidal signal station consisting of a white round stone structure, is situated on the NW extremity of Nakato Shima; signal lights are exhibited at an elevation of 40 m, and an orange light, indicating the position of the station, is exhibited at an elevation of 35 m (see also 7.6).

An **overhead power cable** with a vertical clearance of about 70 m, spans Naka Suidō between the S part of Uma Shima and Nakato Shima. The supporting tower on Nakato Shima stands at an elevation of 107 m and is conspicuous; it is marked by red obstruction lights.

Gōno Ishi, with a depth of less than 2 m, lies within 1 cable E of the E extremity of Nakato Shima.

Mushi Shima (34° 07·1' N, 133° 00·7' E), 54 m high, lies 2½ cables NE of Nakato Shima. **Warabe Iso,** a 3·1 m patch, lies ½ cable offshore close SW of the NW extremity of Mushi Shima. **Ko Mushi Shima,** 36 m high, and **Kenashi Shima,** an islet, lie on a rocky shoal fringing the N side of Mushi Shima.

Higashi Suidō

7.15

Higashi Suidō is the channel between Mushi Shima and Nakato Shima on the W side, and the W coast of Ō Shima on the E side.

Hinai Hana (34° 07·5' N, 133° 01·1' E) lies on the E side of the N entrance to Higashi Suidō.

Leading lights are exhibited from white round concrete towers standing on Hinai Hana; these lights in line bear 122°, and is the lead through the NW approach to Kurushima Kaikyō for vessels proceeding with the tidal stream and therefore passing through Naka Suidō.

Wakame Iso, with a depth of 1·1 m and steep-to on its SW side, lies 1 cable SSE of Hinai Hana.

Bujiro Shō, a steep-to rocky patch with a depth of 3·8 m, lies in the middle of Higashi Suidō, 2 cables E of the E extremity of Mushi Shima.

An **overhead power cable** with a vertical clearance of about 45 m, spans the S part of Higashi Suidō between Nakato Shima and the SW extremity of Ō Shima; the supporting tower on Ō Shima stands at an elevation of 145 m and is conspicuous.

KURUSHIMA KAIKYŌ—SOUTH EAST ENTRANCE

Chart 3604 with plan of Kurushima Kaikyō

7.16

Ōhama tidal signal station (34° 05·2' N, 132° 59·6' E), consisting of a round concrete structure 13 m in height, stands on the coast of Shikoku on the SW side of the SE entrance to Kurushima Kaikyō; signal lights are exhibited at an elevation of 30 m, and an orange light, indicating the position of the station, is exhibited at an elevation of 36 m (see also 7.6).

Landmark. Chikami Yama, 243 m high and a good mark, with some clumps of trees on it, is situated 1 mile WSW of Ōhama tidal signal station.

Jizō Hana (36° 06·4' N, 133° 01·0' E), the SW extremity of Ō Shima, lies on the N side of the SE entrance to Kurushima Kaikyō.

Ryūjin Shima, 9 m high, lies ¼ mile offshore ¾ mile ESE of Jizō Hana; a **light** is exhibited from a black metal framework tower standing on the rock. **Obasama Shima,** 13 m high, lies midway between Ryūjin Shima and the shore N.

Nagaseno (Kagike) Hana (34° 06' N, 133° 02' E) is the S extremity of Ō Shima, and the coast in its vicinity is cliffy. **Kōzō Iso,** drying rocks with a rock 2 m high in the middle, lies 2½ cables SSW of Nagaseno Hana.

Nagaseno Hana tidal signal station consisting of a white tower (square metal framework) stands on the point; signal lights are exhibited on an indicator board at an elevation of 46 m (see also 7.6).

IMABARI KŌ

Chart 3604

7.17

Imabari Kō (34° 04' N, 133° 01' E), a specified port (see 1.64), lies on the S side of the SE entrance to Kurushima Kaikyō; the port is divided into three separate areas:

No. 1 Area, the inner harbour, is situated 1¼ miles SSE of Ōhama tidal signal station (7.16).

No. 2 Area (34° 03·7' N, 133° 01·2' E), a basin lying on the N side of the mouth of **Sōsha Kawa,** 1 mile SE of the inner harbour.

No. 3 Area, embracing the shipyards and anchorage in Hashihama Wan (34° 06·8' N, 132° 58·4' E) is described at 7.11.

Imabari, situated on the N side of Sōsha Kawa, is a large cotton manufacturing city with a population of 114 000 in 1973.

Landmarks. The principal landmarks are:

A prominent power station chimney, standing at an elevation of 67 m near the N end of the city.

The Harbour Office, a 5-storied building with two radio masts on its roof, standing on the W side of the inner harbour.

A prominent building standing on the SE side of the harbour.

No. 1 Area

7.18

The **inner harbour (No. 1 Area)** is protected from E by

a breakwater and is entered from NW; a **light** is exhibited on the head of the breakwater and at the W entrance point of the harbour.

Caution. The inner harbour is congested and numerous ferries and excursion boats are continuously passing in and out of the entrance. Large numbers of fishing boats are likely to be encountered off the harbour particularly at slack water.

A **prohibited area** lies within 1½ cables N and E of the head of the E breakwater.

Temposan Wharf, with a depth of 4·5 m alongside, lies on the SE side of the inner harbour and can accommodate a vessel of 3000 tons. Three piers, and a ferry quay with a depth of 6 m alongside, lie on the SW side of the harbour.

No. 2 Area
7.19

The **basin (No. 2 Area)** situated on reclaimed land on the N side of the mouth of Sōsha Kawa is protected from

E by a short breakwater; a **light** is exhibited on the head of the breakwater.

Kurashiki Wharf borders all three sides of the basin. **No. 1** and **No. 2 Quays** with depths from 6·8 m to 8·5 m alongside, lie on the W side of the basin; **No. 3** and **No. 4 Quays** with a depth of 5 m alongside, lie, respectively, on the S and E sides.

Facilities
7.20

There are offices of the Maritime Safety Agency and Customs in Imabari Kō.

Tugs are based in No. 3 Area but will come to Nos. 1 and 2 Areas on request.

Supplies. Fresh water is available on most quays. There are five oilers.

Communications. There are a large number of ferry services from Imabari Kō to other ports in Seto Naikai and to neighbouring islands.

MIHARA SETO AND APPROACHES

GENERAL INFORMATION
Charts 3603, 3604
7.21

Mihara Seto is the tortuous and narrow passage through the numerous islands lying between the NE part of Aki Nada and the NW part of Bingo Nada.

Tidal streams in the passage are not as strong as those in Kurushima Kaikyō.

Traffic in the strait is considerable and consists of large numbers of local vessels and ferries, large vessels proceeding to and from the port of Onomichi-Itozaki Kō (34° 24' N, 133° 10' E), and vessels towing.

Route. Mihara Seto is approached from SW through Ōge Seto (34° 11' N, 132° 55' E) (7.22); thence the channel leads between Ō Saki Kami Shima and Ōmi Shima; thence between the coast of Honshū and the islands lying to the NE of Ōmi Shima, and finally through Mekari Seto and into Bingo Nada. The strait is about 24 miles long.

The recommended track through Mihara Seto is shown on the charts. A depth of 18 m can be carried through the strait from Ōge Seto, the SW entrance, to Onomichi-Itozaki Kō.

Cautions. Special caution is necessary in the vicinity of the following dangers:

(a) The 4·5 m patch (34° 16·8' N, 132° 58·0' E) (7.24) 3 cables N of Kōdono Shima.

(b) Nōji Tai (34° 19·3' N, 133° 02·5' E) (7.27), with a depth of 1·4 m.

(c) Kami Taka Se (34° 20' N, 133° 04' E) (7.27), with a depth of 3·5 m.

(d) Kakari Se (34° 22·4' N, 133° 08·7' E) (7.30), with a depth of 8·8 m.

Care is also necessary when passing the entrances of the various channels leading off the main channel on account of the tidal streams flowing through them, particularly when passing the entrances of Yanagino Seto (34° 18' N, 132° 58' E) and Hakata Seto (34° 18' N, 133° 02' E).

ŌGE SETO AND THE WEST PART OF MIHARA SETO

Charts 3603, 3604
Ōge Seto
7.22

Ōge Seto (34° 11' N, 132° 55' E), the SW entrance to Mihara Seto, lie between Ko Ōge Shima (6.79) and **Ōge Shima,** ½mile E.

A considerable part of Ōge Shima is cultivated and its summit attains an elevation of 207 m near its N end. The SW part of the islet consists of a small peninsula terminating in **Takenoko Hana** on the W side of which is a very dark cliff; a **light** is exhibited from a white octagonal stone tower standing on the end of the peninsula.

Ōmi Shima, a comparatively large island which is mostly wooded, lies on the E side of the S part of Mihara Seto.

Kanno Mine

Koyoko Shima   *Ōyoko Shima*   *Ōge Shima*   *Nakano Hana Light*

(7.22) Ōge Seto from N, seen from a position about 3 miles NNE of Nakano Hana (34° 13' N, 132° 55' E)

(Original dated prior to 1978)

Nakano Hana to Kōdono Shima

7.23

Nakano Hana (34° 13' N, 132° 55' E), a steep cliff, is the extremity of Ōsaki Kami Shima (6.79) and lies on the W side of the fairway, ¾ mile N of Ōge Shima; a **light** is exhibited from a white round stone tower standing on the point.

Chishago Shō, a rock which dries 3 m and is marked by a **beacon** (red and white in bands), lies 2 cables N of Nakano Hana.

Fuku Shima, a small islet 44 m high, lies on a shoal situated on the E side of the fairway ¾ mile ENE of Nakano Hana. A detached rock, which dries 3·7 m, lies 3 cables SE of Fuku Shima.

Kinoe Kō (34° 14' N, 132° 55' E), a small harbour protected by a breakwater projecting from its N entrance point, lies 1¼ miles N of Nakano Hana; a **light** is exhibited on the head of the breakwater.

Anchorage is afforded in depths from 4 m to 16 m, sand and clay, in the roadstead off the harbour; it is much used by small vessels awaiting a favourable tidal stream through Mihara Seto.

Temman Jetty, with a depth of 3 m alongside, lies on the S side of the S entrance point of the harbour and **Ichikamme Jetty** lies on the N side of the harbour.

Facilities. There is an office of the Maritime Safety Agency in Kinoe Kō. There are shipyards which carry out repairs and build small vessels, situated on the N side of the harbour.

There are scheduled passenger and car ferry services to other ports in Seto Naikai.

Chart 3604

7.24

Mishima Uchi, a shallow bay which is obstructed by mud-flats, lies on the W side of Ōmi Shima. From September to April extensive seaweed and pearl cultivation takes place in the bay.

No. 1 and *No. 3 Light-buoys* mark the channel into **Miyanoura Kō** (34° 14·8' N, 132° 59·5' E), a cove situated near the middle of the E shore of the bay; a jetty with depths from 3 m to 3·5 m alongside and used by the ferry, lies at the SE inner end of this cove.

Ōyoko Shima (34° 15' N, 132° 57' E), on the E side of the fairway, lies across the entrance to Mishima Uchi; at low water it is connected to **Koyoko Shima,** 55 m high, close off its N end.

The NW extremity of Ōyoko Shima is a small thickly wooded peninsula which appears at a distance as a separate islet.

Mebaru Saki (34° 16' N, 132° 57' E) is the NE extremity of Ōsaki Kami Shima and from it a breakwater protecting Mebarusaki Kō (6.84), which lies to the W, extends a short distance NE; a **light** is exhibited from a white round stone tower on the point, and another **light** is exhibited on the head of the breakwater.

Kōdono Shima (34° 16·5' N, 132° 58·0' E), a small islet 47 m high, lies on the E side of the fairway 1 mile E of Mebaru Saki; 1 cable W of it lies a detached rock 3 m high.

A 4·5 m patch marked by a *light-buoy* lies 3 cables N of Kōdono Shima. The channel between Kōdono Shima and the NW end of Ōmi Shima is foul and in its centre is a rock which dries 0·6 m.

Matsu Shima to Oshiyose Hana

7.25

Matsu Shima (34° 18' N, 132° 58' E), on the NW side of the fairway, lies ½ mile NW of **Gōbori Hana** the NW extremity of Ōmi Shima; the islet is 49 m high and has two hills which from SW appear as one.

Kokuno Shima, 83 m high, thickly wooded and round-topped, lies on the N side of the fairway ½ mile NNE of Matsu Shima.

Ōkuno Shima (34° 19' N, 133° 00' E), 107 m high and well-wooded in its N part, lies 4 cables E of Kokuno Shima. A **light** is exhibited from a white round stone tower standing on the S end of Ōkuno Shima; a **beacon** (white octagonal), 6 m in height, stands on a drying rock 2½ cables ENE of the light-tower.

An islet, 11 m high, and a drying rock close SW of it, lie on the S side of the fairway ½ mile SE of Ōkuno Shima Light.

Overhead cables. An overhead cable with a vertical clearance of 54 m, spans the channel to the S of Ōkuno Shima, and another cable with a vertical clearance of 45 m, spans the channel to the N; the pylons supporting these cables are prominent.

7.26

Tadanoumi Kō (34° 20' N, 133° 00' E), protected by breakwaters, lies at the head of a bay situated on the N shore of Mihara Seto, 1¼ miles N of Ōkuno Shima; a **light** is exhibited on the head of the E breakwater. **Ushiga Hae,** a rock which dries 1·8 m and is marked by a white **beacon,** lies 4 cables SE of the breakwater light.

Anchorage in depths from 13 m to 16 m is afforded in the bay fronting Tadanoumi Kō.

7.27

Mekarino Su (34° 19·0' N, 133° 00·5' E), with a depth of 4·7 m, lies on the W part of a bank on the N side of Mihara Seto.

Nōji Tai, with a least depth of 1·4 m, lies 1½ miles ENE of Mekarino Su; a *light-buoy* is moored near the SW end of Nōji Tai.

Uryū Shima (34° 20·3' N, 133° 04·9' E), a red-coloured islet 20 m high, lies on a shoal 2 cables offshore 1½ miles NE of Nōji Tai. **Kami Taka Se,** a detached rock with a depth of 3·5 m, lies close N of the fairway, 3 cables SSE of Uryū Shima.

Clearing line. The S summit of Kosagi Shima (7.28) bearing 045° and open E of Aogi Hana, leads about 2½ cables SE of Kami Take Se.

Kōne Shima, a thickly wooded island, lies on the S side of the entrance to Aogi Seto; a **light** is exhibited from a white round stone tower standing on **Oshiyose Hana,** the N extremity of Kōne Shima.

AOGI SETO

Chart 3604

7.28

Aogi Seto is entered between Oshiyose Hana (34° 20' N, 133° 05' E) and **Aogi Hana** on the N side of the strait, 6 cables N.

Directions. Okō Yama (34° 16' N, 132° 56' E), 261 m high, in the N part of Ōsaki Kami Shima, in line with Gōbori Hana, the NW extremity of Ōmi Shima, bearing 238°, leads through the middle of the S part of Aogi Seto clear of all dangers.

Sagi Shima, on the E side of the fairway, consists mainly of bare granite hills. **Yake Yama,** 277 m high and the summit of the island, and **Inu Yama,** a sharp granite peak 250 m high, situated 4 cables N, are both good marks.

Toramaru Shō, which dries 1·2 m, lies 1 cable NW of **Hoteiiwa Hana** (34° 20·2' N, 133° 06·0' E) situated near the middle of the W side of Sagi Shima. A **light** is exhibited from a red round concrete tower standing on

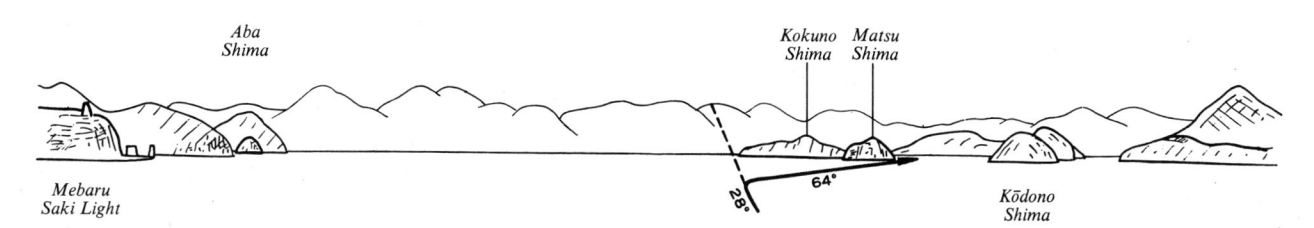

(7.25) Mihara Seto— W entrance from SW, seen from a position close W of
Kōdono Shima *(34°17′N, 132°58′E)*.

(Original dated prior to 1978)

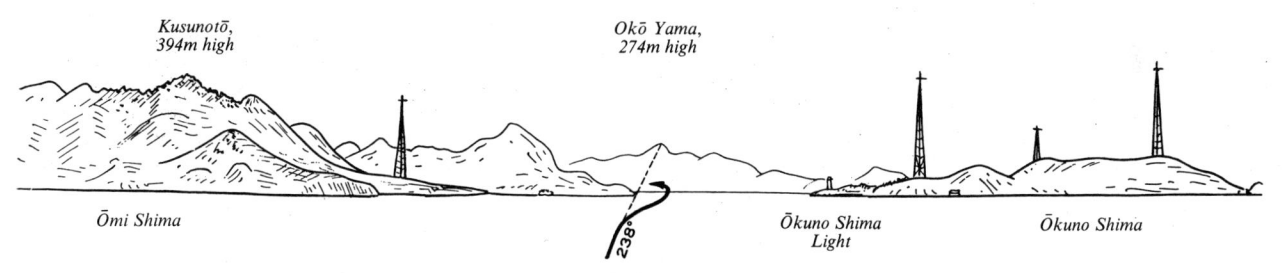

(7.25) Mihara Seto—W entrance from NE, seen from a position about 4½ miles NE of
Ōkuno Shima Light *(34°18′N, 133°00′E)*.

(Original dated prior to 1978)

Toramaru Shō, and there is a prominent monument on Hoteiiwa Hana.

Numerous **fish havens,** charted as obstructions, lie on each side of the fairway in Aogi Seto.

Kosagi Shima (34° 22' N, 133° 06' E), on the SE side of the fairway of Aogi Seto, is separated from the NW end of Sagi Shima by a narrow channel which should not be attempted without local knowledge; on the island are two peaks, the S and highest of which is 75 m high. Four **overhead power cables,** the lowest of which has a vertical clearance of 28 m, span the narrow channel.

A **light** is exhibited from a white round stone tower on the NW end of Kosagi Shima; another **light** is exhibited from a white concrete column on the SE side of the island which illuminates a **beacon** standing on a drying rock $\frac{1}{4}$ cable E.

Charts 694 plan of Itozaki, 3604

7.29

Mihara Wan, the W part of Onomichi-Itozaki Kō (7.31), lies on the N side of the fairway of Aogi Seto and is entered between **Inubōno Hana** (34° 22·5' N, 133° 05·4' E) and **Ropponmatsuno Hana,** $1\frac{1}{2}$ miles ENE.

Landmarks. Inubō Yama, 308 m (1010 ft) high and dome-shaped, lies close inland of Inubōno Hana; an observation platform on its summit is a good mark.

Hata Yama, situated 6 cables SW of Inubō Yama, is 447 m high and shows up well from E; a tower and three pylons stand on its summit.

Hachiga Mine, situated $\frac{1}{4}$ mile NE of Ropponmatsuno Hana, is 429 m (1406 ft) high, thickly wooded, and the highest peak on the E side of Mihara Wan.

7.30

Sukune Shima (34° 22' N, 133° 07' E), a prominent, dark, rounded islet, 29 m (94 ft) high, lies on the S side of the fairway $\frac{1}{2}$ mile E of Kosagi Shima (7.28).

Chōdayū Shō, a group of rocks with a depth of less than 2 m, lies 1 mile ENE of Sukune Shima; a **light** is exhibited from a red round stone tower standing on the rocks. **Okino Sowai** with a depth of 3·7 m, lies $\frac{3}{4}$ cable NNE of Chōdayū Shō.

Hosono Su, a sandbank which dries 0·6 m in places, lies on an extensive shoal situated between Sukune Shima and the NW side of Hoso Shima (7.37), to the S of Chōdayū Shō.

Kakari Se, a rocky patch with a depth of 8·8 m (29 ft), lies nearly in the middle of the fairway, $3\frac{1}{2}$ cables NE of Chōdayū Shō; eddies are formed in its vicinity. Kakari Se has been swept to a depth of 8·3 m and is covered by the red sector of Chōdayū Shō Light between the bearings of 219° and 239°, and by a red light exhibited on Ōhama Saki (7.39) between the bearings of 125° and 130°

ONOMICHI-ITOZAKI KŌ

Charts 3604, 694 plan of Itozaki

7.31

Onomichi-Itozaki Kō, a specified port (see 1.64), lies within harbour limits which enclose Mihara Wan (34° 23' N, 133° 06' E) (7.29) in the W, Onomichi Seto on the N side of Mukai Shima (7.38), and Tosaki Seto (8.35) the E entrance to Onomichi Seto. The harbour is divided into Nos. 1 to 6 Areas with No. 6 Area in the W and No. 1 Area in the E.

Itozaki, on the NE shore of Mihara Wan, is a suburb of **Mihara** which is a manufacturing city; a large number of factories lie along the shore. **Onomichi,** an industrial city, lies along the N shore of the E half of Onomichi Seto and there are extensive shipyards on the S side of the strait opposite the city. In 1973, the combined population of Mihara and Onomichi was 189 000.

Pilotage is not compulsory but recommended. Harbour pilots are available.

Tidal streams. In Onomichi Seto the tidal streams begin as follows:

Interval from HW Onomichi	*Direction*	*Rate Knots*
+ 0200/ + 0100	W-going	$2\frac{1}{2}$
− 0500/ − 0540	E-going	$2\frac{3}{4}$

The tidal streams are influenced by the weather and in particular by W winds.

In Mihara Wan the tidal streams are weak and vary between $\frac{1}{2}$ and 1 knot.

Chart 694 plan of Itozaki

Onomichi-Itozaki Kō—west part

7.32

Mihara Wan (No. 6 Area), in the W part of the port, affords sheltered **anchorage** to vessels according to draught. There are several mooring buoys in the N part of the bay off Itozaki.

Landmarks. See 7.29.

Nuta Kawa flows into the W part of Mihara Wan; quays owned by **Mitsubishi Heavy Industries** lie on reclaimed land on the S side of the mouth of this river.

A buoyed channel, the outer part of which was dredged to 5·4 m in 1972, leads from the NW corner of Mihara Wan to an inner harbour with depths of 3 m; *No. 1 Buoy* and *No. 2 Light-buoy* mark the entrance to this channel. An **overhead cable** with a vertical clearance of 17 m spans the channel near its head.

Moji Shō, with a depth of 0·3 m (1 ft), lies near the edge of the mudbank 1 cable S of the channel entrance; a *light-buoy* is moored close E of the rock.

Itozaki public wharves front the town and are situated about 3 cables E of the entrance to the inner harbour.

In 1979, a breakwater, marked by lights, was under construction close off the NE shore of the bay.

Berths. The principal berths in No. 6 Area are as follows:

Berth & Position	*Length m*	*Depth m*	*Capacity dwt*
Mitsubishi Heavy Industries (34° 22·8' N, 133° 05·5' E)			
Wada No. 1 and No. 2 Quays	205	4–7	3 000
Wada Offing Quay	205	4·5–7·5	7 000
Teijin Quay (34° 23·2' N, 133° 05·6' E)	400	3	500
Itozaki No. 1 Quay (34° 23·1' N, 133° 06·4' E)	135	8	6 000
Itozaki No. 2 Quay (34° 23·1' N, 133° 06·5' E)	185	10 (reported)	10 000

Chart 3604

Onomichi-Itozaki Kō—east part

7.33

Onomichi Seto, the E part of Onomichi-Itozaki Kō, is the narrow strait on the N side of Iwashi Shima (34° 23' N, 133° 10' E) (7.37) and Mukai Shima (7.38).

The fairway leads through the centre of the strait from the W entrance close NW of Iwashi Shima to the E entrance about 5 miles E. Large vessels normally use the W entrance; however to take advantage of the tidal streams, small vessels may well use the E entrance on the flood stream (E-going) and the W entrance on the ebb stream (W-going).

Caution. Traffic entering, leaving and crossing Onomichi Seto is heavy.

Kokujira Shima, and **Ōkujira Shima** (34° 23' N, 133° 09' E) which is covered with trees and is prominent, lie across the W entrance to Onomichi Seto, respectively, 2 cables and 3½ cables NW of the NW extremity of Iwashi Shima. The channel between the coast of Iwashi Shima and Kokujira Shima is foul and that between Kokujira Shima and Ōkujira Shima is narrow and not recommended for large vessels.

A 5·2 m patch lies 4 cables ENE of Ōkujira Shima, and a 4·7 m patch lies 9 cables farther ENE; both close S of the centre line of the strait.

No. 3 Fairway is entered N of Ōkujira Shima and leads N of the 5·2 m and 4·7 m patches, to Onomichi; it passes through Nos. 5, 4 and 3 Areas.

An **overhead cable** with a vertical clearance of 53 m, crosses the strait ¼ mile E of the W entrance.

7.34

The E entrance (34° 24' N, 133° 14' E) to Onomichi Seto is obstructed by shoals, but **No. 1 Fairway,** a buoyed channel about ½ cable wide, leads from the N end of Tosaki Seto (34° 24·0' N, 133° 14·6' E) (8.35) into **No. 2 Fairway,** and joins No. 3 Fairway off Onomichi; it passes through Nos. 1 and 2 Areas.

Onomichi Bridge with a vertical clearance of 35 m, crosses the strait 1 mile W of the E entrance. Traffic **light signals** are exhibited on each side of the bridge as follows:

Signal	Location	Meaning
R	N end of bridge	E-bound traffic
G	S end of bridge	may proceed
G	N end of bridge	W-bound traffic
R	S end of bridge	may proceed
	R = red fixed light	
	G = green fixed light	

An **overhead cable** with a vertical clearance of 40 m crosses the strait close W of the bridge.

7.35

Numerous wharves and piers exist on both sides of Onomichi Seto for the greater part of its length and there are alongside berths for vessels up to 3000 tons. Mooring buoys are available in No. 4 Area for vessels up to 12 000 tons.

Berths. The principal berths in Onomichi Seto are:

Berth & Position	Length m	Depth m	Capacity dwt
Shinhama Wharf			
(34° 23·8' N, 133° 11·3' E)	250	5·5	2000
Nishingosho Wharf			
(34° 23·9' N, 133° 11·5' E)	400	6·5	3000
Ekimae Jetty			
(34° 24·0' N, 133° 11·8' E)	130	5·5	1000
Central Jetty			
(34° 24·3' N, 133° 12·3' E)	135	4·5	1000

7.36

Facilities. There are offices of the Maritime Safety Agency, Customs and Immigration located in the joint Harbour Office situated in Onomichi about ¼ mile W of Shinhama Wharf.

Tugs are brought from other ports when required.

There are five tugs attached to the shipyards. Lighters are available.

Hitachi and **Mukaishima Shipyards** lie on the S side of Onomichi Seto, and **Onomichi Shipyard** on the N side near the E end of the strait; they have numerous dry docks and slipways.

Waste oil disposal facilities are available.

Supplies. Fresh water is laid on to the wharves or can be supplied by waterboat. There are seven oilers.

Communications. There are regular passenger and car ferry and hydrofoil services from Onomichi and Mihara to the neighbouring islands, and to Shikoku.

MEKARI SETO

Chart 3604
Mekari Seto—north west part
7.37

Hoso Shima (34° 22' N, 133° 09' E), with several pointed peaks, is situated on the S side of the NW end of **Mekari Seto.**

Overhead cables. An overhead cable with a vertical clearance of 54 m, spans the strait between **Hosokashira,** the NE extremity of Hoso Shima, and the SW extremity of Iwashi Shima; the pylon (red and white) standing on Hosokashira and supporting the overhead cable, is 82 m in height and a good mark. An overhead cable with a vertical clearance of 31 m, spans the channel between Hoso Shima and the N coast of Inno Shima.

Iwashi Shima, with several granite hills, is situated on the NE side of the fairway of Mekari Seto opposite Hoso Shima.

Landmarks. Nishiiwa Take, 130 m high and the NW'most hill on Iwashi Shima, shows up well from W; **Tono Yama,** 116 m high with a red *torii* on its W side, is the SW'most hill and is prominent.

Numerous **fish havens,** charted as obstructions, lie close off the SW coast of Iwashi Shima.

Ushino Seto, a narrow channel between Iwashi Shima and Mukai Shima to the E, is spanned by a fixed **bridge** near its S end with a vertical clearance of about 13 m.

7.38

Mukai Shima (34° 23' N, 133° 12' E), a large island on the NE side of Mekari Seto, has several granite hills on it.

Landmarks. Takami Yama, 288 m high, lies in the S part of Mukai Shima and is the most prominent hill; a radio mast marked by red lights, stands near its summit.

Ko-takami Yama, 193 m high, lies 6 cables W of Takami Yama and is a remarkable sharp peak which shows up well from a distance.

Mekari Iwa, a group of rocks which dry 1·3 m, lies within 1 cable SSW of **Mekari Hana** (34° 21·8' N, 133° 10·6' E) on the W side of Mukai Shima; a *light-buoy* (red; red light flashing every 3 seconds) is moored close S of the rocks.

Sasa Shima, a rounded grassy islet 13 m high and steep-to on its W and S sides, lies close offshore 8 cables SE of Mekari Hana.

7.39

Inno Shima, a comparatively large thickly wooded island, lies on the SW side of Mekari Seto.

Landmarks. Oku Yama, the summit of Inno Shima, attains an elevation of 392 m near the E coast of the island; it SE side is very steep but on its other sides the slopes are more gradual.

Shirataki Yama (34° 20·5' N, 133° 09·6' E), 226 m high, and **Ryūo San,** 240 m high, lie in the NW part of Inno Shima and have sharp and remarkable bare granite peaks; a shrine stands on the summit of Shirataki Yama.

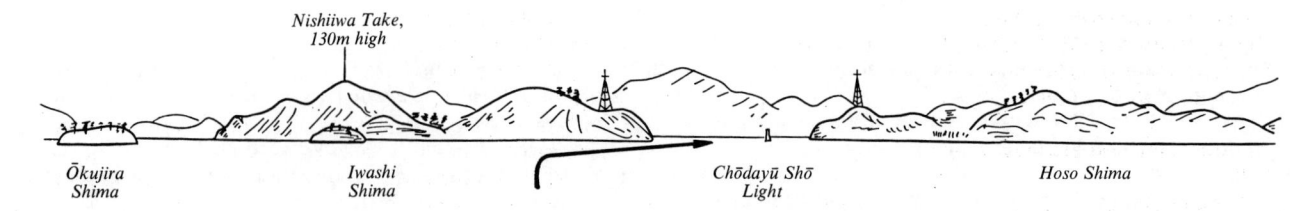

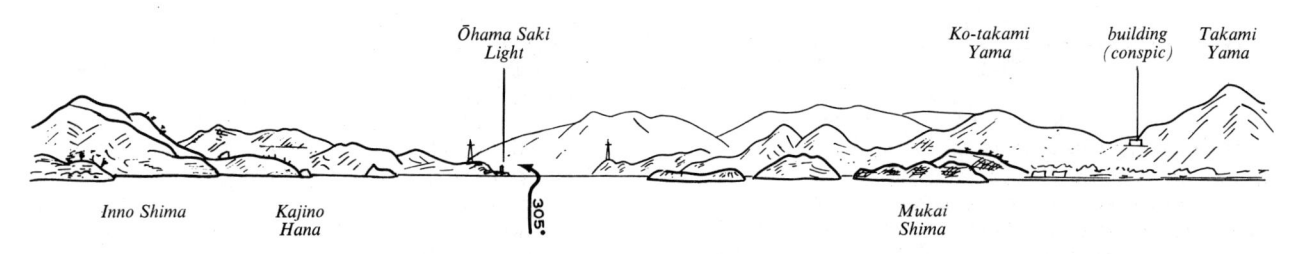

(7.37) Mekari Seto—N entrance, seen from a position about 1 mile WNW of
Chōdayū Shō Light *(34°22′N, 133°08′E)*.

(Original dated prior to 1978)

(7.39) Mekari Seto from SE, seen from a position about 2 miles SE of Kajino Hana
(34°20′N, 133°12′E).

(Original dated prior to 1978)

A **light** is exhibited from a white round stone tower situated on **Ōhama Saki** (34° 21·3' N, 133° 10·6' E); the NE extremity of Inno Shima; an auxiliary **light** is exhibited from the same tower.

In the entrance of the channel between Inno Shima and Hoso Shima to the NW, there are a number of shoals with depths of less than 3 m; **Shijū Shima,** 16 m high, and two drying rocks, lie 1 cable offshore 6 cables WNW of Ōhama Saki.

In 1978, a **bridge** was under construction across the narrowest part of Mekari Seto, close S of Ōhama Saki.

Matsui Dashi, a steep-to shoal with a depth of 9·6 m, lies 7 cables SE of Ōhama Saki; this shoal has been swept to a depth of 8·7 m. **Aka Ne,** a similar shoal with a depth of 9·9 m and swept to a depth of 9·4 m, lies 5 cables farther SE.

Several **submarine cables** cross Mekari Seto from **Kajino Hana,** a cliffy headland on the E coast of Inno Shima, to **Nagaiso Hana** the SW end of Mukai Shima; the landing places of these cables are marked by **beacons.**

Mekari Seto—south east part
7.40

Kannon Hana (34° 21' N, 133° 13' E), the S extremity of Mukai Shima, is a steep cliffy point which rises to a red-coloured bare hill.

Ategi Shima (34° 20' N, 133° 16' E), 2¼ miles SE of Kannon Hana, is a prominent, bare, cliffy islet lying close off the SW extremity of Yoko Shima (8.32).

Tachibanano Su, with a least depth of 5·9 m, lies ½ mile S of Kannon Hana; a *light-buoy* marks its W side.

Morinoseno Su, with a least depth of 1·8 m, lies 6 cables SE of Kannon Hana; a *light-buoy* is moored on both the N and S sides of this shoal. A disused spoil ground lies ½ mile SW of Morinoseno Su.

Charts 3604, 3605
7.41

Hyakkan Shima (34° 18' N, 133° 17' E), at the SE end of Mekari Seto, is a conical islet 70 m high and is a good mark for identifying the E entrance to the strait. A **light** is exhibited from a white round stone tower standing on the summit of the islet.

The fairway passing close N of Hyakkan Shima and leading into the entrance of Mekari Seto, has a least depth of 10 m. Within the entrance, **Bōjino Su,** an extensive shoal with depths from 8·4 m to 9·8 m, lies close to the fairway on the SW side, and a smaller shoal, with a least depth of 8·5 m, lies close on the N side.

ISLANDS AND MINOR CHANNELS NORTH EAST OF KURUSHIMA KAIKYŌ

Chart 3604
7.42

There are several channels between the islands separating Kurushima Kaikyō (34° 07' N, 133° 00' E) from Mihara Seto to the N, but they are mostly narrow and intricate and should not be attempted without local knowledge.

MIYANOKUBO SETO AND HANAGURI SETO

7.43

Miyanokubo Seto (34° 12' N, 122° 04' E) is entered from W between the NW end of Ō Shima (7.1) and the S side of Ōmi Shima (7.22); it is much used by small vessels up to 500 tons passing E/W through Seto Naikai as it is shorter in distance than going through Kurushima Kaikyō (7.1).

A **light** is exhibited from a square concrete tower on **Kayatomari Hana,** the NW extremity of Ō Shima on the S side of the W entrance to Miyanokubo Seto.

Okino Su, with a least depth of 6·4 m, lies in the W approach to the strait 2 miles W of Kayatomari Hana.

An **overhead cable** with a vertical clearance of 41 m, crosses the W end of Miyanokubo Seto close E of Kayatomari Hana; the pylons supporting the cable at each end are prominent.

Hakata Shima, on the N side of Miyanokubo Seto, is separated from the SE end of Ōmi Shima by Hanaguri Seto (7.45). **Hoko San,** the summit of Hakata Shima, is 303 m high, pointed, and remarkable.
7.44

Michika Shima (34° 11·5' N, 133° 04·5' E), 40 m high and flat-topped, lies on the N side of the W entrance to the narrows of Miyanokubo Seto; an **overhead cable** with a least vertical clearance of 36 m, spans the channels on either side of Michika Shima.

A **light** is exhibited from a red concrete tower standing on **Niwatori-ko Shima,** 9 m high and the highest of two rocks lying close off the point 2¼ cables ESE of Michika Shima.

U Shima, 84 m high and densely wooded, divides Miyanokubo Seto into two narrow channels each with a navigable width of about 100 m. The tidal streams in these channels are very strong, sometimes attaining a rate of 9 knots; the passage of either of the two channels should not be attempted without local knowledge.

Funaore Seto or **Arōji Seto** is the N channel and the one used by the majority of small vessels. A **light** is exhibited from a red concrete column standing on the extremity of **Funaore Iwa,** a chain of drying rocks extending 2 cables NE from the N extremity of U Shima.

An **overhead cable** with a vertical clearance of 31 m, spans Funaore Seto.

Kōjin Seto, the channel to the S, is obstructed on its E side by two islets, 25 m and 20 m high, and several rocks, lying close SW of U Shima. **Kōno Se,** with a depth of less than 1 m, and a 7·6 m patch, lie close together in the channel about 3 cables SSW of U Shima.

Mutsuno Hana (34° 11' N, 133° 08' E), the SE extremity of Hakata Shima, lies on the N side of the E entrance to Miyanokubo Seto and is surmounted by a dark conical hill 148 m high. A **light** is exhibited from a red concrete tower on the E extremity of **Mutsu Se,** a reef which extends 2¼ cables E from Mutsuno Hana.

Hanaguri Seto
7.45

Hanaguri Seto (34° 13' N, 133° 04' E) is a narrow channel leading NE and N from the W end of Miyanokubo Seto (7.43) into Hakata Seto. **Ōmi Shima Bridge** with a vertical clearance of about 34 m, spans the channel at its S end; red and green traffic light signals are exhibited on each side of the bridge.

Hanaguri Seto is encumbered with rocks on each side at its narrowest part reducing its navigable width to about 100 m. **Tidal streams** in the strait attain a spring rate of about 7 knots.

Hanaguri Seto is used by ferries and by vessels up to 500 tons, but local knowledge is essential.

A **light** is exhibited from a white round concrete tower standing on a rocky islet situated on the N side of the narrows.

HAKATA SETO

Chart 3604
7.46

Hakata Seto leads SE from the middle of Mihara Seto to Hiuchi Nada and is about 9 miles long.

Tidal streams. At the S entrance to Hakata Seto, between the E end of Hakata Shima (34° 13' N, 133° 09' E) and Tsuba Shima, the spring rate of the tidal stream reaches 5 knots. The rates reach about 3 knots elsewhere in the strait except in the narrows off Tatara Shima (34° 15' N, 133° 03' E) where the rate is 4 to 5 knots. The flood stream (SE-going) is somewhat stronger than the ebb stream (NW-going).

Hakata Seto—north west part
7.47

Ikuchi Shima, on the NE side of Hakata Seto, is a comparatively large island situated SE of Kōne Shima (34° 19' N, 133° 05' E) (7.27); the mountains on it are divided into two groups by a remarkable valley near the middle of the island.

Hyōtan Shima (34° 17' N, 133° 03' E), a small islet 34 m high, lies in the middle of the N end of Hakata Seto; on its summit are two pine trees.

A bank, on the N end of which is situated **Ōtani Iso,** with a least depth of 3·2 m, lies parallel to the SW side of Kōne Shima; a 3·6 m patch lies on the S end of the bank. Two **fish havens** lie within ½ mile S of the S end of this bank.
7.48

Inokuchi Kō (34° 16' N, 133° 03' E), where the **Ōmi Shima Oil Depot** is situated, lies on the NE coast of Ōmi Shima 1 mile SSW of Hyōtan Shima; there are a large number of oil tanks in the vicinity.

Maruzen Sekiyū No. 1 Oil Jetty (34° 15·8' N, 133° 02·8' E) is a T-headed dolphin berth lying close SE of the mouth of **Inokuchi Hon Kawa**; it has a depth of 9·4 m alongside and can accommodate a tanker of 35 000 dwt. There are two mooring buoys off each end of the berth and the jetty is floodlit.

The **tidal streams** on the berth are strong. It is normal to berth head to the stream. A tug is available.

Maruzen Sekiyū No. 2 Oil Jetty (34° 16·0' N, 133° 02·6' E), with a depth of 4 m alongside, lies close N of the mouth of Inokuchi Hon Kawa.

In 1979, a breakwater was under construction to the NW of No. 1 Oil Jetty.

Arrival information. Vessels proceeding to Inokuchi Kō are required to call at Matsuyama Kō or Kōbe Kō for quarantine clearance.

Tatara Saki, a salient point, lies 1 mile SE of Inokuchi Kō; a chain of rocks, some of which dry, extend 2 cables N from the point and **Chitori Ishi,** with a depth of 11·5 m, lies 4 cables N.

A **light** is exhibited from a black round tower with red bands, standing on **Tatara Iso,** a detached rock lying 1½ cables E of Tatara Saki.

Hakata Seto—south part
7.49

Gojunotaka (34° 15' N, 133° 05' E), a steep-to rock with a depth of 5·9 m, lies in the middle of Hakata Seto 1¼ miles SE of Tatara Saki.

Mekari Shō, two rocks with depths, respectively, of 1·8 m and 4·5 m, lies on the N side of the strait ⅓ mile N of **Tayūdono Saki,** the N extremity of Hakata Shima.

Kanzaki Dashi, a rock with a depth of 9·6 m, lies 2¼ cables NW of Tayūdono Saki, and there is a 11·8 m patch of sand and shells 6 cables W of it.

Mekari Shō is the S'most of a number of rocks and shoals lying across the SW entrance of the channel lying between Ikuchi Shima and **Iwagi Shima** to the SE. This channel connects Hakata Seto with Nagae Seto (7.51) and generally has depths of over 10 m in its middle; however, **Tobinoko Shima** (34° 16·6' N, 133° 08·6' E), a rocky islet 24 m high, lies in its narrowest part. The fairway leads SE of the islet but the width is only 80 m.

A **light** is exhibited on the head of a breakwater at **Okogi Kō,** situated at the N end of Iwagi Shima on the SE side of the narrows.
7.50

Kubito Saki (34° 13' N, 133° 09' E), the E extremity of Hakata Shima, lies 2 miles SE of Tayūdono Saki.

Wanwan Se, with a depth of 5·4 m, is the N'most of a chain of below-water rocks extending ⅓ mile N from Kubito Saki; a *light-buoy* is moored on the N side of Wanwan Se.

Akōne Shima, 158 m high and well-wooded, lies close SE of Iwagi Shima and is separated from it by a very narrow channel spanned by two **overhead cables** with a least vertical clearance of 26 m.

A **fish haven,** charted as an obstruction, lies 2¼ cables W of the SW extremity of Akōne Shima.

Iwagi Kō (34° 14·5' N, 133° 09·0' E) protected by a breakwater, lies on the S side of Iwagi Shima. A **light** is exhibited on the head of the breakwater and another **light** is exhibited on the E side of the harbour.

Tsuba Shima (34° 13' N, 133° 09' E) lies close S of Akōne Shima and is separated from it by a narrow channel which is spanned by an **overhead cable** with a vertical clearance of 31 m. The summit of Tsuba Shima, situated near its S end, is 87 m high and faced with a rocky cliff.

The channels between Iwagi Shima and Akōne Shima and between Akōne Shima and Tsuba Shima, are only suitable for small craft.

An **overhead cable** with a vertical clearance of 28 m, spans the S entrance to Hakata Seto between Kubito Saki and Tsuba Shima.

NAGAE SETO AND APPROACHES

Chart 3604
7.51

Nagae Seto lies between the E sides of Akōne Shima (34° 14' N, 133° 10' E) and Iwagi Shima, and the W sides of Sa Shima and Ikina Shima.

Sa Shima (34° 14' N, 133° 12' E) is traversed by hills some of which are covered with dwarf trees and others of bare granite; the summit of the island, 122 m high, lies near its centre.

Ikina Shima lies to the N of Sa Shima and is separated from it by a narrow channel spanned by an **overhead cable** with a vertical clearance of 43 m. The bare white granite hills of Ikina Shima appear from S in strong contrast with the dark forests on Inno Shima farther N.

Two **overhead cables** with a least vertical clearance of 38 m (charted as 33 m), cross Nagae Seto at its narrowest part; two **submarine cables** are laid across the strait and their landing places are marked by **beacons.**

Suzume Shima, 9 m high, and a rocky islet, 16 m high, lie within 1¼ cables W of the W side of the N part of Ikina Shima. A shoal with a least depth of 1·7 m, lies on the W side of the strait 3 cables SE of the N extremity of Iwagi Shima.

The N approach to Nagae Seto leads between Ikuchi Shima and Inno Shima and is spanned by an **overhead cable** with a vertical clearance of about 39 m (charted as 30 m). Several **submarine cables,** their landing places marked by **beacons,** are laid across this strait.

SETODA KŌ AND APPROACHES

Chart 3604
7.52

Setoda Kō (34° 19' N, 133° 06' E) is enclosed by Kōne Shima and Sagi Shima (7.28) and is approached either through Setoda Suidō (34° 18' N, 133° 05' E), a channel between Kōne Shima and Ikuchi Shima, or through channels on either side of Sagi Shima.

Setoda, on the E side of Setoda Suidō, is a popular tourist resort and there is much traffic of small vessels and ferries in and out of the harbour. **Uchino Umi Shipyard** lies on the E side of the N entrance to Setoda Suidō.
7.53

Setoda Suidō has a navigable width of 100 m with depths from 3 m to 7 m; its SW entrance is marked by a *light-buoy* and it is spanned close N of Setoda by **Kōne Bridge** with a vertical clearance of about 23 m and marked by lights. The **tidal streams** in Setoda Suidō reach a rate of about 3½ knots.

The channel between Kōne Shima and Sagi Shima is used by ferries and by vessels proceeding to Uchino Umi Shipyard. A *light-buoy* is moored off the SE end of a narrow middle ground with depths of less than 2 m, lying towards the W side of the channel.

The channel between Ikuchi Shima and Sagi Shima is wide and deep but owing to the shoals in the channel SE and E of Sagi Shima, it is only used by small craft.
7.54

Berths. There is a pontoon jetty with a depth of about 7 m alongside, on the E side of Setoda Suidō close S of the bridge.

A quay with depths alongside from 5·4 m to 7 m is situated in the shipyard about ¼ mile E of the N entrance to Setoda Suidō. No. 1 Dry Dock with a capacity of 37 000 tons lies S of the quay, and there are two other dry docks with a capacity of 4500 tons and 5000 tons, respectively.

Channel east of Sagi Shima
7.55

Nakanomo Su (34° 20' N, 133° 08' E), a bank covered with seaweed and which dries in the centre, lies in the middle of the channel between Sagi Shima and Inno Shima. The N extremity of Nakanomo Su is marked by a *light-buoy*, and there is another *light-buoy* moored 4 cables SSE of the S extremity of the bank.

A *light-buoy* is moored on the E side of the channel which passes E of Nakanomo Su.

Koboso Shima (34° 21' N, 133° 09' E), 48 m high, lies midway between Hoso Shima (7.37) and the NW extremity of Inno Shima; a shoal which dries lies within ¼ mile W of the islet. **Overhead cables** with a vertical

clearance of 33 m, extend from Koboso Shima N to Hoso Shima and S to Inno Shima.

Hakan Shima, 5 m high and fringed with reefs, lies midway between the N extremity of Sagi Shima and Hoso Shima 8 cables E; a **light** is exhibited from a red round concrete tower with black bands standing on the SW end of the islet.

A **light** is exhibited from a white round concrete tower on the NE end of Sagi Shima.

The fairway between the entrance to the N approach to Nagae Seto (7.51) and Hakan Shima nearly 3 miles N, is intricate and many dangers lie in it; it is only suitable for small craft with local knowledge.

YUGE SETO AND NAGASAKI SETO

7.56

Yuge Shima (34° 16' N, 133° 13' E) is separated from the SE coast of Inno Shima (7.39) and the E coast of Sa Shima (7.51) by Yuge Seto; the island is in two parts joined by a low neck. The S part is sparsely covered with pine trees and the N and larger part is mountainous and well wooded, and on it are three prominent peaks; **Mi Yama,** the N'most peak, is 325 m high.

Measured distance. A measured distance, 1852·5 m in length and marked by two pairs of **beacons,** is situated on the SE side of Yuge Shima; the running courses are 053° and 233°.

Anchorage is afforded in depths of about 12 m, mud, in the entrance of a bay on the E side of the low neck joining the two parts of Yuge Shima.

Yuge Seto and approaches
7.57

Yuge Seto is entered from NE between **Miga Saki** (34° 18' N, 133° 13' E), the E extremity of the S part of Inno Shima, and **Umatateno Hana,** the N extremity of Yuge Shima. A *light-buoy*, marking a reef, is moored 2 cables N of Umatateno Hana.

Landmark. Tengu Yama, 207 m high, conical, and with a television tower on its summit, lies in the S part of Inno Shima and is prominent from NE.

Mitsunoshō Wan is situated on the N side of Miga Saki and affords sheltered **anchorage** in depths of less than 6 m, except in E winds. The SW part of the bay lies within the harbour limits of Habu Kō (7.60). A **light** is exhibited on the head of **Hosaki Breakwater** situated in the SW corner of the bay.

The S shore of Yuge Seto between Umatateno Hana and a point 9 cables WSW, is foul for about 2 cables offshore in places.

Fish havens lie on the W side of Yuge Seto close E of the S extremity of Inno Shima.

Aburanookino Ishi, which dries 0·3 m, lies 3¾ cables WSW of **Isega Hana** (34° 16' N, 133° 12' E), the W extremity of Yuge Shima, and is marked close NW by a *light-buoy*.
7.58

The S entrance to Yuge Seto lies between the E side of Sa Shima and the W side of the S part of Yuge Shima; the navigable width of the fairway is reduced to about 1 cable by rocks, close off the E side of Sa Shima, in two places in the narrows.

Two **overhead cables** with a least vertical clearance of 32 m, cross the strait at its narrowest part.

Yuge Kō (34° 15' N, 133° 12' E), protected by breakwaters, lies on the E side of the N entrance to the channel between Sa Shima and Yuge Shima; a **light** is exhibited on the head of the W breakwater.

Nagasaki Seto and Habu Kō
7.59
Nagasaki Seto (34° 16·5' N, 133° 11·0' E), also known as **Habu Kō Fairway,** lies between the SW side of the S end of Inno Shima and the NE side of Ikina Shima. The strait is reduced to a width of less than 1 cable at its S entrance by rocks and shoals on both sides of the channel; the depths in the strait are very irregular and the tidal streams are strong.

7.60
Habu Kō (34° 17' N, 133° 11' E), a harbour well known for its shipbuilding industry and ship repair facilities, lies along the NE shore of Nagasaki Seto; it is an open harbour (see 1.65).

The main part of the **Hitachi Innoshima Shipyard** lies on the NE side of the S end of the strait. Vessels up to 140 000 grt can be accommodated.

There are several mooring buoys off the repair berths.

Another part of the Hitachi Shipyard is situated on the NW side of Yuge Seto, ⅓ mile N of the S end of Inno Shima.

Tokuma Shipyard is situated on the NE side of the N entrance to Nagasaki Seto and can accommodate vessels up to 20 000 grt.

7.61
Facilities. Immigration facilities are available at Habu Kō.

There are four tugs of over 1000 hp for use of large vessels.

Waste oil disposal facilities are available.

Major repairs can be undertaken.

The principal drydocks are:

No.	Length m	Width m	Depth m	Capacity grt
Hitachi Shipyard				
1	175	25·1	6·6	16 000
2	282	46·5	8·8	79 000
3	260	56·7	8·5	69 000
Takuma Shipyard				
1	74·7	10	4·3	1 300
2	134·7	18·6	6·6	8 300

Supplies. Fuel oil can be lightered from the nearest oil terminal.

Fresh water is available at the berths and by water boat.

CHAPTER 8

HIUCHI NADA AND BINGO NADA

GENERAL INFORMATION

Charts 2875, 3604, 3605
8.1

Hiuchi Nada and **Bingo Nada** lie within that portion of Seto Naikai between Kurushima Kaikyō (34° 07' N, 133° 00' E) and Mihara Seto on the W side, and the W end of Bisan Seto (34° 17' N, 133° 33' E) on the E side. Hiuchi Nada is the S part bounded on its S side by the coast of Shikoku; and Bingo Nada is the N part separated from Hiuchi Nada by a chain of islands.

8.2

Routes. The main route through Hiuchi Nada and Bingo Nada from Kurushima Kaikyō (7.1) to the W entrance of Bisan Seto (9.4) is marked by *Bingo Nada Fairway Nos. 1–7 Light-buoys*, about 4 miles apart, and has a minimum depth of 5 m.

The N route from the E entrance of Mekari Seto to the W entrance of Bisan Seto, passes 1 mile N of Hyakkan Shima (34° 18' N, 133° 16' E) (7.41) and joins the main route at *Bingo Nada Fairway No. 7 Light-buoy*.

The recommended tracks to be followed in these two routes are shown on the charts.

The route from the W entrance of Bisan Seto to Niihama Kō (33° 59' N, 133° 17' E) (8.11) leaves the main route at *Bingo Nada Fairway No. 6 Light-buoy* and passes between Eno Shima (34° 10' N, 133° 22' E) and Marugami Shima (34° 09' N, 133° 27' E); it is marked by *Nos. 1–3 Fairway Light-buoys*.

8.3

Fishing. From about April to June, there are **fishing nets** in the vicinity and sometimes across the N route. These nets are indicated by small buoys with flags and flashing lights; it is reported that they are difficult to see when the tidal streams are strong.

Anchorages. In the E part of Hiuchi Nada the depths are nearly everywhere regular. Open anchorage can be obtained almost anywhere but there are many fishing nets and seaweed beds along the coast, some extending up to 1 mile offshore.

Tidal streams. The tidal streams caused by water entering and leaving Seto Naikai through Bungo Suidō and Kii Suidō meet in Hiuchi Nada and Bingo Nada; the positions of the line of division between the E-going and W-going tidal streams varies greatly. Except between the islands the streams are weak, their rates and directions varying remarkably from day to day.

HIUCHI NADA

HIUCHI NADA—WEST PART

Chart 3604

East coasts of Ō Shima and Hakata Shima
8.4

Nagaseno (Kagike) Hana (34° 06' N, 133° 02' E), the S extremity of Ō Shima, is described at 7.16.

Todai Hana (34° 10' N, 133° 07' E), the NE extremity of Ō Shima, is the S entrance point at the E end of Miyanokubo Seto (7.43).

Shikumo Shima, Yoko Shima and **Kamagi Shima** lie on rocky shoals within ¼ mile of the coast off the NE end of Ō Shima.

Hakata Kō (34° 12' N, 133° 08' E) lies on the E coast of Hakata Shima and is entered between Mutsuno Hana (7.44) and **Kanaga Saki,** 1 mile NNE. The bay affords sheltered **anchorage** to small vessels, except in E winds, in depths from 5 m to 10 m, mud and sand.

An inner harbour protected by two breakwaters lies at the head of Hakata kō; a **light** is exhibited on the head of the E breakwater.

Facilities and supplies. There are three small shipyards in the inner harbour; fresh water can be supplied.

There are car ferry services to Onomichi-Itozaki Kō and to Imabari Kō.

Waka Su (34° 12' N, 133° 10' E), a detached bank with a least depth of 7·5 m, lies between 1½ and 2 miles E of the entrance to Hakata Kō; a **fish haven** lies about ½ mile WNW of the bank.

Islands and dangers in the east approach to Kurushima Kaikyō
8.5

Heichi Shima (34° 01' N, 133° 06' E), 95 m high, lies on the S side of the E approach to Kurushima Kaikyō; there is a clump of tall pine trees on its summit and rows of trees on its slopes.

Koheichi Shima, 50 m high, lies close E of Heichi Shima.

Shirakabe Iwa, a remarkable pointed rock 13 m high, lies ½ mile S of Heichi Shima.

Teraga Iso, with a least depth of 4·7 m, lies with its shallowest part 2 miles WNW of Heichi Shima.

Higi Shima (34° 03' N, 133° 06' E), 57 m high and flat-topped, lies 2 miles N of Heichi Shima; a **light** is exhibited from a white column standing near the summit of the island. **Tsubu Shima,** 19 m high, is the highest and N'most of three islets lying close off the NW end of Higi Shima; **Kohigi Shima,** 59 m high, lies 2 cables NE of the island.

Ashika Iso, a rock which dries 2·4 m, lies 1 mile ENE of Kohigi Shima and on it stands a **beacon** (red and black), 8 m in height; a *light-buoy* is moored 2 cables ENE of the rock. **Aino Iwa,** which dries 0·9 m, lies 2 cables SW of Ashika Iso.

Okino Se, an isolated steep-to rock with a depth of 5·8 m, lies 2¼ miles N of Higi Shima. In 1980, Okino Se was marked by a red pillar *light-buoy*.

8.6

Kaji Shima (34° 07' N, 133° 10' E), 78 m high, round-topped and covered with bamboo grass, lies 5 miles NE of Higi Shima.

Shisaka Shima is the collective name of a group of islands lying within 2 miles SE of Kaji Shima.

Nezumi Shima (34° 06' N, 133° 11' E), the SW island in the group, is 48 m high and round-topped.

Ieno Shima lies 1½ cables ENE of Nezumi Shima and is joined to **Mino Shima** close SE by reclaimed land.

Landmark. The tall chimney of the former Sumitomo Metal Works stands at an elevation of 109 m on Ieno Shima and is prominent from a distance.

Bandai Iso, a steep-to rock which sometimes dries, lies 1½ miles SE of Nezumi Shima; a *light-buoy* is moored 1½ cables SE of the rock.

Myōjin Shima, 87 m high and covered with bamboo grass, lies 1 mile NNE of Nezumi Shima.

HIUCHI NADA—SOUTH SIDE
SŌSHA KAWA TO SAIJŌ KŌ

Chart 3604
8.7

The greater part of the coast of Shikoku forming the S shore of Hiuchi Nada is flat and consists mainly of sand and gravel beaches with but few cliffs.

The coast between the mouth of Sōsha Kawa (34° 03' N, 133° 01' E) (7.17) and **Ōsakino Hana,** a point 5 miles SSE which slopes from N to S, is backed by hills.

Landmarks. Karako Yama, an isolated conical hill 105 m high, lies within ½ mile of the coast 2 miles SSE of Sōsha Kawa and is prominent.

Kasamatsu Yama (33° 59' N, 133° 02' E) (Chart 2875), 326 m high, lies 1½ miles W of Ōsakino Hana and from E appears flat-topped.

Tōyo Kō
8.8

Tōyo Kō, consisting of the harbour of Nyūkawa Kō (8.9) and Saijō Kō (8.10), lies in a bight situated between Ōsakino Hana and Niihama Kō, 9 miles E.

8.9

Nyūkawa Kō (33° 57' N, 133° 07' E) lies 3 miles SE of Ōsakino Hana; in the E part of the harbour are situated the factories of **Sumitomo Heavy Industries** and **Sumitomo Tōyo Aluminium.** The harbour consists of two basins separated by an area of reclaimed land.

The commercial and industrial town of **Tōyo** backs the harbour.

Landmarks. A power station chimney (red and white) (33° 55·9' N, 133° 07·1' E) with four stacks, stands at an elevation of 182 m on the W side of the E basin and is the highest of several chimneys in the harbour area.

West basin. The channel leading to the W basin is protected from W by a breakwater, and in 1978, another breakwater was under construction on the E side; a **light** is exhibited on the head of the W breakwater. The channel is marked by a pair of *light-buoys* about 7 cables SW of the head of the W breakwater, and is dredged to a depth of 4·3 m.

East basin. The channel leading to the E basin is marked by two pairs of *light-buoys*, and is dredged to a depth of 5 m. The basin is also dredged to a depth of 5 m

and is spanned by an **overhead cable** with a vertical clearance of 48 m, 3 cables within its entrance, and by another cable with a vertical clearance of about 35 m, farther in.

Berths. Hōjō Quay, with a reported depth of 5·5 m alongside, lies in the SE part of the W basin, and **Outer Harbour Quay,** with a depth of 4·5 m alongside, lies at the root of the W breakwater.

Sumitomo Heavy Industries Quay, with a depth of 5·5 m alongside, lies on the E side of the entrance to the E basin, and **Shikoku Electricity Ferry Quay** lies on the E side of the S end of the basin and has a depth of 5 m alongside.

There are two shipyards in Nyūkawa Kō which can carry out repairs to small vessels. There is a ferry service to Ōsaka Kō.

8.10

Saijō Kō (33° 56' N, 133° 10' E) lies at the mouth of **Honjin Kawa,** 3 miles E of Nyūkawa Kō; **Saijō,** a textile manufacturing town, lies along the banks of the river. There are numerous chimneys and oil tanks on both sides of the inner part of the harbour.

The entrance to the channel leading through reclaimed land to the harbour, is protected on either side by short breakwaters; *No. 1* and *No. 2 Light-buoys* mark the entrance to the fairway through this channel and has depths from 3 m to 4 m.

Leading lights are exhibited from white round towers (triangular topmark) situated at the head of the harbour; the lights in line bear 155° and lead through the fairway.

An **overhead cable** with a vertical clearance of 40 m, spans the harbour 3 cables N of the leading lights.

Berths. Shikoku Electricity Jetties with depths up to 4·5 m alongside, lie on the W side of the harbour, and **No. 1 Landing Jetty** with depths from 3 m to 5 m alongside, lies on the E side of the mouth of Honjin Kawa.

NIIHAMA KŌ

Charts 698 plan of Niihama Kō, 3604
8.11

Niihama Kō (33° 59' N, 133° 17' E), a specified port (see 1.64) and a major industrial harbour, is divided into Niihama Ku (8.12) and Takihama Ku (8.18), the W and E parts, respectively. Niihama Ku is further divided into Nos. 1 to 4 Areas which are indicated on Chart 698.

Niihama, which had a population of 130 000 in 1973, is the centre of the industrial zone that extends along the S shore of Hiuchi Nada and manufactures machinery and chemical products.

Pilotage. Pilotage is not compulsory but is recommended. Harbour pilots are available at the anchorage; 48 hours notice is required.

Tidal streams outside the breakwaters at Niihama Ku are E-going on the rising tide and W-going on the falling tide with a maximum rate of ¾ knot; inside the breakwaters the streams are weak.

Landmarks. Numerous conspicuous factory chimneys, buildings and oil tanks stand on both the W and E sides of Niihama Ku No. 1 Area; in particular the following are good marks:

The tall chimney (red and white) (33° 57·9' N, 133° 15·7' E), with an elevation of 133 m, of the **Sumitomo Chemical Works** on the W side.

A chimney (red and white) (33° 58·4' N, 133° 16·8' E), with an elevation of 123 m, on the E side of the area.

The N side of Miyo Shima (33° 58·6' N, 133° 15·6' E) (8.13) which is reddish brown in colour.

At night the lights of the factories can be seen at a distance.

Anchorages. The **quarantine anchorage,** indicated on Chart 698, is situated in Niihama Ku No. 2 Area; a *light-buoy* is moored on the SW edge of the anchorage.

The **dangerous cargo anchorage** is in No. 3 Area.

Chart 698 plan of Nihama Kō
Niihama Ku
8.12

No. **4 Area** lies on the W side of the harbour area of **Niihama Ku** (33° 58' N, 133° 16' E).

Funagami Iwa (33° 58·2' N, 133° 14·4' E), a rock which dries 2·7 m, is situated in the N part of No. 4 Area; a **light** is exhibited from a red round concrete tower with black bands standing on the rock.

A number of basins, quays and jetties are situated on the W side of reclaimed land bordering the E side of the area.

In 1979, a breakwater was under construction and harbour development work in progress, close W of the S part of No. 4 Area.

8.13

No. **1 Area,** the inner harbour of Niihama Ku, is entered between two breakwaters situated on the E side of the former islet of **Miyo Shima,** 73 m high, flat-topped and thickly covered with trees, and which is joined to the mainland by extensive reclaimed land forming the W side of the inner harbour. A **light** is exhibited at the head of each of the breakwaters.

No. **1 Fairway,** with a least depth of 7·3 m, leads into the inner harbour. No. **2 Fairway,** leading to **Nishi-chō Hakuchi,** branches off from No. 1 Fairway about 5 cables S of the harbour entrance.

An **overhead cable** with a vertical clearance of 48 m in its S part.

8.14

Kokuryō Kawa flows into the sea about 1 mile E of the entrance to the inner harbour and considerable reclamation work has been carried out in the intervening area. A breakwater extends NNE from the E entrance point to Kokuryō Kawa.

Berths and facilities in Niihama Ku
8.15

Berths. The principal berths in Niihama Ku are as follows:

Berth & Position	Length m	Depth m	Capacity tons
Sumitomo Chemicals Kikumoto			
No. 6 Quay (K6)			
(33° 58·8' N, 133° 16·5' E)	200	14	44 000
No. 5 Quay			
(33° 58·5' N, 133° 16·5' E)	Dolphins	6·5	3 000
No. 4 Quay (K4)			
(33° 58·5' N, 133° 16·6' E)	120	9·1–9·4	10 000
Sumitomo Chemicals Ōe			
E No. 4 Quay (O4)	Dolphins	6·4	3 000
(33° 58·3' N, 133° 16·4' E)		(reported)	
Sumitomo Metalworks			
Bekko Quay (B3)	100	10	10 000
(33° 57·9' N, 133° 16·0' E)			

Sumitomo Chemicals Niihama			
Fertiliser Quay (N4)	Dolphins	7·5	5 000
(33° 57·8' N, 133° 15·8' E)			
No. 3 Berthing Quay (N8)	Dolphins	9·4	20 000
(33° 58·0' N, 133° 15·8' E)			
Floating Jetty	60	4–6	2 000
(33° 57·7' N, 133° 15·9' E)			

There are several mooring buoys in No. 1 Area.
8.16

Facilities. Offices of the Maritime Safety Agency, Customs, Quarantine and Immigration are located in the joint Harbour Office situated on **Nishihara Quay** (33° 57·8' N, 133° 16·3' E).

Tugs and lighters are available and there are several harbour lauches.

There are no repair facilities for large vessels.

De-ratting; see 1.70.

Supplies. Fresh water is available at the principal quays and there are two water boats.

Communications. There is a ferry service to Kōbe Kō.

Charts 3604, 2875
Takihama Ku
8.17

Habu Saki (33° 59·5' N, 133° 19·5' E) lies on the E harbour limit of Niihama Ku No. 2 Area; a **light** is exhibited from a white round concrete tower situated on the point. **Habu Yama,** 100 m high, lies close SE of Habu Saki and as the land S of it is low, it appears as an island.

Two **fish havens,** charted as obstructions, lie within ½ mile N of Habu Saki.

Kuro Shima, 49 m high and fringed with rocky ledges, lies close inshore 1 mile ESE of Habu Saki; a *light-buoy* is moored 3 cables NW of Kuro Shima.

Ō Shima, 145 m high with a sharp peak, lies ½ mile NE of Kuro Shima.
8.18

Takihama Ku (33° 59' N, 133° 21' E), which is within the harbour limits of Niihama Kō (8.11), lies between Kuro Shima and Ō Shima and is a timber harbour.

Kajikake, with a depth of 0·3 m, lies 2 cables off the W side of Ō Shima and is marked close NW by a *light-buoy.* A **fish haven** lies 3 cables NW of Kajikake. A red mooring buoy, on which an orange light is exhibited, is moored close SE of the fish haven.

Anchorage. Good anchorage, sheltered from S and W winds, is afforded in the area enclosed by Ō Shima and the coast SW in depths from 5 m to 20 m, mud.

A **submarine cable** is laid between Ō Shima and the coast SW; its landing places are marked by **beacons.**

A small basin with depths from 2 m to 5 m, lies on the SE side of Kuro Shima. **Mikihama Quay,** with a depth of 4·3 m alongside, lies on the S side of this basin.

HIUCHI NADA—EAST SIDE
MISHIMA-KAWANOE KŌ TO MI SAKI

Chart 2875
Mishima-Kawanoe Kō
8.19

Mishima-Kawanoe Kō (34° 00' N, 133° 33' E), an open harbour (see 1.65), lies in the SE corner of Hiuchi Nada and embraces the two harbours of Mishima Kō and Kawanoe Kō; the port is fronted by an extensive area of reclaimed land on which stands an industrial zone containing a number of paper mills.

The towns of **Iyo-Mishima (Mishima)** and **Kawanoe** are both well known for their paper making industries and had a combined population of 75 000 in 1973.

Approaches to Mishima-Kawanoe Kō
8.20
Nabe Iso (34° 01' N, 133° 31' E), a steep-to rock with a depth of 7·8 m (25 ft), lies in the approaches to Mishima-Kawanoe Kō, 1¼ miles NW of the entrance to Mishima Kō; the rock is marked by a *light-buoy* (black and red in bands; red light flashing every 4 seconds) on its E side.

Pilotage. Pilots are available with sufficient advance notice.

Landmarks. Shiro Yama (34° 00·6' N, 133° 34·2' E), 60 m high, and **Iji Yama,** 69 m high, lies close together on the coast in the N part of Mishima-Kawanoe Kō; there is a public park on Shiro Yama which is a good mark from seaward.

A tall chimney (red and white) (33° 59·6' N, 133° 33·3' E), with an elevation of 182 m, stands on reclaimed land in the N part of Mishima Kō and is prominent.

Anchorage. A **quarantine anchorage** is situated on the NE side of the entrance to Mishima Kō.

Mishima Kō
8.21
Mishima Kō (33° 59·7' N, 133° 32·8' E), the SW part of Mishima-Kawanoe Kō, is protected on its W side by a breakwater extending ¼ mile N from the coast, and on its NE side by a large reclaimed area on which stands the **Taiō Paper Mill.** A light is exhibited on the head of the breakwater.

An orange *light-buoy* is moored 1 mile WNW of the head of the breakwater.

Muramatsu Quays lie on the NE and SW faces of the reclaimed area lying on the NE side of Mishima Kō; **East Wharf** lies in the S part of the harbour. There is a dolphin berth with a depth of 9 m alongside projecting N from East Wharf.

Kawanoe Kō
8.22
Kawanoe Kō (34° 01·0' N, 133° 34·5' E) lies at the NE end of Mishima-Kawanoe Kō and consists of a basin protected by two breakwaters and which is entered from N; a light is exhibited at the head of each breakwater. **Higashi Kō Quay** lies on the E side of the outer part of the basin close within the entrance; the inner part of the basin is used by fishing vessels.

Sunasute Iso, with a depth of 4·8 m (16 ft), lies ¼ cable N of the head of the W breakwater, and a **fish haven** with a least depth of 5·5 m (18 ft) lies 1 cable farther N.

Nishi Kō Quays lie on reclaimed land on either side of the mouth of **Kinsei Kawa** which flows into the sea close S of Shiro Yama and 9 cables SSW of the basin at Kawanoe Kō. A *light-buoy* is moored close NNW of Nishi Kō No. 1 Quay situated on the S side of the mouth of the river, and a **fish haven** lies 3 cables NW of Nishi Kō No. 2 Quay on the N side.

Berths and facilities in Mishima-Kawanoe Kō
8.23
Berths. The principal berths in the port, from S to N, are as follows:

Berth & Position	Length m	Depth m	Capacity tons
Mishima East Wharf			
East Wharf Quay	200	4	—
(33° 59·2' N, 133° 33·0' E)			
Taiō Dolphin Berth	—	9	30 000
(33° 59·5' N, 133° 33·1' E)			
Okidai Quay	220	3·5	—
(33° 59·4' N, 133° 33·2' E)			
Muramatsu (SW side)			
(33° 59·7' N, 133° 33·1' E)			
No. 1 Quay	260	6·5–7·5	3 000
No. 2 Quay	385	14–15	—
Muramatsu (NE side)			
(34° 00·0' N, 133° 33·3' E)			
No. 3 Quay	90	5·5–7·5	2 000
No. 4 Quay	260	5·5–7·5	5 000
Nishi Kō No. 1 Quay	480	11·5–12	30 000
(34° 00·3' N, 133° 33·5' E)			
Nishi Kō No. 2 Quay	180	4·5–5	500
(34° 00·5' N, 133° 33·8' E)			
Higashi Kō Quay	210	5	500
(34° 01·1' N, 133° 34·5' E)			

8.24
Facilities. Mishima-Kawanoe Kō is an immigration and quarantine port.

Tugs can be ordered from another port when required. De-ratting; see 1.70.

Supplies. Fresh water is available at the quays. Fuel oil can be supplied with sufficient notice.

Communications. The car ferry from Niihama Kō to Kōbe Kō calls at Kawanoe Kō.

Yoki Saki to Mi Saki
8.25
Yoki Saki (34° 02' N, 133° 36' E), a low point 2 miles NE of Kawanoe Kō (8.22), is at the extremity of a spur sloping down from the hills and in consequence is easy to identify.

Toyohama Kō (34° 04' N, 133° 38' E), a small harbour protected by breakwaters, lies 2¼ miles NE of Yoki Saki; a **light** is exhibited at the head of the W breakwater. In 1977, reclamation work was in progress close S of the harbour.

Chart 3605
8.26
Kanonji Kō (34° 07' N, 133° 38' E) lies 3 miles N of Toyohama Kō (8.25) and is situated within the mouths of **Ichinotani Kawa** and **Saita Kawa. Kotohiki Park,** famous as a tourist resort, lies on the N side of Saita Kawa, the N of the two rivers.

Landmark. Kotohiki Yama, 58 m high and remarkable, lies on the N bank of Saita Kawa ¼ mile within its mouth and is surmounted by a shrine and an observation platform.

Caution. From October to June, shell fish and seaweed beds, extending out to 2¼ miles offshore, are to be found off the coast both N and S of Kanonji Kō.

The part of the harbour which lies in the mouth of Ichinotani Kawa is entered between two breakwaters and is protected from W by a detached breakwater. A **light** is exhibited at the head of each breakwater and at the S end of the detached breakwater.

The outer basin which lies in the mouth of Ichinotani Kawa, has depths of about 6 m and has a wharf with a depth of 4 m alongside, within it.

A breakwater is situated on the N side of the mouth of

Saita Kawa; a **light** is exhibited at the head of the breakwater. The area within the mouth of the river dries.

8.27

Landmark. Tsukumo Yama (34° 09' N, 133° 39' E), a conical hill 153 m high, surmounts a point lying 1½ miles N of Kanonji Kō; it appears as an island from N and on its SW side has a remarkable landslide.

Muromoto Kō, protected by a short breakwater, lies close N of Tsukumo Yama; a **light** is exhibited on the head of the breakwater.

Ō Tsuta Shima (34° 12' N, 133° 38' E), 92 m high, and **Ko Tsuta Shima,** 63 m high, lie close together about ½ mile offshore, 3 miles N of Tsukumo Yama; they are joined to the coast E by banks which dry. A **light** is exhibited on the head of a breakwater at **Nio Kō,** E of Ō Tsuta Shima.

Tenjinno Iso, a steep-to rock with a depth of 7·4 m over it, lies 1¾ miles W of Ō Tsuta Shima.

8.28

Maruyama Shima (34° 13' N, 133° 37' E), 101 m high, lies 1 mile NNW of Ō Tsuta Shima and is joined to the coast NE by a bank which dries; it is thickly wooded, dark and prominent.

Namari Kō (34° 15' N, 133° 35' E), protected by breakwaters, lies in the S bay of **Namari Ura** situated 3 miles NW of Maruyama Shima; a **light** is exhibited at the head of one of the breakwaters.

Mi Saki (34° 15·5' N, 133° 33·7' E) is the W end of a long and narrow peninsula which forms the S entrance point to Bisan Seto; it is thickly wooded and from it a chain of hills, gradually increasing in height, extends 2¼ miles SE to **Shiunde San,** 352 m high, flat-topped and bare. The land close SE of Shiunde San is low and the peninsula on which the hill stands appears from SW as an island.

A **light** is exhibited from a white square concrete tower situated on Mi Saki.

Ogo Ishi consisting of two rocks the highest of which is 2 m high, lies within 1 cable W of Mi Saki.

ISLANDS LYING BETWEEN HIUCHI NADA AND BINGO NADA

Charts 3604, 3605

8.29

Takaikami Shima (34° 11' N, 133° 16' E), 257 m high, lies on the S side of the recommended track through Seto Naikai; its summit, which slopes gradually N and S but falls steeply on its E and W sides, is a sharp and prominent peak. A **light** is exhibited from a white octagonal concrete tower standing on the slopes of the hills on the N side of the island; a **ramark** transmits from the light-tower.

Toyo Shima (34°14' N, 133°16' E) lies on the N side of the recommended track 2 miles N of Takaikami Shima; it has two summits the W and highest of which is 108 m high.

Uo Shima (34° 10' N, 133° 19' E), on which are three hills the two E of which are 169 m high, lies 1½ miles ESE of Takaikami Shima and is much cultivated. **Hyōtan Shima,** 58 m high, lies on the S end of a shallow spit which extends 2½ cables S of Uo Shima; there are a number of tall pine trees on the summit of the islet.

A **fish haven** lies ¾ mile N of the NE point of Uo Shima.

Chart 3605

8.30

Eno Shima (34° 10' N, 133° 22' E), 131 m high, lies 1½ miles ESE of Uo Shima (8.29); its W side is steeply sloping and covered with grass and its N end is low. An islet, 16 m high, lies close off the S end of Eno Shima, and **Yoshita Iso,** with a depth of 1·3 m, lies 5 cables farther SSE.

Marugami Shima (34° 09' N, 133° 27' E), 4½ miles ESE of Eno Shima, is 83 m high and wooded, especially on its N side; except during the fishing season, the islet is uninhabited. **Onko Iwa,** which dries 4 m, lies 4 cables ESE of Marugami Shima.

Chart 2875

Ōmata (Ō Mata) Shima (34° 06' N, 133° 27' E), 55 m (179 ft) high, lies 2½ miles S of Marugami Shima; its N and S sides are thickly covered with pine trees and its flat summit is cultivated. **Komata Shima,** 35 m (116 ft) high to the tops of the trees, lies at the extremity of a reef extending 3 cables SE from Ōmata Shima.

Chart 3605

8.31

Ibuki Shima (34° 08' N, 133° 32' E), a steep-to island, lies 3½ miles ESE of Marugami Shima; its SE part is low and flat but at its NW end there is a wooded steep-sided hill 122 m high. A **light** is exhibited from a white round concrete tower standing on Aka Saki, the S extremity of the island.

A fishing village is situated in the middle of Ibuki Shima, and a basin protected by **Kitaura Breakwater** lies on the N side of the island; a **light** is exhibited on the head of the breakwater.

BINGO NADA

BINGO NADA—NORTH SIDE

Charts 3604, 3605

Approaches to Matsunaga Wan

8.32

Yoko Shima (34° 20' N, 133° 17' E), 257 m high, lies on the N side of the SE entrance to Mekari Seto (7.37); it is covered with pine trees and a group of oil tanks stands on its W side.

Maruzen Sekiyū Dolphin Pier, with a mooring buoy at each end, lies on the S side of the SW extremity of Yoko Shima; it has a depth of 10 m alongside and can accommodate tankers up to 40 000 dwt. The berth is unsuitable during strong winds and heavy seas from S.

Ategi Shima, lying close off the SW extremity of Yoko Shima, is described at 7.40.

A narrow channel, spanned by a swing **bridge** and passable only by small craft, separates Yoko Shima from

Ta Shima to the NE. **Yokota Kō,** protected by a breakwater, lies on the E side of Yoko Shima 3 cables S of the bridge; a **light** is exhibited on the head of the breakwater.

Ta Shima (34° 21' N, 133° 19' E), close NE of Yoko Shima, is divided into two parts by an isthmus; **Taka Yama,** 328 m high, is situated at the SW end of the island.

Hakosaki Kō, protected by a breakwater from which a light is exhibited, lies near the SE extremity of Ta Shima.

8.33

Abuto Seto, between Ta Shima and the mainland of Honshū to the N, is about 2 cables wide at its SE entrance; **Abuto Saki,** on the E side of the entrance, is surmounted by a shrine. A **light** is exhibited from a white concrete tower standing on the point.

Overhead cables with a least vertical clearance of 44 m, span Abuto Seto at its SE entrance.

Tidal streams in Abuto Seto are strong and it should only be used by small vessels with local knowledge.

Three **fish havens** lie on the E side of Abuto Seto within 5 cables N of Abuto Saki; another fish haven lies 7 cables NNW of the point.

Manaita Zowai (34° 22·2' N, 133° 19·5' E), a rock which dries 2·6 m, lies almost in the middle of the channel 2 cables NE of the N extremity of Ta Shima; a **light** is exhibited from a red round concrete tower standing on this rock. The deeper channel is to the S of Manaita Zowai.

Ōno Zowai, a rock which dries, lies in the W entrance to Abuto Seto on the S side of the fairway, nearly 1 mile W of Manaita Zowai; a **light** is exhibited from a red round concrete tower standing on the rock. A shoal with depths of less than 2 m extends 2½ cables SE from Ōno Zowai.

Kurikuwa Zowai, a rock which dries, lies on the N side of the fairway, 7 cables NW of Ōno Zowai; a **light** is exhibited from a red 6-sided concrete tower with black bands standing on the rock.

Chitose Kō (35° 23' N, 133° 18' E), where there is a shipyard, borders the N side of the W entrance to Abuto Seto, to the E of Kurikuwa Zowai.

Katabira Zowai, a drying rock standing on a shoal with depths of less than 4 m, lies in the W approach to Abuto Seto, 1 mile WSW of Ōno Zowai; a **light** is exhibited from a red round concrete tower with black bands standing on the rock.

Chart 3604
8.34

Momo Shima (34° 22' N, 133° 16' E), 183 m high and of reddish brown colour, lies 1 mile N of Yoko Shima (8.32); its W side is precipitous.

Measured distance. A measured distance of 929·6 m, the N and S limits of which are marked by a pair of beacons lies off the SW coast of Momo Shima; the running course is with the 163 m summit 6¼ cables NNW of the NW extremity of Momo Shima, bearing 003°.

Ka Shima, a conical reddish-brown coloured islet, is 102 m high and lies ¼ mile W of Momo Shima. **Okino Taka Sowa,** with a depth of 4 m, lies at the extremity of a reef which dries in places, extending 3½ cables SW from the SW side of Ka Shima.

Shira Ishi, a rocky islet 5 m high, lies 6 cables S of Ka Shima.

Niboneno Sowa, a group of rocks, lies ½ mile W of Ka Shima; the W rock of this group dries 2·4 m and the E

rock dries 1·5 m. A *light-buoy* is moored close E of Niboneno Sowa.

Tosaki Seto and Matsunaga Wan
8.35

Tosaki Seto (34° 23' N, 133° 15' E), the S entrance of Matsunaga Wan, lies between the E extremity of Mukai Shima and the mainland E. **Takoma Sowa,** a rock with a depth of 4·5 m, lies almost in the middle of the channel in the S entrance to the straits; a *light-buoy* is moored close S of the rock.

Landmarks. A cliff at the rocky W entrance point of Tosaki Seto and a clump of pine trees on a hill 3 cables N, are both prominent.

A *light-buoy* (black; white light flashing every 4 seconds) is moored on the W side of Tosaki Seto in its narrowest part.

A **submarine drainpipe** is laid through Tosaki Seto on its E side on the alignment of two beacons (red light flashing), bearing about 002°, situated close together about 6 cables N of the N end of the strait on the mud flats of Matsunaga Wan.

From September to April there are seaweed and oyster beds on either side of Tosaki Seto.

No. 1 Fairway which leads from the N end of Tosaki Seto into Onomichi Seto, is described at 7.34.

Matsunaga Wan (34° 25' N, 133° 15' E), within the harbour limits of Onomichi-Itozaki Kō (7.31), is a landlocked bay to the NE of the E end of Onomichi Seto; the greater part of it is obstructed by shoals which dry but between them there are three creeks suitable from small craft. In 1977, harbour development work was in progress on the W side of the bay.

Anchorage. Matsunaga Wan affords anchorage in depths from 5 m to 10 m in its S part.

Chart 3605
Abuto Saki to Sensui Shima
8.36

Abura Shō (34° 22' N, 133° 22' E) 1 m high, lies 2 cables offshore ¼ mile E of the entrance to Abuto Seto (8.33); a **light** is exhibited from a red round concrete tower with black bands, standing on Abura Shō.

Tsugaru Shima, a wooded islet 15 m high and fringed with rocks, lies ¼ mile ENE of Abura Shō.

Chart 695 plan of Fukuyama Kō and approaches
8.37

Tamatsu Shima (34° 22' N, 133° 23' E), an islet 12 m high, lies 2 miles ENE of the entrance to Abuto Seto and from its E side a breakwater extends 1 cable E; a **light** is exhibited at the head of the breakwater.

Hira Kō, a small fishing harbour protected by breakwaters, is entered close W of Tamatsu Shima.

Tomo Kō, protected by breakwaters and within the harbour limits of Fukuyama Kō, is entered 2½ cables N of Tamatsu Shima; a **light** is exhibited at the head of the E breakwater. There are depths of about 3 m in the harbour but it dries within ½ cable of its W side; there is a landing pier and a jetty in its NE corner.

Anchorage can be obtained off Tomo Kō in depths from 6 m to 9 m, mud, SE of Tamatsu Shima.

Submarine cables are laid from Hira Kō to Hashiri Shima (34° 21' N, 133° 26' E) and a **submarine pipeline** is laid from Tomo Kō to the same island.

8.38

Sensui Shima (34° 23' N, 133° 24' E) lies 3 cables ENE of Tomo Kō; its coasts are cliffy and are fringed with islets and shoals on all sides. A radio tower with a parabolic antennae stands on the summit of the island which is 158 m high.

Benten Shima, a small rocky islet 12 m high, lies in the middle of the channel between Sensui Shima and the mainland; a shrine, illuminated at night, stands on the islet and is a good mark. A rock which dries 2·1 m, lies on the E side of the S entrance to the channel 2 cables SSE of Benten Shima.

Tsutsuji Shima, 24 m high and covered with pine trees, lies on a reef 1½ cables off the SE side of Sensui Shima.

Shirōsaburō Shō, marked by a white **beacon,** lies 1½ cables N of the NW extremity of Sensui Shima.

SOUTH APPROACHES TO FUKUYAMA KŌ

Chart 3605
8.39
Okino Hachikasano Se (34° 19' N, 133° 24' E), a rocky patch with a depth of 14·3 m, lies 3½ miles S of Sensui Shima (8.38) and is marked close SE by a *light-buoy.*

Uji Shima (34° 19' N, 133° 28' E), 117 m high, lies 3¼ miles E of Okino Hachikasano Se; on it are two hills lying E and W of each other.

Chart 695 plan of Fukuyama Kō and approaches
8.40
Hashiri Shima (34° 20' N, 133° 26' E) lies 2½ miles SE of Sensui Shima and its summit, which is situated in its E part, is 179 m high. **Kanayama Hana** is the SE extremity of a small peninsula with a low isthmus at the SE end of the island.

Kajiya Shima, a rocky islet 42 m high to the tops of the trees, lies 4 cables NW of Hashiri Shima.

Hashiri Kō, protected by breakwaters, is situated on the NW side of Hashiri Shima; a **light** is exhibited on the head of the W breakwater.
8.41
A *fairway light-buoy* (34° 21' N, 133° 24' E) is moored in the SW entrance of the channel between Hashiri Shima and Sensui Shima.

Kōno Ishi (34° 22' N, 133° 26' E), 1 m high, lies 1 mile NNW of the N extremity of Hashiri Shima; a **light** is exhibited from a red round concrete tower with black bands standing on the rock.

Hakama Shima, 34 m high and flat-topped, lies 1 mile NE of Hashiri Shima. **Towu,** a rock drying 2·2 m, lies close off the E side of the islet.

Chart 3605
8.42
Ōtobi Shima (34° 20' N, 133° 30' E), 152 m high, lies 2 miles E of Hashiri Shima.

Kobi Shima, 79 m high, lies close NE of Ōtobi Shima and is separated from it by a narrow channel; the W half of this channel is shoal but there is a depth of over 10 m in the E half.

Habu Shima, small, wooded and 56 m high, lies 1¼ miles SSE of Ōtobi Shima; shoals extend 1 cable SW and about 2½ cables NE from the islet.

Misaki Dashi, a steep-to rock with a depth of 3·9 m over it, lies 1 mile NE of Habu Shima.

Mu Shima (34° 18' N, 133° 32' E) lies on the N side of the W entrance to Bisan Seto (9.4) and has a wooded summit 185 m high. A **light** is exhibited from a white round concrete tower situated near the S extremity of

Mu Shima; a **racon** transmits and a fog horn is sounded from the light-tower.

Nezura Iwa, which dries 1·7 m, lies 4½ cables W of the SW extremity of Mu Shima; a *light-buoy* is moored close S of the rock.

FUKUYAMA KŌ

Chart 695 plan of Fukuyama Kō and approaches
8.43
Fukuyama Kō (34° 26' N, 133° 27' E), a specified port (see 1.64), lies in the N part of Bingo Nada; a large industrial complex embracing the **Japan Steel Tubes Steelworks,** lies on reclaimed land at the head of the main channel into the port, on its W side.

Fukuyama which in 1973 had a population of 276 000, lies about 3 miles NW of the industrial complex and is approached through an inner harbour which was formally a canal.

Pilotage is not compulsory but is recommended.

Landmarks. A large number of chimneys and oil tanks, indicated on the chart, are situated in the E part of the Japan Steel Tubes Steelworks and many of them are conspicuous.

A prominent television tower stands at an elevation of 371 m on the summit of Kōno Shima (34° 27' N, 133° 30' E) (8.48).

A **quarantine anchorage** (34° 23' N, 133° 26' E), 8 cables in diameter, lies on the S harbour limit.

Harbour approaches
8.44
Fukuyama Kō is approached by a main channel, 6 miles in length and about 2 cables wide, dredged to a depth of 16 m and marked by *light-buoys.* The entrance to this channel lies 2 miles E of Sensui Shima and close NW of a *light-buoy* moored 2 cables NW of **Shirodashi Iso** (34° 22·2' N, 133° 27·4' E), with a depth of 0·3 m.

No. 1 and *No. 2 Light-buoys,* the outermost pair of channel buoys, are moored 1 mile NW of Shirodashi Iso.

Leading lights are exhibited at the N end of the port; the lights in line bearing 000½° lead through the main channel.

Between *No. 9* and *No. 11 Light-buoys,* a branch channel leads off NW for 2 miles, thence N to the entrance to the inner harbour; it is marked by *light-buoys* and has depths from 10 m to 12 m in its outer part.

Leading lights, in line bearing 300°, lead through the first leg of this channel which is bordered on each side by reclaimed land.

Harbour
8.45
Raw Materials Quay lies along the W side of the N part of the main channel.

South Quay and **Finished Products Quay** lie, respectively, on the NE and E sides of the branch channel. **Japan Chemicals Quay** and **Chūkoku Steel Quay** with depths from 2·5 m to 5 m alongside, lie on reclaimed land on the S side of the channel.

A **signal station** stands at the corner of the reclaimed land close N of the junction of the main and branch channels; berthing signals are made from it.

The **inner harbour** leading to Fukuyama, is narrow and has depths from 2·5 m to 3·5 m; it is spanned near its entrance by an **overhead cable** with a vertical clearance of 68 m, and farther W by a **bridge** with a vertical clearance of about 12 m.

Berths and facilities
8.46

Berths. The principal berths in Fukuyamo Kō are as follows:

Berth & Position	Length m	Depth m	Capacity dwt
Kasoaka Quay			
Pipe Shipment Berth	350	10–11·5	35 000
(34° 28·1' N, 133° 27·5' E)			
Raw Materials Quay (from N to S)			
Berth F	180	11	20 000
E	210	14	70 000
B	280	16	100 000
A	300	17	150 000
L	315	17–18	200 000
M	250	17–17·5	200 000
S	260	12–12·5	35 000
South Quay (from E to W)			
Berth N	180	1·5–6·5	5 000
X, Y	350	12·3–13	35 000
22–24	300	6·5–7	5 000
Finished Products Quay (from S to N)			
Berth 3	145	11–13	35 000
2	230	10·5–13	35 000
1	235	10	20 000
13	90	7	5 000

8.47

Facilities. Offices of the Maritime Safety Agency, Customs, Quarantine and Immigration are located in the joint Harbour Office situated near the entrance to the inner harbour (34° 28·6' N, 133° 24·6' E).

There are five tugs of 3200 hp.

Waste oil disposal facilities are available.

De-ratting; see 1.70.

Supplies. Fresh water is available on the quays. Fuel oil is available with sufficient advance notice.

Communications. There is a **port radio station** at Fukuyama Kō; see *Admiralty List of Radio Signals Volume 6*.

BINGO NADA—NORTH EAST PART

Charts 3605, 695 plan of Fukuyama Kō and approaches
Islands and channels
8.48

Kōno Shima (34° 27' N, 133° 30' E) is joined to the mainland of Honshū NW by reclaimed land the W side of which was, in 1975, being further reclaimed to form the E side of Fukuyama Kō (8.43).

Kōnoshimaseto Kō (34° 27' N, 133° 31' E), a small harbour protected by breakwaters, is situated on the E side of a bay lying on the S side of Kōno Shima; a **light** is exhibited from the head of the W breakwater. There are depths from 2 m to 3 m in the harbour and also alongside a quay on the inner side of the W breakwater.

Landmark. The chimney of the **Kōno Shima Chemical Works,** stands at an elevation of 52 m on the W side of the bay ¼ mile W of the harbour entrance and is conspicuous.

A short breakwater projects ESE from the W side of the bay and a *light-buoy* (black; green light flashing every 3 seconds) is moored off its head; a quay with a depth of about 5 m alongside, lies N of the breakwater and two mooring buoys are moored off it.

Anchorage is afforded in depths from 10 m to 28 m, good holding ground, in the bay but it is exposed to strong winds between SE and SW.

Kurotsuchi Seto lies between Kōno Shima and Taka Shima (8.50) ¼ mile S; there are depths of 7·6 m in its E approach.

A **submarine pipeline** and two **submarine cables** cross the W part of Kurotsuchi Seto.

8.49

Semizo, a narrow channel separating Kōno Shima from the mainland NE, leads to Kasaoka Kō. A *light-buoy* moored off the SE extremity of Kōno Shima marks the entrance to the channel.

The fairway through Semizo is buoyed and dredged to 3 m; a **bridge** with a vertical clearance of 18 m, spans the channel near the N end of Kōno Shima.

Kasaoka Kō (34° 30' N, 133° 30' E), consisting of two basins with depths from 2 m to 3 m, lies near the head of Semizo.

8.50

Taka Shima (34° 26' N, 133° 31' E), 77 m high near its NE end, lies on the S side of Kurotsuchi Seto (8.48); a prominent *torii* stands on the summit of the island.

Myōji Shima, 59 m high, is the largest and middle of three islets lying in the W part of Kurotsuchi Seto close off the NW side of Taka Shima.

Tori Shima, an islet 11 m high, lies 2 cables W of the SW extremity of Taka Shima; a rocky reef extends 3 cables S from Tori Shima and **Hyakken Zowai,** which dries 2·4 m, lies at its S end. A **light** is exhibited from a white round concrete tower on Hyakken Zowai.

Chart 3605
8.51

Shiraishi Seto (34° 25' N, 133° 31' E) lies between Taka Shima and Shiraishi Shimi (8.53) ¼ mile SE and is much used by small vessels proceeding along the S coast of Honshū.

Kotaka Shima, the largest of the islets in Shiraishi Seto, lies 2 cables off the SE side of Taka Shima; it is 40 m high and has some patches of red sand on its S side.

Kogochi Shima (34° 25·0' N, 133° 31·2' E), a rocky islet 29 m high, lies 2 cables S of the E extremity of Kotaka Shima.

An **overhead cable** with a vertical clearance of about 22 m runs from Taka Shima to Kotaka Shima and Kogochi Shima.

Okino Shiraishi, a steep-to white rock 5 m high, lies 2½ cables SSW of Kogochi Shima; a **light** is exhibited from a white round concrete tower standing on the rock.

Caution. Kajikake, a rock with a depth of less than 1 m, lies 1¼ cables SSW of Okino Shiraishi.

Chart 695 plan of Fukuyama Kō and approaches
8.52

Tako Zowai (34° 23·8' N, 133° 29·4' E), a steep-to rock with a depth of 1·6 m, lies in the SW approach to Shiraishi Seto 1 mile WSW of the NW extremity of Shiraishi Shima. **Kanari Shima,** 20 m high, lies 5 cables SSE of Tako Zowai and in between them lie two patches of 7·6 m and 7·3 m, respectively, and a rock which dries 0·2 m.

Kajiko Shima, 38 m high and covered with coarse grass, lies off the SW extremity of Shiraishi Shima, ½ mile SE of Kanari Shima. **Heishō,** a rock which dries 3 m, lies 1¼ cables off the N side of Kajiko Shima.

Chart 3605
8.53

Shiraishi Shima (34° 24' N, 133° 31' E), on the S side of Shiraishi Seto, is 151 m high in its W part; the W side of the island is cliffy and its E part is cultivated.

Shiraishishima Kō, a small inlet protected by a

detached breakwater, lies on the N side of Shiraishi Shima; a **light** is exhibited on the breakwater.

Kitagi Seto (34° 24' N, 133° 32' E) lies between Shiraishi Shima and Kitagi Shima farther SE, and the fairway is about 1½ cables wide at its narrowest part. An **overhead cable** with a vertical clearance of 27 m spans the channel.

Inuno Kashira, a steep-to rock which dries 0·3 m, lies in the SW approach to Kitagi Seto 8 cables SSW of the S extremity of Shiraishi Shima. **Yokobe Shima,** 16 m high and rocky, lies 4 cables ENE of Inuno Kashira.

Tate Shima (34° 24·3' N, 133° 32·4' E), a conical rock 8 m high, lies in the NE entrance to Kitagi Seto; a shoal on which lie some flat rocks which dry 2·1 m, extends 1½ cables NE from the islet.

8.54

Kitagi Shima (34° 23' N, 133° 32' E), the largest of the islands in the vicinity, lies on the S side of Kitagi Seto and can be identified by its remarkable red rocks; it is well known for its stone quarries. **Tako Yama,** the summit of the island, attains an elevation of 226 m near its centre.

Kitagishima Kō (34° 22·5' N, 133° 32·8' E), protected by two breakwaters, lies at the head of the bight on the E side of Kitagi Shima; a **light** is exhibited on the head of the N breakwater.

Anchorage. Temporary anchorage, sheltered from W winds, can be obtained in the bight in depths of about 8 m, mud.

Manabe Shima (34° 21' N, 133° 35' E) lies 8 cables SE of Kitagi Shima; **Shiro Yama,** the summit, attains an elevation of 130 m at the NE end of the island. The coasts of Manabe Shima are mostly cliffy and comparatively steep-to except for a 2·7 m patch in the middle of a bay on the SE side of the island.

8.55

Toi Shima (34° 21' N, 133° 33' E), a small islet covered with grass and 37 m high, lies in the SW approach to the channel between Kitagi Shima and Manabe Shima. A reef on which there are some rocks, surrounds the islet and extends up to 1½ cables from it in places.

Ōzowai, a rock with a depth of 5·9 m, lies 2¼ cables SW of Toi Shima, and **Mefu Iwa,** rocks some of which dry 1·8 m, lies 3 cables NE of the islet.

Ō Shima (34° 22' N, 133° 35' E), 58 m high, lies in the NE approach to the channel between Kitagi Shima and Manabe Shima; it is joined to **Kō Shima,** 63 m high, to the S of it, by a narrow sandy isthmus. Both Ō Shima and Kō Shima are flat-topped.

Modoko Shima, an islet 28 m high, lies 2¼ cables E of Kō Shima.

CHAPTER 9

BISAN SETO

GENERAL INFORMATION

Chart 2875
9.1

Bisan Seto is the main channel leading from the NE side of Bingo Nada to the SW part of Harima Nada and is about 37 miles long; numerous islands and shoals border the channel on either side. The islands in the W part of Bisan Seto are known collectively as **Shiwaku (Shiaku) Shotō.**

Cautions. The traffic in Bisan Seto is heavy and large numbers of fishing vessels may be encountered. Numerous ferries ply between the various ports and harbours on each side of the straits and cross the main traffic routes. Many of the fishing vessels show no lights or will show them only on close approach.

Net fishing is carried out in all traffic routes throughout the fishing season (see 1.6). Nets are set at the turn of the tidal stream and the anchoring position is marked by two white buoys, and at the ends by several white or yellow buoys. When the tidal stream is at strength, these buoys are sometimes difficult to see.

Charts 3605, 1969
9.2

Traffic routes. Traffic routes prescribed by the **Maritime Traffic Safety Law** (1.27), and shown on the charts, are in force in Bisan Seto and are as follows:

Bisan Seto (West)	Bisan Seto South Traffic Route	(9.4)
	Bisan Seto North Traffic Route	(9.5)
	Mizushima Traffic Route	(9.6)

Bisan Seto (East)	Bisan Seto East Traffic Route	(9.48)
	Ukō West Traffic Route	(9.49)
	Ukō East Traffic Route	(9.49)

Pilotage in all traffic routes in Bisan Seto is compulsory for all vessels over 10 000 grt, except for certain exempted Japanese vessels.

Small vessel route. Small vessels proceeding to and from the NE part of Bingo Nada and the NW part of Harima Nada, navigate along the N side of Bisan Seto via Shiraishi Seto (34° 25' N, 133° 31' E), Shimotsui Seto (34° 26' N, 133° 48' E) and Kazurashima Suidō (34° 28' N, 133° 57' E). See also 9.33.
9.3

Regulations. The general regulations for all traffic routes prescribed by the Maritime Traffic Safety Law are given at 1.28. Additional regulations and information are given as follows:

North and South Traffic Routes	(9.7, 9.8)
Mizushima Traffic Route	(9.7–9.9)
East Traffic Route	(9.50)
Ukō West and Ukō East Traffic Routes	(9.50)

Vessels of length 200 m or more may only navigate Bisan Seto traffic routes during daylight hours; transit takes 3–3½ hours. Vessels must enter the traffic route not later than about 4 hours before sunset.

BISAN SETO (WEST)—CENTRAL ROUTES

TRAFFIC ROUTES AND REGULATIONS

Chart 3605 with plan
South Traffic Route
9.4

The W end of **Bisan Seto South Traffic Route** lies 1½ miles S of Futaomote Shima (34° 18' N, 133° 37' E) (9.14) and leads S of Takami Shima and Ushi Shima joining the W end of Bisan Seto East Traffic Route close N of Kosei Shima (34° 22' N, 133° 51' E); *No. 1 Light-buoy* marks the N side of the W end of the route and further light-buoys mark each side.

South Traffic Route has been dredged to a least depth of 12·4 m except for a 11·2 m patch situated 2¼ cables SE of the S extremity of Takami Shima, and there is a dangerous wreck at the junction with Bisan Seto East Traffic Route.

Caution. In 1980, bridge construction work was in progress between the NW side of the reclaimed area extending NE from Shami Shima (34° 20·8' N, 133° 49·4' E) and the S side of South Traffic Route, and in the vicinity of Mitsugo Shima (34° 22·2' N, 133° 49·5' E). **Prohibited areas,** marked by yellow *light-buoys,* had been established.

North Traffic Route
9.5

The W end of **Bisan Seto North Traffic Route** lies ¼ mile N of Futaomote Shima and leads N of Takami Shima and Ushi Shima (34° 21·5' N, 133° 47·0' E) joining the W end of Bisan Seto East Traffic Route close N of Kosei Shima. *No. 2 Light-buoy* marks the S side of the W end of the route and further *light-buoys* mark its N edge.

A depth of at least 17 m can be carried through North Traffic Route; special **caution** is required between the meridians of Ushi Shima and Yo Shima, 2¼ miles NE, where the route is crossed by Mizushima Traffic Route. In addition, the tidal streams are strong and sandwaves are liable to cause changes in depths in this area.

Hon
Shima

Ushi
Shima

Nō Misaki

Takami Shima

Ōzuchi
·Shima

Tadotsu Kō

**(9.4) Bisan Seto South Traffic Route (E-bound), seen from a position about 1 mile SW of
Takami Shima** *(34°18′N, 131°41′E)*.

(Original dated prior to 1978)

Takami
Shimi

Ushi
Shima

Hill,
94m high

Hon Shima

Mitsugo Shima
Light

Nabe Shima

**(9.5) Bisan Seto North Traffic Route (W-bound), seen from a position about 1½ miles E of
Mitsugo Shima Light** *(34°22′N, 131°50′E)*.

(Original dated prior to 1978)

Charts 3605, 695 plan of Mizushima Kō and approaches
Mizushima Traffic Route
9.6

Mizushima Traffic Route extends from near the E end of South Traffic Route (34° 22' N, 133° 49' E), crosses North Traffic Route, and leads through the islands of Shiwaku Shotō to Mizushima Kō.

There is a least depth of 15 m in Mizushima Traffic Route except for a 10·1 m shoal lying 1 mile SW of Nabe Shima (34° 23' N, 133° 50' E); sandwaves with depths of less than 10 m have been reported in the vicinity of this shoal which lies in the most difficult part of Bisan Seto where the traffic routes intersect.

Mizushima Traffic Route is marked on each side by *light-buoys*.

Cautions. From April to August, by day and at night, net fishing is carried out by large numbers of fishing boats in the vicinity of the S end of Mizushima Traffic Route and E of Mukuchi Shima (34° 25' N, 133° 47' E).

Large numbers of small vessels passing through Shimotsui Seto (34° 26' N, 133° 48' E) cross Mizushima Traffic Route close NE of Mukuchi Shima; particular care is needed in this area.

Strong E and W-going tidal streams may be experienced in the traffic route off the W entrance to Shimotsui Seto.

Regulations
9.7

In addition to the general regulations for all traffic routes prescribed by the Maritime Traffic Safety Law (see 1.28), the following regulations are in force for North and South Traffic Routes and for Mizushima Traffic Route:

(a) A vessel navigating in the North Traffic Route shall proceed in a W'ly direction.

(b) A vessel navigating in the South Traffic Route shall proceed in an E'ly direction.

(c) A vessel navigating in the Mizushima Traffic Route shall keep to starboard of the centre line of the route.

(d) A vessel, other than (i) a vessel of length 200 m or more, (ii) a vessel engaged in fishing or other operations, when navigating Mizushima Traffic Route, shall keep out of the way of a vessel navigating North Traffic Route.

(e) A vessel engaged in fishing or other operations, when navigating Mizushima Traffic Route, shall keep out of the way of a vessel of length 200 m or more, which is navigating North Traffic Route.

(f) A vessel, other than a vessel of length 200 m or more, when navigating North Traffic Route shall keep out of the way of a vessel of length 200 m or more, which is navigating Mizushima Traffic Route.

(g) A vessel, other than a vessel of length 200 m or more, when navigating North or South Traffic Routes shall keep out of the way of a vessel of length 200 m or more, which is navigating Mizushima Traffic Route and which intends to turn into North or South Traffic Routes.

(h) Except when a vessel is crossing a traffic route there is a speed limit of 12 knots in the following areas:

   (i) In that part of North Traffic Route between a line drawn 008° from the NE extremity of Ushi Shima (34° 22' N, 133° 47' E), and the E end of that route off Kosei Shima.

   (ii) In that part of South Traffic Route between a line drawn 160° from the SE extremity of Ushi Shima, and the E end of that route off Kosei Shima.

   (iii) Throughout the length of Mizushima Traffic Route.

(i) The draught of tankers on passage between Kurushima Kaikyō Traffic Route (7.2) and Mizushima Traffic Route should not exceed 11 m.

(j) Tankers of length 200 m or more, must have an escorting tug between Kurushima Kaikyō Traffic Route and Mizushima Kō.

(k) In low visibility entry into the traffic routes is restricted as follows:

Type of vessel	*Restriction*
(i) Vessels of length 200 m or more.	Entry prohibited when the visibility in the traffic route is less than 1 mile.
(ii) Vessels of 50 000 grt or more carrying dangerous cargo.	
(iii) Vessels of 25 000 grt or more carrying liquefied gas.	
(iv) Vessels towing or pushing very long tows.	
(v) Vessels carrying dangerous cargo (excluding those in (i), (ii) and (iii)).	Entry prohibited when the visibility in the traffic route is less than ½ mile.

9.8

Signals to be shown by vessels. The chartlet (facing page) of the traffic routes shows the flag signals to be displayed by day and the sound signals to be made at night, by vessels joining or leaving the traffic routes, in order to indicate their intention to other vessels; the sound signals should be made at the positions indicated on the chartlet.

Traffic control in Mizushima Traffic Route
9.9

A **signal station** stands on the SW side of Yo Shima (34° 23' N, 133° 49' E) (9.20) and also on Nishino Saki (34° 26' N, 133° 47' E) (9.40). The traffic in Mizushima Traffic Route is controlled by the following signals shown from these signal stations:

By day	*At night*	*Meaning*
Red light flashing every 2 seconds or black cube	Red light flashing every 2 seconds	N-bound vessels, between 70 m and 200 m in length, wait outside Mizushima Traffic Route
White light flashing every 2 seconds or black cone point up	White light flashing every 2 seconds	S-bound vessels, between 70 m and 200 m in length, wait outside Mizushima Traffic Route

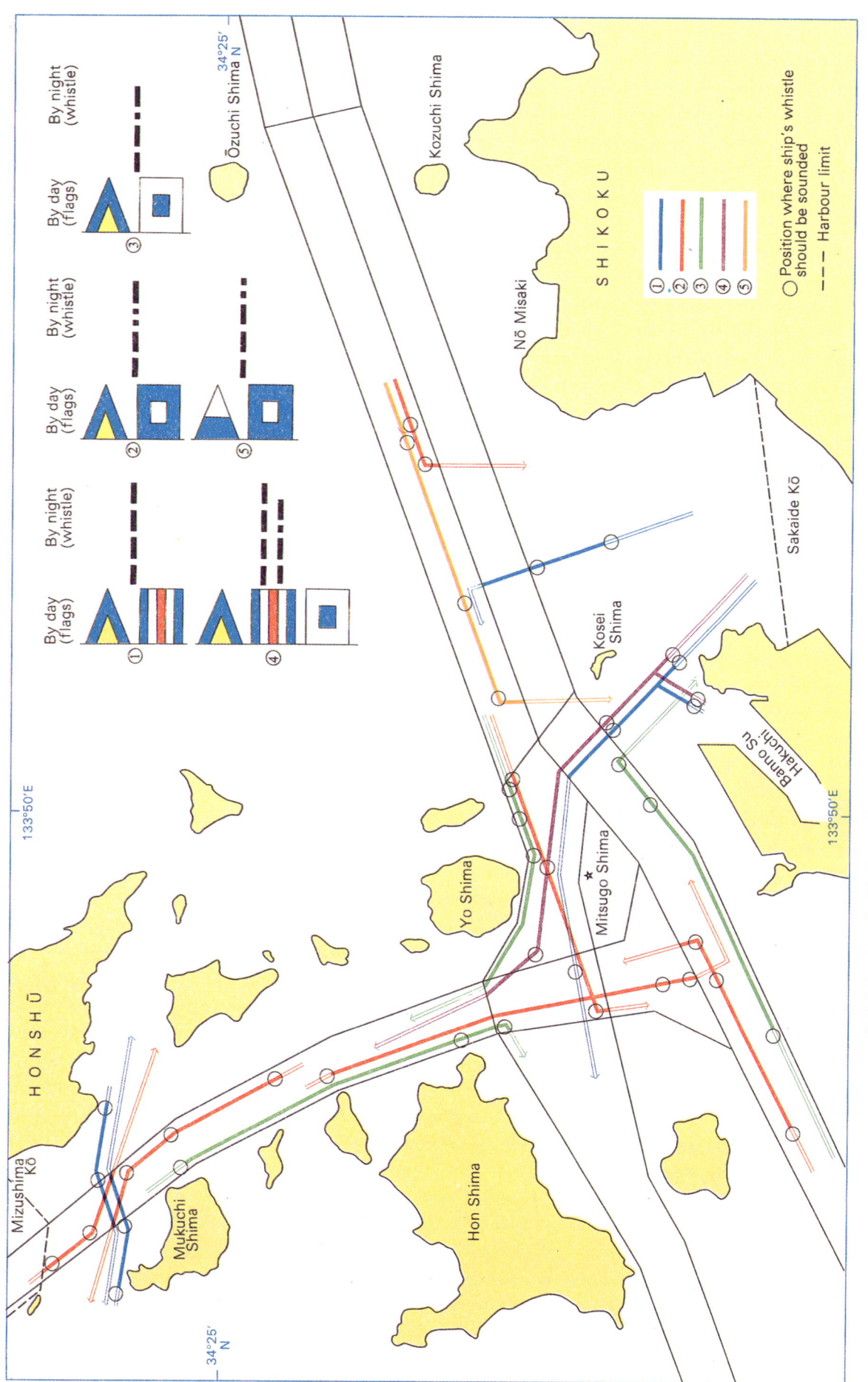

(9.8) Mizushima Traffic Route, Bisan Seto North Traffic Route & Bisan Seto South Traffic Route

If the signal stations are inoperative, traffic control will be exercised by patrol vessels stationed:

close S of Mitsugo Shima (34° 22' N, 133° 49' E)

and

E side of traffic route close within harbour limits of Mizushima Kō.

The patrol vessels will use the following signals:

By day (International Code Flags)	At night (by flashing light)	Meaning
2nd Substitute over Flag L	RZN	N-bound vessels, between 70 m and 200 m in length, wait outside Mizushima Traffic Route
1st Substitute over Flag L	RZS	S-bound vessels, between 70 m and 200 m in length, wait outside Mizushima Traffic Route

Note: The night signals may sometimes be used by day.

In addition to the traffic control signals, the two signal stations will exhibit the following *informatory signals* from an arrow-shaped indicator:

Signal	Meaning
	A vessel of length 200 m or more, will pass through Mizushima Traffic Route in front of the signal station, in the direction of the arrowhead, as follows:
White group flashing light showing 3 flashes of 2 seconds duration, every 13 seconds	Within 3 hours
White group flashing light showing 2 flashes of 2 seconds duration, every 10 seconds	Within 2 hours
White flashing light every 4 seconds	Within 1 hour
White isophase light every 2 seconds	Within ½ hour

ISLANDS AND DANGERS LYING ON THE SOUTH SIDE OF SOUTH TRAFFIC ROUTE

Chart 3605 with plan
9.10
Landmarks. The principal features on the coast of Shikoku to the S of South Traffic Route are:

The white keep of a castle (34° 17' N, 133° 48' E), standing at an elevation of 83 m, in the S part of the town of Marugame; it is conspicuous and floodlit at night.

Iino Yama, the conical summit of which is 420 m (1380 ft) high (Chart 2875), situated 2½ miles ESE of the castle keep, and which is prominent from a distance.

Shōtsūji Yama (34° 19' N, 133° 50' E) situated on the W side of the town of Sakaide and which is 121 m high and has a prominent building on its summit; the lights of the building are a good mark at night.

A power station chimney (red and white) (34° 20·2' N, 133° 50·8' E), with an elevation of 204 m, which is the tallest of several chimneys standing together with numerous oil tanks on reclaimed land within 2½ miles N of Shōtsūji Yama.

9.11
Awa Shima (34° 16' N, 133° 38' E), an island of granite, is situated on the S side of the W entrance to South Traffic Route, 3 miles E of Mi Saki (8.28); it is in three parts connected by low sandy isthmuses. There are summits on each of the three parts and **Shirono Yama,** 222 m high and situated in the S part, is the highest.

Anchorages. There are bays on the N, S and W sides of the island which are known collectively as **Awashima Byōchi.** Anchorage can be obtained in any one of the three bays but that on the W side of the island is exposed and is not recommended.

The most sheltered anchorage is in the S bay either in its inner part, in depths from 5 m to 10 m, or between the bay and the coast of Shikoku to the S, in depths of less than 15 m.

Taishiga Mo, a mudbank with a least depth of 1·8 m, lies across the entrance of the S bay; a nautical college is situated in **Awashima Kō,** a small harbour at the head of this bay.

Anchorage can be obtained in the entrance of **Kita Ura,** the N bay, but local knowledge is necessary.

Extensive fish and seaweed beds are to be found in all three bays from October to April.

Submarine cables, two of which are power cables, and a **submarine pipeline,** are laid from the S coast of Awa Shima to the coast of Shikoku.

Directions. The anchorage in the S bay should be approached from W through the narrow channel between the S extremity of Awa Shima and **Kannon Hana** on the mainland. **Shiogi Yama** (34° 12·4' N, 133° 41·3' E) a prominent conical hill 172 m high, bearing 127°, leads through the middle of this channel.

The E approach to the anchorage is only suitable for small vessels with local knowledge.

9.12
Shishi Shima (34° 16' N, 133° 41' E), ¼ mile E of Awa Shima, is partly wooded and in part cultivated.

Shishino Mosaki, a narrow shoal with depths of less than 5 m, extends 1¼ miles ENE from the NE side of Shishi Shima; the least depth of 2·9 m, lies about 1½ miles from the island.

Okinonaka Se, a sandbank with two heads, extends about 2 miles N from the NE end of Shishino Mosaki; in 1965, the least known depth was 4·2 m. The depths in the shoalest parts of Okinonaka Se are reported to be continually changing under the influence of the tidal streams. *No. 5* and *No. 6 Light-buoys,* marking South Traffic Route, are moored within 4 cables N of the shoalest part of Okinonaka Se.

9.13
Shami Shima (34° 21' N, 133° 49' E), a former island 27 m high, is connected to the NW corner of reclaimed land situated on the W side of Sakaide Kō (9.28). (See also 9.4).

Kosei Shima (34° 22' N, 133° 51' E), 40 m high and covered with pine trees, lies in the approaches to Sakaide Kō at the E end of South Traffic Route; a **light** is exhibited from a white round concrete tower on the N side of the islet.

ISLANDS AND DANGERS LYING BETWEEN SOUTH AND NORTH TRAFFIC ROUTES

Chart 3605 with plan
9.14
Futaomote Shima (34° 18' N, 133° 37' E) lies between

the W ends of Bisan Seto South and North Traffic Routes; it is 23 m high, has two grassy summits and is fringed with reefs. A fairway *light-buoy* is moored 3½ cables W of the islet.

No. 1 Light-buoy, on the N side of the entrance to South Traffic Route, and *No. 2 Light-buoy*, on the S side of the entrance to North Traffic Route, are moored, respectively, 2 cables S and 4 cables N of Futaomote Shima.

Takami Shima (34° 19' N, 133° 40' E), 2½ miles ENE of Futaomote Shima, is cultivated; the conical summit of the island is 298 m high. A sandbank with depths of less than 10 m, lies between Futaomote Shima and Takami Shima; *No. 3 Light-buoy* is moored close S of the shoalest part of this bank.

A **light** is exhibited from a white round concrete tower situated on **Itamochi Hana,** the NW extremity of Takami Shima. A **light** is exhibited from the head of the S breakwater at **Takami Kō** situated at the SE end of the island.

Kojimadashi Se, with two heads the shoalest of which has a depth of 2·7 m, lies 2 miles ENE of Takami Shima.

9.15

Habushi Iwa (34° 20·5' N, 133° 43·0' E), a white rock 2 m high, lies on the S edge of North Traffic Route, 1 mile N of Kojimadashi Se; a **light** is exhibited from a red round stone tower with black bands surmounting the rock.

Okino Su, a long sandbank with a least depth of 2·8 m, extends about 2½ miles ENE from a position 1 mile SE of Habushi Iwa; a *light-buoy* is moored on the N side.

Ushi Shima (34° 21·5' N, 133° 47·0' E) is situated 3½ miles ENE of Habushi Iwa and on it are two prominent hills the E and highest of which is 110 m high.

A **light** is exhibited from a red round concrete tower situated on the head of a breakwater which extends N from the N extremity of Ushi Shima.

9.16

Mitsugo Shima (34° 22·2' N, 133° 49·5' E) is a group of three rocky islets, surmounted by pine trees, lying 2 miles ENE of Ushi Shima. From E or W, the two N'most islets appear to be joined; the NW of these two is 18 m high and the highest of the group. A **light** is exhibited from a white square tower standing on the E side of the NW islet. (See also 9.4).

Mitsugo Sashi, with a least depth of 4 m, lies within ½ mile W of the islets. *No. 4 Light-buoy* is moored 6 cables WSW, and *No. 2 Light-buoy* is moored 4 cables S, of Mitsugo Shima Light-tower.

ISLANDS AND DANGERS LYING ON THE NORTH SIDE OF NORTH TRAFFIC ROUTE

Chart 3605

9.17

Sanagi Shima (34° 20' N, 133° 38' E), 248 m high, lies on the N side of the W end of Bisan Seto North Traffic Route; **Kongō Hana,** its S extremity, consists of a steep-to white cliff about 18 m high.

A **light** is exhibited on the head of a breakwater at **Sanagi Kō** on the E side of the N point of Sanagi Shima.

Ko Shima, 153 m high, conical and wooded, lies ½ mile E of the S end of Sanagi Shima. An **overhead power cable** with a vertical clearance of about 46 m, spans the channel between Sanagi Shima and Ko Shima.

Kawara Su, a bank with depths of less than 5 m which dries in places, extends 2¾ miles E from the E side of Sanagi Shima. *No. 3* and *No. 5 Light-buoys* are moored on the S side of Kawara Su and mark the N edge of North Traffic Route.

Charts 3605, 695 plan of Mizushima Kō and approaches

Ode Shima (34° 23' N, 133° 39' E), a cultivated island, lies 1¾ miles NE of Sanagi Shima; its summit near its N end attains an elevation of 94 m.

Te Shima (34° 24' N, 133° 40' E), situated ¾ mile NE of Ode Shima, attains an elevation of 217 m in its N part; its summit is conical and thickly covered with pine trees. **Takanokoshi Hana,** the NW extremity of the island, is surmounted by a hill 100 m high and prominent; the land SE of it is low and the hill appears from a distance as a detached islet.

Jinbei Zowai, a rock with a depth of 0·6 m over it, lies 2 cables NE of the NE extremity of Te Shima; overfalls are usually formed close to it.

Chart 3605

9.18

Hiro Shima, the largest island in Shiwaku Shotō, is situated with **Haya Saki** (34° 21' N, 133° 42' E), its S extremity, 3 miles ENE of Ko Shima.

Landmarks. Dondoro Yama, the summit of Hiro Shima attains an elevation of 312 m, 6 cables N of Haya Saki and its S face is rocky and precipitous; a pointed hill, 207 m high, situated ½ mile W of Dondoro Yama, shows up well from certain directions.

A **light** is exhibited on the head of a breakwater at **Aoki Kō,** a small harbour on the W coast of Hiro Shima.

No. 7 Light-buoy, moored 7 cables E of Haya Saki, marks the N limit of North Traffic Route.

Anchorage. Temporary anchorage can be obtained in a depth of about 8 m, good holding ground, off **Eno Ura** on the SE side of Hiro Shima. A **light** is exhibited on the head of a breakwater extending from the coast in the E part of Eno Ura.

A **submarine cable** is laid from the W side of Eno Ura to Takami Shima, 3 miles SW.

Charts 3605, 695 plan of Mizushima Kō and approaches

Sono Su, a large sandbank which dries in places, lies in the channel between Hiro Shima and Hon Shima 1¼ miles to the E, with narrow channels on its E and W sides. *No. 2 Light-buoy* is moored off the W side of Sono Su and *No. 3 Light-buoy* off the NW extremity of the bank.

Overfalls occur on the E and W sides of **Hajikami Hana,** the N extremity of Hiro Shima.

Chart 3605 with plan

9.19

Hon Shima lies close NW of the junction of North Traffic Route and Mizushima Traffic Route; its S summit, 203 m high, situated ½ mile NE of **Kabura Saki** (34° 22' N, 133° 45' E), the SW extremity of the island, is a prominent, white, round-topped, rocky point.

No. 9 Light-buoy is moored off **Kuro Hana,** the S extremity of Hon Shima, on the N limit of North Traffic Route.

Charts 3605, 695 plan of Mizushima Kō and approaches

Submarine cables, which cross the traffic routes, are landed at **Shokenbo Hana,** 1¼ miles NE of Kuro Hana; the landing place is marked by **beacons.**

A **light** is exhibited on the head of a breakwater at **Honshima Kō** (34° 22·7' N, 133° 47·3' E), situated close NE of Shokenbo Hana.

Kameyama Hana, the E extremity of Hon Shima, is a cliffy point 20 m high; a rocky patch with a depth of 3·6 m over it, lies 2 cables SSE of the point. *No. 5 Light-*

buoy is moored close E of the 3·6 m patch and marks the NW corner of the junction of North Traffic Route and Mizushima Traffic Route.

Chart 3605 with plan
9.20

Yo Shima (34° 23' N, 133° 49' E) lies close E of the junction of North Traffic Route and Mizushima Traffic Route; its summit, 71 m high, is situated at its NW end and there are several reddish brown-coloured quarries on the island.

A **signal station** consisting of a white building with a flagstaff on its roof, is situated on the SW side of Yo Shima.

No. 6 Light-buoy is moored 3 cables W of Yo Shima

and marks the NE corner of the junction of North Traffic Route and Mizushima Traffic Route.
9.21

Nabe Shima (34° 22·7' N, 133° 49·6' E), a flat-topped islet, lies close SE of the S extremity of Yo Shima; it is comparatively steep-to on its S side but there are reefs and shoals within 1½ cables of its E side.

A **light** is exhibited from a white round stone tower standing on the summit of Nabe Shima; a **racon** transmits from the light-tower.

A breakwater extends N from the N side of Nabe Shima and a **light** is exhibited on its head.

Oyo Shima, 47 m high at its N end, lies 2 cables off the E side of Yo Shima and on it are several brown-coloured quarries; the island is fringed with rocks.

BISAN SETO (WEST)—SOUTH SIDE

TAKUMA KŌ

Chart 3605
9.22

Takuma Kō, an open harbour (see 1.65), comprises the area extending E from **Koda Hana** (34° 14' N, 133° 38' E), a point 4 miles SE of Mi Saki (8.28), and **Midzuide Hana** 3 miles E; the harbour limits are indicated on the chart. The harbour is divided into E and W parts by **Kōya Hana,** a white cliff at the extremity of a peninsula.

A **light** is exhibited from a red round concrete tower standing on **Mitama Iwa,** a reef extending 1 cable N from Kōya Hana.

Pilotage. Pilotage is not compulsory but recommended. Pilots are available in Sakaide Kō (9.28) quarantine anchorage.

Anchorages. A, B and **C** anchor berths are established within ¼ mile N of Kōya Hana and are used by vessels unloading timber; the berths are exposed in strong N winds.

Two **submarine cables,** indicated on the chart, are laid between Kōya Hana and Shishi Shima to the N.
9.23

Takuma Kō—W part. Nabe Iso, a rock with a depth of less than 1·5 m over it, lies 2 cables offshore 1 mile WSW of Kōya Hana. From October to June there are shellfish and seaweed beds within 2½ cables of the shore extending ¼ mile SW from Kōya Hana.

Kōno Shima Chemical Industries Quay, with a depth of 4 m alongside, is situated in the W part of the day, 1¼ miles WSW of Kōya Hana.

At **Suda** situated 1¼ miles SW of Kōya Hana, there is a basin, protected by breakwaters, which is used by ferries to Awa Shima.
9.24

Takuma Kō—E part. Kigasa Shima (34° 15' N, 133° 42' E), 58 m high and thickly covered with trees, lies 1¼ miles ENE of Kōya Hana in the approach to **Takuma Ura,** the E part of Takuma Kō; **Iwa Shima,** flat, rocky and 2 m high, lies 4 cables SW of Kigasa Shima.

The W side of Takuma Ura has been enclosed by an area of reclaimed land and by breakwaters to form a harbour for small vessels and a timber storage area. The fairway to the entrance between the breakwaters has a reported depth of 5·5 m and is marked by a *light-buoy.*

Takum No. 1 Quay, with depths from 5·5 m to 7·5 m alongside, lies within the reclaimed area on the W side of Takuma Ura.

Facilities. There is a Customs Office in Takuma Kō.

Repairs can be undertaken at the **Samuki Shipyard** which has two dry docks, the largest of which has a capacity of 3000 tons.

Tugs are available from Sakaide Kō.

TADOTSU KŌ

Chart 3605
9.25

Tadotsu Kō (34° 17' N, 133° 45' E), entered 4 miles NE of Takuma Kō, lies between large areas of reclaimed land extending ¼ mile NW from the coast; a **light** is exhibited on the head of a short breakwater on the W side of the entrance.

Landmarks. Ōgi Yama (34° 15·9' N, 133° 44·8' E) at the SW end of the harbour, is a prominent isolated hill 91 m high, which is thickly covered with pine trees. A group of oil tanks standing on the reclaimed land on the W side of the entrance is a good mark.

An **overhead cable** with a vertical clearance of about 59 m, crosses the harbour 4 cables within the entrance.

An inner harbour, protected by breakwaters, lies in the SW corner of Tadotsu Kō; a **light** is exhibited at the head of each breakwater.

Directions. Ōgi Yama bearing 158°, leads through to the entrance of the inner harbour.

Berths. The principal berths in Tadotsu Kō are as follows:

Berths & Position	Depth m	Capacity tons
Shōwa Sekiyū Jetty		
(34° 16·4' N, 133° 44·0' E)	7–10	5 000
Nos. 1 and 2 Fitting-out Quays		
(34° 16·6' N, 133° 44·6' E)	6–7	
Nishi-Minato Machi Quay		
(34° 16·3' N, 133° 44·6' E)	6	3 000

Climate. See table at 1.101

Supplies. Fresh water is available at the principal quays.

MARUGAME KŌ

Chart 3605
9.26

Marugame Kō (34° 18' N, 133° 47' E), an industrial

port developed on reclaimed land and an open harbour (see 1.65), is situated 2 miles NE of Tadotsu Kō; the old town of **Marugame** which had a population of 63 000 in 1973, backs the port.

Shimoma Shima (34° 18' N, 133° 47' E), a rocky islet 30 m high, lies close off the NW corner of the reclaimed land and is joined to it by a drying bank. **Kamima Shima,** round-topped, rocky and 35 m high, lies 1¼ miles NE of Shimoma Shima at the NE corner of the harbour limit.

Landmarks. The following objects are prominent:
Marugame Castle (34° 17' N, 133° 48' E) (see 9.10).

A chimney (red and white), with an elevation of 102 m, standing 8 cables N of the castle, near the Harbour Office.

Seven cranes (pale blue, red and white jibs) standing in **Imabari Zōsen Shipyard** close SE of Shimoma Shima.
9.27

The main basin of Marugame Kō is entered 3 cables ENE of Shimoma Shima; the entrance is marked on its W side by a **light** exhibited on the head of a short breakwater, and on its E side by a *light-buoy.*

In 1976, the approach to the basin was dredged to a depth of 13 m and the basin itself had depths from 5 m to 11 m in it.

Another basin with a depth of 5·5 m, lies close NW of a shallow harbour situated to the N of the town. A channel with a dredged depth of 7·5 m in 1976, leads from a position close E of the NE corner of the reclaimed land, to the basin. A **light** is exhibited on the NE corner of the reclaimed land and **leading lights,** in line bearing 155°, lead through the channel.

Berths. The principal berths in Marugame Kō are as follows:

Berth & Position	Length m	Depth m
Shōwa-chō East Quay		
(34° 17·8' N, 133° 46·4' E)	290	7·5–10
Hōrai-chō West Quay		
(34° 18·0' N, 133° 46·8' E)	450	9
Hōrai-chō South Quay		
(34° 17·9' N, 133° 47·0' E)	400	5
Hōrai-chō East Quay		
(34° 18·2' N, 133° 47·3' E)	960	7·5
Public Quay		
(34° 17·6' N, 133° 47·5' E)	540	5·5
Sotobori Quay		
(34° 17·7' N, 133° 47·7' E)	550	1·5–3

Facilities. The Harbour Office is situated at the S end of Sotobori Quay.

There are two dry docks in Imabari Zōsen Shipyard, the largest of which has a capacity of 80 000 tons.

Local weather signals are displayed (see 1.42).

Supplies. There is an oiler.

SAKAIDE KŌ

Charts 694 plan of Sakaide Kō, 3605 with plan
9.28

Sakaide Kō (34° 21' N, 133° 51' E), a specified port (see 1.64), is situated on the E side of reclaimed land extending N and NE from the coast within ⅓ mile of Bisan Seto South Traffic Route. The area is connected at its NW corner to the former island of Shami Shima (9.13) and embraces, at its NE corner, the former island of **Sei Shima,** 111 m high and densely wooded.

Sakaide, which in 1973 had a population of 67 000, is a manufacturing town lying on the S side of the harbour.

Sakaide Kō consists of Banno Su Hakuchi which is entered close W of Sei Shima, and the main harbour to the S, which is separated from Banno Su Hakuchi by a belt of reclaimed land extending SW from Sei Shima. The main harbour is divided into No. 1 and No. 2 Areas.

Pilotage. Pilotage is not compulsory. Pilots are available in the quarantine anchorage between 0700 and 1700.

Anchorage. The **quarantine anchorage,** indicated on the chart, lies in the entrance to the main harbour 1¼ miles E of Sei Shima. Permission to use this anchorage or any other in Sakaide Kō, must be obtained from the Maritime Safety Agency at Takamatsu.

Landmarks. The following landmarks are prominent:
Shōtsūji Yama situated at the root of the reclaimed area on the W side of Sakaide Kō and described at 9.10.

A large number of chimneys and tanks, the positions of which can be seen on the chart, standing on the reclaimed land on each side of Banno Su Hakuchi.

A chimney (red and white) standing at an elevation of 119 m (390 ft) close SE of the SE corner of the quarantine anchorage.

A **signal station** from which traffic and berthing signals for Banno Su Hakuchi are shown, is situated on the N side of Sei Shima.

Banno Su Hakuchi
9.29

Hijiri Iwa, a rock which dries 1·5 m, lies 1 cable off the NW extremity of Sei Shima and is marked close NW by a *light-buoy;* another *light-buoy* marks the N corner of the reclaimed area, 3¼ cables W of Hijiri Iwa.

Banno Su Hakuchi, 3 cables in width and extending 1¼ miles SW, is entered close W of Sei Shima between the two light-buoys; there is a least depth of 12 m in the basin except near its head.

Leading lights are exhibited:
The front light from a white metal framework tower (yellow triangular topmark) standing on the reclaimed area 5 cables WSW of the summit of Sei Shima

The rear light on a gas tank, painted grey, 3 cables S of the front light

The lights in line bearing 181¼°, lead W of Kosei Shima (9.13) and into the basin in a least depth of 13 m.

Sea-berth. Asia Kyodo Sekiyū No. 1 Pier, protected by a submersible oil boom, lies close W of the entrance to Banno Su Hakuchi parallel to the NW face of the reclaimed area; the berth has depths of about 19·5 m alongside and can accommodate tankers up to 100 000 dwt. A **light** is exhibited from the centre of the berth and an auxiliary **light** is exhibited and a fog signal sounded at each end.

A **submarine pipeline** is laid between the berth and the shore SE.

Regulations for Sea-berth. Berthing and unberthing at the dolphin pier is restricted to daylight hours, when the wind speed is less than 20 knots, the tidal stream at the berth is less than ⅓ knot and when the visibility is more than 1 mile. Vessels normally berth on an E-going stream.

When berthing, a vessel from E should take a tug when still E of Oyo Shima (34° 23' N, 133° 50' E), preferably when abeam of Nō Misaki, 3 miles E of Oyo Shima; a vessel from W should take a tug when abeam of Ushi Shima (34° 21' N, 133° 47' E).

When unberthing, a vessel wishing to enter North

Traffic Route should cross South Traffic Route as nearly as possible at right angles from a position close NE of the berth, using tugs as necessary.

A patrol vessel may be provided and other special measures taken to assist the vessel to cross the traffic route. See also traffic route regulations at 9.7 and 9.8.
9.30

Asia Kyodo Sekiyū Refinery stands on the reclaimed land on the NW side of Banno Su Hakuchi, and **Mitsubishi Chemical Industries** on the SE side.

Berths. The principal berths in Banno Su Hakuchi are as follows:

Berth	Length m	Depth m	Capacity dwt
Asia Kyodo-Refinery			
No. 2	100	12·5	75 000
Nos. 3, 6, 7	—	10–10·5	Up to 5 000
No. 5	100	12	75 000
Mitsubishi Chemicals			
A	275	13	115 000
B	200	13	65 000
C	150	12–13	40 000
F–J	—	9–10	3 000
L	100	12	55 000

Main harbour
9.31

The **main harbour** of Sakaide Kō is approached from a position between Nō Misaki (34° 23′ N, 133° 54′ E) (9.52) and a shoal with a least depth of 7·8 m lying ¼ mile E of Kosei Shima; the fairway, with depths of 10 m, lies between *No. 1 Light-buoy* and *No. 2 Light-buoy* moored, respectively, 1 mile E and ¼ mile SE of the summit of Sei Shima.

A channel with depths of less than 10 m lies S of Kosei Shima but the depths are uneven due to sandwaves.

Kawasaki Dockyard lies along the W side of the main harbour.
9.32

Berths. The principal berths in the main harbour of Sakaide Kō are as follows:

Berth & Position	Length m	Depth m	Capacity dwt
Bannosu-Chō (Sei Quay)			
(34° 20·8′ N, 133° 51·7′ E)			
Berth A	315	10·5	10 000
		(Reported)	
Ube Kōsan Dolphins			
(34° 19·6′ N, 133° 51·6′ E)	—	6–7	5 000
Central Wharf			
(34° 19·5′ N, 133° 51·6′ E)			
No. 1	190	9–9·5	15 000
No. 2	160	6–6·5	7 000
West Quay			
(34° 19·5′ N, 133° 51·2′ E)	270	5·5–6·5	3 000

Facilities. Offices of the Maritime Safety Agency, quarantine, customs and immigration are located in the joint Harbour Office situated on Central Wharf.

Tugs and lighters are available.

Repairs of all kinds can be carried out in Kawasaki Dockyard where there are three dry docks with a maximum capacity of 270 000 tons.

Waste oil disposal facilities are available at the Asia Kyodo Refinery.

De-ratting; see 1.70.

Supplies. Fresh water is available on the main quays. Fuel oil can be supplied.

Communications: There is a port radio station at Sakaide; see *Admiralty List of Radio Signals Volume 6*.

BISAN SETO (WEST)—NORTH SIDE

AOSA HANA TO TAMASHIMA KŌ
Charts 3605, 695 plans of Mizushima Kō and approaches
9.33

Routes. Small vessels proceeding along the N side of the W part of Bisan Seto, enter through Shiraishi Seto (34° 25′ N, 133° 31′ E), pass N of the *light-buoy* moored on the N side of **Gantsuga Se** (34° 25′ N, 133° 43′ E), thence between Noji Shotō and Mukuchi Shima (34° 25′ N, 133° 46′ E), cross Mizushima Traffic Route (9.6) and thence through Shimotsui Seto (34° 26′ N, 133° 49′ E) into the E part of Bisan Seto.

Some large vessels bound for Mizushima Kō from W, enter the straits between Manabe Shima (34° 21′ N, 133° 35′ E) and Sanagi Shima, pass within 1 mile N of Te Shima and N of the *light-buoy* moored on the N side of Gantsuga Se, thence between Noji Shotō and Mukuchi Shima and into Mizushima Traffic Route.

Regulations. Vessels of over 100 tons intending to cross Mizushima Traffic Route must display the flag signals and make the sound signals as prescribed in the **Maritime Traffic Safety Law**; see traffic route regulations at 9.7 and 9.8.

Chart 3605
9.34

Aosa Hana (34° 28′ N, 133° 35′ E) lies on the coast of Honshū on the N side of Bisan Seto (West). An isolated hill, 77 m high, standing on the point, and **Aosa Yama,** 250 m high and conical, close NNW, are both prominent from a distance.

Yori Shima, connected to the coast NW of it by reclaimed land, is situated ¼ mile E of Aosa Hana; on it are two hills, the NE and somewhat higher of which is 81 m high, covered with pine trees and a good mark. A sandspit, on which lie three islets surmounted by pine trees, extends 1½ cables S from the S extremity of Yori Shima; a breakwater enclosing a shallow harbour is situated on the NE side of the reclaimed land connecting the island to the mainland.

TAMASHIMA KŌ

Charts 3605, 695 plan of Mizushima Kō and approaches
9.35

Tamashima Kō (34° 31′ N, 133° 40′ E) lies on the W side of **Takahashi Kawa** which flows into the sea 5 miles NE of Yori Shima (9.34).

Landmarks. The following features in Tamashima Kō are conspicuous:

Two power station chimneys (red and white) standing on reclaimed land which forms the E side of the harbour.

Four pylons, three of which are painted red and white,

supporting two overhead cables which span the mouth of the river flowing into the N side of the harbour.

Three pylons (red and white) supporting an overhead cable spanning the mouth of Takahashi Kawa.

No. 1 Light-buoy and *No. 2 Light-buoy,* moored 3½ miles ENE of Yori Shima, mark the entrance to the fairway to Tamashima Kō which has depths from 5·5 m to 6·5 m.

Chart 695 plan of Mizushima Kō and approaches
The fairway into Tamashima Kō leads to **No. 1 Wharf** (34° 30·9' N, 133° 40·6' E) which has depths from 4 m to 5 m alongside; a spoil ground marked by red *buoys* exhibiting orange lights is situated on the E side of the fairway.

A **light** is exhibited on the head of Hachiman Breakwater on the W side of the river mouth in the N part of the harbour.

Tamashima Light is exhibited from a white concrete tower standing at the foot of **Hachiman Yama,** 32 m high, close within and on the W side of the river mouth.

Two **overhead cables** with a least vertical clearance of 31 m, cross the river at its mouth.

In 1978, the S part of the reclaimed land on the E side of the harbour was being extended W towards the fairway; the area was marked by four *buoys.*

Chūkoku Power Station lies in the E part of the reclaimed land on the E side of the harbour. A fairway marked by *No. 2 Light-buoy* and *No. 4 Light-buoy* and with a depth of about 5 m, leads to a basin situated on the S side of the power station.

APPROACHES TO MIZUSHIMA KŌ

Charts 3605, 695 plan of Mizushima Kō and approaches
West approaches to Mizushima Kō
9.36
Shimo Mizu Shima (34° 28' N, 133° 42' E), 3¼ miles NNE of the N extremity of Te Shima (9.17), is dark, 57 m high, and its summit is covered with pine trees.

Shitano Ishi (34° 27' N, 133° 39' E), a detached rock with a depth of 4·5 m over it, lies 2 miles WSW of Shimo Mizu Shima.

Clearing lines. The summit of Ko Shima (34° 20' N, 133° 39' E) in line with the W extremity of Ode Shima bearing about 181°, leads 3 cables W of Shitano Ishi; and the summit of Washu San (34° 26' N, 133° 49' E), on the N side of Shimotsu Seto, in line with the S extremity of Ōbishaku (9.37) bearing about 096°, leads 3 cables S of Shitano Ishi.

Chart 695 plan of Mizushima Kō and approaches
Kami Mizu Shima, 50 m high, red in colour and grassy, lies 9 cables E of Shimo Mizu Shima. **Mezura Shō,** which dries 0·5 m, lies 3 cables W of Kami Mizu Shima.
9.37
Ajiro Shotō (34° 27' N, 133° 42' E), a group of four islets, lies within 1 mile SSE of Shimo Mizu Shima. **Chabin** and **Ōbishaku,** the N and W islets, are each 25 m high and surmounted by a single pine tree; **Ajiro** and **Ko Bishaku,** the middle two islets, are treeless.

Noji Shotō (34° 27' N, 133° 45' E), a group of four islets, lies within 2¼ miles SE of Kami Mizu Shima; a narrow sandbank, with depths of less than 3 m, lies between the group and Kami Mizu Shima. **Shira Iwa,** a white rock with three heads, 3 m high, lies between the two N'most islets.

West side of Mizushima Traffic Route
9.38
Mizushima Traffic Route is described at 9.6 and the regulations for the route are given at 9.7. Hon Shima is described at 9.19.

Mukaekasa Shima (34° 24' N, 133° 47' E), 46 m high, is separated from the NE side of Hon Shima by a shallow bight in which there are oyster beds. **Suzumenoko Shima,** a red-coloured pointed rock, lies close off the N side of Mukaekasa Shima.

Naga Shima, red in colour, lies ½ mile NNW of Mukaekasa Shima; it is 44 m high and has a double summit, the W of which is the highest.

Tidal streams in the vicinity of Naga Shima are strong and cause eddies.

Usu Iwa, which dries 3 m, lies close to the W edge of Mizushima Traffic Route, 2 cables NNW of the SE extremity of Naga Shima.

Takatsuki Iwa, rocky and 2·4 m high, lies at the extremity of a reef extending 1¼ cables WNW of the W extremity of Naga Shima.

Mukuchi Shima (34° 24' N, 133° 46' E), ½ mile NNW of Naga Shima, is covered with pine trees and attains an elevation of 124 m in its S part; a **light** is exhibited from a red round concrete tower standing close off the NW extremity of the island. **Mukuchi Se** with depths of less than 5 m, extends ¼ mile WNW of the W side of Mukuchi Shima.

Charts 3605 with plan, 695 plan of Mizushima Kō and approaches
East side of Mizushima Traffic Route
9.39
Yo Shima is described at 9.20.

Wasa Shima (34° 23·5' N, 133° 48·8' E), 31 m high, lies close off the NW extremity of Yo Shima on the E side of Mizushima Kō Traffic Route.

Ikuro Shima, ¼ mile N of Wasa Shima, is 25 m high and well wooded; the E side of the island is of black rock.

Hitsuishi Shima (34° 25' N, 133° 48' E), close N of Ikuro Shima, is 77 m high near its N end; a cliff formed by quarrying lies on its W side. The N and W sides of Hitsuishi Shima are steep-to except for a rock with a depth of less than 2 m over it, lying 1 cable off the W side.

Shimotsui Seto
9.40
Shimotsui Seto (34° 25·5' N, 133° 48·5' E) is bounded on its S side by the islands of Hitsuishi Shima, Matsu Shima and Kama Shima, and on its N side by the coast of Honshū between Nishino Hana and Kusumino Hana, 1¼ miles ESE.

Shimotsui Seto is deep and about 2 cables wide at its narrowest part; the **tidal streams** in it sometimes attain a rate of 4 knots. Large numbers of small vessels bound E or W along the N side of Bisan Seto use this channel which crosses Mizushima Traffic Route. (See also 9.33.)

Chart 695 plan of Mizushima Kō and approaches
Nishino Saki (34° 26' N, 133° 47' E), with a prominent cliff, lies on the N side of the W entrance to Shimotsui Seto; a **signal station** stands on the point.
9.41
Shimotsui Kō (34° 26' N, 133° 48' E), on the N side of Shimotsui Seto close E of Nishino Saki, consists of a commercial harbour on the W side and a fishing harbour on the E side, of **Gion Hana** on which stands a

prominent building; there are several basins protected by breakwaters in each harbour.

A **light** is exhibited on the W end of a detached breakwater in the commercial harbour; another **light** is exhibited on the head of the W breakwater in the fishing harbour.

Landmark. Washu San, 1¼ miles E of Nishino Saki, is 132 m high and on it stands an observation platform and an hotel.

Chart 3605
9.42

Kusumino Hana (34° 26' N, 133° 50' E) lies on the N side of Shimotsui Seto at its narrowest point; a **light** is exhibited from a black mast on a round concrete base situated on the S extremity of the point.

Landmark. The land between Kusumino Hana and Washu San (9.41) is red in colour and is a good mark for identifying the entrance to Shimotsui Seto from E.

Matsu Shima (34° 25·3' N, 133° 49·2' E) 26 m high, lies on the S side of Shimotsui Seto 2 cables SSW of Kusumino Hana.

Koshiki Iwa, which dries 3 m, **Ō Hadaka Shima,** 12 m high, and **Ko Hadaka Shima,** 6 m high, lie in that order N to S within ¼ mile SE of Matsu Shima.

Kama Shima (34° 25' N, 133° 50' E) lies on the S side of the E entrance to Shimotsui Seto; it is 49 m high at its W end and thickly covered with pine trees. **Muroki Shima,** a reddish almost treeless island, 24 m high, lies on a shoal within 5 cables SE of the S extremity, of Kama Shima. Muroki Shima appears as two islets from certain directions.

A shoal with a depth of 3 m, lies on the NE side of the channel in the E approach to Shimotsui Seto.

A bank with depths of less than 20 m extends SE from Muroki Shima to within ¼ mile of the N limit of Bisan Seto East Traffic Route; depths in the area are likely to change owing to the existence of sandwaves.

MIZUSHIMA KŌ

Chart 695 plan of Mizushima Kō and approaches
9.43

Mizushima Kō (34° 30' N, 133° 45' E), a specified port (see 1.64) and an industrial harbour created by extensive dredging and reclamation, lies at the N end of Mizushima Traffic Route (9.6). The W side of the port consists of a large industrial area, including a steelworks, standing on reclaimed land; the main wharves lie on the E side of this area but there are also wharves on the W side which forms the E bank of Takahashi Kawa (9.35).

The town of **Mizushima** (Chart 2875) lies about 5 miles N of the harbour.

Landmarks. Refineries with numerous chimneys and

tanks stand on each side of the main fairway. Many of the higher chimneys are painted red and white and are conspicuous; their positions can best be seen from the chart.

Pilotage. Pilotage is compulsory. Harbour pilots are available from sunrise to sunset at the quarantine anchorage (34° 26·5' N, 133° 44·5' E).

Anchorage. The **quarantine anchorage,** indicated on the chart, lies close SW of Noji Shotō (9.37) and can be used by vessels up to 50 000 grt. Large vessels may have to wait for a berth or for daylight in Sakate Wan (10.8) at the E entrance to Bisan Seto or off Kobe Kō (12.59).

Vessels are only berthed during daylight hours assisted by two to five tugs.

Mizushima signal station, painted white, stands on the summit of **Takashima** (34° 28·5' N, 133° 45·7' E) on the E side of the main fairway. The following traffic signals are displayed at this signal station:

Signal	*Meaning*
Black cone, point up	Inward bound vessels proceed to berth. Outward bound vessels of
or	over 1000 grt must await further
white light flashing every 2 seconds	signal; smaller vessels may proceed
Black square shape	Outward-bound vessels may proceed. Inward-bound vessels of
or	over 1000 grt must wait outside
red light flashing every 2 seconds	harbour entrance, keeping clear of outward-bound vessels
Two black cones, points together	Both inward and outward-bound vessels of over 20 000 grt must
or	await further signal, inward-bound vessels waiting outside har-
red and white lights flashing alternately every 3 seconds	bour entrance and keeping clear of any outward-bound vessels.
	Vessels of less than 20 000 grt, inward or outward-bound, may proceed
Two black cones, points together, and a red square flag	Entry and departure prohibited except for a vessel specially instructed by the Captain of the Port
or	
red light showing 3 red flashes followed by 3 white flashes every 6 seconds	

9.44

The **main fairway** into Mizushima Kō is entered close within the harbour limit from the N end of Mizushima

Katsura
Shima

Naga Shima   Mukuchi Shima   Mizushima Kō   Nishino Saki   Shimotsui Seto   Hitsuishi Shima

(9.43) Mizushima Kō from S, seen from the Mizushima Traffic Route in a position close SE of Naga Shima (34° 24' N, 133° 47' E)

(Original dated prior to 1978)

Traffic Route; it leads close E of Noji Shotō (9.37), close W of **Katsura Shima** (34° 27·6' N, 33° 45·9' E), 50 m high to the tops of the trees and prominent, and thence to the main wharves on each side of the harbour. The fairway is marked by *light-buoys* and is maintained to a dredged depth of 15·4 m shoaling to 6 m at the head of the harbour.

Anchoring is prohibited in the N part of the main fairway.

The **E fairway,** also marked by *light-buoys,* diverges from the S end of the main fairway and leads E of the shoal water lying S of Katsura Shima, to **Ube Kosan Jetty** (34° 28' N, 133° 46' E) and **Seto Wharves.** The depth in this fairway is over 10 m except for a 9·2 m patch and a 9·8 m patch lying within 1 cable SE of *El Light-buoy.*

Sonayasu Shipyard is situated ½ mile N of Katsura Shima.

9.45

A channel with depths from 10·9 m to 11·5 m and marked on its S side by *No. 1 Light-buoy* and *No. 2 Light-buoy,* branches off from the main fairway close N of Noji Shotō and leads between Kami Mizu Shima and the reclaimed area to the N; it joins a buoyed channel, dredged to depths of 11·5 m and 11 m, which leads to the mouth of Takashi Kawa and to **Kawasaki Steel Shipment Quay** (34° 30' N, 133° 43' E). A breakwater is situated on the N side of the channel NE of Kami Mizu Shima and a **light** is exhibited at its head.

Kawasaki Steel Quays (34° 29' N, 133° 44' E) lie on the SW side of a basin entered on the W side of the main fairway 2¼ miles NNW of Katsura Shima.

There are numerous T-headed piers with mooring dolphins at each end, on the E side of the main fairway and on the W side, N of the basin.

An **overhead cable** with a vertical clearance of 24 m, spans the mouth of Takashi Kawa.

9.46

Berths. The principal berths in Mizushima Kō are as follows:

Berth & Position	Length m	Depth m	Capacity dwt
East side of harbour			
Ube Kosan Jetty	dolphins	11·5	6 000
(34° 27·7' N, 133° 46·2' E)			
Seto Wharves			
(34° 28·0' N, 133° 46·2' E)			
A Quay	200	14	55 000
C Quay	85	14	3 000
Sanoyasu Shipyard			
(34° 28·0' N, 133° 45·8' E)			
E Quay	369	3–5	37 000
S Quay	305	8	190 000
W Quay	475	9–9·5	190 000
Asahi Chemicals			
(34° 28·6' N, 133° 45·5' E)			
C8 Jetty	dolphins	7·5–8·5	10 000
Nippon Mining			
(34° 29·4' N, 133° 44·9' E)			
No. 2 Oil Jetty	dolphins	17	180 000
No. 1 Oil Jetty	dolphins	12	60 000
Mitsubishi Kasei			
(34° 30·1' N, 133° 44·7' E)			
Nos. 1–6 Jetties		4–10	Up to 5 000
Tōkyō Steel			
(34° 30·7' N, 133° 44·6' E)			
A Quay	160	11–11·5	54 000
B, C Quays	300	9·5–10	20 000
East Wharf (Public)			
(34° 31·0' N, 133° 44·5' E)			
Nos. 1–4 Quays	360	5–5·5	2 000
West side of harbour			
Nishi Nihon Grain Centre			
(34° 30·6' N, 133° 44·4' E) dolphins		11·5	60 000
West Wharf (Public)			
(34° 30·4' N, 133° 44·4' E)			
No. 1 Quay	185	9·5	15 000
No. 2 Quay	130	8·5	10 000
Mitsubishi Sekiyū			
(34° 30·0' N, 133° 44·3' E)			
No. 2 Jetty	115	6–8·5	6 000
No. 3 Jetty	115	9–10	4 000
No. 5 Jetty	dolphins	12	45 000
No. 6 Jetty	dolphins	16–16·5	130 000
Kawasaki Steel			
(34° 29·5' N, 133° 43·7' E)			
C4–C5	485	11	30 000
D2–D3	430	10–11	30 000
E1–E2	496	12–15·8	100 000
E3	160	16–17	150 000
F1	320	17	200 000
G	260	16	130 000
Shipment Quay			
(34° 29·9' N, 133° 42·5' E)	720	11	30 000

9.47

Facilities. The offices of the Maritime Safety Agency, Quarantine and Immigration are located in the joint Harbour Office situated at the N end of the harbour.

Tugs up to 3000 h.p. are available.

Waste oil disposal facilities are available.

A dry dock with a capacity of 25 000 tons is situated in Sanoyasu Shipyard. Minor repairs can be undertaken.

Weather signals (1.42) are shown at Mizushima Signal Station.

De-ratting; see 1.70.

Supplies. Fresh water is laid on to the quays. Fuel oil can be obtained.

Communications. A car ferry service to Manugame Kō in Shikoku operates from the E side of the inner end of the harbour.

The nearest airport is at Okayama about 20 miles distant by road.

BISAN SETO (EAST)—CENTRAL ROUTES

TRAFFIC ROUTES AND REGULATIONS

Charts 3605 with plan, 1969
East Traffic Route
9.48

Bisan Seto East Traffic Route, indicated on the charts, extends from the position where North and South Traffic Routes (9.4, 9.5) converge ¼ mile NW of Kosei Shima (34° 22' N, 133° 51' E), to a position 1 mile SSW of Jizō Saki (34° 24' N, 134° 14' E) at the E end of Bisan Seto.

East Traffic Route is generally deep but shoal patches lie in it as follows:

(a) A 19·4 m patch near the centre line 1 mile within the W end of the route.

*Kashiwa
Shima*

*Jizo San,
124m high*

I Shima

*Ogi Shima
Light*

No.4

*Reita
Saki*

(9.48) Bisan Seto East Traffic Route (W-bound), seen from a position about 2 miles ENE of
Ogi Shima Light *(34°26′N, 134°04′E)*.

(Original dated prior to 1978)

*Kozuchi
Shima*

*Nabe
Shima*

*Osakino
Hana*

*Mitsugo
Shima*

Oyo Shima

Ōzuchi Shima

No.2

(9.48) Bisan Seto East Traffic Route (W-bound), seen from a position about 2 miles E of
Ōzuchi Shima *(34°25′N, 133°55′E)*.

(Original dated prior to 1978)

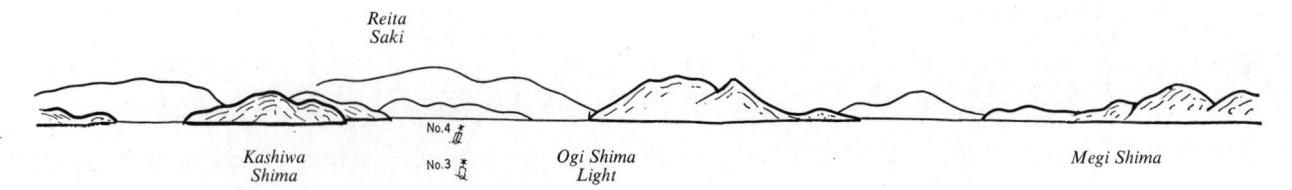

Reita
Saki

No.4

Kashiwa   No.3   *Ogi Shima*   *Megi Shima*
Shima   *Light*

(9.48) Bisan Seto East Traffic Route (E-bound), seen from a position about 4 miles WSW of
Ogi Shima Light *(34°26′N, 134°04′E)*.

(Original dated prior to 1978)

Dan Yama,   *Reita*   *Awara*   *Ogi Shima*
340m high   *Saki*   *Shima*   *Light*

No.4

(9.48) Bisan Seto East Traffic Route (E-bound), seen from a position about 1 mile W of
Ogi Shima Light *(34°26′N, 134°04′E)*.

(Original dated prior to 1978)

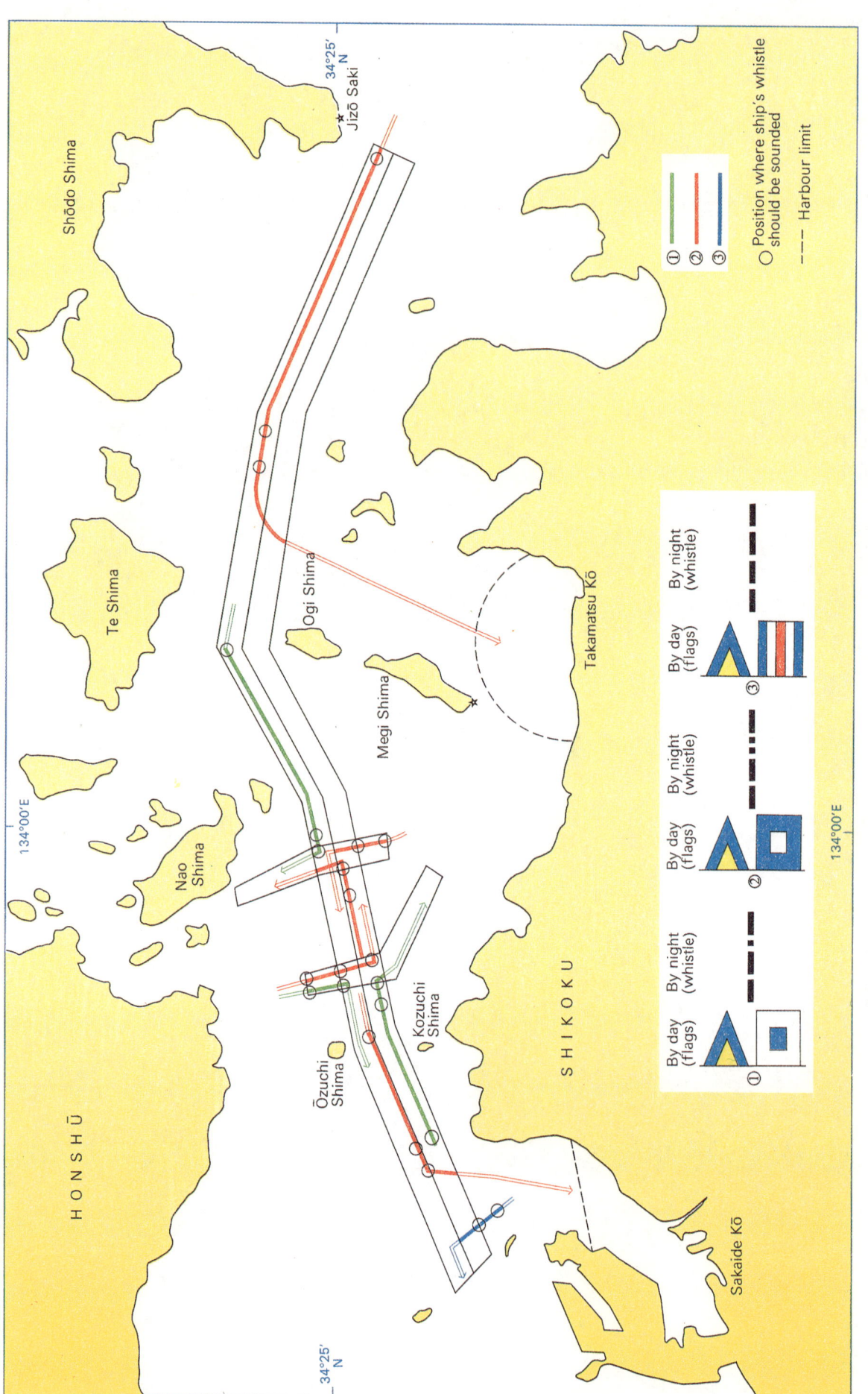

(9.51) Bisan Seto East Traffic Route, Ukō East Traffic Route & Ukō West Traffic Route

Atsusa Iwa and the S side of the island in line with Nō Misaki, bearing 250°, leads 1 cable S of it.

9.53

Kama Se, a narrow sandbank with a least depth of 0·8 m, extends 5 miles E from a position close E of **Ōsakino Hana** (34° 23' N, 133° 56' E), to the S extremity of Megi Shima (9.55).

Caution. Depths are liable to change in the vicinity of Kama Se owing to the existence of sandwaves.

Naka Se, on the S side of Bisan Seto East Traffic Route, extends 3½ miles ENE from a position 3 miles ENE of Ōsakino Hana, to Ogi Shima; it has depths of less than 2 m in places. *No. 2 Light-buoy* marks the W end of Naka Se and also marks the E side of the S end of Ukō East Traffic Route (9.49).

Clearing line. Nō Misaki in line with the S extremity of Kozuchi Shima, bearing 249°, leads at least 4½ cables N of Naka Se.

9.54

Ogi Shima (34° 25' N, 134° 04' E) lies close S of Bisan Seto East Traffic Route and on the W side of the N approach to Takamatsu Kō (9.57); on it are two wooded hills, the N hill is somewhat flat and 213 m high, and the S hill is pointed. A **light** is exhibited from a round stone tower situated on the N point of Ogi Shima.

Ogi Kō, a small harbour protected by two breakwaters, lies on the SW side of Ogi Shima; a **light** is exhibited on the head of each of the two breakwaters.

Doro Se, a detached sandbank with a least depth of 4·6 m over it, lies within 6½ cables E of the E side of Ogi Shima.

Caution. Depths are liable to change in the vicinity of Ogi Shima owing to the existence of sandwaves.

9.55

Megi Shima, a long narrow island on which there are two rounded hills, lies close S of Ogi Shima and is separated from it by **Kamoga Seto**; an **overhead cable** with a vertical clearance of 30 m, spans the channel.

Charts 698 plan of Takamatsu Kō, 3605, 1969

A **light** is exhibited from a white round concrete tower standing on **Hozuchi Hana** (34° 23' N, 134° 02' E), the S extremity of Megi Shima.

Charts 3605, 1969

Megi Kō, a small harbour protected by breakwaters, lies on the SE side of Megi Shima; a **light** is exhibited on the head of the E breakwater.

Masuno Mo, a narrow sandbank with depths from 0·2 m to 5·5 m, lies parallel to and within 1 mile of the E coast of Megi Shima; the bank dries, 4 cables E of Megi Kō.

TAKAMATSU KŌ

Charts 1969, 698 plan of Takamatsu Kō

Approaches to Takamatsu Kō

9.56

West approach. The approach to Takamatsu Kō from W is used by ferries crossing Bisan Seto East Traffic Route via Ukō West and Ukō East Traffic Routes.

S-bound ferries use a channel, marked on each side by a *light-buoy*, across the middle of Kama Se (34° 23' N, 134° 00' E) (9.53); N-bound ferries use the channel between a *light-buoy* marking the E end of Kama Se and the S extremity of Megi Shima.

Takamatsu Central Fairway (34° 23' N, 134° 05' E), leading between Megi Shima and Ō Shima, is the normal route used by traffic from the W-bound lane of Bisan Seto East Traffic Route and traffic bound to and from Shōdo Shima W Fairway (34° 28' N, 134° 08' E) (9.83); it is marked near its S end by *Takamatsu Central Fairway No. 1 Light-buoy* (34° 23' N, 134° 05' E).

The depths on Central Fairway are generally more than 10 m, but in its central part, to the W of Ō Shima, there are scattered shoals with depths from 5 m to 8 m; see 9.63.

Takamatsu East Fairway, the route normally used by ferries and small vessels from the Kōbe/Ōsaka region, lies between Nebutono Hana (34° 23·5' N, 134° 07·5' E) (9.64) and the islands to the N; thence W of Inagi Dashi (34° 28' N, 134° 08' E) (9.62).

Takamatsu Kō

9.57

Takamatsu Kō (34° 21' N, 134° 03' E), a specified port

(9.57) Takamatsu Kō from SW

(Original dated prior to 1978)

(b) An 18·4 m patch, also near the centre line, 2 miles within the W end; sandwaves exist in its vicinity.
(c) Two 19 m (62 ft) patches in the S lane ¾ mile NE of Ogi Shima.
(d) **Taka Se,** a bank with a least depth of 14·6 m (48 ft) in the S lane, 1½ miles within the E end of the route.

The centre line of East Traffic Route is marked by *Nos. 1–7 Fairway Light-buoys*, about 3 miles apart; *No. 4 Light-buoy* has a topmark of two yellow spheres disposed vertically.

Ukō Traffic Routes

9.49

Ukō West Traffic Route, reserved for S-bound vessels, and **Ukō East Traffic Route,** reserved for N-bound vessels, cross Bisan Seto East Traffic Route between *No. 2 Light-buoy* and *No. 3 Light-buoy* NW of Takamatsu Kō (34° 21' N, 134° 03' E). Both these routes are indicated on the charts.

Pilotage. See 9.2

Regulations

9.50

In addition to the general regulations for all traffic routes prescribed by the Maritime Traffic Safety Law (1.28), the following regulations are in force for East Traffic Route and both Ukō Traffic Routes:

(a) A vessel navigating in Bisan Seto East Traffic Route shall keep to the starboard side of the route.
(b) A vessel navigating in Ukō West Traffic Route shall proceed in a S'ly direction.
(c) A vessel navigating in Ukō East Traffic Route shall proceed in a N'ly direction.
(d) Crossing of Bisan Seto East Traffic Route between lines C and D is prohibited except within the area of Ukō West Traffic Route; similarly, crossing is prohibited between lines A and B, except within the area of Ukō East Traffic Route. Lines A, B, C and D are shown on the charts.
(e) A vessel navigating Ukō West or Ukō East Traffic Routes shall keep out of the way of a vessel of length 200 m or more which is navigating Bisan Seto East Traffic Route.
(f) A vessel other than a vessel of length 200 m or more, shall keep out of the way of a vessel of length 200 m or more which intends to turn into Ukō East Traffic Route from Bisan Seto East Traffic Route, or which intends to turn into Bisan Seto East Traffic Route from Ukō West Traffic Route.
(g) Except when a vessel is crossing a traffic route, there is a speed limit of 12 knots in Bisan Seto East Traffic Route between the W end of the traffic route and a line drawn 353° from Ogi Shima Light-tower in the vicinity of No. 4 Light-buoy.
(h) Tankers of length 200 m or more must have an escorting tug between Akashi Traffic Route (10.76) and Mizushima Kō.
(i) In low visibility, entry into the traffic routes is restricted as follows:

	Type of vessel	*Restriction*
(i)	Vessels of length 200 m or more	Entry prohibited when the visibility in the traffic route is less than 1 mile
(ii)	Vessels of 50 000 grt or more carrying dangerous cargo	
(iii)	Vessels of 25 000 grt or more carrying liquefied gas	
(iv)	Vessels towing or pushing very long tows	
(v)	Vessels carrying dangerous cargo (excluding those in (i), (ii) and (iii)	Entry prohibited when visibility in the traffic route is less than ½ mile.

9.51

Signals to be shown by vessels. The chartlet (facing page) of the traffic routes shows the flag signals to be displayed by day and the sound signals to be made at night, by vessels joining or leaving the traffic routes, in order to indicate their intentions to other vessels; the sound signals should be made at the positions indicated on the chartlets.

Cautions. Small vessels often keep close into the headlands and islands in the vicinity of the course alteration points off Ogi Shima (34° 25' N, 134° 04' E), Jizō Saki (34° 25' N, 134° 14' E) and Ōkado Hana (34° 26' N, 134° 20' E).

The ferries crossing the straits from Takamatsu Kō (34° 21' N, 134° 03' E) to Uno Kō are very numerous.

Large numbers of fishing vessels congregate between Ogi Shima and Jizō Saki and often completely block the fairway. Fishing boats with nets are to be encountered principally S of Ōzono Se (34° 25' N, 133° 58' E) and in the vicinity of *Nos. 1, 5* and *6 Fairway Light-buoys.*

BISAN SETO (EAST)—SOUTH SIDE

NŌ MISAKI TO MEGI SHIMA

Charts 3605, 1969

9.52

Nō Misaki (34° 23' N, 133° 54' E), a point situated 2 miles ENE of Kosei Shima (9.13), lies ½ mile S of Bisan Seto East Traffic Route; on it are situated several flat-topped hills the N'most of which is 171 m high and somewhat pointed. There are three remarkable cliffs, formed by landslides, on the W side of the point.

A fish conservation area, marked by three *light-buoys* (orange light) lies ½ mile E of Nō Misaki. **Submarine cables** are laid across Bisan Seto from a position ¼ mile SE of Nō Misaki; their landing place is marked by **beacons.**

Kozuchi Shima, 1½ miles ENE of Nō Misaki, is 111 m high and has a prominent wood on its summit; a **light** is exhibited from a white column situated on the N extremity of the island.

Atsusa Iwa, a detached rock with a depth of 3·4 m over it, lies 5 cables E of Kozuchi Shima.

Clearing lines. The N side of Kozuchi Shima in line with Nō Misaki, bearing 239°, leads 2½ cables N of (see 1.64), lies in **Takamatsu Wan** on the S side of the E part of Bisan Seto and is used extensively by both rail and car ferries plying between Shikoku and Honshū, and by regular shipping services from all parts of Seto Naikai.

Takamatsu, which in 1973 had a population of 286 000, is the administrative centre of Shikoku and also a tourist centre.

The harbour limit of Takamatsu Kō is indicated on the charts.

The inner harbour, protected by breakwaters, is separated from East Harbour by reclaimed land projecting ¼ mile N from the coast.

A fishery harbour, enclosed by reclaimed land and protected by breakwaters, lies 1 mile W of the inner harbour; **Tsuruchi Kō** and **Kosai Kō** both part of Takamatsu Kō, lie, respectively, ¾ mile and 1¼ miles farther W. They are both protected by breakwaters.

Pilotage. Pilotage is not compulsory. Harbour pilots are available from 1 hour before sunrise to 1 hour before sunset.

9.58

Regulations. General regulations prescribed by the Port Regulations Laws are described at 1.37. Local regulations are also in force in Takamatsu Kō and are summarised as follows:

(a) A vessel shall not anchor outside the breakwaters within a radius of 500 metres from the W end of Middle Breakwater (9.59).

(b) A vessel shall not anchor within the harbour breakwaters.

(c) An inward-bound vessel shall give way to an outward-bound vessel.

(d) A vessel shall keep to the starboard side of Takamatsu Fairway (9.59).

(e) All vessels should enter by the W entrance and leave by the E entrance, except that vessels of over 1000 grt may leave by the W entrance.

(f) Vessels leaving by the E entrance must keep clear of Takamatsu Fairway.

(g) A vessel of over 1000 grt intending to leave through the E entrance, shall notify the Captin of the Port by noon the previous day, her ETD. A vessel shall notify the Captain of the Port of any amendment to her ETD without delay.

Signals. Movement control signals are made from a **signal station** situated close to the root of West Breakwater (9.59).

A vessel of over 1000 grt intending to leave the inner harbour by the W entrance should use the following signals:

By day	At night
First substitute over Flag W	If going ahead: 1 prolonged blast on the siren and 1 long flash of a white light, repeated at intervals. If going sternfirst: 3 short blasts on the siren and 3 short flashes of a white light, repeated at intervals

Chart 698 plan of Takamatsu Kō
9.59

The W entrance to the inner harbour lies between **West Breakwater** and the W end of **Middle Breakwater,** and the E entrance between the E end of Middle Breakwater and a short **East Breakwater**; a **light** is exhibited on each side of both entrances, and a fog siren is sounded from the head of West Breakwater.

Ashimachi Breakwater projects 2¼ cables NNE from a position close E of the E entrance to the inner harbour and a **light** is exhibited at its head.

Prohibited area. In 1980, breakwater construction work was in progress to the NW of the head of Ashimachi Breakwater; the area was marked by yellow *buoys* and navigation and anchoring in it was prohibited.

Takamatsu Fairway. A *light-buoy*, moored 4 cables N of the head of West Breakwater, marks the entrance to Takamatsu Fairway leading to the inner harbour through the W entrance; there are depths from 7 m to 10 m in the fairway.

A **direction light** is exhibited in the S part of the inner harbour to facilitate entry through the W entrance.

9.60

Nos. 1, 2 and 3 Quays, used by the rail ferries, are situated on the SW side of the inner harbour. A pair of **leading lights** stand on each of No. 2 and No. 3 Quays; both pairs of lights in line bear 228° and indicate the alignment of the two berths.

No. 1 and **No. 2 Municipal Piers** and **Central Wharf** lie on the S side of the harbour.

An oil depot lies on reclaimed land forming the NE side of the harbour; two piers project from the N side of the reclaimed land and there are several dolphin berths on the S side within the inner harbour.

Shikoku Shipyard lies on the E side of the inner harbour.

The extensive area of reclaimed land projecting N from **Asahi-chō** on the E side of the inner harbour in quayed.

East Harbour (34° 21·0' N, 134° 04·5' E), where there is a ferry pier, lies on the E side of the reclaimed land fronting Asahi-chō.

9.61

Berths. The principal berths in Takamatsu Kō are as follows:

Berth & Position	Length m	Depth m	Capacity dwt
Japan National Railways (34° 20·9' N, 134° 03·0' E)			
1, 2, 3 Quays	—	4·5–5	3 000
Municipal Piers (34° 21·0' N, 134° 03·2' E)			
No. 1	244	4·4–5·5	3 000
No. 2	147	5–6	1 000
Central Wharf (34° 21·0' N, 134° 03·4' E)			
7·5 m Quay	260	6·5–7	3 000
Oil Depot (34° 21·3' N, 134° 03·7' E)			
Piers (2 in No.)	225 (each)	7	2 000
Asahi Chiku			
10 m Quay (34° 21·5' N, 134° 04·0' E)	370	9·5–10	10 000
F-Chiku Quay (N side) (34° 21·6' N, 134° 04·2' E)	660	6–7	3 000
F-Chiku Quay (E side) (34° 21·4' N, 134° 04·4' E)	390	6–7	3 000
East Harbour (34° 21·0' N, 134° 04·5' E)			
Ferry Pier	131	5·5	3 000
5·5 m Quay	90	4	2 000

Facilities. The Harbour Office is situated close S of Central Wharf. There is an Immigration Office.

Repairs can be carried out in the Shikoku Shipyard where there is a drydock of 4000 tons capacity.

Weather signals (see 1.42) are shown at the signal station situated at the root of West Breakwater.

Supplies. Fresh water is available and there are four oilers.

NAGASAKI HANA TO ŌKUSHI SAKI

Charts 698 plan of Takamatsu Kō, 1969

9.62

Nagasaki Hana (34° 23' N, 134° 06' E) is the N extremity of **Ya Shima,** a large island lying on the E side of Takamatsu Wan (9.57) and which is separated from the mainland to the S by a canal. A plateau, 292 m (957 ft) high, covered with pine trees and on which stands an ancient temple, lies in the centre of Ya Shima, and the ruins of a fort stand on Nagasaki Hana. A barren islet, 8 m high, on which stands a solitary pine tree, lies close off Nagasaki Hana.

Inagi Dashi, a sandbank with a least depth of 4 m over it, lies between ½ mile and 1¾ miles SW of Nagasaki Hana; a *light-buoy* is moored near its NE end.

Clearing line. Yatake (Yurubuta) Shima (34° 24·3' N, 134° 06·1' E) in line with the N extremity of Ō Shima, bearing 043°, leads about ½ mile NW of the shoalest part of Inagi Dashi and very close NW of an 8·1 m patch.

Chart 1969

9.63

Ō Shima (34° 24' N, 134° 07' E), on the E side of Takamatsu Central Fairway (9.56), lies 1½ miles NNE of Nagasaki Hana; it is well wooded and is in two parts joined by a wooded sandy isthmus on which stands the chimney of a sanatorium, prominent from both E and W.

Yatake (Yurubuta) Shima, 21 m (68 ft) high and flat-topped, is the largest of three islets situated on the edge of a mudbank which extends 4 cables W from the W side of Ō Shima.

Noyama Dashi, with a depth of 7·3 m (24 ft) over it, lies 5 cables NNW of Yatake Shima; a rock with a depth of 7·8 m (26 ft) lies 4 cables SW of it.

Ōzuchi Dashi, 4 cables SW of Yatake Shima, is a pinnacle rock with a depth of 5 m (16 ft) over it; an 8·2 m (27 ft) patch lies 2 cables W of it.

Matabei and **Oki Matabei,** with depths, respectively, of 2 m (6 ft) and 2·4 m (8 ft) over them, lie on a shoal which extends ¾ mile SW from the SW extremity of Ō Shima.

9.64

Yashima Wan (34° 23' N, 134° 07' E) is entered between Nagasaki Hana (9.62) and Nebutono Hana 1½ miles ENE; it is almost completely obstructed by a mudbank with depths of less than 4 m (13 ft), on which there is a dense growth of seaweed.

Aji Kō, a small shallow harbour protected by two breakwaters one of which is detached, is situated in the NE corner of Yashima Wan; a **light** is exhibited on the head of the N breakwater and at the S end of the detached breakwater.

In 1980, a detached breakwater was under construction ½ mile SW of Aji Kō.

Nebutono Hana, the E entrance point to Yashima Wan, is a low whitish-brown cliff densely covered with pine trees. A **light** which is exhibited from a white round concrete structure situated 1½ cables S of the point and shows over **Shirashi Shō,** 1½ cables to the W. A *light-buoy* is moored 1½ cables NNE of Nebutono Hana.

Kannon Saki (34° 24' N, 134° 08' E), a low rocky point on which stand some pine trees, lies ¾ mile ENE of Nebutono Hana. A spit, with depths of less than 10 m, extends about 3 cables NW from the E side of a small bay lying between the two points; the extremity of the spit is almost always marked by tide rips.

9.65

Ko Kabuto Shima (34° 24·5' N, 134° 07·5' E), a rocky round-topped wooded islet, 41 m (134 ft) high, lies 1 mile N of Nebutono Hana.

Ō Kabuto Shima, 2 cables N of Ko Kabuto Shima, is well wooded and its rounded summit attains an elevation of 76 m (249 ft) to the tops of the trees; a solitary detached rock, 10 m high, lies close off its N extremity.

Kanawa Iwa (34° 25' N, 134° 08' E), 1½ cables NE of Ō Kabuto Shima and close S of Bisan Seto East Traffic Route, consists of two rocks which dry; a **light** is exhibited from a red round concrete tower standing on the W'most of the two rocks.

Inagi Shima, ¾ mile SE of Ō Kabuto Shima, lies on the N side of the E entrance to Takamatsu East Fairway (9.56); two round-topped hills, 57 m (186 ft) high to the tops of the trees, lie in the E part, and the island appears saddle-backed from E and W. A **light** is exhibited from a white round concrete tower standing on the SE end of Inagi Shima.

9.66

Landmarks. Tōmi Yama, 235 m (770 ft) high with a pointed summit, and **Ryūō San,** 238 m (780 ft) high with tall pine trees on its summit, lie, respectively, ¾ mile and 1¼ miles SSE of Kannon Saki (34° 24' N, 134° 05' E) (9.64) and are both good marks.

Goken San, the highest mountain in the vicnity, has a conspicuous rocky summit and attains an elevation of 369 m (1210 ft) 1¼ miles SSW of Ryūō San.

Taka Shima (34° 23' N, 134° 11' E), 1¾ miles E of Kannon Saki is well-wooded and 77 m (252 ft) high to the tops of the trees; shoal banks with depths of less than 10 m (33 ft) extend 3 cables NW and 4 cables SE of the island.

Shido Wan is entered between a point 2 miles SE of Kannon Saki and Ōkushi Saki (34° 22' N, 134° 12·6' E), 2 miles E. The head of the bay is divided into two shallow bays by a small peninsula on which there is a pointed, well-wooded and prominent hill, 99 m (charted as 343 ft) high.

Extensive seaweed and oyster beds lie in the bay, except in the fairways to Shido Kō and Mure Kō.

Shido Kō (34° 20' N, 134° 10' E) lies at the head of the W bay in Shido Wan and is protected by a detached breakwater; a **light** is exhibited on the E end of the breakwater. There are depths of 3 m inside the breakwater and there is a landing jetty with a depth of 2·4 m alongside.

Mure Kō, protected by a breakwater, lies 1½ miles NW of Shido Kō; a **light** is exhibited on the head of the breakwater.

Nagahama Ura, only suitable for small craft, is the E of the two bays at the head of Shido Wan.

Ōkushi Saki (34° 22' N, 134° 13' E), the E entrance point to Shido Wan, lies on the S side of the E end of Bisan Seto; it is 18 m high, wooded and fringed with rocks, and rises to a height of 144 m (472 ft) a short distance SSE.

BISAN SETO (EAST)—NORTH SIDE

KUSUMINO HANA TO INUMODORI HANA

Chart 3605

9.67

Between Kusumino Hana (34° 26' N, 133° 50' E) (9.42) and Hibi Kō 5½ miles ENE, there is a bay which is much encumbered with shoals and drying banks.

The islands and shoals in the E approach to Shimotsui Seto are described at 9.42.

Tateba Shima (34° 27' N, 133° 51' E), lying in the middle of the bay 2 miles NE of Kusumino Hana, is 53 m high, dark, conical and thickly covered with pine trees; the island is somewhat prominent from S.

An extensive mudbank which dries in places, lies on the W side of Tateba Shima and is separated from it by a channel about 3 cables wide. A *light-buoy* is moored at the NE end of this channel. Another channel, about 1 mile farther W and marked at each end by a *light-buoy*, divides the mudbank into E and W parts.

A channel with depths of over 7 m, runs round the bay between the edge of the mudbank and the coast; a rock with a depth of 2·6 m over it lies in the middle of this channel, 1¾ miles NW of Tateba Shima.

Hode Iwa, two rocks 2 m high, lies 6 cables E of the N extremity of Tateba Shima. **Naida Su,** a mudbank which dries, extends about 1 mile E from a position 3 cables S of Hode Iwa; a *light-buoy* moored 2 miles E of Tateba Shima marks the E end of Naida Su.

A shoal bank with depths of less than 2 m in places, extends about 1¼ miles SW of Naida Su; a *light-buoy* is moored on its SW extremity. A stranded wreck lies on the W side of the shoalest part of this bank.

Ajino Kō

9.68

Ajino Kō (34° 27' N, 133° 49' E) lies on the S side of the mouth of **Ō Kawa** 2 miles N of Kusumino Hana; a jetty with a depth of 3 m alongside, is situated at the mouth of the river and there is a fairway leading to it. A *light-buoy* is moored 1 cable N of the head of the jetty.

Kotoura Kō

9.69

Kotoura Kō (34° 28' N, 133° 50' E), 1½ miles ENE of Ajino Kō, consists of two basins separated by **Ganyama Hana**. The W basin is protected by two breakwaters and has a jetty with a depth of about 4 m on its NE side. A **light** is exhibited on the head of the E breakwater, and a *light-buoy* is moored 2 cables S of the entrance to the basin.

Sumitomo Chemical Works lies on the E side of Ganyama Hana, and **Tanoguchi Basin,** protected by two breakwaters and with depths of about 3 m in it, is entered a short distance farther E.

Charts 3605, 1969

Submarine cables are landed on **Shibukawa Beach,** a popular seaside resort, 2½ miles ENE of Tateba Shima.

Charts 694 plan of Uno Kō and approaches, 1969

Hibi Kō

9.70

Hibi Kō (34° 27' N, 133° 56' E), 5½ miles ENE of Kusumino Hana, lies within the harbour area of Uno Kō (9.76). It is protected by two breakwaters and has depths of less than 3 m within it; a **light** is exhibited on the head of each of the two breakwaters.

Landmarks. The chimney (grey), with an elevation of 155 m, of the **Mitsui Metals Refinery** stands on top of a hill 4 cables W of Hibi Kō; a chimney (red and white), with an elevation of 172 m, and another chimney (red and black), with an elevation of 192 m, stand, respectively, 2 cables S and 2 cables E of the refinery chimney. All three chimneys are conspicuous.

Chart 694 plan of Uno Kō and approaches

A timber pond lies at the head of Hibi Kō and there is a small basin, which dries, on its E side.

Timber Wharf, with a depth of 9·5 m alongside and which can accommodate a vessel of 15 000 tons, lies on reclaimed land forming the W side of the harbour entrance. **Mitsui Hibi Wharf,** with a depth of 13 m alongside and which can accommodate a vessel of 20 000 tons, lies on the S side of the reclaimed land close W of Timber Wharf.

Inumodori Hana (34° 27' N, 133° 57' E), situated ¾ mile E of the entrance to Hibi Kō, has a bare brown and rounded summit, 68 m (223 ft) high; a **light** is exhibited from a black round concrete tower standing on the point.

APPROACHES TO KAZURASHIMA SUIDŌ AND UNO KŌ

Charts 3605, 1969

South approach to Kazurashima Suidō and Uno Kō

9.71

Ōzuchi Shima (34° 25' N, 133° 55' E), on the N side of Bisan Seto East Traffic Route, lies 1½ miles N of Kozuchi Shima (9.52) situated on the S side of the route; it is a prominent conical island, 171 m high.

No. 1 Light-buoy is moored on the N edge of Bisan Seto East Traffic Route, ½ mile SE of Ōzuchi Shima.

Ōsono Se, a bank with depths of less than 20 m, extends 4 miles E from Ōzuchi Shima along the N edge of Bisan East Traffic Route. A shallow patch with a least depth of 7·8 m lies 1¼ miles ENE of Ōzuchi Shima and another patch with a least depth of 6·6 m lies 1¾ miles farther ENE. A *light-buoy* is moored on the S side of each of these patches.

Ukō West and Ukō East Traffic Routes (9.49), indicated on the charts, lead across Ōsono Se.

Chart 694 plan of Uno Kō and approaches

9.72

Kōjin Shima (34° 27' N, 133° 58' E), sparsely wooded and 97 m (319 ft) high, lies 8 cables E of Inumodori Hana (9.70). An **overhead power cable,** with a vertical clearance of about 57 m (188 ft), spans the channel between Inumodori Hana and Kōjin Shima; the pylons supporting the cable on each side are painted red and white.

Manaita Ishi, a detached rock which dries, lies ½ mile S of the SE extremity of Kōjin Shima; a **light** is exhibited from a black round concrete tower standing on the rock.

Hokake Ishi, 2½ cables SW of Manaita Ishi, is 1 m (3 ft) high; a red round **beacon,** 9 m in height, stands on the rock.

Nao Shima, close E of Kōjin Shima, is a large hilly island; **Jizō San** (Charts 3605 and 1969), a prominent densely wooded hill, attains an elevation of 124 m near its centre.

Ushinoko Iwa, a rock with two heads which dries

0·7 m (2 ft), lies in the S part of the channel between Kōjin Shima and Nao Shima; a **light** is exhibited from a red round concrete tower standing on the NW end of the rock. The channel lying between Ushinoko Iwa and Kōjin Shima is suitable for vessels with local knowledge.

An **overhead cable** with a vertical clearance of about 27 m (89 ft), spans the N part of the channel between Kōjin Shima and Nao Shima.

9.73

Kazura Shima (34° 28·3' N, 133° 57·3' E), ¼ mile N of Kōjin Shima, is a bare island 104 m (341 ft) high; a **light** is exhibited from a white mast on a concrete base standing on the SE point of the island.

Tobi Su, a rock situated 1¼ cables W of the W extremity of Kazura Shima, stands on a reef which dries and which is steep-to on its W side; a **light** is exhibited from a red round concrete tower standing on the rock.

The **ferry routes** between Uno Kō and Takamatsu Kō (9.57) 9 miles SE, pass E and W of Kōjin Shima and Kazura Shima; S-bound ferries pass W and N-bound ferries pass E, of the two islands.

Kazurashima Suidō, within the harbour limits of Uno Kō (9.76), lies between Kazura Shima and the mainland NW. Vessels proceeding along the S coast of Honshū pass through Kazurashima Suidō and the traffic in the straits is heavy.

North-east approach to Kazurashima Suidō and Uno Kō

9.74

Shimo-karasu Shima (34° 29' N, 133° 58' E), rocky, flat-topped and 27 m (90 ft) high to the tops of the trees, lies on a reef 7 cables NE of Kazura Shima. **Gonin Zowai**, which dries 2·1 m (7 ft) in places, lies within 1¼ cables NE of the islet.

Kami-karasu Shima, rocky, flat-topped and 18 m (59 ft) high, lies 2¼ cables ENE of Shimo-karasu Shima.

Matsu Shima, a rock 5 m (17 ft) high surrounded by reefs, lies on the N side of the NE approach to Kazurashima Suidō, 1¼ cables SE of Kami-karasu Shima; between them is a 2·1 m (7 ft) patch.

Tera Shima, 83 m (273 ft) high, occupies the greater part of a bay on the N side of Nao Shima (9.20); a **light** is exhibited from a red round column standing on the N extremity of the island. **Shiodōshino Seto**, with depths from 3 m to 15 m in its W entrance but shallow in its E entrance, leads between Tera Shima and Nao Shima.

Mitsubishi Metals Mining Refinery stands on the N extremity of Nao Shima on the W side of the W entrance of Shiodōshino Seto.

Mitsubishi Metals Wharf, with a depth of 10 m alongside, lies on the NW side of the refinery; vessels up to 20 000 dwt can be accommodated at this berth. There is a dolpin berth which can accommodate vessels up to 2000 tons, situated on the E side of the refinery.

Takabe Hana (34° 29·3' N, 133° 57·9' E), on the NE side of Uno Kō 3 cables N of Shimo-karasu Shima, is a grey rocky point which rises to **Takabe Yama**, 60 m (198 ft) high.

Yasuno Shima, 30 m (100 ft) high to the tops of the trees, lies 3¼ cables E of Takabe Hana.

Two **submarine pipelines** are laid NW across the strait from the NW point of Nao Shima to the W side of Takabe Hana; the landing places on each side are marked by **beacons**.

Charts 3605, 1969

9.75

Tsubone Shima (34° 29' N, 134° 00' E) lies on the S side of the fairway 1 mile NE of Tera Shima (9.74) and is 75 m high.

Kuōnojōrō Shima lies on the N side of the fairway ½ mile NW of Tsubone Shima; it is 83 m high and both sides of its S summit have been quarried and are of a light brown colour. A **light** is exhibited from a white round concrete tower standing on the SE extremity of the island.

Desaki Uchi, a wide bay lying between Takabe Hana (34° 29·3' N, 133° 57·9' E) (9.74) and De Saki 2¼ miles NE, is much obstructed by islets and shoals and the depths in it are irregular. No attempt should be made to enter this bay without local knowledge.

The entrance to the NE approach to Kazurashima Suidō lies between **De Saki** (34° 30·5' N, 134° 00·5' E), the S extremity of a narrow peninsula extending SE from the coast of Honshū, and the NW side of I Shima (9.80), 6 cables SSE. An islet, 19 m high to the tops of the trees, lies 1¼ cables E of De Saki; two radio towers and a beacon stand on De Saki.

Ōhiru Shima, 26 m high, lies in the entrance to the channel between De Saki and I Shima; a **light** is exhibited from a white metal column standing in the SW part of the islet. A remarkable pointed rock, 10 m high, lies 1 cable N of Ōhiru Shima.

UNO KŌ

Chart 694 plan of Uno Kō and approaches

9.76

Uno Kō (34° 29' N, 133° 57' E), a specified port (see 1.64), lies in Kazurashima Suidō and is used by both rail and car ferries plying between Honshū and Shikoku. See also 9.73.

Uno Kō is the port of the industrial city of **Tamano** which in 1973 had a population of 73 000.

Pilotage is not compulsory but recommended. Pilots are not available after sunset.

No. 1 Pier divides the N part of Uno Kō into two basins; the W basin or inner harbour, has depths from 7 m to 9 m (23–30 ft) over its greater part, and in it lie the public quays.

No. 2 Pier lies on the E side of the E basin; berths in this basin are for the use of Japanese National Railways.

No. 3 Pier lies on reclaimed land which protects a basin with depths of 4 m within it, situated 3 cables SW of the W basin. A prominent chimney, with an elevation of 68 m, stands close N of the pier.

Three pairs of **leading lights** are exhibited on No. 1 Pier, and another pair of **leading lights** are exhibited on No. 2 Pier; these lights indicate the alignment of the berths on these two piers.

Anchorage is **prohibited** in an area, indicated on the chart, S of No. 1 and No. 2 Piers.

Tama Wan lies on the W side of the S part of Uno Kō and the greater part of it shores are occupied by the dry docks and slips of **Mitsui Tamano Shipyard**. A floating dock (34° 28·0' N, 133° 56·5' E) connected to the shore by a jetty, lies in Tama Wan.

9.77

Berths. The principal berths in Uno Kō are as follows:

Berth & Position	Length m	Depth m	Capacity dwt
No. 3 Pier			
(34° 29·1' N, 133° 57·2' E)			
10 m Quay	185	9·5	15 000
5·5 m Quay	90	5·5	2 000

No. 1 Pier (W side)			
(34° 29·3' N, 133° 57·3' E)			
No. 4 Wharf	150	7–8	8 000
No. 5 Wharf	120	5·5–6·5	5 000
No. 1 Pier (E side)			
(34° 29·3' N, 133° 57·4' E)			
No. 1 Wharf	110	5	1 500
No. 2 Wharf	190	8–9·5	10 000
No. 2 Pier			
(34° 29·4' N, 133° 57·7' E)			
No. 1 Wharf	85	5	1 000
No. 2 Wharf	115	8–9·5	3 000

Facilities. Offices of the Maritime Safety Agency, Customs and Immigration are located in the joint Harbour Office situated on the W side of the W basin.

Tugs are available from Mizushima Kō.

Major hull and machinery repairs can be undertaken at the several shipyards where the following docking facilities are available:

Three dry docks with a capacity up to 46 000 dwt
A floating dock with a capacity of 150 000 dwt.

Supplies. Fresh water is available on Nos. 1 and 3 Piers and by water barge. Fuel oil is available.

Communications. The nearest airport is at Okayama about 13 miles distant by road.

ISHIMA SUIDŌ AND APPROACHES

Charts 3605, 1969

9.78

Ishima Suidō (34° 29' N, 134° 02' E), a deep water channel $\frac{1}{4}$ mile wide, lies between I Shima and the W extremity of Te Shima; it leads from the N side of Bisan Seto to the NW corner of Harima Nada.

Harima Nada N Fairway No. 1 Light-buoy (34° 27·5' N, 134° 01·7' E) is moored in the S entrance to Ishima Suidō, and *Harima Nada N Fairway No. 2 Light-buoy* (34° 31·5' N, 134° 02·3' E) is moored in its N entrance.

9.79

Kashiwa Shima (34° 20' N, 134° 00' E) lies $\frac{1}{4}$ mile S of **Tsuno Saki,** the E extremity of Nao Shima; it is 107 m high to the tops of the trees.

Odaka Shima, with two summits the higher of which is 27 m high, lies close off Tsuno Saki.

Teshima Tai, an extensive shoal area with depths of less than 10 m, lies on the E side of the S entrance to Ishima Suidō. The N part of this shoal has depths of less than 5 m and there is a narrow channel between it and the SW coast of Te Shima.

Mukae Shima (34° 28' N, 134° 00' E), on the W side of the S entrance to Ishima Suidō, lies close off the NE side of Nao Shima; it is 35 m high to the tops of the trees and there is a quarry on its SE side.

Ie Shima lies close NW of Mukae Shima and is 71 m high in its NW part; a clump of trees on the summit stands out well.

9.80

I Shima (34° 29' N, 134° 01' E) lies between Ishima Suidō and the entrance to the NE approach to Kazurashima Suidō (9.73); **Dango Yama,** 157 m high, the summit, lies near the middle of the island. **Kurakake Hana,** the S extremity of I Shima, is conical and shows up well from NE; a **light** is exhibited from a white round concrete tower situated on the point.

9.81

Ushirotobi Saki, the W extremity of Te Shima (9.82), lies on the E side of Ishima Suidō; **Uomi Yama,** a prominent pointed hill 102 m high, lies 4 cables E of the point. A rock which dries 1·2 m, lies 1 cable off **Kō Saki** situated 4 cables NNE of Ushirotobi Saki; a *light-buoy* is moored 2 cables NW of the rock.

Ieura Kō (34° 29·2' N, 134° 03·7' E), protected by breakwaters one of which is detached, lies on the NW side of Te Shima, 8 cables E of Kō Saki; a **light** is exhibited on the E head of the detached breakwater.

Dango Se, with depths of less than 10 m and a least depth of 1·3 m near its W end, lies on the E side of the N entrance to Ishima Suidō and extends about 4 miles ENE from a position 1 mile N of Kō Saki. A *light-buoy* is moored on the W end and on the E end (Chart 2875) of Dango Se.

TE SHIMA TO JIZŌ SAKI

Charts 3605, 1969

9.82

Te Shima is situated on the N side of Bisan Seto East Traffic Route (9.48) with **Reita Saki** (34° 27' N, 134° 05' E) its steep-to S extremity, $3\frac{1}{2}$ miles ENE of Kashiwa Shima (9.79).

Landmarks. Dan Yama, the summit of Te Shima, attains an elevation of 340 m near its centre; **Naka Yama,** a prominent pointed hill 204 m high, lies near the S coast $8\frac{1}{2}$ cables SW of Dan Yama.

Chart 1969

Ode (Kote) Shima lies close on the E side of Te Shima and is separated from it by a narrow channel; two **overhead cables** with a least vertical clearance of 42 m, span the channel.

Awara Shima, a conical rock 30 m (97 ft) high, lies $\frac{1}{2}$ mile S of Ode Shima.

Ka Shima, 226 m (740 ft) high, lies close off the W coast of Shōdo (Shōzu) Shima (10.5) and is separated from Ode (Kote) Shima by a narrow channel. **Karamo Sowai,** a detached rock with a depth of 3·7 m (12 ft), lies 5 cables NW of **Tokata Saki,** the W extremity of Ka Shima.

To Ishi, with a depth of 3·7 m (12 ft) over it, lies 4 cables SW of Tokata Saki, and about midway between them is a rock with a depth of less than 2 m. A *light-buoy* (red light group flashing 2 every 6 seconds) is moored $1\frac{1}{4}$ cables NE of To Ishi.

Shōdo Shima W Fairway

9.83

Shōdo Shima W Fairway, with depths from 5 m to 8 m (17–26 ft) in its shoalest part, leads from Bisan Seto, through the channel between Ode (Kote) Shima and Ka Shima, to the NW part of Harima Nada; *Shōdo Shima W Fairway No. 2 Light-buoy* (34° 28·3' N, 134° 08·2' E) is moored in the S entrance of the fairway close SW of Karamo Sowai (9.82). The fairway is entered from N, passing W of *Shōdo Shima W Fairway No. 4 Light-buoy* (34° 30·8' N, 134° 08·5' E) moored 3 cables W of Katsura Shima.

Katsura Shima (34° 31' N, 134° 09' E), 59 m (194 ft) high, lies $6\frac{1}{2}$ cables NNW of **Miyano Hana,** the W extremity of Shōdo Shima.

Okino Shima (34° 31' N, 134° 10' E), close E of Katsura Shima, is separated from the W coast of Shōdo Shima by **Oeno Seto,** a narrow channel in which the tidal streams are strong.

Shikai Kō Light is exhibited on the head of a breakwater off the SE extremity of Okino Shima.

Tonoshō Kō
9.84

Tonoshō Kō (34° 30' N, 134° 10' E), the main part of which lies in the narrow channel between Ka Shima and the W end of Shōdo Shima, is the principal harbour of Shōdo Shima and is extensively used by ferries and fishing boats. **Tonoshō,** the tourist centre of the island, lies at the inner end of the harbour and in 1973 had a population of 23 000.

Tonoshō Kō is approached from Shōdo Shima W Fairway; *Tonoshō Kō Light-buoy* (34° 29·6' N, 134° 10·2' E) marks the entrance to the narrow and shallow fairway leading to the inner end of the harbour. The shores of the channel are fringed with gravel banks and an extensive mudbank is situated at its inner end.

A ferry quay and a hydrofoil terminal are situated on the SW side of the harbour and there are berths for small vessels on the NE side.

Ikeda Wan
9.85

Ikeda Wan is entered between the S extremity of Ka Shima (34° 27' N, 134° 09' E) and Jizō Saki, 5 miles SE.

Anchorage. Ikeda Wan affords sheltered anchorage, except in S winds, in depths from 5 m to 10 m, soft mud, but care is needed as there are fish and seaweed beds situated in many places within the bay.

Yo Shima, a chain of four islets the S and largest of which is covered with pine trees, extends 1 mile S from the E extremity of Ka Shima; the N'most island is joined to Ka Shima by an embankment.

Okino Mo, a narrow detached mudbank, with a depth of 3·7 m (12 ft), on which there is a dense growth of seaweed, lies to the SE of Yo Shima.

Tonoshō Higashi Kō (34° 28·4' N, 134° 11·3' E), consisting of a quay projecting from reclaimed land on the SE side of Ka Shima, is approached through a channel, with a depth of 6 m, entered 2 cables W of the S extremity of Yo Shima. The channel is marked on its W side by *No. 1 Light-buoy* and *No. 3 Light-buoy* and on its E side by two red barrel *buoys.*

There are depths from 3 m to 6 m alongside the quay which can accommodate vessels up to 3000 tons.

9.86

Ikeda Kō (34° 28·5' N, 134° 13·8' E), a small harbour protected by a breakwater, lies in a cove at the head of Ikeda Wan; a **light** is exhibited on the head of the breakwater. **Benten Shima,** a rocky islet 20 m (64 ft) high and sparsely covered with pine trees, lies close S of the E entrance point to the cove.

There is a car ferry service from Ikeda Kō to Takamatsu Kō.

Mito Kō lies in **Kōno Ura** (34° 25·8' N, 134° 14·0' E) situated close within the E entrance point to Ikeda Wan. **Fujino Se,** a sandbank with a least depth of 6·1 m (20 ft),

lies within ¼ mile W of the N entrance point to Kōno Ura.

9.87

Jizō Saki (34° 25' N, 134° 14' E), on the N side of the E entrance to Bisan Seto East Traffic Route (9.48), is the S extremity of Shōdo (Shōzu) Shima; it is faced with high cliffs and is the extremity of a densely wooded promontory which separates Ikeda Wan from Uchino Umi, farther E. The headland is surmounted by a prominent densely wooded hill with two rounded summits, the N and higher of which is 301 m (986 ft) high.

A **light** is exhibited from a white octagonal tower standing on the S point of Jizō Saki; a **racon** transmits and a fog siren is sounded from the lighthouse.

OKAYAMA SUIDŌ AND APPROACHES

Chart 2875
Approaches to Okayama Suidō
9.88

Landmarks. Hachijō-iwa Yama (34° 34·5' N, 134° 01·5' E) 281 m (922 ft) high, is situated on **Koshima Hantō** which forms the SW side of Okayama Suidō (9.90); it has pale red coloured rocky outcrops and is the E summit of the hills in the vicinity. **Tateishi,** a remarkable pointed rock, surmounts a hill 169 m high situated 3 cables SE of Hachijō-iwa Yama.

Kinkō San, 401 m (1316 ft) high, is situated 3 miles WSW of Hachijō-iwa Yama and is the W summit of the hills in the vicinity; a television tower and observation platform standing on its summit are prominent.

9.89

Naga Su (34° 33' N, 134° 04' E), a narrow sandbank with a least depth of 7·4 m (25 ft), is about 2¼ miles long and lies across the approach to Okayama Suidō.

Inushima Shotō lies at the E end of Naga Su 2¼ miles ESE of the entrance to Okayama Suidō and consists of one island and four islets; the depths in the vicinity of the group are irregular and a mudbank with depths of less than 5 m extends 4 cables E from the E side of the group.

Inu Shima, the centre island of the group, is 32 m (106 ft) high and its W half is wooded; six prominent brick chimneys stand in the E half of the island.

Two densely wooded islets lie close off the SW end of Inu Shima, and **Inno Shima,** 38 m high, lies off the NW side. Six white chimneys stand in the S part of Inno Shima and are prominent.

Inu Shima Light is exhibited from a white round concrete tower with red bands standing on **Shira Ishi,** a group of white rocks lying close E of **Okitsuzumi Shima,** the E islet of Inushima Shotō.

Okayama Suidō
9.90

Okayama Suidō is entered between **Kome Saki**

Goken San   *Ryūō San*   *Tōmi Yama*   *Taka Shima*   *Ō Kabuto Shima*

No.7

Ōkushi Saki   *Jizō Saki*

(9.87) E entrance to Bisan Seto from E, seen from a position about 1 mile SE of Jizō Saki (34° 25' N, 134° 14' E)
(Original dated prior to 1978)

(34° 34' N, 134° 03' E) on the W side of the entrance and **Kiriishi (Ishikiri) Hana** on the E side, and leads NW and W into Okayama Kō (9.92). A **light** is exhibited from a white round concrete tower standing on Kome Saki, and there is a remarkable cliff on Kiriishi Hana.

No. 1 Light-buoy (green light, group flashing 3 every 8 seconds) is moored close off the edge of the coastal bank on the W side of the entrance, 8 cables SE of Kome Saki.

Shoals with depths of less that 5 m lie within ⅓ mile NW of Kiriishi Hana; in 1975, it was reported that there was less water in this area.

The fairway from close E of *No. 1 Light-buoy* through the NW leg of Okayama Suidō, lies towards the W side of the channel and has a navigable width of less than 2 cables in places; in 1964, the fairway was dredged to a least depth of 5·5 m.

Tidal streams. Tidal streams in Okayama Suidō are generally weak and even in the entrance to the channel the rate does not exceed 1 knot.
9.91
Yoshii Kawa flows into the N side of Okayama Suidō 1¼ miles NNW of Kome Saki. **Kuban Kō,** a shallow basin protected by breakwaters, lies on the W side of the mouth of Yoshii Kawa; a **light** is exhibited at the head of the E breakwater. Several tall chimneys stand on reclaimed land on the E side of the mouth of the river.

A **light** is exhibited from a black round tower on **Bishago Iwa,** a rock lying near the E edge of a drying shoal which extends E across the mouth of Yoshii Kawa from its W entrance point.

Saidaiji Kō (34° 36·3' N, 134° 02·5' E) lies in Yoshii Kawa, and a narrow channel leads across the sandbar at the mouth of the river to a jetty, with a depth of 2 m alongside, 2¼ miles upstream.

Kogushi Kō lies on the S side of Okayama Suidō opposite the mouth of Yoshii Kawa; vessels up to 3000 tons anchor off this small harbour.

Okayama Kō
9.92
Okayama Kō (34° 36' N, 133° 59' E) lies at the mouth of **Asahi Kawa** which flows into the W end of Okayama Suidō 3 miles W of the mouth of Yoshii Kawa.

The fairway leading to Okayama Kō lies along the S shore of the channel and is marked by *light-buoys*.

An extensive mudbank, the greater part of which dries, lies in the N part of the channel. From September to April seaweed beds are to be found on both sides of the channel.

Tsubushi Shō (34° 36' N, 134° 01' E), a shoal which dries 2·1 m (7 ft), lies on the edge of the mudbank on the N side of the fairway 1 mile W of the mouth of Yoshii Kawa; a **light** is exhibited from a red round concrete tower standing on the shoal.

Hato Shima, 3 cables N of Tsubushi Shō, is an islet 19 m (charted as 73 ft) high to the tops of the trees.

Taka Shima (34° 36·0' N, 133° 59·5' E), a wooded islet, lies on the N side of the fairway 1¼ miles W of Hato Shima and is 26 m (charted as 89 ft) high.

Koshima Wan, a fresh water lake, lies at the W end of Okayama Suidō and is separated from it by a barrier in which there are two sluices which are prominent.
9.93
Takashima quays lie on the E side of the entrance to Asahi Kawa 3 cables W of Taka Shima, and have depths from 3 m to 4 m alongside.

A basin, protected by a breakwater, is entered 1 mile W of the mouth of Asahi Kawa and has quays with depths from 3 m to 5·5 m alongside, on its E side; vessels up to 3000 tons can be accommodated.

There are numerous berths for small vessels in Asahi Kawa between its mouth and **Kyobashi Bridge,** about 2 miles upstream.

An **overhead cable** with a vertical clearance of about 28 m, spans Asahi Kawa close within its entrance.

The industrial and commercial city of **Okayama,** which in 1973 had a population of 485 000, lies on Asahi Kawa about 3½ miles from its mouth.

Facilities. Hospital services are available.

Climate. See table at 1.102.

Supplies. Fresh water is available at the principal quays.

Communications. Car ferries ply between Okayama Kō and Tonoshō Kō situated at the W end of Shōdo Shima.

CHAPTER 10

HARIMA NADA

GENERAL INFORMATION

Chart 2875
10.1

Harima Nada is that part of Seto Naikai lying between the E end of Bisan Seto (34° 24' N, 134° 14' E) in the W, and Awaji Shima in the E; it is bounded on the N side by the S coast of Honshū and on the S side by the E end of the N coast of Shikoku.

The depths in Harima Nada are generally less than 40 m except in the W entrance to Akashi Kaikyō (34° 37' N, 135° 00' E). The S part of Harima Nada is free of off-lying dangers but Ieshima Guntō (10.46), a group of islands, several sandbanks and reefs are situated in the N part.

Routes
10.2

Main route. The recommended track for large vessels between the E end of Bisan Seto (34° 24' N, 134° 16' E) and Akashi Kaikyō, 40 miles NE, is shown on the chart and is marked by *Harima Nada Fairway Nos. 1–6 Light-buoys*, moored 5 to 5½ miles apart. This route is free of dangers and the least depth is 23 m in the vicinity of *No. 5 Light-buoy* (34° 32' N, 134° 45' E).

Cautions. The generally W-going (flood) stream may cause a vessel to be set to the N of the track.

The general E-going (ebb) stream may cause a vessel to be set to the S of the track.

On no account should the red sector of E Saki Light (10.79) be entered until clear of Shikano Se (34° 35' N, 134° 48' E) (10.73).

Fishing. Large numbers of fishing vessels may be encountered between Shikano Se and Awaji Shima to the S; in particular in the periods 0300–0400 and 0700–0900 from March to June. In this vicinity, it is frequently difficult to distinguish the lights of light-buoys from those of the fishing vessels.

Several **fish havens** lie in the vicinity of *Harima Nada Fairway No. 5 Light-buoy*, and within the 20 m depth line off the NW coast of Awaji Shima. See also 10.17.
10.3

N route The route taken by the considerable number of small vessels proceeding E or W through the N part of Harima Nada, is marked by *Harima Nada N Fairway Nos. 3–10 Light-buoys*, moored about 5 miles apart. The depth of water in this route is about 20 m except in its E part where there are depths of about 11 m.

The route passes within 2 miles N of Ieshima Guntō and close N of Shimo Shizumo Shō (34° 42' N, 134° 30' E) (10.50) and Kami Shizumo Shō.

Fishing. Large numbers of net and line fishing boats may be encountered along the route particularly to the N of Tanga (Danga) Shima (34° 40' N, 134° 35' E) and to the E of Kami Shima (34° 41' N, 134° 43' E).

From October to May, seaweed beds are laid along the S coast of Honshū between Ako Kō (34° 44' N, 134° 22' E) and Akashi Kaikyō, around Ieshima Guntō, and in the vicinity of Shikano Se. These beds are marked by buoys exhibiting lights.

Regulations. Vessels carrying a dangerous cargo should have ready emergency towing wires forward and aft when navigating Harima Nada.

Tidal streams
10.4

Tidal streams. The tidal streams in Harima Nada are W-going on the rising tide and E-going on the falling tide, the streams turning about the same time as in Akashi Kaikyō. Except on the N and S sides of Shōdo (Shōzu) Shima and in the W approach to Akashi Kaikyō, the tidal streams are generally weak. Both the directions and rates vary from day to day.

HARIMA NADA—SOUTH PART

EAST APPROACH TO BISAN SETO

Chart 1969
10.5

Shōdo (Shōzu) Shima, the second largest island in Seto Naikai and a well known tourist resort, is situated in the W part of Harima Nada on the N side of the E entrance to Bisan Seto; **Hoshigajō** (34° 39' N, 134° 19' E), the summit, rises to an elevation of 816 m (2680 ft) near the E coast of the island. A mountain, 775 m (2545 ft) high, lies 1½ miles W of Hoshigajō and from it a densely wooded ridge, much of the E side of which is cliffy, extends S towards the S extremity of the island.

A plateau, 462 m (1397 ft) high with cliffs on its S side, lies 5 miles WSW of Hoshigajō and from its foot the land slopes gradually to the head of Ikeda Wan (34° 28' N, 134° 14' E).

Jizō Saki to Ikado Hana
10.6

Jizō Saki (34° 25' N, 134° 14' E), the S extremity of Shōdo Shima and the N entrance point to the E end of Bisan Seto, is described at 9.87.

Uchino Umi, a bay which is a **harbour of refuge** (see 1.67), is entered 2½ miles NE of Jizō Saki and affords sheltered **anchorage** as convenient in depths of about 12 m, mud.

Okino Hanage, a rock which dries 0·6 m (2 ft), lies on the NE side of a small shoal 3¼ cables SW of the wooded

E entrance point to Uchino Umi; a *light-buoy* is moored close NW of the shoal.

Jino Hanage, a rock which dries 0·6 m (2 ft), lies on the S end of a small shoal 5 cables NNE of Okino Hanage; a *light-buoy* is moored close NW of it.

There are pearl and seaweed beds within 1 cable of the shores of Uchino Umi and around Okino Hanage and Jino Hanage.

Uchinomi (Kusakabe) Kō (34° 28' N, 134° 19' E) lies at the head of Uchino Umi; it is a good natural harbour, sheltered from all winds and renowned for its scenic beauty.

Benten Shima lies 2 cables off the middle of the head of Uchino Umi and consists of two wooded islets, the E and somewhat larger of which is 8 m (26 ft) high; the two islets are joined by a reef which dries. In 1978, reclamation work was in progress along the shore E of Benten Shima.

A fish haven lies 8 cables WSW of Benten Shima.

Marugane Quay, with a depth of 5 m alongside, lies on the E side of Uchinomi Kō 3¼ cables SE of Benten Shima; **Yasuda Quay,** with a depth of 4 m alongside, lies 4 cables N of the islet.

Kusakabe pontoon jetty lies 8 cables NW of Benten Shima.

There is a car ferry service from Uchinomi Kō to Takamatsu Kō (9.57).

10.7
Ōfukube Shima (34° 25·3' N, 134° 17·4' E), flat-topped and 56 m (184 ft) high to the tops of the trees, lies on a shoal 1 mile SSE of the E entrance point of Uchino Umi. **Ko Fukube Shima,** conical and 19 m (63 ft) high, is joined to the SE extremity of Ōfukube Shima by a reef which dries.

10.8
Sakate Wan (34° 27' N, 134° 19' E) is entered between the E entrance point to Uchino Umi and Okado Hana, 2¼ miles ESE.

Ko Shima, separated from the E shore of Sakate Wan by a narrow channel, is 48 m (158 ft) high to the tops of the trees and is surmounted by a **beacon**; the sides of the islet are cliffy.

Landmark. Goishi Yama, a sharp prominent peak with many towering crags, attains an elevation of 434 m (1424 ft) 1¼ miles NE of Ko Shima.

Anchorage. Sakate Wan affords anchorage except during SE winds when a heavy sea runs into the bay. Large vessels awaiting berths in Mizushima Kō (9.43), may be found at anchor in Sakate Wan.

Fish havens and **seaweed beds.** There are a large number of fish havens in Sakate Wan, and from October to April there are seaweed beds on the SE side of Ko Shima.

Sakate Kō lies in the NE corner of Sakate Wan and is the second most important harbour in Shōdo Shima after Tonoshō Kō (9.84).

A wharf projects from the N part of the harbour; a **light** is exhibited from a red tower on the W side of the wharf.

Sakate Quay, with depths from 4 m to 6·5 m alongside, lies on the N side of the wharf, and **Sakate No. 2 Quay,** the ferry terminal, lies on the S side.

Sakate Jetty, with depths from 5·5 m to 10 m alongside, lies about ½ cable W of Sakate Quay.

Facilities. The office of the Maritime Safety Agency is located in the Harbour Office situated near the end of Sakate Quay.

Supplies. Fresh water cannot be supplied. Small quantities of fuel oil can be supplied by road.

Communications. There are passenger and car ferry services to several ports in Seto Naikai.

10.9
Ōkado Hana (34° 26' N, 134° 20' E), the SE extremity of Shōdo Shima, is cliffy and wooded; on it are two hills, the S of which is 158 m (518 ft) high and sparsely covered with trees. A **light** is exhibited from a white octogonal tower with a square base standing on the point. There is a **signal station** at the lighthouse, and by day weather signals (see 1.42) are shown from it.

Funoko Shima, a conical island 105 m (345 ft) high and cliffy, lies on the E side of Ōkado Hana and is connected to it by a reef which dries.

Anchorage can be obtained off the N side of Funoko Shima in a depth of about 20 m, but it is exposed NE.

Measured distance. A measured distance, 1899·5 m (6232 ft) in length, lies S of Ōkado Hana and is marked at each end by a pair of **beacons**; the running courses are 086° and 266°.

Ōkushi Saki to Sumiyoshi Hana
10.10
Ōkushi Saki (34° 22' N, 134° 13' E), the S entrance point to the E end of Bisan Seto, is described at 9.66.

Oda Wan is entered between Ōkushi Saki and Umaga Hana 2¼ miles SE; with the exception of **Ikagano Se,** a 10 m (33 ft) sandy patch 1 mile ESE of Ōkushi Saki, the bay is free from off-lying dangers.

Landmark. Hibori Yama, a sharp and prominent wooded peak, rises to an elevation of 184 m (604 ft) 1¼ miles S of Ōkushi Saki.

Umaga Hana, the E entrance point to Oda Wan, is a steep cliffy point on the E side of which are some remarkable white horizontal strata. A **light** is exhibited from a white square concrete tower situated on Umaga Hana.

Anchorage. Oda Wan affords safe anchorage, except during N winds; a good berth is in depths from 7 m to 12 m, mud, with Umaga Hana bearing 066° distant 9 cables.

10.11
Tsuda Wan (34° 18' N, 134° 16' E) is entered 3 miles SSE of Umaga Hana. **Taka Shima,** 42 m (138 ft) high with a rounded summit and covered with a dense growth of bamboos, is the highest of a group of three islets lying within ½ mile E of the N entrance point of Tsuda Wan; **Okino Sowai,** a steep-to rock with a depth of 0·3 m (1 ft) over it, lies 3 cables ENE of Taka Shima.

Unobe Yama, a flat-topped isolated hill 56 m (184 ft) high, rises steeply from the S entrance point of Tsuda Wan; it has a steep cliff on its E side.

Nako Shima, 31 m (102 ft) high with a precipice on its NW side, lies close off Unobe Yama. **Kashirashiro Iwa,** 1 m (3 ft) high, and a rock which dries 2·1 m (7 ft), lie on a shoal within 6 cables E of Nako Shima.

Measured distances of 1930 m and 3995 m, marked by pairs of **beacons,** lie between Umaga Hana and Unobe Yama; the running courses are 134° and 314°.

Anchorage. Tsuda Wan affords anchorage except with winds between NNE and ESE when a heavy sea runs into the bay; the best berth is in a depth of 11·5 m, mud, with Nako Shima bearing 160° and **Ametaki Yama** (34° 17' N, 134° 14' E), 253 m (830 ft) high, bearing 230°.

From October to April, seaweed beds are situated inside Tsuda Wan and care is needed when anchoring.

Tsuda Kō lies at the inner end of Tsuda Wan and affords good anchorage for small vessels in W winds within the harbour limit. There are a number of factories on the shore of the harbour.

There is a basin enclosed by two breakwaters at the head of the bay; a jetty with a depth of 3 m alongside is situated in the basin.

10.12

Umashino Wan (34° 17′ N, 134° 18′ E) is entered between Kashirashiro Iwa (10.11) and **Sumiyoshi Hana,** 1½ miles SE; the shores consist of sandy beaches separated by rocky headlands.

Marugame (Marugamidan) Shima, a round-topped islet 68 m (223 ft) high, and **Me Shima,** flat-topped and 44 m (145 ft) high, lie on a spit extending 4 cables NNE of Sumiyoshi Hana.

Kino Shima, round-topped and 31 m (102 ft) high to the tops of the trees, lies near the middle of Umashino Wan 5½ cables W of Sumiyoshi Hana; its seaward side is cliffy.

Anchorage. Umashino Wan affords anchorage in a depth of about 9 m, mud, either 3 cables W of Kino Shima or in greater depths N of the islet.

In 1979, a breakwater was under construction in the W part of the bay.

SHIKOKU—NORTH EAST COAST

Chart 2875

Matsubara Ura to Senokata Hana

10.13

Matsubara Ura lies between Sumiyoshi Hana (34° 16·5′ N, 134° 18·5′ E) (10.12) and **Kabukoshi (Kaburakosi) Saki,** surmounted by an isolated hill with a pointed summit, 3¾ miles ESE.

Futago Shima, ½ mile NE of Kabukoshi Saki, consists of two rocky islets surmounted by pine trees, which are both 26 m (84 ft) high. Vessels should pass to the N of the two islets.

Hitotsu Shima, a rocky islet 21 m (68 ft) high and densely covered with pine trees, lies 1 mile NNW of Futago Shima and has some high rocks on its N side.

Anchorage is afforded in Matsubara Ura in offshore winds and the holding ground is good.

Sanbonmatsu Kō (34° 15′ N, 134° 21′ E), situated in Matsubara Ura, is a small harbour which is much used by small vessels loading sand, gravel and cement.

Landmarks in the vicinity of Sanbonmatsu Kō are:

A prominent chimney, standing 3½ cables SE of the head of the W breakwater, which has an elevation of 30 m.

A silo close WSW of the head of the breakwater which is a good mark when entering harbour.

Seaweed beds. From October to April, there are seaweed beds within 1 mile offshore on both the E and W sides of Sanbonmatsu Kō.

Harbour. Sanbonmatsu Kō is protected by three breakwaters. A **light** is exhibited at the head of the W breakwater and at the NW end of the detached breakwater.

Within the breakwaters depths are less than 7 m and there is a basin with depths of less than 4 m at the inner end of the harbour.

A quay on the W breakwater has a depth alongside of 5 m.

Shirotori Kō situated in the SE part of Matsubara Ura 1½ miles E of Sanbonmatsu Kō, has a breakwater from the head of which a **light** is exhibited.

10.14

Hiketa (Hikeda) Hana (34° 14′ N, 134° 25′ E) lies 2¼ miles SE of Kabukoshi Saki (10.13) and is the extremity of a small peninsula on which there are a number of round-topped hills. A **light** is exhibited from a white round concrete tower standing on the point.

Mitsu Shima and **Okino Shima,** each 37 m (120 ft) high and covered with pine trees, lie close together 1½ miles E of Hiketa Hana. **Benten Shima,** 1½ cables W of Mitsu Shima, is 1·5 m (5 ft) high; 2 cables SW of it there is a rock awash.

From March to November fishing nets are laid within 1¾ miles NNE of Okino Shima.

Hiketa (Hikeda) Wan is entered between Hiketa Hana and a point 4 miles E; in its W part there is a sandy beach and in its E part the hills slope down to the shore.

Anchorage. Anchorage is afforded in Hiketa Wan in depths from 9 m to 16 m; in places where the bottom is mud, the holding ground is good. Care is needed to avoid fishing nets and seaweed beds which are to be found in all parts of the bay at most times of the year.

Hiketa Kō, protected by breakwaters, lies in the NW corner of Hiketa Wan; a **light** is exhibited on the head of each of the breakwaters.

Orino Kō (34° 12·5′ N, 134° 29·0′ E) situated on the E side of Hiketa Wan, has a breakwater from which a **light** is exhibited.

10.15

Awata Kō (34° 13·3′ N, 134° 33·0′ E) situated 3½ miles E of Orino Kō, has a breakwater from the head of which a **light** is exhibited.

Hiude Ura is entered 1 mile E of Awata Kō. **Anchorage** is afforded to small vessels with local knowledge, off the entrance to Hiude Ura in depths of 20 m; the greater part of the bay is shoal.

10.16

Kitadomarino Seto (34° 14′ N, 134° 36′ E), about 1½ miles long, is entered 1½ miles ENE of Hiude Ura and is the N end of Muyano Seto (11.25).

Kitadomari Light is exhibited from a white round concrete tower standing at the head of a breakwater on the W side of the N entrance to Kitadomarino Seto.

A **bridge** with a vertical clearance of 23 m, spans Kitadomarino Seto ¼ mile within the N entrance.

Shimada Shima lies on the E side of Kitadomarino Seto at the N end of Muyano Seto and forms the W side of the N approach to Naruto Kaikyō (11.70).

Senokata Hana is the N extremity of Shimada Shima; reefs and shoals extend about 1 cable N from the point.

Landmark. Kanekakematsu Mori, situated in the N part of Shimada Shima, is a conspicuous hill, 167 m high, with a wooded summit.

AWAJI SHIMA—NORTH WEST COAST

Charts 2875, 3614

10.17

The NW coast of **Awaji Shima,** lying between Naruto Kaikyō (34° 15′ N, 134° 39′ E) and Akashi Kaikyō, forms the E shore of Harima Nada. Between Kariko Saki (34° 20′ N, 134° 42′ E) and Ei Saki, 11 miles NE, the coast consists mainly of sandy beaches with some cliffy headlands backed by flattish hills; from Ei Saki to E Saki, 12 miles farther NE, the coast is generally cliffy.

Landmarks. Jōryuji Yama (34° 30′ N, 134° 55′ E), 515 m high, lies in the N part of Awaji Shima and there are several peaks to the W of it; on the summit of the

W'most peak, 248 m high, there are some remarkable trees.

Senkōji (Saki) Yama attains an elevation of 448 m near the centre of the island and is somewhat prominent.

Ōhira Yama, 2¾ miles E of Maruyama Saki, the W extremity of Awaji Shima, is 172 m high and has some remarkable pine trees on its summit.

From October to May, **seaweed beds** are laid within 1½ miles of the NW coast of Awaji Shima; the beds are marked by *buoys* exhibiting flashing lights.

Chart 2875

Yoroi Saki to Ei Saki

10.18

Yoroi Saki (34° 16' N, 134° 40' E), on the E side of the N approach to Naruto Kaikyō (11.70), lies 3 miles NE of Senokata Hana (10.16) and is a cliffy point.

Maruyama Saki, the W extremity of Awaji Shima, is a small but prominent peninsula with a low sandy isthmus; its flat summit is 23 m high covered with pine trees, and from certain directions it appears as an island.

Benten Shima, pointed, well wooded and 34 m high, lies close off the S extremity of Maruyama Saki.

Maruyama Kō, protected by breakwaters, lies close S of Maruyama Saki; a **light** is exhibited on the head of the W breakwater.

Anchorage is afforded in a depth of about 10 m, mud, 3 or 4 cables from the shore off Maruyama Kō.

Hanatsura Hana lies 1¾ miles NNE of Maruyama Saki; S of it the coastal range terminates in cliffs but N of it the coast consists of low sandhills.

10.19

Kariko Saki (34° 20' N, 134° 42' E), 50 m high and with some pine trees on it, lies 2¾ miles NNE of Maruyama Saki and is fringed with black rocks extending a short distance offshore.

Minato Kō, situated 2 miles E of Kariko Saki, consists of a basin lying within the mouth of **Mihara Kawa;** a **light** is exhibited at the head of the E and the W breakwater which lie one on each side of the mouth of the river.

In 1978, an outer harbour enclosed by two breakwaters was under construction on the W side of the basin.

There is a narrow channel over the bar at the mouth of Mihara Kawa with a depth of about 3 m. Caution is necessary when crossing the bar during strong W winds.

Anchorage, sheltered from winds between E and S, can be obtained in depths from 13 m to 15 m, mud, off the mouth of Mihara Kawa.

Fish havens, fixed fishing nets and seaweed beds lie in the approaches to Minato Kō and care is needed when anchoring.

Chart 3614

10.20

Torikai Kō (34° 22' N, 134° 45' E), protected by a breakwater, lies 2½ miles NNE of Minato Kō (10.19); a **light** is exhibited on the head of the breakwater.

Tsushi Kō, a small harbour protected by a breakwater, lies 3 miles NNE of Torikai Kō; a **light** is exhibited on the head of the breakwater.

Myōjin Hana, 2¼ miles NNE of Tsushi Kō, is a white cliffy point with a dense growth of trees on its upper part; it is joined to the mainland by a narrow isthmus and appears as an islet from some directions.

Yamado Kō (34° 26·8' N, 134° 48·1' E), close N of Myōjin Hana, has a breakwater from the head of which a **light** is exhibited.

Ei Saki, a bluff 40 m high, lies 1½ miles NNE of Myōjin Saki.

Ei Kō to E Saki

10.21

Ei Kō (34° 28' N, 134° 50' E), a small harbour protected by a breakwater, lies ½ mile E of Ei Saki; a **light** is exhibited on the head of the breakwater.

Gunke Kō, protected by a breakwater, lies 1¼ miles ENE of Ei Saki; a **light** is exhibited on the head of the breakwater.

Murotsu Kō, a small harbour protected by breakwaters, lies 4¼ miles NE of Ei Saki; a **light** is exhibited on the head of the W breakwater.

Ikuwa Kō, protected by breakwaters, lies 1 mile ENE of Murotsu Kō; a **light** is exhibited on the head of the W breakwater.

Fish beds, marked by metal piles exhibiting lights (yellow flashing), lie between Murotsu Kō and Ikuwa Kō.

Asano Kō (34° 32' N, 134° 55' E), a small harbour protected by breakwaters, lies nearly 1 mile ENE of Ikuwa Kō; a **light** is exhibited on the head of the N breakwater.

Two mooring buoys (red), each of which can accommodate a vessel of 5000 tons, are moored close NE of the entrance to Asano Kō.

Yoko Se, a spit with a least depth of 1 m, extends ¾ mile SW from a position 1 mile NE of Asano Kō.

Anchorage can be obtained during offshore winds, in depths from 11 m to 14 m, mud and good holding ground, on the bank N of Yoko Se.

10.22

Toshima Kō (34° 33' N, 134° 56' E), a small harbour protected by breakwaters, lies 1½ miles NE of Asano Kō; a **light** is exhibited on the head of the N breakwater.

A jetty projects 1½ cables from the shore about 3½ cables W of the root of the N breakwater and a red **light** is exhibited on its head. A pier, from the head of which two orange **lights** are exhibited, lies 1½ cables NE of the N breakwater.

E Saki, situated at the N end of Awaji Shima, 4½ miles NE of Toshima Kō, is described at 10.79.

HARIMA NADA—NORTH WEST PART

SHŌDO (SHŌZU) SHIMA—NORTH AND EAST COASTS

Chart 2875

Shōdo (Shōzu) Shima—north coast

10.23

Kabura Saki (34° 31·3' N, 134° 10·5' E) is the W'most point on the N side of Shōdo (Shōzu) Shima; the depths in its vicinity are irregular and it should not be approached within 4 cables.

Chiburi Shima, 31 m (103 ft) high, lies ½ mile W of Kabura Saki; numerous rocks lie within 2 cables of its SW side. A **light** is exhibited from a white round concrete tower standing on the NE point of Chiburi Shima.

Ko Shima, 33 m (charted as 99 ft) high and covered with pine trees, lies 3¼ miles E of Kabura Saki; the narrow channel between it and the coast of Shōdo Shima is deep.

Myōken Saki, a steep-to wooded point, lies 5 miles ENE of Kabura Saki.

10.24

Ōbe Wan (34° 33′ N, 134° 17′ E) is a bay lying between Myōken Saki and a point 1¾ miles E. **Ō Shima,** 7 cables NE of Myōken Saki, is 29 m (93 ft) high and covered with pine trees; it is the outermost of a group of above-water rocks connected by shoals.

A *light-buoy* marks the E extremity of the rocks extending ½ mile E of Ō Shima, in the approach to Ōbe Wan.

Ko Shima, wooded and 34 m high, lies close inshore 8 cables ESE of Ō Shima and between them is a mudbank with depths of less than 10 m.

Anchorage. Ōbe Wan affords temporary anchorage to small vessels, in depths from 5 m to 7 m, about midway between Ō Shima and Ko Shima.

From October to April, there are **seaweed beds** in the vicinity of Ko Shima.

Ōbe Kō, a basin protected by breakwaters, lies ½ mile S of Ō Shima and has depths of about 3 m; a **light** is exhibited on the head of the E breakwater.

Shōdo (Shōzu) Shima—east coast

10.25

Fuji Saki (34° 34′ N, 134° 21′ E) is the NE extremity of Shōdo Shima and is surmounted by a prominent wooded peak.

Kanaga Saki, 3 cables SE of Fuji Saki, is an islet 104 m (charted as 349 ft) high which is joined to a point SW of its W end by a bank of gravel which dries.

Fukuda Wan (34° 33′ N, 134° 22′ E) is entered between Kanaga Saki and **Ko Shima,** an islet 41 m high, 1 mile S.

O Iso, a rock with deep water within ½ cable of it on all sides, lies in the E approaches to Fukuda Wan, 1 mile ESE of Kanaga Saki. A **light** is exhibited from a red round concrete tower with black bands standing on O Iso.

Manaita Iwa, with a depth of 2 m (6 ft) over it, and **Hinden Iwa,** which dries 0·6 m (2 ft), lie about midway between O Iso and Ko Shima. A *light-buoy* is moored close SE of Hinden Iwa.

Anchorage. Anchorage is afforded in Fukuda Wan, sheltered from all but E winds, in a depth of about 20 m. A **fish haven** lies 1½ cables N of Ko Shima.

Fukuda Gyokō, protected by breakwaters, lies at the inner end of Fukuda Wan; a **light** is exhibited on the head of the N breakwater.

10.26

Nakase Iwa (34° 30′ N, 134° 34′ E), a detached rocky patch with a least depth of 1·6 m (5 ft) over it, lies 2 miles offshore 3 miles SE of Fukuda Wan.

Mizunoko Iwa, a detached steep-to rock 2·5 m (8 ft) high, lies 1 mile SE of Nakase Iwa; a *light-buoy* is moored close SE of the rock.

Charts 1969, 2875

Tachibana Wan (34° 29′ N, 134° 21′ E) lies 3 miles N of the SE extremity of Shōdo Shima. **Jō Shima,** 51 m (166 ft) high, lies close off the N entrance point and helps to identify the bay from seaward.

Anchorage. Tachibana Wan affords sheltered anchorage, except during E winds when a heavy sea runs into the bay, in a depth of about 15 m, mud.

There are a number of **fish havens** in the bay.

Ōkado Hana, the SE extremity of Shōdo Shima, and Funoko Shima, are described at 10·9.

USHIMADO KŌ AND KINKAI WAN

Chart 2875

Approaches to Ushimado Kō

10.27

Yomogi Saki (34° 36′ N, 134° 08′ E) lies on the W side of the main entrance to Ushimado Kō which is situated in the NW part of Harima Nada; a **light** is exhibited from a white round concrete tower standing on the point. A *light-buoy* (black; white light quick flashing every 6 seconds) is moored on the N side of the entrance 2½ cables SW of Yomogi Saki.

Kuro Shima (34° 35·8′ N, 134° 09·7′ E), 32 m high and surmounted by a wood of tall pine trees, lies 1 mile E of Yomogi Saki; it is the E'most and largest of three islets which are connected by a drying shingle bank. A mudbank extends W from the W'most islet leaving a channel about 3 cables wide between its W edge and Yomogi Saki.

Mae Shima is situated with its W extremity 3 cables N of the E end of Kuro Shima; its summit attains an elevation of 137 m (451 ft) in its E part. A **light** is exhibited from a white round concrete tower on **Jono Hana,** the N extremity of the W end of Mae Shima.

Ki Shima lies 2½ cables S of the E part of Mae Shima and on it are two hills each surmounted by a row of pine trees. A **light** is exhibited from a white round concrete tower standing on the S side of Ki Shima.

Ao Shima, a treeless islet 30 m (100 ft) high, is situated 4 cables NE of Ki Shima; between the two islands there are several reefs and rocks.

The channel between Ki Shima and Mae Shima, NW, is deep but narrow and the tidal streams in it are strong.

Ushimado Kō

10.28

Ushimado Kō (34° 37′ N, 134° 10′ E) lies between the mainland and the bank on which are Kuro Shima (10.27) and Mae Shima. The harbour is divided into E and W parts by a point on which the town of **Ushimado** stands.

Ushimado Seto, 1 cable wide, connects the two parts of the harbour, but the fairway is so reduced by shoals that it is only suitable for small craft; the tidal streams in the channel are strong.

An **overhead cable** with a vertical clearance of 31 m, spans Ushimado Seto.

Landmarks. A building stands on the summit of **Hachiken Iwa Yama** (34° 37·5′ N, 134° 09·5′ E), 166 m (charted as 552 ft) high, situated to the N of the town.

A pagoda stands in the W part of the town, ¾ mile SE of Hachiken Iwa Yama.

Directions. Ushimado Kō is entered from SW; Hachiken Iwa Yama, bearing 026° ahead, leads 1 cable E of Yomogi Saki. When the S extremity of Ki Shima is in line with the N extremity of Kuro Shima, bearing about 101°, the pagoda, bearing 054° ahead, leads N of a *light-buoy* marking the NW edge of a mudbank extending W from the W end of Mae Shima.

When the E extremity of Kuro Shima bears 144°, a course of 074°, with the point on the N side of Ushimado Seto ahead, will lead to the **anchorage.** Anchor in depths from 14·6 m to 16 m when the W extremity of Mae

Shima bears 164°. Owing to the strength of the tidal stream, vessels should moor.

The least charted depth in the SW entrance to the harbour is 5·3 m (18 ft).

10.29

A boat harbour with depths from 2·1 m to 3·6 m, protected by a detached breakwater, is situated on the N side of the W part of Ushimado Kō. A **light** is exhibited on the E end of the detached breakwater.

There are berths for small vessels in both parts of the harbour; the E part affords good shelter during strong W winds.

Kinkai Wan

10.30

Kinkai Wan (34° 38' N, 134° 11' E), a shallow bay with depths of less than 5 m, is entered 1¼ miles N of the NE extremity of Mae Shima (10.27).

Kami Ikada, a rock 2 m high, lies nearly 1 mile E of the S entrance point to Kinkai Wan; a **light** is exhibited from a black round concrete tower with red bands standing on the rock.

Nezu Shima, 134 m high with pine trees on its summit, lies 2¼ cables NW of Kami Ikada and a 2·7 m (9 ft) patch lies between them.

Shimo Ikada, a rock 2 m high, lies 5¼ cables SE of the S entrance point to Kinkai Wan, and within 2 cables NW of it are other rocks one of which dries 1·8 m (6 ft).

Landmark. Takatsubo Yama rises to an elevation of 142 m on the N entrance point to Kinkai Wan; it is surmounted by a clump of tall pine trees and is a prominent mark.

A cove that affords shelter to small craft, except with onshore winds, lies 1 mile NE of the N entrance point to Kinkai Wan.

KATAGAMI KŌ AND APPROACHES

Chart 2875

Approaches to Katagami Kō

10.31

Naga Shima (34° 41,'N, 134° 15' E) is situated on the W side of the approach to Katagami Kō and is separated from the mainland by a very narrow and shallow channel. It is a narrow island from 61 m to 98 m high covered with pine trees; it is in two parts joined by a low isthmus near its centre and appears as two islands from a distance.

Kōno Shima, 147 m (483 ft) high, flat-topped and treeless, lies close N of the E part of Naga Shima and is separated from it by a narrow channel. **So Shima,** close N of Kōno Shima, is 127 m (418 ft) high and treeless.

Mushiage Wan, a bay with depths of less than 5 m, lies between the N side of Naga Shima and **Tsurumi Hantō,** the part of the mainland to the N. **Ōbano Se,** a rock awash, lies in the middle of Mushiage Wan.

Mushiage Wan, a bay with depths of less than 5 m, lies between the N side of Naga Shima and **Tsurumi Hantō,** the part of the mainland to the N. **Ōbano Se,** a rock awash, lies in the middle of Mushiage Wan.

Landmarks. Three peaks, the highest and W of which attains an elevation of 266 m (874 ft), are situated on Tsurumi Hantō and are conspicuous.

10.32

Ōtabu Shima (34° 41' N, 134° 18' E), 40 m (133 ft) high and surmounted by a few pine trees, lies on the E side of the approach to Katagami Kō, 8 cables E of the E extremity of Naga Shima (10.31).

Kakui Shima, the largest of the islands in the approaches to Katagami Kō, lies with its W end 2 miles NNW of Ōtabu Shima; its summit, which lies near its centre, is 218 m (charted as 713 ft) high, round-topped and prominent. A **light** is exhibited from a white round concrete tower standing on **Unoishi Hana,** the SE extremity of Kakui Shima.

Kashira (Tō) Shima (34° 42·0' N, 134° 17·8' E), between Ōtabo Shima and the W end of Kakui Shima, is 57 m (185 ft).

Hadaka Iwa, 4 m high, and a group of other rocks some of which dry, lie nearly midway between Kashira Shima and Kōno Shima (10.31), ¼ mile W; *No. 1 Light-buoy* is moored on the E side of these rocks and marks the W side of the fairway (10.33).

Tsuru Shima, 36 m (charted as 159 ft) high and treeless, lies 1 mile NE of Ōtabu Shima; a rock, 14 m high, lies close off its S extremity.

Anchorage is afforded to small vessels in a depth of 7 m, mud, in the area enclosed by Ōtabu Shima, Kashira Shima, Kakui Shima and Tsuru Shima.

Caution. Care is needed to avoid two **submarine cables** and a **submarine pipeline** which are laid down between Kashira Shima and Ōtabu Shima, and a **submarine cable** between Ōtabu Shima and Tsuru Shima.

10.33

Hinase Kō (34° 43·5' N, 134° 16·3' E), protected by breakwaters, lies in an inlet on the mainland 1 mile NNW of the W extremity of Kakui Shima (10.32); a **light** is exhibited on the head of the outer breakwater.

Hinase Kō is part of Katagami Kō and is a terminal for a car ferry service to Ōbe Kō (10.24) on the N side of Shōdo Shima.

Large numbers of fishing stakes, oyster beds and seaweed beds are situated in the approaches to Katagami Kō.

Channels to Katagami Kō

10.34

Between the islands in the approaches to Katagami Kō and the mainland there are numerous narrow channels but the majority of them are only suitable for small vessels with local knowledge.

The main channel to Katagami Kō is about 7 miles long and is entered between Naga Shima and **Ko-Aka Ishi** (34° 41·0' N, 134° 17·4' E), a rock 2 m high, lying 2 cables W of Ōtabu Shima. A *light-buoy* is moored at the entrance to the channel ¼ mile SSE of the E extremity of Naga Shima, and thereafter the fairway is marked by *light-buoys* and *buoys*.

The channel, with depths from 3·5 m to 6 m, leads W of Kashira Shima (10.32) and E of Hadaka Iwa, N of So Shima and thence through Katagami Wan (10.35).

Caution. The fairway is very narrow in places and shelves steeply on either side.

Tōbi Bridge (34° 42·8' N, 134° 14·1' E), with a vertical clearance of about 29 m, spans the channel between the NE extremity of Tsurumi Hantō (10.31) and the coast to the N.

Hinase Kō (10.33) is approached from W of Kakui Shima; the channel along the N side of Kakui Shima, which leads to the harbour from E, is narrow and shallow and can only be used by small craft.

Katagami Kō

10.35

Katagami (Katakami) Kō (34° 44' N, 134° 11' E) lies at the head of **Katagami Wan,** a shallow inlet which is entered ½ mile NW of So Shima (10.31). The main channel to the harbour is described at 10.34.

Mae Shima (34° 43·2' N, 134° 13·0' E), an islet 56 m high, lies in the middle of Katagami Wan, and S of it is the entrance to **Tsurumi Kō** which is part of Katagami Kō. A **light** is exhibited from a red concrete tower with black bands situated on **Takagono Shō,** a drying rock lying close E of the N entrance point to Tsurumi Kō.

A public wharf with a reported depth of 4 m alongside, lies on the N side of the channel ½ mile WNW of Mae Shima and can accommodate vessels up to 1000 tons.

There is a roadstead with depths from 5 m to 6 m, and a berthing wall, at the head of Katagami Kō.

The city of **Bizen** at the inner end of the harbour has a flourishing pottery industry.

AKŌ WAN

Chart 2875

10.36

Akō Wan (34° 43' N, 134° 22' E), with depths of less than 5 m, is entered between the SE extremity of Kakui Shima (10.32) and Toriage Shima, 1¾ miles ENE. **Toriage Shima,** 16 m high and sparsely covered with pine trees, lies close off the edge of the sandbanks at the mouth of **Chigusa Kawa.**

Akō Kō lies at the mouth of **Ōtsu Kawa** which flows into the head of Akō Wan and is an industrial harbour in which lie the quays of the **Mitsubishi Cement Works.**

Akō, which in 1973 had a population of 48 000, lies on the W bank of Chigusa Kawa and is an industrial town and tourist centre.

Landmarks. A cliff on the W side of the entrance to Akō Kō is a good mark for identifying the harbour from a distance.

The chimney (red and white), with an elevation of 100 m, of the cement works on the E side of the mouth of Ōtsu Kawa, is a good mark.

The **fairway** leading to the cement quay in the W part of the harbour is about ¾ cable wide with depths from 7·5 m to 8 m. It is entered between *No. 1* and *No. 2 Light-buoys* moored 8 cables W of Toriage Shima and is marked by *light-buoys* farther in.

Leading lights, privately maintained, exhibited from posts (red and white in bands; white triangular topmarks), in line bearing 000°, lead to the quay. The 100 m cement works chimney lies nearly between the leading lights and they are sometimes difficult to see.

A turning area at the inner end of the harbour has a depth of 5·5 m and is marked by *buoys*.

A large number of fishing nets and seaweed beds lie on both sides of the fairway leading to Akō Kō.

10.37

Berths. The principal berths in Akō Kō are as follows:

Berth & Position	*Length* m	*Depth* m	*Capacity* tons
Public Quay			
(34° 43·8' N, 134° 22·6' E)	100	7·5	—
Mitsubishi Cement			
(34° 44·6' N, 134° 22·2' E)			
Dolphins	—	7·5	7000
Quay	581	3·5–7·5	7000
Mitsubishi Electrical			
(34° 44·6' N, 134° 21·7' E)			
Jetty	—	5·5	2000
Harima Tiles			
(34°44·6' N, 134° 21·9' E)			
Quay	—	—	4500

Facilities. Fresh water is available at the Mitsubishi Cement dolphin berth.

MI SAKI TO ITSU WAN

Chart 2875

10.38

Between Mi Saki (34° 44' N, 134° 25' E) and Itsu Wan, 6¼ miles ENE, there are three bays; Sakoshi Wan (10.40), Aioi Wan (10.41) and Murotsu Wan (10.44).

Mi Saki and Sakoshi Wan

10.39

Mi Saki, 1¼ miles ENE of Toriage Shima (10.36), is the S extremity of a hilly promontory on the SE side of the delta of Chigusa Kawa. A **light** is exhibited from a white octagonal concrete tower standing on the headland on which there is also a shrine.

Landmarks. There are many hotels in the vicinity of Mi Saki and at night their lights stand out well from a distance.

Misaki Iwa, a rock 1 m high, lies 2 cables S of Mi Saki; a **light** is exhibited from a black round concrete tower with a stone base standing on the rock.

10.40

Sakoshi Wan (34° 45' N, 134° 27' E) is entered 2 miles NE of Mi Saki (10.39); reefs lie within 3½ cables S of the W entrance point to the bay.

Ika Shima, close to the W part of the N shore of Sakoshi Wan, is 59 m high to the tops of the trees and densely wooded. **Nabe Shima,** in the NE corner of the bay, is 28 m high and sparsely covered with pine trees.

Anchorage. Sakoshi Wan affords anchorage as convenient in depths of about 6 m, mud. Oyster beds and seaweed beds are to be found in the bay.

Sakoshi Kō, lying NW of Iki Shima, has depths from 4 m to 5 m and has a landing jetty.

Aioi Wan or Aioi Kō

10.41

Kazura Shima (34° 45' N, 134° 28' E), well wooded and 37 m high to the tops of the trees, lies in the middle of the approach to Aioi Wan, ¾ mile SE of **Kama Saki,** the E entrance point to Sakoshi Wan (10.40); a **light** is exhibited from a white round tower standing on the summit of the island. A reef with a depth of less than 2 m over it, extends 1 cable N of Kazura Shima.

Aioi Wan or **Aioi Kō** (34° 46' N, 134° 28' E), a narrow inlet extending N for 1½ miles, is entered between Kama Saki and **Kanega Saki,** 1 mile E; it is an open harbour (see 1.65). **Kimi Shima,** 1½ cables S of Kanega Saki, is 30 m (charted as 87 ft) high to the tops of the trees and sparsely covered with pine trees.

Aioi Wan is bounded on three sides by hills and has depths from 6 m to 8 m. The **Ishikawajima-Harima Shipyard,** where there are a number of building slips and dry docks, is situated on the W side of the inlet.

Landmarks. A 3-storied building standing on the top of a hill on the E side of the harbour entrance is prominent from a distance.

A radio tower, painted white, stands on a hill 180 m

high, situated on the W side of the inner end of the harbour.

Pilotage is not compulsory but if required pilots are only available from sunrise to ½ hour before sunset.

10.42

Leading lights, privately maintained, are exhibited from a pair of masts (red and white in bands; triangular top-mark) standing on a hill in the N part of the harbour; in line they bear 353½° and lead into the inlet.

Kasamatsu Iwa, 2 m high, lies within ½ cable of the E shore of the inlet, 1¼ miles N of Kazura Shima (10.41).

Kabe Shima (34° 46·7' N, 134° 28·3' E), a rock 1·5 m high, lies about 2 cables offshore 8 cables farther N; a **light** is exhibited from a red round concrete tower with black bands standing on the rock. A rock with a depth of 4·5 m over it, lies ¼ cable S of Kabe Shima.

10.43

Anchorages. Anchor berths are established as follows:

	From Kabe Shima	
Berth	*Bearing*	*Distance*
A	250°	350 m
B	217°	730 m
C	205°	1250 m

The greater part of the W side of Aioi Wan consists of private shipyard quays with depths from 6 m to 7 m alongside.

Kaikin Jetty, with a moveable floating caisson near its middle, links the N and S sides of the inner end of the harbour. The part of the harbour beyond the jetty is generally shallow and is restricted to vessels under 1000 tons.

Overhead cables with a least vertical clearance of 31 m, span the harbour in the vicinity of Kaikin Jetty.

Facilities. There are customs and immigration offices in **Aioi** which lies at the head of Aioi Wan.

There are several tugs belonging to the shipyard.

The principal dry docks in the Ishikawajima-Harima Shipyard are as follows:

	Length m	*Width m*	*Depth m*	*Capacity tons*
No. 1	238·1	35·0	9·0	43 300
No. 2	151·5	20·7	6·4	9 600
No. 3	340·0	56·0	8·0	150 000

All types of fitting out and repair work can be undertaken.

Communications. The nearest airport is at Ōsaka, 50 miles E.

Murotsu Wan

10.44

Murotsu Wan (34° 45' N, 134° 27' E) lies on the E side of the entrance to Aioi Wan (10.41); its shores are free from off-lying dangers but from October to December, seaweed beds are to be found in the N part of the bay.

Murotsu Gyokō, protected by a breakwater, lies in a small inlet on the E shore of Murotsu Wan; a **light** is exhibited on the head of the breakwater.

Karani Shima, a group of three islets, lies within 1½ miles S of the entrance to Murotsu Wan. **Okino-karani Shima,** the S'most, is 20 m (67 ft) high, flat-topped and densely wooded.

Nakano-karani Shima, 1 cable NNE of Okino-karani Shima and joined to it by a reef, is 20 m high to the tops of the trees.

Jino-karani Shima, the N'most islet in the group, lies 3½ cables NNE of Nakano-karani Shima, is thickly wooded and 39 m (charted as 80 ft) high to the tops of the trees.

Itsu Wan

10.45

Itsu Wan is entered between the E entrance point to Murotsu Wan and the mouth of Naka Kawa, 3 miles E.

Iwami Kō (34° 47' N, 134° 32' E), protected by a breakwater, lies at the head of Itsu Wan; a **light** is exhibited on the head of the breakwater.

Landmark. Naboriiwa Yama, 143 m high, lies close to the coast ¼ mile SE of Iwami Kō; it is sparsely covered with pine trees and a large rock stands on its summit.

Anchorage. Good but open anchorage can be obtained in the entrance to Itsu Wan in depths from 5 m to 8 m.

A **submarine cable area,** indicated on the chart, extends S from the E side of Itsu Wan to Ieshima Guntō.

IESHIMA GUNTŌ

Chart 2875

10.46

Ieshima Guntō, consisting of four large islands and many smaller ones, extends from Komatsu Shima (34° 37·2' N, 134° 25·5' E) in the W, to Kami Shima (34° 41·0' N, 134° 43·0' E) in the E.

Harima Nada N Fairway (10.3) leads between Ieshima Guntō and the S coast of Honshū.

10.47

Matsu Shima (34° 36' N, 134° 29' E) is the largest of the S'most group of islets in Ieshima Guntō; it is 87 m (charted as 274 ft) high to the tops of the trees and well wooded. A **light** is exhibited from a white round concrete tower standing on the SW point of the islet.

Ōdono Se, with a depth of 0·4 m (1 ft), and **Dekisōno Se,** with a depth of 1·2 m (4 ft), lie, respectively, 3½ cables ENE and 4 cables WSW of Matsu Shima.

Mitsugashira Shima, 46 m (153 ft) high, and **Katsura (Kaisura) Shima,** 40 m (133 ft) high, are, respectively, the W'most and N'most of a group of five islets lying within 1 mile W and N of Matsu Shima.

No attempt should be made to pass between any of the islets of this group as the channels are foul.

10.48

Inge Shima (34° 39' N, 134° 26' E), the W'most of the larger islets in Ieshima Guntō, is situated 3¾ miles NW of Matsu Shima; it is 75 m (charted as 241 ft) high and a **light** is exhibited from a white octagonal tower standing near the centre of the islet.

A chain of islets and reefs extends 1¾ miles SSW from Inge Shima to **Komatsu Shima** which is 31 m (100 ft) high with some bushes on it.

No attempt should be made to pass between any of the islets and reefs in this chain.

10.49

Nishi Shima (34° 39' N, 134° 29' E) is the largest island in Ieshima Guntō; its coasts are considerably indented and have many white cliffs. The summit, in the SW part of the island, attains an elevation of 275 m (charted as 894 ft) and has a remarkable pyramid shaped rock on its N slope.

Bōze (Bose) Shima, 103 m (charted as 330 ft) high in its W part, is connected to the SE extremity of Nishi Shima by a narrow neck of sand which dries.

Anchorage. Anchorage is afforded in depths from 16 m to 20 m between the NW side of Bōze Shima and the E side of Nishi Shima, but care must be taken to avoid **Uchi Shizumo Shō,** with a depth of 1·2 m (4 ft) over it, lying 5½ cables W of the N extremity of Bōze Shima. Furthermore, fish beds lie between Uchi Shizumo Shō and the coast of Nishi Shima, and in the inner part of the anchorage.

A **light** is exhibited on the head of a breakwater at **Bōze Kō,** a small fishing harbour on the NW coast of Bōze Shima.

Jaka Shima, 106 m (346 ft) high, lies ¼ mile SW of Bōze Shima; the passage between the two islands is foul.

Tako (Taka) Shima, Kuro Shima and **Yano Shima,** lie in that order from S to N within ¾ mile of the E side of Bōze Shima.

10.50

Ie Shima (34° 40' N, 134° 32' E), the principal island of Ieshima Guntō, lies 1 mile NNW of Bōze Shima and is 141 m (charted as 454 ft) high. A **light** is exhibited from a white round concrete tower with a square base, standing on **Ozaki Hana,** the N extremity of the island.

Ieshima Kō, protected by breakwaters, lies in a bay on the NE side of Ie Shima; a **light** is exhibited on the E breakwater.

Anchorage. Small vessels can obtain anchorage, sheltered from winds from all directions except NE, in the bay outside the breakwaters. Two **submarine cables** are landed close within the E entrance point to the bay.

Shimo Shizumo Shō and **Kami Shizumo Shō,** with depths of 4·6 m (15 ft) and 1·4 m (4 ft), respectively, lie close together 1¼ miles NNW of the NW extremity of Ie Shima. The SW side of Shimo Shizumo Shō and the NE side of Kami Shizumo Shō are each marked by a *light-buoy*.

A **fish haven,** marked by a spar *buoy* (orange; orange light) lies 1½ miles NE of Ozaki Hana and close S of Harima Nada N Fairway.

Clearing lines. Ozaki Hana in line with the summit of Tanga (Danga) Shima (10.51), bearing 127°, or in line with the summit of Kurakake Shima (10.52), bearing 090°, leads ½ mile NE and ½ mile S, respectively, of Shimo Shizumo Shō and Kami Shizumo Shō.

10.51

Tanga (Danga) Shima (34° 40' N, 134° 35' E) lies ¾ mile E of Ie Shima and has two summits, the W of which is 219 m (720 ft) high; there are white cliffs on its coast. A **light** is exhibited from a white octagonal concrete tower standing on the S side of the W summit at an elevation of 231 m.

Uwa Shima, consisting of two islets close together the highest of which is 33 m (charted as 113 ft) high, lies ¼ mile N of the N extremity of Tanga Shima.

Ka Shima, 56 m (185 ft) high and consisting of three islets joined by a sandy beach, lies 6 cables SE of the S extremity of Tanga Shima.

Ko Ikari, a rock drying 0·6 m (2 ft), lies 1½ cables E of the E extremity of Tanga Shima. **Ō Ikari,** a rock 1 m (3 ft) high, lies 8 cables ENE of the same point. A *light-buoy* is moored close NW of Ō Ikari.

Futon Shima, an islet 42 m (charted as 142 ft) high, lies 1 mile NE of Tanga Shima; a rock, 18 m high, lies close S and is joined to Futon Shima by a drying bank.

10.52

Kurakake Shima (34° 41' N, 134° 38' E), 1½ miles ENE of Futon Shima, consists of two hillocks joined by a low neck; the E and somewhat higher hillock is 63 m (206 ft) high. A **light** is exhibited from a white round concrete tower with red bands standing on the W hillock of Kurakake Shima.

Charts 2875, 3614

Kami Shima (34° 41' N, 134° 48' E), the E'most islet in Ieshima Guntō, lies 3½ miles E of Kurakake Shima; its rounded summit is 43 m (142 ft) high. A **light** is exhibited from a white hexagonal metal framework tower situated near the summit of the islet.

Numerous rocks lie off the N and S extremities of Kami Shima which should not be approached within 3 cables.

A **fish haven,** marked by a spar *buoy* (orange; orange light) lies 1 mile NE of Kami Shima.

Jino (Tino) Ishi, a rock with a depth of 12 m (39 ft) over it, lies 7 cables SW of Kami Shima and 1 mile NNW of *Harima Nada N Fairway No. 9 Light-buoy* (10.3).

A **fish haven,** charted as an obstruction, lies 3 cables E of Jino Ishi.

10.53

Measured distances. Measured distances of 3745·1 m and 1855·5 m are established S of Ieshima Guntō; they are marked as follows:

W end—Matsu Shima Light in line with beacon on Katsura Shima.

Centre—Two beacons on Bōze Shima in line

E end—A beacon on Tako Shima in line with a beacon on Kuro Shima.

The running courses are 082° and 262°.

HARIMA NADA—NORTH EAST PART

HIMEJI KŌ

Charts 698 plan of Himeji Kō, 2875

10.54

Himeji Kō, a specified port (see 1.64), extends from the mouth of Naka Kawa (34° 45' N, 134° 34' E) to Mega Hakuchi, 7½ miles E; the port is backed by the **Harima Industrial Zone** in which there are a number of power stations and large factories.

The port area of Himeji Kō, described at 10.56 to 10.62, is divided from W into Nishi Ku, Aboshi Ku, Hirohata Ku, Shikama Ku and Higashi Ku; the limits of these harbours are indicated on Chart 698. Each harbour is divided into No. 1 and No. 2 Areas.

Himeji, a leading industrial and commercial city, lies near the centre of the **Harima Plain,** about 4 miles NE of the port; in 1973 it had a population of 423 000.

Himeji Castle, one of the most famous castles in Japan, stands in the middle of the city and can be seen at a distance from certain directions.

Pilotage. Pilotage is not compulsory but recommended. Pilots can be arranged through the Naikai (Inland Sea) Pilots Association (see 1.24). Harbour pilots are available at the anchorage from 1 hour after sunrise to 1 hour before sunset.

Landmarks. Numerous chimneys, some of which are composite 3-stack chimneys, and tanks stand along the frontage of Himeji Kō and their positions can best be seen on Chart 698; several of the higher chimneys are painted red and white, and are marked by red obstruction lights.

The chimney of the **Peretto Factory** (34° 46·3′ N, 134° 37·0′ E) standing on the W side of the entrance to Hirohata Ku, has an elevation of 216 m and is the highest in the vicinity.

10.55

Sea-berth. The **Idemitsu Kōsan Sea-berth** (34° 42·6′ N, 134° 39·9′ E), a lighted mooring buoy, lies in the outer harbour 2¼ miles S of Shikama Ku in a depth of 20·2 m. Vessels up to 200 000 dwt can use the berth.

Anchorage. Anchorage can be obtained as convenient as close as possible to the port according to draught.

Caution. A **submarine oil pipeline,** indicated on the charts, is laid from Idemitsu Kōsan Sea-berth to the mouth of Ichi Kawa 3¼ miles N.

Chart 698 plan of Himeji Kō
Nishi Ku
10.56

No. 1 Area of **Nishi Ku** lies at the mouth of **Naka Kawa** (34° 45′ N, 134° 34′ E) and is used mainly for the shipment of timber. The basin is entered between two breakwaters; a **light** is exhibited at the head of each breakwater.

New Wharf, with a depth of 10 m alongside, lies on the E side of the entrance to the basin.

A lock leading to a timber pond is situated on the E side of the basin. **Lights** are exhibited from a mast at the lock entrance as follows:

Red light   Lock closed
Blue light   Lock open

Three mooring buoys lie in the basin and can accommodate vessels up to 9 m draught.

Aboshi Ku
10.57

No. 1 Area of **Aboshi Ku** is situated across the mouths of **Ibo Kawa** and **Ōzumo Kawa** (34° 46·0′ N, 134° 36·5′ E).

Aboshi Breakwater lies on the W side of the E entrance channel which has a depth of 5·5 m in it. A **light** is exhibited on the head of the breakwater, and *No. 2* and *No. 4 Light-buoys* mark the E side of the channel. The channel leads to **Yoshima Landing Quay,** with depths from 3 m to 5 m alongside.

Nihon Chemical dolphin berths, with a depth of 5 m alongside, lie on the W side of the mouth of Ibo Kawa, 1 mile WSW of Aboshi Breakwater.

Hirohata Ku
10.58

No. 1 Area of **Hirohata Ku** consists of a large basin bordered on its S side by areas of reclaimed land. **Hirohata East Breakwater** (34° 46′ N, 134° 38′ E) extends SW from the SW corner of the reclaimed area on the E side of the entrance to the basin; a **light** is exhibited on the head of the breakwater.

Hirohata Fairway, dredged to a depth of 17 m, is entered between *No. 1* and *No. 2 Light-buoys* (see Chart 2875) moored 2 miles SSW of the head of Hirohata East Breakwater, and leads towards the entrance to the basin; the fairway is marked on each side by further *light-buoys.*

Genryo Raw Material Quay, with a depth of 17 m alongside, and which can accommodate a vessel of 100 000 grt, lies on the W side of the entrance to the basin.

Leading lights, exhibited from a pair of white metal framework towers (white triangular topmarks), in line bearing 000°, lead through the narrow entrance channel, which has a least depth of 13·2 m, and into the basin.

A **signal station,** from which private berthing signals are made, is situated on the W side of the entrance to the basin.

10.59

Berths. The principal berths in No. 1 Area of Hirohata Ku, owned and controlled by the **Shin-Nippon Steel Company,** are as follows:

Berth	Length m	Depth m	Capacity dwt
Tsuruta Quay			
10, 11	350	8·5–9·5	20 000
Central Quay			
8, 9	315	10–13·5	76 000
Kamoda Quay			
3–7	720	6·5–7·5	10 000
Yumesaki Quay			
1, 2	280	7·5	7 000
Higashihama Quay			
A1, A2	350	7–11	30 000
Limestone Quay			
	55	8	6 500

Shikama Ku
10.60

No. 1 Area of **Shikama Ku** consists of a basin lying at the mouth of **Suga Kawa** (34° 47′ N, 134° 40′ E).

The approach channel to the basin, dredged to a depth of 12 m, is entered between *No. 1 Light-buoy* and *No. 2 Light-buoy* and leads between **Shikama W Breakwater** and **Shikama E Breakwater**; a **light** is exhibited on the S end of each breakwater, both of which are detached.

In 1978, reclamation work marked by towers and buoys, was in progress on each side of the entrance.

Two mooring buoys lie in the middle of the basin and can accommodate vessels up to 7·7 m draught. An **overhead cable** with a vertical clearance of 42 m, crosses the E corner of the basin.

A channel with a depth of 7·6 m and marked by *No. 1* and *No. 3 Light-buoys*, is entered close N of Shikama W Breakwater and leads into **Senba Kawa.**

Berths. The principal berths in No. 1 Area of Shikama Ku are as follows:

Berth & Position	Length m	Depth m	Capacity dwt
Nakashima Wharf			
(34° 46·3′ N, 134° 39·8′ E)	390	0·5–4·5	2 000
Shikama Quay			
(34° 46·7′ N, 134° 39·6′ E)			
3–6	690	9·5–10	10 000
7	240	12	30 000
Kansai Electricity Quay			
(34° 46·5′ N, 134° 40·2′ E)	200	6–7·5	12 000
Nippon Steel Quay			
(34° 46·7′ N, 134° 40·2′ E)	200	7·5–8·5	10 000
Senba Kawa Quay			
(34° 46·5′ N, 134° 39·4′ E)	360	6	2 000

Higashi Ku
10.61

No. 1 Area of **Higashi Ku** consists of a basin which lies on the E side of the mouth of **Ichi Kawa** (34° 46′ N, 134° 41′ E). The entrance to the basin is protected by **West Outer Breakwater, East Breakwater** and **West Breakwater**; a **light** is exhibited on the SE end of West

Outer Breakwater and on the head of East and West Breakwaters.

In 1978, reclamation work and the construction of an LNG installation, were in progress on the E side of East Breakwater.

East Fairway, dredged to a depth of 14 m, is entered between *No. 1* and *No. 2 Light-buoys*, moored ¼ mile S of the head of East Breakwater, and leads between the breakwaters towards the basin.

A **signal station** from which private signals are made, is situated on East Breakwater. An orange flashing light, exhibited at the signal station, indicates that a vessel carrying liquefied gas is either entering or leaving the harbour.

Berths. The principal berths in Higashi Ku are as follows:

Berth	Length m	Depth m	Capacity dwt
Himeji LNG Berth			
	dolphins	14	125 000
Idemitsu Oil Refinery			
1	190	6–7	3 000
2	—	5·5	3 000
3	dolphins	12	50 000
4, 5	—	6–7	Up to 4 000
LPG Jetty	—	5·5	3 000

10.62

Mega Hakuchi (34° 46' N, 134° 42' E), a small shallow harbour protected on its W side by a reclaimed area, lies in the NE corner of Higashi Ku; it is only suitable for small craft of less than 3 m draught.

A *light-buoy* marks the W side of the approach to Mega Hakuchi. An **overhead power cable** with a vertical clearance of 38 m, spans the entrance to the harbour.

A **fish haven** lies ¼ mile S of the entrance to the harbour.

Facilities at Himeji Kō
10.63

The offices of the Maritime Safety Agency, Customs and Immigration are located in the joint Harbour Office situated at the N end of Shikama Quay in Shikama Ku (10.60).

Tugs and lighters are available in Hirohata Ku and Shikama Ku.

Repair facilities are available in Shikama Ku for small vessels but there are none for large vessels.

Waste oil disposal facilities are available in Higashi Ku.

There is a hospital in the Shin Nippon Steelworks in Hirohata Ku.

Supplies. Fresh water and fuel oil can be supplied in all the harbours. Fresh water is laid on at the principal berths.

Communications. There is a regular shipping service to Ieshima Guntō (10.46) and a car ferry service to Shōdo Shima (10.5).

The nearest airport is at Ōsaka, 40 miles E.

Chart 2875
10.64

Between Mega Hakuchi and Iho Kō (10.66), 3½ miles ESE, lie the mouths of several rivers in which there are harbours available to small craft only.

Yagi Kō (34° 46·1' N, 134° 43·5' E) lies ¼ mile E of the E harbour limit of Himeji Kō and is protected on its W

side by a short breakwater on which a **light** is exhibited.

Landmark. A grey cliff, 68 m high, lies on the E side of the harbour entrance.

HIGASHI—HARIMA KŌ

Chart 3614
10.65

Higashi-Harima Kō, a specified port (see 1.64), extends from close W of Iho Kō (34° 45' N, 134° 45' E) to Futami Kō, 7½ miles SE, and in conjunction with Himeji Kō (10.54), serves the Harima Industrial Zone.

The harbour limit of Higashi-Harima Kō embraces Iho Kō (10.66), Takasago Kō (10.67), Befu Kō (also known as Kakogawa Kō) (10.69) and Futami Kō (10.71).

The industrial cities of **Takasago** and **Kakogawa** lie on each side of Kako Kawa, and in 1973 had a combined population of 223 000.

Pilotage. Pilotage is not compulsory but recommended. Pilots can be arranged through the Naikai (Inland Sea) Pilots Association (see 1.24). Harbour pilots are available at the anchorage from sunrise to sunset.

Landmarks. Several chimneys stand along the frontage of Higashi-Harima Kō and some of them are conspicuous; their positions can best be seen on the chart.

A factory with a pale green roof stands close NE of the root of the E breakwater (34° 41·6' N, 134° 50·6' E) at Befu Kō.

Anchorage. Anchor berths have been established as follows; bearing and distance from Befu Kō W Breakwater Light (34° 41·6' N, 134° 50·1' E):

Berth No.	Bearing	Distance
1	255°	3·5 miles
2	237°	3·7 miles
3	239°	2·9 miles
4	228°	3·3 miles

Iho Kō
10.66

Iho Kō (34° 45' N, 134° 46' E) lies at the mouth of **Arai Kawa** and is formed by two areas of reclaimed land, one on each side of the river mouth. A short breakwater is situated on the E side of the entrance.

A **light** is exhibited on the W side of the entrance to Iho Kō, and another **light** is exhibited on the head of the breakwater.

An **overhead power cable** with a vertical clearance of 47 m, spans Arai Kawa close within its mouth.

Berths. Dengen Kaihatsu Quay, with a depth of 7 m alongside, lies on the E side of the reclaimed land on the W side of the entrance to Arai Kawa; vessels up to 5000 dwt can be accommodated. **Kansai Electricity** dolphin berth, with a depth of 8 m alongside, lies on the W side of the reclaimed land.

Mobil Oil Jetty, with a depth of 6 m alongside, and **Iho Quay,** with a depth of 4 m alongside, lie upstream on the W bank of Arai Kawa, respectively, ¼ mile and 1¼ miles from the mouth of the river.

Takasago Kō
10.67

Takasago Nishikō (34° 44·2' N, 134° 47·3' E), an L-shaped basin with depths from 2·7 m to 7·6 m, lies nearly 1¼ miles SE of Iho Kō and is entered between two short breakwaters; a **light** is exhibited at the head of the W breakwater.

Takasago Kō (34° 43·8' N, 134° 48·1' E), a small artificial harbour protected by two breakwaters, lies on the W side of the mouth of **Kako Kawa,** 1 mile SE of Takasago Nishikō; a **light** is exhibited at the head of each breakwater. There are depths from 6·4 m to 7·3 m in the outer part of the harbour, and from 3 m to 4 m in the two inner basins.

A *light-buoy* is moored 3 cables S of the entrance to Takasago Kō; several **fish havens** lie within 4 cables S and ¼ mile SW of the light-buoy.

Caution. Depths of less than 5 m lie on the E side of the approach to Takasago Kō between the light-buoy and the entrance; care is needed in strong S to W winds or when the tidal stream is E-going.

Kako Kawa has a bar and can only be entered by small craft.

10.68

Berths. In Takasago Nishikō, **Kanebuchi Chemicals W** dolphin berth with a depth of about 6·5 m alongside, lies on the E side close within the entrance; **Takasago W Quay,** with a reported depth of 5·5 m alongside, lies in the inner part of the basin.

In Takasago Kō, **Kanebuchi Chemicals E** dolphin berth with a depth of 7 m alongside, lies on the W side; **Takasago Quay,** with a depth of 4·3 m alongside, lies in the NE part of the harbour.

Befu Kō
10.69

Befu Kō (34° 42' N, 134° 50' E), also known as **Kakogawa Kō,** lies 2¼ miles SE of Takasago Kō and is entered between two breakwaters; a **light** is exhibited at the head of each breakwater.

Kōbe Steelworks stands on reclaimed land on the W side of Befu Kō.

The **fairway** to Befu Kō is dredged to 17 m and is marked by *light-buoys*; *No. 1* and *No. 2 Light-buoys*, the outermost pair, are moored 1¾ miles SW of the entrance to the harbour.

A bank with a least depth of 11·6 m and a sandwave area, lies 2 miles S of the entrance to the fairway.

Leading lights, privately maintained, are exhibited from white columns (red triangular topmarks), standing at the head of the harbour; in line bearing 022¼°, they lead through the harbour entrance.

Befu Nishikō W Breakwater (34° 42·9' N, 134° 48·6' E) lies on the E side of the mouth of Kako Kawa and protects **West Quay** which lies on the W side of Kōbe Steelworks; a **light** is exhibited on the S end of the breakwater. The approach to West Quay is marked by a pair of *light-buoys*.

10.70

Berths. The principal berths in Befu Kō are as follows:

Berth & Position	Length m	Depth m	Capacity dwt
Kōbe Steelworks			
(34° 43' N, 134° 50' E)			
East Quay (E2–E5)	1150	4–17	Up to 160 000
South Quay (S1, S3)	820	3–12	Up to 25 000
West Quay (W1–W5)	1430	5–12	Up to 35 000
West Quay (W6)	275	12	Up to 55 000
LPG Jetty			
(34° 42·0' N, 134° 49·9' E) dolphins	14–17		Up to 70 000

Harima Public Wharf			
(34° 42·3' N, 134° 51·2' E)			
1, 2	970	5·5–8	Up to 5 000
3, 4	665	10	Up to 30 000
Tōa Quay			
(34° 41·7' N, 134° 50·6' E)	150	4–4·5	3 000

Futami Kō
10.71

Futami Kō (34° 41' N, 134° 53' E) lies 2½ miles E of the entrance to Befu Kō and is a small harbour with depths from 2 m to 3 m, protected by breakwaters. A **light** is exhibited on the head of the W breakwater.

Extensive reclamation work has taken place between Befu Kō and Futami Kō; in 1974, a basin E of Befu Kō was being developed.

A **light** is exhibited from a survey platform standing 4¼ cables SSE of Futami Kō W Breakwater Light.

Facilities at Higashi-Harima Kō
10.72

The offices of the Maritime Safety Agency, Customs and Immigration are located in the joint Harbour Office situated at the N end of Kōbe Steelworks East Quay in Befu Kō (10.69).

Tugs are available.

Waste oil disposal facilities are available in Takasago Kō (10.67).

Supplies. Fresh water is available on all the principal quays. Fuel oil is available.

Communications. The nearest airport is at Ōsaka, 30 miles E.

WEST APPROACHES TO AKASHI KAIKYŌ

Chart 3614
10.73

Shikano Se (34° 35' N, 134° 48' E), on the N side of Harima Nada Fairway in the W approach to Akashi Kaikyō, is a narrow rocky ridge about 3 miles long covered with sand and shingle; it has a least depth of 2·2 m. A *light-buoy* is moored off the middle of the S side of Shikano Se.

A bank with depths of less than 20 m lies to the W of Shikano Se and is marked at its W end by a *light-buoy*.

Matsuo and **Takakura Se** (34° 36·5' N, 134° 52·5' E), detached shoals with depths of 7·6 m over them, lie to the E of Shikano Se; a *light-buoy* is moored on the E side of Takakura Se.

Sandwaves exist in the vicinity of Takakura Se.

Shikano Se, Matsuo and Takakura Se are all covered by the red sector of an auxiliary **light** on E Saki (10.79).

Murotsuno Se, on the S side of Harima Nada Fairway, is a sandbank which lies almost parallel with Shikano Se and has a least depth of 8·3 m.

Clearing line. Hachibuse Yama (34° 38' N, 135° 06' E) (12.65) bearing 069° and slightly open N of E Saki, leads about midway between Shikano Se and Murotsuno Se.

The part of the NW coast of Awaji Shima which lies on the S side of the W approaches to Akashi Kaikyō is described at 10.20 to 10.22.

10.74

Eigashima Kō (34° 40' N, 134° 55' E), a small harbour protected by a breakwater, lies on the N shore of the W approaches to Akashi Kaikyō, 1 mile SE of the E limit of

Higashi-Harima Kō (10.65); a **light** is exhibited on the head of the breakwater.

Seaweed cultivation areas lie within 1½ miles NW and 3 miles SE of Eigashima Kō. Numerous steel piles, 1 m in height, stand up to 8 cables offshore in these areas; their seaward limit is marked by steel posts exhibiting red fixed lights.

The coast between Eigashima Kō and the mouth of Akashi Kawa (10.81) 3¾ miles SE, is fringed with shoals with depths of less than 5 m which extend about 3 miles offshore in places. The S edge of these shoals is steep-to and extends 3½ miles WSW from the mouth of Akashi Kawa.

Kantama Se, with a least depth of 5 m, lies on the W edge of these shoals and is marked on its SW side by a *light-buoy.*

Numerous **fish havens** lie W and N of Kantama Se within 3½ miles.

AKASHI KAIKYŌ

REGULATIONS AND GENERAL INFORMATION

Chart 3614
10.75

Akashi Kaikyō (34° 37' N, 135° 00' E) is the strait leading from the NE corner of Harima Nada into the NW side of Ōsaka Wan. The strait itself is deep and free from dangers but care is needed owing to the tidal streams (10.78) which in places set across the fairway.

Cautions. The fairways through Harima Nada and the route from the Kōbe/Ōsaka area and from Tomogashima Suidō, converge in Akashi Kaikyō and consequently the traffic, consisting of vessels of all types and sizes, is very heavy; the strait is considered to be one of the most congested sea areas in Japan.

In 1976, over 1800 vessels were passing through Akashi Kaikyō daily, the busiest periods being 0400–0500 and 1000–1100. Ferries run continuously across the strait between Akashi Kō and Iwaya Kō.

Particular care is necessary in the W approaches to the straits in the vicinity of Shikano Se (34° 35' N, 134° 48' E), and in the E entrance, in the area S of Hira Iso (34° 37' N, 135° 04' E), where large numbers of fishing vessels are likely to be encountered.

At night, the dazzle of the shore lights along the coast in the vicinity of Akashi Kō (134° 38' N, 135° 00' E), may make it difficult to distinguish the navigation lights of other vessels.

Traffic routes and regulations
10.76

A traffic route prescribed by the **Maritime Traffic Safety Law** and shown on the chart, is in force in Akashi Kaikyō.

Regulations. The general regulations for all traffic routes prescribed by the Law are given at 1.28. Additional regulations for Akashi Kaikyō are as follows:

(a) A vessel shall keep to the starboard side of the centre line of the traffic route; the centre line is marked by *Akashi Kaikyō Fairway Nos. 1–3 Light-buoys.*

(b) In low visibility, entry into the traffic route is restricted as follows:

Type of vessel	Restriction
(i) Vessels of length 200 m or more	Entry prohibited when the visibility in the traffic route is less than 1 mile.
(ii) Vessels of 10 000 grt or more carrying a dangerous cargo	
(iii) Vessels towing or pushing very long tows	

Signals to be shown by vessels. The charlet (facing page) of the Akashi Kaikyō Traffic Route shows the flag signals to be displayed by day and the sound signals to be made at night, by vessels in the traffic route or crossing between Akashi Kō and Iwaya Kō.

10.77

Recommended Traffic Separation Scheme. The 5th Regional Maritime Safety Headquarters requests that vessels comply with the following instructions when passing through Akashi Kaikyō:

(a) A vessel of 30 000 grt or more, and a vessel of 10 000 grt or more carrying a dangerous cargo, should employ a pilot.

(b) Vessels of 5000 grt or more should navigate as follows:

E-bound vessels. Vessels from Himeji Kō and Higashi-Harima Kō and other vessels from NW intending to enter the traffic route should pass S of Point B, marked by *Akashi W Fairway Light-buoy* (34° 36·3' N, 134° 56·9' E).

Vessels leaving the traffic route and proceeding towards Kōbe Kō or Ōsaka Kō, should pass S of Point A, marked by *Akashi E Fairway Light-buoy* (34° 34·9' N, 135° 05·0' E).

W-bound vessels. Vessels intending to enter the traffic route from E should pass N of *Akashi E Fairway Light-buoy* marking Point A.

(c) Vessels of 10 000 grt or less carrying dangerous cargo, should not enter the traffic route when the visibility in the straits is less than 1 mile.

(d) Vessels carrying dangerous cargo should have ready emergency towing wires forward and aft.

Tidal streams
10.78

Tidal streams. In Akashi Kaikyō the tidal streams flow as follows:

Time	Direction	Max rate
About 3 hours after LW to about 3 hours after HW	W-going	5–6 knots at time of HW
About 3 hours after HW to about 3 hours after LW	E-going	5–6 knots at time of LW

Slack water lasts from 10–30 minutes.

The maximum rate of either stream is experienced in the middle of the strait over about ⅓ of its width.

The E-going stream is stronger off E Saki than on the N side of the strait.

The W-going stream is stronger on the N side of the strait than off E Saki.

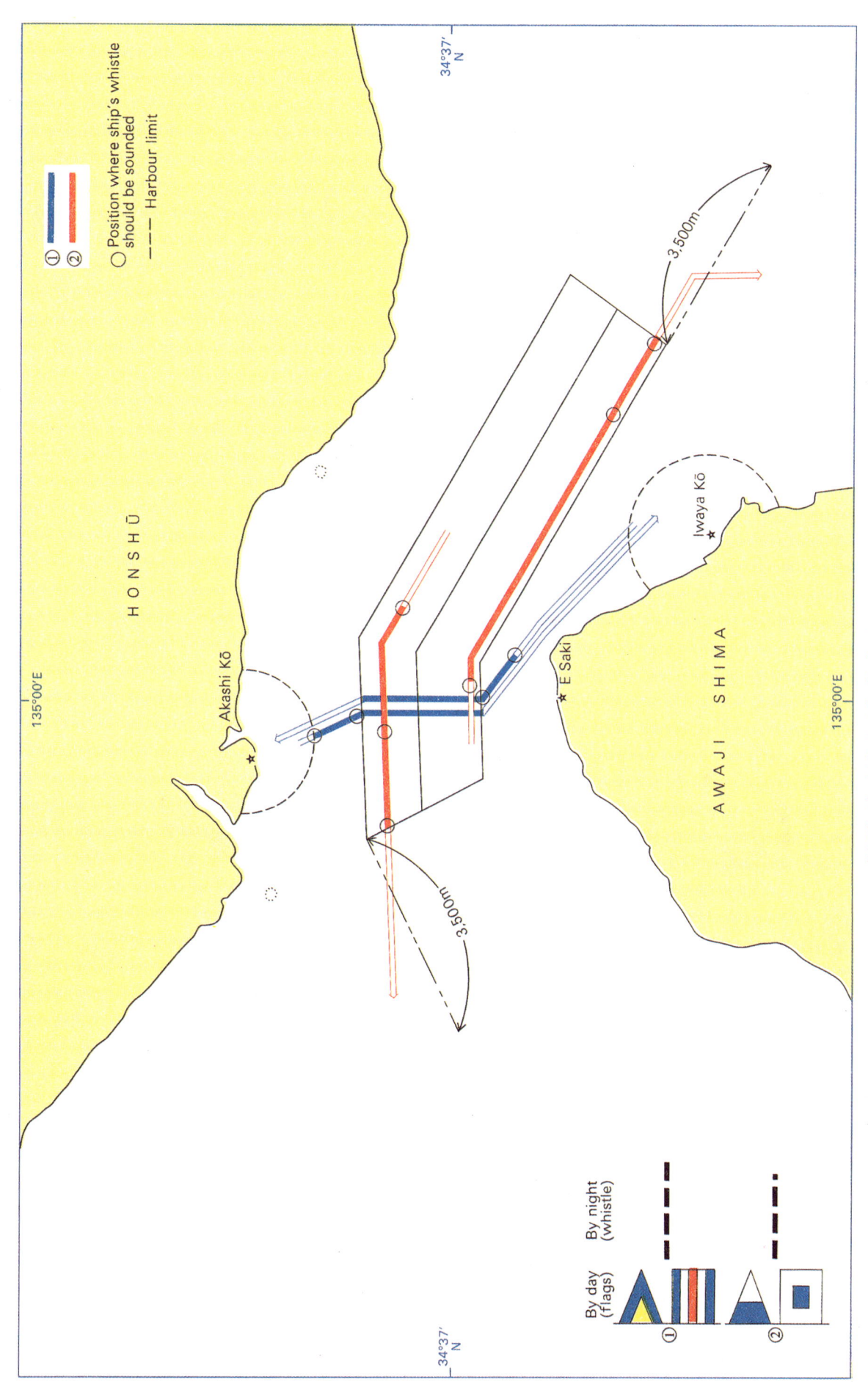

Position where ship's whistle should be sounded
Harbour limit

① ②

HONSHŪ

135°00'E

Akashi Kō

34°37'
N

34°37'
N

135°00'E

AWAJI SHIMA

E Saki

Iwaya Kō

3,500m

3,500m

34°37'
N

By day
(flags)

By night
(whistle)

①

②

(10.76) Akashi Kaikyō Traffic Route

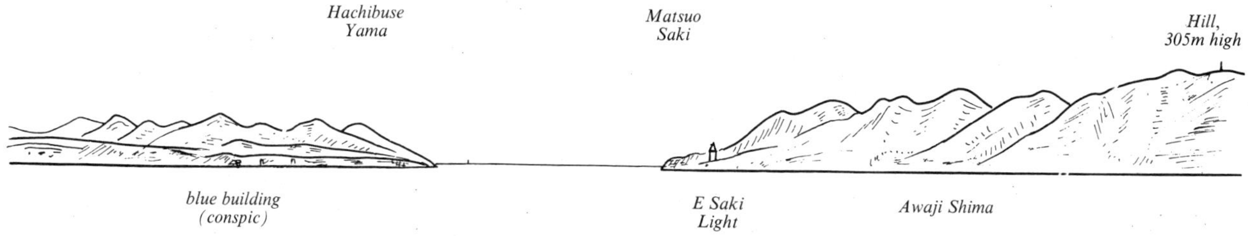

Hachibuse
Yama

Matsuo
Saki

Hill,
305m high

blue building
(conspic)

E Saki
Light

Awaji Shima

(10.75) Akashi Kaikyō *(34°37′N, 135°00′E)* from W.

(Original dated prior to 1978)

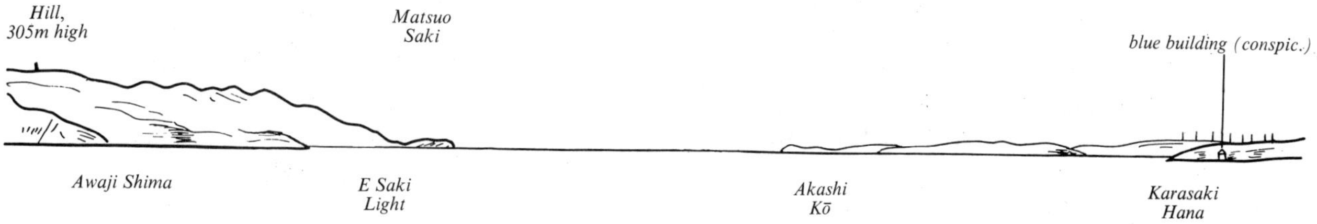

Hill,
305m high

Matsuo
Saki

blue building (conspic.)

Awaji Shima

E Saki
Light

Akashi
Kō

Karasaki
Hana

(10.75) Akashi Kaikyō *(34°37′N, 135°00′E)* from E.

(Original dated prior to 1978)

Eddies and counter-streams may be experienced as follows:

N side. Between Akashi Kō and Karasaki Hana and near Hiro Iso (34° 37' N, 135° 04' E).

S side. Either side of Matsuo Saki.

AKASHI KAIKYŌ—THE NARROWS

Chart 3614
South side
10.79

E Saki (34° 36' N, 135° 00' E), near the N extremity of Awaji Shima, lies on the S side of Akashi Kaikyō. A **light** is exhibited from a white round stone tower standing on E Saki, and an auxiliary **light** is exhibited from the same tower.

A **ramark** transmits from E Saki Light-tower.

Matsuo Saki, a low, thickly wooded, sandy point, ½ mile ENE of E Saki, is the N extremity of Awaji Shima. Two radio towers, 124 m in height, stand on Matsuo Saki and are marked by red obstruction lights.
10.80

Iwaya Kō (34° 35' N, 135° 02' E), 1¼ miles SSE of Matsuo Saki, is a small harbour used by the ferries from Akashi Kō, and as a sheltering place for small vessels up to 200 tons.

Iwaya Kō is protected by breakwaters and is divided into an outer and inner harbour. The outer harbour, which lies on the E side, is entered between the W end of a detached breakwater and the head of an E breakwater; a **light** is exhibited on each side of the entrance.

Anchorage. Good anchorage can be obtained in a depth of 15 m, about 3 cables N of the entrance to Iwaya Kō, but it is dangerous in strong NE winds.

Fish havens lie 7 cables N of the harbour.

There are depths of about 3·5 m in the outer harbour; quays with depths from 3 m to 4 m alongside, lie on both its E and W sides. A passenger terminal building stands on the E side of the harbour.

North side
10.81

Hayashi Kō (34° 38' N, 134° 58' E), a small harbour protected by breakwaters, is situated on the N side of Akashi Kaikyō close NW of the mouth of **Akashi Kawa**;

a **light** is exhibited on the head of the W breakwater.

Semento Iso, a narrow shoal 9 cables in length with a least depth of 1 m, lies parallel with the coast and ¼ mile offshore, S of Hayashi Kō. The W and E ends and the S side of this shoal are marked, respectively, by a *light-buoy*.
10.82

Akashi Kō (34° 38' N, 135° 00' E), ¼ mile E of the mouth of Akashi Kawa, is protected by breakwaters and is divided into an outer and inner harbour; **lights** are exhibited on the ends of the W, E and S breakwaters.

Landmarks. A 6-storied building, which is prominent, stands on reclaimed land on the E side of the harbour; a television tower and advertising tower stand close W of it.

An observatory standing ¼ mile NE of the harbour is conspicuous.

Akashi Kō is used by the ferries plying across Akashi Kaikyō to Iwaya Kō, and as a sheltering place for small vessels up to 100 tons.

The industrial city of **Akashi,** with a population of 216 000 in 1973, backs the harbour and forms the W end of the Ōsaka/Kōbe Industrial Zone.

Caution. Care is needed when approaching the entrance to Akashi Kō as the tidal streams across the approach are strong, and small vessels passing through Akashi Kaikyō, pass close across the entrance to avoid the strength of the tidal stream in the main part of the strait.
10.83

Tarumi Kō (34° 37' N, 135° 03' E), a small harbour protected by breakwaters, lies 3¼ miles ESE of Akashi Kō; a **light** is exhibited on the head of the W breakwater.

Seaweed beds in which there are numerous steel pipes, lie close in to the shore within 2 miles WNW of Tarumi Kō.

Landmarks. A number of conspicuous buildings, the position of which can be seen on the chart, stand near the coast in the vicinity of Tarumi Kō.
10.84

A **light** is exhibited from a black round concrete tower with red bands standing on **Hira Iso** (34° 37' N, 135° 05' E) situated on the N side of the E entrance to Akashi Kaikyō.

A 2·4 m patch lies close W of Hira Iso and is marked, respectively, on its W and N sides by a *light-buoy*.

CHAPTER 11

KII SUIDŌ

GENERAL INFORMATION

Chart 951
11.1

Kii Suidō, which is the S approach to the E end of Seto Naikai, lies between the E coast of Shikoku and the mainland of Honshū farther E. The seaward approach to the strait is described in *Japan Pilot Volume II*.

Kii Suidō is entered from S between Kamoda (Komoda) Misaki (33° 50' N, 134° 45' E) and Hino Misaki, 16 miles E. Naruto Kaikyō (34° 14' N, 134° 40' E) (11.59) in the NW corner of the strait, leads into Harima Nada, and Tomogashima Suidō (34°16' N, 135° 00' E) (11.72), in the NE corner, leads into Ōsaka Wan.

The **Maritime Traffic Safety Law** (see 1.27) is applicable within Seto Naikai, N of a line joining Kamoda Misaki and Hino Misaki.

Directions for Kii Suidō
11.2

Large vessels bound for Ōsaka Wan from SE should pass at least 2 miles off Hino Misaki (33° 53' N, 135° 03' E) and shape course to pass through Yura Seto (34° 16' N, 134° 59' E), the W of the two channels in Tomogashima Suidō.

Cautions. In addition to the large number of vessels on passage through Kii Suidō and which round Hino Misaki, numerous small vessels are likely to be encountered rounding the point close inshore; fishing vessels congregate off Hii Wan, 2 miles N of the point.

Numerous **fish havens,** indicated on the chart, lie off the coast on the E side of Kii Suidō.

Care is needed to avoid being set towards the Honshū coast between Hino Misaki and Tomogashima Suidō; at night, vessels should keep within the arc of visibility (273°–172°) of Hino Misaki Light.

The traffic of small vessels and ferries crossing Kii Suidō E/W is very heavy.

11.3

Approaching Kii Suidō from SW, vessels should round I Shima (33° 51' N, 134° 49' E) about 4 miles off and shape course for Yura Seto. In the S approach to Yura Seto, this course will cross the track of S-bound traffic and care is needed.

The passage between Kamoda Misaki and I Shima is used by small vessels but it is encumbered with rocks and should be avoided by vessels without local knowledge.

11.4

The route through Naruto Kaikyō into Harima Nada shortens the distance by about 40 miles compared with that through Tomagashima Suidō, Ōsaka Wan and Akashi Kaikyō, but the strait is narrow with very strong tidal streams and should be avoided by large vessels and by vessels without local knowledge.

Tidal streams
11.5

In a position 2 miles W of Hino Misaki, the tidal streams are as follows:

Interval from local HW	Direction	Rate
– 0200	N-going	1 knot
+ 0400	S-going	—

Broken water may be encountered off Hino Misaki, particularly when a N wind meets the tidal stream flowing out of the bay on the S side of the cape.

KII SUIDŌ—WEST SIDE

TACHIBANA KŌ AND APPROACHES

Chart 951
11.6

Kamoda (Komoda) Misaki (33° 50' N, 134° 45' E), I Shima and the dangers between them, are described in *Japan Pilot Volume II*.

Tsubakidomari Ura
11.7

Tsubakidomari Ura (33° 50' N, 134° 42' E), a long and narrow inlet, lies on the N side of the promontory terminating in Kamoda Misaki and affords good shelter to small vessels with local knowledge.

Maiko Shima, 84 m high, forms the N entrance point to Tsubakidomari Ura; the S side of the island is fringed with sandbanks extending 1½ cables offshore in places and the channel S of it is considerably obstructed by reefs. **Naka Bae,** which dries 0·2 m, lies near the middle of the channel and is marked on its N side by a *light-buoy* (black; green light group flashing 2 every 6 seconds); there are depths from 7 m to 10 m in the passage N of the light-buoy.

The N channel into Tsubakidomari Ura lies between the W end of Maiko Shima and **Karimata Saki,** 4 cables W; the width of this channel, which has a depth of over 20 m, is reduced by reefs on either side to about 2 cables. A **light** is exhibited from a white round concrete tower situated on Karimata Saki.

Tachibana Ura
11.8

Tachibana Ura (33° 53' N, 134° 43' E) is entered between Karimata Saki (33° 50·5' N, 134° 43·4' E) and **Tōjinba Kaku,** 3¼ miles NNW; and in it lie numerous islands and islets.

Tachibana Kō, a developing industrial port and an open harbour (see 1.65), lies at the inner end of Tachibana Ura. The city of **Anan,** which in 1973 had a population of 62 000, lies on the N side of the inlet.

Landmarks. Ishōgamori Yama, 180 m high and densely wooded, lies 1½ miles W of the head of Tachibana Ura and is a good mark.

Tsuno Mine, 3 miles N of Ishōgamori Yama, is 299 m high with a sharp peak surmounted by a temple.

Weather signals (see 1.42) are displayed on Tōjinba Kaku.

Approaches to Tachibana Kō

11.9

Nono Shima (33° 51' N, 134° 43' E), 83 m high and covered with bushes, lies close inshore on the S side of the entrance to Tachibana Ura; from it a chain of detached reefs extends about 1¼ miles N. **Tobi Shima,** a conical islet 29 m high, and **Hadiki Shima,** a rock 7 m high, are situated on these reefs.

Funa Iso, consisting of two rocks about 1 m high, lies on the N side of the entrance to Tachibana Ura, 2 miles N of Nono Shima; a **light** is exhibited from a white round concrete tower standing on the N of the two rocks.

Urume Shima (33° 51·5' N, 134° 41·3' E), a conical islet 45 m high to the tops of the trees, lies 1¼ miles WNW of Nono Shima. **Taka Shima,** 83 m high and sparsely wooded, lies ½ mile W of Urume Shima. **Kokatsu Shima** lies ½ mile W of Taka Shima and is 75 m high.

Naga Shima, a long and narrow islet lying E/W and 40 m high to the tops of the trees, is situated ½ mile NNW of Taka Shima; a **light** is exhibited from a white round concrete tower standing on the E end of the islet.

11.10

Pilotage is not compulsory. If required the pilot will embark off the entrance to Tachibana Ura. Vessels usually anchor first off Shimotsu Ku (11.44), 25 miles NE, to obtain pratique.

Directions. From NE, the track leads as follows:

Urume Shima (11.9) ahead bearing 223° until Funa Iso bears 270° and is in line with **Takasaki Yama** (33° 53·4' N, 134° 41·1' E), 80 m high, flat-topped and covered with trees, lying 1 mile W; thence with the summit of Kokatsu Shima ahead bearing 242° until Urume Shima bears 152°; thence with **Okonai Yama** (33° 51·8' N, 134 °37·7' E), 137 m high, situated on the W side of the inlet, ahead bearing 262°; thence to the harbour.

From E, the track leads as follows:

Takasaki Yama in line with Funa Iso ahead bearing 270° until the light-tower on Ao Shima (33° 55·3' N, 134° 43·3' E) bears 000°; thence with the summit of Kokatsu Shima ahead bearing 242°, and thence as previously directed.

Caution. In the passage between Funa Iso and the reefs which extend N from the S entrance point to Tachibana Ura, Hadiki Shima should be given a berth of at least ½ mile.

Anchorage. Good anchorage is afforded in a depth of 10·5 m, mud and good holding ground, about mid way between Taka Shima, Kokatsu Shima and Naga Shima. The anchorage is exposed to NE winds.

Harbour

11.11

There is a reclaimed area W of Naga Shima on which stands **Shikoku Electricity Power Station** with a number of chimneys of which the most prominent has an elevation of 201 m and is painted red and white.

The channel leading to the S part of the reclaimed area is marked by *light-buoys* and has a least depth of 10 m.

Nippon Denkō Quay (33° 52·1' N, 134° 39·4' E), with depths from 10·5 m to 11 m alongside and which can accommodate a vessel up to 30 000 dwt, lies on the S side of the reclaimed area; a dolphin stands at each end of the berth.

Shikoku Electricity Nos. 1–3 Jetties (33° 52·6' N, 134° 39·5' E), with depths from 5·5 m to 7·5 m alongside, lie on the NE side of the reclaimed area and can accommodate vessels up to 5000 tons.

West Shore Quay (33° 52·0' N, 134° 38·6' E), with a depth of about 5·5 m alongside, lies to the W of the reclaimed area.

Facilities. Tugs are available from Komatsushima Kō (11.16) when required. There are four lighters.

Minor repair facilities are available.

Supplies. Fuel oil can be ordered from elsewhere. Fresh water is only available from shore hydrants.

Communications. There is a regular ferry service to I Shima (11.6).

TOMIOKA KŌ

Chart 951

11.12

Tomoika Kō (33° 55' N, 134° 42' E) lies at the mouth of **Naka Kawa** 4 miles NNE of Tachibana Kō (11.8).

Approaches

Ao Shima (33° 55·3' N, 134° 43·3' E), 54 m high and saddle-backed, lies 3 cables E of the entrance to Naka Kawa; it is dark and densely wooded and is the largest and N'most of several islets in the vicinity. A **light** is exhibited from a white round concrete tower standing on a hill in the SW part of Ao Shima.

Mitsu Ishi, 6 m high, lies at the extremity of a chain of rocks extending 3 cables E from the NE extremity of Ao Shima; a 2 m patch lies 1 cable NE of Mitsu Ishi.

Nakatsu Shima, 51 m high, lies 3 cables S of Ao Shima.

Maru Shima, 71 m high with steep cliffs, lies ¾ mile SSW of Ao Shima.

A **light** is exhibited on the head of a breakwater, 2¼ miles NNW of Ao Shima. A tower (red and white), 150 m in height and marked by red lights, stands near the root of the breakwater.

Landmark. A chimney (white) stands at an elevation of 94 m on the S bank of Naka Kawa about ¾ mile within its entrance, and is a good mark.

11.13

Pilotage. The pilot for Tomioka Kō boards at Komatsushima Kō (34° 02' N, 134° 37' E).

Directions. The main fairway leading to the entrance to Naka Kawa is between Nakatsu Shima (33° 55·0' N, 134° 43·4' E) and Maru Shima, but care is needed to avoid a rock with a depth of less than 2 m, lying 1 cable E of Maru Shima, and the rocks, which dry, extending 2 cables SW from Nakatsu Shima; there are depths from 16 m to 19 m in this fairway.

No attempt should be made to pass between Maru Shima and the coast W as the area is encumbered with rocks.

From the N, vessels of under 90 m in length, normally approach the entrance to the river in the channel between Ao Shima and the head of the N breakwater.

Harbour

11.14

Training walls have been constructed on each side of the mouth of Naka Kawa; a **light** is exhibited on the head of the N training wall. A breakwater extends 4½ cables E from the coast, 2 cables N of the N training wall.

There is a least depth of 6 m as far as the quay at Tomioka Kō but the navigable width between the training walls at the entrance is very narrow.

Kanzaki Quay, with depths from 3·5 m to 4·5 m alongside, lies on the S side of Naka Kawa close W of the root of the training wall, and can accommodate a vessel of 2000 tons.

Facilities. There is a Customs Office in Tomioka Kō.

Supplies. Fresh water is laid on to the quay. Fuel oil can be supplied by road.

APPROACHES TO KOMATSUSHIMA KŌ AND TOKUSHIMA KŌ

Chart 3615 plan of Komatsushima Kō and Tokushima Kō
11.15

Wadano Hana (34° 00' N, 134° 38' E), a low wooded sandspit, forms the SE arm of the entrance to Komatsushima Kō; a **light** is exhibited from a white square concrete tower standing near the N extremity of the spit.

Okino Se, a steep-to rock with a depth of 3 m over it, lies nearly 3 miles NNE of Wadano Hana; it is marked by breakers when there is any swell.

Okame Se, a group of rocks some of which dry, lies 1¼ miles N of Wadano Hana; a **light** is exhibited from a red round concrete tower with black bands standing on Okame Se. An observation tower (metal framework) exhibiting a **light** is situated ½ mile E of Okame Se.

Landmarks. A silo stands ¼ mile S of Wadano Hana and is the most conspicuous object in the area.

A fire lookout stands in Komatsushima 2 miles W of Wadano Hana and is conspicuous.

Two radio towers, 20 m in height, stand in the harbour area of Komatsushima Kō.

Bi San (34° 04' N, 134° 32' E) (Chart 951), 290 m high, is situated in the W part of the city of Tokushima; two radio towers and a pagoda from which a light is exhibited, stand near its summit and are prominent.

Pilotage is not compulsory. If required pilots are available and will board ¼ mile NW of Wadano Hana except in bad weather when they will board inside No. 3 Area (11.17).

Vessels usually anchor first off Shomotsu Ku (11.44), 27 miles ENE, to obtain pratique.

KOMATSUSHIMA KŌ

Chart 3615 plan of Komatsushima Kō and Tokushima Kō
11.16

Komatsushima Kō (34° 00' N, 134° 37' E), a specified port (see 1.64), is entered between Wadano Hana (11.15) and **Ō Saki** a well defined headland, 2¼ miles NW. The harbour is divided into Nos. 1, 2 and 3 Areas which are indicated on the chart.

Komatsushima Kō is the main port on the E coast of Shikoku and is extensively used by shipping to and from Kōbe and Ōsaka. In 1973, the town of **Komatsushima** had a population of 43 000.

Nos. 3 and 2 Areas
11.17

The main part of Komatsushima Kō is contained in **No. 3 Area; No. 2 Area** lies in the NW corner of the harbour.

Nei Hana (34° 01' N, 134° 36' E), 1¼ miles NW of Wadano Hana, is sparsely wooded and a red-coloured cliff is situated on the headland immediately N of it. **Komatsushima Kō Light** is exhibited at an elevation of 91 m from a white concrete column standing on top of a hill 3 cables W of Nei Hana.

Hino Mine, 134 m high and 1 mile WNW of Nei Hana, together with other hills in its vicinity, are dark in appearance.

A **light** is exhibited from a red round concrete tower standing on **Taka Sone** situated 1½ cables E of Nei Hana.

Kigi Su, a group of four rocks the largest of which is 12 m high, lie on a shoal 3 cables NNE of Nei Hana.

Komatsushima Ko No. 1 and *No. 2 Light-buoys,* moored 1 mile W of Wadano Hana, mark the entrance to the approach channel to No. 1 Area, the inner harbour.

Kanaiso Wharf lies on reclaimed land on the NW side of the mouth of a river which flows into the S part of No. 3 Area. The wharf is approached by a channel, with depths from 8 m to 9 m and marked by two pairs of light-buoys; *Kanaiso No. 1* and *No. 2 Light-buoys,* the outermost pair, are moored ¼ mile SW of Wadano Hana.

Anchorages. Anchorage is afforded in depths from 8 m to 13 m outside the detached breakwater protecting No. 1 Area.

At the time of a typhoon, sheltered anchorage can be obtained to the SW of Wadano Hana in depths from 7 m to 8 m, mud; however care is needed as there are seaweed beds and fixed fishing nets off the W side of Wadano Hana.

A **dangerous cargo** anchorage lies in No. 2 Area.

No. 1 Area
11.18

No. 1 Area, protected by three breakwaters the middle one of which is detached, lies on the NW side of Komatsushima Kō; a **light** is exhibited at each end of the detached breakwater and at the head of the S breakwater.

Within the breakwaters, a fairway with depths from 9 m to 10·5 m in its greater part, leads NW from the entrance between the S end of the detached breakwater and the head of the S breakwater, to the berths on **Shinkō Wharf** on the W side of the harbour.

Nos. 1 and 2 mooring buoys, suitable for vessels of 6 m and 7 m draught, respectively, lie in the N part of No. 1 Area.

Anchorage can be obtained in No. 1 Area in depths from 8 m to 10 m.

Berths and facilities
11.19

Berths. The principal berths in Komatsushima Kō are as follows:

Berth & Position	Length m	Depth m	Capacity dwt
Shinkō Wharf			
(34° 00·5' N, 134° 35·7' E)			
Shinkō Jetty	150	about 8	10 000
N Quay	218	6·5	3 000
S Quay	221	6·5–7·5	3 000
Public Ferry Jetty			
(34° 00·3' N, 134° 35·7' E)	130	6–6·5	3 600
Kanaiso Wharf			
(33° 59·6' N, 134° 37·0' E)			
No. 1 Quay	170	9	10 000
No. 2 Quay	200	9	15 000

Kokusaku Pulp Jetty
(33° 59·3' N, 134° 36·9' E)   60   7·5   5 000

11.20
Facilities. The offices of the Maritime Safety Agency, Customs and Immigration are located in the joint Harbour Office situated on the S side of S Quay (34° 00·4' N, 134° 35·6' E) in No. 1 Area.
Two tugs and two lighters are available.
Minor repairs can be undertaken.
Supplies. Fuel oil can be supplied. Fresh water is laid on to the main quays and there is a water barge.
Communications. There is a regular ferry service to Ōsaka Kō. Tokushima Airport is situated 10 miles N of Komatsushima Kō.

TOKUSHIMA KŌ

Chart 3615 plan of Komatsushima Kō and Tokushima Kō
11.21
Tokushima Kō (34° 03' N, 134° 36' E) lies within the mouth of **Shinmachi Kawa** which flows into the sea 2 miles N of Komatsushima Kō (11.16). The approaches to the harbour are described at 11.15.
The city of **Tokushima** lies about 2 miles upstream and in 1973 had a population of 243 000.
Tokushima Kō is protected from seaward by **Tsuda Outer Breakwater** (34° 02·5' N, 134° 36·4' E), ¼ mile long and detached, and by a breakwater on the N side of the river mouth. A **light** is exhibited on each end of Tsuda Outer Breakwater and on the head of the N breakwater.
No. 2 Light-buoy is moored 2 cables NW of the N end of Tsuda Outer Breakwater.
A timber pond and timber storage area, the entrance to which is protected by breakwaters, lie on the S side of the mouth of Shinmachi Kawa. Extensive laver beds lie to the N of the N breakwater.
Shinmachi Kawa has been dredged to a depth of 5 m as far as **Suehiro Bridge,** with a vertical clearance of 21 m, situated 1¼ miles upstream. The channel within the river is marked by *light-buoys.*
Leading lights, in line bearing 308°, are exhibited from masts (white triangular topmark) standing ¼ mile WNW of the head of the N breakwater; they lead towards **Okino Su Ferry Berth.**
An **overhead cable** with a vertical clearance of 34 m, spans the river a short distance below the bridge.
11.22
Berths. The principal berths in Tokushima Kō are:

Berth & Position	Length m	Depth m	Capacity dwt
Ocean/Tōkyō Ferry Quay			
(34° 02·8' N, 134° 35·6' E)	130	5·5–6	7000
Tsuda Quay			
(34° 02·8' N, 134° 35·4' E)	270	5·5 reported	2000
Okino Su Ferry Berth			
(34° 03·2' N, 134° 35·2' E)	98	8	2700
Okino Su Quay			
(34° 03·2' N, 134° 35·0' E)	108	2–5	2000

In 1979, **Tsuda Timber Quay** with a planned depth of 10 m alongside and suitable for vessels up to 10 000 dwt, was under construction on the S side of the entrance to the river 1¼ cables SSW of the head of the N breakwater.
Climate. See table at 1.103.
Supplies. Fresh water is available on the main quays.

Communications. There are regular car ferry, hydrofoil and hovercraft services to Kanmon Kō, Kōbe Kō, Ōsaka Kō and Tōkyō Ku.
Tokushima Airport is situated 5 miles N of the port.

YOSHINO KAWA TO ŌISO SAKI

Charts 3615 plan of Komatsushima Kō and Tokushima Kō, 951
11.23
Yoshino Kawa (34° 04' N, 134° 36' E), the largest river in Shikoku, flows into the sea 1¼ miles NNE of the entrance to Tokushima Kō (11.21). A *light-buoy* is moored about 1 mile off the entrance to the river.
Chart 951
The coast between the mouth of Yoshino Kawa and Ōiso Saki 7 miles NNE consists of sand or shingle; inland is the delta of Yoshino Kawa. The river discharges such large quantities of silt that its mouths are constantly changing.

Imakiri Kō (34° 06' N, 134° 37' E), 3½ miles NNE of Tokushima Kō, lies in **Nagahara Kuchi.**
A training wall lies on each side of the entrance; a **light** is exhibited at the head of the N training wall.
An **aero light** is exhibited from a metal framework tower at **Tokushima Airport** situated about ½ mile inland, 1¼ miles N of Imakiri Kō.
11.24
Awazu Kō (34° 08' N, 134° 37' E) lies in **Awazu (Awatsu) Kuchi,** 2½ miles N of Imakiri Kō. A breakwater extends NE from the S bank of the river and a **light** is exhibited on its head.
Matsushiga Quay with a depth of 5·5 m alongside, lies on the S bank of the river about ½ mile W of the head of the breakwater. A fairway, about 120 m wide, leading from the entrance of the river to this quay, is reported to be dredged to 5·5 m.
Landmarks. Three tall cranes (red and white) stand in the **Awazu Shipyard** on the N bank of the river opposite Matsushiga Quay, and are prominent.

Ōiso Saki (34° 11' N, 134° 39' E) is surmounted by a conical grassy hillock from which a range of hills, covered with pine trees, extends nearly 1 mile W to **Myōken Yama,** 61 m high; a tower which is illuminated at night stands on Myōken Yama.
A **light** is exhibited from a white round concrete tower situated on Ōiso Saki; a group of hotels stands on a hill lying between the point and Myōken Yama.
Okame Iso, a detached shoal on which lie some rocks awash, is situated 3 cables E of Ōiso Saki; a **beacon** (metal mast, white ball topmark) stands on these rocks. An auxiliary **light** on Ōiso Saki Light-tower shows over Okame Iso.

MUYANO SETO AND MUYA KŌ

Charts 951, 694 plan of Naruto
Muyano Seto
11.25
Muyano Seto (34° 11' N, 134° 38' E) is the narrow channel, on either side of which are extensive saltpans, which separates Ōge Shima (11.61) and Shimada Shima (10.16) from the NE extremity of Shikoku; it is entered from S between Ōiso Saki (11.24) and the S end of Ōge Shima. Owing to the shoals in both the E and N entrances, and to the tidal streams which attain a rate of

5 knots, the channel is only suitable for small vessels up to about 300 tons with local knowledge.

The N end of Muyano Seto leads through Kitadomarino Seto (34° 14' N, 134° 36' E) (10.16) and into Harima Nada.

Uchi Umi is a salt water lagoon enclosed by Ōge Shima and Shimada Shima; the W entrance to this lagoon is situated near the middle of the E side of Muyano Seto and is shoal.

Horikoshi Suidō (34° 14' N, 134° 37' E), the NE entrance to Uchi Umi which leads into the N part of Naruko Kaikyō, is only about 30 m wide with depths of less than 2 m; the tidal streams in the strait are so strong that boats can only pass through at slack water.

Muya Kō

11.26

Muya Kō (34° 11' N, 134° 38' E) lies in the S part of Muyano Seto close within its E entrance. The harbour affords sheltered anchorage with good holding ground to small vessels.

Landmarks; see 11.62.

The city of **Naruto,** which in 1973 had a population of 63 000, lies on the S side of Muyano Seto.

A rubble breakwater extends 1½ cables N from Oiso Saki (34° 10·6' N, 134° 38·6' E); a bank, with depths of less than 5 m, extends about 3 cables NNW from the head of this breakwater and forms a bar across the E entrance to Muya Kō. A pile stands on the bank close N of the leading line.

Sengoku Su, a sandspit with a depth of less than 2 m, extends about 6 cables E from **Tōmino Hana** (34° 10·9' N, 134° 37·5' E), the S extremity of Ōge Shima.

Naka Se is a reef lying in mid-channel 2½ cables SE of Tōmino Hana; a **light** is exhibited from a red round concrete tower standing close S of the reef.

Leading lights, exhibited from a pair of white round concrete towers with red bands (white triangular topmarks), are situated on the S side of the entrance 1¼ cables WSW of Naka Se Light-tower; in line they bear 253¼°.

In 1976, the lights led over the bar in a least depth of 4 m; they lead S of Naka Se Light-tower.

Cautions. The position of the outer edge of Sengoku Su is liable to alter owing to shifting sand. In strong S winds a confused sea may be encountered over the bar.

From April to October many excusion boats are to be found in the vicinity of Naka Se and it is reported that difficulty in manoeuvring is frequently experienced in consequence.

11.27

Konarato Bridge, painted red, spans Muyano Seto 7 cables NW of Tōmina Hana; there are two navigational spans, each about 80 m wide, the N having a vertical clearance of 23 m and the S of 16 m.

An **overhead cable** with a vertical clearance of 26 m, spans the strait about 1 mile W of the bridge. An **overhead cable** with a vertical clearance of 25 m, spans **Muya Kawa** which flows into the S side of Muyano Seto.

Berths. Okazaki Jetty, from which excursion boats run to view the tidal flow in Naruto Kaikyō, has depths from 2·5 m to 3·5 m alongside and is situated on the S shore of the harbour 1¼ cables SW of Tōmino Hana.

Kuwashima Wharf, with depths of less than 4 m alongside, lies along the W side of Muya Kawa about ½ mile from its mouth.

Naruto Ferry Terminal, with depths from 2·5 m to 3·5 m alongside, lies 2½ cables SE of the S end of Konarato Bridge. There are passenger and car ferry services to Fukura Kō (34° 14' N, 134° 43' E) on Awaji Shima.

KII SUIDŌ—EAST SIDE

HINO MISAKI TO OURA SAKI

Chart 951

11.28

Hino Misaki (33° 53' N, 135° 04' E), the SW extremity of a cliffy promontory, lies on the E side of the S entrance to Kii Suidō; it is described in *Japan Pilot Vol II.*

Landmark. Hino Yama attains an elevation of 202 m, 3¼ cables NE of Hino Misaki and is a prominent mark.

Several rocks, the outermost of which is **Ōkura Baie,** 20 m high, lie within 1½ cables of Hino Misaki. **Kajitori Shō,** which dries 0·6 m and is steep-to on its seaward side, is situated 4½ cables NNW of Hino Misaki.

Hasedeno Hana, fringed with rocks extending 1 cable offshore, lies 1½ miles N of Hino Misaki; it is surmounted by **Hokotsuku Yama,** a pointed and prominent hill, 100 m high and covered with trees.

Hii Wan

11.29

Hii Wan (33° 55' N, 135° 04' E) is entered between Hasedeno Hana and **Oura Saki,** a low flat cliffy projection, 1½ miles N. At the head of the bay are three arms of which the central one is **Hii Kō,** which is suitable for small vessels except that it is exposed to W winds.

Naka Iso, a group of rocks the highest of which is 2·5 m high, lies in the middle of Hii Wan; a **light** is exhibited from a red round concrete tower with bands standing on the rocks.

Ao Kō, protected from N by two breakwaters, lies in the S part of Hii Wan; a **light** is exhibited at the head of each breakwater.

YURA KŌ

Chart 951

11.30

Yura Kō (33° 57' N, 135° 06' E) is a **harbour of refuge** (see 1.67) and is administered by the harbour authority at Wakayama-Shimotsu Kō (11.37). Except in SW winds, the harbour affords sheltered anchorage in its inner part to vessels up to 3000 tons in depths from 9 m to 13 m, mud and good holding ground. Many vessels seek shelter in Yura Kō during the typhoon season.

The **Mitsui Yura Shipyard,** which can accommodate vessels up to 300 000 tons, is situated in Yura Kō. The town of **Yura** lies at the head of the inlet.

Approaches

11.31

Ichino Bae (33° 56' N, 135° 04' E), 4 m high, is the

outermost above-water rock on a shoal spit extending 4 cables NW from a point 3½ cables NE of Oura Saki (11.29), and is the S entrance point to Yura Kō. A **light,** privately maintained, is exhibited from a red metal frame work tower on Ichino Bae.

Shimoyama Hana, 1¾ miles NNE of Ichino Bae, is a rugged point which attains an elevation of 118 m, 2 cables within its extremity, and is the N entrance point to Yura Kō.

Hijiki Shima, 35 m high, steep-to and precipitous, lies ¼ mile W of Shimoyama Hana and is the outermost of several islets off the point.

Ari Shima (33° 56·7' N, 135° 04·6' E), pointed and 71 m high, lies almost in the middle of the entrance to Yura Kō; a **light** is exhibited from a white round concrete tower situated on the SW side of the islet. The W side of Ari Shima is precipitous but a shoal with a depth of 3·7 m at its extremity, extends 2 cables E from its NE point; *No. 1 Light-buoy* and *No. 3 Light-buoy* are moored, respectively, close S and close E of this shoal.

Landmarks. A silver painted radio tower stands on the S side of Yura Kō, 1½ miles E of Ari Shima. A similar tower stands on **Kasane Yama,** a smooth rounded hill 263 m high, on the N side of the inlet.

Pilotage. The berthing master boards off Ari Shima. Berthing is carried out both by day and at night.

Harbour

11.32

Leading lights. There are two pairs of privately maintained leading lights for Yura Kō; they lead through the principal channel S and E of Ari Shima to the inner part of the harbour.

Katakui Leading Lights (metal columns, white triangular topmarks), the outer pair, stand on **Katakui Saki,** 5¾ cables SE of Ari Shima Light-tower, and in line bear 097°.

Kasane Yama Leading Lights (metal columns, white triangular topmarks), the inner pair, stand close S of Kasane Yama, 1¼ miles ENE of Ari Shima Light-tower, and in line bear 041°.

A **light** is exhibited from a red metal framework tower standing on **Muronoki Hana** (33° 56·8' N, 135° 05·5' E) situated 6 cables NE of Katakui Saki.

Anchorage. A good berth is in a depth of about 11 m with the N extremity of Ari Shima in line with a rock, 6 m high, situated 3½ cables SSE of Kasane Yama, bearing 252°, and the E entrance point of a cove on the N side of the harbour 4½ cables ENE of Kasane Yama, bearing 336°. Small vessels can obtain shelter from all winds in the cove.

Pearl beds, and from October to April seaweed beds, lie in the waters round Ari Shima and in several areas on both sides of the inlet.

11.33

Yura Kawa flows into the head of the harbour; a breakwater extends W from the S side of the river mouth, and a basin used by fishing vessels is entered on the N side.

Landmarks. Two radio towers stand on the E side of a boat harbour situated on the S side of the mouth of Yura Kawa.

Mitsui Yura Shipyard Jetty projects W from the shore on the N side of the river mouth; it is 320 m long and has depths from 9 m to 9·8 m alongside. A dry dock owned by the shipyard lies close N of the jetty.

Facilities. The dry dock has a length of 350 m, a width of 65 m and a depth over the sill of 10 m. Repairs to vessels of up to 175 000 dwt can be carried out.

Six tugs of up to 3000 hp are available.

Supplies. Fresh water is available on Mitsui Yura Shipyard Jetty. Fuel oil and stores can be obtained from Wakayama (11.37).

YUASA WAN AND APPROACHES

Chart 951

11.34

Shira Saki (33° 58' N, 135° 04' E), 1 mile NNW of Shimoyama Hana (11.31), is faced with a whitish grey cliff and is prominent; from it a range of hills rises gradually to the rocky summit of **Kuro Yama** which attains an elevation of 254 m, 1½ miles E of the point.

Tachigo, a rock lying in the N part of **Ohiki Ura,** 4½ cables ESE of Shira Saki, is 61 m high, white, pointed and prominent.

Ashika Shima, 4 m high and steep-to on its W side, lies 4 cables W of Shira Saki; a **light** is exhibited from a red round concrete tower with black bands standing on the rock.

11.35

Yuasa Wan is entered between Shira Saki and **Miyazakino Hana (Miya Saki),** a steep headland densely covered with pine trees, 6 miles N; a **light** is exhibited from a white square concrete tower situated on the W end of the headland. Two pine trees on top of a hill, 88 m high, situated 4 cables SE of Miyazakino Hana are prominent.

Kuro Shima (34° 00' N, 135° 06' E), 2 miles NE of Shira Saki, is 126 m high, precipitous and prominent, and is the highest of several islets which lie in the S part of Yuasa Wan.

Taka Shima, 110 m high and cliffy, lies 1 mile NE of Kuro Shima and has a rounded summit near its W end which is remarkable.

Karumo Shima, 2½ miles NE of Kuro Shima, consists of two islets the highest and S of which is 41 m high; above-water rocks extend 1½ cables N from the W end of the S islet.

Oba Se, steep-to with a depth of 0·6 m over it, lies in the middle of Yuasa Wan nearly 2 miles N of Kuro Shima. **Sono Se,** with a depth of 7·3 m, lies ¾ mile SE of Oba Se. **Sogami Se,** awash in places, lies 1¾ miles NE of Oba Se.

Caution. A large number of **fish havens** lie in Yuasa Wan, and three lines of fixed fishing nets extend from the N shore of the bay. From October to April there are seaweed beds in the bay.

Anchorage. Small vessels can obtain temporary anchorage, sheltered from W winds, in depths from 12 m to 15 m, mud, off a bight on the E side of Taka Shima. Sheltered anchorage is also afforded in depths from 12 m to 15 m on the SE side of two steep-to brown rocks, 20 m high, which lie 4 cables offshore ¾ mile NE of Karumo Shima.

11.36

Yuasa-Hiro Kō (34° 02' N, 135° 10' E) lies at the head of Yuasa Wan and is protected by two breakwaters; a **light** is exhibited on the head of each breakwater.

There are depths of less than 5 m within the breakwaters; a landing jetty for use by small vessels is situated in the harbour.

WAKAYAMA-SHIMOTSU KŌ

GENERAL INFORMATION

Chart 3615

11.37

Wakayama-Shimotsu Kō (34° 12' N, 135° 08' E), a specified port (see 1.64), lies in the N part of the E side of Kii Suidō. The port is divided into five areas which from S to N are:

Arida Ku (34° 05·5' N, 135° 06·5' E) (11.40)

Shimotsu Ku (34° 07·0' N, 135° 08·0' E) (11.44)

Kainan Ku (34° 08·5' N, 135° 11·5' E) (11.49)

Wakayama Ku (34° 13' N, 135° 08' E) (11.51)

Outer Harbour

The harbour limits of these areas are shown on the chart.

The three cities of **Arida, Kainan** and **Wakayama,** which in 1973 had a combined population of 471 000, and the town of **Shimotsu,** lie along the shores of the port.

A petro-chemical factory zone with large groups of refineries is situated in Arida Ku and Shimotsu Ku, and a large industrial zone lies in Kainan Ku.

11.38

Landmarks. The following objects in Wakayama-Shimotsu Kō are conspicuous:

The oil tanks (silver painted) and chimneys in the Tōa Nenryo Refinery (34° 07' N, 135° 07' E) (11.43) on the S side of the entrance to Shimotsu Ku; the tallest chimney (red and white, with flare) in this group stands at an elevation of 161 m.

Two 2-stack composite power station chimneys (red and white), with an elevation of 184 m, standing on the N side of the entrance to Kainan Ku (34° 09' N, 135° 11' E).

An observation tower standing on Takozuchi Yama (34° 11' N, 135° 10' E), 152 m high, situated on the N side of Wakaura Wan.

A group of chimneys in Sumitomo Steel Mills on the E side of Kita Ku (34° 14' N, 135° 08' E); the tallest chimney (red and white) has an elevation of 124 m, and a gasometer (red light), with an elevation of 100 m, stands 4 cables NNW of it.

A 3-stack composite power station chimney (red and white; red light) standing at an elevation of 80 m, close N of Kita Ku.

Pilotage. Six pilots are available from 1 hour after sunrise to 1 hour before sunset. Normally pilots board in the quarantine anchorage, but for vessels entering harbour without need of pratique, they will board in the approaches to the harbour in which the vessel is to be berthed.

Pilots will board vessels bound for the Tōa Nenryo Pier No. 0–1 (34° 06·5' N, 135° 06·8' E) or the Fuji Kōsan Ōsaki Sea-berth (34° 07·8' N, 135° 07·4' E) in the quarantine anchorage or in the area N of these berths. Two pilots are compulsory for vessels over 30 000 tons.

Pilots will board other vessels over 30 000 tons in an anchorage designated by the Captain of the Port.

Quarantine anchorage. The quarantine anchorage for all harbours within Wakayama-Shimotsu Kō is in the S part of the port off the entrance to Shimotsu Ku (34° 07' N, 135° 07' E); it is indicated on Chart 3615, plan of Shimotsu.

11.39

Weather. In winter when the monsoon wind is strong, a swell will be experienced in all harbour areas. Shimotsu Ku is well sheltered from S winds but Tōa Nenroyo Pier No. 0–1 is exposed to SE squalls blowing from the mountains behind.

The outer harbour of Wakayama-Shimotsu Kō is exposed from winds from SW to WNW.

Typhoons. When the centre of a typhoon passes to the W of the port, winds are strong from the S to SW; after the passage of the typhoon, the winds are strong from the W.

At the time of a typhoon, large vessels in Arida Ku, Shimotsu Ku and Kainan Ku are recommended to seek shelter in Wakaura Wan (34° 10' N, 135° 10' E). Large vessels in Wakayama Ku should proceed to Ōsaka Wan and seek shelter off Hannan Kō (34° 28' N, 135° 21' E).

Tidal streams. The tidal streams in Wakayama-Shimotsu Kō set mainly N or S, but they are weak. In the vicinity of the quarantine anchorage at the time of HW and LW at Shimotsu Ku, the stream is, respectively, N-going and S-going at a rate of ½–1 knot.

ARIDA KU

Chart 3615 with plan of Shimotsu

11.40

Arida Ku (34° 05' N, 135° 06' E) lies in the S part of Wakayama-Shimotsu Kō between Miyazakino Hana (Miya Saki) (34° 04' N, 135° 05' E) (11.35) and the N end of Jino Shima, 3 miles NNE; the harbour is divided from S into Nos. 3, 2 and 1 Areas which are indicated on the chart.

Approaches

11.41

Okino Shima, lying 1¼ miles offshore 2 miles N of Miyazakino Hana, is 92 m high, barren and round-topped; a **light** is exhibited from a white square concrete tower situated on the W side of the island.

Jino Shima, between Okino Shima and the mainland, attains an elevation of 115 m near its SW end; its W side is a high cliff fringed with reefs and rocks.

No. 3 Area

Arida Kawa which has a total length of over 80 miles, flows into **No. 3 Area** about 1 mile NE of Miyazakino Hana, but its entrance is shoal. In 1978, a breakwater was under construction on the S side of the mouth of the river.

A boat harbour is situated on each bank of Arida Kawa close within its mouth.

Chart 3615 plan of Shimotsu

No. 2 Area

11.42

Nabe Iso lies in the N part of **No. 2 Area** and 3 cables S of Jino Shima (11.41); it has depths from 0·9 m to 1·2 m. A *light-buoy* is moored close SW of Nabe Iso.

A large **fish haven,** indicated on the chart, lies between Nabe Iso and the S side of Jino Shima.

Kenashi Ishi, 11 m high, and a 4·3 m patch, lie close together on the edge of the shore bank 3 cables SE of Nabe Iso.

A basin, protected from W by a breakwater, lies in the S part of No. 2 Area; a rock, 1 m high, lies close off the head of the breakwater.

Public Quay with depths from 3·8 m to 5·6 m alongside, lies on the E side of the basin.

No. 1 Area
11.43

The channel through **No. 1 Area** between Jino Shima and the mainland is marked by *light-buoys*; a red *buoy* (red light) is moored in the bay situated on the E side of Jino Shima.

Tōa Nenryo Pier No. 0–1 lies off the **Tōa Nenryo Refinery** situated on the mainland opposite Jino Shima. The berth can be used by tankers up to 236 000 dwt and with a draught of 18·5 m. Vessels are secured to dolphins and mooring buoys off each end of the jetty. There is a submersible oil boom at the berth.

Directions. Vessels proceeding to Tōa Nenryo Pier No. 0–1 should approach from N; there are depths of at least 19·5 m in the approach. Berthing is only carried out at slack water and tug assistance is necessary. Tankers are required to make a sternboard to the berth, berthing starboard side-to.

Anchorages. Anchorage is afforded close NW of *No. 3 Light-buoy* in a depth of about 20 m, but care is needed as the bottom consists of a shallow layer of sand over rock.

Temporary anchorage, sheltered from W winds, can be obtained in depths from 10 m to 15 m off the bay on the E side of Jino Shima but the tidal streams are strong.

SHIMOTSU KU

Chart 3615 plan of Shimotsu
11.44

Shimotsu Ku is entered between **Kannon Saki** (34° 07' N, 135° 07' E), on the N side of Tōa Nenryo Refinery (11.43), and **Tsubune Hana** ¼ mile NNE. A **light** is exhibited from a white round concrete tower situated on Tsubune Hana; a number of large and prominent oil tanks (white) stand close E of the light-tower.

Pilotage. Pilotage is not compulsory but recommended. Pilots are available in the quarantine anchorage (see 11.38).

Landmarks. See 11.38.

Approaches
11.45

The approach course for Shimotsu Ku from W leads through the quarantine anchorage situated ½ mile W of the entrance to the harbour; traffic is heavy in the vicinity of the anchorage and many vessels may be found at anchor.

Fuji Kōsan Ōsaki Sea-berth (34° 08' N, 135° 07' E) lies close N of the entrance to Shimotsu Ku and can accommodate tankers up to 245 000 dwt and with a draught of 24 m. The berth consists of nine dolphins and is 400 m in length; a **light** is exhibited at the centre of the berth and at each end, and a fog horn is sounded. A **submarine pipeline** is laid from the berth to the shore and a **submarine power cable** is laid between the dolphins.

Harbour
11.46

Shimotsu Fairway, with a least depth of 14 m and a navigable width of about 250 m, leads to the quays at the inner end of Shimotsu Ku.

Directions. Entering the fairway from seaward, steer 123° with the summit of **Sotose Yama** (34° 06·5' N, 135° 08·5' E), 42 m high, situated on **Ushiga Kubi** at the inner end of the harbour, ahead.

North side. Kajitori Ne, with a least depth of 1·2 m, lies within 1 cable of the shore 1½ cables SSE of Tsubune Hana (11.44); it is marked by a red *buoy* on its W side. An auxiliary **light,** mounted on Tsubune Hana Light-tower, shows over Kajitori Ne.

Ōsaki Ura, with depths from 5 m to 10 m, lies on the N side of Shimotsu Ku and affords **anchorage** to small vessels except in strong S winds. A **light** is exhibited on the head of a short breakwater situated near the head of Ōsaki Ura; pearl beds are situated in the cove.

Kamanoshita Breakwater extends 1 cable SSW from the N shore of Shimotsu Ku; a **light** is exhibited on the head of the breakwater.

South side. Numerous piers and dolphin berths serving Tōa Nenryo Refinery, extend E from Kannon Saki (11.44) along the S side of the harbour.

Ushiga Kubi Breakwater extends NNE from Ushiga Kubi; another breakwater extends NE from the W entrance point of a boat harbour on the SW side of Ushiga Kubi. A **light** is exhibited at the head of each breakwater.

Maruzen Refinery in which there are numerous tanks and chimneys, lies at the inner end of Shimotsu Ku.

Berths and facilities
11.47

Berths. The principal berths in Shimotsu Ku are as follows:

Berth & Position	Length m	Depth m	Capacity dwt
Tōa Nenryo Refinery			
W2, W3, W4 Jetties (34° 06·8' N, 135° 07·5' E)	—	6–7·4	2 000
E1 Jetty (34° 06·7' N, 135° 07·9' E) dolphins		13·5	70 000
Ōsaka Cement Jetty (34° 06·6' N, 135° 08·3' E)	70	6·5–7	3 000
Maruzen Refinery (34° 06·7' N, 135° 08·8' E)			
Nos. 3, 6, 7 Jetties	—	3–5·5	3 000
No. 5 Jetty	dolphins	10·5–11	50 000
Fuji Kōsan Refinery			
Ōsaki Shipment Jetty (34° 07·5' N, 135° 07·7' E) dolphins		7·5	6 200

There are a number of mooring buoys in the harbour.

Facilities. Offices of the Maritime Safety Agency, Customs and Immigration are located in the joint Harbour Office situated in the SE corner of Shimotsu Ku.

There are three small shipyards and minor repairs can be carried out.

Tugs are available and will join in the quarantine anchorage.

Waste oil disposal facilities are available in each of the three refineries.

Supplies. Fresh water and oil fuel are available by barge and oiler. Water is laid on to the principal berths.

WAKAURA WAN AND KAINAN KU

Chart 3615 with plans of Shimotsu and Wakayama
Wakaura Wan
11.48

Wakaura Wan, situated in the Outer Harbour area of Wakayama-Shimoku Kō is entered between **Ara Saki** (34° 08' N, 135° 08' E) and **Saika Saki,** a steep, cliffy headland, 3¼ miles NNW. A **light** is exhibited from a white round concrete tower standing on Saika Saki.

Four precipitous islets lie within 4 cables W of Saika Saki, the outermost of which is 37 m high to the tops of the trees.

Landmarks. See 11.38.

Anchorages. Anchorage is afforded in Wakaura Wan in depths from 5 m to 20 m, soft mud and good holding ground, but strong winds from between S and W send in a heavy sea.

Shiotsu Hakuchi lies on the S shore of Wakaura Wan 2¼ miles E of Ara Saki; it affords anchorage in a depth of about 6 m, and a pier projects from its W side.

Wakaura Gyokō (34° 11' N, 135° 10' E), a small fishing harbour on the N side of Wakaura Wan, affords a sheltered anchorage in W to N winds but room in the harbour is limited; a **light** is exhibited on the head of the W breakwater at Wakaura Gyokō.

Chart 3615
Kainan Ku
11.49

Kainan Ku (34° 09' N, 135° 11' E) is situated in the SE corner of Wakaura Wan and is approached through a buoyed channel dredged to a depth of 12 m. *No. 1* and *No. 2 Light-buoys*, the outermost pair of buoys, are moored 2 miles ENE of Ara Saki.

Pilotage. See 11.38. Pilotage is not compulsory; if required pilots board at the entrance to the buoyed channel.

Harbour. The harbour is entered between two short breakwaters; a **light** is exhibited on the head of each breakwater.

An **overhead cable** with a vertical clearance of about 52 m, spans the entrance to the harbour. The cable is supported at each end by a tower (metal framework; red and white), 127 m in height.

Two chimneys (see 11.38) of the **Kainan Power Station** and a number of oil tanks, stand on reclaimed land on the N side of the harbour; the **Kihoku Industrial Zone** in which stands the **Sumitomo Steelworks,** lies to the E of the power station.

Fuki Kōsan Refinery, in which there are a number of chimneys and oil tanks, lies at the inner end of the harbour.
11.50

Berths. The principal berths in Kainan Ku are as follows:

Berth & Position	Length m	Depth m	Capacity dwt
Fuji Kōsan No. 9 Jetty			
(34° 08·5' N, 135° 12·1' E) dolphins	13		78 000
Sumitomo Kainan Kokan Wharf			
(34° 08·7' N, 135° 11·7' E)	360	11–12	20 000
Kainan Power Station Jetties			
(34° 08·8' N, 135° 11·6' E) dolphins	6·3–6·5		5 000

Facilities. Tugs are available. Minor repairs can be carried out.

Supplies. Fuel oil and fresh water are available.

WAKAYAMA KU

Chart 3615 plan of Wakayama
11.51

Wakayama Ku (34° 13' N, 135° 08' E), consisting of two main harbours, lies at the mouth of **Kino Kawa** which flows into the NE part of Wakayama-Shimotsu Kō, 2 miles N of Saika Saki (11.48).

Landmarks. Wakayama Castle (34° 13·4' N, 135° 10·6' E) surmounts an isolated hill, 40 m high, in the centre of the city. See also 11.38.

Weather signals (see 1.42) are shown from the observatory standing on a low hill about ¼ mile W of Wakayama Castle.

Pilotage. See 11.38. Pilotage is not compulsory but is recommended; if required pilots board in the anchorage off Wakayama Ku.

Anchorages. Anchor berths for vessels over 30 000 tons in Outer Harbour are established as follows:

A berth	34° 12·3' N,	135° 06·3' E
B berth	34° 12·8' N,	135° 06·0' E
C berth	34° 13·3' N,	135° 05·6' E
D berth	34° 13·7' N,	135° 05·3' E

Other vessels should anchor in position 34° 13·5' N, 135° 06·5' E, or farther inshore.

Harbours
11.52

No. 1 Area (34° 12·8' N, 135° 08·5' E) or **Wakayama Hon Kō** lies on the S side of the mouth of Kino Kawa and is protected by two breakwaters; a **light** is exhibited on the head of each breakwater.

Leading lights are exhibited from white round concrete towers (white triangular topmarks) situated on the S side of the inner harbour; in line bearing 066°, they lead through the entrance into No. 1 Area.

An observation tower (red and white framework), marked by red flashing lights, stands 2¼ cables SW of the head of the S breakwater.

Foreign Trade Quay lies on the S side of this harbour and there is a ferry berth 2 cables N of it.
11.53

Minami Ku, a timber harbour protected by an auxiliary breakwater about 1¼ miles long, extends S from No. 1 Area. The entrance to the harbour is between the NW end of the auxiliary breakwater on which a **light** is exhibited, and the head of the S breakwater of No. 1 Area.

Three pairs of mooring buoys, each pair providing head and stern moorings for a vessel up to 35 000 dwt, are situated in Minami Ku.

A timber pond and an inner harbour protected by breakwaters, lie on the SE side of Minami Ku.
11.54

No. 2 Area lies at the mouth of Kino Kawa. The sandbanks at the mouth of the river are liable to alteration and only small vessels with local knowledge can enter. **Kino Kawa Mouth Quay,** with depths from 2 m to 3·5 m alongside, lies on the N side of the river close within its entrance.
11.55

Kita Ku, a private harbour for the use of Sumitomo Steel Mills, is entered 1 mile NNW of the mouth of Kino Kawa and is protected by two breakwaters; a **light** is exhibited at the head of each breakwater.

A detached breakwater lies close W of the head of the W breakwater; a **light** is exhibited on its W end. A **prohibited area** extends S from the detached breakwater.

Kita Ku Fairway, a buoyed channel 1¼ cables wide and dredged to 14·6 m in 1970, leads to the harbour entrance; *No. 1* and *No. 2 Light-buoys*, the outermost pair of buoys, are moored ¼ mile WNW of the entrance.

A **signal station** is situated 1 cable NW of the root of the N breakwater. Berthing signals are displayed at the signal station.

Traffic signal. A black cube displayed at the signal station indicates that a large vessel is underway inward or outward bound.

Nos. 1 and **2 Dolphin Berths,** one of which is a LPG berth, lie on the W side of the harbour on the inside of the S breakwater.

Sumitomo Metals Quay lies on the NE' side of the harbour.

Nos. 1, 2 and 3 mooring buoys are situated in the S part of the harbour.

No. 1 and **No. 2 Inner Harbours** lie, respectively, at the S and N ends of Kita Ku.

Berths and facilities
11.56

Berths. The principal berths in Wakayama Ku are as follows:

Berth & Position	Length m	Depth m	Capacity dwt
No. 1 Area			
Foreign Trade Quay	370	8·5–9·5	15 000
(34° 12·7' N, 135° 08·7' E)			
Onoda Cement Jetty			
(34° 12·8' N, 135° 08·8' E) dolphins		7	3 000
No. 1 Quay			
(34° 13·1' N, 135° 09·2' E)	201	5–6·5	3 000
Kita Ku			
No. 1 Dolphin Berth			
(34° 13·8' N, 135° 07·4' E) dolphins		12	20 000
No. 2 Dolphin Berth			
(34° 13·7' N, 135° 07·5' E) dolphins		12	20 000
Sumitomo Metals Quay			
(34° 14·0' N, 135° 07·8' E)			
Berth A	172	4–10·3	20 000
B	365	9·5–14	90 000
C	274	14	70 000
D	215	12–14	40 000
E	218	12	20 000
F	186	10	20 000
G	80	5·5–10	1 500
Kita Ku (No. 1 Inner Harbour)			
W Quay			
(34° 13·5' N, 135° 07·8' E)	185	5·5–6	3 000
Kita Ku (No. 2 Inner Harbour)			
E Quay			
(34° 14·5' N, 135° 07·3' E)	372	5·5–7·5	5 000
N Quay			
(34° 14·5' N, 135° 07·1' E)	306	5·5–6	3 000

11.57

Facilities. The office of the Maritime Safety Agency, Customs and Immigration are located in the joint Harbour Office situated in No. 1 Area close S of No. 1 Quay (34° 13·1' N, 135° 09·2' E).

Tugs are available. Repairs can be undertaken.

There are hospital facilities in Wakayama.

De-ratting; see 1.70.

Climate. See table at 1.104.

Supplies. There is a water boat and four oilers. Fresh water is laid on to the main quays.

KII SUIDŌ—NORTH END—STRAITS

Chart 951
11.58

The N end of Kii Suidō is divided by the S part of Awaji Shima forming two exit channels. Naruto Kaikyō (34° 14' N, 134° 39' E) (11.59), the NW exit, leads to Harima Nada and lies between the islands off the NE end of Shikoku and Awaji Shima.

Tomogashima Suidō (34° 16' N, 135° 00' E) (11.72), the NE exit, lies between the SE end of Awaji Shima and the W coast of Honshu.

NARUTO KAIKYŌ

Chart 694 plan of Naruto
General information
11.59

Naruto Kaikyō (34° 14' N, 134° 39' E), in the NW corner of Kii Suidō, is narrow, the tidal streams strong, and the traffic, particularly at slack water, heavy; in 1976, an average of 670 vessels a day were passing through the straits. The route is best avoided by large vessels and by vessels without local knowledge.

Naruto Kaikyō is about ¼ mile wide at its narrowest part and this is further divided into two channels by reefs; the E channel being only passable by small craft.

Caution. In 1980, construction work was in progress on a bridge across Naruto Kaikyō; see 11.69.

Tidal streams. There are inequalities in the twice daily N-going and S-going streams in Naruto Kaikyō; generally the inequalities are greater in the N-going than in the S-going stream.

Rates up to 11 knots are experienced in the narrowest part of the straits, the strongest streams being downstream of Ō Naruto.

The sea is usually smooth in the main stream but eddies and whirlpools are generated on each side of it. In the narrows the largest whirlpools occur on the W side of the main stream when S-going, and on the E side when N-going.

After the stream in the narrows has turned from S to N, a weak S-going stream may continue to run for up to 1 hour in the area S of the narrows. Similarly, a weak N-going stream may continue to run in the area N of the narrows after the stream has turned from N to S.

Directions for Naruto Kaikyō
11.60

All vessels, other than small craft, passing through the straits should use Ō Naruto (11.69) the channel on the W side of Naka Se (34° 14·1' N, 134° 39·4' E).

As a result of observations over a period of 15 days in winter, it was ascertained that vessels with a speed of 8 knots or more, could pass through the straits at the following times:

With a following stream:
at any time
Against the stream:
(i) for 3 days at Neaps—at any time

(ii) for 3 days at Springs—1 hour before to ¼ hour after slack water

(iii) on other days—at all times except for a period of 1–3 hours when the stream is at its maximum strength.

From whichever side the narrows are approached, vessels should get on to the line of mid-channel (352°/172°) when at least 1 mile away. Care should be taken to identify the main stream and to keep in the middle of it.

Approaching the narrows, it is important to identify Naka Se (34° 14·1' N, 134° 39·4' E) (11.68).

11.61

In bad weather, particularly during strong S winds or when the tidal stream is against the wind, a confused sea runs right across the strait and the line of the main stream may be obscured; in such circumstances it is recommended that no attempt should be made to pass through the strait.

A good lookout should be kept for vessels approaching from the other direction as meeting in the narrows should be avoided. A vessel proceeding through the strait against the tidal stream and seeing another vessel approaching from the other direction, should wait until the other vessel has passed through the narrows.

At or near slack water, the traffic of small vessels, ferries and excursion boats in the vicinity of the straits is heavy, and fishing boats are likely to be encountered.

Naruto Kaikyō—south approach

11.62

Ōge Shima (34° 13' N, 134° 38' E), the greater part of which is wooded, forms the W side of the S approach to Naruto Kaikyō; the E coast of the island consists of dark rocks and sandy beaches.

Landmarks. Tōmi Yama, close N of the S extremity of Ōge Shima, is conical and 79 m high; a white observation platform stands on its NE slopes.

Nodamaru, 202 m (662 ft) high, in the S part of Ōge Shima, and **Shishimaino Taka,** 162 m (532 ft) high, in the N part of the island, are two prominent hills.

Ochikubo Se (34° 12' N, 134° 38' E), a rocky patch with a depth of 3·1 m (10 ft) over it, lies 3½ cables off the central part of the E coast of Ōge Shima.

Chart 951

11.63

Shio Saki (34° 11' N, 134° 44' E), the SW extremity of Awaji Shima, lies on the E side of the S approach to Naruto Kaikyō; on it is a grassy conical hillock from which a range of hills extends E.

Charts 951, 694 plan of Naruto

Chika Zono, with a depth of 10·9 m (36 ft), and **Taka Zono,** with a depth of 11·6 m (38 ft), lie close together 1½ miles W of Shio Saki; the sea breaks over them in bad weather.

Akaiwa Bae, a detached 5 m (16 ft) patch, lies near the edge of the coastal bank 1 mile NW of Shio Saki.

Kourano Hana (34° 13' N, 134° 42' E) lies 2½ miles NW of Shio Saki and between them is a bight with a sandy beach. **Mizutani Yama,** with twin peaks the highest of which is 141 m (461 ft) high, lies close to the coast ½ mile N of Kourano Hana.

There are always tide rips off Kourano Hana.

Chart 694 plan of Naruto

11.64

Tsurushima Hana (34° 14' N, 134° 42' E) lies 1½ miles N of Kourano Hana; rocks, marked by a concrete **beacon,** 2 m in height, extend about 1 cable SW from the point. A **light** is exhibited from a white round concrete tower situated on Tsurushima Hana.

Okikarumo Shima, 37 m (123 ft) high, lies within 4 cables of the coast ½ mile W of Tsurushima Hana; rocks, the outermost of which dries 1·2 m (4 ft) and on which stands a concrete **beacon,** 2 m in height, extends about 1 cable SSE.

Clearing line. Kanekakematsu Mori (34° 14·5' N, 134° 36·8' E) (10.16) in line with the outermost above-water rock close off To Saki (11.68), bearing 276°, leads about ½ cable S of the rocks extending SSE of Okikarumo Shima.

Fukura Kō

11.65

Fukura Kō (34° 15' N, 134° 43' E), entered close S of Tsurushima Hana, affords sheltered anchorage and is used by vessels awaiting a favourable tidal stream through Naruto Kaikyō. There is a car and passenger ferry service to Muya Kō (11.26) on Shikoku, and it is a tourist harbour from which excursion boats run to view the tidal flow in Naruto Kaikyō. A large number of hotels stand around the harbour.

Fukura Kō is divided into two parts by a line of breakwaters lying on a shallow bar which extends across the harbour ¼ mile within its entrance.

Kemuri Shima, 45 m high and conical, and **Susaki Shima,** 9 m (31 ft) high and flat, lie at the N end of the bar. A **light** is exhibited from a white round concrete tower standing on the E side of Kemuri Shima; a stone embankment lies on the S and W sides of Susaki Shima.

Anchorages. Anchorage is afforded in a depth of 12·8 m, mud and good holding ground, about 4 cables S of Kemuri Shima; it is exposed to W winds but heavy seas are seldom experienced.

Vessels awaiting the turn of the tidal stream in Naruto Kaikyō, are reported to obtain good temporary anchorage near the harbour entrance.

Small vessels up to 250 tons can obtain anchorage in depths from 6 m to 12 m, mud, in the inner part of the harbour.

11.66

A narrow channel leading to the inner part of Fukura Kō leads between Kemuri Shima and Susaki Shima and has a least depth of 4·5 m. Care is needed in using this channel as it is tortuous and shoal water extends W from Susaki Shima.

The town of **Fukura** lies on the N side of the inner part of the harbour. **Fukura Jetty,** with a depth of about 4 m alongside, and a ferry terminal jetty, lie off the front of the town and are protected by a breakwater.

In 1977, harbour works were in progress on the SE shore of the outer part of the harbour.

Naruto Kaikyō—the narrows

11.67

Naruto Kaikyō at its narrowest part lies between **Mago Saki** (34° 14·2' N, 134° 38·8' E), the NE extremity of Ōge Shima (11.62), and To Saki, ¾ mile E. Mago Saki is thickly wooded and its SE side is fringed with a rocky shoal which extends 2 cables offshore. A **light** is exhibited from a white square concrete tower on Mago Saki. In 1980, this light was obscured between the bearings of 305° and 314° due to bridge construction work (11.69).

Hadaka Shima, rocky, wooded and 23 m (74 ft) high, lies on the shoal extending from Mago Saki, 1½ cables

SSE of the light-tower. A shoal with a depth of 2·8 m(9 ft), lies 1 cable E of the islet.

Tobi Shima, rocky, wooded and 35 m (116 ft) high, lies 3½ cables SSE of Hadaka Shima and is fringed with rocks and shoals on all sides extending about ¾ cable offshore.

Nakano Se, with a depth of 6·7 m (22 ft) over it, lies 6½ cables S of Hadaka Shima.

Stranded wrecks lie in the vicinity of the NE coasts of Hadaka Shima and Tobi Shima.

11.68

To Saki (34° 14·3' N, 134° 39·7' E), on the E side of the narrowest part of Naruto Kaikyō, is the extremity of a high, narrow, cliffy projection which extends ¾ mile SW from the coast of Awaji Shima. A shoal on which are two rocks, 6 m high, extend 1 cable SW from the headland. A **light** is exhibited from a white square concrete tower situated on To Saki.

Naka Se, 1 m high, lies 2 cables SW of To Saki; from it reefs and shoals extend 1¾ cables SSW and 1 cable NNE. An auxiliary **light** mounted on To Saki Light-tower shows over Naka Se.

11.69

Ō Naruto, the channel between Hadaka Shima and Naka Se, is about 3 cables wide but owing to the whirlpools and tide rips on either side, its navigable width is only about 1 cable.

Ko Naruto, the channel between Naka Se and To Saki, has a navigable width of about ½ cable and the depths in it are less than 5 m.

In 1980, construction work on **Ō Naruto Bridge** was in progress on both sides of Ō Naruto. A temporary metal framework tower for use in connection with the construction work, stands on Hadaka Shima and on Naka Se; a flashing orange light is exhibited on each tower and a fog signal (bell) is sounded from the tower on Naka Se.

An **overhead power cable** with a vertical clearance of 32 m (105 ft), crosses Naruto Kaikyō from Mago Saki to To Saki. The metal towers supporting the ends of the cable are marked by red obstruction lights and are prominent.

An **overhead cable** with a vertical clearance of 19 m, spans the channel between To Saki and Naka Se.

Naruto Kaikyō—north approach

11.70

Kameura Kō (34° 13·7' N, 134° 37·5' E) is a harbour protected by a breakwater which has been constructed on the N coast of Ōge Shima (11.62) 1 mile WSW of Mago Saki; a **light** is exhibited on the head of the breakwater. It is a tourist harbour from which excursion boats run to view the tidal flow in Naruto Kaikyō; there is also a hydrofoil service to Kōbe Kō.

Kameura Quay, with a reported depth of 5·5 m alongside and which can accommodate vessels up to 2000 tons, lies in the basin.

Omoi Saki (34° 15' N, 134° 37' E), the NE extremity of Shimada Shima (10.16), lies 1½ miles NW of Mago Saki. Overfalls are always experienced within 3 cables of the coast in the vicinity of this point.

A **fish haven,** charted as foul, lies in the N approach of Naruto Kaikyō 1 mile NE of Omoi Saki.

Okino Shima (34° 15' N, 134° 40' E) lies close inshore on the E side of the N approach to Naruto Kaikyō; it is 25 m (83 ft) high and a few trees stand near its centre. Reefs and rocks extend from it about 1 cable SE and ½ cable W.

Anaga Ura is a bay between Okino Shima and Yoroi Saki (10.18), 1 mile NNW. **Anchorage** is afforded in Anaga Ura in depths from 11 m to 22 m, but owing to the tidal eddies anchor cables are very liable to fouling.

AWAJI SHIMA—SOUTH COAST

Charts 951, 3615

11.71

The S coast of Awaji Shima between Naruto Kaikyō and Tomogashima Suidō is almost strait and mainly cliffy; there are no dangers more than ¼ mile offshore but there are numerous **fish havens,** indicated on the charts, off the coast and around Nu Shima.

Landmarks. Flat-topped hills, 500 m to 600 m high, extend along the S coast of Awaji Shima and from a distance appear as a high almost level ridge with a blunt horn at each end. **Yuzuraha Yama** (34° 13' N, 134° 49' E), 608 m high, lies at the W end of the ridge and **Kashiwabara (Kashiwa) Yama** (34° 17' N, 134° 54' E), 570 m high, at the E end.

Nu Shima (34° 10' N, 134° 49' E), a thickly wooded island 117 m high near its SW end, lies 1½ miles off the S coast of Awaji Shima; a **light** is exhibited from a white round concrete tower standing on the E side of the island.

A harbour, protected by two breakwaters, lies on the NW coast of Nu Shima; a **light** is exhibited on the head of each breakwater.

TOMOGASHIMA SUIDŌ

Chart 3615

11.72

Tomogashima Suidō (34° 17' N, 135° 00' E), the strait between the SE extremity of Awaji Shima and the coast of Honshū, is divided into three passages by **Tomoga Shima,** a group of three islets. Large vessels on passage to and from Ōsaka Wan use Yura Seto (11.73), the W and main channel.

Oishino Hana (34° 16' N, 134° 57' E), on the W side of Tomogashima Suidō, is well-wooded, steep and cliffy; a **light** is exhibited from a white round concrete tower standing on the headland, and a conspicuous white house is situated close by. An auxiliary **light** is mounted on Oishino Hana Light-tower and shows over a reef 1½ cables SE.

Naruyama Shima, a long, low and narrow island covered with shrubs, is situated on the W side of the strait, to the N of Oishino Hana; a **light** is exhibited from a white round concrete tower standing on **Taka Saki,** the S extremity of the island, and there is an hotel on a hill at the N end.

A **light** is exhibited from a **beacon** standing on the NE edge of a shoal bank extending ½ mile E from Naruyama Shima, 8 cables NNE of Taka Saki.

Yuro Kō which lies on the W side of Naruyama Shima, is described at 12.4.

11.73

Yura Seto (34° 17' N, 134° 59' E), the W'most channel of Tomogashima Suidō, has a navigable width of about 1½ miles and the only danger is the shoal bank extending E from Naruyama Shima (11.72).

Okino Shima, the W'most of the islets forming Tomoga Shima, is situated on the E side of Yura Seto; the islet is densely wooded with the exception of its barren summit which attains an elevation of 119 m in its

W part. A **light** is exhibited from a white round stone tower standing on the W point of Okino Shima.

Tora Shima, a small islet, lies close off the NE extremity of Okino Shima and is connected to it by a causeway.

Nakano Seto, a narrow channel obstructed by reefs, lies between Tora Shima and **Jino Shima,** the E'most of the islets forming Tomoga Shima. A **light** is exhibited from a white octagonal concrete tower standing on the E end of Jino Shima.

Kadano Seto, between the E extremity of Jino Shima and the coast of Honshū, has a navigable width of about 3 cables.

Takura Saki (34° 16' N, 135° 04' E), on the E side of Tomogashima Suidō, forms the N entrance point of Wakayama-Shimotsu Kō (11.37); a **light** is exhibited from a white round concrete tower standing on the headland, and an auxiliary **light** mounted on the light-tower, shows over a white column standing on a rock 300 m NNW.

A number of **fish havens,** indicated on the chart, lie off Takura Saki and around the islets of Tomoga Shima.

Kada Kō, which lies 1 mile N of Takura Saki, is described at 12.10.

11.74

Recommended Traffic Separation Scheme. A vessel navigating Yura Seto (11.73) is requested by the 5th Regional Maritime Safety Headquarters to keep to the starboard side of the channel and not less than 150 m distant from the meridian of 134° 59·0' E when between the parallels of 34° 15·7' N and 34° 17·7' N.

A vessel N-bound through Ōsaka Wan and a vessel approaching Yura Seto from N, should leave *Sumoto Offing Light-buoy* (34° 21·1' N, 135° 00·7' E) on her port hand.

Pilotage in the traffic separation scheme is strongly recommended (see 12.3).

Traffic. In 1976, 580 vessels a day were on average passing through Yura Seto; the peak period being between 1200 and 1400, the times between which large vessels tend to use the channel.

Small vessels generally use Kadano Seto; in 1976, 360 vessels a day were on average using this channel. In low visibility many groundings are reported to take place on the S side of Takura Saki and the NE coast of Jino Shima.

Many fishing vessels of all sizes may be encountered in the vicinity of Tomogashima Suidō.

CHAPTER 12

ŌSAKA WAN

GENERAL INFORMATION

Charts 3615, 3614, 2875
12.1
Ōsaka Wan, the E'most part of Seto Naikai, is oval-shaped and about 35 miles in length. No islands or outlying rocks lie within the bay, but the traffic consisting of all types of vessels is very heavy and many vessels will be found at anchor in the N part of the bay.

Landmarks and aspect. The principal features are described in the following paragraphs:
On the west side
Awaji Shima (10.17) is mountainous with hills sweeping down to the coast.
Senkōji (Saki) Yama (10.17) lies near the centre of the island.
Myōken Yama (34° 30' N, 134° 57' E) is 519 m high.
Some red cliffs in the vicinity of U Saki (34° 34' N, 135° 02' E) (12.9) are prominent.
On the north side
The N side of Ōsaka Wan is backed by a range of mountains extending NE. **Rokkō San** (34° 46' N, 135° 16' E), 931 m (charted as 3067 ft) high, is the highest peak in this range; an hotel and other buildings stand on its top.
Kabuto Yama, 3¼ miles E of Rokkō San, is 308 m high, thickly covered with pine trees and dark in appearance, and is prominent.
On the east side
The **Hanshin Industrial Zone,** in which the two large ports of Kōbe and Ōsaka are situated, extends along the NE shore of Ōsaka Wan. A number of conspicuous chimneys, towers and tanks stand in this area; see also 12.16, 12.28, 12,37 and 12.60.
The **Ōsaka Plain** is situated on the E side of the bay but the hills behind it are distant.
12.2
Offshore dangers. Many wrecks and obstructions, indicated on Chart 3614, lie in the NE part of Ōsaka Wan.
A laver nursery (34° 33' N, 135° 12' E), marked by numerous *light-buoys* (orange light, synchronised flashing every 3 seconds), is established from October to May near the middle of the bay. Further beds, and also **fish havens,** are to be found within ¼ mile of the shore along the E coast of Awaji Shima.
An **observation tower** (34° 26' N, 135° 14' E), from which a **light** is exhibited, lies 3 miles off the SE shore of the bay. In 1980, it was reported that construction work on a new international airport was in progress in the area between the tower and the coast to the SE.
Tidal streams. Except in the N approaches to Tomogashima Suidō (34° 17' N, 135° 00' E) and the E approaches to Akashi Kaikyō (34° 37' N, 135° 00' E), the tidal streams are weak in Ōsaka Wan but the direction and rate varies markedly from day to day.

Pilotage
12.3
Limits. The pilotage district of Ōsaka Wan extends over an area bounded by the following lines:
South limit. A line joining Shio Saki (34° 11' N, 134° 44' E) and Mitsuga Saki (34° 09' N, 134° 49' E), thence 090° 10 miles and 020° 7 miles to Takura Saki (34°16' N, 135° 04' E).
West limit. The E coast of Awaji Shima from Shio Saki (34° 11' N, 134° 44' E) to U Saki (34° 34' N, 135° 02' E), thence 090° 3½ miles and 000° 3½ miles to the N shore of Ōsaka Wan.
North east limit. A line joining the extremities of the outer breakwaters of Kōbe Kō and Ōsaka Kō.

Boarding points are as follows:
(a) In the area 7 miles S of Tomogashima Suidō (34° 17' N, 135° 00' E)—Ōsaka Wan pilots board inward-bound vessels arriving from S.
(b) In the area 4 to 5 miles SSW of Kōbe Light (Wada Misaki) (34° 39' N, 135° 10' E)—Naikai (Inland Sea) pilots replace Ōsaka Wan pilots in vessels proceeding W through Akashi Kaikyō.
(c) In vicinity of the quarantine anchorages serving the ports of Kōbe, Nishinomiya, Amagasaki and Ōsaka—harbour pilots replace Ōsaka Wan pilots.
When in bad weather a pilot is unable to board at the boarding point, alternative arrangements will be notified by radio.
Ōsaka Wan pilot boats have red hulls, with either BAYPILOT ONE, TWO or THREE in white on each side. They are equipped with R/T.
Procedure. Information required by the Ōsaka Wan pilotage association and procedure to be followed are as follows:
(a) Send ETA at Tomogashima Suidō pilot station, 12 hours and 6 hours in advance, stating:
(i) Vessel's name
(ii) Grt and deepest draught
(iii) Last port and destination
(iv) Agent's name
(b) When within VHF radio range, confirm ETA with Kōbe Port Radio or pilot boat
(c) Report any defects in machinery or equipment.

Regulations
Vessels carrying a dangerous cargo should have ready emergency towing wires forward and aft when navigating Ōsaka Wan.

ŌSAKA WAN—WEST SIDE

Chart 3615
Yura Kō
12.4

Yura Kō (34° 17' N, 134° 57' E), a fishing base, lies on the W side of Tomogashima Suidō and is protected on its E side by Naruyama Shima (11.72).

Imakawa Kuchi, the S entrance to Yura Kō, lies close W of Taka Saki the S extremity of Naruyama Shima; it has depths of about 2·5 m and is only suitable for small craft.

Shinkawa Kuchi, the N entrance, lies 2 cables W of **Ume Saki** the N end of Naruyama Shima; it is about $\frac{1}{4}$ cable wide and has a depth of about 4 m.

Naruyama Breakwater extends N from the E entrance point of Shinkawa Kuchi; a **light** is exhibited on the head of the breakwater.

Anchorage. Sheltered anchorage is afforded to small vessels in Yura Kō in depths from 2 m to 10 m, sand and good holding ground. In strong SE winds a large number of small vessels seek shelter in this anchorage.

Yura lies on the W shore of the harbour and has a flourishing fishing industry and is a tourist resort. A basin protected from E by two breakwaters, lies in the N part of the town.

Yura Jetty, with depths from 3·5 m to 4·5 m alongside, lies close S of the basin and is used by ferries plying across Tomogashima Suidō to Fuke Kō, 9$\frac{1}{4}$ miles ENE.
12.5

A direction light is exhibited from a position close S of **Miyasaki Hana** situated 3 miles NNW of Yura Kō.

Charts 3615, 3614
Sumoto Kō
12.6

Sumoto Kō (34° 21' N, 134° 54' E), the principal harbour on the E coast of Awaji Shima, lies at the mouth of **Sumoto Kawa,** 1 mile NW of Miyasaki Hana; it consists of an outer and inner harbour.

Sumoto, which in 1973 had a population of 46 000, lies to the W of the harbour; it is the largest town on Iwaji Shima and is a tourist centre and a popular seaside resort.

The **outer harbour,** protected by two breakwaters, is entered 3$\frac{1}{4}$ cables SE of the mouth of Sumoto Kawa and has depths of less than 5 m within it; a **light** is exhibited at the head of each breakwater. A **fish haven** lies $\frac{1}{4}$ cable N of the head of the N breakwater.

Kansai Kisen Quay, with depths from 4 m to 4·5 m alongside, lies on the NW side of the outer harbour, and **Sumoto City Jetty**, with a depth of 4·5 m alongside, lies on the SW side.

The **inner harbour,** protected by two breakwaters, is entered between the entrance to the outer harbour and the mouth of Sumoto Kawa and has depths of less than 5 m within it; a **light** is exhibited at the head of each breakwater.

Landmark. A chimney with an elevation of 132 m, stands at the inner end of the inner harbour and serves as a good head mark for entering the harbour.

Quays with depths from 2·5 m to 4 m alongside, lie on the S and W sides of the inner harbour.
12.7

Takenokuchi Gyokō, protected by two breakwaters, is entered 3 cables N of the mouth of Sumoto Kawa; a **light** is exhibited on the head of the N breakwater. A car ferry terminal is situated within the basin.

A **fish haven** lies 1 cable ENE of the entrance to Takenokuchi Gyokō.

Supplies. Fuel oil can be supplied at the quays in the inner harbour of Sumoto Kō.

Communications. There are regular passenger and car ferry services to Kōbe Kō, Yura Kō and Fuke Kō.

Chart 3614
Tsuna Kō
12.8

Tsuna (Tuna) Kō is the collective name for the small harbours of **Shiota Kō, Shizuki Kō, Ikubo Gyokō** and **Sano Kō** which lie in line within 2$\frac{1}{4}$ miles NNE of Shiota Kō (34° 24·6' N, 134° 54·1' E). In 1978, work was in progress to construct a large scale port by reclaiming the land in between these harbours.

Each of the four harbours is protected by breakwaters and has berthing facilities; a **light** is exhibited on the head of each breakwater.

A quay, with a depth of 5·5 m alongside, and public landing piers, lie in Shizuki Kō. A high speed ferry service runs from this harbour to Nishimomiya Kō (34° 42' N, 135° 21' E), 28 miles NE.

Measured distance. A measured distance of 1874·3 m and marked by a pair of **beacons** at each end, lies between Ikubo Gyokō and Sano Kō; the running course is 033°.

Kariya Kō to U Saki
12.9

Kariya Kō (34° 30·5' N, 134° 59·5' E), a small harbour protected by breakwaters, is situated 4 miles NE of Sano Kō (12.8); a **light** is exhibited on the head of the S breakwater and the N head of the E breakwater.

Landmark. A prominent white chimney stands on the W side of Kariya Kō.

Ura Kō (34° 32' N, 135° 00' E), a small harbour protected by two breakwaters, lies 1$\frac{1}{4}$ miles NNE of Kariya Kō; a **light** is exhibited on the head of each of the breakwaters.

A number of *light-buoys* and *buoys* are moored within $\frac{1}{4}$ mile of the coast between Kariya Kō and Ura Kō.

A ferry harbour lies between two areas of reclaimed land $\frac{1}{4}$ mile NE of Ura Kō; a **light**, privately maintained and for the use of the ferries, is exhibited on the head of a short breakwater on the S side of the harbour entrance.

U Saki (34° 34' N, 135° 02' E), 2$\frac{1}{4}$ miles NE of Ura Kō and 1 mile S of Iwaya Kō (10.80), is faced with a remarkable red cliff and is fronted by an area of reclaimed land.

A **tower,** marked by red lights and from which a fog signal is sounded, stands 2 cables offshore, $\frac{1}{4}$ mile N of U Saki.

ŌSAKA WAN—EAST SIDE

KADA KŌ TO TANNOWA KŌ

Chart 3615
12.10
    Kada Kō (34° 17' N, 135° 04' E), a small bay, lies on the E side of Tomogashima Suidō (11.72); a **light** is exhibited on the head of a short breakwater on the S side of the bay.
    Anchorage. Kada Kō affords anchorage in depths from 7 m to 11 m about midway between its entrance points.

Fuke Kō
12.11
    Fuke Kō (34° 19' N, 135° 08' E), consists of three parts namely;
        Tanikawa Hakuchi (12.12).
        Tanagawa Hakuchi (12.12).
        Fuke Hakuchi (12.13).
    It is used by ferries plying to Tokushima Kō (11.21) in Shikoku and to harbours in Awaji Shima.
    Landmarks. A power station chimney (red and white), 202 m in height, and a group of tanks, stand on reclaimed land projecting NE from the shore close E of **Kannon Saki** (34° 19·3' N, 135° 07·7' E); another power station chimney (red and white), 152 m in height, stands 3 cables SSE of the first chimney. These two chimneys and the tanks are prominent from a distance.
    Misaki Tourist Tower (34° 19·6' N, 135° 09·8' E), painted white and which is prominent, stands 4 cables E of **Naga Saki,** the E entrance point to Fuke Kō.

    A number of **fish havens,** indicated on the chart, lie in the approaches to Fuke Kō.
12.12
    Tanikawa Hakuchi, entered 2½ cables WSW of Kannon Saki, is a long narrow basin used as a yacht harbour and by small fishing boats. An observation tower, marked by a red light, stands close NW of the entrance to this basin.

    Tanagawa Hakuchi, the main roadstead of Fuke Kō, lies between the reclaimed land E of Kannon Saki, and Naga Saki.
    A stony patch with a least depth of 2·7 m lies in the middle of the entrance to Tanagawa Hakuchi and is marked close SW by *No. 1 Light-buoy.*
    A spit with depths from 1·2 m to 4·4 m, extends ¼ mile NNE from the end of a short breakwater projecting from the shore on the S side of the roadstead, 2 cables SE of the reclaimed land; the extremity of the spit is marked by *No. 2 Light-buoy.*
    Several **fish havens** lie in the E part of Tanagawa Hakuchi.
    Dolphin berths, with depths from 8 m to 8·5 m alongside, lie on the NE and SE sides of the reclaimed land and can accommodate vessels up to 5000 tons.
    Anchorage. In strong S winds a large number of small vessels seek shelter in the W part of Tanagawa Hakuchi.
12.13
    Fuke Hakuchi, protected by two breakwaters, lies in the SE corner of Fuke Kō; a **light** is exhibited on the head of each breakwater. There are depths of about 4 m in the W part of the harbour but the E part is shallow.
    Leading lights are exhibited from aluminium masts (triangular topmarks) situated on the SE side of Fuke Hakuchi; in line bearing 140°, these lights lead into the

harbour towards **No. 5 Quay** used by the ferry to Tokushima Kō (11.21).
    Nos. 1–4 Quays, with depths from 3 m to 4 m alongside, lie on the S side of Fuke Hakuchi.
    A basin enclosed by two breakwaters, lies 2 cables NE of Fuke Hakuchi; in 1978, a quay was under construction in the SW part of this basin.

Charts 3615, 3614
Tannowa Kō
12.14
    Tannowa Kō (34° 20' N, 135° 11' E), protected by two breakwaters, lies 2 miles ENE of Fuke Kō (12.11); a **light** is exhibited on the head of the W breakwater.
    The approach channel to Tannowa Kō is marked by a pair of *light-buoys.*
    In 1979, a detached breakwater was under construction ¼ mile E of the harbour.

HANNAN KŌ

Chart 2287
12.15
    Hannan Kō (34° 27' N, 135° 22' E), a specified port (see 1.64), is situated in the middle of the E side of Ōsaka Wan and embraces the former harbours of Izumi-Sano, Kaizuka and Kishiwada. The port extends from its SW harbour limit to the mouth of Ōtsu Kawa (12.20) 6 miles NNE, and is divided from S to N into Nos. 3, 2 and 1 Areas; the harbour limits are shown on the chart.

Approaches
12.16
    Landmarks. The following objects along the shore of Hannan Ko are conspicuous:
    A radio tower (34° 27·2' N, 135° 22·1' E) (red and white), with an elevation of 86 m, marked by a red obstruction light.
    The keep of **Kishiwada Castle,** 3 cables NE of the radio tower, with an elevation of 40 m.
    A group of oil tanks, painted silver, 1¼ miles N of the radio tower.
    Several chimneys, indicated on the chart, situated in No. 1 Area, the N part of the port.
    Pilotage. Pilots of the Naikai (Inland Sea) Pilots Association will come from Kobe Kō and board in the quarantine anchorage.
    Anchorage. The **quarantine anchorage** (34° 28·0' N, 135° 20·5' E), indicated on the chart, lies in the middle of No. 2 Area close within the W harbour limit.
    Caution. A wreck with a depth of 6·4 m over it, lies 1½ miles WSW of the quarantine anchorage.
    In 1980, detached breakwaters were under construction in No. 2 and No. 3 Areas between the quarantine anchorage and the shore; **prohibited areas** marked by *light-buoys* (light flashing orange) and survey towers, had been established in the vicinity of these breakwaters.

No. 3 Area
12.17
    Izumi-Sano Fairway, with depths from 11·4 m to 13·4 m, lies in **No. 3 Area** and leads from N to a basin protected by a detached breakwater in **Izumi-Sano Chiku** (34° 26' N, 135° 20' E). The fairway is marked by

two pairs of *light-buoys*; the outer pair are moored 1¼ miles N of the entrance to the basin.

A **light** is exhibited from the NE end of the detached breakwater. There are depths from 11·4 m to 13·3 m in the entrance, and of 7 m in the basin.

Sano Gyokō (34° 25·0' N, 135° 19·2' E), a fishing harbour protected by breakwaters, lies close within the SW limit of Hannan Kō; a **light** is exhibited on the head of the W breakwater.

No. 2 Area
12.18

Kaizuka Chiku (34° 27' N, 135° 21' E), 2 miles NE of Izumi-Sano Chiku (12.17), and **Kishiwada Chiku,** 1¼ miles farther NE, are both situated in No. 2 Area.

The two harbours are entered, respectively, SW and NE of **West Breakwater,** ¼ mile long and at each end of which a **light** is exhibited. In 1978, the area between this breakwater and the harbour front SE, was being reclaimed.

Kaizuka Offing Breakwater, on the head of which a **light** is exhibited, forms the W side of the entrance to Kaizuka Chiku basin.

A fishing harbour protected by two breakwaters lies in the E part of Kishiwada Chiku; a **light** is exhibited on the head of each breakwater. There is a depth of about 5 m in the entrance and from 5 m to 11·5 m in its central part; the harbour affords sheltered **anchorage** to small vessels.

No. 1 Area
12.19

Kishiwada Fairway, with depths from 10·8 m to 14 m, lies in **No. 1 Area** and leads from N into Mokuzai Chiku; *No. 1* and *No. 2 Light-buoys,* situated 2¼ miles NNE of the quarantine anchorage, mark the entrance to the fairway.

In 1978, reclamation work was in progress on the E side of Kishiwada Fairway and a **prohibited area** had been established.

Mokuzai Chiku (34° 29' N, 135° 22' E) is protected on its W side by **New West Breakwater;** the harbour is entered between the N head of this breakwater and a short breakwater extending from the SW corner of a reclaimed area in which there are two large timber ponds. A **light** is exhibited at each end of New West Breakwater and at the head of the short breakwater.

Four pairs of head and stern mooring buoys lie in Mokuzai Chiku and are suitable for vessels of 10 m draught.
12.20

Kishiwada Gyokō, a small fishing harbour with depths

from 3 m to 6 m, lies in the SE corner of the inner end of Mokuzai Chiku.

Tadaoka Chiku, with depths from 2 m to 4 m, lies on the S side of the mouth of **Ōtsu Kawa** (34° 30' N, 135° 23' E) which flows into the sea on the N limit of Hannan Kō.

Berths and facilities in Hannan Kō
12.21

Berths. The principal berths in Hannan Kō are as follows:

Berths & Position	Length m	Depth m	Capacity dwt
No. 3 Area			
Fuji Seiyū Jetty			
(34° 25·6' N, 135° 19·4' E) dolphins	12·5		10 000
Ensuiko Seito Quay			
(34° 25·7' N, 135° 19·5' E)	100	12	10 000
South Quay			
(34° 25·3' N, 135° 19·5' E)	220	5·5	—
Middle Quay			
(34° 25·4' N, 135° 19·7' E)	800	4–5·5	—
North Quay			
(34° 25·6' N, 135° 19·8' E)	220	about 7	—
No. 2 Area			
Kaizuka Nos. 1 and 2 Quays			
(34° 27·1' N, 135° 21·3' E)	750	6·5	12 000
Hannan No. 1 Landing Jetty			
(34° 27·4' N, 135° 21·8' E)	570	about 4	—
Tokuyama Seikon Jetty			
(34° 28·2' N, 135° 22·2' E) dolphins	7·5		4 000
No. 1 Area			
Idemitsu Kōsan N Jetty			
(34° 28·6' N, 135° 22·2' E) dolphins	about 6		3 000
Kishiwada No. 1 Quay			
(34° 28·5' N, 135° 22·7' E)	185	10	15 000
Kishiwada No. 15 Jetty			
(34° 28·4' N, 135° 22·8' E)	290	about 4	—

12.22

Facilities. The office of the Maritime Safety Agency, Customs and Quarantine are located in the joint Harbour Office situated in No. 1 Area at the inner end of Mokusai Chiku.

Tugs, which operate both in Hannan Kō and Ōsaka Kō, are based in Sakai-Senboku Ku (12.28), in between the two ports.

There is a shipyard for small vessels.

Supplies. Fresh water is laid on to the principal wharves and there is one water boat.

ŌSAKA KŌ

GENERAL INFORMATION

Charts 3614, 2279, 2287
12.23

Ōsaka Kō (34° 35' N, 135° 25' E), one of the great ports of Japan, lies in the NE corner of Ōsaka Wan; it is a specified port (1.64) and is divided into the two separate harbours of Sakai-Senboku Ku and Ōsaka Ku. The harbour area of the whole port extends from the N limit of Hannan Kō (12.15) to the E limit of Amagasaki Kō (12.53), 10 miles NE; the harbour limits are shown on the charts.

Ōsaka, which in 1973 had a population of 2 807 000, is the second largest city in Japan and is the commercial, industrial and administration centre of W Honshū; it is an amalgamation of the cities of Ōsaka, **Sakai, Takaishi** and **Izumi-Ōtsu.**
12.24

Weather. In summer, with steady land and sea breezes, the weather is generally fine. In winter, a strong W wind may be persistent bringing in a sea. See also **climatic table** at 1.105.

Caution should be exercised when approaching Ōsaka Kō in the early morning for the visibility is usually greatly reduced by mist and the entrance is not easily identified; the position of the harbour can however often be estimated by the flow of out-going traffic.

Landmarks. See 12.28 and 12.37.

12.25

Pilotage. Pilotage in Ōsaka Kō is not compulsory but is recommended. Berthing is carried out by day only.

Pilots board as follows:

(a) Vessels requiring pratique—in the quarantine anchorage (34° 37' N, 135° 23' E).

(b) Vessels proceeding to berths in Nos. 4, 5 and 6 Areas of Sakai-Senboku Ku—off the entrance to Hamadera Fairway (34° 33' N, 135° 20' E).

(c) Vessels proceeding to berths in Nos. 1, 2 and 3 Areas of Sakai-Senboku Ku—off the entrance to Sakai South Fairway (34° 37' N, 135° 21' E).

(d) Vessels proceeding to berths in Ōsaka Ku—off *Ōsaka No. 1* and *No. 2 Light-buoys* (34° 38' N, 135° 23' E).

Ōsaka Harbour Radar. A radar station is situated on Central Pier (34° 39' N, 135° 26' E) (12.37) in Ōsaka Ku. Radar advice on vessel's position and movements of other vessels, may be obtained on request when within 4 miles of the station for vessels under 1000 tons and within 8 miles for vessels over 1000 tons.

12.26

Anchorages. The **quarantine anchorage** used by vessels bound for either Sakai-Senboku Ku or Ōsaka Ku is situated on the N side of Sakai South Fairway (34° 37' N, 135° 23' E).

Anchor berths, allocated by the Captain of the Port, are established as follows; vessels should not anchor without his permission:

Anchor Berth		*Bearing/distance from Hamadera North Breakwater Light (34°33·3' N, 135° 24·7' E)*	
No. 6 Area	1	231½°	5820 m
	2	240°	6030 m
	3	246°	6360 m
	4	253°	6760 m
No. 7 Area	1	325½°	5820 m
	2	320½°	5170 m
	3	314°	4580 m
	4	306½°	4070 m
	5	296°	3660 m
	6	284°	3365 m
	7	319½°	6260 m
	8	314½°	5690 m
	9	308°	5190 m
	10	300½°	4720 m
	11	291½°	4370 m
	12	281°	4160 m
	13	214½°	6850 m
	14	309½°	6300 m
	15	303½°	5830 m
	16	296°	5430 m
	17	288°	5020 m
	18	279½°	4930 m
	19	290½°	6000 m
	20	282°	6120 m
	21	305°	6750 m
	22	297°	6600 m
	23	288½°	6780 m
	24	281°	7120 m
	25	309°	7430 m
	26	301½°	7410 m
	27	294°	7530 m
	28	286½°	7740 m
	29	280°	8080 m
	30	305°	8270 m
	31	298°	8290 m
	32	291½°	8440 m
	33	285°	8690 m
	34	279°	9100 m
	35	274°	9500 m

Anchor berth signals. When a vessel is proceeding to an anchorage, she should display the Answering Pendant above the numeral pendants indicating the number of the anchor berth.

Prohibited areas. See 12.38.

12.27

Regulations. General regulations prescribed by the Port Regulations Law are described at 1.37. Local regulations are also in force and are summarised as follows:

(a) A vessel of over 500 grt shall use two anchors unless otherwise permitted by the Captain of the Port. However this shall not apply to a vessel anchoring outside the breakwaters unless deemed necessary by the Captain of the Port.

(b) A vessel of over 10 000 grt intending to use Hamadera Fairway (12.31) shall notify the Captain of the Port by noon the day before arrival, her ETA at the entrance to the fairway, or, if leaving the port, her ETD.

(c) A vessel of over 3000 grt intending to use Sakai South Fairway (12.32) shall notify the Captain of the Port by noon the day before arrival, her ETA at the entrance to the fairway, or, if leaving the port, her ETD.

(d) A vessel of over 5000 grt intending to use South Harbour Fairway (12.41) shall notify the Captain of the Port by noon the day before arrival, her ETA at the entrance to the fairway, or, if leaving the port, her ETD.

(e) A vessel shall notify the Captain of the Port of any amendments to her ETA or ETD without delay.

(f) A vessel overtaking another vessel in a river or canal in Ōsaka Kō, shall indicate her intention by making the following sound signals:

Overtaking to starboard	1 prolonged blast followed by 1 short blast.
Overtaking to port	1 prolonged blast followed by 2 short blasts.

SAKAI—SENBOKU KU

Charts 2279, 2287

General information

12.28

Sakai-Senboku Ku (34° 34' N, 135° 24' E), an industrial and commercial port, forms the S part of Osaka Kō and is divided into Nos. 1–7 Areas; its harbour limits are indicated on the charts. See also 12.23–12.27.

The port is divided as follows:

Outer Harbour	Nos. 6, 7 Areas
and from S to N	
Ōtsu Minami Hakuchi and Ōtsu Hakuchi	No. 5 Area
Hamadera Hakuchi	No. 4 Area
Nishi Hakuchi	No. 3 Area
Minami Hakuchi	No. 2 Area
Kita Hakuchi	No. 1 Area

Landmarks. Two conspicuous radio towers with elevations of 173 m and 151 m, stand 2¼ miles and 3 miles, respectively, E of the entrance to Ōtsu Minami Hakuchi (34° 31' N, 135° 23' E) the S'most harbour in Sakai-Senboku Ku.

Numerous conspicuous chimneys and gas tanks stand in the harbour area and their positions can be seen on the charts. Among the most conspicuous and highest are:

The six chimneys of the **Sakai Steam Power Station** standing in an E/W line close SW of Minami Hakuchi (34° 34' N, 135° 27' E); the W'most two have an elevation of 184 m and are painted red and white.

A conspicuous chimney (red and white), with an elevation of 182 m, standing in the **Shin Nippon Steelworks** (34° 36' N, 135° 27' E), 2 miles N of Sakai Steam Power Station, and two conspicuous gasometers, each with an elevation of 107 m and marked by red lights, standing 4 cables farther N.

Outer Harbour—Nos. 6 and 7 Areas
12.29

The outer harbour of Sakai-Senboku Ku is divided by Hamadera Fairway (12.31) into **No. 6 Area** in the S and **No. 7 Area** in the N.

Kansai Oil Jetty (34° 33·5' N, 135° 24·4' E) with a depth of 20 m alongside, projects 3 cables WSW from the shore on the N side of the entrance to Hamadera Hakuchi. It is protected by a submersible oil boom.

Chart 2287
Ōtsu Minami Hakuchi and Ōtsu Hakuchi—No. 5 Area
12.30

Ōtsu Minami Hakuchi (34° 31' N, 135° 23' E) and Ōtsu Hakuchi (34° 32' N, 135° 24' E) which comprise **No. 5 Area,** lie in the S part of Sakai-Senboku Ku and are separated by an area of reclaimed land known as **Sukematsu Wharf**; a channel spanned by **Izumi-Ōtsu Bridge** with a least vertical clearance of 15 m, connects the two harbours.

Ōtsu Minami Hakuchi, the S of these two harbours is entered between two breakwaters; a **light** is exhibited on the head of each breakwater. The approach channel to the harbour is marked on its SW side by *No. 2* and *No. 4 Light-buoys* and has depths from 11 m to 13·4 m.

Ōtsu Hakuchi, the N harbour, is entered between *S1* and *S2 Light-buoys* and there is a least depth of 13·6 m in the entrance channel.

Hamadera Hakuchi—No. 4 Area
12.31

Hamadera Hakuchi (34° 33' N, 135° 25' E) comprises **No. 4 Area,** the central part of Sakai-Senboku Ku, and is entered between short breakwaters; a **light** is exhibited on the head of each breakwater.

Hamadera Fairway, about 3¼ miles long, leads through No. 6 Area of the outer harbour to Hamadera Hakuchi and is dredged to a depth of 16 m. The fairway is entered between *No. 1* and *No. 2 Light-buoys* (34° 33' N, 135° 20' E) and is marked on each side by further pairs of light-buoys.

Anchorage is **prohibited** in Hamadera Fairway.

Hamadera signal station stands at the root of the N breakwater and from it are displayed anchoring and berthing signals.

A number of dolphin oil berths lie on the N side of Hamadera Hakuchi and an LNG jetty lies on the S side close within the entrance to the harbour.

Chart 2279
Nishi Hakuchi, Minami Hakuchi and Kita Hakuchi—Nos. 3, 2 and 1 Areas
12.32

Sakai South Fairway, about 4¼ miles long and buoyed, leads from the S part of the outer harbour of Ōsaka Ku to three basins in the N part of Sakai-Senboku Ku. The fairway is entered between *No. 1* and *No. 2 Light-buoys* (34° 17' N, 135° 21' E) and its outer part is dredged to 14 m.

At *No. 7 Light-buoy*, 2 miles within its entrance, the fairway divides; **Sakai North Fairway,** dredged to a depth of 14·2 m, leads E to the entrance to Kita Hakuchi (12.33) and to **Yamato Kawa**; the inner part of Sakai South Fairway, dredged to a depth of 10·3 m, leads SE to the entrances to Nishi Hakuchi and Minami Hakuchi. These fairways are marked by *light-buoys*.

In 1978, a detached breakwater was under construction 2 cables S of the junction of Sakai North and South Fairways.
12.33

Nishi Hakuchi (34° 35' N, 135° 25' E), comprising **No. 3 Area,** has depths from 9 m to 12 m; on its E side are several berths used for the unloading of dangerous cargoes.

Sakai signal station is situated at the E entrance point of Nishi Hakuchi and from it are displayed traffic control and berthing signals.

Minami Hakuchi (34° 35' N, 135° 27' E), comprising **No. 2 Area,** has depths from 15 m to 17 m except for a shoal with depths from 9·2 m to 9·5 m in its entrance.

Ōhama Wharf, a public quay, lies in the NE part of Minami Hakuchi and the two dry docks of the **Hitachi Zōsen Shipyard** lie on the W side of the basin.

Kita Hakuchi (34° 36' N, 135° 26' E), in **No. 1 Area,** has depths from 15 m to 16·5 m. A **signal station** stands on a short breakwater on the S side of the entrance to the basin.

Shin Nippon Steel quays lie on the S and E sides of Kita Hakuchi.

Charts 2279, 2287
Berths and facilities in Sakai-Senboku Ku
12.34

Berths. The principal berths within the basins of Sakai-Senboku Ku are as follows:

Berth & Position	Length m	Depth m	Capacity dwt
No. 5 Area			
Shiomi Wharf			
(34° 30·3' N, 135° 23·2' E)			
No. 2 Quay	—	10	—
No. 3 Quay	370	10	18 000
No. 4 Quay	260	7·8	5 000
No. 5 Quay	—	12	—
Komatsu Wharf			
(34° 30·6' N, 135° 24·3' E)			
No. 2 Quay	390	6·1–7·5	6 000
Nippon Cement Jetty			
(34° 31·4' N, 135° 25·6' E) dolphins		8·5	10 000
Fujita Kōgyo Quay			
(34° 31·3' N, 135° 25·0' E)	119	15	15 000
Kyōa Oil Jetties			
(34° 31·5' N, 135° 24·6' E) various	various		Up to 5 000
No. 4 Area			
Ōsaka Gas Izumi LNG Jetty			
(34° 32·9' N, 135° 25·0' E)	125	15	64 000

Kyōa Oil Jetty
  (34° 32·3' N, 135° 25·2' E)   355   16–17   150 000

Mitsui Tōatsu Fertiliser Jetty
  (34° 32·4' N, 135° 25·6' E)   415   14–18   66 000

Ōsaka Gas—LNG Jetty
  (34° 32·7' N, 135° 25·8' E) dolphins   14–16   54 000

General Oil—Crude Jetty
  (34° 33·0' N, 135° 26·1' E) dolphins 16·5–17 160 000

General Gas Jetty
  (34° 33·1' N, 135° 26·4' E)   —   16   160 000

Marubeni Oil Jetty
  (34° 33·4' N, 135° 26·2' E) dolphins   14–16   50 000

No. 3 Area

Ube Kōsan Cement
  (34° 34·4' N, 135° 25·4' E)

D Jetty	dolphins	11–11·5	20 000
A2 Jetty	dolphins	11–11·5	12 000

Kansai Sekiyū Dangerous Cargo Jetties
  (34° 34·4' N, 135° 25·8' E)   —   7–8   Up to
                                                  5 000

No. 2 Area

Ōsaka Refinery
  (34° 34·9' N, 135° 26·2' E)

No. 1 Jetty	150	11	25 000

Hitachi Zōsen Shipyard
  (34° 34·8' N, 135° 26·4' E)

N Quay	590	7–8	170 000
E Quay	340	7–11	200 000

Ōhama Wharf
  (34° 35·2' N, 135° 27·3' E)

No. 4 Quay	165	8–5	12 000
No. 5 Quay	370	10	18 000

Shiohama Wharf
  (34° 35·2' N, 135° 27·9' E)

No. 1 Quay	120	7	5 000

No. 1 Area

Shin Nippon Steel
  (34° 35·7' N, 135° 26·7' E)

Ore Quay	600	14·5	80 000
Coke Quay	dolphins	4–6	3 000

Ōsaka Gas
  (34°36·0' N, 135° 26·6' E)

Coal Quay	400	11–12·5	55 000

12.35

Facilities. Offices of the Maritime Safety Agency, Customs and Immigration are located in the joint Harbour Office situated at the S end of Minami Hakuchi (No. 2 Area).

There are numerous tugs and lighters.

The two dry docks in the Hitachi Zōsen Shipyard have the following particulars:

	Minimum Length m	Minimum Width m	Depth m	Capacity tons
No. 1	400	55	6·5	90 000
No. 2	380·6	63	12·5	400 000

Waste oil disposal facilities are available.

ŌSAKA KU

Chart 2279
General information
12.36

Ōsaka Ku (34° 38' N, 135° 24' E), which lies in the delta of **Yodo Kawa,** forms the N part of Ōsaka Kō and is divided into Nos. 1–8 Areas; its harbour limits are indicated on the chart. See also 12.23–12.27.

The port consists of Outer Harbour (Nos. 7 and 8 Areas), and from S to N, South Harbour (No. 5 Area), Inner Harbour (Nos. 1–4 Areas) and North Harbour (No. 6 Area).

An industrial zone, in which lie a number of mineral, chemical and steel works, extends along the front of the port. In 1978, further development work was in progress in Nos. 5, 7 and 8 Areas.

12.37

Landmarks. Numerous chimneys, gas tanks, bridges and towers stand in the harbour area and their positions can be seen on the chart. Among the most conspicuous and highest, from S to N are:

The **Kansai Power Station** chimney (red and white), with an elevation of 52 m, standing on the S bank of the mouth of **Kizu Kawa** (34° 37·1' N, 135° 27·6' E).

Minato-Ōhashi Bridge (34° 38·5' N, 135° 26·5' E) (12.46), painted red, spanning Inner Harbour in No. 3 Area.

The tower, with an elevation of 48 m, of the Ōsaka Harbour Radar Station (12.25) standing on Central Pier in No. 2 Area.

A group of oil tanks, painted white, on the W side of Umemachi Basin (34° 39·3' N, 135° 25·2' E) (12.45) in No. 2 Area.

A group of gas tanks standing on each side of Shōrenji Kawa (34° 40·3' N, 135° 25·8' E) (12.49) which flows into the head of North Harbour in No. 6 Area.

ŌSAKA KU—OUTER HARBOUR

Chart 2279
12.38

Outer Harbour, comprising **No. 7** and **No. 8 Areas,** is the area within the harbour limits and outside the breakwaters extending from the N limit of Sakai-Senboku Ku to the mouth of Nakashima Kawa about 5 miles N.

Prohibited areas. An extensive prohibited area marked by towers, lights and buoys, lies on the N side of the entrance to Inner Harbour; a similar area lies on the S side of South Harbour South Breakwater. Both areas are indicated on the chart.

Sakai South Fairway (12.32) is entered in the S part of Outer Harbour and the quarantine anchorage (12.26) lies on the N side of the fairway.

12.39

Shin-Yodo Kawa, Kansaki Kawa and **Nakashima Kawa** flow into the N part of No. 8 Area. A *light-buoy* is moored 3 cables SW of the point (34° 41' N, 135° 25' E) separating the mouths of Shin-Yodo Kawa and Kansaki Kawa.

The entrance to Nakashima Kawa is approached through a buoyed channel leading through Amagasaki Kō (12.55). **Nippon Tsūun North Harbour Wharf,** with depths from 11·5 m to 12 m alongside, lies on the E bank of the mouth of this river.

Submarine cables, marked by lights on piles, are laid in the SW approaches to Shin-Yodo Kawa.

ŌSAKA KU—SOUTH HARBOUR

Chart 2279
12.40

South Harbour, comprising **No. 5 Area,** is entered between **South Harbour South Breakwater** and **South Harbour North Breakwater**; a **light** is exhibited on the head of each breakwater.

No. 2 Light-buoy (34° 37·7′ N, 135° 22·7′ E), moored near the NW corner of the quarantine anchorage, is the outer of three light-buoys marking the S side of the channel, dredged to 12 m, leading through the entrance and into South Harbour.

Nankō North Wharf and **Liner Wharf** lie, respectively, on the NW and SE sides of a basin forming the NE arm (34° 38′ N, 135° 25′ E) of South Harbour.

Prohibited areas. In 1977, prohibited areas, where construction work was in progress, had been established on the N side of **Nankō South Wharf** and the S side of **Nankō Middle Wharf.**

12.41

South Harbour Fairway, with depths from 7·2 m to 12 m, is entered 8 cables ESE of the head of South Breakwater and leads between Nankō South Wharf and Nankō Middle Wharf into the two basins situated in the SE corner of South Harbour.

Traffic signals are displayed from **South Harbour (Nankō) signal station** situated on the S extremity of Nankō Middle Wharf.

Traffic through South Harbour Fairway is controlled by the following signals shown from the signal station. The signals consist of a flashing light shown by day and at night; by day, a shape is displayed in addition:

Light, shape	*Meaning*
White light flashing every 2 seconds; black cone, point up	Inward-bound traffic and outward-bound vessels under 500 grt may proceed
	Outward-bound traffic of over 500 grt stop and await further signal
Red light flashing every 2 seconds; black square	Outward-bound traffic and inward-bound vessels under 500 grt may proceed
	Inward-bound traffic of over 500 grt stop outside the fairway and await further signal
White and red lights flashing alternately every 3 seconds; black drum	Inward-bound vessels under 5000 grt may proceed
	Inward-bound vessels over 5000 grt stop outside the fairway and await further signal
	Outward-bound vessels over 5000 grt stop and await further signal
Light exhibiting 3 red flashes and 3 white flashes every 6 seconds; drum above red flag	All traffic prohibited except the one vessel permitted by the Captain of the Port

Traffic regulations. Vessels are required to comply with the following regulations in South Harbour Fairway:

(a) A vessel entering or leaving the fairway shall keep clear of a vessel in the fairway.
(b) A vessel meeting an oncoming vessel shall keep to the starboard side of the fairway.
(c) Overtaking or proceeding abeam of another vessel in the fairway is not allowed.

12.42

A channel spanned by **Kamome Bridge** (34° 36·5′ N, 135° 25·5′ E) with vertical clearance from 7 m to 11 m and marked by lights, connects South Harbour with Sakai North Fairway (12.32); a similar channel, spanned by two bridges with a least vertical clearance of 10 m, leads into No. 4 Area of Inner Harbour. Both channels may be used by small vessels.

ŌSAKA KU—INNER HARBOUR

Chart 2279
12.43

Inner Harbour, comprising Nos. 1–4 Areas, the limits of which are shown on the chart, is entered between **Inner Harbour North Breakwater** (34° 38·3′ N, 135° 24·0′ E) and **Inner Harbour South Breakwater**; a **light** is exhibited on the head of each breakwater.

Naikō (Inner Harbour) Fairway leads through the entrance into the harbour and is marked at its seaward end by *Ōsaka No. 1* and *No. 2 Light-buoys* moored 6 cables WSW of the entrance; it has depths from 9·6 m to 13·5 m in it.

Ajikawa Fairway, with depths of about 12 m, leads NE from the E end of Naikō Fairway towards the mouth of Aji Kawa.

Kanmon signal station stands on the head of Inner Harbour North Breakwater and from it are displayed anchoring and berthing signals.

No. 1 Area
12.44

Nos. 1–4 Dolphin Berths lie in **No. 1 Area** on the N side of Naikō Fairway close within the entrance of the harbour; **No. 5** and **No. 6 Dolphin Berths** lie on the S side of the fairway.

Nos. 1 and 2 mooring buoys lie in the SE part of No. 1 Area.

No. 2 Area
12.45

Umemachi Basin with **Umemachi West Wharf** on its W side, is situated on the N side of **No. 2 Area.**

Aji Kawa, with depths of about 10 m, lies in the NE part of the No. 2 Area and numerous berths lie on both banks of the river. **Sakurajima Quay** and **Umemachi Quay** lie on the N side of its mouth.

Aji Kawa signal station (34° 39·3′ N, 135° 26·1′ E) is situated on the S bank of Aji Kawa near its mouth.

Central Pier is situated at the E entrance point of Aji Kawa and the tower of the harbour radar station (12.25) stands near its head. Cambers from which **lights** are exhibited, face the shore both N and S of the pier.

No. 3 and No. 4 mooring buoys lie in the SW part of No. 2 Area.

No. 3 Area
12.46

Minato-Ōhashi Bridge (34° 38·5′ N, 135° 26·5′ E) with a vertical clearance of 49 m, spans **No. 3 Area**

about ¼ mile SE of Central Pier. The fairway is marked by lights on each side of the bridge as follows:

    (a) centre of fairway—green light
    (b) each edge of fairway—orange light
    (c) each end of the bridge outside the navigable channel—red light.

Nos. 1, 2 and 3 Piers lie on the NE side of No. 3 Area, and **Shirmashi Kawa,** in which there are several berths, forms the E arm of the area.

No. 4 Area
12.47

Nos. 1–5 Container Terminals extend along the W side of No. 4 Area. Nos. 18–26 mooring buoys are situated in the middle of the area.

Two cambers, on which **lights** are exhibited, face the E side of the area. **Kizu Kawa signal station** is situated at the entrance of a canal close SE of the S of the two cambers.

Kizu Kawa, in which are situated Kansai Power Station (34° 37·1' N, 135° 27·5' E) and several shipyards, flows into the S part of the area and is marked on its N side by a *light-buoy.* The river is spanned by two **overhead cables** with a least vertical clearance of 53 m, and a **bridge** with a vertical clearance of 30 m.

ŌSAKA KU—NORTH HARBOUR

Chart 2279
12.48

North Harbour, comprising **No. 6 Area,** lies between Inner Harbour and the mouth of Shin-yodo Kawa (12.39) 1¼ miles N, and has three entrances.

The **S entrance,** with a least depth of 9·8 m and leading from Inner Harbour, lies between the E end of Inner Harbour North Breakwater (34° 38·8' N, 135° 24·8' E) (12.43) and the S extremity of Umemachi West Wharf. *No. 2 Light-buoy* is moored close off the end of North Breakwater and a **light** is exhibited on the head of a short breakwater projecting from the S extremity of Umemachi West Wharf.

The **W entrance** to North Harbour lies between **North Harbour South Breakwater** (34° 39·1' N, 135° 24·5' E) which projects 4 cables N from Inner Harbour North Breakwater, and **Middle Breakwater;** a **light** is exhibited at the head of each breakwater.

The approach channel to the W entrance lies between a prohibited area (12.38) on the S side and reclaimed land on the N side and is marked by *light-buoys. No. 1* and *No. 2 Light-buoys* (34° 39·5' N, 135° 23·1' E), the outer pair, are moored 1¼ miles W of the entrance between the breakwaters. There is a least depth of 9·6 m in the approach channel.

The **N entrance** to the harbour is approached through a channel, with a depth of about 5 m, lying between reclaimed land on its S side and a prohibited area on its N side. A **light** is exhibited on the N extremity of the reclaimed land (34° 40·2' N, 135° 24·3' E) and also on the head of **North Breakwater** which forms the N side of the entrance.

12.49

There are depths from 9·8 m to 11 m in the S part of North Harbour shoaling to 7·3 m in the N part; **Shōrenji Kawa** flows into the N end of the harbour.

Nos. 21–28 Dolphin Berths lie along the W side of North Harbour. **No. 1 Quay** and **Tatsumi Wharf** lie on the N side of a basin on the E side of the harbour, and there are a number of berths on both banks of Shōrenji Kawa.

ŌSAKA KU—BERTHS AND FACILITIES

Chart 2279
12.50

Berths. The principal berths within the harbours of Ōsaka Ku are as follows:

Berth & Position	Length m	Depth m	Capacity dwt
Outer Harbour (*No. 8 Area*)			
Nippon Tsūun North Harbour Wharf			
(34° 41·7' N, 135° 24·7' E)	256	11·5–12	20 000
South Harbour (*No. 5 Area*)			
J Quay			
(34°36·5' N, 135° 24·6' E)	720	12	30 000
Ferry Wharf No. 7			
(34° 37·0' N, 135° 25·1' E)	260	8·5	—
A, B, D, E Quays			
(34° 36·6' N, 135° 25·8' E)	—	5–7·5	3 000
Ferry Wharf Nos. 1–6			
(34° 37·0' N, 135° 26·0' E)	—	6–7·5	Up to 8 000
Liner Wharf			
(34° 37·7' N, 135° 24·8' E)	1600	10	15 000
R Quay			
(34° 37·8' N, 135° 24·6' E)	850	10–12	—
Inner Harbour (*No. 1 Area*)			
Dolphin Berths Nos. 1–4			
(34° 38·7' N, 135° 24·5' E)	—	10	10 000
Dolphin Berths Nos. 5, 6			
(34° 38·2' N, 135° 24·6' E)	—	12–14	20 000
Inner Harbour (*No. 2 Area*)			
Umemachi West Wharf			
(34° 39·2' N, 135° 25·2' E)	670	7–12	Up to 30 000
Umemachi Quay			
(34° 39·1' N, 135° 25·5' E)	395	9·5–12	10 000
Sakurajima Quay			
(34° 39·3' N, 135° 25·7' E)	530	10	10 000
Central Pier			
(34° 38·9' N, 135° 25·8' E)			
North Quay	210	11	13 000
South Quay	210	10	10 000
Timber Wharf			
(34° 38·4' N, 135° 25·9' E)	630	11·5–13	10 000
Aji Kawa No. 1 Quay			
(34° 39·5' N, 135° 26·6' E)	320	9·5–10	10 000
Aji Kawa Nos. 2, 3 Quays			
(34° 39·8' N, 135° 27·0' E)	540	9·5–10	10 000
Ōsaka Silo Quay			
(34° 39·7' N, 135° 26·9' E)	dolphins	10·5	13 000
Inner Harbour (*No. 3 Area*)			
Nos. 1, 2, 3 Piers			
(34° 38·6' N, 135° 26·6' E)	—	5·5–10	Up to 10 000
No. 10 Quay			
(34° 38·9' N, 135° 27·8' E)	617	5–8·5	Up to 7 000
Inner Harbour (*No. 4 Area*)			
Container Terminals			
(34° 38·0' N, 135° 26·6' E)			
Nos. 1–5 Quays	1370	12	25 000
Dolphin Berth No. 13			
(34° 37·3' N, 135° 26·9' E)	—	12·5	10 000

Nakayama Steel W Main Wharf
(34°37·4' N, 135° 27·2' E) 260 12 25 000
Kansai Power Station Quay
(34° 37·2' N, 135° 27·5' E) 200 9·5–10 7 000

North Harbour (No. 6 Area)
Dolphin Berths Nos. 21–28
(34° 39·5' N, 135° 24·8' E) — 7–11 Up to 10 000
No. 1 Quay
(34° 39·6' N, 135° 25·4' E) 250 8·5–10 10 000
Tatsumi Wharf
(34° 39·7' N, 135° 25·6' E) 105 6 10 000
Sumitomo Steel Centre Quay
(34° 40·3' N, 135° 25·5' E) 100 6 2 500

12.51

Facilities. Offices of the Maritime Safety Agency, Customs, Quarantine and Immigration are located in the joint Harbour Office situated at the root of Central Pier (34° 39' N, 135° 26' E).

A British Consul resides in Ōsaka (see 1.73).

Numerous tugs, lighters and harbour launches are available.

Waste oil disposal facilities are available at the mouth of Shōrenji Kawa in North Harbour.

There are several hospitals and seamen's homes in Ōsaka.

De-ratting; see 1.70.

Major hull and machinery repairs can be undertaken. The principal dry docks, situated near the mouth of Kizu Kawa (34° 37·4' N, 135° 28·2' E), are as follows:

	Length m	Width m	Depth m	Capacity tons
Hitachi Shipyard				
No. 1	193·2	25·0	8·1	24 000
No. 2	167·0	23·0	6·2	10 000
Fujinagata Shipyard				
No. 1	128·9	18·4	6·3	5 000
No. 2	154·7	20·1	8·2	10 000
Namura Shipyard				
No. 1	178·0	26·8	6·4	7 000
No. 2	140·0	20·0	6·5	9 000
Sanoyasu Shipyard				
No. 1	145·2	20·8	4·1	10 000
No. 2	106·6	16·4	3·7	3 700

Climate. See table at 1.105.

Supplies. Fuel oil can be supplied. Fresh water is laid on to the principal quays and there are several water boats.

Communications. There is a port radio station at Ōsaka; see *Admiralty List of Radio Signals Volume 6*.

Numerous passenger and car ferry services ply to ports in Shikoku and Kyūshū.

Ōsaka International Airport is about 15 miles (1 hour by road) from the port.

AMAGASAKI KŌ AND NISHINOMIYA KŌ

GENERAL INFORMATION

Charts 2279, 2265

12.52

Amagasaki Kō (34° 41' N, 135° 23' E) (12.53) and Nishinomiya Kō (12.57) 2¼ miles NW, lie in the NE corner of Ōsaka Wan between the two large port complexes of Ōsaka and Kōbe; they are part of the Hanshin Industrial Zone.

Nishinomiya Breakwater (34° 40·4' N, 135° 21·0' E) extends about 2¼ miles W from a position on the NW side of the buoyed approach channel to Amagasaki Kō; a **light** is exhibited on the SE head of the breakwater. In 1978, the W end of the breakwater was still under construction and was marked by orange lights.

A disused spoil ground with numerous depths of 8·5 m, lies between Nishinomiya Breakwater and the entrance to Nishinomiya Kō, 2 miles N.

AMAGASAKI KŌ

Chart 2279

12.53

Amagasaki Kō, the limits of which are shown on the chart, lies between the mouth of Nakashima Kawa (34° 41' N, 135° 24' E) (12.39) and the mouth of Muko Kawa, 1¼ miles W; it is an open harbour (see 1.65). Shōge Kawa and Yomoge Kawa, with their branch canals and channels, discharge into the harbour.

Amagasaki, which had a population of 537 000 in 1973, is an important industrial city; it has a thermal power station and large factories which includes a steelworks.

Landmarks. The following features in Amagasaki Kō are conspicuous:

The composite chimney (red and white), with an elevation of 151 m, of **Kansai Power Station** (34° 41·4' N, 135° 23·4' E); six chimneys, each with an elevation of 65 m, stand in line 2 cables NNE of it.

A chimney (red and white), with an elevation of 93 m, and another chimney (red and white), with an elevation of 149 m, standing, respectively, 3 cables W and 9 cables NE of Kansai Power Station.

A gas tank (black), with an elevation of 96 m, standing 8 cables N of the power station.

Pilotage. Pilotage in Amagasaki Kō is not compulsory. Vessels requiring pratique can embark the pilot either in the Ōsaka Kō or the Kōbe Kō quarantine anchorage; otherwise a pilot can be embarked off the entrance to the approach channel (34° 39' N, 135° 21' E).

12.54

Channels. The approach channel to Amagasaki Kō leads from SW and is marked by three pairs of *light-buoys*; it has a depth of 12 m. *No. 1* and *No. 2 Light-buoys*, the outer pair, are moored nearly 1¼ miles SW of the E end of Nishinomiya Breakwater (12.52).

South Breakwater, which is detached, lies across the front of the harbour; a **light** is exhibited at each end of the breakwater.

The harbour is entered between the W end of South Breakwater and the head of **West Breakwater**. A **light** is exhibited on the head of West Breakwater, and in 1977 extensive reclamation work was in progress to the SW of this breakwater.

A channel dredged to 10 m leads from *Naruo Light-buoy*, moored 4¼ cables NNE of the E head of Nishinomiya Breakwater, to an **anchorage,** and to No. 1

and No. 2 mooring buoys in the mouth of **Muko Kawa.**

12.55

Harbour. Within the breakwaters in the vicinity of *No. 8 Light-buoy* (34° 41·0' N, 135° 23·3' E), the channel divides; two branches lead NNE, one to a basin on the W side of an artificial island on which stands Kansai Power Station and the other to a basin on the E side of the island; the third branch leads to berths on the E side of **Higashi Kaigan** and to Nippon Tsūun North Harbour Wharf (12.39) on the E side of the mouth of Nakashima Kawa.

All three branches are marked by *light-buoys* and have a least depth of 10 m, but they are narrow in parts.

Two floodgates giving entry to **Shōge Kawa** and **Yomoge Kawa** lie at the head of the E basin; passage through these gates is limited to vessels up to 870 tons.

Traffic signals are displayed at each gate.

12.56

Berths. The principal berths in Amagasaki Kō are as follows:

Berth & Position	Length m	Depth m	Capacity tons
Kobe Steel			
Ogimachi Jetty			
(34° 41·3' N, 135° 23·1' E)	250	12	35 000
Ōhama Quay			
(34° 41·8' N, 135° 23·4' E)	360	8·5–10	10 000
Kansai Power Station			
Amagasaki No. 2 Quay			
(34° 41·7' N, 135° 23·4' E)	180	10–11	10 000
Higashi Kaigan			
Nos. 1, 2, 3 Public Quays			
(34° 41·4' N, 135° 24·0' E)	—	10	10 000
Daikyō-Kyōdō Sekiyū Jetty			
(34° 41·1N, 135° 24·1' E)	160	10·5–11	—
Mobil Oil Jetty			
(34° 41·2' N, 135° 24·3' E) dolphins		10·5–12	—
Sumitomo Metals Quay			
(34° 41·4' N, 135° 24·4' E)	320	5	—

Facilities. The office of the Maritime Safety Agency is situated in the vicinity of Ogimachi Jetty.

Tugs are available from either Kōbe Kō or Ōsaka Kō and are normally used by vessels over 5000 tons.

Supplies. Oil fuel and fresh water are available.

Communications. Amagasaki Kō is covered by Ōsaka port radio station.

NISHINOMIYA KŌ

Charts 2265, 2279

12.57

Nishinomiya Kō (34° 43' N, 135° 21' E) lies 2¼ miles NW of Amagasaki Kō (12.53) and fronts the city of **Nishinomiya** which in 1973 had a population of 373 000; it is a noted *sake* distilling centre. **Ashiya,** a large residential area, lies at the foot of Rokkō San (12.1), 2 miles W of Nishinomiya.

Landmarks. Kabuto Yama (12.1), an isolated mountain 308 m high, is situated 3 miles N of Nishinomiya and is easily identified.

Four spherical gas tanks which are conspicuous, stand ½ mile NNE of the entrance to the harbour.

Pilotage. Pilotage is not compulsory. Vessels requiring pratique can embark the pilot either in Ōsaka Kō or the Kōbe Kō quarantine anchorage; otherwise a pilot can be embarked off the entrance to the approach channel to Amagasaki Kō (34° 39' N, 135° 21' E).

12.58

Harbour. Nishinomiya Kō is protected by breakwaters. In 1980, construction work and reclamation was in progress between the harbour entrance and the mouth of Muko Kawa (12.54), 2 miles SE.

In 1980, large scale harbour development work was in progress between the W breakwater and the E limit of Kōbe Kō, 1¼ miles WSW; the work extends up to 1 mile offshore and was marked by platforms exhibiting orange lights, and by *light-buoys* (orange light).

An **anchorage,** with depths from 4 m to 7·5 m, good holding, lies in the NW part of the harbour; a **yacht basin** (34° 43·1' N, 135° 20·3' E) lies in the W corner.

Imatsu Hakuchi (34° 43·0' N, 135° 20·8' E) lies at the mouth of **Higashi Kawa** which flows into the E part of the harbour. **Public Quay,** with a depth of 4 m alongside, extends SE from the E entrance point to Imatsu Hakuchi.

KŌBE KŌ

GENERAL INFORMATION

Charts 2265, 3614

12.59

Kōbe Kō, a specified port (see 1.64), lies on the N shore of Ōsaka Wan; extensive development has much enlarged the port which is protected by breakwaters extending from Wada Misaki (34° 39' N, 135° 11' E) (12.67) to the E limit of the harbour, 6 miles ENE.

Kōbe Kō is one of the largest ports in Japan and is an important international trading centre. A major feature of the port is Port Island (12.69), an artificial island connected to the mainland by a bridge and which affords quays for contained ships and for regular shipping services. In 1980, a similar artificial area known as Rokkō Island (12.75), was being reclaimed 1½ miles E of Port Island.

Kōbe, together with the four cities of Ashiya, Nishinomiya, Amagasaki and Ōsaka, forms a contiguous urban area along the NE shore of Ōsaka Wan. Kōbe had a population of 1 340 000 in 1973.

Kōbe Kō is divided into Nos. 1–6 Areas, the limits of which are shown on Chart 2265.

12.60

Landmarks. Kōbe Light (34° 38·7' N, 135° 10·2' E) (12.67), standing 1 mile W of Wada Misaki, serves as a good head mark when approaching Kōbe Kō from S. Wada Misaki signal station (12.67), a white building, is situated 3 cables E of Kōbe Light.

In 1980, it was reported that the word MITSUBISHI painted on the sea wall about ½ mile E of Kōbe Light, was a good mark when approaching the quarantine anchorage (12.62) from S.

Trade Centre Building (34° 41·1' N, 135° 12·2' E),

118 m in height and marked by a red obstruction light, stands on the N side of No. 2 Area and is conspicuous.

A **light** is exhibited from a glazed black metal framework tower standing on the roof of the **Oriental Hotel**, 3 cables W of the Trade Centre Building.

Port Tower, 102 m in height and painted red, stands on Naka (Central) Pier in the NW corner of No. 2 Area; the tower is floodlit at night.

Eight cranes, painted red, stand on the Container Wharf on the W side of Port Island.

Three chimneys (red and white), the highest of which has an elevation of 120 m, stand in No. 1 Industrial District (34° 42' N, 135° 15' E) on the N side of No. 5 Area and are conspicuous.

A power station chimney, with an elevation of 63 m, stands near the SW extremity of No. 3 Industrial District (34° 42' N, 135° 17' E) on the N side of No. 6 Area and is conspicuous.

12.61

Cautions. There are many wrecks and obstructions in the approaches to Kōbe Kō; their positions and the depths over them may be seen on the charts.

At night, the lights of buoys marking the fairways and the lights on breakwaters are not easy to distinguish against the background of shore lights; they may also be obscured by the many vessels likely to be at anchor off the harbour.

The harbour is used by a large number of ferries; passenger ferries entering and leaving harbour will be encountered in Nos. 1 and 2 Fairways (12.70) and car ferries in Higashi-Kōbe Fairway (12.77).

Pilotage. Pilotage in Nos. 1, 2, 5 and 6 Areas, within the breakwaters, is compulsory. Pilots board in the vicinity of the quarantine anchorage. Pilots are available only between sunrise and 1 hour before sunset for berthing.

12.62

Anchorages. The **quarantine anchorage,** indicated on the charts, is situated in No. 3 Area close SW of Wada Misaki.

There are anchorages for vessels carrying **dangerous cargoes** in Nos. 4, 5 and 6 Areas.

Anchor berths are allocated by the Captain of the Port and vessels should not anchor without his permission.

The following anchor berths have been established:

South of No. 1 Breakwater

Anchor Berth	Bearing/distance from No. 1 South Breakwater Light (34° 38·9' N, 135° 12·4' E)	
S1	251°	980 m
S2	240°	500 m
M1	213°	1300 m
M2	176°	1000 m
M3	189°	1850 m
M4	165°	1800 m

South west of No. 6 Breakwater

Anchor Berth	Bearing/distance from No. 6 Breakwater Light (34° 40·1' N, 135° 14·9' E)	
S3	238°	2100 m
S4	238°	1650 m
S5	235°	1150 m
M5	222°	2650 m
M6	214°	1950 m
M7	196°	1300 m
M8	171°	1860 m
L1	205°	3250 m
L2	192°	2500 m

South of No. 7 Breakwater

Anchor Berth	Bearing/distance from No. 7 Breakwater Light (34°39·9' N, 135° 15·4' E)	
S6	090°	1100 m
S7	088°	1600 m
S8	085°	3200 m
M9	094°	2500 m
M10	099°	3300 m
M11	091°	3950 m
L3	118°	2000 m

North of No. 7 Breakwater

Anchor Berth	Bearing/distance from No. 7 Breakwater Light (34° 39·9' N, 135° 15·4' E)	
M12	032°	1550 m
M13	049°	2200 m
M14	057°	2820 m
M15	063°	3550 m
	Bearing/distance from Higashi-Kōbe signal station (34° 42·1' N, 135° 17·8' E)	
F1	139°	750 m
F2	152°	1200 m
F3	157°	2150 m
F4	115°	1150 m
F5	133°	1500 m
F6	144°	1900 m
F7	153°	2650 m

Anchor berths are designated as follows:

S	for vessels under 130 m in length.
M	for vessels under 200 m in length.
L	for vessels under 300 m in length.
F	for car ferries.

12.63

Regulations. General regulations prescribed by the Port Regulations Law are described at 1.37. Local regulations are also in force in Kōbe Kō and are summarised as follows:

(a) A vessel of over 5000 grt intending to use Higashi-Kōbe Fairway (34° 42' N, 135° 18' E), shall notify the Captain of the Port by noon the day before arrival her ETA at the entrance to the fairway, or, if leaving the port, her ETD. A vessel shall notify the Captain of the Port of any amendment to her ETA or ETD without delay.

(b) A vessel of over 500 grt shall use two anchors unless otherwise permitted by the Captain of the Port. However this shall not apply to a vessel anchoring outside the breakwaters unless deemed necessary by the Captain of the Port.

(c) A vessel of over 500 grt, when leaving harbour or shifting berth, shall display flags of the International Code of Signals to indicate the fairway it is intended to use, as follows:

No. 1 Fairway	1st Substitute
	over
	No. 1 Pendant
No. 2 Fairway	1st Substitute
	over
	No. 2 Pendant
No. 3 Fairway	1st Substitute
	over
	No. 3 Pendant

(d) Vessels of less than 1000 grt may not use Nos. 2

and 3 Fairways without the permission of the Captain of the Port.
(e) Anchoring is prohibited in the fairways.
(f) A vessel approaching Kawa Saki (34° 40·1' N, 135° 11·5' E) in No. 2 Area, either from W or from N, shall sound one prolonged blast at frequent intervals until she has passed the point.

12.64
Typhoon precautions. At the time of a typhoon, the Captain of the Port will issue instructions. Generally, medium-sized vessels from 2000 to 3000 tons should anchor within the breakwaters or seek shelter in Uchino Umi (10.6) on the SE side of Shōdo Shima, 48 miles WSW; large-sized vessels should either anchor or heave-to outside the breakwaters.

KÔBE KÔ—NO. 3 AND NO. 4 AREAS

Charts 3614, 2265
No. 3 Area
12.65
No. 3 Area embraces the area between the W limit of Kōbe Kō to a line drawn SE from the E end of No. 1 Breakwater, about 6 miles E.
Landmarks. Hachibuse Yama (34° 38' N, 135° 06' E), 246 m high, rises steeply from the coast at the W extremity of No. 3 Area; it is the end of a range of mountains which extends NE inland of Kōbe. A white building, from which a white light is exhibited, is situated near the summit of Hachibuse Yama.
Outer Suma Tower, on which a **light** is exhibited, stands 2 cables offshore ¼ mile SE of Hachibuse Yama; the tower is connected to the shore NNW by a bridge.

Chart 2265
12.66
Suma Beach Park which embraces a yacht basin, fishing centre and an aquarium, lies at the mouth of **Myōhōji Kawa** (34° 38·3' N, 135° 08·2' E), 1½ miles E of Outer Suma Tower. A **light** is exhibited from the E end of a detached breakwater lying across the mouth of the river.
No. 3 Area oil depot with numerous tanks, lies on the E side of the mouth of Myōhōji Kawa; several short piers with depths from 6 m to 10 m alongside, project from it.
Sea-berths. Two sea-berths, each consisting of four mooring buoys and each connected with the shore by a **submarine pipeline** which is marked at its head by a *buoy*, lie off No. 3 Area oil depot. Vessels up to 180 m in length and 9 m in draught can be accommodated at the W berth, and up to 230 m in length and 11·3 m draught at the E berth.
Tug assistance is required for berthing at these two berths and pilotage is compulsory.
Nagata Basin (34° 38·6' N, 135° 09·2' E) lies on the E side of No. 3 oil depot; a **light** is exhibited on the head of a short breakwater at the W entrance point of the basin.
12.67
Karumo Shima (34° 38·7' N, 135° 09·8' E), an artificial island, lies ¼ mile E of Nagata Basin; channels leading to the mouths of **Shinminato Kawa** and **Shin Kawa** lie on either side of the island.
Kōbe Light (34° 38·7' N, 135° 10·2' E) is exhibited from a white round concrete tower standing on the E entrance point of the channel on the E side of Karumo Shima.
Wada Misaki signal station stands 3 cables E of Kōbe

Light and from it are displayed anchoring and berthing signals.
Wada Misaki (34° 39' N, 135° 11' E) lies on the W side of No. 1 Fairway at the W entrance to No. 2 Area; a **light** is exhibited on the head of **Wada Breakwater** which projects E from the point.

No. 4 Area
12.68
No. 4 Area lies on the S side of the Port Island between a line drawn SE from the E end of No. 1 Breakwater (12.69) and a line drawn SSE from the head of No. 6 Breakwater (12.72).
Port Island Sea-berth, with depths from 12 m to 12·5 m alongside, lie on the S side of Port Island and is connected to it by a jetty; a **light** is exhibited on the end of the berth.

KÔBE KÔ—NO. 2 AND NO. 1 AREAS

Chart 2265
No. 2 Area
12.69
No. 2 Area, protected from S by **No. 1 Breakwater,** lies in the W part of Kōbe Kō inner harbour and is bordered on its E side by **Port Island;** a **light** is exhibited at each end of No. 1 Breakwater.
No. 1 South Breakwater, which is detached, lies close SE of the E end of No. 1 Breakwater and is connected to it by a bridge; a **light** is exhibited on the S end of the breakwater.
No. 2 Breakwater extends S from the S extremity of Port Island, and a **light** is exhibited on its head.
12.70
No. 1 Fairway leads N into No. 2 Area between Wada Breakwater (12.67) and the W end of No. 1 Breakwater, and towards Naka (Central) Pier. Between the breakwater heads there is a depth of 13·9 m but the fairway is shoal on each side; inside the entrance, the fairway has depths from 8·7 m to 12 m.
No. 2 Fairway leads N into No. 2 Area between the E end of No. 1 Breakwater and the head of No. 2 Breakwater, and towards Shinko Nos. 2 and 3 Piers. Between the breakwaters there is a depth of 13·4 m; inside the entrance the fairway narrows and has depths of about 12 m.
A number of mooring buoys lie within No. 1 Breakwater between Nos. 1 and 2 Fairways and are suitable for vessels from 8 m to 11 m draught.
12.71
Kawa Saki (34° 40·1' N, 135° 11·5' E) lies on the W side of No. 2 Area, 1 mile N of No. 1 Breakwater. **Kawa Saki signal station** stands on the point.
Mitsubishi Heavy Industries Shipyard, in which there are several dry docks and building slips, lies on the N side of Wada Misaki; **Kawasaki Heavy Industries Shipyard** occupies the greater part of Kawa Saki.
A number of piers project from the shore on the W and N sides of the area, and there is a container wharf on the W side of Port Island.
Kōbe Bridge with a minimum vertical clearance of 15 m, connects the NW extremity of Port Island to Shinko No. 4 Pier to the N.

No. 1 Area
12.72
No. 1 Area lies on the NE side of Port Island and is enclosed by **No. 4** and **No. 5 Breakwaters** on its N side

and by **No. 6 Breakwater** on its S side. A **light** is exhibited at the E end of both No. 5 and No. 6 Breakwaters.

The inner part of No. 3 Fairway (12.74) leads between a *light-buoy* moored off the W end of No. 5 Breakwater and **No. 3 Breakwater** which projects from the NE corner of Port Island; a **light** is exhibited at the head of No. 3 Breakwater.

Nos. 31–34 mooring buoys lie in the NE part of No. 1 Area.

12.73

A number of berths lie along the N side of Port Island and in the two basins on the E side of the island. A **prohibited area** marked by *light-buoys* has been established along the S side of the S of these two basins.

A channel dredged to 12 m leads from the NW end of the inner part of No. 3 Fairway towards the piers in the NW part of the area.

Maya Bridge (34° 41·5' N, 133° 13·1' E) with a least vertical clearance of 14 m, connects Shinko Wharf to Maya Pier situated in the N part of the area.

KŌBE KŌ—NO. 5 AND NO. 6 AREAS

Chart 2265
No. 5 Area
12.74

No. 5 Area lies to the E of Nos. 1 and 4 Areas and extends from the S harbour limit to the N shore of the inner harbour.

A **wave observation tower** (34° 38·7' N, 135° 16·8' E), 9 m high, stands at the SE corner of No. 5 Area and is marked by orange lights; a **light** is exhibited from the tower.

No. 3 Fairway leads between a detached breakwater lying to the SE of the head of No. 6 Breakwater (12.72) and the W end of **No. 7 Breakwater** which extends 2¼ miles ENE; a **light** is exhibited on the W end of No. 7 Breakwater. There are depths from 11·3 m to 12·8 m in No. 3 Fairway and its S entrance is marked by *No. 3 Light-buoy*.

The inner part of No. 3 Fairway in No. 1 Area is described at 12.72.

Traffic regulations. Vessels are required to comply with the following regulations in No. 3 Fairway:
  (a) A vessel entering or leaving the fairway shall keep clear of vessels in the fairway.
  (b) A vessel meeting an oncoming vessel shall keep to the starboard side of the fairway.
  (c) Overtaking or proceeding abeam of another vessel is not allowed.

12.75

Nadahama Channel, marked by *light-buoys*, leads to **Kōbe Steelworks** wharves (34° 42' N, 135° 15' E) in the N part of No. 5 Area. *No. 1* and *No. 2 Light-buoys*, at the entrance to the channel, are moored ¼ mile N of the head of No. 6 Breakwater.

Leading lights exhibited from towers (red triangular topmarks) stand in **No. 1 Industrial District** at the N end of Nadahama Channel and in line bear 358°; there is a least depth of 13·1 m on the leading line.

A buoyed channel with a least depth of 11 m, branches E from the N end of Nadahama Channel and leads to berths in **No. 2 Industrial District** and to the N side of Rokkō Island (34° 41' N, 135° 16' E).

In 1980, **Rokkō Island** was under development and an extensive reclamation area extended 2 miles E of Nadahama Channel and 1 mile offshore. A **prohibited area,** the limits of which were marked by *light-buoys*, had been established to facilitate reclamation work.

Rokkō Bridge with a vertical clearance of 14 m, connects the N side of the Rokkō Island reclamation area to No. 2 Industrial District.

12.76

Maya Pier lies in the NW part of No. 5 Area, N of No. 5 Breakwater.

Nos. 21 and 22 head and stern mooring buoys lie 2 cables N of No. 5 Breakwater; a number of dolphin berths lie on the N side of the breakwater.

No. 6 Area
12.77

No. 6 Area lies to the E of No. 5 Area and extends from the S harbour limit to the N shore of the inner harbour.

Higashi-Kōbe Basin (34° 42·5' N, 135° 17·5' E) lies on the N side of the area and is entered through **Higashi-Kōbe Fairway.** The fairway is approached through a channel leading E of No. 7 Breakwater (12.74) and marked by *Nos. 1–4 Fairway Light-buoys*; *No. 1 Fairway Light-buoy* is moored 1¼ miles S of the E end of No. 7 Breakwater.

Light-towers marking the E limit of the construction of Rokkō Island lie on the W side of the approach channel.

There is a least depth of 12 m in Higashi-Kōbe Fairway and from 6 m to 9 m within the basin.

Wharves used by the ferries lie on the N side of the basin.

12.78

Traffic signals are displayed from **Higashi-Kōbe signal station** situated on the SW corner of **No. 4 Industrial District** on the E side of Higashi-Kōbe Fairway.

Traffic through the fairway is controlled by the following signals shown from the signal station. The signals consist of a flashing light shown by day and at night; by day, a shape is displayed in addition:

Light, shape	*Meaning*
White light flashing every 2 seconds; black cone, point up	Inward-bound traffic and outward-bound vessels under 500 grt may proceed. Outward-bound traffic of over 5000 grt stop and await further signal
Red light flashing every 2 seconds; black square	Outward-bound traffic and inward-bound vessels under 500 grt may proceed. Inward-bound traffic of over 500 grt stop and await further signal
White and red lights flashing alternately every 3 seconds; 2 black cones, points together	Both inward and outward-bound vessels of over 5000 grt stop and await further signal, inward-bound vessels keeping clear of outward-bound vessels. Vessels of under 5000 grt, inward or outward-bound, may proceed
Light exhibiting 3 red flashes and 3 white flashes every 6 seconds; 2 black cones, points together, above red flag	All traffic prohibited except the one vessel permitted by the Captain of the Port

KŌBE KŌ—BERTHS AND FACILITIES

Chart 2265
Berths
12.79

The principal berths in Kōbe Kō are as follows:

Berth & Position	Length m	Depth m	Capacity tons
No. 3 Area			
Nippon Gatex Jetty			
(34° 38·6' N, 135° 09·4' E)	100	9	20 000
Shell Oil Jetty			
(34° 38·4' N, 135° 08·7' E)	120	5·5–11	8 000
No. 2 Area			
Hyōgo No. 3 Pier			
(34° 39·6' N, 135° 11·1' E)			
Berth T	150	8·5	5 000
U	250	6·5–7	6 000
Hyōgo No. 2 Pier			
(34° 39·7' N, 135° 11·2' E)			
Berths Q, R, S	435	4·5–9	Up to 10 000
M, N, O	435	8·5	Up to 10 000
Hyōgo No. 1 Pier			
(34° 39·8' N, 135° 11·3' E)			
Berths I–L	435	6–9	Up to 10 000
A–G	620	6–7·5	5 000
Takahama Quay			
(34° 40·6' N, 135° 11·3' E)			
Berths A, B	325	6·5–8	8 000
C	190	6·5–7·5	8 000
Naka (Central) Pier			
(34° 40·7' N, 135° 11·4' E)			
Berth A	200	4–8·5	8 000
B	150	8	10 000
Shinko Wharf			
(34° 40·8' N, 135° 11·9' E)			
No. 1 Pier	—	8·5–9	8 000
No. 2 Pier	—	8–9	8 000
No. 3 Pier	—	8·5–10	Up to 10 000
No. 4 Pier—W side	—	8·5–11	15 000
Port Island—Container Wharf			
(34° 39·6' N, 135° 12·3' E)			
PC1–5	1450	11·5–12	25 000
No. 1 Area			
Shinko Wharf			
(34° 41·1' N, 135° 12·5' E)			
No. 4 Pier—E side	—	8·5–11·5	20 000
No. 5 Pier	—	8–11	Up to 20 000
No. 6 Pier	—	10	15 000
No. 7 Pier	—	10–11·5	Up to 20 000
No. 8 Pier	—	9·5–10·5	10 000
Mitsui Pier			
(34° 40·9' N, 135° 12·4' E)	—	9–9·5	10 000
Maya Wharf			
(34° 41·5' N, 135° 13·6' E)			
No. 1 Pier—W side	590	9·5–10	Up to 20 000
No. 1 Dolphin Berth			
(34° 41·0' N, 135° 13·6' E)	—	9·5–10	14 000
Port Island—N side			
(34° 40·7' N, 135° 13·0' E)			
PC6	300	11·5–12	25 000
PL1–3	600	11–11·5	15 000
Port Island—E side			
PC7–9	900	12	25 000
PL4–8	1000	12	15 000
PL9	300	11–12	25 000
PL10–15	1200	11–12	15 000
No. 5 Area			
Maya Wharf			
(34° 41·5' N, 135° 13·6' E)			
No. 1 Pier—E side	400	10–10·5	Up to 20 000
No. 2 Pier	—	9·5–10	Up to 20 000
No. 3 Pier	—	9–10	Up to 20 000
No. 4 Pier	—	9–11	Up to 20 000
Nada Wharf			
(34° 41·8' N, 135° 14·1' E)	645	3·5–4·5	2 000
No. 2 Dolphin Berth			
(34° 41·0' N, 135° 13·7' E)	—	9·5	14 000
Nos. 3–8 Dolphin Berths			
(34° 40·9' N, 135° 14·0' E)	—	9–10·5	14 000
No. 2 Industrial District			
(34° 42·0' N, 135° 15·8' E)			
Mitsubishi S Jetty	dolphins	12	28 000
Shōwa Industries	dolphins	12·5	40 000
Tomen Silo	dolphins	12–12·5	45 000
Kōbe Silo	dolphins	12–13	—
Rokkō Island Quay			
(34° 41·6' N, 135° 15·8' N)			
Berths F–I	—	10	—
No. 6 Area			
Hanshin Silo Jetty			
(34° 42·0' N, 135° 17·0' E)	240	13	—
Japan Port Industries Jetty			
(34° 42·0' N, 135° 17·2' E)	300	10·5–11	—
Higashi-Kōbe Ferry Wharf			
(34° 42·7' N, 135° 17·3' E)			
Nos. 1–4 Piers	625	5–7	Up to 6 000
Konan Jetty			
(34° 42·1' N, 135° 17·9' E)	220	12	—

Facilities
12.80

The office of the Maritime Safety Agency is located in the Harbour Office (34° 41·0' N, 135° 11·6' E) situated at the N end of No. 2 Area. There are offices of quarantine, immigration and customs elsewhere in the port.

A large number of tugs, equipped for fire fighting, are available. They normally join vessels entering harbour at the entrance of the fairway.

Vessels over 500 grt are obliged to use tugs in accordance with the following scale, subject to the pilot's discretion:

Tonnage grt	Tugs required* Wharf/Dolphin	Double buoy mooring
Under 3 000	1 small	—
3 000–5 000	1 small, 1 medium	1 medium
5 000–7 000	1 medium	1 medium
7 000–10 000	1 medium, 1 large	1 large
10 000–40 000	2 large	1 large
Over 40 000	3 large	—

Vessels of 10 000 to 40 000 tons berthing at a single buoy mooring require 1 medium or 1 large tug.

*Large tug   2000 hp or more
Medium tug 1000 to 2000 hp
Small tug   less than 1000 hp.

There are numerous lighters and launches.

12.81

Docks. Major repairs can be undertaken. The principal docks are as follows:

No.	Type	Length m	Width m	Depth m	Capacity tons
Mitsubishi Heavy Industries (34° 39' N, 135° 11' E)					
1	Floating	95	5	11·7	4 000
2	Floating	209·5	33·6	14·5	32 000
3	Floating	175·3	29·2	13	20 000
4	Dry	301·5	43·7	9·5	85 000

Kawasaki Heavy Industries (34° 40' N, 135° 11' E)					
1	Dry	161	23·5	6·5	10 000
2	Floating	94	16	11·1	3 000
3	Floating	172·8	28	12·7	13 000
4	Dry	215	33·5	7·6	30 000

Waste oil disposal facilities are available in Mitsubishi and Kawasaki Shipyards and at the Kōbe City waste oil disposal jetty situated in the W part of No. 3 Area.

De-ratting; see 1.70.

Weather signals (1.42) are shown at the following stations:

The observatory, situated 6 cables NW of the root of Naka (Central) Pier.

Roof of the Harbour Office (34° 41·0' N, 135° 11·6' E).

Shinko No. 5 Pier signal station (34° 40·9' N, 135° 12·6' E).

Climate. See table at 1.106.

12.82

Supplies. Fuel oil supply facilities are available at Port Island Sea-berth (12.68). There are several oilers.

There are four waterboats and fresh water can be supplied at the principal quays.

Communications. There is a port radio station at Kōbe Kō.

There are passenger and car ferry services to many ports in Seto Naikai.

Ōsaka International Airport is about 18 miles from the port.

INDEX

PUBLICATIONS OF THE HYDROGRAPHIC DEPARTMENT

A complete list of the Sailing Directions, Charts and other works published by the Hydrographer of the Navy, together with a list of Agents for their sale, is contained in the "Catalogue of Admiralty Charts and other Hydrographic publications," published annually. The list of Agents is also promulgated in Admiralty Notice to Mariners No. 2 of each year, or it can be obtained from:

The Hydrographic Department,
Ministry of Defence,
Taunton, Somerset
TA1 2DN

Printed in the United Kingdom
for UKHO by The Bath Press